THEATRE ON THE EDGE:

NEW VISIONS,
NEW VOICES

THE APPLAUSE CRITICS CIRCLE

ALARUMS & EXCURSIONS by Charles Marowitz

THE COLLECTED WORKS OF HAROLD CLURMAN
edited by Marjorie Loggia & Glenn Young

THE GRAHAM GREENE FILM READER
edited by David Parkinson

IN SEARCH OF THEATER by Eric Bentley

LIFE OF THE DRAMA by Eric Bentley

MAD ABOUT THEATRE by Richard Hornby

SHAW ON MUSIC edited by Eric Bentley

THEORY OF THE MODERN STAGE
edited by Eric Bentley

THE WORLD OF GEORGE JEAN NATHAN
edited by Charles Angoff

Forthcoming

THE COLLECTED THEATER CRITICISM
OF JOHN GASSNER

THEATRE ON THE EDGE:
NEW VISIONS, NEW VOICES

Mel Gussow

APPLAUSE
NEW YORK • LONDON

An Applause Original

Theatre on the Edge: New Visions, New Voices
© 1998 by Mel Gussow
ISBN 1-55783-311-7

Library of Congress Cataloging-in-Publication Data

Gussow, Mel.
    Theatre on the edge : new visions, new voices / Mel Gussow.
        p.   cm.
    Collection of essays written over the past thirty years.
    ISBN 1-55783-311-7 (cloth)
    1. Drama.   2. Theater.   I. Title.
    PN1655.G85   1998
    792--dc21   97-28474
                                                         CIP

The material in this book that originally appeared in *The New York Times* is reprinted by permission of *The New York Times* © Copyright 1970-1997 by The New York Times Company.

British Library of Congress in Publication Data
A catalogue record for this book is available from the British Library.

APPLAUSE BOOKS   A&C BLACK

211 West 71st Street   Howard Road, Eaton Socon
New York, NY 10023   Huntington, Cambs PE19 3EZ
Phone (212) 496-7511   Phone 0171-242 0946
Fax: (212) 721-2856   Fax 0171-831 8478

First Applause Printing, 1998

FOR ANN AND ETHAN

CONTENTS

A Rich Crop of Writing Talent Brings New Life to the American Theater: August 21, 1977 ... What is a Regional Play?: October 14, 1979 ... Beastly Happenings on Broadway: October 28, 1979 ... Epic Dramatization of a Dickens Novel: July 6, 1980 ... Is Theater All a Juggling Act?: May 14, 1981 ... Daredevil Musical Provides Some Novel Credits: August 10, 1982... On Late Curtains, Blabs and the British: September 9, 1984 ... Grit and Wit Made Ruth Gordon a Star: September 8, 1985 ... The Curtain Rises on Kelp Lasagna and Chopped Liver: February 26, 1986 ... Hazards of the Trade: Fish and Flying Pickles: March 6, 1986 ... Character Actors: Bright Perennials of British Theater: July 27, 1986 ... On the Stage or Screen, Charisma Sells Tickets: August 10, 1986 ... A Play That Never Played by Two Masters of Satire: Feburary 8, 1987 ... A Virtuoso Who Specializes in Everything: August 23, 1987 ... Plays Considered During a Needed Intermission: September 20, 1987 ... For Yuppies on Stage, a Time for Reflection: January 1, 1989 ... Encore! From Stage to Screen: February 1, 1989 ... When Writers Turn the Tables Rather than the Other Cheek: July 16, 1989 ... Hot in London: Play and Weather: August 28, 1989 ... The Season's Hot Playwright: George S. Kaufman in Revival: February 19, 1990 ... Luring Actors Back to the Stage They Left Behind: January 7, 1991 ... On the London Stage, a Feast of Revenge, Menace and Guilt: July 31, 1991 ... Clurman on Theater with Sweep and Passion: April 6, 1994 ... Design Marches On: the Prague Quadrennial: October 1995 ... When Playwrights Cross (or Crisscross) the Footlights: February 5, 1996 ... Actors Theater of Louisville: The Plays Tell the Tale: March 1996 ... The Not-So-Accidental Recognition of an Anarchist: October 15, 1997 ... A Second 'Godot' for Peter Hall: December 18, 1997

Ingmar Bergman ... Peter Brook ... Joseph Chaikin ... Martha Clarke ... Tadeusz Kantor ... Mabou Mines ... Andrei Serban ... Julie Taymor ... Deborah Warner ... Robert Wilson

FOREWORD

When James Agate was reviewing theater for the Sunday Times in London, he said that he would prefer to be remembered as a critic who would never let anything second-rate get past him. Harold Hobson, his successor at the Times, responded that, in contrast, he would rather be a critic "who never failed to recognize anything that was first-rate, however bizarre it may have appeared." Proving his point, Hobson was primarily responsible for establishing the reputation in England of Samuel Beckett and Harold Pinter. I would certainly agree more with him than with Agate. History was Hobson's reward, as it also was for Harold Clurman, who, in a similar fashion, was the most astute of American theater critics.

Unquestionably a critic should point out the meretricious, and it is important not to overpraise good intentions, but it is essential to point out the meritorious and to identify artists of promise. This calls for openmindedness as well as foresight. One of the most damaging things for a critic is have an agenda, hidden or otherwise - one strike against Kenneth Tynan, among others. While praising John Osborne for his social awareness, Tynan was restrained in his enthusiasm for Beckett, even to writing a lame parody of *Krapp's Last Tape* and *Endgame* in lieu of a review.

I have sought out theater of great diversity, from the Ridiculous to the sublime, and even found moments of the sublime in the Ridiculous. The double meaning of the title of this book is intentional: theater on the edge and the critic alert for the possibility of new visions and new voices. Often one finds them in the most unusual circumstances: in a dusk to dawn vigil with Robert Wilson; a visit to Ossining to see prison theater (and the discovery of the incipient talent of an inmate named Miguel Piñero), at the Temple of Dendur in the Metropolitan Museum of Art for an evening of Noh. My theater travels have taken me to New York's waterfront, streets and parks (often with Anne Hamburger's En Garde Arts) as well as to traditional venues; to regional companies across America and to out of the way spaces in London and Paris. A special citation should go to Ellen Stewart, empress of La Mama, without whom this would be a far less rewarding occupation. While seconding Hobson in matters Beckettian and Pinteresque, I would also note my early identification of the value of the work of Sam Shepard,

Lanford Wilson, Richard Foreman, Charles Ludlam, David Mamet, Beth Henley, Martha Clarke, Bill Irwin, Julie Taymor, Whoopi Goldberg, Spalding Gray, Mac Wellman, David Ives and many others.

In hindsight, one can see that occasionally artists have been underrated and a few have been overpraised. Some have simply fallen short of their potential. I have always tried to avoid pre-judgments and to keep myself open to new experiences, which might come from any direction. Having generally dismissed *The International Stud*, an early play by Harvey Fierstein, I was startled to see it in revised form as one third of *Torch Song Trilogy*, and to realize that this was an important dramatic event.

Contrary to popular opinion, the power of critics is more in discovering work than in disparaging it. Critics (in consensus) can close shows in the commercial arena; more importantly, reviews can also help plays and playwrights find a wider audience. Shepard and Mamet are two of the more obvious examples. In terms of impact, I probably had the most immediate effect with a review of a New York Shakespeare Festival production of *The Comedy of Errors* in Central Park. I criticized June Gable for swiveling "around stage as if she were trying to parody Rita Moreno in *The Ritz*, a play by Terrence McNally then on Broadway. In response, Ms. Gable sent me an impolite letter quickly followed by an abject apology, saying that my review had prompted the producers of *The Ritz* to hire her as Ms. Moreno's replacement. Ms. Gable's conclusion: "So I can truly say that I got my job through the New York Times."

Some people have not been so conciliatory. Irate letters and telephone calls (from playwrights and mothers of playwrights) are to be expected, but threats against one's life are rare. As recorded in an essay in this book, once at a dinner party I found myself choking, and a playwright seated next to me saved my life by giving me the Heimlich maneuver. This was, I suggested, a singular event in the relationship between playwrights and critics, the first instance of a playwright saving a critic's life. I toasted the writer by saying that I would not reveal her name so as not to lower her reputation in the eyes of her colleagues, adding that she would of course never receive a negative notice from me. There was a postscript to this near catastrophic event: a letter arrived from a reader declaring herself as a victim of one of my reviews, and adding with malice: "You were lucky you weren't sitting next to me at that dinner party. I would have let you choke and take my chances with your successor." The letter was signed anonymously "Woman Playwright." Such are the hazards of criticism.

Artists crave admiration and, for some, a single negative review can obliterate previous praise. There are also some playwrights who challenge the idea of a critic not of their race or gender reviewing their work. I consider all such questions insupportable. A perceptive critic should feel no restrictions about what he or she can review.

My first theater review was of a student production of *Summer and Smoke* at Middlebury College and I still think that Barbara Fitzgerald's performance as

Alma Winemiller was in a class with that of Geraldine Page at Circle in the Square. Later, when I was studying at Columbia University's Graduate School of Journalism, I spent all my free time in the theater. That year, more than any other, shaped my perspective on theater, away from the commercial and toward the experimental. It was the year that *Waiting for Godot* opened on Broadway. By showing my student I.D. I was admitted free. Without prior knowledge, I saw - and enjoyed - a play that was to change the course of contemporary theater. My enthusiasm about *Godot* encouraged me to think about criticism as a possible profession. Seeing the play again and again in different productions, including the definitive German-language version directed by the author, I came to believe that it was, in fact, the seminal theatrical work of the last half of this century, as *The Cherry Orchard* was for the first half of the century.

Drafted into the army, I was eventually sent to Heidelberg, Germany, where I became the editor of an army newspaper, and assigned myself to review local cultural events. On leave, I went to London for the first time, where I immersed myself in the English theater, beginning with Peter Brook's historic production of *Titus Andronicus*, starring Laurence Olivier, Vivien Leigh and Anthony Quayle. The night that I was there, Winston Churchill was also in the audience. Years later, theatergoing in England became at least an annual experience. Whenever I think of the most significant theatrical events, many of them are English, including the premiere of the Royal Shakespeare Company's production of *The Life and Adventures of Nicholas Nickleby* and John Dexter's National Theater production of Brecht's *Galileo*, Michael Gambon's breakthrough performance.

At Newsweek magazine, I reviewed movies as well as plays - before there were bylines in that province of group journalism. Because of space limitations, we were encouraged to be pithy, and to offer a "summing up" after the review that would, in effect, make the review unnecessary. I made my Broadway "debut" when the resident drama critic, T. H. Wenning, an admirable man of the theater and a very good friend, became gravely ill, and asked me to fill in for him and review a new play that we had just seen at its opening. The play was Edward Albee's *Who's Afraid of Virginia Woolf?* In retrospect, that review, with its space limitations, only begins to deal with the depth of the play and its impact on the American theater.

After Albee, the deluge. Without byline, I continued reviewing for Newsweek. When I first began writing for the New York Times, newspapers still held to an opening night deadline. This meant that critics would rush back from the theater, often as late as 9:30 P.M., write a review in an hour's time and have it edited and locked in print by 11. This was unfair to most of the plays. On the other hand, one's adrenalin was up, and some of the work did not need the extra time. When the preview system was instituted, the deadline was delayed for at least one day - a much saner system.

I have written several thousand reviews for the New York Times and many for other publications (including American Theater and Playboy as well as Newsweek) and for WQXR radio and briefly on Channel 13 during a newspaper strike. When the Times computerized and (unwisely) stopped adding to its collection of clippings, it allowed the writers to reclaim their bylines from the morgue. My large file box of clippings, indexed by year, has been the primary source of this book. To wade through such a mass of material is to re-view one's past (the dreadful evenings as well as the salutary ones), and to wonder how I managed to have something to say about so many productions. With her customary incisiveness, my wife Ann collaborated with me in the selection and the editing. For her, this was a case of double jeopardy. She not only saw a greater share of the shows, she had to relive the reviews.

Certain critics are so compulsive about advancing their opinion that they would review anything (a cat caught up a tree as well as in a Lloyd Webber musical). Sometimes, in rereading my words, I realized that I also might be subject to that charge. Some of the plays reviewed were, in short, catastrophes. On the other hand...Because this is a sampling, one has had to be judicious. Certain events and reviews that seemed consequential in their time dwindle with age; others achieve a new or a renewed importance. Some artists are not represented simply because of space limitations. Trying to limit the number of pieces for each artist has led to a certain arbitrariness on my part. In the case of Ludlam that has been especially difficult. Over several decades, I reviewed every one of his plays, and feel an eternal debt to him. His flamboyant theatricality seemed to awaken critical creativity (as well as a penchant for punning). Something similar could be said about Tom Stoppard.

Since most of my reviewing has been away from Broadway, a few playwrights have eluded my criticism. I have seen but not generally reviewed the work of August Wilson and Neil Simon, to name two, although I have written about them in other contexts. I remember hearing that Louis La Russo III, a playwright with a brief Broadway career, had said on the radio that I was one of his favorite critics. The key to his praise was that I had never reviewed his work. I saw no reason to do otherwise and alter our excellent relationship.

Many of the artists whose work I reviewed favorably have gone on to win Pulitzer Prizes and MacArthur awards. Three times I was a member of a jury to name the Pulitzer Prize for drama. The other judges and myself readily agreed on Lanford Wilson (for *Talley's Folly*) in 1980 and Beth Henley (for *Crimes of the Heart*) the following year, and the journalistic board approved our choice. However, in 1986, when I was chairman of the jury, my fellow jurors (Edwin Wilson and Bernard Weiner) and I unanimously selected Robert Wilson for *The Civil Wars*, which at that point had been presented in Cambridge, Mass., but not yet in New York. As a conceptualist and performance artist, Wilson did not fit the traditional Pulitzer role of playwright. It was our idea to widen the range of this prestigious award. To our chagrin, the journalistic board preemptorily rejected our nomination - and did not award a Pulitzer in drama that year. This was the last time that I was asked to serve on a Pulitzer jury. Parenthetically, when I was president of the New York Drama Critics Circle, the Times requested that its critics stop participating in the annual voting of awards for that group, on the grounds that their individual opinions should not be submitted to a homogeneous process, homogeneous of course being a code word for democratic. I therefore became the Circle's first non-voting president, a fact that I acknowledged when I presented the annual awards.

One of the obvious problems of the profession is that a critic is called upon to see the same play again and again, and still has to have something to say about it. I have seen and reviewed *Hamlet* more than any other play. Instead of printing all or many of those reviews (that would comprise a small book), I have chosen several, one a brief essay about the variety of interpretations of the play (including three productions with women in the title role). Without counting, I would think that other Shakespeare plays would follow numerically, along with *Waiting for Godot*. A selection of my Beckett reviews appears in my book, "Conversations with and about Beckett." Here the author is represented by his obituary, which, as with the obituaries of Jean Genet and Eugene Ionesco, also acts as a career appraisal. It was interesting to realize how often I reviewed certain actors, such as Daniel Gerroll, Joe Grifasi, Stephen Mellor, J. Smith-Cameron, Mary Layne and Black-Eyed Susan. Since the reviews of their performances are favorable, that says something about their versatility as well as their productivity.

Along the way there have been some surprises. Rereading my review of Ingmar Bergman's production of *A Doll's House*, I realized that his willful Nora was actually a precursor of the one played by Janet McTeer in Anthony Page's production. I had forgotten that I had reviewed *Score*, which I characterized as "the first nude sex play whose action takes place in Queens." In that negative review, I did not mention any of the actors by name, apparently as an act of discretion. This means that among the unmentioned was a young man named Sylvester E. Stallone, who was perhaps making his Off Broadway debut. Similarly I omitted Richard Gere from a review of *A Midsummer Night's Dream* and overlooked Christopher Reeve in his debut at the Circle Repertory Company (how was that possible?), but soon made up for that in his subsequent appearances on stage. I did notice Demi Moore (also at the Circle Rep) in a play called *The Early Girl*, and singled her out for praise. She was, of course, already in the nude. Visits to the Juilliard Theater Center and Yale Repertory Theater uncovered such newcomers as Kevin Kline, Meryl Streep, Sigourney Weaver and Henry Winkler (who at that stage of his career seemed to specialize in playing old men). The premiere of *The Idiots Karamazov* at Yale represented something of a bonanza; the discovery of Ms. Streep and the authors Christopher Durang and Albert Innaurato. Then there was Macauley Culkin, a tiny showstopper in his debut onstage at the Ensemble Studio Theater.

Some special place should be reserved for a show called *Claptrap*. Ostensibly a spoof of *Deathtrap*, it opened in June of 1987 at the Manhattan Theater Club.

MEL GUSSOW ∾ XV

Featured in the cast of five were Nathan Lane and Cherry Jones, who were soon to be recognized as two of the finest actors of their generation. This was relatively early in their careers, and they were trapped in a show that, as I suggested in my review, succeeded in living up to--or, rather, down to--its title. Significantly, the plot centered around a funeral, and it seemed overly concerned with vegetables. Mr. Lane had to wrestle with another actor over a head of iceburg lettuce, and Ms. Jones wore two carrots in her hair. The review ended, "The perishable dialogue is unwittingly filled with self-criticism, as in the reference to 'one meaningless experience seen from every possible point of view.' Watching the play, one is reminded of David Mamet's observation that the time one spends in the theater is deducted from our total lifetime allotment. *Claptrap* steals two hours." What I did not fully realize was how much the play shortchanged its actors. Later, when I wrote a piece about Cherry Jones and her extraordinary performance in *The Heiress*, she told me that the production of *Claptrap* hand been "fraught from beginning to end." She said that she walked on stage with egg on her face: "You didn't acquire it in the course of the evening." She remembered that Lynne Meadow, the theater's director, "begged people to come back after intermission: that took chutzpah, because she knew it was not going to get any better." Mr. Lane later said that after one performance he sat outside the theater sunk in misery. Terrence McNally came up to him and told him how much he admired his talent and hoped that one day he would appear in one of his plays. The actor looked up and said, "How about today?"

Reviewing an early Lampoon Lemming show, I proclaimed a comic actor named John Belushi as the evening's discovery. Years later, Belushi told me that was his favorite review and he carried it around with him in his wallet. He and others have died prematurely, including Charles Ludlam, Miguel Piñero, Susan Kingsley, David Warrilow, Dennis McIntyre, Anthony Holland, Ethyl Eichelberger and Percy Granger. Each is a distinct loss for the theater.

One of the many reasons I admired Harold Clurman was that he was one of the few critics who was also a first rate director and knew a great deal about the practical side of the theatrical profession. On several occasions, I stepped behind the footlights, taking comedy classes with Bill Irwin (for my New Yorker Profile about him) and joining an acting workshop led by Ludlam. These proved to be a great help, especially when writing about comedy. I remember with particular pleasure one woman of the theater saying that she had heard that I did something funny with a top hat in Mr. Irwin's class. Later, at an evening of foolery from Bob Berky, I was chosen, anonymously, as a volunteer from the audience and found myself on stage, and at the mercy of the clown in a comedy sketch. The audience laughed at "us." Is there a clown or at least a performance artist behind every cool critical facade?

Then there was the time that a casting agent called to ask me to audition for a cameo role in a movie. He explained that the role was that of a tyrannical high school teacher who is hated by all his students. In a crucial scene, he is killed by an arrow. The movie people thought it would be interesting if this villainous role was played by a critic. I suggested that they call John Simon. It turned out that they had called John Simon, but he had apparently rejected the opportunity because the character had no dialogue. Out of curiosity, I went to the production office, where I was interviewed and given a copy of the script. To my dismay, I realized that the author was a playwright whose work I had reviewed none too favorably. In his screenplay, he described the teacher as an "evil guy" with a "cruel" smile. That sounded suspiciously like a spurned playwright's portrait of a critic. Suddenly the scenario was clear. Get the critic on set, point an arrow at him - and really kill him. Before the role was not offered to me, I decided that it was not within my range as an actor.

Once I was the victim of plagiarism. I had written enthusiastically about Al Carmines's nostalgic musical, *A Look at the Fifties*, when it was first done at the Judson Poets Theater. A year later the show opened at the Arena Stage in Washington. My review had begun: Forget *Grease*, Good-by *Bye Bye Birdie*, and let's hear a locomotive cheer from *The Last Picture Show*. The fifties musical is here.'" The reviewer for the Georgetowner, a periodical in Washington, cavalierly appropriated my lead and most of the rest of my review. What hurt even more than the plagiarism was the liberty he took with my words. His version read: "You can forget *Bye Bye Birdie*, *Goodbye Columbus*, *Grease*, and all those '7-Up' commercials on t.v."

In terms of authorship, it should be left to the reviewer to repeat his or her own words. Reading mine again, I was struck by the repetition of certain adjectives. In retrospect, it is difficult to think that so many plays could have been compelling, so many actors virtuosic, so many performance artists paradigmatic. A computer zeroing in on my work might also enumerate the many references to the Marx Brothers, Beckett and Bunraku. For reasons of space, the pieces have occasionally been pruned. The evenings of discovery are counterbalanced by those plays that offer the familiar and the formulaic. For obvious reasons, most of the reviews in this collection are of works that I have admired. That does not mean that they are representative of a critic's nightly life. A few of the pieces could be described as critical profiles. A close reader of this book will find one entry that qualifies neither as a review or as an essay. I laugh every time I read it and simply wanted to see it in print again. Call it a public performance.

INTRODUCTION: VISIONS AND VOICES

"The essence of theater," said Peter Brook, "is within a mystery called 'the present moment.'" That moment, he explained, "releases the hidden collective potential of thought, image, feeling, myth and trauma," and it is powerful as well as dangerous. Experiencing a work by Robert Wilson, Ingmar Bergman or by Brook himself - one can feel the surge of something almost supersensory. Drawing from and unifying various arts, both graphic and dramatic, these artists and others can change the way we look at theater. They are in striking contrast to the predictability of so much in the theatrical mainstream. Paradoxically, it is in this experimental arena that artists have been most responsive to the extraordinary social, cultural and technological changes that have occurred as the world speeds toward the millenium.

In the last three decades, Broadway has retrenched and retreated. In the 1940's, 50's and 60's, it was a home for challenging work by such playwrights as Tennessee Williams, Arthur Miller and Edward Albee, a place where producers could take chances and where previously unknown writers could make overnight reputations. While trying to attract an even more popular audience, the commercial theater began marginalizing itself into a home for cinematic style musicals, some of them, in fact, stage versions of movie musicals. In this way, Broadway paralleled the decline of Hollywood where big budget, star-driven action movies forced the independent cinema into a world, or rather a niche of its own. Subsequently, the serious work - dramatic, and, occasionally, musical - began almost entirely in non-profit venues.

Off Broadway theaters including the Circle Repertory Company, the Manhattan Theater Club and Playwrights Horizons became seedbeds of new talent. Led by Ellen Stewart at La Mama, Off Off Broadway - an unaffiliated collection of coffee houses, storefronts and lofts - offered a stage to experimental artists from here and abroad. Through the Next Wave Festival at the Brooklyn Academy of Music, Harvey Lichtenstein introduced American audiences to the most innovative international talent in theater (as well as music and dance). Regional theater, as exemplified by the Hartford Stage Company, the Yale Repertory Theater, the Arena Stage in Washington and the Goodman Theater of

Chicago, welcomed new writers and, in many cases, new forms of theater. For many years, the regional theater has been our national theater.

With the exception of the work by Neil Simon, David Mamet and August Wilson, and plays with proven success in London, new plays are no longer done with any regularity on Broadway. Wilson himself is something of an anomaly. His plays arrive there only after a long tryout period through regional theaters. Even then, despite the quality of the effort and the awards that the playwright achieves, the work struggles to survive. Similarly, the musicals of Stephen Sondheim, the only major American composer to have a continuing career on Broadway during this time, are now nurtured in workshops and regional theaters before chancing mass exposure. It is possible that August Wilson and Sondheim will eventually join David Mamet, Sam Shepard and Lanford Wilson whose work is largely done away from Broadway.

At the same time that Broadway was in sharp decline artistically, the experimental theater reached out to engage new visions and new voices. The "visions" are generally those of directors, the "voices" those of playwrights, but there is an overlapping when the writer (such as Richard Foreman) is also a director and a conceptualist. On the other hand, some of the most original artists like John Kelly and John Jesurun would not accurately be identified as writers. In his multimedia plays, Jesurun shatters artificial walls, so that actors playing characters on stage interact with characters on a movie or a television screen. In one of his most innovative pieces, *Everything That Rises Must Converge*, he whirled the set around like a giant spinning top, creating alternative perspectives for the audience.

It is several steps from Jesurun to Spalding Gray, who sits at a table as he leads the audience through his often disabling misadventures as actor, traveler and worrier. Gray is himself emblematic of the seismic shifts in the theater. Working as an actor with the Wooster Group, he began by appearing in plays in which he would deliver soliloquies from his past, scenes that in their precision and humor were the opposite of the inchoate ramblings that surrounded them. Soon, Gray omitted the play and just did the monologues, moving from the Performing Garage to Lincoln Center. Whether facing 100 or 1000 or having his story preserved on film, Gray has not changed: the theater has changed to accommodate him and his audience. He is only one of many exemplars of the individual's art, which is itself one of the healthier signs in the contemporary theater. There are critics and theatergoers whose moans are audible when they confront a single performer on stage, as they wonder where the conflict, action and scenery have gone. There are, of course, one-man shows that are stifling in their solipsism: people we would avoid at a party cornering us with their harangues. But there can be genius in this form, depending on the imagination of the actor-author. Fred Curchack and Robert Lepage are the inverse of those Broadway shows which through technological advances try to overwhelm an audience with special effects.

Although Bill Irwin often interacts with a sidekick on stage, the root of his performance is himself as a clown. From the time that he first stepped into a theatrical trunk and walked down inside it as if descending the stairs in a lighthouse, one knew there was brilliance afoot. Speaking of feet, there is Irwin in his lean shoes, tilting as far forward as gravity (or his balance) will permit, while keeping all comedy in his mind's eye, or, one might say, in our eye's mind. He tricks our sight, making a theatergoer wonder at his perspective. Is there really a bump in the floor? If not, why does Irwin keep tripping over the exact same spot? He is the paradigm of postmodern New Vaudeville, even as he pays homage to Buster Keaton and other great clowns.

Innovators of this period have roots reaching back to Surrealism and to Artaud. In their art, the past is very much intertwined with the present. Many owe a debt to Samuel Beckett, and New Vaudeville was certainly inspired by old vaudeville. Were Bert Lahr alive today, he might be considered a New Vaudevillian. But the artists are very much of their times and they are often more responsive to their times than one might normally think. It is often said (inaccurately) that Robert Wilson's art is all images and no ideas. Certainly the visual is the strongest element in his work, whether he is doing an original piece or reinterpreting an opera. One cannot read a Wilson text and have a proper understanding of how the piece appears in performance. But there is a firm intellectual, if not an ideological base to his work, and there is commentary on the life and times of Sigmund Freud, Albert Einstein and other objects of his explorations. There is no more political theater writer than Mac Wellman, whose every work accosts conservatism and normalcy, which is why he has had such a running battle with Jesse Helms and other self-proclaimed protectors of public morality.

Integral to all this is the question of performance art, a variety of theater that is as nebulous as Orion. Trying to define it, the Cambridge Guide to American Theater says, "A performance art work can occur anywhere and be of any duration. It can also be entirely conceptual and exist only in the mind." Or, more importantly, one can only experience it in the moment. It can be taped or filmed but the recorded experience will never equal the live one, the direct encounter between the theatergoer (who can be enlisted as a participant) and the artist. In the land of performance art, the sui generis is king.

For all the emphasis on performance art, the period has also seen the emergence of important new playwrights. In the 1960s, Sam Shepard and Lanford Wilson arrived on the scene, both from the heartland of America: Shepard, the balladeer of folk heroes, including rock stars and gamblers; Wilson, the poet of wistful dreams and failed illusions. Before following their individual paths, Shepard and Wilson were endemic to Off Off Broadway. Their plays were done for small audiences at places like Caffe Cino, La Mama and Theater Genesis. Soon they began commanding a larger, but no less intense following, Shepard in regional as well as New York theater, Wilson largely through the Circle Repertory Company. Until it ended in 1996, the Circle, as led by Marshall W. Mason, was one of the principal discoverers of new American plays. If Wilson's colleagues did not often write on his level, at least many had promise and their work was presented under the best possible circumstances. The Circle contributed not only playwrights but also designers and actors, and a theatrical genre. Labeled lyrical realism, the plays may have derived from a traditional base, but they were bold in terms of subject matter, as in Wilson's *The Fifth of July*, which was one of the earliest intelligent treatments of the aftermath of the Vietnam war.

The Circle Rep was not the only significant theater to close during this time. Some simply suffered from a natural attrition, but others left a vacuum. At the same time, new companies sprang up: the New York Theater Workshop, the Atlantic Theater Company, the Blue Light Theater, the Vineyard Theater, the Drama Department and the New Group, proving that talent sometimes can rely on itself, if the commitment and a sense of direction are firmly in place. By devoting an entire season to a single playwright, the Signature Theater Company shifted the emphasis away from the individual play to the body of work, and gave theatergoers a full sampling of such writers as Romulus Linney and Horton Foote.

As always, the demands of maintaining a profession drew writers, directors and actors to movies and television. There was not ample work for them in the live theater, at least not if they wanted to stay in New York. Just as actors have long periods of unemployment, there are few fulltime playwrights, as many combine creative roles, writing screenplays, directing, teaching, or, in several cases, acting. Sam Shepard balanced his career as a movie actor with his role as a playwright, and continued to probe deeply into the malaise of the American family, where identity could shift on a whim. Returning home after a long absence, a son is not recognized. Nor does he recognize his roots. He is a stranger in his past. The titles of Shepard's visceral plays are filled with words like buried, curse and lie. He is a truth salvager but in a world spinning out of control (like Jesurun's free-flying set), it is difficult to distinguish verity from mendacity. With an idiosyncratic ingeniousness, Wallace Shawn turned the tables on seemingly familiar characters, so that theatergoers found themselves listening to - and caught up by - determinedly wrong-headed people.

It was David Rabe, who staked out war as his dramatic territory, showing us the terror of men in battle and men after battle. Eventually he was to move to the war at home and in *A Question of Mercy* to AIDS and assisted suicide. Gay writers like Tony Kushner and Larry Kramer had a crucial impact on contemporary theater, but gay issues were no longer their exclusive province. Many of the finest women playwrights wrote in a style that might have once been categorized as masculine. Would one ever think of describing a male playwright as feminine? From males and females, across the board, there was a breaking of fences (and of lances). Subject a play to a blindfold test, and one might easily mistake the gender or race of the author, except perhaps for David Mamet.

Mamet strode in from Chicago, with a distinctively urban, male voice, creating a street patois of his own as the repressed in society took to cheating and petty crime to improve their position and their self-worth. Mamet's eye matched

Mamet's ear, for conjuring the precisely revealing image, the moment when "God forbid the inevitable should occur." Repeatedly, the playwright caught his characters off guard, as if they did not know they were creatures of Mamet. Despite his hard-edged veneer, he could also have his reflective side, looking back ruefully on the terrors of childhood. The new Chicago, fresh as a breeze off Lake Michigan, has both a spontaneity and an immediacy, a tradition passed along from the Second City to the Steppenwolf Theater Company.

August Wilson found in the history of blacks in America rising and falling patterns of behavior, as people moved off the land and into the city, taking with them their music and their myths. With the focus moving away from Broadway, artists of various backgrounds, ethnicities, attitudes and predilictions enhanced the theater. The early plays of Ed Bullins and Amiri Baraka were a harbinger, leading all the way to Suzan-Lori Parks, who in her jaggedly poetic plays sees the black experience through a kaleidoscope darkly. At the same time, Hispanic-American writers from Miguel Piñero (a former prison inmate who embodied his own message) to Eduardo Machado recognized the importance of the individuality of their experience (universality could come naturally). With a prismatic sense of irony, David Henry Hwang looked at the adjustment difficulties of immigrants in America. One of many firm believers in non-traditional casting, Tisa Chang, head of the Pan Asian Repertory Theater, discovered new writers and also had classics of Western theater played out by Asian-American actors.

One of the most significant changes was the opening of opportunities for women. In 1972, six women playwrights whose work was largely non-naturalistic banded together in an alliance to encourage productions of plays by themselves and their peers, and also to expand women's opportunities as directors, designers and producers. That collective, the Women's Theater Council, did not endure, but gradually female artists began to proliferate. They found their individual way in the theatrical landscape, inspired by the Actors Theater of Louisville's annual New Play Festival, Julia Miles's Women's Project and Productions and the Susan Smith Blackburn Prize.

Marsha Norman explored the psyches of a former inmate and a determined suicide and Beth Henley and Jane Martin used down-home regional humor to uncover the latent dreams of women entrapped in a familial or marital environment. Other writers searching for greater truth looked to illness, illegal immigration, bigotry, bias and misogyny through the ages. In common with Rabe, Lavonne Mueller scrutinizes men at war. Naomi Wallace takes an uncompromising approach to such unlikely subjects as the slaughterhouse and the black plague. With her fantasist's view of history repeating itself, Caryl Churchill fastforwards across the centuries. They and others banish theatrical stereotypes. When the Women's Project celebrated its 20th anniversary in 1997, I moderated a panel of female playwrights and asked them if there were any areas of self-censorship, in other words, if any taboos still existed. Most of them responded that if they felt a subject was considered taboo, that was precisely when they chose to write about it.

Charles Ludlam - actor, playwright and clown, and Ridiculous in all his guises - was the self-styled "scourge of human folly." Recycling culture from the past, he created a body of work that could be called *Detritus Regained*. Drawing from popular culture and classic forms (puppetry, commedia dell'arte) he made contributions that were substantive as well as stylistic. Puppetry itself became a valuable arm of the avant garde, with Theodora Skipitares and Julie Taymor employing it as an extension of their skylarking imagination. Taymor's trajectory from experimental theater to the most popular form of entertainment (her stage musical version of Disney's animated cartoon, *The Lion King*) proves that innovative artists can help to alter public perception. Using techniques perfected in works like *Juan Darien*, Taymor takes advantage of Hollywood's bottomless resources for her own dazzling purposes. She is the first to make this transition into the public consciousness, but Robert Wilson, Bill Irwin, Martha Clarke and others also have that potential.

Artists from abroad have made their own definable impact, and can stand as icons to American experimentalists. In Sweden, Ingmar Bergman, a rare director with brilliant careers both in film and on stage, took a radical approach to Strindberg, Ibsen and O'Neill. In England, Deborah Warner boldly reinterpreted Shakespeare while also allowing a space to speak for itself, as in her *St. Pancras Project*, a journey in which, one by one, theatergoers walked through an abandoned hotel that had been reactivated with sounds and suggestions of events. This was a clear case of a "sight" (as well as "site") specific environment. Though rooted in Paris, Brook continues to have a worldwide influence with his ongoing investigations of the theatrical past, from Shakespeare to Beckett, at the same time that he found inspiration in literary and folkloric sources.

There are people who try to reinvent theater and there are others who deconstruct it, and the line of demarcation is not always easily identifiable. Often it is simply a matter of taste, but one litmus test should be the question of replacement. Is the director simply smashing icons or is there a valid purpose behind the maneuver? Peter Sellars straddles the question. His work with opera has a clarity of purpose even when it diverges drastically from the original: he retains the score. In theater, however, he turns cavalier, as in the destructive production he entitled *A Seagull*, as if he needed to distinguish it from anything remotely resembling Chekhov. In contrast there are venturesome ensemble groups such as Mabou Mines, which unearthed new forms of drama in prose works by Beckett and in the mythification of figures in history and Greek tragedy.

Just when one might have thought that language had been banished, or at least submerged, along came Mac Wellman, David Ives and Eric Overmyer, with their word-spinning circumlocutions about the wayward world we live in. Through them and others we can sense an arc of history. Wellman tracks Dracula swooping down over the New York theater, Ives spoofs the creative process itself, as in *Words Words Words*, in which a gaggle of typewriting monkeys accidentally lurches into lines from Shakespeare, and Overmyer soars through the cultural cosmos with gun and chimera.

Even as explorations continue to take place, there is a discouraging downside, as art is victimized by economics and politics, as the National Endowment for the Arts is assaulted by politicians and as corporate sponsors diversify away from the arts. For some, art is seen as a subversive act, not worthy of public support. The reduction in funding is matched by the timidity of producers and artistic directors, who look for a safety net and are fearful of taking chances. Even in the non-profit theater, experimentation can be supplanted by expediency. Increasingly, regional theaters clone productions of last year's Off Broadway hit. One hopes that in the future there will still be a universe of possibilities for emerging artists. Although theater remains the most collaborative of art forms, it is only through the boldness of individuals that new visions can be seen, new voices can be heard and creativity achieved.

1

ESSAYS AND NOTEBOOKS

A RICH CROP OF WRITING TALENT BRINGS NEW LIFE TO THE AMERICAN THEATER: AUGUST 21, 1977

The American theater is being revitalized by a prolific band of adventurous new young playwrights. Away from the spotlight, working Off Off Broadway and in regional and institutional theaters, they have been sharpening their talents and expanding their possibilities. Late last season, four new playwrights - Michael Cristofer, David Mamet, Albert Innaurato and Christopher Durang - made an impact on the public consciousness. Cristofer's *The Shadow Box* won the Pulitzer Prize and the Tony Award as Best Play. Mamet's *American Buffalo* was named Best American Play of the Year by the New York Drama Critics. Innaurato had two plays produced commercially, *The Transfiguration of Benno Blimpie* and *Gemini*. Durang's *A History of the American Film* had three consecutive, different productions in major regional theaters.

The four men are on the crest of a wave that is buffeting theatrical tradition. For years, new American plays have been, if not exactly anathema, at least a rare commodity. But the theater is changing; it is becoming more hospitable to experimental work.

Ntozake Shange's *For Colored Girls Who Have Considered Suicide/When the Rainbow is Enuf*, which began in a bar on the Lower East Side, is a Broadway success. David Rabe's *Streamers*, a long-run at Lincoln Center, was followed by a profitable Broadway revival of his first play, *The Basic Training of Pavlo Hummel*, starring Al Pacino. Sam Shepard had premieres of three different new plays at the Yale Repertory Theater, McCarter Theater in Princeton and the Royal Court Theater in London. The Manhattan Theater Club ended an outstanding season with Richard Wesley's memorable new work, *The Last Street Play*, a sensitive, humane drama about an over-the-hill street gang surviving on memories of vainglorious days.

These plays - and many others - do not exist in a vacuum. They come from a definable place, and the playwrights have open-ended futures. These are not one-play writers - a home run and back to the dugout - but artists with staying power and growing bodies of work. Apparently, they also have a commitment to the theater. Though occasionally they have been drawn to other pursuits - Wesley, for example, wrote movie comedies for Sidney Poitier and Bill Cosby - live theater is their primary arena for creativity.

Many of them have plays on tap for next season. Wesley's *The Last Street Play* is planned for Broadway, where it may prove to be the first black drama in recentyears to appeal to a broad cross-section of the theatergoing audience. Mamet's *A Life in the Theater,* a joyful look at the artifice of acting and of living, will open Off Broadway in a production starring Ellis Rabb. Durang's *American Film,* a satiric cavalcade of movie myths with an enormous popular potential, may be on Broadway in the spring. Among his many offerings, Joseph Papp has scheduled a new Shange play, *A Photograph,* at the Public Theater. Ronald Ribman's *Cold Storage,* presented last season at the American Place, is now in line for Broadway.

The weather has changed. In America, as in England, there is now opportunity for new playwrights. Broadway is not the new writer's only choice, and, in fact, it may not be his first choice. In terms of technical facility, artistic imagination and quality of performance, enriching - and often more advantageous - productions can be found at the Mark Taper Forum, the Arena Stage in Washington and the Manhattan Theater Club, to name only three outlets.

The emergence of new dramatists in the 1970's is part of a much larger picture. The theater has fragmented and diversified - and in the process it has been strengthened. The American theater is more than Broadway; it is national. The process has been a gradual one.

Led by Tennessee Williams and Arthur Miller, the 1950's promised to be a golden age of American playwriting - but became only a golden age of Williams and Miller. When Edward Albee astonished Broadway in 1962 with *Who's Afraid of Virginia Woolf?* it looked as if he might be an advance scout for an entire expedition of experimentalists from Off Broadway. He was the first - and also the last. Williams, Miller and Albee remain our three name playwrights. Those who attempted to follow Albee found the atmosphere increasingly inhospitable - and in some cases their own talent was lacking. Economics shriveled Off Broadway and forced Broadway to concentrate on musicals, light comedies and pre-sold successes.

The next tide of dramatic writing came Off Off Broadway, in an unaligned array of coffeehouses, churches and lofts. Lanford Wilson and Sam Shepard were - and still are - the two most talented members of this movement. Far from commercial pressures, they wrote plays, actively participated in productions - and never stopped writing. Off Off Broadway was receptive to newcomers with new ideas. Simultaneously, the regional and institutional movement began to expand. Taking a cue from Off Off Broadway, these subsidized theaters deepened their interest in new plays. What first was tokenism - one original work to arouse a subscription audience - in many theaters became a major drive.

A number of companies, such as Joseph Papp's Public Theater and Gordon Davidson's Mark Taper Forum, began scaling production to suit a play's needs - from staged readings to workshops to full performances. The lesson learned was that plays need nurturing and shaping. The traditional Broadway tryout route often had the opposite effect: plays altered, abused or abandoned - wrecks on the way to the automobile graveyard.

Instead of having to wait for a producer to option his play, a writer now has options: somewhere he can find a theater interested in his work. Like David Mamet, he can even start his own theater; the St. Nicholas in Chicago, co-founded by Mamet, is a prime producer of his plays. Or he can gather actors and have a reading in his living room. Annually he can submit a play to the Eugene O'Neill Playwrights Conference in Waterford, Conn., and, if he is lucky, his play will be presented there in the summer. Frequently, the O'Neill ignites a chain reaction, as do such places as the New Dramatists Committee and the Ensemble Studio Theater.

The route can be circuitous, but the result can be a Broadway production, after a play has been seasoned in many other situations. For example, in several months Innaurato's *Gemini* went from a weekend showcase at Playwrights Horizons to the PAF Playhouse in Huntington, L.I. (a small regional theater run by a playwright, Jay Broad, and producing only new plays) to the Circle Repertory Theater Off Broadway, and then to Broadway - always improving but not drastically changing.

Naturally some writers find a particular company more conducive than others and become - in fact or in principle - resident playwrights: Lanford Wilson at the Circle, Ray Aranha at Hartford Stage, Preston Jones at the Dallas Theater Center, Michael Cristofer at the Mark Taper. Foundation grants frequently tie a writer to a company, which can be profitable to both parties.

It would be difficult, if not foolhardy, to attempt to draw a group profile of the playwrights of the 70's. They come from diverse backgrounds. They write in a variety of styles and cannot be grouped under an single label. They are not Angry Young Men - even black playwrights have moved a step beyond radicalism - although they are concerned about their civilization and environment. These are not Absurdists (although some of the plays are absurd) and Albee, Beckett and Pinter are among the primary influences.

The work ranges from the poetic naturalism of Lanford Wilson to the vaudeville travesties of Christopher Durang. David Mamet brings new and original characters into the theater and Sam Shepard re-creates old ones, mythologizing gangsters as well as cowboys and rock stars. The stoops and poolhalls of urban America form an impressionistic foreground for Richard Wesley's studies of black disorientation. In a harsher, more staccato vein, Ed Bullins - by now almost a father figure to other black playwrights - chronicles the black migration from country to city. In her blistering theatrical poetry, Ntozake Shange is passionately concerned with the frustrations of her triply deprived minority: the black woman artist. Miguel Piñero's eye is on the street corner and prison dayroom where recidivism is a fact of life. Ray Aranha discovers demons in our past, while Phillip Hayes Dean finds them knocking at the door. The diversity can be demonstrated within an individual's work. Albert Innaurato, for example, has swung from the Kafkaesque abyss of *Benno Blimpie* to the high spirits of *Gemini*.

In a special category are the directors who also function as playwrights -

Richard Foreman with his Ontological-Hysteric explorations of the inner space of his own daily life; JoAnne Akalaitis's contrapuntal investigations of the connective tissue between the literary and the theatrical; Robert Wilson's sculptural and architectural time-expansions.

Many of these people are in their late 20's and early 30's, a decade younger than most of their British playwright peers. They were children in the 1950's, adolescents in the 1960's. having largely missed the parades of 60's political activism, they find no need to fall into reactionary passivism. They are individuals, not responsive to groups (although many feel a kinship with their fellow playwrights).

The one war that that they all know is Vietnam. David Rabe, who experienced it first hand, deals directly and forcefully with Vietnam as an act of conscience. Richard Wesley in *Strike Heaven on the Face* dealt with it less directly; this was a drama about a war hero driven to homicide. Why does he kill? To many of these writers, violence is not so much inexplicable as inevitable. Why does Teach (Robert Duvall) strike the young man in *American Buffalo* - a blow of such willful intensity that it causes the audience to shudder? Why is the jolly sergeant slain in *Streamers?* Frustration, anguish and rage push characters past limits. Many of them are searching for a situation in which they can function. As in *The Last Street Play*, it is a quest for turf as much as it is for identity. Pavlo Hummel does not enlist as an act of patriotism but because of his need for army-as-family. In Rabe's *Sticks and Bones*, the subject is family-as-army, the embattled American household. Many of these are family plays - with a difference. In place of Albee's sardonic *American Dream* we have the horrifying American nightmare of *Benno Blimpie*, where suppressed thoughts become a direct blow on an adolescent's psyche.

One strong unifying factor is their sense of humor; even the apocalypse can get a laugh. Mamet's wit comes in the use of language, and anyone doubting that should not miss his buoyant *A Life in the Theater.* Lanford Wilson's humor is dry and gentle, whereas Sam Shepard's is rollicking. One of the most exuberant plays of recent years is Oyamo's *The Juice Problem*, about a black electrical repairman who turns on his clients (a comedy that is yet to have a New York production). Before it ends tragically, *The Last Street Play* reminds me of Fellini's *I Vitelloni.* In both works, young toughs flex their bravado but are frightened to death of an aimless future.

Remember Randall Kim as a burglar handcuffed to a radiator in Steve Tesich's *Nourish the Beast*, a helpless victim of the insanely overbearing good will of a modern American family? In Michael Weller's *Moonchildren*, collegians perfect the art of the put-on, blatantly lying - a crescendo of illusions to avoid facing reality. The convict in Miguel Piñero's *Short Eyes* makes us share his laughter as he recounts a masturbatory fantasy.

Of all the new writers, Durang is perhaps the most overtly comic. His most titanic comedy is *A History of the American Film*, which asks if movies were our only artifact, what would we know about our civilization? The play, at its base, a serious commentary on our society, could be called *A Film of American History.*

Of all the new writers, David Rabe is perhaps the most overtly tragic. But does anyone remember how much we laughed during the first half of *Streamers* - before it became a bloodbath?

Periodically, people ask, often on these pages, where the new playwrights are. Some weeks ago, Benedict Nightingale, an English critic, had an answer: in England. Certainly there is an abundance of gifted English playwrights, and I greatly admire many of them. But it is presumptuous for an Englishman living in England to pontificate about the paucity of new American writers. Of course, apart from Wesley, Innaurato, Rabe, Mamet, Cristofer, Shepard, Durang, Wilson, Shange, Bullins, Ribman, Tesich, Piñero, Dean, Aranha, Weller, Jacker, McNally, Medoff, Guare, Jones, Linney and Oyamo, we have almost nobody.

WHAT IS A 'REGIONAL' PLAY?: OCTOBER 14, 1979

The death of Preston Jones at the age of 43 represents a loss for the American, as well as regional, theater. When his *A Texas Trilogy* opened on Broadway in 1976, it was greeted with skepticism and even hostility. These were three overlapping, realistic plays about life in a small Texas town - and the consensus seemed to be: small town, small drama. The plays closed precipitously, and Mr. Jones returned to Dallas to continue writing plays and acting for his home company, the Dallas Theater Center.

The odd fact was that *A Texas Trilogy* traveled well almost everywhere it went - except New York. The plays have been presented successfully at theaters around the country and in London. Clearly, there is something that we missed in New York, but that speaks to a wider constituency. Perhaps we were the ones who were provincial. I do not know how much of the New York reaction was a result of the pre-opening fanfare that compared this promising playwright to Eugene O'Neill and Tennessee Williams. If we had quietly come across one of the plays - I thought that *The Oldest Living Graduate* was the most interesting - in an unheralded production at the Circle Repertory Company, we might have felt differently about the playwright. We might have had the same sense of discovery as we did with the early work of Lanford Wilson, and with the first plays by Mark Medoff and Edward J. Moore. In the spotlight of Broadway, with the added burden of three successive openings, only a triple masterpiece could have survived. It would be premature to make an assessment of Mr. Jones's career. One would have to see more of his plays - and producers are not anxious to do them in New York -and to reconsider the trilogy. But perhaps it is time for us to reevaluate our attitude toward him and related writers.

It was Mr. Jones's fate to be categorized - and diminished - as a regional playwright. The word "regional," as applied to theaters as well as to playwrights, is generally considered to be pejorative. In popular usage, it not only means local, but limited, and even rural. This is despite the fact that regional theaters have pro- liferated in cities from Washington, D.C. to Seattle. In addition, many of the more significant new American plays of recent years have originated at these the- aters - David Rabe's *Streamers*, David Mamet's *American Buffalo*, Michael Weller's *Loose Ends*, Michael Cristofer's *The Shadow Box*, to name just a few. Of course, there is a difference between these plays and *A Texas Trilogy*. They are not inte- gral to their theater of origin. *Streamers*, which began at the Long Wharf, could have been created for the Mark Taper Forum. In common, these plays were first produced at regional theaters, but they are not, definably, regional plays - works that derive from a local source.

An important question is whether a play moves beyond its source or remains landlocked in an insular enclave. Just as David Storey's plays about Yorkshire coal mining families transcend the author's North Country of England, many of America's regionalists - through specificity of landscape, language and character - arrive at general truths about human behavior.

In a recent article, Variety reported that the most produced contemporary playwright in regional theater is Tennessee Williams, followed by Lanford Wilson and Sam Shepard, all three of whom draw inspiration from a particular geo- graphic base - Mr. Williams from the South, Mr. Wilson and Mr. Shepard from the Midwest. In contrast, Arthur Miller, farther down the Variety list, writes plays with apparent universality, but with unspecified roots.

Although Mr. Wilson is not affiliated with a regional company - all of his plays have been done first at the Circle Repertory Company, a New York equiva- lent of a regional theater - he is an outstanding example of a writer who is nour- ished by an environment. His current trilogy, which began with *Talley's Folly* and *The Fifth of July* and will conclude this season with *The War in Lebanon*, takes place over a period of years in and around one family home in Lebanon, Missouri, which happens to be the birthplace of the author. One might surmise that the "war" in Lebanon is that favorite Wilson conflict between tradition and progress. In many of his plays, from *The Hot l Baltimore* to *The Fifth of July*, characters try to reject the past, to replace it with a future that may be progressive but is also im- personal. In Mr. Wilson's *The Mound Builders*, his most metaphorical play, the past becomes a battleground between archeologists and land developers, between pre- servers and destroyers. In his defense of our country - its tradition as well as his- tory - Mr. Wilson is, along with Mr. Shepard, an ecologist.

Theaters as well as writers are still self-conscious about wearing the label "re- gional." Many companies prefer to think of themselves as resident theaters, which is a questionable title. If these companies are resident, it implies that others are transient. Some prefer to be called repertory theaters, which is often a misnomer. Few have permanent troupes of actors or perform plays in rotation, both of which are prerequisites for repertory. Perhaps it is time to reclaim the word regional -

meaning, residing in, and responsive to, a specific community, but cognizant of a more comprehensive artistic responsibility.

BEASTLY HAPPENINGS ON BROADWAY: OCTOBER 28, 1979

After years of obscurity and second-class citizenship, animals are making a comeback in the American theater, reminding audiences of the golden age of animal acting. With renewed vigor, our furred and feathered friends are frequenting audition rooms and rehearsal halls in search of that dream role that can turn a household pet into a household word. Before Sandy made his debut in *Annie*, he was on his way to the dog pound and to probable extinction. Now he has a dressing room and an understudy, a high salary, his own house in Glen Rock, N.J., and he has sold the television rights to his autobiography. There are 10 Sandys in touring companies and, unlike Annies, Sandys never seem to get too old for the part. Broadway's Sandy has already outlasted three Annies.

This year's Tony - or Sandy? - for best animal performance should go to Louie, a springer spaniel starring in *Sugar Babies*. Louie is the dog half of a venerable vaudeville act making its Broadway debut. With his partner, Bob Williams, Louie was supposed to make his Broadway debut several seasons ago in *Hellzapoppin*, but the show closed in Boston. Jerry Lewis never made it to Broadway, but Louie did. In *Sugar Babies*, the dog is considered irreplaceable; for the road company of the show, producer Harry Rigby is thinking about substituting a seal act.

The substitution would undoubtedly be met with a protest. This is the dog role in *Sugar Babies*, and to fill it with a creature of a different species is blatant discrimination. Is there no other dog qualified for the spot? Is there no other Spot qualified to be the dog? Think of all the countless canines who would roll over and play dead for a chance to star opposite Mickey Rooney. Ever since *National Velvet*, he has been a trainer-figure in the world of animals.

There are also 14 doves in *Sugar Babies*, although there were only 12 doves when the show was in Philadelphia. One assumes that the Mark Hellinger Theater is, under union contract, a 14-dove house. Perhaps a pair of bird-walkers sits downstairs under the stage and plays cards during the performance. One of the original 12-dove cast, unhappy with his role in *Sugar Babies*, flew the coop in Philadelphia. He soared out of a window and was last seen headed for a Marlboro sign. That dove has gone commercial.

Mr. Rigby seems to be engaged in a one-man campaign to revive old musicals and to increase career-opportunities for animals. A dog played opposite Debbie Reynolds in Mr. Rigby's production of *Irene*, and in *Good News* the boards were trod by a dog, duck, llama and skunk, which was not good news for the maintenance crew. An elephant was fired on the road after two performances, apparently because he upstaged his co-star, Alice Faye. The elephant decided not to take the matter to arbitration.

The success story of this season may be Hermione, a funny duck in *Scrambled Feet*, the Off Broadway comedy revue about the theater. Hermione was rescued from a poultry market and now shares billing and curtain calls with four human actors. Interestingly, today's successful animal actors do not have to fall back on stereotyped routines and audience expectations. Hermione does not have to quack in order to get laughs. Despite his partner's pleading, Louie the dog never performs a trick. He wins the audience with acting technique, reaching far back to his pup-hood to find a sense memory that will help him present an indelible portrait of a deadpan dog.

Up to now, the theater, unlike the cinema, has not been particularly hospitable to horses, although there is a horse in the stage version of *Snow White* at the Radio City Music Hall. Perhaps it is the sheer size of the animal that limits its opportunities on stage. But horses figure prominently in dramatic literature. In *Equus*, the horsiest show since *Three Men on a Horse*, actors cantered and pranced, and a real horse never had a change to neigh for a part. When the Chelsea Theater Center mounted its production of Tolstoy's *Strider: The Story of a Horse*, in an overt disregard of equine rights, an actor, Gerald Hiken, was chosen to play the title role. No consideration was given to background and experience, and Mr. Hiken was surrounded by a pack of actors and actresses pretending to be a team of horses. The idea of American actors playing Russian horses is damaging to international relations. However, the Russians have been slow to recognize our copyright laws, and perhaps it is only fitting that we should be slow to recognize the thespian talents of their animals. Besides, think of the expense that would entail if one tried to airlift horses from Moscow. And, once faced with the improved chances for artistic fulfillment, any horse with sense might defect.

The issue of actors playing roles that should be reserved for animals is a serious one. As opportunities in the theater expand, more and more animals will prepare to enter show business, and then find that some doors will remain closed. Opponents of full utilization of our animal resources may point to tradition: animals are for circuses, actors are for the theater. But let a lion try to do a highwire act and the Wallendas would be up in arms. Tradition also means that certain specific roles are ritualistically filled by humans. One of the leading characters in *Peter Pan* is Nana, the St. Bernard, a shaggy symbol of caninely love and affection; yet, the character is always played by a human in hair suit. This is a role well within the range of Sandy and Louie.

Similarly, in Charles Ludlam's fable *The Enchanted Pig*, pigs are played by people. Any actor thinks he can put on a porcine face and play a pig. Ridiculous! Ever since Miss Piggy became a movie star - positive proof that there is more in a pig than meets the sty - pigs have risen in the national estimation. But real pigs, pigeonholed by preconceptions, have not yet left the barnyard.

Cats have also not been in great demand, although one, a cat named Uncle Elizabeth, did play an important role in the musical *I Remember Mama*. As the pet of Liv Ullmann's youngest daughter, the cat had to act out a death scene worthy of Camille, and then come back to life. It was a difficult role, but the cat was up to the challenge, transcending all his or her previous performances.

Chickens have probably been the least fortunate actors in the American theater. As plucky as they are sensitive, they are simply not accepted as professionals. Typecast as street fighters, they are like athletes turned artists. One cannot forget their natural bailiwick. You can take a chicken out of a coop, but you can't guarantee residuals. The original chicken who started in *The Best Little Whorehouse in Texas* - was pecked to death by his jealous understudy, who had spent too many hours watching reruns of *All About Eve* on television. Three chickens, all unbilled, have since played the part in *Whorehouse*. The search continues for the perfect pullet, or poulet for the French company.

Any day an enterprising American producer will bring over a London hit with an animal in the cast. Depending on the role, it may be advisable to employ an English animal; one would not want to take a chance on losing authenticity. In some cases, the role could be recast with an American animal, but many eligible candidates would not have the proper training or breeding, particularly if they are playing Shakespeare. With American dogs, their Bard is worse than their bite. Applying the criteria of Actors Equity, animals would have to be stars of international stature in order to work on the American stage. Such a rigid doctrine would exclude many collies, setters and Cheshire cats that have a particular affinity for their native culture. Equity's response, of course, would be that the policy should be reciprocal - kit for cat, or, what's sauce for the English goose is sauce for the American gander. Equity would probably also be firm about protecting animals from showcase productions, insisting that they receive 20 percent of a theater's annual budget. Anything else would be chicken feed.

The theater is an insecure business and, in common with all actors, animals are subjected to the whim of producers, the guile of directors and the ire of critics (although few critics have been known to attack a pet performance). One season's star is next season's goat, and one season's goat is next season's white elephant. One of the most disciplined goat performances in recent Broadway history was given last year in *Carmelina*. While this musical was trying out, as the book was reworked and songs were rewritten, there was one major constant: the goat honed his performance as the show moved to Broadway. *Carmelina* closed and everyone including the goat lost his job, but unlike his co-stars, the goat was not eligible for unemployment insurance. As George Orwell might have said, some actors are more equal than others.

EPIC DRAMATIZATION OF A DICKENS NOVEL: JULY 6, 1980

LONDON - The Royal Shakespeare Company's production of Charles Dickens's *Nicholas Nickleby* is a monumental theatrical experience. Performed in two parts in alternating repertory over a period of eight and one half hours, the play, as adapted by David Edgar, synthesizes the book's 65 chapters into five densely textured, incident-filled acts. Every major character in the novel is represented on stage - some 150 played by 45 quick-changing actors.

Instead of dramatizing a portion of the novel, or limiting the scope to the dramatic high points as in the movies based on Dickens, the company has undertaken the more difficult task of consuming the entire text and recreating it as an epic play.

This is as close to a complete *Nicholas Nickleby* as one could imagine within the boundaries of theatrical artifice. A collaborative venture among the actors, the adaptor and the company-directors, Trevor Nunn and John Caird, it is a kind of live *Masterpiece Theater* mini-series - and something more.

Most of the dialogue is direct from Dickens; it is ornate without being fustian. Wisely, Mr. Edgar has also retained a taste of the original descriptive text. In an exemplary use of the Story Theater method, actors issue occasional commentary on their actions and those of others, underscore attitudes and stitch transitions. As chorus, singly and in unison, the company characterizes " this wilderness of London," where wealth and poverty stand side by side. The play does not shortchange Dickens's pronounced social conscience, showing, among other things, how the burden of money affects those who need it as well as those who have it.

Essential to this compassionate collage is the contribution of the designers, John Napier and Dermot Hayes, who have reconstructed the interior of the Aldwych Theater, sending a ramp through the orchestra, building catwalks around the balcony, and filling the stage with bridges and staircases so that it looks like an arcaded city street. Interspersing actors with stagehands and using sliding platforms, the directors orchestrate scene changes with a logistical felicity that borders on the awesome.

This is one environmental production that really profits from that approach. Before the play begins, actors amble through the audience, passing out crumpets along with conversation. During the performance, there is direct, spontaneous reaction from theatergoers. Actors make entrances from the theater's exit doors and, when not participating, they watch the action from parapets and also mingle on stage as part of the hubbub of London.

Using improvisatory techniques, the actors hold chairs and march in close order-drill miming an omnibus and then, almost without pause, they swivel and use the chairs to simulate a night at the opera. Coaches clatter, a horse rears up on its hind legs - and all through the magic of theatrical ingenuity. Lights change from ominous urban gloom to the warmth of a homey hearthside. Repeatedly, we catch the characters not posing but composed for a group portrait; it is almost as if there is a lithographer at work just offstage.

The changes in character tumble by so quickly that we often lose sight of the identity of individual actors behind wigs, beards and costumes. A cross-check in the program - four pages for the cast - clarifies some of the astonishing transformations.

The production is a paradigm of the art of transformation - from actors into a diversity of characters, from theater today into England of the 1830's, from narrative into drama. The work has an authenticity that surpasses that in any other stage adaptation of Dickens that I have seen. The wretchedness of actual conditions is juxtaposed next to the remembered bliss of "bygone days and childhood times." Dastardly evil is vanquished by selfless heroism. The latter is, of course, incarnated by the title character.

Facing penury with his widowed mother and his beautiful sister Kate, young Nicholas is forced to seek protection from his rich uncle Ralph, a cold and cunning usurer who takes advantage of the vulnerability of his relatives. Nicholas is sent off to be assistant master in a Yorkshire school that is as horrid as a medieval prison and Kate is offered up by her uncle as enticement to jaded and rapacious London aristocrats. Nicholas's awakening to injustice is a stroke of lightning. He suddenly whips the inhumane schoolmaster and runs away in company with the forlorn Smike, the outcast who becomes his devoted Sancho Panza.

As in the novel, there are subplots within subplots, some of which could have been plays by themselves - Nicholas's peregrinations with Mr. Crummles's provincial theatrical troupe; Kate's woeful employment at a millinery company; the contented Cheeryble brothers, a pair of Saint Nicholases in a counting house; even the minor saga of Nicholas's platitudinous mother and her daintily amorous exploits.

The script seems to omit nothing, but it does make minor alterations and elisions. We see Kate take a more active role than in the book; she accompanies her brother on some of his journeys and is more self-possessed and assertive.

There is one notable addition. Where Dickens simply alluded to Nicholas playing Romeo with that provincial troupe, the R.S.C. closes the first half of its *Nicholas Nickleby* with a hilarious, rewritten version turning tragedy into joy, with all the slain (except for Tybalt) miraculously returning to life.

In the course of the two parts, there are a few random references that have a special contemporary meaning. For example, Mr. Crummles regrets the defection of some of his actors to a theater "hard by the bank at Waterloo." presumably an early 19th-century equivalent of the R.S.C.'s competitor, the National Theater.

The changes are all in the interest of playfulness. Repeatedly, the R.S.C. tries to alleviate the work's potential heaviness. This is not a musical, but it has incidental music and occasional songs. A number of scenes are offered simultaneously. Reading Dickens, we frequently face an interlude of several chapters before arriving at an earlier conclusion. On stage, one "chapter" is counterpointed with another.

The production is dominated by Roger Rees as Nicholas, a marathon challenge for an actor and one that he meets without faltering. He has the necessary intensity and impulsiveness; chance carries the character from one act of passion to another. Mr. Rees keeps Nicholas highstrung, as if he is about to be overwhelmed by his own idealism. Only he and David Threlfall as Smike do not double in roles.

Mr. Threlfall has to externalize as well as internalize his character. Outwardly, he is deformed - a body twisted in knots - a mouth constantly agape. Inwardly, he is saintly. As played by this young Englishman, Smike becomes a country cousin to *The Elephant Man* - and an equally gripping characterization. As Kate, Susan Littler projects a sense of insulted innocence and also of resilience. Nothing can deflect her, or her resolute brother, from their convictions.

The gallery of villainy moves from John Woodvine's imperious uncle, whose mind is totally obsessed with money, to Ben Kingsley's Fagin-esque schoolmaster, with Lila Kaye as his sadistic wife and Suzanne Bertish as his smug, drab daughter. The mercurial Miss Bertish also plays Juliet to Nicholas's Romeo and a cackling crone.

Representing the other side of humanity is Edward Petherbridge as Newman Noggs, the uncle's clerk, a former gentleman who has fallen on hard times, an eminently decent soul who, though sometimes dimmed by alchohol, never diminishes in gallantry. More than anyone, Newman manipulates the happy ending. Moving at sharp angles, shadow boxing his frustration, cracking his knuckles in despair at his master's vileness, Mr. Petherbridge delivers the play's most indelibly Dickensian performance.

Among the many other outstanding members of the ensemble is Bob Peck, who artfully switches back and forth between the haughty malice of the suave Sir Mulberry Hawk and the rustic heartiness of the honest Yorkshire lad, John Browdie.

Each half of the play is self-sustaining and can be seen separately. The second half begins with a speedy recapitulation of the preceding events. However, for maximum enjoyment the work should be seen in sequence in its entirety. I saw it all in one day, at a matinee and an evening performance, beginning at two P.M. and ending at 11:30 P.M, with an hour for dinner. My feeling at the end of the doubleheader was one of satisfaction, not satiety.

As the actors took the last of many curtain calls, it appeared as if they were as reluctant to leave our company as we were to leave theirs. Even though all wrongs were righted and all plot strands were knitted neatly together, one still hoped that there could be more to the story, which is, of course, the reaction we have when we read the book. The R.S.C.'s *Nicholas Nickleby* is a great novel turned into grand theater.

IS THE THEATER ALL A JUGGLING ACT?: MAY 14, 1981

Tossing a tennis ball up and down in one hand, Michael Davis says, "It's not what you do, but how you do it." Mr. Davis is joking, but he is also clearly a man of style. He is an inspired juggler-comic - a distinguished hyphenate once worn by W.C. Fields. Mr. Davis survived the wreckage of the short-lived *Broadway Follies* and has gone on to assume a featured role in *Sugar Babies.* How is the newcomer faring in his second Broadway show of the season? A deadpan comedian in broad, burlesque surroundings, he is next to last on the bill, a choice spot, the vaudeville equivalent of batting third in a baseball lineup. He has 13 solo minutes in the spotlight, time to offer a distillation of the Davis art.

Walking on stage with the timidity of another Smothers Brother, he illustrates the range of the juggler: he juggles water (splash, splash, splash go his hands in a wash basin) and then switches from comedy to a death-defying stunt. He tosses three wicked weapons in the air - a machete, an ax and a meat cleaver. In this particular case, it's what you do and how you do it. While the arsenal is still flying - a large vicious circle - he looks helplessly at the audience in the hope that some stranger may be able to give him guidance on how to end the dangerous routine without losing a limb. If you think you see him accidentally drop an item, he says, it is an optical illusion. Mr. Davis is so nimble with his hands and so quick with his timing that his whole magical act seems like an optical illusion.

❖ ❖ ❖

If you liked *Sugar Babies,* you will still like *Sugar Babies.* Mickey Rooney and Ann Miller are performing with their customary gusto, with Mr. Rooney zipping through a cavalcade of burlesque routines, including a stint dressed as a woman. In costume, Mr. Rooney is a short knobby-kneed witch in a fright-wig. Actually, this is one of the actor's most appealing impersonations, and it immediately brings to mind the company called "Bloolips," which is performing the transvestite musical *Lust in Space* to appreciative fans at the downtown Orpheum Theater. In costume, the Bloolips, who are six Englishmen, are no more feminine than Mr. Rooney, though some of them would stand a better chance of winning a beauty contest.

Just as *Sugar Babies* represents the indigenous American tradition of burleque, *Bloolips* is an example of English music-hall comedy. The show is longer than it need be, and its ragtag story line about a trip to the moon is a slim excuse for tom-foolery. But the Bloolips are bizarrely funny. It's not what you do, but how you do it. They tap-dance with clattering precision, harmonize with old-sounding tunes and never forget the parodistic nature of their endeavor, imitating everyone from dimwitted ingénues to flamboyant femmes fatales. The costumes, as devised by the company, are an unfashion show of unparalleled tackiness. One Bloolip is a twin for old Miss Havisham in *Great Expectations*, even down to his/her gray/whey face; there is a chorus line of cheeses (from cottage to gorgonzola), and there is one outfit so encumbered with objects that it becomes a collage of consumables, making its wearer look like an animated grocery cart.

As we watch the all-male cast in its plasticized plumage and garish makeup, we realize that the Bloolips are not female impersonators so much as circus clowns. The jokes, by the way, are no more or less suggestive than those in *Sugar Babies*. In each case, one might say that the entertainment is a triumph of talent over material.

Ian McKellen's recent single performance of his one-man show, *Acting Shakespeare*. was a triumph of talent and material. Mr. McKellen did his solo act one evening, after a matinee of *Amadeus*, for the benefit of the Shakespeare Globe Theater Center of London. It was truly an astonishing performance - comical, tragical, historical, critical and anecdotal. Mr. McKellen is an actor-scholar. He took Macbeth's "tomorrow and tomorrow" soliloquy and gave it a thick Scots burr, turning it into a comic monologue. Then he parsed the same speech for meaning, analyzing it with the erudition of an Oxford don. Finally, he spoke it, beautifully, in the context of the play, surrounded by other soliloquies.

Often, one-man shows are dry and self-indulgent; Mr. McKellen's show was a feat of acting. He played Prince Hal and Falstaff each impersonating Henry IV, did both Romeo and Juliet, and told tales about Shakespeareans from Burbage through Olivier. When John Gielgud was asked by a young actor for advice on how to play Lear, Mr. McKellen reported, Sir John said, "Find a small Cordelia."

For two hours at the Broadhurst Theater, the actor enraptured his audience, which gave him one of this season's few deserved standing ovations. If there is any doubt that Mr. McKellen is the natural heir to Laurence Olivier, *Acting Shakespeare* is the final proof.

Actors are indefatigable, even as fate and casting agents buffet them into as-suming alternate occupations. There are actor-waiters, bartenders, typists, cab-drivers, house cleaners and salesmen. One actor-waiter zoomed from serving fettucine Alfredo to playing opposite Richard Burton in *Equus* on Broadway.

For some actors, part-time pursuits can become running roles in their lives. One experienced actor is a successful dealer in rare books. Others take up such skilled professions as house painting, cabinetmaking, catering and carpentry. I know a team of actor-carpenters, who are both fine actors and fine carpenters. Once, when they were installing a bookcase in our apartment, the telephone rang, and one of them obligingly answered it. It was a critic friend of mine. Hearing his name, the actor introduced himself and reminded him that in one review he had said that his performance should be "enshrined within a national theater." Briefly buoyed by that memory, the actor returned to his hammering.

At a neighborhood market, there is a young man with a most unusual alternate occupation; he is an actor-butcher. Between auditions, he works at the meat counter, or, if you will, between trimming and weighing, he reads for roles in the theater. He is eager and intelligent and, doubtless, he is a good actor. He is certainly a good butcher, and he is proud of his extra talent.

When he has to fill in "work experience" on his actor's resumé, he writes "meat-cutting," which must give producers and agents faint heart. His current ambition is to win a role in the projected Broadway musical version of Arnold Weinstein's *The Red Eye of Love*. The play takes place in the world's largest meat supermarket. The central character and the tap-dancing chorus are all butchers.

When I mentioned the existence of an actor-butcher to one playwright, he suggested that a more apt hyphenate would be a critic-butcher. Obviously he was speaking from his own experience on the firing line; critics have been known to wield a cleaver. I would suggest that playwright-butcher might be an equally apt hyphenate. A dramatist who is educated in the art of butchering might learn to trim the fat from his prose, pare the gristle of his plot and keep his thumb off the script.

DAREDEVIL MUSICAL PROVIDES SOME NOVEL CREDITS: AUGUST 10, 1982

There are two novel credits in the program for Des McAnuff's *The Death of von Richthofen as Witnessed from Earth*, a daredevil musical at the Public Theater. The credits are "Automation and Flying Rigs by Feller Precision Inc." and "Dog by Fred Nihde." One assumes that Feller Precision is the Feller scene shop, a primary builder of traditional, three-walled stage rooms and that concern is now apparently making an advance into the aerospace industry.

As designed by Douglas W. Schmidt, *von Richthofen* takes lavish advantage of all sorts of flying and falling devices. The baron himself (John Vickery) climbs into a mockup of a World War I fighting plane, which looks like a mechanical mutation of a praying mantis, and he flies 10 feet off the ground. There is also a scene in the basket of a flying balloon (several seasons ago at the Yale Repertory Theater in *An Attempt at Flying*, there was an actual hot-air balloon on stage).

At various moments in *von Richthofen* an aviator floats down to his death and a field soldier rises into the sky while playing a piano. At one point, Mr. Vickery appears to levitate, a magic trick for which one could perceive no wires. Mr. Schmidt is a proved master at such technological wizardry. He placed a railroad car on stage for *The Crazy Locomotive* (directed by Mr. McAnuff at the Chelsea Theater Center) and was the inventor of the mad doctor's laboratory in the play *Frankenstein*. When *von Richthofen* closes, the scenery could be transplanted to the Smithsonian Institution's Air and Space Museum, to be on exhibition along with such American classics as the Spirit of St. Louis and the Starship Enterprise.

Mr. Nihde's Dog fits more naturally under the category of properties (for critics it is often as difficult to differentiate between scenery and properties as it is between direction and performance). The dog is a large inanimate wolfhound, the baron's pet, which sits silently on stage for the entire evening, with his tail tied to a desk with a red bow. For the record, its name is Moritz, not Snoopy. As for the actors, it is one thing to be upstaged by animals and children, quite another to be upstaged by a stuffed dog.

To move from taxidermy to horticulture, aficionados of anthropomorphism should luxuriate in the musical *Little Shop of Horrors*, which recently reopened Off Broadway at the Orpheum Theater after a previous engagement at the WPA. This is a diabolical musical about a killer cactus that wants to eat New York. The centerpiece of the evening is the plant itself, named Audrey II. It is designed and manipulated by Martin P. Johnson, who served his apprenticeship with such puppeteers as Bil Baird and Jim Henson and continues to play Mr. Snuffleupagus on *Sesame Street*. Nourished by a diet of human blood, the plant grows larger and larger until it occupies the entire stage and threatens to devour the audience. Is Audrey II scenery, a prop or a costume? I prefer to think of it as a floral arrangement.

From hothouse Audrey, we can move around the world to Ming Cho Lee's flash-frozen setting for Patrick Meyers's *K2*, a play about mountain climbers that was presented last spring at the Arena Stage in Washington. For this adventure, the designer created an astonishingly lifelike glacier. A chill ran through the theater every time the actor Stephen McHattie had to climb straight up the icy wall. Late in the play an avalanche on stage frightened theatergoers in the front rows.

After my review of *K2* appeared, I received a call from the Syracuse Stage Company, which was offering its own production of the play, on a lower budget, in a stylized setting. This version apparently met with the playwright's approval because it put the emphasis on his words rather than feats of daring by actors. In all fairness to Mr. Meyers, it is difficult to imagine *K2* without a mountain. To rephrase F. Scott Fitzgerald's famous dictum, scenery is character.

∽

ON LATE CURTAINS, BLABS AND THE BRITISH: SEPTEMBER 9, 1984

Once while I was writing a theater review on a computer, the words began to disappear and, in a matter of seconds, the entire review was replaced by a long scroll of question marks. This was the critic's nightmare - as compared to the actor's nightmare, in which the actor forgets his lines in the middle of a play and wonders what he is doing on stage. The incident left one awestruck. It was as if someone had questioned the review, the point of view, the play being discussed and the critic's very existence. That day the Force was not with me. Since then, I have been on the alert when confronting a computer, so it was without surprise the other day when a terminal began talking back - asking questions instead of creating question marks. The cross-examination dealt with audiences, actors and the audio-visual aspects of being in a theater; in other words, we never got past the letter "A," before I purged the interrogation.

Q: Why is it that plays in New York never begin at the announced time? The curtain goes up at least five, usually 10 and sometimes as much as 30 minutes late.

A: Theaters are trying to measure the audience's threshold of patience. It is the theatrical equivalent of the stress test some expensive restaurants inflict on their customers. How much bad service are you willing to put up with in order to have the privilege of paying top dollar for an evening of indeterminate pleasure? Short shows are historic late-starters, just to assure that all plays will end at exactly the same time - doubling the difficulty of finding a taxicab after the curtain.

Q: Why are intermissions so long?

A: Intermissions are like school fire drills. They are to test the accessibility of exits, to determine how quickly one could leave a theater in case of emergency. The answer is, very slowly, up the center aisle.

Q: If you were a civilian rather than a critic, what guidelines would you use in deciding what shows to see?

A: One guideline that I would not use would be quotations from critics in advertisements and on billboards outside of the theater. They are often misrepresentations of what critics have actually written. Producers have special sonar equipment that can scan reviews and obliterate all negative comment. What is left is an abundance of honorific adjectives (riveting, exhilarating, marvelous) without reference to a context. Shake them up in a jar, add a twist and serve cold. If one wrote that an actor was "astonishing" - that adjective will undoubtedly be used to describe the entire show. There is also a special electronic switch that inserts a period before every critical "but." This button is commonly know as the Qualifier Deterrent. No buts about it. Critics' quotations are referred to as blurbs; as reworked in the interest of salesmanship they should be called blabs. Once I had the temerity to refer to a work as "the best American play of the season," and received a call from someone associated with the show who asked if it would be all right to alter the quote to "the best American comedy of the season," because the world "comedy" sells more tickets than "play."

Q: What does a producer do when all the reviews are negative but he still wants to keep the show running?

A: As David Mamet said in a different context in *American Buffalo*, "God forbid the inevitable should occur." In that case, the producer takes a simple statement of fact from a review, a description, follows it with an exclamation point and tries to pretend that it is a blab, as "An evening of poetry!," followed by the critic's name. Producers in London do not face this problem.

Q: Why not?

A: Because there are more critics in London, and there is always someone who writes something favorable about a show. If in doubt there is the Daily Mail. "I loved it, Daily Mail" must be permanently set in type at British advertising agencies. Because there is no statute of limitations on quotations, they live forever, and, occasionally, so does the show. *No Sex Please, We're British* has been running so long in London that it is on tourist maps along with Madame Tussaud's Wax Museum. Outside its current theater - it is trying to play all of the theaters in its journey around the West End - is my favorite critic's quotation: "The audience were falling about." What audience - and when? The image I have is of a grand prix tournament of Chinese gymnasts. On cue, all of them fall out of their seats. Now representing the United States in the Olympic synchronized rolling-in-the-aisle competition is last Saturday's matinee audience at *Noises Off*. Perhaps that ancient, now arthritic, original opening-night audience at *No Sex Please, We're British* continues to free-fall about in space.

My second favorite West End quotation appears outside the theater where *The Real Thing* is playing. The quote reads, "I was knocked for six!" Upon investigation, I discovered that this was a pithy way of saying, "I was so overwhelmed by the experience of seeing the play that I felt as if I were a cricket ball knocked out of the park." What is most unusual about the expression is the use of the first person. Imagine an American critic writing about *The Real Thing* - or anything "I was hit for a home run."

Speaking of English audiences, that reminds me of a story. Through a computer error, for one performance of a current London production of a major American musical, the same seat location was accidently printed on every single ticket in the house. Just think - more than 1,000 people sitting, spoon style, in each other's lap, teetering 10 times as high as Big Ben. God forbid the inevitable should occur and a theatergoer should decide to fall about.

Q: In their reviews, why don't critics mention audience reaction? If the audience enjoys a show, shouldn't that fact be recognized in the review?

A: Is the audience enjoying the show or has the producer papered the house with laughers - or are the backers simply laughing at the absurdity of ever recovering their investment? Is the laughter the real thing or the flash-frozen variety? Besides, each theatergoer has his own taste. One man's meat is another man's poisson. A critic is in the house to offer his assessment, not that of the man dozing in the seat next to him.

Q: What should actors do if an accident occurs in the course of a performance?

A: Ignore it, unless it happens on stage. At a recent performance of a comedy, one of the actors suddenly discovered that the waistband of his trousers was stuck in the back of his chair. Discreetly he tried to reach behind him and extract it, but he was unsuccessful. I couldn't stop staring at him, and then started to wonder if his role called for him to stand up soon. If so, the evening would really become a farce - a large, portly actor walking around at a stoop with a chair stuck to his seat. Fortunately, another actor noticed his dilemma, and, arising from his chair, he went over to his colleague and carefully extracted the caught clothing. Then he patted the old fellow on the back as if to say it was all part of the performance. There was a collective sigh of relief in the house.

When I saw Paul Scofield in the original production of *Amadeus* at the National Theater, at one point he choked on a piece of pastry - as you remember, Salieri was a compulsive eater of desserts. One of the character's quick-thinking servants scurried off stage and returned with an impromptu glass of water. Eventually the actor regained his composure, but the incident disturbed the audience's concentration. When *Amadeus* arrived in New York with Ian McKellen, the pastry had been replaced by a dish of custard. Mr. McKellen did not choke.

Q: Do British actors regain their equilibrium more quickly than their American cousins?

A: Quite - even off stage. Sir John Gielgud is legendary for his absent-mindedness, and his quick recovery - albeit with an unconscious lack of tact. The classic Gielgud-ism, as best recounted by John Mortimer, concerns a luncheon that Gielgud had with Edward Knoblock, in his time a well-known playwright who was commonly regarded as a dull man. Someone passed by their table and Gielgud commented, "He's the biggest bore in London - with the exception of Edward Knoblock." Then, realizing who was next to him, he apologized, "Not you. I meant the other Edward Knoblock."

GRIT AND WIT MADE RUTH GORDON A STAR: SEPTEMBER 8, 1985

The Ruth Gordon that America cherished for almost three-quarters of a century began in 1911 at the Colonial Theater in Boston. Miss Gordon was fond of telling the story, and, along with so many of her stories, it could serve as an inspiration to all aspiring young actresses. Hazel Dawn was playing in *The Pink Lady*, and sitting in the Colonial balcony was Ruth Gordon Jones from Quincy, Mass. She saw Miss Dawn - and she loved her - and she also heard "my voices." As Miss Gordon recalled, about those voices, "Joan heard hers at Domremy, mine came through at the corner of Boylston and Tremont, Boston, Mass. My voices said go on stage, Ruth, go on stage! Be an actress!"

Miss Gordon was never one to disregard a good suggestion, and, taking the ethereal advice, she plunged into a career that was to carry her to the top of several professions. At first, it was not easy - actually, it never was easy. She was not beautiful or glamorous and had neither the voice nor the stature for tragedy. She was also totally without experience and connections in the business. What she had was determination - in Miss Gordon's case, a far more apt word than ambition.

Most of all, she desperately wanted to be an actress and, for her, being an actress did not mean waiting to be discovered but seizing every opportunity and disregarding every discouragement. From her Broadway debut in 1915 as Nibs in *Peter Pan*, until her death Aug. 28 at 88, she never stopped working. In fact, when she died she still had four movies to be released. When she was not acting, she was writing - stage plays, screenplays in collaboration with her husband Garson Kanin and memoirs. Most important, she was being Ruth Gordon, which was a calling unto itself.

Though Miss Gordon acted in plays by Shaw long before she did *Mrs. Warren's Profession* at Lincoln Center, she never took the time to distinguish herself in classics, except for a brief two-year flourish in the late 1930's. In quick order, she played Mattie Silver in *Ethan Frome*, Mrs. Pinchwife in *The Country Wife* (both at the Old Vic and on Broadway) and, to top it all off, Nora in *A Doll's House* in an adaptation by her friend Thornton Wilder. Opening night of *A Doll's House* was, she said, "the absolute peak of my career. I went to bed with the highest heart in the whole world."

For reasons that have more to do with the limitations of the American theater than with her talent, she did not play many of the roles she was capable of playing. Had she been English, she might have gone on to become an Edith Evans or a Peggy Ashcroft. There were of course several individual triumphs - her Natasha in *The Three Sisters*, her definitive Dolly Levi in *The Matchmaker* (the first time I saw her perform on stage). But in recent decades her appearances in plays were fleeting, or at least the plays were fleeting. One remembers vividly her mother in Lillian Hellman's savage but anarchic comedy, *My Mother, My Father and Me*." One wished that Miss Gordon, as dramatist, could have done a rewrite on that play.

In what could be called her middle period, the roles that suited her did not exist in abundance, and she was apparently aware of her own acting range. Because she was brilliant as Nora did not mean she should do Hedda Gabler. Her Serena Blandish did not qualify her for Lady Macbeth. As an actress - on film as on stage - she was at her finest in comedy. That is not to say she was a comedienne, though detractors might have regarded her as such. What she did was character comedy, and it is our loss not to have seen her in Sheridan and Goldsmith as well as Christopher Durang. Her comic style came to be so definable as to be idiosyncratic. She was a great personality actress.

Miss Gordon attacked her own writing with the same persistence and dedication she brought to acting. Every time you enjoy Spencer Tracy and Katharine Hepburn sparring in *Adam's Rib* and *Pat and Mike*, remember who created their characters and wrote their witty dialogue. Ruth Gordon and Garson Kanin's contribution to the symbiosis of the Tracy-Hepburn team is inestimable.

There were two other important aspects to Miss Gordon's writing career, the first as a playwright. On the Gordon scale of productivity, her playwriting was a minor element - by my count, three original plays, one adaptation and a play that never reached fruition - but at least two plays, *Over Twenty-One* and *Years Ago"* bear reconsideration. It was clear from a recent viewing of the film version of her youthful memoir, *Years Ago*, called *The Actress* (starring Spencer Tracy as the father and Jean Simmons as the daughter) that this is an endearing romantic comedy of adolescent longing. With all the unearthing of early Philip Barry and George Kelly, it is time that the theater looked again at early Ruth Gordon. Her books included, most notably, *My Side*, an exhilarating non-stop monologue as memoir.

Her talk, in person as in print, was inimitable. Last year, in one of many honors that seemed to strike her weekly from the time she became an octogenarian, the Players toasted her with an evening. After all the testimonials from her admiring peers, she took center stage and told, with variations, the story of how she left Quincy for the Never-Never Land of Broadway, how doors were slammed in her face (she opened them), how she survived and, finally, thrived. Self-taught and self-made, she learned about life and learned about theater. She created herself as an actress. As she told her story, it was evident that if there ever were a solo performance artist, it was Ruth Gordon.

I regret that I missed most of her greatest stage performances, but, along with others, I was to rediscover her as a character actress in the movies. I am not exactly sure how that career began, but, in a swarm, she made scores of movies, *Rosemary's Baby*, *Where's Poppa?*, *Harold and Maude*, and became a cult star. How many First Ladies of the theater can make that claim - and make no mistake, even without playing Medea, she was a First Lady of several stages.

Fifty-three years after the American Academy of Dramatic Arts dismissed her from its ranks for showing no promise, the organization honored her. She addressed the graduating class: "The last time I was at the Academy, the president said, 'We feel you're not suited to acting. Don't come back.' Well, you see who's standing here. And on that awful day when someone says you're not pretty, you're no good, think of me and don't give up!" When, at 72, she won an Academy

Award for *Rosemary's Baby*, she said, "I can't tell you how encouraging a thing like this is." She meant it.

I recall traveling with the Kanins to Quincy for a citywide celebration on Miss Gordon's 80th birthday. Thanking her hometown, she reminisced about her birth, then laughed and corrected herself. Her memory began, she said, when she was four. "That was 1900 and I got organized. I knew I was going to have the damnedest great things happen to me." At her death, friends referred to a light going out. Actually, an entire theatrical galaxy had been extinguished. As she once said, "If you live long enough, you are your work and your work is you." The memories of stage performances, her movies, screenplays, plays and books and, most of all, her life as theater endure.

THE CURTAIN RISES ON KELP LASAGNA AND CHOPPED LIVER: FEBRUARY 26, 1986

Although the current theatrical season has not yet provided much food for thought, it has given considerable thought to food. On stages all over New York, breakfast, lunch and dinner are being served along with beer, wine, schnapps, tea in a glass and blue tropical drinks with or without tiny umbrellas. Caterers and chefs should demand program credit. It has almost reached the point where one cannot tell a show without a menu.

The obsession reflects the interests of a public that is captivated by the theatricality of the dining experience, by designer restaurants where presentation is as important as the food. People demand sizzle in their fajitas - show business for their money. In the theater, it may be an attempt to win back an audience that prefers to spend its entertainment dollar (or $100) eating rather than watching. Both *Tamara* and *Tony 'n' Tina's Wedding* capture two segments of the population by serving dinner along with drama. In the other examples of theater of food, the theatergoer becomes a voyeur. Only the aroma passes his way.

The daily special in the trendy cafe in Richard Greenberg's *Eastern Standard* is grouper tortellini. While waiting for her swordfish without butter in the equally upscale restaurant in Wendy Wasserstein's *Heidi Chronicles*, a character concentrates on the power side of her power lunch. Everything from tuna melt to kelp lasagna is tossed into the comedy wok at *The Kathy and Mo Show: Parallel Lives*. Bill Bozzone's one-act *Good Honest Food* takes the audience into the world's dingiest coffee shop, where insults are the plat du jour and the customer is always wronged. The carefree waitress worries only that a diner may prove to be a designated critic from Gourmet magazine. In another one-act, David Ives's *Seven Menus*, there is a food therapist in the cast of eaters.

Led by these shows and *Cafe Crown*. which looks back at the golden age of Yiddish theater of food, the hyphenated actor-waiter has been blurred. This season there are almost as many actors working as waiters on stage as there are waiters in restaurants hoping to be actors. More and more there are opportunities for someone to practice both professions without changing costume. With the proper union credentials, an actor could move directly from Orso to Broadway (and back again). What is learned while waiting can be used while acting, and vice versa.

Except for the waiters, most of the characters in these shows could be described by the Y word. They are passing 30, are upwardly mobile and dine out when they are not taking out or sending out for food. This partially explains the restaurant setting in the plays; that is where the playwrights are watching the prototypes of their generation. David Mamet, from a slightly older group, does not usually set his plays in restaurants, although the first act of *Glengarry Glen Ross* takes place in a Chinese restaurant. But Mr. Mamet often writes them there, which is why he entitled his collection of essays *Writing in Restaurants*.

Sam Shepard, on the other hand, is obsessed by food, especially artichokes - for throwing (in *Curse of the Starving Class*), not for eating. Bananas and artichokes share the spotlight in Mark Harelik's *Immigrant*. The title character, a fruit and vegetable peddler, sells the first, but gives away the second, saying that if a customer can figure out how to cook the strange vegetable, she can keep it. Not long ago, Calvin Trillin (in his one-man show) was demonstrating that comedy is chicken à la king. He decided that all America's unconsumed chicken à la king was locked up in silos in the Midwest.

The proliferation of theater of food began last season with Lanford Wilson's *Burn This*, in which the leading male character was the maitre d' and chef of an epicurean restaurant (the title of the play did not, however, refer to food). The characters in Terrence McNally's *Frankie and Johnny in the Clair de Lune* both work in the same restaurant, Frankie as a waitress, Johnny as the chef - and in every performance he chops, dices and cooks on stage.

In *Cafe Crown*, the scene is the Cafe Crown (in real life, the Cafe Royale), where actors schmooze between plays and collect heartburn. When the show closes, Bob Dishy, who leads the team of waiters, would have no trouble finding a role in a restaurant. In fact, *Cafe Crown* could be that restaurant. Santo Loquasto's set so lovingly reproduces the ambiance of the original that, should the show sag at the box office, the set could open for business. Along with Mr. Loquasto, Edward T. Gianfrancesco, the resident designer at the WPA Theater, is an artist at creating richly detailed realistic settings. Mr. Gianfrancesco's current one is a Texas bar in Larry L. King's *The Night Hank Williams Died*, the play that sets this season's record for beer consumed in performance (and not a potato chip in sight). Some years ago, a downtown bar presented a season of plays that were situated in bars, beginning with an evening of Eugene O'Neill's sea plays. Other bar plays include *The Iceman Cometh*, *The Time of Your Life*, *The Hostage* and *The Sea Horse*. One set serves all.

Theater of food is at least as old as Shakespeare. Food dominates plays as diverse as *The Taming of the Shrew* (poor Kate, who would eat anything, is served nothing) to *Titus Andronicus* (don't ask what's on the menu). Falstaff had his favorite tavern, and was famed as a capon carver. Chekhov's characters have a craving for herring, vodka and tea from the ubiquitous samovar, Schnitzler's people idle in Viennese cafes, and Shaw and Wilde serve tea and cucumber sandwiches. But in Ibsen and Strindberg hardly anyone ever eats. Although there is a country feast in *Peer Gynt*, no one has time for breakfast in *A Doll's House*, and there is nary a nibble in the kitchen of *Miss Julie*. In America, the tradition - more at home than in a restaurant - can be traced back to popular fare of the 1930's and 1940's as exemplified by such family plays as *Life With Father* and *I Remember Mama*, *Awake and Sing!* and *Ah Wilderness!* (people always sat on three sides of a dining table and faced the audience). The cycle was carried out by *Dinner at Eight* and *The Man Who Came to Dinner*, though neither of them put much stock in actual food.

Especially in WASP society, drinks delay dinner, as in *The Cocktail Party* and the current *Cocktail Hour*, by A.R. Gurney, author of *The Dining Room*. Almost every play at the Pan Asian Repertory Theater has an obligatory eating scene, and on every opening night there is a Pan Asian banquet in the lobby. Last June, Theodora Skipitares presented a puppet version of *The History of Food*, from the nutritionist's point of view. The show was provocative, but the food was unappetizing - the Pilgrims ate rubber turkey.

The Hall of Fame for Food Onstage would include the cornflakes in Harold Pinter's *Birthday Party* ("Are they nice?" "Very nice."); the marshmallows consumed by Carol Channing in the Harmonia Gardens scene in *Hello, Dolly!*; the meat pies in *Sweeney Todd*, and the pasta in Albert Innaurato's *Gemini* ("I'll just pick."). Both Neil Simon and Alan Ayckbourn are fond of food humor but usually avoid actual eating, except in Mr. Ayckbourn's *Table Manners*.

With all the food being cooked and consumed on stage, there is no longer such a thing as a starving actor - unless he has something against grouper tortellini or chopped liver.

HAZARDS OF THE TRADE: FISH AND FLYING PICKLES: MARCH 6, 1986

Stung by criticism, actors, playwrights and directors have been known to respond with brickbats - or worse. As ire rises, an uncontrollable desire for vengeance takes possession and otherwise mild-mannered people move to the state of high dudgeon. Those engaged in the craft of criticism have all been subjected to outraged letters and telephone calls, and some have been slapped or punched in public or had foodstuff flung in their faces. Occasionally, a messenger arrives bearing objects expressing derision.

One such parcel arrived several years ago addressed to a theater reviewer on this newspaper. Inside was a large, wet fish, an obvious comment on what was, in hindsight, a rather gentle remonstration in print. It was a fishy case of overkill. When the critic's emissary refused to accept the unwanted gift, an office receptionist daringly took the catch home, cooked it and ate it. Against all odds, he lived.

Recently I was on the receiving end of a different odoriferous package. After I had criticized an actress's performance, she sent me roses. A note attached said, "Thinking of you." What, I wondered, was she thinking of me. Fish I can understand, but roses remain a puzzlement. Perhaps the actress was trying to neutralize negative waves, sending a bouquet in order to disarm future criticism.

In common with theatergoers, whom they sometimes resemble, critics can be pelted in the course of a performance. Two shows this season sought comic resolution in a free-for-all of flying objects. In Larry Ketron's *Fresh Horses*, which closed last weekend at the WPA, a group of young people, pigging out on junk food, suddenly began throwing marshmallows at one another until the stage was filled with a carpet of the squishy morsels. Ted Tally's *Little Footsteps* (at Playwrights Horizons) climaxes with an angry young mother besieging her prodigal husband with a shower of disposable diapers and cotton balls. In both plays, actors on stage and theatergoers in the front rows ducked for cover - and there was extra work for stagehands. Because the plays were Off Broadway, one assumes the company thriftily reused the airy arsenal.

As Stewart Klein, the drama critic for Channel 5, reminded me, a number of seasons ago there was an Off Broadway play in which the actors had a picnic on stage, complete with delicatessen. At a press performance, a pickle hurtled into the audience and struck a critic. Edith Oliver, who reviews Off Broadway for The New Yorker, was heard advising her wounded colleague, "Throw it back. I wouldn't let an actor throw a pickle at me." In the second act, a plate of potato salad flew off the stage and landed in a soggy heap in the lap of another critic. Ms. Oliver asked that second colleague, "Would you like a pickle with your potato salad?"

I never fail to be fascinated by the consumption of food and drink on stage in performance. Eating is not necessarily compatible with acting, and there is always the danger of choking. So far as is known, there has been no case of the Heimlich maneuver in mid-performance, but it remains a distinct possibility. Intrepid actors drink gallons of colored liquids and eat even the most unappetizing substitute substances with imaginary relish.

In the aforementioned *Little Footsteps*, Thomas Toner has to engorge a plateful of pathetic looking sandwiches while keeping up a steady stream of conversation. On the other hand, sometimes stage food can look good enough to eat. Such was the case with *Caligula* at the Circle Repertory Company. In this studiously anachronistic version, Caligula ordered out for Chinese food, which arrived post-haste (were there bicycles in ancient Rome?) and piping hot, in cardboard cartons, complete with chopsticks. Unfortunately, there were no fortune cookies. If there were, one fortune might have read, "Disarm criticism. Send roses."

In the art of stage dining, an acme of sorts is reached in Alan Arkin's revival of *Room Service* at the Roundabout Theater. The eating scene is a centerpiece of all *Room Service* productions as well as of the Marx Brothers movie version. The starved, indigent theater people in this backstage comedy finally are enabled to avail themselves of their hotel's room service. They sit at a table and stuff their faces with everything edible and potable in sight. At the Roundabout, Keith Reddin outdoes all of his farcical colleagues by downing, chug-a-lug style, a large pitcher of milk - twice on matinee days.

The peril of theatergoing was illustrated at a recent performance of *Jerry's Girls*. Catching up with that musical on a Sunday afternoon, I was immediately aware of a foul smell pervading the theater. Many theatergoers left their seats in the middle of the performance while other sedentary patrons remained uncomfortably in place. Near the end of the first act, the show was halted and the announcement made that there was a plumbing problem in the basement.

Before one could say Environmental Protection Agency, a team of fire engines arrived and an inspection was made. The musical briefly resumed, then canceled the second act, inviting theatergoers to return on a day when the air was clearer. The aroma was, it seemed, even more noxious backstage. An actor's life is not a bed of roses.

A most curious theatrical incident occurred earlier this season - and no matter how the story is told it sounds callous. It happened during the first act of a performance of *Hay Fever*. While Rosemary Harris and family were quietly cavorting on stage, a portly theatergoer sitting on an aisle rose to allow her husband to leave his seat. To facilitate his return, she tried to shift into his place. Accidentally, she sat down not on his seat but on the floor and found herself wedged between the rows. She appeared to be unhurt but was unable to extricate herself. A neighbor tried to assist her to her feet.

Slowly, the eyes of nearby theatergoers turned from the stage to the woman. As if watching someone who had just slipped on a banana peel, they began to laugh helplessly. Laughter soon spread to all surrounding rows and giggling ascended into a laughing mania. Eventually the woman regained her seat and settled down to enjoy the rest of the show. Since then I have wondered what the actors thought. Clearly, they could not see the wedged woman, but they certainly could hear the laughter. They must have been puzzled as to why a rather innocuous scene in the play drew such an appreciative response - never to be repeated in the course of the engagement.

CHARACTER ACTORS: BRIGHT PERENNIALS OF BRITISH THEATER: JULY 27, 1986

At one point this summer, Vanessa Redgrave, Albert Finney, Maggie Smith, Glenda Jackson, Roger Rees and Jane Lapotaire were all appearing in plays in London. The fact that these stars were on stage says something about the health of the English theater - a vitality that continues despite a paucity of interesting plays and a preponderance of over-produced musicals. After several weeks of theatergoing in London, one begins to think that the English theater is the English actor, and nowhere is there a greater indication of that than in the performance of Bill Fraser in the West End revival of J.B. Priestley's 1938 comedy, *When We Are Married.* Mr. Fraser is a paradigm of the art of the English character actor.

As this 78-year-old actor provokes his first wave of laughter at the Whitehall Theater, one simultaneously hears the rustle of programs as visitors to England try to ascertain his identity. In England he is a popular figure through his work on television as well as in movies and plays (he was one of the judges on the television series, *Rumpole of the Bailey*). Mr. Fraser has only a few scenes in *When We Are Married*, but each is priceless, and his performance - by any measure except length - is one that clearly deserves the label virtuosic.

The play is a minor Priestley farce, and one would hate to see it performed by a lesser company of players. Fortunately, the director, Ronald Eyre, has assembled a splendid cast, consisting of some of the most amusing character actors available. For Americans, perhaps only Prunella Scales (who delights television audiences as Sybil Fawlty in *Fawlty Towers*) and Patricia Routledge (who has starred in a number of New York musicals, including *The Pirates of Penzance*) would be recognizable. In unison, the actors have taken Priestley by the hand and, without altering the dialogue or the period (the early 20th century), made him alive in 1986 - no small theatrical feat. The contrivances of the farce prove to be no hindrance.

Three middle-aged couples, who were married on the same day 25 years ago, meet for a combined anniversary, only to discover that they were never married. The parson who performed the ceremony, they are told, lacked the proper credentials. A stuffed shirt explodes, a battle-ax backs down, a worm turns and everyone is beset by chagrin, embarassment and regret. Eventually each is also struck by hindsight. They are tantalized by the thought of an apparently illicit, though long-running, relationship and by the fact that they are, in effect, unhitched. "Would it be too late to start over?" is a question that shares center stage with "What will the neighbors think?"

In its day, the comedy may have had a certain social relevance as Priestley considered the gradations of ethical conduct and snobbery in a provincial Yorkshire town. Today those specifics matter far less than the characters, each of whom is given full comedic dimension in performance. Deservedly sharing top billing with those who have larger roles is Mr. Fraser, who plays Henry Ormonroyd, a photographer covering the anniversary for a local gazette. In his sack suit - it looks as if it had never been pressed - as he gazes quizzically around him, he appears to have wandered in from a different play. Humor often derives from his absentmindedness. In that sense and others, he reminds one of Sir Ralph Richardson, who, though a star, was always a character actor.

In one scene, the sad-eyed Mr. Fraser sinks into a sofa. He is as silent as a pillow, which, at the moment, he resembles. Sipping a glass of whiskey, he listens to a pert young maid giddily recite poetry. As her monologue continues, he closes his eyes, momentarily drifting into a reverie. While his eyes are closed, the young woman is called away from the stage, and Elizabeth Spriggs, the quintessential harridan, enters and coincidentally stands in the spot vacated by the maid. We smile as we wait for Mr. Fraser to open his eyes, and, when he does, his reaction - a succession of cascading double takes - is uproarious. He stares at Ms. Spriggs in amazement and then mulls over the startling transformation. The laughter builds until the actor finds the perfect finish, darting a small, very suspicious look down at his whiskey glass. If ever a theatergoer were drawn to that physically impossible maneuver of rolling in the aisles, it would be while watching Mr. Fraser try to come to terms with the apparition.

In order to determine how much of the scene was the work of the actor and how much it was the work of the playwright, I looked at the text of the play and discovered that every bit of it was in the performance. The stage directions indicate that the maid leaves the stage and the harridan stands in her place. Ormonroyd is "astonished" to see her there. For the actor playing the part, the only other guidance is the suggestion that the character is "bewildered." Bewilderment has never had such hilarious nuances.

Similar instances of Mr. Fraser's artistry can be found throughout the play. With little aid from the playwright, he has created a droll character, and we find ourselves looking forward to his reappearance. The play ends with the audience wanting more of Henry Ormonroyd. It would be unfair, however, to slight his fellow actors. Together they form an ensemble, yet, as is often the case in England, this is not a permanent acting troupe. Perhaps English actors share some ineffable "Humour," in the Jonsonian sense of the word, that allows them to tune in to each other's reactions, without prior acclimatization.

Special mention should be made of several others, in particular, Ms. Scales (as the most dignified of the wives) and James Grout (as a bluff country squire). In recent seasons, Mr. Grout has clearly displayed his own versatility in roles as varied as John Gielgud's butler in *Half-Life*, as an ambitious teacher in *Quartermaine's Terms* and, last season, as the vicious Boss Finley in *Sweet Bird of Youth*. Playing a small role as a gossipy servant in *When We Are Married* is Patricia Hayes. In the program we are told that in the original 1938 production, she created the role of the young maid - a cycle that is a further indication of the durability of the English character actor.

Every season the London stage is brightened by actors such as Michael Bryant, Colin Blakely, Michael Gambon and Edward Petherbridge. Some have moved on to stardom, but they reappear, apparently without damage to their egos, in supporting roles. Mr. Bryant, for example, is in *Dalliance*, Tom Stoppard's adapation of Schnitzler at the National Theater, investing a small role with a touching gentility. Though Mr. Gambon plays the great classic roles, he was seen, up to his old character-actor artistry, as the sympathetic zookeeper in the film, *Turtle Diary*.

It is interesting to note that many English character actors have become better known to American audiences through their appearances in movies or on television (a path that brought us Alec Guinness and Robert Morley). More recently, television has been the medium for pleasurable encounters with Ms. Scales, Penelope Keith, Wendy Craig and Leo McKern. Visitors to London, familiar with their faces, seek them out on stage.

The fact that actors can so easily shift from stage to screen helps to assure the continuity of their careers. Between films, an English actor can often find a stage role to fill out a season. In New York, an actor with similar intention is forced to be bi-coastal. England, of course, has a greater sense of acting tradition. Not a season goes by without a full share of revivals of Shaw, Coward and Wilde as well as Shakespeare. One additional hallmark of the English actor is the apparent willingness with which he will replace someone in a play. There is every indication that *When We Are Married* is settling in for a long run. New actors eventually will join the troupe and, one assumes, they will have a comparable talent. There may even be an actor capable of duplicating Mr. Fraser's success, though, in that one case, I would tend to think that the actor was irreplaceable.

ON THE STAGE OR SCREEN, CHARISMA SELLS TICKETS: AUGUST 10, 1986

Even before it opened at the Public Theater, *Cuba and His Teddy Bear* sold out its entire engagement, and continued to do extremely good business when it transferred to Broadway. The reason is simple; the star of the Reinaldo Povod play is Robert De Niro, who has demonstrated his remarkable talent and his popularity in a score of films. The fact that the play received mixed reviews does not seem to matter an iota to his admirers. They want to see Mr. De Niro act on stage (and a certain number also want to see his co-star, Ralph Macchio) - and they are not disappointed. By no means is this a star turn. Although he has not acted in the theater for many years and has never before appeared on Broadway, Mr. De Niro has an immediate, visceral presence, endowing his character, that of a New York drug dealer with strongly paternal instincts, with a dimension almost equal to that of his film roles.

Mr. De Niro's performance adds further certification to his position as one of our most creative actors. Unlike the great Hollywood actors of the 1940's who often played themselves , projecting performance through an assertion of personality. Mr. De Niro changes markedly from role to role. Sometimes, as in *Raging Bull*, there is a physical transformation as well. More often, the change is emotional, as he moves from the avenging *Taxi Driver* to the guileful Don Corleone in *Godfather II* to the politically minded priest in *True Confessions* - these and other characters were all embodied by Robert De Niro. For such a relatively young actor, his is a large and varied filmography.

Why Mr. De Niro is the most magnetic drawing card in a drama on Broadway, at least since Dustin Hoffman returned in *Death of a Salesman*, says something about his own stature; in a general sense it also says something about the relationship between actors and audiences. Even with economic strictures and career obligations, actors can challenge themselves in the legitimate theater - and audiences will rush to see certain performers. Charisma still sells tickets.

Years ago, movie stars such as Henry Fonda and Katharine Hepburn returned to the stage with some regularity. Among younger performers, there has been a clearer division between movies and theater. An actor worked principally in one or the other; stage was one of several routes to film, and it could also serve as a retreat or a renewal if a movie career was fading. A new cycle may have begun when Al Pacino ventured on Broadway in David Rabe's *Basic Training of Pavlo Hummel*, reviving and, to a certain extent, reinterpreting a contemporary play. It might be said that Mr. Pacino tapped a new Broadway audience, or recovered one that had been lost to the movies. Theatergoers followed him, several seasons later, when he brought back David Mamet's *American Buffalo*, a play that had already had a previous Broadway run (starring Robert Duvall). The matching of actor and play was harmonious, which was not the case when Mr. Pacino played *Richard III* on Broadway (a pairing that was far more successful in a prior, more intimate, Boston production).

Like Mr. Pacino, Mr. Hoffman began as a stage actor, working his way up from Off Off Broadway. He, too, had been absent from the theater for a number of years and chose to return in a revival of a contemporary drama, in his case, *Death of a Salesman*. Although Willy Loman might seem at a great distance from Mr. Hoffman's other roles, the actor has always specialized in character parts, many of them wildly divergent from his public image (from the crippled Ratso Rizzo in *Midnight Cowboy* to *Tootsie*). One might say that each of the three actors was thoughtful in his choice of roles to play.

The appearance on Broadway of a De Niro, Pacino or Hoffman is something quite distinct from the traditional casting of a television star in a stage vehicle. In the latter case, the assumption often is that television popularity is transferable to theater (as, some would think, it is also transferable to movies). Experience tells us that if people can watch a performer every week on a home screen, they will not necessarily go to a theater to see him in person. The exceptions, of course, are musical stars and comedians. For Mr. De Niro, Mr. Pacino and Mr. Hoffman, there is an extra sense of anticipation when one of them decides to work in the theater, and when the actor steps on stage, there is an excitement that is converted to electricity.

For each of the three, the appearances have been at a financial loss and, at least overtly, at a career sacrifice. It meant putting aside film work for the duration of the engagement, although in Mr. Hoffman's case, the filming of *Death of a Salesman* for television also added a financial enrichment. Clearly there was something more important - an affirmation of theatrical roots, a need to provide oneself with a challenge - that impelled them back on stage. One assumes that all three profited from the experience, as did theatergoers, and that they will return in other shows.

What it takes is a certain commitment of an actor's time and talent along with appropriate and imaginative casting. One of the more interesting aspects of Mr. De Niro's appearance is the apparently organic quality of the engagement, with a limited run extended by popular demand. Mr. De Niro is proving, as Mr. Pacino and Mr. Hoffman did before him, that an actor need not sign away a full year of his life in order to fortify himself artistically. Between films, he can return to the stage - and then decide whether or not an extension is warranted. As with Mr. Hoffman, Mr. De Niro could consider filming *Cuba and His Teddy Bear*, further expanding the play's audience and its income.

Their success should encourage other actors to follow their lead, especially those who also began their careers on stage, actors such as Paul Newman, Robert Redford, Warren Beatty, Robert Duvall, Meryl Streep and Jane Fonda, as well as such musical performers as Barbra Streisand and Julie Andrews. In the right play or musical, each should find an enthusiastic reception. Imagine, for example, Mr. Newman in O'Neill (if it had not been done so recently, *Long Day's Journey into Night* would have been a venturesome selection). In her days at the Yale Repertory Theater, Ms. Streep was celebrated for her command of comedy, a side of her talent that has been too little explored in films. Certainly there are plays by Barry and Behrman, to say nothing of Molière, that would profit from her eccentric humor.

Mr. Hoffman and Mr. Duvall might discover an affinity for Ibsen; one could envirion these two acting friends sharing the stage in *The Wild Duck*-- or in *Waiting for Godot*, as they once did years ago at the Theater Company of Boston. Although Jack Nicholson has worked only in movies, one suspects that his intuitive style would transfer easily to the theater. As for Mr. Redford or Mr. Beatty, it has been several decades since the two appeared on Broadway, Mr. Beatty in William Inge's *Loss of Roses*, Mr. Redford in *Barefoot in the Park*. The next new play by David Mamet, Michael Weller or John Guare could provide an incentive for a return. Faye Dunaway is demonstrating her continuing popularity, as well as her artistry, in the London production of *Circe and Bravo* by Donald Freed.

On the musical side, Ms. Streisand could move on to *Gypsy*. Although she trained Off Broadway, played a supporting role in *Fiddler on the Roof* and has performed concert shows on Broadway, Bette Midler has not yet headlined a Broadway musical comedy. At the memorial service for Alan Jay Lerner, Julie Andrews, with her lilting voice, was a striking reminder of Broadway musicals at their best. What an asset she would be in a revival of *Kiss Me Kate*.

A few of our most talented performers, including Glenn Close, William Hurt and John Malkovich, have never left the stage and still have managed to have flourishing movie careers. In this regard, Kevin Kline could serve as a role model to his peers, pairing a *Big Chill* or a *Sophie's Choice* with a *Henry V* or a *Hamlet*. He has shown that with careful planning and dedication, it is possible to be both a movie star and a leading actor on stage.

A PLAY THAT NEVER PLAYED, BY TWO MASTERS OF SATIRE: FEBRUARY 8, 1987

The title page of the play is tantalizing: *Even Stephen*, by S.J. Perelman and Nathaniel West. One can easily imagine the cross-breeding of talent - Mr. Perelman, the quintessential humorist, Mr. West the tragicomic chronicler of the corruptibility of man. Combine the effervescence of Mr. Perelman's New Yorker spoofs, or his zany Marx Brothers screenplays, with Mr. West's mordant novel, *The Day of the Locust*, and you have an idea of the potential of their collaboration.

However, reading the play, one is quickly aware of the pitfalls of shared authorship, even when it involves such estimable artists. With two of the most celebrated American theatrical partners, Moss Hart and George S. Kaufman, the division of responsibility was clear; Mr. Kaufman's primary role was as inspirer and editor. With Mr. Perelman and Mr. West, apparently there was more of a duplication of roles. In their individual work, both were masterly at writing dialogue and each had a sharp satiric sense. In retrospect, one could surmise that neither was comfortable in the guise of a Kaufman, picking the lint off the prose and, in effect, directing the play while it was still in process.

As best friends and brothers-in-law (Mr. Perelman was married to Mr. West's sister, Laura), both had a high regard for each other's work. But their art remained separate, except for the play they wrote together in 1934. *Even Stephen*, which has never been produced, recently came to light in a collection of Perelman and West papers and books sold to Brown University by Mr. Perelman's son and daughter.

The play is not the neglected masterwork one would have hoped for, but it should be of interest to admirers of both authors.

In emulation of the Broadway comedies of its time (especially those written by George S. Kaufman), *Even Stephen* attempts to be both satirical and farcical. The heroine of the play is Diana Breed Latimer, a best-selling author of romantic fiction, the Judith Krantz of her day. The character is based on a teacher that both writers knew at Brown University, where they were undergraduates. Mrs. Latimer is in residence at a quiet New England women's college to research her next work, a novel about the sexual escapades of young women on campus. To a certain degree, the play foreshadows Mary McCarthy's novel, *The Group*; coincidentally, both the fictional Mrs. Latimer and Miss McCarthy went to Smith College.

The escapades are a figment of Mrs. Latimer's Gothic imagination, a fact that does not stop her from telling a local reporter that, "in the hothouse atmosphere of a women's college," vice "spreads like a giant creeper twisting and torturing the lives of its unfortunate victims." The novelist fancies herself as a kind of American Zola, even to using the expression, "J'accuse." On campus, she becomes entangled with a poetically inclined young professor, his idealistic fiancée, a mad scientist and others. Several of the characters seem to have leaped into print from Mr. Perelman's rapier pen, others are stereotypes from plays and fiction of the time. Mr. West's hand is less in evidence.

The most Perelmanian of the lot is Marcel Schwartz, Mrs. Latimer's publisher, an unscrupulous bookman whose taste is pulpable. In one of the play's funnier moments the novelist and the publisher argue the merits of two psychologists. Mrs. Latimer says, "Braunstein found that sexual frustration could be detected by the use of a series of small rubber hammers," and Schwartz responds, "Kessler can do it without hammers."

Schwartz is a role that could have been designed for Groucho Marx. In fact, it would not be twisting the play too much to imagine Margaret Dumont as Mrs. Latimer, Zeppo as the headstrong young professor and Harpo, of course, as the mad scientist. Perhaps Chico could have played the newspaper reporter. One trouble with the script, however, is that it takes itself too seriously. It is not content with being a campus comedy, but tries to be Romantic and Meaningful.

The play begins on a sardonic note with the publisher intimidating his timid press agent and otherwise expressing his arrogance (he steals a book title from a would-be child author). Some of the early scenes at college have the verve of *The Male Animal*, but the plot is soon thickened with threats of homicide. By the third act, "Even Stephen" loses its sense of humor. Perhaps if the authors had more than a nibble from Broadway, they might have pitched into a rewrite, but, as it was, they were met only by discouragement. Though the premise is dated in the day of *Animal House* high jinks, it may have had a certain pertinence in its time. Given the authors' track record, it is surprising that the play did not have more of a hearing in the 1930's.

Actually, in 1938, Mr. West did have a play on Broadway, *Good Hunting*, a comedy about World War I written in collaboration with Joseph Shrank, and dismissed by Brooks Atkinson in The New York Times as "nitwit theater." Burned by that experience, Mr. West turned his attentions further to the movies. In 1939, according to Mr. West's biographer, Jay Martin, the novelist referred to *Even Stephen* as "a dead noodle," and borrowed some of the jokes for a movie he was writing.

Mr. Perelman, on the other hand, seemed to retain his hope for *Even Stephen*, updating it after Mr. West's death in 1940. Throughout his life, he hoped to have another Broadway success to equal the 1943 Kurt Weill musical *One Touch of Venus*, for which he wrote the book in collaboration with Ogden Nash. When Marlene Dietrich, the first choice to play Venus, turned down the show as "too sexy and profane," the title role went to Mary Martin. The performance certified her stardom.

With the exception of *One Touch of Venus*, Mr. Perelman was an unlucky playwright. Two plays that he created with his wife, *All Good Americans* and *The Night Before Christmas*, were Broadway failures, and his own play, *The Beauty Part*, had the misfortune to open during a newspaper strike in 1962. *Sweet Bye and Bye*, a musical he wrote with Mr. Nash, Vernon Duke and Al Hirschfeld, closed in Philadelphia, "like a 10-cent mousetrap," said Mr. Perelman.

In the Brown University collection, catalogued by Andreas Brown of the Gotham Book Mart, there are snippets from other Perelman theatrical works in progress, including notes for "an Arthur Murray musical"; a suggestion by Mr. Perelman to himself that he should write a play about his move from New York to London, and a summary of a show about "a dynasty of exterminators" in Grand Central Terminal. Most extensively, there is an outline for *White Rhino*, a musical comedy he and Mr. Nash were planning to write about hunting in East Africa.

The genesis of *White Rhino* was an "all-girl safari" Mr. Perelman had written about for The New Yorker in 1954. (With the author participating, this more properly should have been labeled an almost-all-girl safari.) In the Nash-Perelman version, a woman who works in the credit department of Abercrombie & Fitch organizes the safari and finds her life and travels complicated by the interference of several white hunters. A famous writer named Hannibal Fargo also stops by, a character patterned after Ernest Hemingway.

The show was supposed to have intimations of *Moby Dick*, as it followed one hunter's obsessive search for the title animal. Fargo points out that the story is an improvement over Melville's because it "has women in it." About 10 years after their first discussion, Mr. Perelman and Mr. Nash returned to the show, renaming it *Kilimanjaro* and inserting a "Liz Taylor movie-actress type" who is in quest of a cheetah (very unlike a whale). Along with other Perelman theatrical projects, *White Rhino*, also known as *Kilimanjaro*, was never completed.

It was the theater's loss. The humorist (who died in 1979) had an intuitive theatricality and a talent for dialogue that was equal to that of such successors as Woody Allen and Tom Stoppard. Shunned by Broadway, he occasionally toiled in Hollywood, where he wrote *Monkey Business* and *Horse Feathers* for the Marx Brothers and won an Academy Award for his screenplay for *Around the World in 80 Days*. Despite those successes, he was totally dismissive of the screenwriting profession. He once compared it to "herding swine," as an occupation that "makes the vocabulary pungent but contributes little to one's prose style." Characteristically, he also maintained his objectivity about his career in the theater. As he once wrote about himself, "Retired today to peaceful Erwinna, Pennsylvania, Perelman raises turkeys which he occasionally displays on Broadway."

A VIRTUOSO WHO SPECIALIZES IN EVERYTHING: AUGUST 23, 1987

LONDON - In London in the summer of 1976, I was disappointed to learn that Alan Bates, the star of Simon Gray's *Otherwise Engaged*, had left the cast and had been replaced by an actor named Michael Gambon. As it turned out, the relatively unknown Mr. Gambon was splendid in the role of the coolly unemotional publisher. However, I had no idea that in scarcely more than 10 years he would rise to the very peak of his profession. Role for role, pound for pound, Michael Gambon is, arguably, the finest actor in the English theater.

Ask English actors which colleague they most admire and many would name Mr. Gambon. Americans who have not recently visited the National Theater of the Royal Shakespeare Company on their home ground and who know their English theater largely from those plays that are exported to Broadway might well question the claim. Mr. Gambon has not yet appeared on the American stage - apparently he has had neither the time nor the occasion - a major loss for our theater.

He is a stage actor who never stops challenging himself and his audience and who swings gymnastically from the weightiest of classics to sardonic contemporary comedies. Not only is he a master at Shakespeare, he is one of England's foremost interpreters of the plays of Alan Ayckbourn, Simon Gray and Harold Pinter. As proof of his range, this summer he has been performing three widely diverse roles in repertory at the National - Eddie Carbone in *A View from the Bridge*; Sprules, the clownish butler in the 1920's farce, *Tons of Money*; and a perplexed middle-class entrepreneur in Mr. Ayckbourn's new play, *A Small Family Business*. *A View from the Bridge*, as directed by Mr. Ayckbourn, has been such a success at the National that in the fall it will move to the West End. Later in the season, Mr. Gambon will act in *Uncle Vanya*.

As is customary with this extraordinary actor, he is almost unrecognizable from role to role. Mr. Gambon has always had the ability to transform himself into people apparently distant from his own personality, but Eddie Carbone must be counted as a major leap. This 46-year-old Englishman is totally convincing - and more - as Arthur Miller's Italian-American longshoreman. From the moment he walks on stage, with a movement that is both graceful and lumbering, he is Eddie Carbone on the hoof, a man who, in the actor's interpretation, is almost too large for his body. With his sweeping gestures - the way he embraces his niece or coaxes the immigrant Rodolpho into a boxing match - he seems to encompass everything in sight. Emotionally as well as physically he is bone-crushing. He delivers the kind of dangerous performance once associated with Marlon Brando.

Theatergoers seeing Mr. Gambon for the first time in *A View from the Bridge* will be startled to see him in *Tons of Money* (as adapted and directed by Mr. Ayckbourn). In this creaky farce, he plays a small, supporting role, and wins the evening's heartiest laughs. Standing at a perpetual tilt, with his back hunched, he could be a good-natured Quasimodo. He always seems to be leaning against a door or against another actor - as each is about to give way. This is a subtle, though occasionally boisterous performance, filled with mirthful invention. The fact that he has only a few scenes does not detract from the dimension of his performance.

As another change of pace, on alternate nights, he turns into Mr. Ayckbourn's Jack MacCracken, who takes over the *Small Family Business* and finds himself surrounded by increasingly greater family corruption. By Gambon standards, MacCracken is a bland character; the actor imbues him with substance. These three faces of Mr. Gambon are enough to certify his versatility, but one alters that word to virtuosity when we consider his other accomplishments. In previous seasons, as Brecht's Galileo and as King Lear, he had the classical grandeur of Laurence Olivier. At other times, he has displayed a comic eccentricity like that of Ralph Richardson.

As a young engineer turned actor, he was discovered by Olivier who brought him into the National Theater. Several years ago, I asked Olivier about Mr. Gambon and he replied, "He was one of my 'old boys' at the National. I started him in almost walk-on parts." He added, with evident admiration, "He's a very important actor now." Mr. Gambon's Galileo and Lear, the first in 1981 at the National, the second in 1982 at the Royal Shakespeare theater in Stratford-on-Avon, were titanic characterizations - and a turning point in his career. Suddenly, people realized that his clown-size comedic talent was only one aspect of a multi-faceted theater artist. The following year he played Antony to Helen Mirren's Cleopatra for the Royal Shakespeare Company in London. It was astonishing to look at any of the three performances and to realize that there was also a Pinter-Gray-Ayckbourn actor within the epic framework.

One key to his artistry is that he has always been a character actor rather than a leading man. From an early age, he has played roles older than his years, a fact that is helped by his robust, leonine physique. Although he played the role of the husband in *Betrayal*, later interpreted on the screen by Jeremy Irons, he has not generally been cast in romantic leads. Actually, I would think that nothing is beyond his grasp. The breadth of his talent raises him above many actors of his age. Ian McKellen excels at Shakespeare (as does Mr. Gambon), but he has not yet appeared in many modern plays. Conversely, Alan Bates and Albert Finney, who have had great success in modern plays, have not fully conquered the classics. Other estimable artists lack Mr. Gambon's gift for farce.

Though his reputation has been growing by the year on the London stage, Mr. Gambon has made only a few films (upstaging Ben Kingsley and Glenda Jackson as the kindly zookeeper in *Turtle Diary*). However, Dennis Potter's recent English television mini-series, *The Singing Detective*, suddenly turned him into a household name in Britain. One would hope that those households that have tuned in Mr. Gambon will also see him act in the theater.

In an interview in the current issue of Drama, an English magazine, Mr. Gambon characterized his technique, as "almost like method acting." Before going on stage, he said, "I stand there trying to find the center of the character. Sometimes, you don't find it and you get by on a sort of sense-memory of what it was like when it worked. But I know when I've got him. I finish with my heart pounding, feeling as if I've been running..." If Marlon Brando had continued to work in the theater, he might have developed into an American Michael Gambon.

PLAYS CONSIDERED DURING A NEEDED INTERMISSION: SEPTEMBER 20, 1987

MONHEGAN ISLAND, Me. - While watching the last rays of New York theater this summer - *Sherlock's Last Case*, *Henry IV, Part I* and *Bunker Reveries* - it struck me (no revelation) that those of us who work in the critical profession spend entirely too much time viewing. Almost every evening and on occasional matinee days, we are in the dark looking at actors trying to inject life into sometimes inert objects. When there is an off night, a night away from the theater, a drama critic can often be found at the movies or the dance - in other words, seeing something in a related performance art. Actually my last summer theatrical experience was at a rock concert - David Bowie's final New York performance at Madison Square Garden, which, as some might say about experimental theater, was visually arresting although somewhat lacking in intellectual content.

Sherlock, *Henry IV* and *Bunker Reveries* all suffered in comparison with their antecedents. Charles Marowitz's assault on Conan Doyle - clearly a case of character assassination - was the least Holmesian visit to Baker Street, and that includes those World War II movie updatings that brought Basil Rathbone's powers of ratiocination to bear against the Nazis. The disdain of Mr. Marowitz (a critic!)

for his hero was obvious. There was, in fact, only one moment that left a lingering impression. That was when Frank Langella, as the Holmes in question, sauntered to his private bar and took two fine-stemmed wine glasses in one hand, palm down, and, switching both glasses to an upright position poured wine into each. This was indeed a clever oenological trick and, practicing it, I have managed to shatter a few glasses.

Henry IV, Part I, which ended Joseph Papp's 25th season at the Delacorte Theater in Central Park, was undercast and undernourished. Only Donald Moffatt as Falstaff deserved praise. The critics' preview took place on a night that threatened, but did not deliver, rain. If a baseball game goes five innings before it rains it is, of course, declared an official contest. By the bottom of the fifth of *Henry IV*, the game was already over - and Shakespeare was the loser. As with *Sherlock*, *Henry IV* was overshadowed by many other productions bearing the hero's name, many of which had been performed by the New York Shakespeare Festival itself.

David Shaber's *Bunker Reveries*, last of the old season at the Roundabout, or perhaps the first of the new season, was an attempt at a theatrical roman à clef about Richard Nixon and John Mitchell. However, it was both too close and too far from its source. Despite the name changes and the program disclaimer, the characters were instantly identifiable, but proved to be less dramatically interesting than the real thing.

After those three shows, it was time, critically speaking, for an intermission, a respite from viewing. As in the past, the choice of a retreat was a particular, secluded island off the coast of Maine, where one spends the daytime out of doors and evenings reading and conversing by gaslight. In a theatrical sense, this is a dry island. Nothing entertaining is offered, although some years ago there was a slide show on the art of lobstering that sold out all the seats in a one-room schoolhouse. There have also been occasional confrontational games of charades.

Within memory, there has never been a play staged in these environs, though there have been sporadic concerts. According to The Camden Herald, the play *Greater Tuna*, that perpetual touring show, can be seen (or missed) on the mainland. The only plays on the island are on the bookshelves. For stimulation, one can read a day-old newspaper, catch the daily game of volleyball or croquet or watch a roof being shingled. Every few year, a chimney sweep, piano tuner or tree pruner disembarks - and immediately gathers an attentive audience to watch an artisan and a true island celebrity practice his trade.

Actually, the island lost its principal link with theatricality when Zero Mostel died. A longtime summer resident, he himself was a performance event of a kind. Walking to meet the mail boat, still the major local social activity, he was inexhaustibly expressive and amusing, whether he was talking about the theater, the island art scene or the world at large.

Years ago, when Clifford Odets was already famous, he summered here, and an islander was heard to say, "If he has any talent, Monhegan will bring it out." Several other playwrights have quietly courted their muse, but the island is not known for the writers who have been in residence. Rather, it has served as a home for painters, who have been coming since the time of Rockwell Kent and George Bellows. Most of the artists are friends and they can be mutually supportive, but they can also be each other's harshest critics, reminding one of Simon Gray's published statement that the last person he would want to review one of his plays would be a fellow playwright. He would prefer, he said, to have it reviewed by his greengrocer or "even" by a drama critic.

For that drama critic - for any critic - time in the sun (or even in the fog) can be illuminating. Sitting on a porch, we watch the sun set, and never cloud our minds with thoughts about theater. Time to go inside now and try that trick with the wine glasses. I wonder: Was that in the script or was it created by Frank Langella, or his director?

FOR YUPPIES ON STAGE, A TIME FOR REFLECTION: JANUARY 1, 1989

In the theater, as in life, people have been discovering that the fast track can be a treadmill. They are forced to confront what could be called the Yuppie Trauma: early success leading to young-life crisis. If you rise to the top of a profession before you are 30 - as stockbroker, movie producer, publisher, theater director - burnout may result when you are 30 something.

Increasingly on stage - and in films and on television - the Yuppie Trauma has become a subject for dramatic and comedic contemplation as audiences are asked to understand the vicissitudes of being young and prosperous. For many, sympathies stop short; in a world beset by terrorism, acid rain, hunger and earthquakes, the problems of young upwardly mobile careerists seem marginal, perhaps even incomprehensible. But our concern can of course be deepened by the seriousness of the artistic approach. Coincidentally, the three most striking new plays I have seen so far this season deal revealingly with the subject: Richard Greenberg's *Eastern Standard*, which opens at the Golden Theater on Thursday after its engagement at Manhattan Theater Club; Wendy Wasserstein's *The Heidi Chronicles* at Playwrights Horizons, and Dennis McIntyre's *National Anthems*, presently at the Long Wharf Theater in New Haven.

Each of the plays takes a disparate view of the brat race, but in common the authors are able to hold their characters at arm's length, to be ironic as well as sympathetic. None of them accepts any pretension; all are concerned with broader, human issues, such as the loss of individualism in the cogs of the system. For these three thoughtful playwrights, yuppies are a microcosm of an endangered society. They are just succeeding earlier and crashing more quickly. In each case, the message is enhanced in the delivery. The playwrights have been given assured productions in which the actors mirror the perspicacity of the plays.

The perspective is partly a reflection of the playwrights' ages. Ms. Wasserstein is 38; Mr. McIntyre, 46. The youngest of them, Mr. Greenberg, is 30 and he is the one most deeply immersed in the world and speaks from front-line experience. He has already explored the subject in a number of plays. In his melancholic *Life Under Water*, adolescents idle richly in the Hamptons before swimming in the mainstream. *The Maderati* was a gleeful assault on the glittering celebrity of publishing, posing the question, "What does being good have to do with getting published?" In the hilarious one-act *The Author's Voice*, Mr. Greenberg carried the premise into surrealism. A handsome, suave new novelist has all the qualities for success - except for the fact that he has absolutely no talent. The actual author, his ghostwriter, could be Quasimodo's identical twin. He is confined in a locked room, from which he secretly produces the author's art. Personality, self-presentation, sex appeal are all important conditions of yuppiehood.

Then there is the reverse side: sudden, sometimes insincere, altruism. The high-flyers in *Eastern Standard* have a spasm of self-doubt and social remorse. Stephen (Dylan Baker), the central character, is an architect who designs high-rise monoliths all over Manhattan, until he realizes the social responsibility he bears. He is urban blight. His girlfriend, Phoebe (Patricia Clarkson), a stockbroker, finally faces the fact that her co-workers may be evil (and that she shares in the complicity). Drew (Peter Frechette), an artist and the most naturally cynical in the group, feels that his peers, the Julian Schnabels and the David Salles, are on "the cutting edge of the passé" - and where does that leave him?

The characters respond by inviting a homeless person to the Hamptons. Responding to their innate hypocrisy, the bag lady steals their valuables. Possessions are themselves amulets of success, as in Mr. McIntyre's *National Anthems*. In that bitter play, Arthur and Leslie Reed (Tom Berenger and Mary McDonnell), a wealthy Midwestern couple, buy the brand names and memorize the buzz words of their times. Their lifestyle is a glossy photographic spread in House & Garden magazine. They do not simply have a stereo; they have a Bang & Olufsen music system with RL140 speakers. In their driveway is a silver BMW, which the husband is thinking of upgrading to a Porsche.

The Reeds are startled from their false paradise by a visit from a confrontational neighbor, Ben Cook (Kevin Spacey). After a late-night housewarming party, he unloads an unwelcome wagon of disparaging remarks about the complacent couple, their life and their unseen friends, all of whom seem to spend their time hang-gliding, ice-boating and making money. For a long stretch the hosts are unfailingly courteous - company manners even for the unmannerly. The living room war begins with the neighbor's casual assault on the expensive Milanese furniture and continues with a bruising scrimmage of tackle football. That neighbor, who is a fireman, eventually poses his sense of civic duty opposite their acquisitiveness and quest for status.

That fireman would have been far more gracious to the heroine of Ms. Wasserstein's play. Heidi (Joan Allen) is a good girl of the 1960's, someone who demonstrated for feminism, campaigned for Senator Eugene McCarthy and could be enlisted in any ecological emergency. In her personal life, she is wary about settling for any prescribed goal, whether it is marrying well or seeking worldly advantage. Meanwhile her friends are leaping prematurely into positions of prestige and power. A faithless lover and former liberal activist ends up publishing a trendy magazine called Boomer. One could imagine the characters in all three plays sitting down with the latest issue of Boomer to see how the other fellow got there first, if indeed he did.

Heidi herself is an art historian, woefully aware of the neglect suffered by women artists who painted in secrecy. An epiphany comes to her in an aerobics class, where she is surrounded by overachievers in mind and body. Cowed by her sisters, but not blaming them for her depression, Heidi feels stranded, and almost out of ideals. She finds a renewed strength in her independence, in her willingness to forego competition in the mainstream. She also achieves an additional sense of purpose by adopting a child, adding single motherhood to her other concerns.

Similarly, in *Eastern Standard* the characters look to marriage for stability - to coupling and to friends as family (a recurrent theme in many yuppie plays). The Reeds in *National Anthems* have no such solace - not even intimate friends to keep their fireside warm. When the neighbor leaves, after his anguished recounting of his own failed attempt at heroism, the couple's elegant home is in disarray. The host and hostess sit silently, at the end of a siege.

Though it begins with wry humor, *National Anthems* has the most mordant conclusion. That is not to suggest that the other two plays end on an upbeat note. Each leaves theatergoers - and the other characters in the plays - in a state of sobering inquietude. For Heidi, motherhood is more of a challenge than a solution. In *Eastern Standard*, the architect and the stockbroker may marry as planned, but the stockbroker's brother is, as we know, dying of AIDS. The anguish of AIDS is also a backdrop in *The Heidi Chronicles*, as the heroine's gay soulmate (Boyd Gaines), a successful pediatrician, confronts losses in his own life.

These three plays deal directly with the yuppie experience, but each raises more universal issues that are also reflected in current works on other stages. The suburban club world of A.R. Gurney, Jr.'s *Cocktail Hour* is very far removed from yuppiedom, but the hero's primary concern - how to justify his life to his parents - is something that would be immediately recognized by his younger compatriots in the plays by Mr. Greenberg and others.

Craig Lucas's *Reckless* deals with characters of a similar age, but of a different social standing. They do, however, face related problems such as entrapment by apparent comfort. In this fanciful comedy, a husband takes out a contract on his wife's life (partly because she talks too much) and them warns her of the danger. She leaves home on Christmas Eve in search of sanctuary, self and fulfillment which is, of course, also Heidi's aim.

Last season, in *Serious Money*, Caryl Churchill decried the quick-rich life in London's financial world. Howard Korder's *Boy's Life* of last spring was a pre-yuppie comedy about rampant young Sybarites who, one assumes, will soon stop the partying and dive into the marketplace.

More and more films and television programs are also charting the upward - and sometimes immediately downward - mobility of early risers, as in *Broadcast News*, *Wall Street* and almost anything starring Michael J. Fox (*The Secret of My Success*, *Bright Lights, Big City*). One could trace an arc from *The Graduate* in 1967 to *Working Girl* in 1988 (both Mike Nichols films), marking each as endemic of its time.

In *The Graduate*. Benjamin Braddock (Dustin Hoffman) is beset by a man boasting of the supremacy of plastics and the young man reacts with irony. Were that movie to be made today, Benjamin might be the head of a plastics empire, edging his elders into early retirement. In *Working Girl*, Tess (Melanie Griffith), as a Cinderella secretary, outwits all suppressive opposition, those who are male, those who are older and, most tellingly, her immediate superior (Sigourney Weaver), who is the same age. Ms. Weaver's character is the ultimate yuppie, and, as such, is a sister to Phoebe in *Eastern Standard*, although, we are led to believe, Phoebe eventually comes to her senses and realizes the shallowness of her world while Ms. Weaver scurries to get back on the track after her derailment.

On television, there is *thirtysomething*, in which couples try to have it all, and often do, but at great personal expense. Watching these characters try to balance family and career, one thinks of Ms. Wasserstein's Heidi as a new single mother, soon to search for daycare. If she brings the baby to the office, Heidi would turn into Diane Keaton in the movie *Baby Boom* (briefly a television situation comedy), in which the simple fact of parenting makes it difficult for a woman to continue as an executive.

Many television sitcoms are lightheaded to the point of being frivolous; a laugh track can certainly mitigate against social concern. In contrast, *Eastern Standard*, *The Heidi Chronicles* and *National Anthems* are witty comedies with a socially redemptive purpose, and each is written from a mature perspective. Avoiding sentimentality and free from a facile resolution, the playwrights treat the Yuppie Trauma with trenchancy. At the end of *Eastern Standard*, Stephen toasts his friends and the "sadly infrequent - accidental - happiness of all the rest of our lives." And in a typical Greenberg coda, the wine they drink turns out to be sour.

⟿

ENCORE! FROM STAGE TO SCREEN: FEBRUARY 1, 1989

In the decades when there was an active, self-starting Broadway theater, successful musicals and plays - especially those by Tennessee Williams - were almost unfailingly transformed into Hollywood movies. But in recent years, Broadway and Hollywood have generally regarded each other at a cool, bicoastal distance.

The principal reason is the change in the theater itself. Increasingly, there has been a shift from Broadway to Off Broadway and regional theaters, where new plays can be more specialized and, in some cases, less subject to the broad popular appeal demanded by Hollywood. With the exception of Neil Simon, playwrights have stopped moving between the theater and the movies with any regularity, although a number of playwrights (including David Mamet, Sam Shepard, Michael Weller and John Patrick Shanley) have become productive screenwriters.

However, there have been indications of a rediscovery of theater as a source for films, beginning with Beth Henley's *Crimes of the Heart* and Charles Fuller's *Soldier's Play*. Eric Bogosian's *Talk Radio*, Harvey Fierstein's *Torch Song Trilogy* and Christopher Hampton's *Liaisons Dangereuses* (retitled *Dangerous Liaisons*) are now in movie theaters.

All these plays-into-movies began their lives in Off Broadway or regional theaters, except for *Liaisons*, which was first presented on one of the Royal Shakespeare Companys's small stages. The new Hollywood interest in theater is in creating a kind of Off Broadway film. Movies of Ms. Henley's *Miss Firecracker Contest* and Robert Harling's *Steel Magnolias* are awaiting release, and Alfred Uhry's *Driving Miss Daisy* is being filmed. In the past, the traffic has been two-way, with movies like *Forty-Second Street* and *La Cage aux Folles* being turned into Broadway musicals.

No matter what the source, the problems of screen adaptation remain the same. The danger, of course, is of adding atmosphere for its own sake, attempting to dramatize something better left to the imagination, or enlisting inappropriate stars in pursuit of name recognition on the marquee.

When Elia Kazan decided to film *A Streetcar Named Desire*, his initial plan was to visualize scenes that were only talked about in the play. As he recalled in his memoirs, when it came time to shoot, he realized that "the force of the play had come precisely from its compression, from the fact that Blanche was trapped in those two small rooms." Everything that he had done to "open up" the play had "diluted its power." His response was to jettison the screenplay and to "photograph what we'd had on stage, simply that."

The movie *Streetcar* is both a record of the stage performance and an object lesson to anyone attempting to capture a play on film. The principle of *Streetcar* works best with plays that are equally claustrophobic. *Long Day's Journey Into*

Night and *Who's Afraid of Virginia Woolf?* are examples. To that list, one could add *Talk Radio.*

On stage, *Talk Radio* locked us into a broadcasting studio where we witnessed the harrowing on-the-air disintegration of the talk-show host Barry Champlain (Mr. Bogosian). That studio was Barry's cocoon, and within it he was totally in control. Calls came in and, with a press of a button, he could guillotine a listener in midsentence.

In Oliver Stone's expansive and reductive film version (written in collaboration with Mr. Bogosian), we see Barry out in society. At a basketball game he is verbally and physically attacked by irate listeners. In person he is unable to cut off his antagonists; he loses the self-willed authoritarianism so essential to his character.

When Barry is in the studio, which he is for most of the picture, the director zooms in on his facial features and circles him restlessly with the camera, using a swivel technique that pretends camera movement is dramatic action rather than distraction. Years ago Sidney Lumet did something similar in his movie of *Long Day's Journey Into Night.* One would hope there is no restlessly circling camera in the movie of *Steel Magnolias*, inspecting every pore on every face in the small-town beauty salon.

The decision with *Torch Song Trilogy* was to "open it up" and include more scenes in the transvestite nightclub where the play's central character (played by Mr. Fierstein) works. In reducing the four-hour play to a movie less than two hours long, the movie makers have sacrificed some of the most moving moments between Mr. Fierstein and his adopted son. (In substitution, in an attempt to open up the play, the actor rushes off to the son's school wearing outrageous flip-flopping bunny slippers.)

Because of its opulent period settings, *Liaisons* lends itself more naturally to screen adaptation. What was stylized on stage - all the seductions seemed to take place in the same boudoir - is realistically detailed on screen. The film's director, Stephen Frears, has also managed to retain Mr. Hampton's wit and the decadence that acts as a kind of claustrophobic curtain. Of the three current plays-into-movies, *Dangerous Liaisons* is easily the most astute (except for that new title, which makes the Hampton adaptation sound like a sequel to *Fatal Attraction*).

The three movies share a frankness of language. The end of censorship is one reason for the resurgence of plays-into-films. Historically, plays were sanitized for the screen. One remembers the opposition faced by Otto Preminger in his attempt to have the word "virgin" used in his film version of *The Moon is Blue*." Shirley Clarke's controversial movie of Jack Gelber's *Connection* made it possible, many years later, for producers to plan films of Lanford Wilson's *Burn This* and David Mamet's *Glengarry Glen Ross*, outspoken plays that would not have been permissible on screen in the heyday of Hollywood.

Still, even with the threat of censorship, Hollywood managed to produce with authenticity films of Tennessee Williams plays like *Streetcar* and *Baby Doll* (directed by Mr. Kazan) and *Suddenly Last Summer* (directed by Joseph L. Mankiewicz), as movie makers found ways to outwit restrictive codes.

The move from stage to screen is, I think, more hazardous than the move from page to screen. The physical limitations of the stage can, in certain circumstances, be an asset, as with such highly theatricalized plays like *Amadeus*, which call for a leap of faith on the part of the audience. Through their length and breadth, novels can lend themselves more readily to adaptation and interpretation. To my eyes, Lawrence Kasdan's film condensation of *The Accidental Tourist* is more faithful to the eccentric spirit of the Anne Tyler novel than Mr. Stone's film of *Talk Radio* is faithful to the obsessiveness of the Eric Bogosian play.

Looking back, the finest plays-into-films have been those adapted from Shakespeare: Lord Olivier's trilogy, Mr. Mankiewicz's *Julius Caesar*, Orson Welles's *Chimes at Midnight* and *Throne of Blood*, Akira Kurosawa's version of *Macbeth*. I am not sure what that proves except that Shakespeare, in imaginative directorial hands, can be remarkably cinematic.

WHEN WRITERS TURN THE TABLES RATHER THAN THE OTHER CHEEK: JULY 16, 1989

From the playwright's point of view, critics occupy a special place in hell - somewhere between the eighth and ninth circles, between the hypocrites and the spreaders of false doctrines. For the playwright, the critic is the most dispensable person in the theater - unless he offers unstinting praise. In response to negative reviews, the playwright can sulk, grumble, complain by telephone or mail - or he can write a play about the experience. That last recourse has been taken by, among others, Peter Nichols, Terrence McNally, A.R. Gurney and Albert Innaurato, who, earlier this season, in *Gus and Al*, demonstrated the lengths to which a playwright could go in reaction to reviews.

In the play, a character bearing the author's name time-traveled to turn-of-the-century Vienna in order to seek commiseration in the company of his artistic idol, Gustav Mahler. "Al" read excerpts from the dire notices of his last play to "Gus," who said, in effect, you think you got bad reviews? Then Mahler read back excerpts from his. Posterity, of course, caught up with Gustav Mahler, and, one might hope, such will also be the case with Albert Innaurato.

Mr. Innaurato approached the trauma with unabated wryness. Other playwrights have been provoked to acts of vituperation and even violence. Jack Kirkland was so furious at Richard Watts's review of his adapation of John Steinbeck's *Tortilla Flat* (in 1938) that he punched the critic. His mistake was to deliver the blow in a public bar frequented by Mr. Watts's colleagues, who, with uncharacteristic critical compassion, rushed to his defense, pummeling the playwright as they had previously done in print.

Such was not the case many years later, when David Storey, stung by reviews of his play, *Mother's Day*, cuffed Michael Billington in the bar at the Royal Court Theater. In contrast to their American cousins, Mr. Billington's colleagues watched the fracas with detachment (or was it cowardice?). Some may even have taken notes. (English critics always take notes.) As for the critic under fire, he responded in cool journalistic fashion by calling a press conference. Arguing ad hominem, Mr. Storey, a rugged ex-rugby player, responded by saying that critics should be in better physical shape if they planned to challenge playwrights in print.

As a drama critic, I have never been assailed in public, but, along with my colleagues, I have had a full share of fierce, even vengeful, retorts from irate dramatists and their relatives.

Historically, the relationship between critics and playwrights has been conducted at pen's length, although the pen has often been dipped in venom. Critics can of course be at fault, having misjudged masterpieces from *Peer Gynt* to *Waiting for Godot*. As long ago as 1662, Samuel Pepys attacked *Romeo and Juliet* as "the worst" play he had ever seen in his life, an assessment he appeared to contradict six months later, when he decided that *A Midsummer Night's Dream* was "the most insipid, ridiculous play that ever I saw in my life." Pepys was astigmatic in matters Shakespearean, a congenital weakness shared by Tolstoy and Shaw. Chekhov was nonplused - although amused - by Tolstoy's comment to him that his plays were "even worse" than Shakespeare's.

Shaw spoke from a special interest as Shakespeare's putative rival. This led him to declare in a letter to Ellen Terry (who was about to play Imogen in *Cymbeline*), that Shakespeare was "as dead dramatically as a doornail." In his subsequent review of that production, he said that *Cymbeline* was "for the most part stagey trash of the lowest melodramatic order, in parts abominably written, throughout intellectually vulgar." Fifty years later, as a final act of belittling the Bard, he rewrote the last act of *Cymbeline*, a rare example of a man merging roles as critic and playwright.

Sean O'Casey, the self-styled "flying wasp" of playwright-critics, was infuriated by James Agate, the reigning English reviewer of his time, and his furor was directed against Agate's attitude toward Eugene O'Neill as well as O'Casey. Agate dismissed *Strange Interlude* as "rotten and morbid with decay," at the same time he was praising *Musical Chairs*, a play never heard from again, as "the best first play written by an English playwright during the last forty years." To Agate, it was "a little masterpiece." O'Casey felt, to say the least, that the critic had mixed up masterpieces.

In his home country, O'Neill had his share of detractors as well as admirers.

Alexander Woollcott called *Mourning Becomes Electra* "that glum three-decker," as if it were a thick and inedible club sandwich (Woollcott often used food imagery, a reflection, one assumes, of his own considerable avoirdupois). The critic perhaps least appreciative of O'Neill in his time was J. Ranken Towse of the The New York Evening Post. Just the sound of the name, J. Ranken Towse, could make a playwright quake. The only more threatening appellation for a critic might have been A. Toxen Worm, who, however, worked on the other side of the fence, as a press agent.

After O'Neill had won two Pulitzer Prizes, Towse had the temerity to dismiss *The Hairy Ape* as "an exceedingly promising juvenile work." To give Towse his due, he praised *Beyond the Horizon* as a work of "uncommon merit," words that were outdistanced by the fulsome prose of the briefly appreciative Woollcott, who took a characteristically gourmand view of the play, saying that it was "so full of meat that it makes most of the remaining fare seem like the merest meringue."

The most discouraging review for *Beyond the Horizon* came not from a critic but from an actor, the author's father, James O'Neill, who said, "It's all right, Gene, if that's what you want to do, but people come to the theater to forget their troubles, not to be reminded of them. What are you trying to do - send the audience home to commit suicide?" Perhaps the older O'Neill, along with Agate, would have preferred *Musical Chairs*.

Praise from a critic can be diminished by the quality of his writing. (Playwrights might take exception to that premise.) Here is George Jean Nathan on O'Neill: He "alone and single-handed waded through the dismal swamp lands of American drama, bleak, squashy and oozing sticky goo, and alone and single-handed bore out of them the water lily that no American had found before him." It was a long squashy crawl from Woollcott's meringue to Nathan's bog, but O'Neill survived both.

By 1933, O'Neill had concluded that the more he read of critics, "either pro or con, past and present, the wearier feeling I get that all they say is something between them and their trade, but, so far as the reality of my play goes, totally irrelevant, except as box office help or hindrance." O'Neill remained grudging in his attitude toward critics throughout his career, even though Nathan and others were counted among his close friends. When the New York Drama Critics Circle was founded in 1939, the playwright was asked to provide a welcoming statement. He wrote, with considerable self-consciousness, "It is a terrible, harrowing experience for a playwright to be forced by his conscience to praise critics for anything ... There is something morbid and abnormal about it, something destructive to the noble tradition of what is correct conduct for dramatists."

O'Neill's contemporary, Maxwell Anderson, was not as polite. He accepted the Critics Circle's first award for *Winterset*. Ten years later, when critics panned his play *Truckline Cafe*, he took an advertisement in The New York Times, in which he labeled the critics the "Jukes family of journalism, who bring to the theater nothing but their own hopelessness, recklessness and despair." Anderson never won another Critics Circle prize. In the 1940's, the advertisement for one-self - from Elmer Rice as well as Maxwell Anderson - was the resort of the rich playwright.

In a collection of interviews with David Savran (published by Theater Communications Group), 20 of our most prominent playwrights line up to throw bricks at critics. Of the people interviewed, only two, August Wilson and Charles Fuller, seem prepared to allow for the critic's right to practice his profession. Playwrights who owe their careers largely or partly to receptive critics are totally dismissive of their role, and the general feeling is that one less-than-enthusiastic review negates years of encouragement. For these writers, critics are promotional -or nothing.

Typical of the reaction is David Henry Hwang's statement, "Individual critics are useful mainly from a commercial standpoint. If you get a good review, you can use it on an ad." And, as others indicate, even if you get a bad review, you can extract a favorable adjective from it and turn it into a blurb.

Critic-bashing continues to be a popular sport among playwrights, and, for a critic, there seems no way to avoid the assault. The guest speaker at my son's graduation was Jules Feiffer. After discussing the perils of being both a playwright and a cartoonist, he took a parting shot at the playwright's favorite pariah. He said that he did not like to be judged by people he would not want to have dinner with.

At a recent dinner, I happened to be seated next to a playwright. In the middle of a stimulating conversation with her, I suddenly found myself choking. Silently I signaled my evident distress. Without hesitation, the playwright leaped into action and applied the Heimlich maneuver. This was, I submit, a singular event in the relationship between critics and playwrights, the first recorded instance of a playwright saving a critic's life. I will not name the writer for fear of ruining her reputation in the eyes of her colleagues. Need I add that it is unlikely she will ever receive a bad review from this critic?

HOT IN LONDON: PLAY AND WEATHER: AUGUST 28, 1989

LONDON - On one of the hottest nights of the summer, the tiny pub theater in the East Dulwich Tavern was filled to overflowing. Without a hint of air-conditioning or ventilation, the temperature rose as if someone were turning up the steam in a sauna. The play, *In Lambeth*, written and directed by Jack Shepard, dealt with a meeting between William Blake and Tom Paine, after Paine had helped foment the American Revolution.

The first act took place in Blake's garden in Lambeth, where we encountered Blake and his wife (Michael Maloney and Lesley Clare O'Neill), up a tree, naked.

When Paine (Bob Peck) arrived for an unexpected visit, the Blakes remained unclothed for a time, then with the announcement of a chill in the air, the couple went indoors to dress - to the sound of laughter from the uncomfortable theatergoers.

In Lambeth is an informative and thought-provoking dialogue about the uses of revolution, and the varieties of radical commitment. The cross-purposes of art and politics are scrutinized by the two contrasting Englishmen and by Mrs. Blake, who can say - ingenuously, not condescendingly - to their guest, "And what were you doing in America?" To which the play's Paine answers forthrightly, "Fighting the war of independence."

All three performances added luster to the work, especially so in the case of Mr. Peck, celebrated for his doubling as the villainous Sir Mulberry Hawk and the heroic John Browdie in Nicholas Nickleby. He has the zeal to play Paine and the boldness to do it for two sweltering weeks on the Fringe, far away from the center of London theater. One reason for Mr. Peck's appearance in such offbeat surroundings is that, in common with the playwright, he lives in nearby Dulwich. Because of the critical and audience response, it is expected that In Lambeth will return, presumably in less humid circumstances.

The weather - the warmest in 13 years - and repeated transit strikes were blamed for a drop in London box-office receipts. Trying to combat that loss, box-office personnel in at least one theater were told to lie when asked if the theater was air-conditioned. As theatergoers discovered, one could count on coolness only at the institutional theaters, the National, the Royal Shakespeare Company, and - a refreshing newcomer to audience comfort - the Royal Court.

The theaters themselves remain London's pride, even as one is occasionally threatened, as in New York, by urban redevelopers. They are jewelbox reminders of English theatrical history. I thought I had been in all the active West End houses, but, sitting in the Strand (the play was Much Ado About Nothing) I realized that I had never been in this splendid theater before. The reason was self-evident. For 10 years the Strand was the home of No Sex Please, We're British.

As it turned out, In Lambeth was one of the few rewarding new plays of the summer, along with Richard Nelson's Some Americans Abroad (at the Royal Shakespeare Company). Another recent Royal Shakespeare opening proved to be less auspicious - the London premiere of Robert Holman's Across Oka. The play is an ornithological epic, centering on an almost extinct crane whose eggs are transported across continents (and the Oka preserve in the Soviet Union). A Russian scientist is trying to propagate the bird, but makes the mistake of entrusting the eggs to two teen-age boys, who, as the audience suspects, will soon shatter their Anglo-Soviet détente. Though high-minded, the play manages to be both predictable and unbelievable.

The most powerful contemporary play, though not a new one, was Tom Murphy's Whistle in the Dark, which, in the Abbey Theater production, was presented at the Royal Court as part of the London International Festival of Theater. Written in 1960, when Mr. Murphy was 25 years old, the play has lost none of its riveting sense of menace. This is an excoriating drama about family and country, offering an uncompromising harsh group portait of Irishmen at war with themselves. The Carneys are a family of braggarts and brawlers, brought up by their father to battle one another but never to question his authority. Beneath the father's prideful boasts, he is a coward, and his sons are in various ways failures.

Garry Hynes's volatile production begins in chaos, as the men of the family crowd the stage. Once the emotion subsides, the individual identities emerge - the eldest brother, who is regarded as an intellectual but is as ineffectual and as cowardly as his father; and his brutish brothers, who live by their wits and their fists.

The most moving in a fine cast was Sean McGinley as the one brother who, beneath his vulgarity, has the strongest sense of fidelity and family. When the father (Godfrey Quigley) blathers excuses for not joining his sons in their blood feud against their rivals, Mr. McGinley signals with his silence that he understands the deficiencies and the self-defeats of the warring Carneys.

Though only a guest production, *A Whistle in the Dark* seems a definitive Royal Court play of the naturalistic school, reminiscent of the early work of John Osborne and David Storey. Mr. Murphy, an unjustly neglected playwright, has written a dozen plays in the intervening years, few of which have been presented in the United States.

A minor theatrical contretemps arose when it was reported in the London newspapers that Col. Muammar el-Qaddafi had claimed that Shakespeare was an Arab and that his real name was Sheik Zubayr, a reference to a seventh-century convert to Islam. Actually, Colonel Qaddafi had simply repeated a joke he had first made in a speech last year, but Elizabethan scholars were quick to take up their Shakespeares and to reiterate counterclaims that Bacon, Marlowe and the Earl of Oxford were the real authors of Shakespeare's plays.

Should Colonel Qaddafi's candidate be certified, it would, of course, necessitate a name change for the Royal Shakespeare Company. It would become the Royal Sheik Zubayr Company - the R.S.Z.C.

THE SEASON'S HOT PLAYWRIGHT: GEORGE S. KAUFMAN IN REVIVAL: FEBRUARY 19, 1990

George S. Kaufman began his life in the theater in his early 20's working for a small summer stock company in Troy, N.Y. He quit after one week, sending his father a telegram that said: "*Last Supper* and original cast wouldn't draw in this house."

Almost immediately, his career began to improve. Before the decade was over, he had his first Broadway hit. Eventually, he became the most successful man in the American theater as the co-author of more than 40 plays and musicals and as a director.

He was very much a man of his times, the 1920's and 30's, a witty sage of the Algonquin Round Table who never lost his sense of acerbity. For many, that is the Kaufman that survives: Kaufman the quotable, the critic in life, the man who said about one play, "I saw it under adverse conditions; the curtain was up," the man who declared that satire was what closed Saturday night and then did his best to disprove his dictum.

This is the centennial year of George S. Kaufman's birth and all sides of him are being celebrated. Curtains and glasses are being raised to the Great Collaborator, and his plays are being revived at theaters across the country. Almost 30 years after his death, Kaufman has become one of the most produced playwrights of the season.

The essence of Kaufman's work was in partnership with others, which is one of the problems in evaluating his artistic contribution. Is it Kaufman being cele-brated, or Moss Hart, Edna Ferber and Marc Connelly, or, in the case of his films, the Marx Brothers? It comes as no surprise to realize that Kaufman was only as good as his collaborators, though their work could also fluctuate. With Hart, he wrote *The Fabulous Invalid* as well as *You Can't Take It With You*; with Ferber, *This Land Is Bright* as well as *The Royal Family*. One of his failures, *The Good Fellow*," was written with Herman Mankiewicz, who then went on to write *Citizen Kane*.

The question that will probably never be answered is the division of credit. One naturally assumes that the satiric thrusts should be attributed to Kaufman, the characterization to Hart, the romance to Ferber. It is said that Kaufman left the room while Ferber wrote the love scenes in *Stage Door*. But from *Merton of the Movies* to *The Butter and Egg Man* (the one play he wrote by himself) to *June Moon* and *Once in a Lifetime*, the typical hero was a lovable rube from the sticks. Could Kaufman the sarcastic have been a secret sentimentalist?

For all his apparent dominance, he was always quick to share credit, chal-lenging the assumption that Ferber was "some sort of cook's assistant in the preparation of these little dishes and that I dash them off single-handed." He as-serted clearly that their plays were "collaborations in every sense of the word, from beginning to end." His co-authors returned the credit. In his autobiogra-phy, *Act One*, Hart said that "such success as I have had in the theater is due in large part to George Kaufman." As partial - if accidental - demonstration of that fact, Hart's best plays were those written with Kaufman.

The Kaufman-Hart Pulitzer Prize winner, *You Can't Take It With You*, has never gone out of public favor and, with justification, remains Kaufman's most popular work. This season, *The Man Who Came to Dinner* was revived by both the Royal Shakespeare Company in London and the Arena Stage in Washington, which is now presenting *Merrily We Roll Along*, the Stephen Sondheim musical based on the Kaufman-Hart play of the same name.

The Solid Gold Cadillac (written with Howard Teichmann) was at the Yale Repertory Theater, *George Washington Slept Here* (with Hart) and *The Butter and Egg Man* were presented at other regional theaters and a new version of *Dinner at Eight* (with Ferber) appeared on television. *June Moon*, Kaufman's sole collaboration with Ring Lardner was a success last summer at Alan Ayckbourn's theater in Scarborough, England. But except for a Manhattan Punch Line series of readings of Kaufman plays, his work has been absent from New York during his 100th year.

In re-viewing Kaufman, there are occasional surprises. At the Royal Shakespeare Company, *The Man Who Came to Dinner* seemed dated, but, watching the film version with Monty Woolley re-creating his stage role as Sheridan Whiteside, one enjoyed his excessive exertion of egotism, as well as the oddity of Jimmy Durante cast as Banjo, the character patterned after Harpo Marx. Last season, in his production at the Long Wharf Theater in New Haven, Arvin Brown demonstrated that *Dinner at Eight* could have a life outside the all-star M-G-M movie, although the recent television adaptation demonstrated that the opposite was also possible.

Kaufman wrote eight shows with Connelly, the same number as he did with Hart, but they appear to revive less well. In recent years, both *Dulcy* and *Merton of the Movies*, two of their biggest Broadway successes, were brought back with pallid results.

The one collaboration that may have been underrated was that with Morrie Ryskind, who worked with Kaufman without credit on the Irving Berlin musical *The Cocoanuts*, and who later co-authored *Animal Crackers* for the Marx Brothers. The team of Kaufman and Ryskind also wrote the book for the Gershwin musical *Of Thee I Sing* (Kaufman's second Pulitzer Prize winner) and its sequel, *Let 'Em Eat Cake*. Mr. Ryskind's talent came to mind while watching the film *Stage Door*, which he and Anthony Veillers adapted from the play by Kaufman and Ferber.

The film is definitely an improvement over the play, partly because of the appealing performances by Katharine Hepburn, Ginger Rogers, Lucille Ball, Eve Arden and Ann Miller early in their careers, but also because the adapters strengthened the characters and their relationships in this theatrical boarding house. Both the play and the movie are filled with tart backstage dialogue. According to Malcolm Goldstein, who wrote a biography of Kaufman in 1979, Kaufman himself preferred the film, though he referred to it as *Screen Door*.

Despite the relative brevity of his career in Hollywood, films are a substantial part of the Kaufman legacy, beginning with the three films he wrote for the Marx Brothers, *A Night at the Opera*, *Animal Crackers* and *The Cocoanuts*. The stage versions of the last two were recently revived at the Arena Stage and proved to be evergreen, without the presence of the Marx Brothers but guided by the ingenious directorial hand of Douglas C. Wager.

Kaufman collaborated with Robert E. Sherwood on the story for *Roman Scandals*, a silly Samuel Goldwyn musical in which Eddie Cantor was transported back to ancient Rome. At least one line in that movie has a Kaufman ring, a glum-faced Goldwyn slave girl saying, "To me all life is comedy."

Though he directed 40 plays, he directed only one film, *The Senator Was Indiscreet*, a political spoof written by Charles MacArthur. Kaufman and MacArthur were apparently not the closest of colleagues, but this would have seemed to be a natural partnership, with MacArthur's big-city newspaper know-how encouraging the sardonic side of Kaufman, himself a former drama editor and critic for The New York Times. It was Kaufman who directed the Broadway premiere of *The Front Page*, by MacArthur and Ben Hecht.

Politics and theater remained Kaufman's two principal subjects for satire. In *The Senator Was Indiscreet*, one can detect a Kaufman touch in the portrait of the flagrantly incompetent Senator (William Powell) who can think of only one other position that requires no talent or experience: President of the United States.

Three Kaufman plays, in diverse revivals, have provided unfailing entertainment: *The Royal Family*, *Once in a Lifetime* and, especially, *You Can't Take It With You*. Recently, at an evening at the Players honoring Kaufman, there was a reading of the final scene in *You Can't Take It With You*, when the two disparate families come together in amity. Without sets, costumes or context, the scene was moving as always.

In looking at Kaufman, one must keep a sense of perspective. His work was never as ambitious or as serious as that of Eugene O'Neill or Clifford Odets, whose careers overlapped with his. He admired O'Neill, but he mocked Odets in *Stage Door* as a pompous artist who says: "I don't think in terms of material success. Who cares whether a play makes money! All that matters is its message!" Of course, those lines could have been written by Edna Ferber.

As a director, Kaufman chose not to challenge himself by doing weightier plays than his own. As Harold Clurman said, "He knew his own worth. He was a superb craftsman within his own orbit, a master of theatrical skills, including a keen perception of his audience's proclivities and requirements."

Though he was to achieve some of his greatest successes writing books for musicals and as director of *Guys and Dolls*, he never fully trusted himself in musical matters. It was Kaufman, after all, who persuaded Irving Berlin to cut "Always" from the score of *The Cocoanuts*. His first suggestion was to alter the lyric to the more realistic "I'll be loving you Thursday."

LURING ACTORS BACK TO THE STAGE THEY LEFT BEHIND:
JANUARY 7, 1991

Before he charmed movie audiences, Macauley Culkin, the 9-year-old star of the high-grossing comedy *Home Alone,* had a brief though notable career on the New York stage. In 1987, at the age of 6, he acted in *Afterschool Special,* a surrealistic one act by Keith Reddin, in the Ensemble Studio Theater's annual marathon of short plays.

In this demented domestic comedy, he was hilarious as a child who was blamed by his parents for assorted acts of mischief committed by the Big Squirrel, a clown-size mutant with a malevolent streak. While getting the little boy in trouble, the Big Squirrel was also having a dalliance with the child's mother.

The Reddin play could be considered a prelude to *Home Alone,* in which Master Culkin outwits everyone, his parents as well as a pair of inept burglars. Show business is business, and the young actor evidently has found more opportunity in the movies than on stage.

Though the path from stage to screen is unusual for someone that young, it has been a standard route for many more mature actors. Kathy Bates, who was justly acclaimed for her fiendish performance as a Stephen King figure of witch fulfillment in the movie *Misery,* preceded her movie stardom with a distinguished career on stage. In New York, she was the suicidal daughter in Marsha Norman's *'night, Mother* and the drab waif-like waitress in Terrence McNally's romantic comedy *Frankie and Johnny in the Clair de Lune.* In both cases, she was not chosen to play her role in the film versions: in *'night, Mother* she was replaced by Sissy Spacek and for *Frankie and Johnny* the role is to go to Michelle Pfeiffer (who should find it a challenge to portray drabness).

For a number of years, Ms. Bates has been a favorite of theatergoers Off Broadway and in regional theaters, especially at the Actors Theater of Louisville in Kentucky. It was there that she created the role of an unsuccessful weight watcher in Mary Gallagher's *Chocolate Cake* and gave a mordant performance in Frank Manley's *Rain of Terror.* In the Manley black comedy, she took murderous revenge on an intruder who held her and her husband hostage in their trailer home. As with Macauley Culkin's battle against the Big Squirrel, this could be considered as a pre-run for her current movie hit.

With Hollywood success there will naturally be attempts at typecasting. Undoubtedly, Ms. Bates will be deluged with offers to play murderers, though her range runs widely from Sam Shepard comedy to tragedy. Because of his age, Macaulay will probably have less of a problem in this area, but after the inevitable sequel (or sequels) to *Home Alone,* it may be hard for him to choose roles of a quietly contemplative nature.

Reflecting on these careers brings to mind countless actors seen in their earliest stage work long before they made an impact on the moviegoing public, a list that includes Dianne Wiest, Joe Mantegna and Glenn Close, among those appearing prominently in current films. Coincidentally, most began in comedy.

While still a student at the Yale Graduate School of Drama, Meryl Streep was featured in a number of roles in professional productions at the Yale Repertory Theater. She made her first vivid impression as a caricature of the translator Constance Garnett in the musical *The Idiots Karamazov* by Christopher Durang and Albert Innaurato.

Even at that early stage, it was evident that Ms. Streep had a command of accents as well as characters, and within several years she was playing leading roles in Shakespeare in Central Park (*The Taming of the Shrew* and *Measure for Measure*). But Hollywood has been slow to recognize her comic instincts, which were partly revealed in her most recent film, *Postcards from the Edge*. In that Mike Nichols movie, she demonstrates her musicality, no surprise to early Streep watchers, who heard her sing onstage in Brecht and Weill's *Happy End* and Elizabeth Swados's *Alice in Concert*.

While Ms. Streep was already a star at Yale, schoolmates like Sigourney Weaver were relegated to lesser roles. Ms. Weaver found a home at the Yale Cabaret, often in company with Mr. Durang. Movie audiences may think of her as the heroic space pilot in the *Alien* action series or as the stalwart Dian Fossey in *Gorillas in the Mist*, but my earliest - and most memorable - image of her is as a promiscuous nymphet in Mr. Durang's tipsy travesty *Titanic*.

Several years ago before the Streep era at Yale Rep, there was a versatile young actor who specialized in character parts, some of them old men. Imagine the surprise when Henry Winkler received his first fame as the adolescent Fonz on the television show *Happy Days*.

In an earlier period Off Broadway, both Dustin Hoffman and Al Pacino gave breakthrough performances in comic roles, Mr. Hoffman as a cockney in Henry Livings's *Eh* and Mr. Pacino as a street tough in Israel Horovitz's comedy of menace *The Indian Wants the Bronx*.

Although Mr. Hoffman has moved back and forth between comedy and drama in the movies, Mr. Pacino's gift for comedy has been tapped less frequently (*Dog Day Afternoon* was one example). *Dick Tracy* reminded audiences of his talent for caricature and mimicry as he spoofed a gallery of villains including his own *Scarface*. By the end of 1990, Mr. Pacino was back in more familiar trappings as Michael Corleone. Watching him in *The Godfather Part III*, one was reminded of his stage performances in Shakespeare. His final howl of grief is Lear-like, as befitting a godfather who has divested himself of his empire and who has to face the loss of a favored child.

Mr. Pacino's *Richard III* failed on Broadway, but in its first version in Boston, it was a most visceral - and darkly comic - interpretation. At the time, it seemed a step toward a possible Shakespearean career and the eventual goal of a Pacino

King Lear, which will probably exist only as an undercurrent in a Francis Ford Coppola film.

ON THE LONDON STAGE, A FEAST OF REVENGE, MENACE AND GUILT: JULY 31, 1991

LONDON - Tyranny, torture and vengeance were the subjects of plays here this summer as England's continuing concern for political theater assumed a global perspective. On various London stages there were outspoken plays from Chile, the Soviet Union and Trinidad, among other countries. England itself was represented by a brief sketch by Harold Pinter entitled *The New World Order*, inspired by the war in the Persian Gulf. The intentionally ironic title of that piece resonated in a number of other works that questioned the results of sweeping geopolitical changes as well as revisionist history.

By far the most powerful of the plays was Ariel Dorfman's *Death and the Maiden*, in the upstairs studio space at the Royal Court Theater. Through the years, the Royal Court has itself been a frequent setting for plays that address challenging issues by playwrights from John Osborne through Caryl Churchill and Timberlake Wertenbaker.

The new drama by Mr. Dorfman, an exiled Chilean novelist and playwright who lives in the United States, was the centerpiece of a monthlong political minifestival within the annual London International Festival of Theater. Through the cooperative efforts of the Royal Court and the National Theaters, *Death and the Maiden* was paired with a series of curtain-raisers. I saw it with *The New World Order*.

It was Mr. Pinter who was instrumental in bringing the Dorfman play to the attention of the Royal Court. His own sketch, offering a variation on themes of oppression evoked in his *One for the Road* and *Mountain Language*, set the ominous tone for the main play.

As tautly directed by Lindsay Posner and acted by a cast of three headed by Juliet Stevenson, *Death and the Maiden* proved to be a play of ideas in the guise of a political thriller. In it, Mr. Dorfman illuminates both the psychopathological results of torture on an individual and the corruptive effects of years of tyranny on a country's psyche.

"People can die from an excess of truth," warns a cautious liberal lawyer (Bill Paterson). He has just been appointed to a presidential commission investigating violations of human rights in a country like Chile. But as the lawyer's wife (Ms. Stevenson) responds, the only way to salvage their communal soul is to face the truth of the past, regardless of the consequences. She speaks from her own excru-ciating experience as a victim of torture during the country's days of repression.

She has carried the psychological devastation of her ordeal with her for more than 15 years, even as the country has changed leadership. Democracy promises a new order, but having endured tyranny, she knows how easily it can return. Suddenly, the doctor who was her primary assailant re-enters her life, or so she thinks. She had been blindfolded during the interrogation and can only identify him through his voice and his mannerisms. Confronting him in the present, she plots a savage course of revenge.

Once past the contrived beginning - the doctor is introduced in an act of peacetime good samaritanism - the play moves through twists and turns, riveting the audience for an unrelenting 90 minutes. The suspenseful, cat-and-mouse drama is deepened by the political arguments, as conscience collides with tempo-ral justice, as a desire for retribution conflicts with moral responsibility.

Though the play deals with a South American situation, it achieves a univer-sality that extends beyond the political into an area that is movingly personal. Watching Ms. Stevenson take the law into her own hands, one thinks of the an-guish felt by victims of rape and other crimes who are unable to prove their case in court.

One of the many paradoxes of the play is that the husband's human rights commission will limit itself to people who have died, implying that only death can certify true victimization. As the wife wonders, in any new world order what will happen to the walking wounded and the permanently impaired, like herself? Wisely, Mr. Dorfman leaves conclusions open, in a play that audiences will carry out of the theater and into life.

On this small stage, all three actors deliver knife-edge performances, Mr. Paterson as the temporizing husband, Michael Byrne as the captor turned terri-fied captive and, most important, Ms. Stevenson as the avenging angel, a woman whose sanity is at stake along with a country's future. Coming after her deeply moving performances in recent London seasons as Hedda Gabler at the National Theater and opposite John Malkovich in *Burn This, Death and the Maiden* consol-idates her position as one of the most extraordinary of young English actresses.

CLURMAN ON THE THEATER, WITH SWEEP AND PASSION: APRIL 6, 1994

Harold Clurman always had stage presence, whether he was teaching, talking or simply going to the theater. Wherever he went, he was accompanied by a sense of theatrical history, which was as endemic to his personality as his silver-tipped cane and black velour hat. For most of his life, he undertook two potentially adversarial careers, as director and as drama critic, roles that in Clurman's case were complementary. This means that he was an astute observer of major artistic events as well as a participant in them, beginning with the founding of the Group Theater in 1931.

His memoir, *All People Are Famous*, was a step removed from autobiography. It was, he said, "about myself through others." One might suggest that the posthumous new book, *The Collected Works of Harold Clurman* (Applause Books), is about Clurman through the plays he saw. It is literally the story of his life in the theater.

Although the material is only a third of his journalistic output during 60 years, the book is as large and as heavy as an unabridged dictionary. Faced with such an immense tome, Clurman would have exclaimed, "Too big!" which is approximately what he wrote about the original Broadway production of the musical *Candide*.

The Collected Works of Harold Clurman could have been called "The Collected Words of Harold Clurman": 1,101 pages of Clurman speaking out about theater and other arts. In contrast to other collections of criticism, the book sweeps across the 20th century, offering a panoply of theater in Clurman's time. As one might expect, the book resonates with passion. Here, as in the classroom, is Clurman agitated, with his almost messianic attitude. As he said: "I'm not interested in changing someone's opinion. I want to change people." Although he was known as an outspoken zealot, he insisted that he had been shy as a youth. Shy Clurman seems like an oxymoron. He wrote as he talked: at the top of his voice.

For most of his years as a critic, he reviewed theater in the obscurity of The Nation. Many of his friends did not read his reviews until they were anthologized, but they always knew what he thought: he told them, sometimes commenting on a play on the night of its performance. He would identify the Odetsian ancestry of a provocative drama by a black author, or reach back for a reference to Stanislavsky during a performance of a play by Chekhov. He would be so convincing in his creation of a dialogue between the two Russian artists that one would wonder if he had been the third party to the conversation. Despite his volubility, he was hesitant about discussing a play with strangers. Once a theatergoer came up to him at intermission and asked what he thought of the show. "I haven't seen it yet," he said firmly.

Some of those who criticized him when he was alive thought he was too closely affiliated with the theater to be objective in his assessments of his colleagues. Actually he was highly subjective in his objectivity. As he said, "The fact that I am engaged in active stage work does not render me either timid or indulgent or resentful, malicious and vindictive," adjectives that he regarded as antithetical to the craft he practiced in print. "It makes me scrupulous and responsible." He criticized without fear or favoritism, even if it meant crossing swords with a friend like Elia Kazan.

Because he was a theater practitioner, Clurman was that rare critic who had no difficulty distinguishing between script and production, direction and performance. In a conversation at the end of the book, Kenneth Tynan declares that Clurman's single best review was of *A Streetcar Named Desire*. To condense a career to one review seems foolhardy, but rereading his "Streetcar" notice, it is easy to agree with the assessment.

What makes it such a brilliant review is that unlike his peers, he understood how Mr. Kazan's powerful production actually distorted the focus of the play. By tilting the drama in favor of Marlon Brando in the role of Stanley Kowalski, the director encouraged theatergoers to regard Blanche DuBois "as a deteriorated Southern belle" rather than "as the potential artist in all of us," as someone who is "defeated because everything in her environment conspires to degrade the meaning of her tragic situation."

Naturally, Clurman had blind spots. Although he had a fondness for vaudeville and in particular for the Marx Brothers ("absolute idiocy" as a "deliberate style"), his reviews of Broadway musicals were at least several beats less enthusiastic than those of other critics, as was the case with his response to *Brigadoon*," *Kiss Me Kate*, *West Side Story* and *Fiddler on the Roof*. About *Carousel*, he said, "I am certainly not its best audience since songs that go 'This was a real nice clam bake' fail to melt me."

Whenever possible he would couch his most negative criticism in ironic humor. Early in Alfred Lunt's career, he praised him as "more subtly and richly endowed" than Laurence Olivier, but without Olivier's opportunity to explore his range. Years later he said about Lunt and his wife, Lynn Fontanne, that they had "retired to the stage," adding that "this superb couple have been gradually converting themselves into museum pieces." Explaining his curt dismissiveness of bad plays, he said: "There is little point in specifying exactly how rotten an egg is. It is enough to say that it is inedible."

As a critic in the contemporary theater, Clurman was always forward looking, even when a playwright's philosophy was different from his, as was the case with Samuel Beckett. He was an early champion of Edward Albee and an artful analyzer of Bertolt Brecht, whom he called a "kind of Gothic primitive, in whom a rude simplicity is coupled with a shrewd mentality." He could be instructive to other critics, as in his suggestion that they might "mistake a play's materials for its meaning." This was, he said, "as if an art critic were to say that Cézanne's painting is about apples." An enemy of the snap judgment, he resolutely took a longer view. He was extremely reluctant to use the word great, reserving it for masterpieces like *King Lear*.

The Collected Works intentionally omits excerpts from several of his books, including *The Fervent Years* (his definitive history of the Group Theater), while finding room for discoveries: the diary of his trip to the Soviet Union in 1935, an account of a revealing visit to Charles Chaplin in Switzerland and a dialogue with Louis Sheaffer. In that wide-ranging conversation, he recalls that at 19 he cut a class at Columbia University to go to the first performance of Eugene O'Neill's *Beyond the Horizon*. As the "first successful attempt to write an American tragedy," it was, he said, "the most important moment in the American theater."

Because of its bulk, the book is more suitable for browsing than for nonstop reading, but one is quickly recaptured by the nimbleness of Clurman's mind and the clarity with which he expressed himself. In reviewing a collection of Henry James's criticism, he said, "To serve as something beyond a privileged press agent with a fancy vocabulary, the theater critic must be an artist, a historian and a philosopher." Clurman was all three.

DESIGN MARCHES ON: THE PRAGUE QUADRENNIAL: OCTOBER 1995

PRAGUE - The Prague Quadrennial, the World's Fair of theatrical design and architecture, has been held in this architectural gem of a city every four years since 1967. Over the years, the PQ (as it is commonly known) has drawn together theater professionals from around the world competing for awards in scenic design, costume design and theater architecture. The PQ has gone through the Prague Spring and the Velvet Revolution and a change in national identity from Czechoslovakia to the Czech Republic. As the Czechs have embraced democracy (and capitalism), art has been a consistent, stabilizing force. This does not mean that the Quadrennial is above politics. Each country is free to express political and social concerns through its art: Croatia's exhibit, for example, was about the restoration of theaters damaged during the war. The PQ, which is open to the public, also functions as an international convention in which designers from various countries can meet and exchange ideas.

This year I was one of eleven judges, an ecumenical gathering of experts from the Netherlands, Russia, Hungary, Korea and other countries. Despite minor differences, there was general agreement on important issues, and by the end of our deliberations, we were amiably exchanging addresses and toasting the PQ with Becherovka, the Czech liqueur.

With more than 40 nations, each represented by an exhibit that could fill a room of a museum, this was the largest Quadrennial yet. For a first-time visitor, the initial impression was overwhelming - a splendiferous array of designs for a universe of theater: classical, modern, post-modern, operatic, dance. I had recently been to Ming Cho Lee's annual Clambake in New York, his grand portfolio review of stage design in which the graduating students from across the country display their work. The PQ was the Clambake 20 times over, and adjoining it was a student show that in some cases equaled the professionals. There was also a wide-ranging photographic display of the design artistry of Josef Svoboda.

Taken together, the three exhibitions gave a comprehensive view of the current state and the future of theatrical design.

More than anything, PQ '95 offered persuasive proof that theater design is an advancing art, elevated by energy and imagination, irrevocably allied with new developments in the visual arts and apparently undeterred by questions of economics. Seeing the designs in models, drawings and photographs, one wanted to see the productions themselves: the tilted world of Ibsen's *Lady from the Sea* as designed by Hartmut Meyer (Germany); *Wozzeck* in Hildegarde Bechtler's wasteland environment (Great Britain); Jose Carlos Serroni's stark vision of *Happy Days* (Brazil) and the opera, *The Dream*, as imagined by Korea's Dong-Woo Park, who used picture frames and screens as scenic devices.

This year's theme, "In Search of Stage Space," was eloquently illustrated by the gold-medal-winning exhibit from Great Britain, which emphasized the varieties of stages in that country, from formal theaters to found spaces for environmental productions. Through the use of models, the exhibition documented the transfer of an exuberant production of *The Beggar's Opera* from the Swan Theater's thrust stage at Stratford-upon-Avon to the black box Pit at London's Barbican.

Although Brazil did not emphasize the PQ's central theme, it had the most theatrical exhibit, as three of its designers, Serroni, Daniela Thomas and Jose de Anchieta, demonstrated the breadth and the vividness of their art. Colorfully evocative, the Brazilians gave visitors and judges a sense of euphoria. For its conceptual boldness, Brazil was a clear winner of the top prize, the Golden Triga (or chariot).

In contrast to the expansiveness of Brazil, Poland seemed locked in a dark expressionist mode. One of the judges announced he was so moved by the Polish exhibit that he cried every time he visited it. I had a far more pragmatic reaction: in order to avoid stepping into a pool of water, I was careful not to stray from the dirt path that led through the dungeon-like labyrinth. The Polish exhibit had none of the haunting theatricality of the work of the late Tadeusz Kantor, and was brightened only by an island theater at the center of the exhibit. Proving that less can be less, a Swiss house built to explore Faust and the *Tragedy of Human Inadequacy* turned out to be merely an exercise in carpentry.

Far more effective was the Netherlands' sound and light show using light as scenery. The artful Japanese pavilion was an island of peace and solitude. Spain, the winner of the gold medal for costume design, delighted visitors with a continuous showing of a video of the opening of the Olympic Games in Barcelona in 1992. At first, the German exhibit seemed overly rigid, with its metal staircases and floors, looking like an enlarged erector set. But careful scrutiny made it clear that the Germans had pristine, highly individualized visions; some of these designs could be matched imaginatively with the work of Robert Wilson. Instead of singling out one designer, we decided to give the entire German team (Frank

Honig, Robert Ebeling, Hartmut Meyer and Peter Schubert) the gold medal for scenic design.

The United States, which had won the Golden Triga in 1987, displayed designs by Tony Walton, William Ivey Long, Robert Israel, George Tsypin, Anne Hould-Ward and Gabriel Berry. Berry, whose work I have admired since she designed the costumes for Charles Ludlam's *The Enchanted Pig*, was awarded a silver medal for her contribution to experimental theater. In direct contrast, another silver went to Finland's Anna Kontek for her opulent gowns for Stravinsky's *Nightingale*. Along the way, there were several discoveries, including scenic designers from Belorussia and Latvia.

The Russian exhibit had its own sense of novelty. The floor was covered with leaf-like contact paper. Hanging from the walls were dozens of field jackets, with an array of hats affixed to the ceiling. Partly this represented the design for a play entitled *Goodbye America!*, but it had the unfortunate effect of looking like an Army surplus store. One judge wanted to check and see if Russia had his size jacket in stock.

Repeated visits brought surprises and, occasionally, a change of mind. The Swedish exhibit seemed striking, a tall tower of 30 stage models by one designer, Soren Brunes. Although one might credit him for versatility as well as productivity, it was evident that there was a definite streak of pretension. One of his models featured an immense ball poised on top of a staircase, ready to roll down and crush a small human figure. This was not a design for the myth of Sisyphus, but for a production of *Death of a Salesman*. In refreshing contrast, the Swedish exhibit in the student show, designed by students who had trained with Brunes, was simply a glass-enclosed room, like a sound studio, filled with croquet-size plastic balls. To a background of rock music, visitors were invited to dive in and swim with the balls, as if this were a pool for thought. Naturally this was one of the most popular exhibits, a meeting place and jumping off spot for young people (and even judges).

The presentation of the prizes at the grand Valdstejn Palace was televised; it would be impossible to imagine anything similar happening in the U.S. With jury duties done, we immersed ourselves in Prague, a most theatrical city, and its environs. On a final group outing to the picturesque 13th-century town of Cesky Krumlov some three hours outside of the city, we toured a private castle theater that dates back to the 18th century. It is one of three surviving baroque theaters in Europe (the other two are in Sweden), and although performances have not been given there for many years, the theater is scheduled to undergo restoration. As we watched, the scenery was changed, with powerful winches and pulleys moving into action. The audience applauded. It was announced that our visit would have to be brief because every time there were people in the theater, the temperature and humidity rose fractionally and endangered the original designs. Amazingly, the scenery has survived in place for centuries, lending a sense of permanence to what otherwise might be regarded as an evanescent art.

WHEN PLAYWRIGHTS CROSS (OR CRISSCROSS) THE FOOTLIGHTS: FEBRUARY 5, 1996

Question: What do Athol Fugard, Harold Pinter, Sam Shepard, Christopher Durang, Alan Bennett, Wallace Shawn and William Shakespeare have in common?

Answer: They are all actors as well as playwrights: not one-shot, let's-do-it-for-the-fun-of-it actors, but professionals who have spent a substantial amount of their time and earned a substantial amount of their income from performing. The latest playwright to join this band of hyphenates is Jon Robin Baitz, who makes his acting debut in Henry Jaglom's new film, *Last Summer in the Hamptons*. Taking no chances, Mr. Baitz plays a successful playwright very much like himself; he acts with such verisimilitude that, should he so choose, he may have a second career ahead of him.

The other playwrights on that initial list (W.S. excepted) have wandered widely in their roles, appearing in their own plays and also in plays and movies by others. They have portrayed playwrights and actors as well as secret agents (Mr. Bennett) and Santa Claus (Mr. Durang). Often they have tailored roles to suit their own sensibilities.

They have acted out of curiosity, necessity, egotism or frugality (it can save a salary). Where once they might have bolstered their income by writing screenplays, now many of them double as actors. Some playwrights, weary of working in isolation, cannot help themselves; they are drawn to the spotlight. Others learn more about writing plays by being involved in the performance process.

In his recent play, *Valley Song*, Mr. Fugard portrayed two characters, one of whom was a man of mixed race.

Mr. Pinter began as an actor in English repertory. In his newly activated acting career, he has gone from the role of the keeper of a madhouse in a London revival of his play *The Hothouse* to a role as a man from MI5 in the film version of the spy story *Breaking the Code*. He seems to specialize in sinister characters of all stripes.

In direct contrast, Mr. Shepard is a movie star of heroic stature, filling the screen in films from *The Right Stuff* to *The Pelican Brief*. And he is not the only actor to win a Pulitzer Prize for Drama; the honor also belongs to George S. Kaufman, Charles Gordone, Jason Miller, Michael Cristofer and Robert Schenkkan.

Mr. Shawn may be the busiest acting playwright, with a play opening soon at the Royal National Theater in London and a prolific career as a comic character actor. Even when he is not seen, he is heard, currently as the voice of a dinosaur in *Toy Story*.

Mr. Durang, in addition to appearances in his own plays - most memorably as the Infant of Prague in *Laughing Wild* - has a whole cabaret career as the center-piece of a troupe called Chris Durang and Dawne (Dawne is two people). He is also the author of *The Actor's Nightmare*, a comedy sketch about an actor who finds himself onstage and does not know why he is there. *The Playwright's Nightmare*, yet to be written, might be about a playwright who finds himself onstage in one of his own plays, and does not remember his lines. But couldn't he improvise? Presented with that thought, Mr. Pinter, for one, is horrified. When an author's own words are at stake, improvisation is not improvement.

Mr. Bennett began as an actor and author in *Beyond the Fringe*, then moved on to write *The Madness of George III* and other works while still retaining the pre-rogatives of a performer. Now he follows other actors in roles of his own creation.

Often actors have sidestepped into playwriting: Harvey Fierstein, Steve Martin, Eric Bogosian, Samm-Art Williams, Laurence Fishburne, Keith Reddin. Then they are faced with the decision of which profession takes precedence. Clifford Odets was an actor in the Group Theater before he became that com-pany's house playwright. Alan Ayckbourn and David Mamet both started as ac-tors, then chose to remain offstage, devoting themselves to directing as their alternative theatrical profession.

Shakespeare was first, but it is a tradition honored through the centuries by playwrights from Molière to Charles Ludlam, each of whom became the essential interpreter of his own work. Noël Coward occupied a special category, writing from life and setting the tone for each of the characters he played. Anyone who follows him is shadowed by the Coward image.

Many women have contributed to both arenas: Anna Deveare Smith, Ntozake Shange, Catherine Butterfield, Susan Miller, Karen Finley. Beth Henley was once an actress, and Elaine May wears a triple crown as actress, playwright and screen-writer. But where are you, Wendy Wasserstein, Marsha Norman and Caryl Churchill?

Sometimes acting can begin as an afterthought. In an alcoholic daze, Brendan Behan blundered onto the stage during the Broadway run of *The Hostage* and in-terrupted the performance. He was, of course, discouraged from making other ap-pearances. Tennessee Williams temporarily took a stool as a barfly during the Off Broadway run of his *Small Craft Warning*, though he wisely kept his distance from more demanding roles.

Ibsen steered clear of playing the title role in *The Master Builder*; Strindberg never attempted "The Father", and Chekhov did not play Astrov, although all three roles had their roots in the playwrights' lives. Among contemporary play-wrights. Arthur Miller, Edward Albee, John Guare, Tom Stoppard and Neil

Simon remain prominently non-stagestruck. Perhaps each is waiting for an irresistible offer.

ACTORS THEATER OF LOUISVILLE: THE PLAYS TELL THE TALE: MARCH 1996

Stretched out on a series of connecting tables in the lobby of the Actors Theater of Louisville was an entire library of plays: Pulitzer Prize-winners, steps in promising directions, forgotten names. Not all of these works were performed at the Humana Festival of New American Plays, but all were written by festival playwrights. The array of scripts provided striking evidence of how, for 20 years, Actors Theater has been a prolific provider of new plays -more than 200, almost all of them mounted for the festival in their premieres.

Other organizations have, of course, specialized in new work. The Brooklyn Academy of Music's Next Wave Festival brings an international array of experimental theater to New York. The Signature Theater in New York devotes an entire season to a single playwright (coincidentally, the first two Signature choices, Romulus Linney and Lee Blessing, were Louisville regulars). Manhattan's Ensemble Studio Theater offers an annual marathon of one-act plays. But Actors Theater is unmatched in its record of discovery.

For the company to have sustained its creativity through the seesaw theatrical economies and politics of the past two decades is itself an achievement. Under the leadership of Jon Jory, the festival has taken its place as a central showcase of new writing, annually attracting hundreds of theater professionals to Louisville for an exhilarating weekend of uninterrupted theater viewing. One charge, generally raised by people who have not been to Louisville, is that the work is provincial. In fact, the work is indigenous, but it is not insular. Playwrights like Linney and Beth Henley defy the label of regionalism: In their plays, local color rises to national character. At its best, the festival provides a cross-section of the concerns of theater artists in America.

Through the years, many of the playwrights have changed, as has the diversity of the audience. There are still foreign visitors, but no longer does a platoon of English critics arrive in an airbus, put up at the Galt House (a kind of all-American theme park hotel) and then send word back to England about what's hapening in the American theater. Despite the "cast" changes, the event continues to serve as convention and floating colloquy. People gather at the theater bar between shows and compare notes; critics suddenly find themselves confronting playwrights, and vice versa; everyone has an opinion, and one person's favorite provokes another's fury.

At the 1979 festival, I argued vigorously with another New York critic who was unable to see the value in *Crimes of the Heart*, Beth Henley's breakthrough. At this year's gathering, Richard Christiansen, the astute critic of the Chicago Tribune, confessed that at the very first festival, which consisted of just two plays, he had preferred John Orlock's *Indulgences in the Louisville Harem* to D.L. Coburn's *The Gin Game*.

Year after year, for 16 of the 20 festivals, I have been in Louisville for a play-packed weekend, seeing eight or more shows, sometimes (fueled by an endless supply of coffee) as many as four a day. One encouragement has been the knowledge that Mary Bingham, the doyenne of the Louisville newspaper empire, was also going through the annual marathon. Well into her eighties, she attended all the plays (we would compare notes over dinner). The stamina of the audience is a match for the adrenalin of the actors, who rush from stage to stage, and for the inventiveness of Paul Owen, who designs all the festival's scenery.

A few conclusions based on the two decades of festival going: Jory's primary contribution has been the discovery and nurturing of new female playwrights, each of whom has a distinct voice. Led by Marsha Norman, Beth Henley and Jane Martin, the list also includes Wendy Kesselman, Mary Gallagher, Emily Mann, Shirley Lauro, Jane Anderson and Joan Ackermann. This year, Naomi Wallace is a significant addition. The festival has given center stage to such striking new actresses as Susan Kingsley and Kathy Bates, both of whom were in the original production of *Crimes of the Heart*, and increased opportunities for such veteran actresses as Anne Pitoniak and Adale O'Brien. It has given free reign as directors to Anne Bogart, Lisa Peterson, Gloria Muzio and Mary Robinson.

This is not to suggest that men have been neglected, but in the long run, they have played a subsidiary role. Curiously, many of the male playwrights discovered in Louisville seem to have had a more difficult time sustaining a playwriting career (I am thinking of James McLure and John Pielmeier, among others), whereas the women, beginning with Norman, Henley and Martin, have amassed a full body of work. And while actresses have repeatedly demonstrated their virtuosity, some of the actors simply seem to repeat themselves. This year, when Frederic Major, ATL's ubiquitous character actor, referred to himself as a "bull of a man" as a guard in Naomi Wallace's *One Flea Spare*, I had a sudden flash of memory of him at Festival Eight as a Hemingway-esque white hunter announcing, "I am as virile as a bloody bull."

Almost every year is marked by a theme or motif, sometimes paralleling public events, sometimes simply a coincidence. During one festival, there was so much murder and mayhem on stage (seven deaths, an attempted suicide and other threats of violence) that a sign indicating that there would be a gun fired during the performance remained permanently posted. The Year of the Dog (animals howling in the night on the prairie) was followed by the Year of Garbage, trash-filled stages that turned Paul Owen into a designer-scavenger. Family matters were so pervasive in the early years that an English critic defined the typical festival play as four-people-sitting-around-a-dining-room-table-talking (for variety, sometimes the play moved to the front porch). Occasionally the naturalism has been steeped in mysticism, and one year was marked by an excess of medical equipment on stage (a tip of the hat to the Humana Foundation?).

In 1996, characters incessantly searched for identity, as if it were a handbag misplaced in the cloakroom. In plays dealing with dysfunctional relationships of the sibling and marital variety, inapproachable objects met irresistible forces, sometimes to the sound of offstage music. In that sense, this season was a throwback to Festival Ten, when the dominant theme was the self-regarding philosophy of "I think, therefore I am," which I characterized as a case of putting Descartes before the house.

Conceptually, the festival tripped twice in 20 years, in both cases over commissions, with a series of flaccid adaptations of novels and with a misguided attempt to turn celebrated theatrical novices (Jimmy Breslin, William F. Buckley, Jr.) into playwrights, a policy that was subsequently reversed. Buckley is the only ATL playwright to fly in 50 of his friends for a preview, a greater distinction than the espionage play he unveiled on stage. Undaunted by his experience, Breslin returned in Festival Twenty with a 10-minute doodle about Newt Gingrich, and demonstrated that in the intervening years he had learned nothing new about playwriting.

The disappointments are far overshadowed by the surprises. In 1979, there was Beth Henley. Two years later, the actress Lisa Goodman delivered a breathtaking 17-minute monologue called *Twirler*, about the fine art and metaphor of baton twirling. At that point, the author of *Twirler* was anonymous; it was not until the next year with *Talking With* that she became pseudonymous. While others searched for the writer's identity, Romulus Linney (himself a festival favorite) aptly suggested that *Twirler* was "handed down from heaven by Flannery O'Connor." Ms. Martin's subsequent plays - rambunctious comedies, confrontational dramas about public issues and this year's wry anti-romance *Jack and Jill* - have underscored the breadth of her talent.

A few Louisville plays have become major successes in New York (*Crimes of the Heart, Agnes of God, Getting Out*) while others have failed there, sometimes because of productions that were inferior to the original (e.g., José Rivera's *Marisol*). Some valuable plays remain in Louisville or on a national circuit without ever reaching New York, starting with Ms. Martin's *Cementville* and *Keely and Du*, and including Horton Foote's *Courtship*, Eduardo Machado's *In the Eye of the Hurricane* and Barbara Damashek's *Whereabouts Unknown*.

One reason for the limited number that have transferred is that Jory has tended to favor shorter works which are more difficult to move. He has in fact been in the forefront of those who honor the one-act, and its cousin, the 10-minute play, as amusingly represented this year by David Henry Hwang and Tony Kushner. Kushner's *Reverse Transcription* lasted 20 minutes, proving that a 10-minute play is whatever one makes it.

Even as the quality of the writing varies, the directing and acting are generally of the highest caliber. When a production falters, it is something of a shock. This was the case this year with *One Flea Spare* (one of several Louisville plays to win the Susan Smith Blackburn Prize). An unsparing and poetic look at four people isolated during a 17th-century epidemic, the play suffered by being miscast in a pivotal role and by being staged arena-style. At its core, this is the equivalent of a prison play. One should have felt confined with the characters, as occurred previously with Linney's *2*.

Naturally, theatergoers were divided about the plays. I thought the three most stimulating this year were by women, beginning (despite the production) with *One Flea Spare*. Wallace, a Kentucky native, is a bold new playwright with an eye for the humanity behind historical subjects. *Jack and Jill* was a shrewdly observant and poignant chronicle of an impossible relationship. In Anne Bogart's *Going, Going, Gone*, two couples bantered Albee-style through a quintessential cocktail party, the subject being quantum mathematics - call it *Who's Afraid of the Big Bang?"* The funniest short play was Hwang's 10-minute puncturing of ethnic stereotypes, *Trying to Find Chinatown*. There is always an audience favorite, and this year, it was Joan Ackermann's *The Batting Cage*, a shaggy family comedy about sisters as rivals.

While Broadway tries, of course, to regain its disappearing audience by narrowing its perspective, the Actors Theater of Louisville remains expansive - an extended family of playwrights that has become a long-running source of theatrical vitality.

THE NOT-SO ACCIDENTAL RECOGNITION OF AN ANARCHIST: OCTOBER 15, 1997

When Dario Fo was awarded the Nobel Prize in Literature last week, it was the first time the honor had been given to an actor and clown. Mr. Fo is, of course, also a playwright, but it is as a performer of his own comedies that he has achieved his greatest international celebrity. His primary distinction is in combining all his diverse theatrical roles - he is also a director and designer - into a single act of comic self-creation.

For more than 40 years, he has been a court jester, a professional gadfly with a stinging sense of satire, attacking corruption, greed and hypocrisy, especially in high places. As a mime and mimic, he is a throwback to the guillari, medieval strolling players, but with a very contemporary political purpose.

Next to such esteemed Nobel laureates as Samuel Beckett and Luigi Pirandello, Mr. Fo seems like an alien, even an accidental choice. His response was characteristic: He said that to be in their company gave him "a certain sensation." One can imagine that the sensation was a combination of disbelief and pride, seasoned by a hearty Fovian laugh, an awareness of the irony of it all.

By recognizing Mr. Fo, the Swedish Academy expands the boundaries of literature and underscores the immediacy of theater. It legitimizes the world of performance and recognizes the contribution of comedy, and, in particular, of political satire. All outspoken monologuists, clowns and cartoonists should be aware of the importance of the award. Jonathan Swift takes his position in the pantheon with Shakespeare.

Mr. Fo has written more than 40 plays, some in collaboration with his wife, Franca Rame. Three of them (*Accidental Death of an Anarchist, We Won't Pay! We Won't Pay!* and *About Face*) and his one-man show *Mistero Buffo (Comical Mystery)* are the cornerstones of his career, but none of the work is a sacred text, least of all to the author. Those who stage his plays are encouraged to take liberties, as Mr. Fo does when he performs them. *Accidental Death* would have been duck soup to the Marx Brothers.

His work is not easy to translate or to perform, which is why his plays have had such mixed success in the United States. On Broadway, *Accidental Death* lost the sheer zaniness that another version had in London. On the other hand, the Off Broadway production of *We Won't Pay*, a scathing broadside about consumerism, seemed as relevant as it must have been in Italy; and the Yale Repertory Theater version of *About Face* was a delirious animated cartoon. Mr. Fo partly solves the language problem by performing *Mistero Buffo* in a language called grammelot, doubletalk that could have been ciphered by Sid Caesar.

One of the oddities of his career is that he is a fringe experimental artist with enormous popular appeal, at last in Italy and other European countries. He has appeared in football stadiums, circus tents and public squares as well as in intimate theaters. He is always dedicated to destroying the fourth wall of theater. Bringing his art to the people, he is the performance artist as populist.

It was not surprising that the award was greeted with astonishment by the Roman Catholic Church. Years ago, the Vatican called *Mistero Buffo* the "most blasphemous show in the history of television." He has also been attacked by the Italian Communist Party. With Mr. Fo, few take a neutral position. Throughout his life, he has thumbed his nose at tradition and offended sensibilities as his God-given right. Those who disparage him overlook his effervescent wit and his moral purpose. At heart, he is a social reformer. In common with the character of the Fool in *Accidental Death*, he throws all secret files out the window and proclaims that "justice has arrived."

In 1984, when he was finally allowed to come to the United States after twice being denied a visa on political grounds, he said to me, "I came without a sense of euphoria, with the nonchalance of a slave who has become free." He denied that he was anti-American, saying that he had always criticized "all people who are in charge of any country."

It is no great leap of the imagination to suggest that if earlier Nobel electors had been as free-spirited and open-minded as current members of the academy, radical writers like the futurist poet and playwright Vladimir Mayakovsky might have won the literature prize. The award widens the door for this and related honors to other innovative theater artists.

Although Mr. Fo had apparently been nominated (by Simone de Beauvoir and Alberto Moravia) as early as 1975, his name would probably not have appeared on many short lists of the most deserving candidates, alongside V. S. Naipaul, William Trevor and Mr. Fo's friend and countryman Umberto Eco, among others. In the world of theater, playwrights like Athol Fugard, Fernando Arrabal and Harold Pinter would certainly merit the most serious consideration. But taken on its own terms, the naming of Mr. Fo is an act of boldness. In elevating a grand clown, the Swedish Academy reveals that it has an irreverent sense of humor.

A tantalizing question remains as to what Mr. Fo will say in his acceptance speech. How can he, or anyone, follow the eloquence of William Faulkner? When he plays Stockholm, will he perform a new version of *Mistero Buffo*, and, if so, will members of the august academy, his captive audience, collapse in helpless laughter?

Perhaps he will begin with one of his favorite quotations from Mayakovsky: "The end of satire is the first alarm bell signaling the end of real democracy." Then, dashing in and out of guises, using his expressive face and body and speaking in grammelot so that everyone can understand him, he might improvise. That would surely be a Nobel first, like the winner himself.

A SECOND 'GODOT' FOR PETER HALL: DECEMBER 18, 1997

London - The first English-language production of *Waiting for Godot* opened in London in the summer of 1955. The director, Peter Hall, then 24, was just out of university. This year, 42 years later, Mr. Hall staged his second production of the Beckett play, starring Ben Kingsley and Alan Howard, and in many respects it was in striking contrast to the original.

In 1955, the cast was recruited from the secondary ranks of British actors after Alec Guinness, Ralph Richardson and other stars proved to be unavailable. The theater was The Arts Theater Club, a small West End stage on which Mr. Hall had agreed to present a series of plays. The opening, as he recalled, was a vociferous event. When Gogo said, "Nothing happens, nobody comes, nobody goes. It's awful!" a theatergoer shouted, "Hear! Hear!" Most critics echoed that reaction, except Harold Hobson, who wisely predicted that the play might "securely lodge in a corner of your mind for as long as you live."

Despite the otherwise adverse reception, London was soon, in Mr. Hall's words, gripped by "Godot mania." The play changed the director's life as well as that of the playwright and eventually was recognized as the pivotal dramatic work of the latter half of the century. Mr. Hall went on to become the head of England's two major institutional theaters, the Royal Shakespeare Company and the National Theater. Later he formed his own company to produce seasons of classics in repertory. This year he presented 13 plays at the Old Vic, and his new version of *Godot* was greeted with enthusiasm by the critics. The closing night - which I attended - became a celebratory event.

Staged with artful fidelity, the revival was exhilarating in all areas: performance, direction and design. I had the distinct feeling that many in the audience, especially the contingent of schoolchildren, were encountering *Godot* as a fresh experience. They laughed frequently and acted with surprise at the first entrance of Pozzo and Lucky. Undoubtedly, some of them were unsure whether or not Godot would arrive.

The audience response was true and accurate. This was a clear, precise and uncluttered performance. The stage was empty except for a tree and a rock. There was no massive sand pit filled with relics, such as marred Mike Nichols's Lincoln Center revival. The two leading actors exceeded even their own high level of previous accomplishment. As intended, Mr. Kingsley's Gogo was earthy, practical and comically dour, with the body language of a Buster Keaton, while Mr. Howard's Didi was aloft, adrift in the ether of his sanguineness and always ready with a joke or a philosophical observation, gamely pretending he was on a holiday. They were a beautifully synchronized team, as vaudevillians and as men at wit's end caught in the act of waiting.

Agilely adopting Irish accents, they immersed themselves in their characters, playing them for all their irony. They were actors as clowns, relishing the physical comedy as well as the verbal byplay. Lines that apparently struck theatergoers in the 1950's as unintentional self-mockery provoked a cascade of laughter, as when Gogo grumbled that there was no lack of void. There was definitely no lack of comedy or tragedy in the production, a fact that was illustrated by Denis Quilley's amusingly bombastic Pozzo, a ham actor at heart, and Greg Hicks's hapless Lucky.

Because this was the last night of *Godot* in the final week of Mr. Hall's residency in the Old Vic, a long line of people had stood outside the theater in the rain waiting for the possible return of tickets. At intermission, two theatergoers talked, as if in an act of discovery, about the religious symbolism in the play, and at the end, after the actors were greeted with cheers, one young woman said to a friend that she must read the play. She did not say, reread it.

In the program, the director put the play in historical perspective. He questioned the assumption that the opening of John Osborne's *Look Back in Anger* in 1956 represented "the reinvention of British theater." As significant as that play was in its time, he said that, as a revolution, it was "faintly parochial, which *Godot* wasn't." In contrast, *Godot* remains "a poetic masterpiece transcending all barriers and nationalities."

Mr. Hall's original idea was to take this production to New York, where it would have been the first Broadway *Godot* since the underappreciated debut of the play in 1956, but those plans were shelved after Mr. Kingsley decided to honor another acting commitment. Should Mr. Hall restage the play on Broadway, it would apparently be without Mr. Kingsley and Mr. Howard, which would be a loss for the actors as well as for American audiences.

During his recent seasons, Mr. Hall has freely alternated Shakespeare with modern classics and occasional new plays. His success has been mixed, but the principle behind his company remains not only viable but vital. Mr. Howard did *King Lear* as well as *Godot*, and Michael Pennington, Geraldine McEwan, Felicity Kendal and others were able to challenge themselves in a diversity of plays.

The Old Vic, a theater rich with history reaching back to 1818 and to its glory days under the guidance of Lilian Baylis in the early 20th century, was the ideal setting for such an undertaking. Ending Mr. Hall's tenancy, David and Ed Mirvish, the Canadian owners of the Old Vic, have put the building up for sale. There is the possibility that it will be turned into a showplace for touring entertainments or worse. At the closing night of *Lear*, Mr. Hall came out on the stage and expressed his dread that the theater might become a tourist attraction "along the lines of the London Dungeon."

Whatever the fate of the Old Vic or of Mr. Hall's company, one will remember the director's return to *Godot* as the finest production of the play since Beckett's own German-language version in 1977.

2

DIRECTORS

INGMAR BERGMAN

MISS JULIE: JUNE 12, 1991

It is a midsummer night and the light through the windows of the kitchen has an unnatural glow. In the course of Ingmar Bergman's staging of Strindberg's *Miss Julie*, that light will go through many subtle changes, counterpointing the emotional turbulence of the characters. Their duel is a class war as well as a fierce battle of the sexes.

Despite all the portent, the play never loses its personal dimension, its sense of wounds mutually inflicted. Strindberg called *Miss Julie* a naturalistic tragedy, a fact that has never been so evident as in Mr. Bergman's stunning production. This is the opening play of the Royal Dramatic Theater of Sweden's all too brief season at the Brooklyn Academy of Music.

As the production flawlessly unfolds on stage at the Majestic Theater, one necessarily thinks of Bergman films like *Persona*, in which the director confines disparate characters in domestic disharmony. Though the play remains firmly fixed within that kitchen, there is a feeling of life outside the room. *Miss Julie* is commonly regarded as a small-scale intimate drama. The director enlarges its dramatic vision so that the audience more clearly understands the psychological and societal forces that drive the title character to her destructive acts.

Initially, we see only the inhabitants of the kitchen: Jean, the valet, and Kristin, the cook. Jean (Peter Stormare) exudes fastidiousness. Pouring himself a glass of wine, he pretends to be both servant and master, and, after a sip, he offers himself an approving glance. Except for the accident of his birth, he could be an aristocrat. Later we will see that Miss Julie (Lena Olin) has a vulgarity that would be unacceptable in the servant class. Kristin (Gerthi Kulle) is quietly submissive in the background, demeaning herself to Jean's wishes.

Gunilla Palmstierna-Weiss's pale setting is perfect - everything neatly arranged in a pristine, painterly environment. Suddenly Miss Julie enters, her red dress and her forthright manner a brusque intrusion on the placidity of the room. Ms. Olin brings with her a swirl of sensuality and immediately embarks on the seduction of Jean. But which one is the predator? Both could answer the call, as each is, to use the title of a related Strindberg drama, "playing with fire."

Ms. Olin is a glamorous figure and she and Mr. Stormare are mutually attracted - with good reason. They are so evenly matched that a newcomer to the play might not be aware which character is the stronger. Although Miss Julie grasps control of her fate, it is Jean who will survive the "spell of this magical night."

Theatergoers can hear the dialogue in English on headsets, although, without the translation, one is still aware of the themes - of submission, dishonor and revenge, of the urge but not the will toward flight. Even in moments of silence, the production never loses its highly charged intensity.

Just as the play alternates currents, Ms. Olin is mercurial as Miss Julie. She is demanding in her approach to Jean, yet at odd times seems almost unsure of herself, summoning demons she is unable to control. The actress offers a beautifully seductive, virtuosic performance, one that translates in any language.

Mr. Stormare, who played the title role in Mr. Bergman's version of *Hamlet* several seasons ago at the Brooklyn Academy, also reveals the breadth of his artistry. His Jean is cool in his arrogance and childlike about receiving his due, whether it is the admiration of Kristin or a fulfillment of a youthful dream of paradise on earth. Jean can seem stiff and fussy. Mr. Stormare keeps him aggressively masculine and also locates the self-mocking humor, as in his response to Miss Julie's suggestion that death may be his solution. "Die?" he says, dismissing the notion. "That's stupid. I'd rather start a hotel."

In a role that is often neglected, Ms. Kulle offers a proud and watchful portrait of Kristin. She endures indignities, while shrinking from all of Ms. Olin's patronizing overtures. Because the actress is herself attractive, she poses more of an alternative to Miss Julie than in many productions.

The director devises an evocative variation on the servants who dance onstage in a mime show. Instead of having them represent a joy of life, they are all self-indulgently drunk, falling over themselves like figures in a Breughel canvas.

The production runs almost two hours rather than the author's suggested 90 minutes. Mr. Bergman has slightly expanded the text by inserting a passage cut by Strindberg. But the primary reason for the length is that the director, with his cinematic eye, takes time for subtext, using the kitchen as an active presence and dramatizing mood along with character. This is an eloquent performance of a masterwork, in every sense a transcendant evening of theater.

⌘

LONG DAY'S JOURNEY INTO NIGHT: JUNE 17, 1991

Ingmar Bergman's version of *Long Day's Journey Into Night* is an evening of anguished cries and fearful whispers, in which the troubled Tyrones haunt one another with specters from the past. In this Swedish-language production, the director has made minor alterations in the text, but has kept the powerful core of O'Neill's masterpiece intact.

In contrast, Eimuntas Nekrosius's Lithuanian-language production of *Uncle Vanya* is an eccentric adaptation, like no other version of the play one has seen - or that Chekhov could have imagined. This State Theater of Lithuania production is earnest in its eagerness to be unconventional and unerring in its ability to be digressionary.

Both plays are part of the New York International Festival of the Arts.

Coming after the Royal Dramatic Theater of Sweden presentation of *Miss Julie* last week, *Long Day's Journey* proves that Mr. Bergman is as attuned to O'Neill's ruefulness as he is to Strindberg's mordancy. While retaining the Irish-American sensibility of the original, the director has added a few unobtrusive Swedish touches (in setting and costumes). Stripping the play of excess trappings, he and his designer, Gunilla Palmstierna-Weiss, have unmoored it on a platform, a simulated island representing a sparsely furnished Tyrone parlor. At significant moments, striking cinematic images are projected in the background: the exterior of the home, a Mark Rothko-like window and the fog itself. Without losing its naturalism, the play gains in symbolic resonance.

Under Mr. Bergman's brilliant direction, the actors become a close-knit chamber quartet, led by Bibi Andersson, who uncovers a great emotional range in the role of Mary Tyrone. She brings with her a fragile beauty as well as a profoundly poetic sense of the mother's loneliness.

Even when she is offstage, as in most of the final scene, one is aware of her luminous presence and of the meaningfulness of her character to the other members of the family. When she is onstage, the others cannot stop watching her, looking futilely for a ray of hope in a sky fogged with despair.

Though Jarl Kulle begins too effusively as James Tyrone, he soon fills the role with an actorial authority, striking profiles and launching into speeches in the manner of a man who has spent his life onstage and is compulsively theatrical even in life.

Peter Stormare, who played the valet in *Miss Julie* and the title role in Mr. Bergman's *Hamlet*, continues to demonstrate his virtuosity, with a lyrical and very natural approach to Edmund. He makes a sometimes subordinated role seem more consequential. It is impossible to watch any performance of Jamie Tyrone without thinking of Jason Robards, who created the role and left his signature on it. Thommy Berggren moves in a disparate direction, emphasizing the character's flashiness as a helpless habitue of seedy bars and bordellos. Their late-night battle is, as it should be, a revelation for both brothers.

The production stresses the emotional turmoil and the bonds within this divisive family, as each character longs to be loved and respected by the others. Frequently, they embrace as if reaching for a cohesiveness that can never exist because as Mary Tyrone observes: "The past is the present. It's the future, too."

Although the production runs nearly four hours, the intensity of the performance is unabating. The opposite is true of Mr. Nekrosius's three-and-a-half-hour *Uncle Vanya*. It seems endless.

The Lithuanian *Vanya* takes place in an indeterminate environment that could be an anteroom to *Grand Hotel*. It begins not, as in the original, with the old nurse serving tea from a samovar but with her reclining on a chair and Astrov singeing her with flames in an apparent attempt to cure some unnamed malady. Then the doctor rolls up one sleeve and a leg of his trousers, as if he is about to give himself a double dose of drugs. Next, he lifts a doorstop-size weight above his shoulders.

All these early morning activities do nothing except to delay the play. Subsequent divergencies are for undefined dramatic and political purposes, as the director apparently tries to equate the Professor's domination of the household with the Soviet repression of the Baltic states.

When Astrov tells Yelena about his environmentalist concerns, he shows her minuscule maps, holding them up with tweezers, in the manner of a dentist displaying X-rays of teeth. It is possible that this is meant as a symbolic commentary on a country's shrinking resources. More likely it is a commentary on a director's overreaching imagination and his disregard of Chekhovian context. Despite all the directorial proclamations and critical attempts at exegesis during the play's international tour, the political statements seem superimposed rather than organic.

In what would have been news to the author, the play is presented as a black comedy. It is not clear what is intended to be comic and what is unintentionally amusing. Sonya, for example, is weighted by two thick ugly braids of hair that hang down almost to her toes. When Yelena says politely that she has beautiful hair, the line becomes laughable. The servants have been transformed into clowns, skating onstage in slippery shoes and pummeling their masters in their own private revolution.

Because of the directorial concept, experienced actors are led into prodigal paths, where it is difficult to measure performance. The Professor is smug to the point of being supercilious. Still there is no justification for having the actor walk at a perpetual tilt or to have him tied up at the end of the play, like a carpet awaiting shipment.

When he is not lifting weights, Kostas Smoriginas can be found shooting Vanya's pistol and crawling around the stage under the cover of an animal skin, all of which may add to Astrov's world weariness. Two performances are as pointed as they are authentic. Juozas Pocius is amusing as homely old Waffles, and in the title role Vidas Petkevicius demonstrates an empathetic understanding of Vanya's desperation. Around them is an ersatz experimentalist environment.

With his expansive vision, Mr. Bergman illuminates O'Neill's universality while Mr. Nekrosius takes a deconstructionist and reductive approach to Chekhov.

A DOLL'S HOUSE: JUNE 20, 1991

Nora in Ingmar Bergman's astonishing production of *A Doll's House* is charmingly seductive, intelligent and beautiful. In the director's interpretation and in Pernilla Ostergren's masterly portrayal, she is not a frivolous child-wife, but a willful woman and a mine of emotional resources. This seemingly revisionist approach to Ibsen's classic does not negate any of Nora's acknowledged traits, but it probes deeply into her psyche.

In every sense, Mr. Bergman's version makes the play even more relevant to contemporary society. Traditional revivals emphasize Nora's ingenuousness and her husband's small-minded vindictiveness. In this production, both characters are more complex and unpredictable. The Torvald of Per Mattsson is certainly an egoist, but he is also very much a banker on the rise and someone who is fiercely protective of his image.

One of the director's many contributions is to locate and dramatize the passion in the Nora-Torvald relationship. This Nora is far more than a coquette. She is a highly sensual woman with a sense of vanity and a determination to achieve her goals.

Ms. Ostergren's performance, along with those of Lena Olin in *Miss Julie* and Bibi Andersson in *Long Day's Journey Into Night*, the previous Bergman productions at the Brooklyn Academy of Music, remind one of the director's cinematic success with roles for actresses. In the case of each play, a woman becomes by far the dominant figure.

The production of *A Doll's House* is searingly intense and filled with Bergmanesque images and directorial surprises. Using a Swedish translation by Klas Ostergren (translated into English over headsets), Mr. Bergman has re-ordered the text and in some areas applied a scalpel, while remaining faithful to Ibsen. In his adaptation, the director has removed the minor household characters and replaced the three Helmer children with one, a girl, who is used for symbolic as well as narrative purposes.

A Doll's House takes place, as does Mr. Bergman's version of *Long Day's Journey*, on an island-like platform, which is sparsely and imaginatively furnished by Gunilla Palmstierna-Weiss. Instead of the one set of the original play, there is a succession of three rooms - parlor, dining room and bedroom, for a climactic scene that as much as anything on stage testifies to Mr. Bergman's inspiration.

There are moments that cause the audience to gasp, as when Krogstad, furious at Nora's resistant manner, strikes her on the shoulder, physicalizing his fury at her and at the injustice he thinks has been inflicted on him. Repeatedly and with great effectiveness, there are visceral representations of inward emotions.

Moving a step away from naturalism, the production is as stylized as a Bergman film. That platform set is backed by a large photograph of the interior of the Helmer home, a picture that itself resonates with significant detail. When the actors are not participating in a scene, they sit on either side of the platform, as silent witnesses to what is occurring at center stage. When they enter a scene, it is without introduction. There are no transitions, just quick cinematic cuts, capturing the cross-currents of conflict that permeate this household.

Ms. Ostergren, who was Ophelia in Mr. Bergman's *Hamlet*, is a radiantly expressive actress, combining intimacy with boldness, as in her tarantella. Lifting her skirts high above her knees, she dances with ferocity on top of a table, threatening to be swept away in a dance of death. Mr. Mattsson, dazzled by his wife, is a handsome, elegant Torvald, but with an insidiousness that would make him an uncomfortable companion and employer.

Erland Josephson is equally fine as Dr. Rank. In his characterization, the doctor has an air of vulnerability as well as authority, as he succumbs to Nora's sly charms. Their flirtation is made more flagrant and gives a clearer picture of why the doctor has become a ubiquitous guest in this house.

Mr. Bergman's most radical stroke is reserved for last. He splits the final act in two, so that the showdown between Nora and Torvald takes place in their bedroom, where a now rebellious and triumphant wife assails her husband, who has been aroused from his bed. He is amazed at the violence of her reaction. When he declares, "No one sacrifices his honor for love," Ms. Ostergren exudes confidence as she says, simply, "Thousands of women have."

As Ms. Ostergren's Nora abandons her marriage, it is impossible to believe there is the slightest hope for "a miracle" of reconciliation. That door slam reverberates more conclusively than in other productions of the play.

With *A Doll's House* following *Miss Julie* and *Long Day's Journey*, it is evident that the visit of Mr. Bergman and the Royal Dramatic Theater of Sweden is the most memorable theatrical event of the New York International Festival of the Arts - and of the theater season.

⤴

PEER GYNT: MAY 13, 1993

In his vision of *Peer Gynt* (at the Brooklyn Academy of Music), Ingmar Bergman interprets the Ibsen epic as both dream play and clown play. Searching for a key to unlock this awesome poetic drama, the director finds it in Peer's childhood fantasies, the dreams that he shares with his mother. To a background of trolls and international intrigue, the title character acts out one man's lifelong quest for spiritual self-awareness.

Coming after Mr. Bergman's highly politicized *Hamlet* and his revelatory season of Strindberg, Ibsen and O'Neill at the Brooklyn Academy, *Peer Gynt* reaffirms his position in the pantheon of experimental theater artists. In his 70's he retains a youthful brashness. His *Peer Gynt* is a fabulistic folk tale filled with visual richness and an ebullient sense of comedy. His first production of the play in 1957 was apparently stark and simple. It starred Max von Sydow, who had recently appeared in *The Seventh Seal*, which might have been considered a cinematic companion piece.

With the new *Peer*, one thinks at first of *Fanny and Alexander*, as the title character is projected back to his youth. In this case there is only a family of two, expressing an emotional and intellectual bond. As Peer spins his fanciful tales, his mother is his audience, encouraging him even while she accuses him of lying, as in his story of a wild ride on a reindeer's back.

Peer is a natural storyteller and in Borje Ahlstedt's extraordinary performance, he is also a clown, a boisterous bad boy whose boastfulness is matched by his insecurity. With his round, ruddy face and stocky build, Mr. Ahlstedt has a comedic look. That fact makes him an easy object for ridicule by wedding guests in a neighboring town and in the troll kingdom where he is mocked for being the only creature without a tail.

In Mark Lamos's version of the play at Hartford Stage, Richard Thomas was a kind of anti-Hamlet, a man of action who refused to be introspective. Derek Jacobi's performance in a chamber production at Stratford-on-Avon was closer to that of Mr. Ahlstedt but with less of an emphasis on the character's self-mocking drollery. In Mr. Ahlstedt's portrayal, Peer becomes a tragic clown who will try anything on a dare. What he cannot do he will pretend to have done. Improvising his life with an irrepressible spontaneity, he soon finds that he has undermined all chance for happiness or stability.

Mr. Bergman has chosen to begin the play inside the mother's cottage rather than on a wooded hillside. As Peer embarks on his adventures, the home - with its artfully burnished look - remains in place. It is the backdrop for all his travels, which occur on and around a suspended platform. The production was originally conceived for a small studio stage at the Royal Dramatic Theater of Sweden, but, by sending a ramp into the audience, the director has managed to evoke an intimacy in the vastness of the BAM Opera House.

As it is raised and lowered, the platform achieves its own physicality. Peer peeps over it, rolls down it and hides behind it. Soon the platform becomes the mountain kingdom swarming with grotesque trolls. The production is filled with indelible stage pictures. In one nightmare, Peer is surrounded by a chorus of bowler-hatted clowns, Chaplining his image to infinity. Later when he becomes a world traveler and king of capitalism, he is faced by a frieze of mountebanks.

In the middle section of the play, there is momentary stasis, as Peer seems to repeat himself in contrasting situations: on the North Africa coast, in the desert. This section is itself a sandtrap for directors, and Mr. Bergman does not elude all obstacles. There are, however, striking images: a man as ostrich springing across the stage; a madhouse tableau with Napoleon, Icarus and an Egyptian mummy competing for attention like lunatics in *Marat/Sade*.

When Peer is back at sea, the platform becomes a ship, rolling in a tempest. We hear the deep rumbling of waves threatening to drown the prodigal. Back in his homeland, Mr. Ahlstedt adds a moving Beckettian dimension to his performance. While looking for a witness to his humanity, he sits on the ground in a daze and watches the whirl pass by. There is more than a measure of Beckett's Gogo in this characterization, as he elucidates man's helplessness in confrontation with his fate.

His life is inextricably bound up with women, with his mother (Bibi Andersson, in a powerful matriarchal performance) and with his beloved Solveig (the beautiful Lena Endre). Like Ulysses's Penelope, Solveig waits a lifetime for her lover's return.

The play is wordy and for those who do not understand Swedish, headsets are a necessary guide. Lars Forssell's Swedish version, translated into English, has an overlay of anachronisms. Although one would prefer a text more dutiful to the original, there is a hearty line of malicious humor, as in the Troll King's decision to try the life of an actor. "I hear they're looking for regional types," he says, and adds, "There must be a role for an old troll."

Peer Gynt is followed next week by Mr. Bergman's production of Yukio Mishima's *Madame de Sade*. As with the director's other visits to the Brooklyn Academy, this is an essential theatrical experience.

MADAME DE SADE: MAY 22, 1993

By staging a production of astonishing lucidity and theatricality, Ingmar Bergman has reinvented Yukio Mishima's *Madame de Sade*. In his hands, it becomes a political power play as well as a shocking discourse on the guises of evil. Written in 1965, five years before Mishima's ritual suicide, the play is about the Marquis de

Sade "as seen through women's eyes." De Sade never appears on stage, but we hear in grotesque and sometimes glowing detail about the paradoxes of his perversity.

Mishima, who evidently identified with de Sade, paired opposites: the sacred and the profane, the beautiful and the horrific. The greater truth about the character of de Sade is that he is whatever the women and the world want him to be. For one of the women he is a lovable vampire. At the end of the play there is the suggestion that his decadence has not only destroyed women but may also have contributed to the French Revolution.

The idea of a play about France written in Japanese and intended to be played by Japanese actresses and now performed in Swedish by the Royal Dramatic Theater of Sweden poses a multinational picture of Babel proportions. Banish all such thoughts when confronting Mr. Bergman's version.

On every count - acting, design, script interpretation and directorial conceptualization - Mr. Bergman grasps the quintessence of the play and of de Sade's mania. In two previous New York productions, most recently in 1988 at the Pan Asian Repertory Theater, *Madame de Sade* seemed to be a sequence of stilted conversations that kept eluding the central issue. The opposite turns out to be true. Although it remains a play of ideas with little overt action, it surges with dramatic intensity. Mr. Bergman can do more with the sudden flash of a fan than other directors can with a crescendo of violence.

Sadism is approached through elegance. The women in the play - three real people, de Sade's wife, her mother and her sister, and three imagined by the author - are in an 18th century drawing room. Even as they talk about de Sade's debauchery, they mind their courtly manners.

Gradually each character is realized with a searing identity, always in relation to de Sade himself, who is imprisoned during the 18 years of the play. His wife (Stina Ekblad), a symbol of marital devotion, is swept away by her own delusory dreams in which her husband has a satanic saintliness. Demanding decorum, her mother (Anita Bjork) is de Sade's most malevolent critic, but she practices her own stratagems of deceit as she plots to end her daughter's marriage. Radiating sensuality is Countess de Saint-Fond (Agneta Ekmanner), who would like to become a female de Sade. Acrimony arises as each battles for domination and as morality bows to self-interest. The work shares a period and subject matter with *Marat/Sade* and *Les Liaisons Dangereuses*.

The director orchestrates the warring emotions as well as the movements of the cast. Like Tissot paintings come to life, the elegantly costumed actresses perform with balletic magnetism, shifting positions for a pas de duel. They communicate their feelings with their eyes and their voices, which we hear in synchronization with the simultaneous translation over headsets.

These are marvelous actresses who can isolate defining characteristics in a gesture, the way, for example, the sister displays her vanity in her confident stride.

Often they seem to simulate animals in the wild, as in the pantherlike grace of Ms. Ekmanner. In one scene, Ms. Bjork and Ms. Ekblad, unable to resolve their mother-daughter conflict, tear at each other in anger and frustration. Mr. Bergman discloses intimacy between women in *Madame de Sade* with the same perceptiveness that he brought to *Persona* and *Cries and Whispers*.

As de Sade's imprisonment continues, the mood and environment alter. The play takes place on an open set framed with arches, through which we see the outline of a Japanese cherry tree, a rare Oriental touch. In the second act, this emblematic image is replaced by a flame-red sky and in the third by billowing clouds (backed by the sound of wind). From drawing room reflectiveness, the play moves to revolution. At the same time, the wife's period dress is replaced by a stark, ascetic cloak. Eventually the least important character turns out to be pivotal. The housekeeper has been watching and waiting (in both senses), and after the revolution begins, she becomes a gathering storm and threatens to take center stage.

Mishima said he had written the play to solve the mystery of Madame de Sade, wondering how a woman totally dedicated to her husband during his confinement could immediately abandon him on his release. In Mr. Bergman's sublime version, the steps on that path are clarified. To use the author's words in a different context, the director has "unlocked a strange door on a sky full of stars." From his films, this play and his other productions at the Brooklyn Academy, it is evident that no other director has achieved such brilliance both on screen and on stage.

PETER BROOK

TIMON OF ATHENS: AUGUST 10, 1975

PARIS - The biggest dramatic hit in Paris this past season was *Timon d'Athènes*, Peter Brook's startling new version of Shakespeare's *Timon of Athens*, performed in French (in an adaptation by Jean-Claude Carrière) by an international cast at Théâtre des Bouffes-du-Nord, a shattered shell of a theater in a working-class section of Paris. The choice of the play, the language and the location were all considered decisions on Mr. Brook's part.

Clearly the Bouffe-du-Nord was the play's natural environment. Following a fire, the theater remained unused for 25 years - until Mr. Brook discovered it: a "lost" theater for a "lost" play. Instead of reconditioning the building, Mr. Brook left it untouched - a scarred, battered hulk. During the play's run, it was a cracked-mirror image of the depleted civilization depicted on stage. Backless hard bleachers occupied what once was the orchestra (cheap seats for the masses). The more expensive and comfortable, but less choice, seats were in the balcony - removed from the center of the action.

The play was performed informally in and out of the audience, on a flat space backed by a cavernous pit. Entrances and exits were made as if up from and down to nether regions, and occasional soliloquies and dialogues were delivered from toweringly high promontories - gaping wounds in the walls - by actors who looked like victims waiting to be evacuated from a disaster. In the first act, which takes place in Athens, the staging, by design, was simple but basically naturalistic. The second act, Timon's exile, was stark, barren and metaphysical. Mr. Brook created a dry Beckettian desert inhabited by a hermit Timon.

In Mr. Brook's hands, *Timon of Athens*, seemingly a most uncontemporary play - why should we care if the richest man in Athens swings impulsively from open-handed philanthropy to total misanthropy? - becomes enormously relevant. And Mr. Brook manages this without imposing a joltingly "modern" interpretation.

Mr. Brook's Timon faces, in the director's phrase, "the profound liberal dilemma." His entire life is his supposed altruism, his indulgence not only of his friends but of passing acquaintances. Timon is an easy mark. When he is disappointed and disillusioned, he veers suddenly off the track, removes himself from his shallow civilization and retreats. He becomes, in a sense, a Thoreau of Athens, or, perhaps more to Mr. Brook's political point, a kind of Eugene McCarthy after being rebuffed by the electorate. Defeated, this Timon hastily blames the system, rather than searching himself for weaknesses of leadership.

Even for Mr. Brook, who in the past specialized in form-upsetting productions of Shakespeare, *Timon* is an unusual venture. It is, in fact, something of a synthesis of his work at the Royal Shakespeare Company and at the International Center. I saw the production on the closing night of its current Paris engagement (a superlative performance that was recorded on film for French television). It probably will be performed again this coming season, for this is a landmark production, one that measures up to the director's other significant collaborations with Shakespeare: his Beckett-like *King Lear* and his magical *A Midsummer Night's Dream*. In terms of taking a lesser Shakespearean play and transforming it into something major, Mr. Brook himself compares it with his productions of *Titus Andronicus* (with Laurence Olivier) and *Measure for Measure* (with John Gielgud).

COMEDY, TRAGEDY AND 'MYSTICAL FANTASY' FROM PETER BROOK: MAY 25, 1980

Peter Brook's season at the La Mama Annex, consisting of four plays in repertory, represents the culmination of his years of experimentation with his Paris-based company, the International Center for Theater Research. The plays, drawn from widely divergent sources, are essential experiences for anyone concerned with the progress of innovative theater.

On one comic double bill are *L'Os*, a primitive African folk fable about envy and greed, and Mr. Brook's uproarious escapade based upon Alfred Jarry's *Ubu*, which provoked riots in Paris in 1896 and which has come to be acknowledged as the harbinger of modern absurdist comedy. Another presentation is *The Ik*, an adaptation of *The Mountain People*, Colin Turnbull's anthropological study of a North Ugandan tribe - a harrowing investigation of a people forced into degradation. The final play, the zenith of the Brook season, is *The Conference of the Birds*, based on a 12th-century Persian poem about a spiritual quest for a purpose in life.

Comedy, tragedy and a magic carpet of mystical fantasy - the contrasting evenings are filtered through Mr. Brook's vision of what theater can be, and they are united by a performance technique that has been taught and nurtured within an ensemble of extraordinary actors.

Before the plays opened at La Mama, it was suggested that critics attend the events in sequence and that they approach them as a body of work. It is hoped that, given the time and the availability of tickets for the engagement, theatergoers will also follow that suggestion. Not only are the plays thematically connected, but they also follow a natural progression. The director thinks of them, appropriately, as a trilogy.

L'Os is a prelude not only to *Ubu* but to all of the plays - a tale about a man so obsessed with his own pride, possessions and appetites that he sacrifices his humanity and, eventually, even his life. *Ubu* is an attack on the barbarism of civilization. A mock Macbeth, the scoundrel Ubu plots to kill a king and to steal a kingdom. In the process he destroys his countrymen as well as enemies. After Ubu has satiated his desires, the nation is destitute.

Struggling to survive in a post-*Ubu* wasteland are *The Ik*, a people feeding off each other as if they were carrion. For this tribe, evicted from its homeland, wrenched from its way of sustenance - the Ik are hunters who are forced to be farmers - all bonds have been removed. No feelings of kindness or kinship continue to exist. The only lingering desire is for acquisition. Malice and selfishness become the ruling order.

What follows after the dark tragedy of *The Ik* is the quest of *The Conference of the Birds*. A nation of birds, emblems for nomadic and fallible man, seeks salvation. Led by a guiding bird called the Hoopoe, they cross seven dangerous valleys in a journey to find their true king, who is neither an evil Ubu nor a redeeming god, but themselves. The Hoopoe forces his followers to look into the mirror of their lives, to find man's fate in man's soul. Mr. Brook's journey ends on a note of hope: Ik-ness is not inevitable.

In his work, the director has tried to shatter all preconceptions as to what constitutes a stage - and what constitutes theater. His current season takes place in a room as large and as barren as a warehouse. Avoiding artifice, the plays draw deeply from the imagination of the director, the actors and the audience. Together we fill in the empty space. What Mr. Brook offers is not minimal, but maximal theater.

"Nothing is as dangerous as standing still." The line is spoken by Natasha Parry in *The Conference of the Birds*. The actress happens to be married to the director, a fact that underscores the aptness of the line, as applied to his life's work or to the play itself. In his artistic restlessness, Mr. Brook might be compared to a whirling dervish. Not content with being England's foremost director of Shakespeare, he staged his radical productions of *King Lear* and *A Midsummer Night's Dream* and moved on to Paris with his new company. Since then, with occasional steps back into the traditional repertory - last season with *Antony and Cleopatra* at the Royal Shakespeare Company - he has been concerned with theater as an art of distillation.

We begin this current three-part adventure in an empty space, which, with an absolute minimum of production detail, becomes the Africa of *L'Os* and the Poland of *Ubu*. Mr. Brook's *Ubu* is strewn with bricks - enough to build a small chimney - and two industrial spools, one large, one small, the kind used for coiling cables. The spools become tables, platforms and thrones. At one point the larger spool becomes a deadly comic vehicle, rolling like a chariot over a track of people. Later, the heads of Ubu's victims peer comically over the edge of the spool, like disembodied corpses rising from their grave. When Ubu's guests arrive for dinner, he serves them bricks instead of veal and chicken, and the actors savor them as if they were delicacies. Teeteringly, Ubu steps onto a single brick representing the highest mountain cliff. In this and countless other instances we are reminded of Mr. Brook's instinctive sense of comedy.

For *The Ik*, in simulation of the African landscape, the floor is covered with earth, raked into paths and patterns. For *The Conference of the Birds*, the company brushes the ground clean and spreads it with flowing Oriental carpets, wall to wall and floor to ceiling. The actors, who, up to now, have been garbed in homespun, don elegant robes and gowns. They carry and sometimes they wear exotic Balinese masks. The setting is exquisite, and even the lighting, which had been unvarying in its intensity, changes subtly from scene to scene. There is more extensive use of music. That remarkable percussionist, Toshi Tsuchitori - a deus ex machina of elemental sounds - is joined by a violinist and flutist.

The actors cover their hands with carved heads of birds - fist puppets - and, gracefully arching their arms under their voluminous garments, they strut balletically and even seem to fly. As we watch, they become omniscient owls, an ostrich who has strode across the desert (the ostrich's head is the gnarled end of a long branch), a caged parrot, and a phoenix rising from the ashes. The actors are expert at mime and movement; it is as if they have joined the Bunraku theater both as puppeteers and as puppets, turning their own bodies into winged creatures. At the same time, many members of the ensemble have a verbal felicity. Bob Lloyd plays the birds' leader with an articulateness worthy of Shakespeare.

Over three evenings, we witness the diversity of the actors' talent. Andreas Katsulas's Ubu is a kind of comic caveman, Sid Caesar as Fred Flintstone. In *The Ik*, Mr. Katsulas is the inquiring Colin Turnbull, suddenly thrown into a looking-glass world. In *The Conference of the Birds*, he is a one-man aviary; in his finest plumage, he parades across the stage as a pampered peacock. The actors are exemplary communicators: Malick Bowens and Yoshi Oida as best friends turned jealous rivals in *L'Os*; Bruce Myers as a hopelessly deceitful Ik guide; Miriam Goldschmidt as the maneuvering Ma Ubu; Harold Baines and Mark Morris as two small Ik children who easily emulate their parents' inhumanity.

In words and gestures, the company transmits what might be termed Brook's Universal Language. Years ago in Shiraz, together with the poet, Ted Hughes, the director tried to invent a language called Orghast, which was so guttural as to seem non-verbal. He has apparently shelved Orghast, but not his search for a way to transcend linguistic barriers. In *Ubu*, the actors speak a frappé of emphatic schoolboy French punctuated by explanatory bursts of English. This has the double effect of elucidating the dialogue and of commenting ironically on the action. *The Ik* is in English, with a leavening of Ik, or pseudo-Ik, for enrichment. *The Conference of the Birds* is in English and in bird sounds. All the plays can be easily understood, as they have been wherever the Brook troupe has traveled, from African villages to its theater in Paris.

Sightlines are excellent at La Mama, but it should be noted that most of the seats are backless and that it becomes very warm in the theater. This is especially true during the first two evenings, when the audience as well as the actors are bathed in a relentless stream of light. This apparent lack of comfort seems to be a hallmark for Mr. Brook. One watched his version of *Timon of Athens* in Paris sitting - and sweltering - on the narrowest and hardest of benches. In all respects, this director likes to challenge rather than to cosset an audience.

If one can attend only one of the events, the choice would be *The Conference of the Birds*. Those who saw the work in its earlier version in 1973 at the Brooklyn Academy of Music should be astonished by the change. A preliminary and rudimentary workshop sketch has been transmuted into an evening of grandeur. On the final day all four plays will be presented in their proper sequence - a marathon expedition in company with the genius of Peter Brook.

THE CHERRY ORCHARD: AUGUST 9, 1981

PARIS - In his 38 years as a director, Peter Brook has often altered our way of looking at theater. His production of *A Midsummer Night's Dream* banished the fairy dust encrusting the text and turned the play into a bright, white acrobatic carnival. With *Marat/Sade*, audience and actors were confined in the insane asylum at Charenton for an evening of revolutionary theater. His production of *Timon of Athens* in Paris turned Timon into the equivalent of a modern political exile, scuttering crablike into the desert. Last year at La Mama, Mr. Brook took us on a mystical journey to ancient Persia in the epic *The Conference of the Birds*. Working with both his international experimental company and the Royal Shakespeare Company, staging plays from Persepolis to Broadway, Mr. Brook has remained unpredictable. The range of his work is perhaps unmatched by that of any other contemporary director but until recently he has neglected one major area of theater: naturalism. His striking version of *The Cherry Orchard*, performed in French in Paris, rectified that oversight.

In the center of the stage was a large carpet, and on it were placed several cushions and a few straight-backed chairs. Natasha Parry, playing the elegant Mme. Ranevskaya, returning to her country estate, swept on stage and sat in one of those hard chairs. In the classic Brook sense, this was a "free carpet show," Chekhov stripped of ornamentation and affectation; there was not even a semblance of a tree in sight. The actors were thrown back on the words, as adapted by Jean-Claude Carrière, and on their own resources. In lieu of scenery, the costumes were elaborate; each summarized its character. The few remaining properties assumed even greater metaphorical significance - the bouquet of keys that Varya, Ranevskaya's adopted daughter, wore at her waist became the badge of her office as supervisor of the family estate. When she flung them at the estate's new owner, the outsider, Lopakhin, it was as if she were challenging him to a duel.

The production was not a reinterpretation in the manner of Andrei Serban's version at Lincoln Center, but a return to Chekhov's own vision. The evening was comic without being farcical, and it was immensely human - and an authentic ensemble piece. Other productions have centered on the conflict between Ranevskaya and Lopakhin, treated as a representative of the aggressive working man on the move. Without overlooking Ranevskaya's commanding presence - even in this version, she was always surrounded by her entourage - Ms. Parry emphasized her charm, femininity and fragility. This was a glamorous woman who needed to be taken care of. In his essay on Chekhov, Vladimir Nabokov describes the Chekhovian intellectual, but he could have been speaking about Ms. Parry's Ranevskaya as someone "who combined the deepest human decency of which man is capable with an almost ridiculous inability to put his ideals and principles into action." Gracefully, Ms. Parry captured her character's helplessness and her generosity of spirit. Niels Arestrup's Lopakhin was not the boorish rustic we often find in productions of *The Cherry Orchard*, but a man of considerable sensitivity. When Trofimov tells him that he has the hands and the soul of an artist, the remark should not seem humorous or gratuitous. Lopakhin has suppressed the lyrical side of himself, but the instinct is there. In Mr. Arestrup's portrayal, we saw a man lacking in table manners but not in taste or in sympathy. Instead of wondering, as we sometimes do, why Varya wants to marry such an oaf, we wondered why he wanted to marry her, a pale reflection of Ranevskaya. Mme. Ranevskaya's brother, Gaev, shooting billiard balls into imaginary side pockets, has been portrayed as a doddering old simpleton. In a performance of remarkable tenderness, Michel Piccoli restored him to his position as an aging innocent and seraphic wastral, frittering away his life and his sister's resources. He is simply unable to function in a real world; even if he had the money, he would never be able to buy the estate. When the estate is lost, he offers his sister immediate consolation, trying to soothe her because he knows that her heart is breaking.

Even the minor characters achieved an inner importance - the maid Dunyasha, flirting with the idea of freedom, and Yasha, the big-city servant with illusions of position, already boasting a cigar and a bowler hat. In the final act - the play was staged without intermission - the carpet was thrown back and the stage was emptied of its few accoutrements. The house was ready for abandonment, and for formal old Firs, the most dignified member of the family. Exquisitely personified by Robert Murzeau, he delivered his final lines not as the last words of a man about to be entombed, but almost in a whisper, a quiet verbalization of the offstage cry of the falling trees. As an era ends, Firs remains an afterthought. Paradoxically, this revival of a well-known classic became, in Mr. Brook's hands, one of the most original events of the theater season.

JOSEPH CHAIKIN

THE SERPENT: A CEREMONY: JUNE 2, 1970

From the middle of life, "a stop between open and closed," Joseph Chaikin's Open Theater reflects on our beginnings. *The Serpent* is the group's eloquent reexamination of Genesis. What does *The Serpent* say about Genesis? That man created God to set limits on himself. That Cain meant to kill Abel, but not to cause his death. That events in Genesis will be re-enacted until the end. That no one really knows what happened in the beginning.

Mostly *The Serpent* doesn't say; it shows. This is "a ceremony," but the actor-authors are not high priests. They are superbly disciplined artists who are very aware of their own mortality.

The play begins in the audience at the Washington Square Methodist Church. Actors sit silently in the aisles, then delicately begin rubbing sandpaper blocks together, clacking wood rods, blowing whistles. Slowly the sound becomes more insistent, pervasive, rhythmic, and finally musical - until the entire church is filled.

One is engaged and entertained, then realizes that this is not only the beginning of the ceremony, but perhaps also a metaphorical representation of the creation of the world. The most provocative thing about *The Serpent* is that its many levels of approach and meaning are enticing and open-minded.

Three actors carry a dead girl on stage (there is, by the way, no scenery). The first word spoken is "Autopsy" - one indication, I believe, that the Open Theater's later *Terminal* had its origins within *The Serpent*. Death is one of the many themes in *The Serpent* - also, love, hate, revenge - all of which could give birth to individual ensemble works.

Having achieved verbalization the actors retrace themselves (as they do repeatedly), returning to sounds, then back to words, until they appear to have created their own language, sometimes identifiable, sometimes not. There is more "language" in *The Serpent* than in *Terminal*. "Words and structure" are by Jean-Claude van Itallie. There are scenes and, one might say, even a plot. There are commentaries and dialogue, and much of it is startling, such as a counterpointed conversation between two women in which each follows every statement, (some prophetic, some outrageous) with a fixed grin.

First the primordial ooze, then crawling creatures. Slithering snakes become a tree of serpents. There are only five actor-snakes; they seem like hundreds. As they enmesh themselves, they dart their tongues and shower Eve with temptations. They are not so much evil, as tempting - and maliciously amusing. The temptation is so exuberant that the banishment from Eden seems, in contrast, even more terrifying than one might imagine. Not fire and smoke, but a rising chant of "Accused! Accused! Accused!"

Abel's death is staged as a ritual with Cain reflexively going through the motions (almost slow motion: down comes the arm, up goes the elbow) until the murder itself. Cain himself is the most surprised at the finality of the act.

While the "begats" are being recited, the Open Theater performs a mass orgy, ending in mass orgasm. In *Zabriskie Point*, a quite similar (although naked) Open Theater display of carnal passion seemed merely ridiculous, here it is intentionally ironic and absurd, as if to say, isn't copulation what was really behind all those begats?

The Serpent is the most fully formed piece in the Open Theater's current repertory. *Terminal*, which by contrast seems serial and somewhat rough-edged, has images that I found even more haunting. Each in its own way is a unique and enormous theatrical experience.

If you intend to witness the Open Theater before it disappears again, a word of caution: The crowds at Washington Square Methodist are thick and clamorous, and the seating is very limited.

MARTHA CLARKE

THE GARDEN OF EARTHLY DELIGHTS: APRIL 5, 1981

Martha Clarke's dramatization of Hieronymus Bosch's painting *Garden of Earthly Delights* is an inspired synthesis of the visual and the performing arts. A production of the Music Theater Group/Lenox Arts Center, the ensemble performance piece opened last night at St. Clement's.

As conceived and directed by Ms. Clarke, the evening transports us into a universe that is wordless but filled with spiritual and sensual imagery. Because Ms. Clarke is leading a small company (seven including herself plus three musicians who also take part in the performance), this is necessarily a chamber version of Bosch's densely populated panorama. What the evening lacks in expanse, it more than makes up for in creativity.

Ms. Clarke comes to experimental theater from the world of modern dance. She was a member of the Pilobolus Dance Theater and is co-founder of Crowsnest, and most of her cast has had experience in one or both of those companies. The approach is, first of all, choreographic, as the troupe instills kinetic life into the dreamlike images of Bosch's altarpiece.

This is not a cycle of tableaux vivants, but a free-form theatrical interpretation. Ms. Clarke takes an idea or a posture from the painting and elaborates on it; a stance becomes a motif. The show draws on mime, and is enriched by Richard Peaslee's vibrant score. Additional dramatic effect is supplied by Paul Gallo's lighting, substituting for scenery.

With the implementation of mechanical devices, the evening becomes a flight of fancy, as actor-dancers are borne aloft, swirling in seraphic patterns. With the agility of aerialists, they appear to levitate, performing cartwheels in space. Her long hair streaming, Margie Gillis dances airs-above-ground as well as onstage.

Without neglecting the artist's gift for the grotesque, Ms. Clarke stresses the beauty of Bosch's landscape. In an impressionistic view of the painting, the accent is on the innocence rather than on the sinfulness of earthly delights. With textual assistance from Peter Beagle, the director has turned the triptych into a four-part invention, moving from the Garden of Eden to the Garden of Earthly Delights and pausing to insert the Seven Deadly Sins before ending the journey in Hell.

The effect of the insertion of the sins is to illustrate the duality of the pleasure garden. In Ms. Clarke's version, the blissfulness continues after the fall, but the attitude eventually coarsens as the characters are caught up in the grossness of civilization.

The show is labeled a work in progress, and there is still artistic progress to be made in the conceptualization of the sins; they lack the precision of other aspects of the presentation. There is, however, a dramatic unity to the event, one that clearly derives from collaborative vitality.

As Adam and Eve discover each other in a graceful pas de deux, we hear the musical equivalent of a zephyr, which grows into a chorus of angels. Counterpointing the narrative, Mr. Peaslee's score becomes discordant, and then cacaphonous as a musician pursues a sinner with a kettle drum as a battering ram. At other equally striking moments, musicians play the pipes of Pan and a chiming carillon. With the addition of masks and horns, the actors assume other guises - as trees, floating islands and mythological beasts.

In her previous performance piece, *A Metamorphosis in Miniature*, Ms. Clarke transformed Kafka into a choreographic oratorio. Venturing into the graphic arts, she and her collaborators have "painted" a visionary theatrical canvas.

MARTHA CLARKE SPEAKS THE LANGUAGE OF ILLUSION

In *The Garden of Earthly Delights*, Ms. Clarke dramatized the Hieronymus Bosch triptych, just as in *Vienna: Lusthaus*, she dramatizes the atmosphere and character of fin de siècle Vienna. In each case, a theatergoer experiences - rather than simply watches - a performance art piece and receives emanations that are both visceral and visual. Each play lasts only 60 minutes, but is a full theatrical event, dense with voluptuous imagery. Both are haunting dreams that unify theater, dance, music and fine art. They were originally produced by Lyn Austin's Music Theater Group/Lenox Arts Center, and, in an extended engagement, *Vienna: Lusthaus* can now be seen at the Public Theater.

Dancer-actors, supported by wires, flew over the stage and the audience in *The Garden of Earthly Delights*. They dipped and floated as if they were heavenly bodies released in space. The balletic movements seemed like airs-above-ground, those wondrous flying steps made by Vienna's Lippizaner horses, whose grace belies their size. That image of horses pausing and then cantering in midair is re-evoked in *Vienna: Lusthaus*. In the new work, an actor prances on stage, arching his legs as he kicks them, tossing his head from side to side. It may take a moment to realize that he is miming a Lippizaner. Ms. Clarke does not underscore this or other images, and if one blinks or looks at a program, one may miss a transformation. As with *The Garden of Earthly Delights*, *Vienna: Lusthaus* demands - and earns - the audience's total concentration.

Vienna was the city of Schnitzler's witty comedies, Klimt's sensuous nudes; it was the city of Johann Strauss, Freud and Adolf Hitler, a city, in other words, of astounding contradictions. Vienna combined the noblest artistic aspirations with nightmarish political realities. As Ms. Clarke has observed, it represented the "end of the old world" and the birth of "20th-century art, philosophy and psychology." As a theatrical conceptualist, she has bound all her thoughts and impressions (and research) into a seamless collage, a series of living tableaux with text that capture the decadence as well as the beauty. Always behind the beauty, one feels the imminent dread, yet decadence has never seemed more beautiful.

Between the audience and the action is a scrim, which distances the play and endows it with a mistiness. It is as if we are watching *Vienna: Lusthaus* through the sheerest lace - a haze of memory. The scrim also acts as frame for Ms. Clarke's stage pictures. The walls of the set are at a tilt, slightly disorienting the audience. As actors appear, the effect is like that of *The Cabinet of Dr. Caligari*. We may not be in Vienna; this could be a madhouse. Or, this could be the madhouse of Vienna. That suspicion is deepened by extracts from the text (prepared by Charles Mee, a playwright and historian), which moves from an elegant world of Viennese waltz and opera to intimations of repressive force. Borrowing from Freud's letters and his own dreams, Mr. Mee tells us about a woman who "let her mind wander for a moment, and she walked right out through an open window and fell to her death." Stories are elliptical but enticing, and they flow smoothly through the accompanying photographs-in-life.

On one level, *Vienna: Lusthaus* is a gallery of pictures, both rapturous and ethereal. Costumed in petticoats, actresses rush to summer rooms for afternoon slumber. Nude, both sexes converge; they are life models in loving poses. We are not voyeurs, but viewers in an animated art gallery. Without imitating Klimt, the piece evokes his essence. Watching the play, I was reminded of an exhibition I saw in Paris of paintings by Klimt, Kokoschka and Schiele, with works that, in some cases, managed simultaneously to project an innocence and a carnality. Though it has no narrative line, *Vienna* accumulates drama. We are swept along in this lusthaus, or pleasure pavilion, until one receives a vision of vertiginous days in Vienna.

Ms. Clarke began her career as a dancer and choreographer. She moved into theater several seasons ago with *A Metamorphosis in Miniature*, a cameo oratorio based on Kafka - a small but striking show in which the late actor, David Rounds, went through his own amazing stage metamorphosis. *The Garden of Earthly Delights* was a far larger canvas.

Moving from the literary to the painterly, Ms. Clarke applied the same artistic principle. She never mimics her source; instead she synthesizes herself with it. It is an intuitive rather than an intellectual response. In effect, Bosch grew wings. The author-director offered specific Boschian impressions of the Garden of Eden, the Garden of Earthly Delights, the Seven Deadly Sins and Hell, while also allowing her own imagination to wander. Through her we could see the duality of the Garden of Eden, in which bliss survived the fall. Coarseness arrived with the entrance of civilization. The idea of a pleasure garden returns in *Vienna: Lusthaus*, but we can feel the decay in process, the evil that was soon to become a visceral reality.

In both *Earthly Delights* and *Vienna*, Ms. Peaslee as composer and Paul Gallo as lighting designer - and also, in the case of *Vienna*, to Robert Israel for his sets and costumes. In *Vienna*, Mr. Peaslee takes his first familiar waltz step, then moves into a pastiche score that achieves its own Viennese and Peaslee identity. As for Mr. Gallo, as he demonstrated with *Earthly Delights*, he is a theatrical master of chiaroscuro.

Just as one should view *Vienna* within the context of Ms. Clarke's other work, one must approach it within a theatrical genre. With her theater of images and illusions, she is closely allied with Robert Wilson, Ping Chong, the Mabou Mines and other experimental innovators, some of whom (such as Meredith Monk) also come from dance. The work is, in the best sense, multimedia, with one medium reinforcing the other. Though several of these artists have also worked with film and television, their stage pieces exist only in performance. By necessity, the audience is its own recording device, storing up impressions. A piece is bound to provoke a different reaction from different people. For some curious reason, it seems that theater people rather than dance people feel the greater affinity for Ms. Clarke's work. Perhaps those in dance are too conscious of the uses of movement while those in experimental theater are more inwardly attuned to receiving a cumulative image and can luxuriate in Ms. Clarke's creative encounters with writers, artists and cities.

TADEUSZ KANTOR

LET THE ARTISTS DIE: OCTOBER 20, 1985

In his analysis of the performance art of Tadeusz Kantor, Jan Kott speaks of his Polish countryman as a creator of "a theater of essence." With Kantor, he explains, "essence is the aftermath... as final as the Last Judgment." It is "a trace, like the still undissolved imprint of a crustacean on stone." Kantor's archeological imprint is transmitted through images, transporting us to a world in which the dead play restless roles.

In *The Dead Class*, a dirge for pre-World War I Poland, the dead return, en masse, to their childhood schoolroom where they pose as for a post-mortem reunion photograph. In *Wielopole Wielopole*, a play that takes its title from Kantor's hometown, and deals partly with the Holocaust, a regiment of soldiers killed in action marches, without expression, across the stage. In Kantor's new play, *Let the Artists Die*, once again we see a legion of the doomed, in dull silver uniforms and with gray faces, looking like a corps of ghosts of Hamlet's father. Dominating their cortege is a towering skeleton of a horse that could itself be a relic of the apocalypse.

As written, designed and directed by Kantor, and as performed by the members of his Cricot 2 company, the three plays are linked as a trilogy about the artist's life within the history of Poland. They are, at the same time, intensely autobiographical and speculative about cognitive memory. The new work (at La Mama Annex) shares with its predecessors a marked concern for history, but, perhaps more than anything, it is a contemplation of Kantor's own mortality.

The director himself is on stage for the entire performance as observer and conductor. To some theatergoers, his presence may seem an intrusion. Rather, I regard it as an affirmation of what might be called his esthetic attachment. There is no distancing of the artist from his work. He is not simply playing a role, he is orchestrating his memory into action. The play is his dream and we become fellow voyagers. With his mournful face - as downcast a look as that of Buster Keaton - he watches silently from the sidelines, and occasionally steps in to cue the music or to signal a shift in scene. In performance, Kantor becomes our conduit to his consciousness.

Even if one reads the detailed summary in the director's *Guide to the Performance*, for sale in the lobby, the play can seem cryptic. It is not easy to ascertain exactly the substance of any individual event, and the work does not have the rich iconographic texture of the two earlier Kantor pieces. But *Let the Artists Die* has an emotional, visual and aural immediacy. It could be approached as movement theater, a kinetic museum installation or an animated tableau of images and impressions. Performed in Polish, the play is less concerned with words than with signposts of behavior. Among other things, it illuminates aspects of heroism.

At the core of the work are two historical characters. Veit Stoss, a 15th-century artist who created the altarpiece at Krakow's St. Mary church, returned late in life to his home in Nuremberg and was subjected to a brutal facial disfigurement. Marshal Joseph Pilsudski, who fought for Poland during World War I, was a great national patriot. Artistic integrity and selfless patriotism - and the price that is paid for each - are honored through the mind and memory of Kantor as native son.

Both characters are represented on stage as forces of resistance. The artist wears a scarf over his face concealing his scars; he sweeps through the action as a figure of fate. The marshal is seen in several semblances, as a 6-year-old boy and as an adult riding the skeletal horse. The small boy is also a reference to Kantor's own youthful aspirations, playing soldiers long before he ever thought about playing theater.

The evening begins as a mass for the recently dead; as in Kantor's other work, the play is saturated with religious and funereal imagery. A door is opened and, to the tune of martial music, men in tails and bowler hats lay a corpse to rest in a room filled with crosses. The room is also, perhaps, a prison. Placed in a bed, the dead man returns to life and becomes an observer at his own funeral. He is played by two actors, identically costumed and mustached. According to the director, one is the deceased, the other is his "author," this makes for a receding perspective of mirror images. The dead man and his double are evocations of twins that appear in *Wielopole Wielopole*. They are deadpan clowns, sharing the same narrow bed and quizzically scrutinizing one another. In both plays, the twins have the cock-eyed look and spasmodic movements of silent film comedy. Though the plays deal with mordant issues, they are not without leavening humor.

In *Let the Artists Die*, characters and scenes disappear and reappear. Images become motifs, and incidents are interspersed with a recurrent parade - including a hanged man sitting in a closed cubicle, a card-player/pimp, a prostitute sinuously striding around the stage. The parade is the equivalent of a clown walka-round in a circus. At such moments, *Let the Artists Die* bears a relationship to the work of Fellini, especially in his autobiographical *8 1/2*, with its clown-tragic view of the artist at wit's end.

It is difficult to know all Kantor has intended, and there is the distinct possibility that he himself is not entirely cognizant of the effect of his work. He has said that the play is not so much a matter of choice as of chance, though it would be ingenuous to regard it as an improvisation. It is carefully conceived and artfully implemented by his company of actors. The evening leads to a mass crucifixion - characters are clamped and immobilized in odd devices of torture - and the construction onstage of a symbolic version of Veit Stoss's altarpiece. The child's go-cart, the skeletal horse, planks, tables and boxes are regrouped and propped up. Found objects become a sculptural monument of civilization. As with Kantor's other pieces, *Let the Artists Die* has spiritual connotations; man dies but values endure. Although he uses the images of death, his work has an almost serene attitude toward the lessons of the past.

MABOU MINES

JOANNE AKALAITIS

DRESSED LIKE AN EGG: MAY 17, 1977

In its theatrical adventures, the Mabou Mines has specialized in compact performance pieces - a few actors, a single set - with astonishingly complex results.

The company's adaptations of Beckett are exquisite cameos; they could be staged in a shadow box. In the Mabou Mines series of "animations," it is the setting that is animated; the actors are almost extensions of the scenery. Occasionally, the company has unleashed its ingenuity on a large canvas, as in the gym-size spectacular *The Saint and the Football Players*.

Dressed Like an Egg, the new Mabou Mines piece, an ensemble collaboration designed and directed by JoAnne Akalaitis, is a consolidation and a culmination of all of the group's previous experimentation. It makes the intimate stage at the Public Theater's new Old Prop Shop theater seem infinite.

This is an exhilarating, multi-dimensional experience that is indebted to painting and sculpture, as well as to dance, music and theater. Ms. Akalaitis's numerous artistic accomplices include the painter Nancy Graves, the composer Philip Glass and the sculptor Ree Morton, who died recently.

The piece is "taken" from the writings of Colette - taken and transformed. Ms. Akalaitis has created visual counterpoint to spoken words, somewhat in the manner of the company's Beckett evenings. This is an elaboration on Colette, an adaptation that is as interpretative as choreography.

This is not a stage biography of the novelist, although it covers some of the same territory as Elinor Jones's play, *Colette*. There are recognizable Colette guideposts - her bulldog (a lifelike, inanimate replica constructed by Toby Grant), her plush boudoir, her nights in bed and in music-hall varieties. Just as Beckett's texts became a diving board for Mabou Mines's imagination, Colette's works send the group spiraling into a dizzying circle of mysterious sensations. This is a vision of Colette's world, as filtered through the sensibility of Ms. Akalaitis, her four company-performers and their team of collaborators.

The actors take turns at playing Colette, weaving a tapestry of her characters. Though the actors are exceptional - particularly the silver-voiced David Warrilow and the enticing Ellen McElduff - the performance is less evocative than the stage design.

What Richard Foreman has done with string - splicing his stage into playing areas, fields of perception - the Mabou Mines now does with curtains. There is one long curtain in front of the stage - the footlights are set in seashells - which briskly sweeps open to reveal a lavish interior landscape of fin de siècle France, then narrows down like a camera shutter to reveal pinpoint pictures. In a narrow aperture under a wide curtain, two dancers tap, but we see only the shoes, illuminated by light bulbs in their high heels. Then each pair is replaced - suddenly, as if on a puppet stage - by men's two-toned shoes.

Repeatedly, the show takes us by surprise with its stage pictures: a hip-deep bathtub is filled with steaming water from a kettle, the smoke swirling into rhythmic patterns; a single beam of light, as thin as a crack, strikes the stage as if the sun had just entered a jet-black cave; an actress moves off stage, but her costume remains in place, a stiff-backed object like a Claes Oldenburg sculpture.

The evening is a jack-in-the-box of visual delights, embellished by Mr. Glass's tingling sound. Actors, scenery, props, light and music are all implements for manipulation - and for exploration. *Dressed Like an Egg* is dipped in the lush romanticism and sensuality of Colette.

⤳

LEE BREUER

THE GOSPEL AT COLONUS: NOVEMBER 12, 1983

Playing a preacher in a black Baptist church, Morgan Freeman steps in front of his congregation and announces, "I take as my text this evening the Book of Oedipus," and, in context, his statement is as natural as if he had said, "the Book of Job." In *The Gospel at Colonus*, Lee Breuer as adapter-director and Bob Telson as composer show us how Oedipus was transfigured by his suffering and became the saintliest of sinners.

An unlikely but inspired marriage of Sophocles and gospel songs, *The Gospel at Colonus* is at the Brooklyn Academy of Music as part of the academy's Next Wave Festival. The work is on the crest of that wave, inundating the audience with jubilant music and soulful testimony about the power of redemption.

As a risk-taking theatrical conceptualist, Mr. Breuer has sometimes been charged with distorting classics. In this case, he remains faithful, although not subservient, to his source, and gives an immediacy to Greek tragedy. Both the spoken words and the gospel lyrics by Mr. Breuer and Mr. Telson) are adapted from Sophocles in the Robert Fitzgerald and Dudley Fitts translations - with the addition of an occasional hallelujah. It is surprising how organically *Oedipus* can fit within the framework of a gospel musical, the cadenced lyricism of Sophocles merging with Mr. Telson's rhapsodic rhythms.

There are some 60 performers on stage, filling a grandstand that would not be out of place at Shea Stadium. Individually and in unison, this is a heavenly choir, a feeling that its enriched by the stage setting designed by Alison Yerxa - a celestial cyclorama of sky-flying seraphs. The band is split in two, with half in a pit on stage, half high in a perch.

The evening has the shape of a church service, with hymns, prayers, tableaux, a sermon and a final benediction. Mr. Freeman plays the minister, narrator and dramatic voice of Oedipus. Oedipus in concert is sung by Clarence Fountain, who is blind, backed up by his group, the Five Blind Boys of Alabama. The effect, as intended, is as if five Ray Charleses were singing Oedipus, adding a reality and a depth of field to the tragedy.

Other roles are also doubly cast, with the words spoken by actors and with lyrics sung by members of celebrated gospel groups, including Brooklyn's own Institutional Radio Choir. When Oedipus is welcomed as an exile in the strange land of Colonus, Martin Jacox, whose voice is a vocal equivalent of a whirling dervish, urges the Original Soul Stirrers into a kind of gospel contest with the Blind Boys of Alabama. Each one tops the other and reaches toward ecstasy.

For all the moments of exaltation, the show never forgets to be playful. When Oedipus's traitorous son Polyneices (Kevin Davis) arrives to patch things up with his father figure, he directly addresses the audience, "I'll tell you why I came," and he does. During the self-serving monologue, Sam Butler plays a low-down guitar in the pit band, and then looks up and wins a laugh with the comment, "He's so slick!"

Just as Mr. Davis captures the son's guile, Isabell Monk has the intensity for Antigone, Jevetta Steele is a touching Ismene (her song "How Shall I See You Through My Tears" is one of the show's soaring numbers) and Carl Lumbly and Robert Earl Jones are fiercely matched opposites as Theseus and Creon, respectively. It should be sufficient to say about Mr. Freeman that he has the authority to play the title role in a dramatic production of *Oedipus*.

With his home company, the Mabou Mines, Mr. Breuer has often worked on a small scale with unlimited inventiveness, as in *A Prelude to Death in Venice* and *Sister Suzie Cinema*, the doo-wop chamber musical that he and Mr. Telson presented several seasons ago at the Public Theater. *The Gospel at Colonus*, which began as a pilot project, is now on a grand scale. Logistically, it is almost the equal of a Robert Wilson opera epic. Because of the size of the company and the complexity of the production, there are occasional slow stretches in performance. However, as a work of musical theater, the evening is truly blessed, in its adapter-director, composer and cast.

After Oedipus's death comes an apotheosis. Swaying multitudes of gospel singers, led by the clarion voice of Joyce Taylor, exhort "Lift Him Up," and the stage threatens to lift off from its moorings, joining the show in an evangelical musical flight.

ANDREI SERBAN

FRAGMENTS OF A TRILOGY - THE TROJAN WOMEN: DECEMBER 31, 1975

Following a tour of Europe and the Mideast, Andrei Serban has returned to the United States with his versions of Greek classics, two of which, *The Trojan Women* and *Electra* are being performed on weekends at La Mama Annex under the title *Fragments of a Trilogy*. This Rumanian-born director's daringly experimental work is clearly in a class with that of Peter Brook and Jerzy Grotowski. It is nothing less than a reinvention of theater.

Euripides and Sophocles speak to us in our language (in translation) about an ancient time and timeless themes. Mr. Serban's heretical response to these towering classics has been to banish words. His plays are performed in ancient Greek (and also in Latin and other unrecognizable languages), in throaty and gutteral raspings that have no relevance to speech as we know it today.

What is lost is a certain specificity of character (we are not always sure who is speaking to whom), psychological shadings and lyricism. But what is gained is immense. Mr. Serban's plays are excavations deep into the human heart.

Nonverbal theater has never seemed so searingly evocative. The plays communicate directly with cries, whispers, silences, looks and images. The images are unforgettable: Helen stripped, shorn of her hair, smeared with offal and ravished; a child encaged like a captured beast on the way to slaughter; a suicide rolling in ritualistic slow motion down an incline, weaving her body in exquisite patterns like an angel tumbling from the heavens.

These visions would be powerful even if removed from us on a proscenium stage or in a film. Mr. Serban's innovation is to turn the entire theater into a stage and to involve the action with the audience.

Together with the actors, we walk into the theater space and the play begins to explode all around us - on platforms, in rolling carts, above our heads on promontories, on stairways, occasionally even on the stage. The technique has been used before, most prominently by Luca Ronconi in *Orlando Furioso*, but what seemed a carnival-like contrivance from Ronconi, seems inspired in the hands of Mr. Serban.

As the actors charge among us, as Elizabeth Swados's music throbs in the background, we feel almost as if we are witnesses at the fall of Troy (and at Troy would we have understood the language?). The play becomes credible, and also symbolic and impressionistic. This is an interpretation, a variation on a classic theme, as if the director were choreographing or composing piece of theater. *The Trojan Women* is designed as "an epic opera," and the composer is symbiotic with the director. Ms. Swados's music is inextricable from the event. With its eerie pulsating rhythms, it seems to derive from the fall of Troy itself.

Having witnessed the savaging of a people, for the second half of *The Trojan Women*, we sit on benches and watch the final devastation of a nation, the banishment of womankind as it is herded out of the arena.

Following a long intermission, the actors return to play *Electra*. Again we are seated - two long peninsulas of people divided by the distilled essence of *Electra*. The characters introduce themselves, their names the only words we recognize in the evening.

Electra is even more deeply symbolic and personal than *The Trojan Women*. A live dove and a live snake represent polarities. There is a draped, roving spirit of the dead Agamemnon, as well as a blind Oedipus. Axes are raised for murder. In contrast to the opening epic, this is an intimate, impacted cry of agony. The acting, particularly by Priscilla Smith as Electra, is almost unbearably intense.

At the end, with Clytemnestra and Aegistus dead and Agamemnon revenged, the chorus surrounds Electra and rings clarion notes on individual bells - a peal of rebirth and renewal.

On opening night, Ellen Stewart, the guiding mother of La Mama, joined the chorus with her own bell (which she customarily rings before performances). The moment was a celebration, the evening a fulfillment of Ms. Stewart's monumental efforts in sustaining and expanding theater. A collaboration across countries, spanning the barrier of language, *Fragments of a Trilogy* is pure and phenomenal.

⟳

JULIE TAYMOR

JUAN DARIÉN: MARCH 16, 1988

In the distance on the deep St. Clement's stage, there is a tiny church, and, as we watch, the church windows crumble and the building itself seems to disintegrate. Suddenly, lush foliage descends until the stage becomes a jungle. Strange serpentine creatures slither through the vines and leaves. Lizards fly, accompanied by frenzied night sounds. A mother tiger is slain and her cub stands forlornly in the wilderness.

Then, as quickly as it appeared, the jungle disappears and moving toward us is an entire hill town, dotted with houses and with a road winding to a graveyard at its peak. Later, the windows of the houses will be illuminated with interior dramas and, along the road, we will spy a miniature funeral procession. But in the opening moments of *Juan Darién*, the polarities of the story are set: faith and superstition, civilization and savagery.

What follows is an astonishing array of images, in stage pictures and music, telling us the fabulous story of a tiger cub transformed into a boy and forced to pay tragic consequences. Watching it, one is fearful that Julie Taymor and her collaborator, Elliot Goldenthal, will lose their footing in the entanglement of the jungle. That they do not is a tribute to their combined creativity and to the orchestrated energies of their actors, puppeteers and musicians, whose many roles are intertwined. Behind their masks, the performers are not always individually identifiable; Thuli Dumakude and Lawrence A. Neals Jr. as a mother and the boy who was a tiger carry most of the acting burden - and each offers a moving portrayal.

The exceedingly complex environment is at the root of the performance piece, and the primary credit for it goes to Ms. Taymor. She is responsible for the puppets and masks as well as the concept, and she is also co-designer of the elaborate sets and costumes with G.W. Mercier. Ms. Taymor has always been an accomplished puppeteer and designer, but her past efforts have not adequately prepared us for this artistic adventure.

Until now, she has had difficulty dealing with text and, in fact, has done her most imaginative work when she subordinated her own authorial instincts to those of others (such as Andrei Serban and Elizabeth Swados). Here, acting as director and co-author (with Mr. Goldenthal), she has banished spoken words from her play (based on a story by the Uruguayan writer Horacio Quiroga). In addition, the lyrics to Mr. Goldenthal's haunting score are sung in Latin and Spanish. Unencumbered by words, the play draws its power from the symbiosis of design, movement and music, melding diverse performance art forms and transforming the St. Clement's stage into a living theatrical organism.

On one level, the show is an interpretive anthology of puppet arts - monumental mourners reminiscent of Bread and Puppet Theater parables, beasts that move Bunraku-style - tantalizing shadow puppets, and, in a brief moment of ecstasy, an aurora borealis of butterflies. At one point, a walking puppet stage appears. On the outside is a schoolhouse and, swinging around, the puppeteer reveals a classroom in which children misbehave as in a Punch and Judy show. The masks on the actors are themselves objects of exhibition quality. Many are as totemic as Mayan sculptures, and, to lighten the journey, some are satiric, such as the schoolmaster, whose head is topped with an open book, parted in the middle with the pages flapping like a loose toupee.

Juan Darién, a production of Lyn Austin's Music Theater Group, is not simply an exercise in scenic ingenuity, but a compelling narrative dense with Latin American mysticism and dealing with the beast within man and the man within beast. The subjects under scrutiny include mother love and bereavement, the primitiveness of the natural world and the malevolence of those who are unknowing. The play, which the authors regard, accurately, as a "carnival mass," is filled with the darkest doubts about our survivability.

Everything leads inexorably to an eerie, climactic image as a skeletal figure of Death, stalking the magical landscape, moves into a final danse macabre. In her previous theatrical work, Ms. Taymor has dealt with the theme of transformation but never with the artistic assurance and breathtaking intensity of *Juan Darién*.

DEBORAH WARNER

THE ST. PANCRAS PROJECT: A FANTASTIC WALK: AUGUST 14, 1995

LONDON - One by one, at pre-arranged intervals of 10 minutes, theatergoers were led into the labyrinth of the long-abandoned Midland Grand Hotel, a cas tle-size Victorian building adjoining St. Pancras Station. Following a narrow white tape on the floor, the equivalent of the yellow brick road in *The Wizard of Oz*, each visitor roamed alone through the endless corridors and took part in the reawakening of a classic architectural relic. Deborah Warner had mapped the tour and, in collaboration with her designer, Hildegard Bechtler, had prepared the rooms of the hotel as if for an extensive series of museum installations. Strange things were in the air and underfoot.

As created and directed by Ms. Warner, *The St. Pancras Project: A Fantastical Walk* was a highlight of LIFT, the international experimental theater festival that is held in London every summer. Because of the privacy of each person's visit to the environmental project and the brevity of the run, only several hundred people could attend. But for those who did, the event was mesmerizing. Christo wrapped the Reichstag in Berlin and, conversely, Ms. Warner unwrapped the Midland Grand Hotel in London.

The magnificent hotel, designed by Sir George Gilbert Scott in 1873, has been closed since 1935, but despite the disuse and the disrepair, it exuded elegance. Beneath the grime and flaking paint could be seen elaborate filigree; serpentine creatures embraced over an archway. Blink, and one could envision the hotel in its heyday at the turn of the century, as travelers from the provinces arrived wide-eyed at the terminus of the Midland Railway.

Walking down a winding staircase fit for Norma Desmond, a theatergoer had a feeling of the lost grandeur. A bellboy rushed by like a Mad Hatter, put down two leather suitcases and disappeared. Later, a chambermaid in a long black dress appeared and hurried away in alarm. A corridor of closed doors was lined with high-button shoes, pumps and boots waiting to be shined. Next to them were scores of silver trays set for English breakfast, complete with copies of the morning newspaper. (Oddly, there was also a full tray at the door of the Gentleman's room.) If a buzzer sounded, the entire hotel might spring to life.

Through open doors, rooms became landscapes. One room looked as if it had been set by Magritte: a suit jacket hanging on the outside of an armoire, with a hat on top; three 78 r.p.m. records on the floor; the sound of a music box in the background. A larger room - honeymoon suite? - was completely carpeted with grass, and a watering can sat at the entrance. All it needed was Manet, for a picnic.

Sounds were overheard: in a tiny servant's room on the top floor there were cries of tearful remorse. High over an air shaft, a caged canary sang. Echoes, whispers; was that the rumble of a suddenly activated elevator? Imagine an interactive version of the movie *Grand Hotel*, and one would have a glimmer of the startling effect of *The St. Pancras Project*.

In the basement, there was a sign, *Danger, Rats*, and a guard on duty (before entering the building, theatergoers had to sign insurance liability waivers, a first even for environmental theater). The air was dank, the atmosphere dungeonlike, except in a large storage room where a dirt floor was piled high with crisp white linen, enough sheets and towels to fill a wing of the hotel. Call it a sculpture: white on blight. Imaginative juxtaposition is the key to Ms. Warner's art.

Exiting after about 50 minutes, a visitor wondered if this was theater. It had no script, no dialogue, no beginning, no end, no real performance and an audience of one. But it was a world of theatrical images, a mysterious dream trip to the Victorian past. At first, Ms. Warner tried to find a text to go with the building. Then she realized that the building would speak for itself.

During an auspicious season, Ms. Warner was also the director of *Richard II* at the Royal National Theater. In a bold stroke of casting, Fiona Shaw played the title role. The reasoning: sex is not a motivational issue in *Richard II*, as it is in *Hamlet* and *Richard III*. As Ms. Warner pointed out, the character is somewhat feminine, a fact that has led some actors - not Ms. Shaw - to portray him as effeminate.

Her hair cropped short, Ms. Shaw played Richard as a man, without altering her voice, without the artifice that often encumbers an actress attempting male Shakespearean roles. In league with her director, she plunged so deeply into the character and his political conflict with Bolingbroke that theatergoers could be unconcerned with questions of gender. As performed by Ms. Shaw, Richard is a petulant, insufficient king, a man in thrall to his own helplessness. In keeping with the role, her Richard was less domineering than her Hedda Gabler.

The actress was surrounded by a dynamic ensemble, including David Threlfall as Bolingbroke and Michael Bryant as the aged Duke of York. *Richard II* was at the Cottlesloe, the National's smallest theater, and it was staged corridor-style, with the audience on two sides of the stage looking down, as if watching a duel. The director proved that an actress, at least an actress with Ms. Shaw's clear-sighted intelligence, could play the tormented monarch. Together they invigorated a play that in lesser hands can seem wordy rather than eloquent.

It must be said that the Warner approach does not always work. Last year, in an attempt to reinterpret Samuel Beckett's *Footfalls*, she turned the Garrick Theater into a madhouse-like environment and placed Ms. Shaw on the edge of the balcony, where she paced back and forth and grimaced her anguish. But one *Footfalls* is far outweighed by Ms. Warner's *St. Pancras Project*, by her success with Shakespeare (*Titus Andronicus* and *King John* as well as *Richard II*) and by her sense of theater as a primal experience.

In common with Americans, the English have an appetite for environmental productions, just as they do for walk-through installations in art museums, like the recent "Rites of Passage" exhibition at the Tate Gallery. In New York, Anne Hamburger is the principal theatrical environmentalist, with her En Garde Arts company presenting site-specific plays in the unlikeliest of places: the meat market district, on piers and most recently on Wall Street, with *J.P. Morgan Saves the Nation*. London is filled with directors who willfully involve the audience in the action. With undue discretion, the English call these shows promenade productions. What a misnomer!

No theatergoers saunter in their finery or amble from scene to scene. In the course of a performance, they are moved, displaced (sometimes rudely) by the actors, and if the elderly chance to sit down on the edge of scenery for a moment's rest, they risk being stepped on. One English theatergoer defines promenade as a euphemism for audience discomfort.

But depending on the play - and the production - a promenade can have an almost tactile immediacy. This was the case with a recent production of Martin Sperr's *Hunting Scenes From Lower Bavaria* at the Gate, a pub theater on London's Fringe. Written in 1966, *Hunting Scenes* looks back in horror on Germany immediately after World War II, when citizens of one small Bavarian town confront economic deprivation by persecuting their neighbors.

In the playwright's view, the townspeople are mean and malicious. They are prejudiced against any outsider, especially a young gay man who dares to assert his individuality in a place that values conformity. The play is strong meat, made stronger by Dominic Cooke's production. Standing on the earth-covered floor, the audience was enveloped by vengefulness and violence. At the end of the performance, when one character in the play expressed his longing for the return of Hitler, there was a perceptible chill in the audience, a collective witness to the rise of neo-Nazism.

ROBERT WILSON

EINSTEIN ON THE BEACH: NOVEMBER 28, 1976

At exactly 11 P.M. last Sunday evening a pillar of white light rose from the stage at the Metropolitan Opera House and disappeared slowly into the sky. A few minutes later a spaceship landed, an intricate three-story assembly humming with light and sound. As the lights formed labyrinthine patterns of dots, blinking and changing like a panoply of fireworks, clocks in glass coffins began to levitate and a weightless spaceman flew across the stage. This was the climax of a mystical, monumental theater piece, *Einstein on the Beach*, the Robert Wilson-Philip Glass opera, which had its American premiere at the Met.

It was an auspicious opening, first of all because of the work's location at the prestigious Met. Abroad, particularly in France where this opera had its world premiere last summer, the playwright-director-designer ("Bobwilson," as he is called) is as popular as he is experimental. Here, up to now, his art has generally been considered as special. The 4,000 people who crammed into the Met on

Sunday, most of whom stayed for the nearly five-hour epic gave the cast and the authors a thunderous ovation at the end of the performance.

Partially, of course, Wilson ovations are a gesture of audience relief and euphoria as when dawn broke over his 12-hour spectacular *The Life and Times of Joseph Stalin* at the Brooklyn Academy of Music. *Einstein* is considerably shorter and less demanding than *Stalin* (next to it, it might be considered austere), but it still needs a certain indulgence and suspension of traditional theatrical expectation.

Einstein has nothing to do, literally, with a beach (except for the frequent presence on stage of a large white conch shell). "On the beach" is meant in the apocalyptical sense. This is a dream-like pattern of landscapes and images, suggested by Einstein's life and times. The play parallels his lifespan - from steam engine to rocket ship - and symbols and signs are drawn from his biography (such as his fondness for trains and boats), but this is an impressionistic portrait in which drama is only one of many ingredients. As with all works by Wilson, *Einstein* is an anthology of the arts.

Despite aleatory aspects, there is a strict structural form, coordinated through theater, music, dance and design. The play is divided into four acts, interwoven with five "knee plays," small choreographic connectives. In those four acts, four images occur, reoccur, alter and synthesize: a train becomes a building, a courtroom becomes a bed and a jail, a field is surmounted by a spaceship (and then the stage becomes the interior of the spaceship). Transformation is one key to the mysteries of the evening. Just as scenery metamorphoses, people change and words find new forms. The lyrics are numbers and solfège syllables (do-re-mi) - eminently suitable to the mathematical bedrock of the subject - and they are repeated until they create their own throbbing musical language.

Gradually, as we are taken hostage by the sway of movement, stasis and repetition, we catch motifs, for example, geometric shapes. The vertical beam of light that "paints" itself as backdrop for the first-act steam engine reappears like that monolith in the movie *2001*, a shimmering link to an elusive and illusory world. In the courtroom scene, the beam lies horizontally; it is a bed of light. Later it is that ascendant fluorescent pillar. Circles are matched: clocks, compasses, the sun, an eclipse. A triangle of string is lifted and transported across the stage.

The images are also gestural. A man writes on the air with imaginary chalk; he is a mathematician making calculations. The movement, brisk, even feverish, is repeated by witnesses in court, dancers at a gallop, and finally by a solitary figure in a window at the pinnacle of a building. It is clearly a mathematics institute, where he is solving universal riddles as a crowd watches from below.

Symbolically, everyone is Einstein - dressed in suspenders and overalls - but there is one principal Einstein, a violinist in white wig and mustache, who sits for much of the play on the apron of the stage and obsessively fiddles. The opera could be happening in his mind; it accompanies his music. This is a dream of Einstein, an evolving exercise in time and space relations.

A word about time: Wilson's body clock is slow. Minutes equal hours. This is ... slow motion. Repetition can be enervating, particularly when the dialogue is intentionally banal. Our brains survive this ennui because there is a calculated design (the opera is a suspension bridge) and because of the professionalism of the performance. For example, the dancer Lucinda Childs as a droning trial witness ("I was in this prematurely air-conditioned supermarket....") becomes a rhythmic encapsulation of all tiresome court proceedings. While she is delivering her litany, justice is sleeping.

Einstein is serious, but it does have leavening moments. Dancers in the field - jumping and leaping - become a whirl of pastoral ebullience. A boy (10-year-old Paul Mann) on a high promontory scales paper airplanes; they gracefully dip and fall. Sometimes our eyes seem to deceive us. Did I see a silver spoon sailing into space?

The opera has a full score played by Mr. Glass and a small, industrious orchestra and sung by a chorus and the principals. I will leave the analysis of the harmonic structure to the composer and to the music critics, except to say that the score is insistent, ear-piercing and, ultimately, as hypnotic as the play itself. Mr. Glass has aptly described his music as sounding like "the motor on a space machine." There is an eerie, other-worldly quality that occasionally makes us feel that we are on Mars rather than at the Met. Actually, when Glass and Wilson first decided to collaborate, the composer suggested that they write a science-fiction opera, and, to an extent, that is what they have done, particularly in the final act. The interior of the spaceship is an astonishing act of theater, a living machine-as-body. In the end, *Einstein on the Beach* itself seems less a play or an opera than an organism with its own pulsating heartbeat.

HAMLETMACHINE: MAY 25, 1986

The plays by Heiner Müller are as dense as they are brief - shell fragments fired into our collective psyche. This East German playwright subscribes to the theory that "theater is a laboratory for the social imagination," and, in *Hamletmachine*, he deconstructs Shakespeare in order to contemplate and comprehend the disintegration of civilization. Hamlet's madness becomes Mr. Müller's obsession, and he sees in it, in particular, a reflection of Germany today. For the author's English translator, Carl Weber, *Hamletmachine* is "probably Müller's most complicated text, and the most difficult to decode." It is also, one might add, almost impossible to stage. What do you do, for example, with a stage direction that says that

Hamlet "steps into the armor, splits with the ax the heads of Marx, Lenin, Mao. Snow. Ice Age?"

Two seasons ago, the play had its New York premiere at the Theater for the New City, in a production that disregarded much of Mr. Müller's text and turned the work into a monotonous monodrama. It was with trepidation as well as anticipation that one approached Robert Wilson's version of *Hamletmachine*," presented by the New York University undergraduate theater department. Politics has not been Mr. Wilson's primary metier; his work can be as textually slight as it is visually inspired. He and Mr. Müller have collaborated before (on *The Civil Wars*), but this is the first time that Mr. Wilson has staged a previously produced play by the dramatist and it is also, for him, a rare attempt at interpreting a contemporary text.

The Wilson-Müller *Hamletmachine* turns out to be a compatible harnessing of two disparate artists - a playwright passionately concerned with his times and a theatrical conceptualist who operates on a rarefied esthetic plane. The play is a powerful stimulus to Mr. Wilson's own creativity, pulling him into the arena of political consciousness. Acting as "decoder," Mr. Wilson filters Mr. Müller's fragmented, Dadaesque script through his own phantasmagoric imagination. We hear Mr. Müller's voice; we see Mr. Wilson's vision. Both run on simultaneous tracks. At the outset, it should be pointed out that, as with the play itself, the production poses obstacles. For the audience, it does not have the relief of the director's spectacular architectural stage pictures (as in *The Life and Times of Sigmund Freud* and *Einstein on the Beach*). This is more of a chamber work, intense, distilled, often in slow motion, often in no motion - a small still life with silent scream, until the climax when that scream becomes an ear-piercing reality.

In its published version, the Müller play barely fills six pages, representing, in the author's words, "the shrunken head of the Hamlet tragedy." Merging Müller and Shakespeare, the play uses some stage directions as dialogue and creates a collage of horrific events. The Wilson variation runs more than two hours without intermission, which means that at least three quarters of the work is Mr. Wilson's invention, beginning with a dreamlike prelude. The prelude establishes the director's presence and introduces semblances of the characters: Ophelia in white; Hamlet in black leather jacket and jeans; a top-hatted apparition with coal-black face (the Ghost as chimney sweep?). Others are not so easily identifiable. At the center of the stage in a swivel chair is an elderly woman in a gray wig that sheds the dust of mortality whenever she moves. She is as wizened as a character in a late Beckett play. Perhaps she is Gertrude, or Mother Europe, herself. Sitting at a long table are three women, matched automatons, who choreographically imitate each other's movements. As a chorus, they could be a substitute for the three television screens suggested in the text, or they could represent the witches from *Macbeth*.

In the play and in the performance, there is a repeated converging of *Hamlet* and *Macbeth*. Mr. Müller has said that his Ophelia is intended as a criticism of

Hamlet, and in that regard he has allied her with the German terrorist, Ulrike Meinhof. The character recites a Müller variation of Lady Macbeth's "unsex me here," before speaking the words of one of Charles Manson's "family": "When she walks through your bedrooms carrying butcher knives you'll know the truth."

By the author's design, Ophelia shares center stage with Hamlet, and, in Mr. Wilson's production, their lines, given equal weight, are distributed among various actors. The effect is to surround the audience with a collage of words, fragmented and distorted from Shakespeare ("Something is rotten in this age of hope"). As an overlay, we hear the wail of dogs and the caw of carnivorous birds, a one-finger piano rendition of the Peggy Lee tune, "Is That All There Is?" and a crescendo of Schubert. Tableaux shift from the calmly composed to the viscerally reactive.

One of the playwright's scenes is interpreted on film. As we watch, the faces projected are transformed into apes and then, as on a computer screen, into a Cubist canvas. Flames leap up on screen, evoking an image - in my mind - of the burning Reichstag, firebombing and nuclear holocaust. The subject under scrutiny is terrorism in all its guises, from assassination to genocide. The subtext is how mankind is inured to horror, which becomes a news break between television commercials. At one point, Ophelia intones, "Give us this day our daily murder."

While not alleviating the playwright's bitterness, the director succeeds in objectifying it. Repeatedly, he changes the audience's perspective, reordering scenery (a picket fence, a tree, a table), playing scenes against blank screens facing different directions. The result is itself a kind of Cubism, so that even as we sit still we seem to be viewing the events from alternate angles. Instead of disembodying the text, Mr. Wilson places it within an environment that is as eye-impelling as it is mind-provoking.

One aspect of the production is of additional interest - the use of N.Y.U. theater students as performers. Previous Wilson pieces have been presented by professional actors and dancers as well as by members of his floating ensemble of disciples. As it turns out, the ingenuousness of the student actors is an asset. One can feel a trustfulness - and a truthfulness - as they allow themselves to be maneuvered through the Wilson landscape, as, for example, one young man, a Mercury-like runner, has to balance on one leg for an extended period. There is no assertion of actors' personality, yet they do not remain simply a scenic element. They are expressive within the context of the Wilson-Müller universe.

The theater itself is minuscule, with seats for 74 and a stage the size of a small classroom. Mr. Wilson, who has presented epics on the stages of the world's great opera houses, is equally adept in these confined quarters. Physically as well as intellectually, he proves to be an adaptive artist. With a slightly larger production budget, he might even be able to find a Wilsonian way to visualize the author's request for "Snow. Ice Age."

THE KNEE PLAYS: DECEMBER 4, 1986

The Knee Plays by Robert Wilson and David Byrne are presented as the American section of *The Civil Wars*, Mr. Wilson's monumental, multilinear extravaganza. However, in keeping with the global aspect of the complete epic, the work is decidedly international - with a specific Japanese flavor. In fact, one could regard this as a Wilsonian ascent into Orientalism, as his *Noh Plays*, with more than a touch of Bunraku and Kabuki. As seen in its New York premiere Tuesday at Alice Tully Hall, this is an eclectic piece, filled with visual puns. It is one of Mr. Wilson's most sheerly enjoyable and accessible works.

The 13 vignettes that comprise *The Knee Plays* are meant to be joints or connectives between the long acts of *Civil Wars*. Extracted from the cycle and put together into an evening lasting 100 minutes, the "opera" is not simply a series of interludes. Instead, it is like an acrostic puzzle, a riddle that, once solved, assumes a new shape and significance. Parenthetically, the Knee Plays themselves have preludes, which perhaps one could call Elbow Plays.

At the core of the work is the art of transformation. Puppets become people and people, in masks, become puppets. A tree turns into a house, which turns into a boat. From the boat evolves a book, which then becomes a tree. Each object is represented by square modules - a cross between children's building blocks and Japanese screens - which regroup themselves into different arrangements. There are patterns within patterns. The tree is T-shaped. Struck by lightning, it becomes a tipped tree (or T). Later its foliage or wings are clipped and it sails to sea.

Orchestrating the regrouping is an elegant company of white-garbed dancers. Silently, they shift the scenery, manipulate the puppets, Bunraku-style, and achieve a life within the rebus of Mr. Wilson's fervid imagination. At the same time, a jazz band plays Mr. Byrne's score, infectious New Orleans-style music - slow drags and street arches - and an offstage narrator speaks a stream of Mr. Byrne's words.

Though the piece is decidedly abstract, there is a story line, dealing with the life cycle through history, from the tree of life through Noah's ark and onward to Admiral Perry's opening of Japan and to the American Civil War. But to be overly conscious of narrative is to miss some of the intuitive surprise of the expedition.

Things are seldom what they seem to be. Nor are they necessarily congruent with Mr. Wilson's storyboard reproduced in the program. I am still wondering where the promised lion was in the first play; perhaps it was subliminal. Other figures are self-evident: a golden-hued robot, a pterodactyl puppet, a mound of Japanese baskets that becomes self-animating, a child with a Buddha head who closes the evening by reading a book of the tree.

Geometric shapes - light forms - congregate, as if gathering for a meeting. At times they resemble a Mondrian canvas in motion. Then, suddenly, a rear screen is ablaze with Miro-like swirls. Each theatergoer will have his own impressions of the stage pictures. The eighth Knee Play is summarized as "the boat hull sinks below the sea." In actuality, there is a simulated underwater ballet - a restless cinematic sea projected on the screen and sensuous dancers (as fish or waves?) rippling on stage.

Suzushi Hanayagi's choreography is as integral to the piece as Mr. Byrne's music and Mr. Wilson's tapestry of images, and an additional asset is Heinrich Brunke's palette of lighting effects, which finds infinite shadings in the black and white design. Only Mr. Byrne's words (spoken by Matthew Buckingham) remain quizzical, although they seem generally to deal with matters of time and travel. As passengers, we sit back and let our senses luxuriate in a pristine performance-art journey.

WHEN WE DEAD AWAKEN: FEBRUARY 16, 1991

CAMBRIDGE, Mass. - Ibsen's final play, *When We Dead Awaken*, is one of his most adventurous and intensely personal works. As the author intended, it is a "dramatic epilogue" to his naturalism and a return to the poetic symbolism of earlier plays like *Peer Gynt* and *Brand*. In it, an artist, a surrogate for Ibsen, suffers "remorse for a forfeited life."

Because of its allusiveness and its epic canvas, the play leaves ample room for directorial imagination. This is strikingly true in the case of Robert Wilson, in his first attempt at Ibsen (at the American Repertory Theater). As a conceptualist, Mr. Wilson might find himself confined by the domesticity of *A Doll's House*. But *When We Dead Awaken* acts as inspiration to his brand of theatrical magic realism.

The words are Ibsen's (in translation); the images and the interludes belong to Mr. Wilson. This is an interpretation, not a deconstruction of a text. The director's perambulations do not obscure Ibsen's unrelenting exploration of the agony of an aged, depleted artist. Though the production has a few rough edges, especially of a technical variety, it represents a creative collaboration between the director and the playwright, and between the director and his partner in design, John Conklin.

The protagonist of the play is a sculptor named Rubek, who has channeled all his passion into his sculpture and in the process has compromised his own genius. Late in life, cynical about worldly success, he torments himself with what he has lost - in particular, the woman who was the model and muse of his youthful endeavors.

At a coastal spa, Rubek and his young wife, Maya, exude the boredom of a sterile marriage. They are Ibsen characters embarking on a Strindberg marital dance of death. Suddenly the model appears, aged and burdened by disillusionment. While hewing to Ibsen's play, Mr. Wilson approaches the characters as figures on a shifting metaphorical landscape. The play expands in length as well as in imagery: the Wilson version adds more than 30 minutes.

In keeping with the barrenness of the central couple, the resort of the first act is a cracked-earth wasteland; in the background we hear crashing waves, the first evidence of Hans Peter Kuhn's vivid score of sounds. The characters then move to a forboding mountaintop, heightened by two towering cliffs.

Rubek sits in a huge spidery chair that looks like a throne designed by Giacometti. From there he looks down on his wife standing before a bright blue ribbon of light representing a stream. Maya places a shoe in the stream and it magically floats away. The stage picture is mesmerizing; each time the curtain rises, there is a scenic transformation.

The spirit that most affects the landscape is that of Ingmar Bergman, in his own epic phase, as in *The Seventh Seal*, not least of all because Death is a lingering presence. A Bergman *When We Dead Awaken* might approximate aspects of the Wilson version. There are no trees in sight, only stone, earth and ice, signifying the harsh, jagged view of people enthralled by their fate.

Alvin Epstein is a brooding Rubek, haughtily dismissive of his wife. As played by Stephanie Roth, the wife has the mercurial unpredictability of Hedda Gabler (who was also trapped in an impossible marriage of her own choosing). The model is an enigmatic force, doubly so in Mr. Wilson's conception. She is symbolically portrayed by two actresses, old and young, Elzbieta Czyzewska and Sheryl Sutton. Her shadow (and protector) is now her alter ego.

As one has come to expect from Mr. Wilson, the acting is highly stylized, voice and gesture burnished with a tinge of Kabuki. What at first is disconcerting becomes ritualistic as the director tries to choreograph the characters' inner emotions. Maya's willfulness, for example, comes out in sudden, almost violent mood swings.

For all the seriousness of effort, the production repeatedly uncovers a troll-like comedy within Ibsen, as in the conception of the bear hunter who seduces Maya. He is intended as a crude, natural man, almost a beast. As played with diabolical humor by Mario Arrambide, he becomes a satyr, down to his cloven hoof. His roguish abandon is the opposite of the sculptor's rigid repressiveness.

In the third act, as the characters head toward a threatening glacier, Mr. Wilson's invention momentarily flags, and there is a brief dramatic letdown. Flames spark unconvincingly before the final coup de théâtre, as the earth is struck by the rumble of an avalanche.

In characteristic fashion, Mr. Wilson has devised three short Knee Plays or entr'actes, which are presented in front of the curtain while the scenery is being changed. The legendary tap-dancer Charles (Honi) Coles sings sweet and sad blues of his own composition, often in harmony with the other actors. Mr. Coles appears fleetingly in the play itself as a hotel manager. Though the Knee Plays have nothing to do directly with Ibsen, they are a kind of contemporary evocation of the love the characters have denied themselves. These interludes could be excised, but we would miss Mr. Coles's engaging essence.

In the play, Mr. Kuhn's score, the lighting, scenery and performance all unite in a daring attempt to scale a craggy, neglected masterwork.

Simultaneously with the play's production, there is a retrospective exhibition, "Robert Wilson's Vision," at Boston's Museum of Fine Arts. In a series of walk-in installations, one can examine more closely the designs, sculptural objects, masks and puppets from the director's onstage dream world.

The exhibition echoes with memories of Wilson plays and operas, including an electronic panel from *Einstein on the Beach*, a simulation of a spaceship that seems about to take flight. Visiting the museum and the American Repertory Theater, one experiences the double-edged nature of Mr. Wilson's work: the theatricality of his art and the visual splendor of his theater.

THE CLARK KENT OF MODERN THEATER: JAN. 6, 1994

In Robert Wilson's loft in TriBeCa, everything is exactly in place: furniture, sculpture and artifacts from his operas and plays. Bare light bulbs glare down on a carpetless concrete floor. By his design, there are no doors in the apartment, only passageways 20 inches wide. The effect is that of a post-modern museum. Moving among his possessions and identifying them, Mr. Wilson is a walking Acoustiguide, stopping longer before some displays for more extended commentary.

Years ago, when his father visited the apartment, he asked him how he could live there. "It's like being in prison," his father said. "None of the chairs are comfortable." His son replied, "Comfort is a state of mind."

Robert Wilson himself is a state of mind. At 52, this native of Waco, Tex., is a towering figure in the world of experimental theater and an explorer in the uses of time and space onstage. For more than two decades, he has been animating his astonishing visions. Transcending theatrical convention, he draws in other performance and graphic arts, which coalesce into an interated tapestry of images and sounds. To some, the choices may seem arbitrary; in fact, Mr. Wilson is a paradigm of precision, finding a direct linkage between idea and execution.

His neat Clark Kentish appearance belies the phantasmagoric images he creates on stage. Tall (6 feet 4 inches), infinitely polite and well groomed, he has a penchant for wearing conservative blue suits. He has always been "rather formal" in the makeup of his art and in his personal habits. Even when he was in art school, he always wore a suit. He adds by way of explanation, "Magritte painted in a suit and tie."

Despite the formality of his home, he seems at ease there; he has invented an environment to suit his temperament. He points to a metal, non-loungeable chair and says it is a litter for Amfortas in the *Parsifal* he directed in Hamburg, Germany. Nearby are a Frank Lloyd Wright chair and table, and King Lear's shoes from a production he staged in Frankfurt.

In a narrow corridor separating his bedroom and living room, shelves are closely aligned with curios: Thai, American Indian, Etruscan, Spanish, pre-Columbian and a nest of sculptured hot dogs from an opera he did with Allen Ginsberg. Like items in a Joseph Cornell box, these diverse pieces achieve a unity within the Wilson collection. It is his specific intention that objects in his theater should not be decoration; they are meant to have an artistic life of their own.

Moving past a window with a sweeping vista of the Hudson River, he looks toward a sanitation department building and says that he reproduced a version of it in *Einstein on the Beach*. At least in this one instance, that Philip Glass-Robert Wilson opera directly imitated life. "The world's a library," he says, indicating that ideas for image come from his window, his travels, his dreams.

As an innovator, he puts his signature on everything he does, including his two recent Paris successes, *Madame Butterfly* and his dramatization of *Orlando*, and *The Black Rider*, the antic expressionistic entertainment he wrote with Tom Waits and William Burroughs (presented at the Brooklyn Academy of Music). He quotes Marcel Breuer as saying that a single Breuer chair encapsulates all his esthetics, the same esthetics that go into designing a city. Similarly, one of the galvanized pipe chairs that he designed for *Einstein on the Beach* captures the quintessence of Wilson. A surrealist might regard them as a totemic self-portrait.

Mr. Wilson is the most successful American director in Europe, working in all the major theaters and opera houses in France, Italy and Germany. In addition, as an artist, he sells originals and limited editions of his furniture, sculpture and drawings, priced from $4,500 to $80,000. His sculptural installation won the Golden Lion last summer at the Venice Biennale.

His art has expanded and deepened, encompassing grand opera as well as reinterpretations of great dramatic literature. At the same time, in his original pieces he continues his investigation of history, science and cultural identity. In his boldness, he remains an iconoclast, shattering preconceptions and heightening perceptions. The key to his art is in counterpoint. He juxtaposes the unexpected: a period opera staged in a modern setting, or as he says, a computer rather than a candelabra sitting on a baroque commode. "Our theatrical language has been limited by literature," he said. "That is not to say that words are unimportant. But the 'visual book' doesn't have to be subservient to what you hear."

Although it will come as a surprise to many people, he thinks of himself as a classicist, reinventing the past by asking questions. "The reason we work in the theater is to ask, 'What is it?,' not say what it is," he says.

Standing before a Man Ray photograph of Gertrude Stein and Alice B. Toklas, he quotes the photographer's advice to him: "Don't give up your roots in America." Mr. Wilson has heeded that warning, despite the fact that is difficult for him to find the financial support to work in the United States. He has become a confirmed New Yorker, but because of the demands of his career he was able to be here only three days in the last year. Like an opera singer, he is booked for the next four years, and most of his work will be in Europe.

This year he will be busy restaging operas at the Opera Bastille in Paris, and preparing new works that include his own one-man *Hamlet*. The next collaboration between him and Mr. Waits will be based either on the Bible (Mr. Wilson's choice) or on *Frankenstein* (Mr. Waits's choice). Among his major projects is a gigantic sculpture park he is designing for Paris. "It will go alongside the new national library and will be about the size of three football fields, with a giant chair, 50 meters high, and 30-some-odd-bronze camels in a pool of water." Another principal concern is an international arts center he plans to open in Water Mill, L.I. It would serve both as a Wilson library and as a place to develop projects in various performing and visual arts.

In Europe, he is a personage. When he was in the house for a performance of his stunning production of *The Magic Flute* in Paris, the audience rose at the end of the opera to chant, "Vilson! Vilson!" A four-and-a-half-hour documentary about him was recently shown during prime time on French television. In America, however, he is still considered an outsider. For example, in 1986, this writer was chairman of a jury that unanimously nominated him for the Pulitzer Prize for drama for his epic play, *The Civil Wars*. The supervisory board of journalists and educators exercised its right to reject the selection; no drama award was given.

For years, Mr. Wilson was detached from Texas, and he has not even the barest trace of a Texas accent. Partly because of an association with the Alley Theater in Houston, he has an increasing affinity for his home state.

Although he is often surrounded by associates, he remains something of a loner. Wherever he is, he sets up an office, working during breaks in a performance. He works late, often to 2 or 3 A.M. Then he gets up at 9, and while taking a bath listens to tapes (currently, of himself reading *Hamlet*, to learn the lines). Swimming is his primary athletic activity.

His work uses state-of-the-art advances in sonar, laser and video equipment, but he is mechanically inept. He is unable to work his VCR, a tape recorder or even his answering machine. Others carry out his explicit directives. His New York office houses his archives and handles the practical as well as the business side of his life. In common with his home, it is ultramodern.

Since he is habitually late for appointments, his staff automatically sets his schedule accordingly, knowing that he operates on his own interior clock. A compulsive illustrator, he is always story-boarding his thoughts as well as his plays. He thinks in stage pictures. As he says: "I can't talk without drawing. It's a way of speaking for me."

High on the list of artists he admires are Merce Cunningham, John Cage and George Balanchine - along with Jack Benny, for his timing as well as simplicity. "He could do nothing; it was everything," he says. Watching Benny, he adds, "is like waiting for the toast to pop out of the toaster: you know it's going to pop up but you don't know when." He is also a fan of Buster Keaton, Charles Chaplin (who saw *Deafman Glance* twice) and Bill Irwin - old and new vaudevillians.

In his own work, he has often confronted the charge that events proceed too slowly, as in *The Life and Times of Joseph Stalin*, which ran 12 hours, dusk to dawn. The first time his sister saw one of his plays, he asked her if she could have identified it as his work if she did not know he was the author, director and designer. She said yes, "because it was too slow."

Explaining his relationship to time, he admits: "Often I take much more tiii-iime than one would normally take to do something. I...slow...it...down, and then sometimes Ispeeditup."

3

PLAYWRIGHTS

EDWARD ALBEE

WHO'S AFRAID OF VIRGINIA WOOLF?: OCTOBER 29, 1962

In his shorter plays, *The Zoo Story* and *The American Dream*, Edward Albee revealed an uncommon talent for taking a commonplace situation and twisting it into something almost surrealistic, which shocked and amused, but did not always move its audience. Albee's new play runs three times as long as his earlier ones. The style is the same, but the result is a play that is not only shocking and amusing, but is also as emotionally shattering, in its own way, as Eugene O'Neill's *Long Day's Journey Into Night*.

Who's Afraid of Virginia Woolf? - Albee's first Broadway offering - takes the form of a conversation piece. The setting is the book-lined living room of a faculty home on a college campus, and the conversation goes on for three and a half hours at a small party after a large party given by the president of the college.

The mistress of the house, Martha (Uta Hagen), is the daughter of the president, and she is a strident, brassy harpy, as crude (and as funny) as she is loud. She despises her husband for his weaknesses and herself for knowing those weaknesses. "You never mix," she accuses him. "You just sit around and talk." George (Arthur Hill), a history professor, is Martha's handpicked failure of a husband, ineffectual in life, but never tiring of mind-to-mind combat with his wife. Where Martha is brutal on a grand scale, slashing large gaps in his ego, George's lance strokes are quick, sharp, and low, and in the end the more damaging.

Their two guests for the evening are Nick (George Grizzard), a new young biology instructor, and his childlike wife, Honey (Melinda Dillon). At first Nick seems an innocent, no guile and less wit, but soon he reveals himself as a man who knows what he wants and will do anything to get it. Nick is almost - but not quite - a match for George and Martha; Honey is a match for no one. Midst all the fury, she drinks and dances, the most disengaged of the four. She is never quite sure what is going on and when she suspects, she forces it from her mind. As George divulges to the assembled company the painfully embarrassing story of Honey's false pregnancy that led to her marriage - to Nick's horror, since he told George the story in confidence - Honey says, quiveringly, "That story sounds familiar."

Albee's characters are playing The Game of Truth - comically, corrosively, horribly, vengefully - and for keeps, stripping away all illusions until they expose the raw bone of reality. And then, once at the bone, they attack the marrow. Much of what they say would be offensive out of context, but the spoken vulgarities lose their shock impact when placed alongside the unspeakable marital and mental cruelties.

Virginia Woolf is a splendidly acted, electrically staged (by Alan Schneider), brilliantly original work of art - an excoriating theatrical experience, surging with shocks of recognition and dramatic fire. It will be igniting Broadway for some time to come.

FERNANDO ARRABAL

AND THEY PUT HANDCUFFS ON THE FLOWERS: OCTOBER 19, 1971

Four years ago Fernando Arrabal, who has lived in France since 1955, revisited his native Spain, was arrested and charged with blasphemy and calumny, and spent 24 days in jail. During his imprisonment he observed political prisoners "guilty" of crimes of opinion. From this experience he wrote *And They Put Handcuffs on the Flowers*, a harrowing and disturbing work of art.

The Off Off Broadway Extension theater has performed a theatrical coup by presenting the first United States production of *Handcuffs*, and by persuading the author to direct the play himself.

Steel bars clang. An ear-punishing horn bleats. The theater is a prison. Three men are confined inside a cell. One has been made mute by his imprisonment. He paces the cell, squaring the corners, his hand tremblingly fixed to his mouth as if in search of a voice. The others are on the edge of madness.

The three remember and fantasize. They leave their cell to become other characters or themselves in fantasy. There are occasional "love dreams" and flashes of bitter humor, but mostly the prisoners enact nightmares of psychological bestiality, physical torture and sexual abuse. Before long we have not only an excruciating picture of the prisoners but also a history of this prison's depravity, and an indictment of a dictatorial nation.

The play's structure is loose and episodic, and the narrative is further interrupted by ritualistic announcements blandly recited by an actor dressed as a girl. Harsh prison noises collide with church music. The fact that the Extension theater is in a church is emphasized, as is the fact that the tyranny the playwright is condemning is taking place in a religious state.

The title of the play, according to Arrabal, was a statement made by Garcia Lorca in despair just before he was murdered. The most haunting image in the play is not the handcuffed flowers, but the condemned man whose face is masked with a dog's muzzle, forcing his mouth to remain open, while prohibiting even a cry of pain or protest at execution.

In the past, Arrabal's plays have seemed dryly intellectual and self-consciously poetic, but this time he has forsaken mannerisms. The evening is discomforting, almost unbearable. Some people will be offended, even disgusted. But it is powerful - the playwright's own unmuzzled cry in favor of freedom.

As director, Arrabal has extracted the last ounce of bile from the play. With the aid of Lois Messerman as interpreter, he leads his cast with a precise regard for the drama's violent rhythms.

The roles are extremely demanding, and the actors take no shortcuts. Ron Faber, James Richardson and Lazaro Perez have a fiendish, almost self-injurious, identification with their characters. Mr. Faber gives the most penetrating performance.

Natalie Gray, Ellen Schindler, and Muriel Miguel are potent as the wives and whores, and Bruce Levine, as the head of The Movement, and late-arriver in the cell, has the final and most outrageous moment of an outraged play.

Before the performance the audience is admitted one by one to a dark theater. As I entered, I was accosted by an usher - or was it an actor? - who grabbed me in a hammerlock. As it turned out, the gesture was unnecessary. The play provides its own hammerlock.

AMIRI BARAKA

SIDNEE POET HEROICAL: MAY 21, 1975

In its own way, *Sidnee Poet Heroical* by Imamu Amiri Baraka (LeRoi Jones) is as scandalous as *Macbird.* This exuberant comedy, written in 1969 but for obvious reasons - too hot to handle - not produced until now (by the Henry Street Settlement's New Federal Theater), permits the author to express himself simultaneously as artist and activist.

His hero, Sidnee Poet, is an untutored West Indian black man who immigrates to the United States and decides to become a movie star. "I'm going to make it," he says modestly, "because I'm big and black and handsome. I'm a great actor, even a great person."

Sidnee's sidekick is an equally confident and ambitious calypso singer who wears his bright red shirt open below the navel. One does not have to know that character's name - Lairee Elefant - to ascertain his prototype.

These two portraits of famous blacks are malicious, even savage, but the characters have a redeeming charm - in the conception and in the performances by Neville Richen (as Sidnee) and Count Stovall (as Lairee).

The play is not just a theatrical equivalent of a roman á clef, but also a devastating commentary on the image of the American black in popular culture, the image demanded by whites and delivered, to order, by blacks. Sidnee Poet is heroical because society needs him to be heroical.

The author's criticism - and the play is an act of criticism as well as a piece of theater - is not directed so much against a specific personality as against a role (and movie roles) thrust upon him. He is projected toward his fate.

In a series of acidulous parodies (on film and live), Mr. Baraka spoofs Sidnee's movies. The black convict looks out, first, for his white brother (boos from the audience). The black carpenter dances with nuns. The "nigger helper" aids a blind girl. A black woman pleads, "I need help, too," and he spurns her with, "You're not blind! Those other folks need the help."

Guess who's coming to dinner? One look at her daughter's stunning fiancé, and the mother (a neat Katharine Hepburn imitation by Lynn Singer, the only actual attempt at impersonation) says ecstatically, "Ah wince in pure sexual joy." And one wonders, why shouldn't she be attracted to Sidnee?

Nuns and blind girls keep popping up in strange places. It is the serene emasculation of the black man that inspires Mr. Baraka to his greatest causticity. But the character has no time to worry about his image. On occasion, he bursts into song, at one point putting on top hat and tails to proclaim happily: "I'm making it. I'm making it."

Eventually, Sidnee becomes so integrated that he turns white, which he tries to cover with make-up. Lairee is revealed as the true cynic. "The whole damn thing is whiteness," he says, and when his friend rejects the "choice" movie role of White Pongo (who seems closer to King Kong than the Noble Savage), Lairee eagerly embraces it.

In the second act, the play slows down and grows didactic, but it leads inevitably to Sidnee's awakening. "This is a life of love and struggle," he says. "Our life is our art," and he begins to take stock of his reality - and to become truly heroical.

Acting as his own director, Mr. Baraka succeeds in getting this unwieldy play on stage (no small accomplishment) and extracts sharp performances from minor players as well as from the lead actors. But the film clips are too cursory, and the production is rudimentary. The play does not yet fully realize its potential. It would also be interesting to see it filtered through another director's sensibility.

Sidnee Poet is a corrosive indictment of an American dream - and the plundering of that dream by the expectations of society. It makes us realize what a loss it was for the American theater when Mr. Baraka turned his attention primarily to political activism.

ERIC BOGOSIAN

TALK RADIO: MAY 29, 1987

Imagine Lenny Bruce at the height of his notoriety becoming a popular talk show host -and you may begin to have an idea of the whiplash intensity and black, hard-edged cynicism of Eric Bogosian's *Talk Radio*. With his new play, opening last night at the Public Theater, Mr. Bogosian takes a long leap from performance artist to playwright.

In his previous one-man shows, such as *FunHouse* and *Drinking in America*, Mr. Bogosian played a gallery of characters of his own creation - Hollywood agents, rock stars and street derelicts - with a deftness that moved beyond satire. In *Talk Radio*, conceived in collaboration with Tad Savinar, he plays just one character, but he is surrounded by people, seen and unseen, in his orbit. Depending on one's point of view, he is either a pilot fish or a piranha.

Mr. Bogosian is Barry Champlain, a composite of all the early morning and late night talk jockeys who specialize in subversive radio. But he is a man with his own, diabolical presence. As written and played by Mr. Bogosian, Barry Champlain is malicious to his marrow. For several hours every night, he sits in a studio in Cleveland, taking calls from listeners and handling them with the dispatch of a sushi chef. If someone is boring or objectionable, Barry pushes a button and cuts him off the air in mid-sentence. When met with abuse, he responds with even greater abuse. No one can top him for an insult.

As the play begins, the program is on the eve of going national and the producer (Mark Metcalf) is worried that the host will offend sponsors, although offensiveness is of course the essence of Barry's method. He excoriates everyone, while denouncing the dismal state of the world and asserting his own godlike loftiness. As he says, "This decadent country needs a loud voice - and that's me."

Who listens to Barry Champlain? Insomniacs, we are told, "nut jobs and psychos," neo-Nazis, the lonely and the desperate. Night after night, Barry pushes them to the breaking point, as he plays analyst, confessor and devil's advocate. On the air, he often infiltrates the listener's subconscious, prodding a guest to reveal secrets, promising friendship and love and then, suddenly, severing the relationship. In confrontation, he can seem as savage as an executioner.

One hysterical phone-in cries that his girlfriend has just overdosed and, without a blink, Barry calls him a liar. The switchboard lights up with concerned callers, wondering how he could be so brutal. The truth is the young man has lied. Later, invited to come to the studio, he turns out to be a weirdo off-the-wall, played by Michael Wincott as a frenetic jangle of nerves.

Most of the other characters - dozens of them - remain unseen, bizarre voices in the night. But there are also tangible people in Barry's circle, including his producer, an awed assistant (John C. McGinley) and a sexy girl Friday (Robyn Peterson). Each steps forward and, in a spotlighted monologue, pictures another aspect of Barry's career.

There is a breathlessness about the performance, despite the brief, non-broadcast interludes. Mr. Bogosian's energy as an actor is as unrelenting as his writer's imagination. As we watch in fascination, one must ask if he is not merely an aberration. In common with the subsidiary characters, we are alternately captivated and repelled by his personality. Barry Champlain is a fact, etched from life. He and his counterparts can exercise an influence to the point of Big Brother mind control. Conceivably, he could even lead a revolution - and, as he says, the world he is attacking is troubled to the point of madness.

As director, Frederick Zollo has given the play a broadcasting authenticity, setting it within the equivalent of a hi-tech bunker. *Talk Radio* does not waste words or time. Though the background is radio, the evening becomes visual and visceral. This is not because of Mr. Savinar's unnecessary slide projections (they are a minor distraction), but, primarily, because of Mr. Bogosian's own expressive unpredictability as an actor. His voice has the brittle clarity of a man compelled to communicate in the dark. Speaking on his phone, he looks possessed. In character, he represents danger, a threat to complacency and sanctity.

Behind the callousness runs a streak of self-hate and behind that there is a curious kind of honesty. Mr. Bogosian's Barry Champlain backs his audience into a corner and forces it to face itself. When he ridicules a sponsor or assails a phone-in pervert, he is vicariously filling a role for his listeners, who urge him to greater excess.

Necessarily, he is trapped by his own excess. He is, to use one of the plays many violent images, like "a train out of control." How long can Barry Champlain's center hold? A crackup will come, but not before we have been taken for a mordant, midnight ride.

BERTOLT BRECHT

NO PLAYS NO POETRY BUT PHILOSOPHICAL REFLECTIONS PRACTICAL INSTRUCTIONS PROVOCATIVE DESCRIPTIONS OPINIONS AND POINTERS FROM A NOTED CRITIC AND PLAYWRIGHT: MARCH 31, 1988

As director, Anne Bogart has had the ingenious notion of staging Bertolt Brecht's theories rather than one of his plays. In collaboration with member of three experimental troupes, Otrabanda, the Talking Band and Ms. Bogart's Via Theater, she is presenting a collective performance piece with a self-descriptive title.

Behind that lengthy title, the work (at the Ohio Theater) is both a non-play of ideas and a playful act of literary criticism. The object of the criticism is Brecht himself who is spoofed at the same time he is admired. Appropriately, the style is that of a funhouse or Brechtian theme park. Call it Alienation World. With its disrespect, *No Plays No Poetry* is the opposite of the eulogistic anthology, *Brecht on Brecht*. Because of all the author's built-in contradictions, the show could be regarded as *Brecht Against Brecht*.

The environmental evening begins with Paul Zimet as a sideshow barker. The saturnine actor does not look remotely like Brecht but, more than any of his colleagues, he captures the author's arrogant intellectualism and derisive humor. Puffing a cigar and blowing bilious clouds of smoke and sarcasm at the audience, he savagely attacks everyone from Aristotle onward, including Shakespeare, Shaw and Stanislavsky. Slinking around the theater he gradually begins to resemble Peter Lorre, a sinister image that seems curiously in keeping with the subject.

Repeatedly the audience is encouraged to wander in various directions. We can choose from an array of instructive events, such as a one-woman clown show by Tina Shepard. Spinning a globe, she imitates Brecht imitating Chaplin imitating Hitler. At the same time, in the corner of the warehouse-sized space, Jonathan Fried offers a yawning rendition of "great moments from that play *Hamlet*."

Necessarily some of this is nihilistic knockabout comedy, and some of it is overtly casual commentary. In either case, it is informative, and Brecht himself might have been forced to approve. As Walter Benjamin observed, Brecht considered all charges against him to be complimentary, even the accusation that he was a theatrical troublemaker and saboteur.

Drawing from Brecht's theoretical writings and criticism, including the *The Messinkauf Dialogues*, the company explains and explores the author's concept of epic theater, the alienation effect and his manipulative attitude toward actors. He warned actors never to identify with the characters they created. Lines are intentionally - and with humorous result - spoken out of context. Sipping champagne and seemingly about to step into a tango, a man and a woman exchange Brechtian manifestos as if they are Noël Coward epigrams. Occasionally the actors assemble into a brass band and march through the theater playing music with a Kurt Weill tinge (written by Neal Kirkwood and Harry Mann).

Though some of the maneuvers are digressionary, the 70-minute show does not overstay its welcome and, in Brechtian fashion, the actors retain their skepticism. At no point do they try to ennoble the author but continue to confront him on his own disputatious terms. In contrast to other environmental shows this season (*Tamara, Tony 'n' Tina's Wedding*), *No Plays No Poetry* offers no dinner no drink. It alone provides food for thought.

ED BULLINS

THE TAKING OF MISS JANIE: MARCH 18, 1975

In his provocative new play *The Taking of Miss Janie*, at Henry Street Settlement's New Federal Theater, Ed Bullins sees the nineteen-sixties as a time when many blacks were seeking peaceful assimilation and many whites proudly vaunted their liberalism as a ticket to the black world - blacks wanting to be like whites, whites wanting to be liked by blacks.

To Miss Janie, an ingenuous California coed, blacks (at that time they were still called Negroes) are an exotic, endearing race. She is like a missionary in colonial Africa, sowing good will, good works and nonsense. In the play her opposition is represented by a stiff-backed fanatical black militant, who is a nationalist before it is popular. "I'm just trying to be black in this white wilderness!" he roars at the patronizing invader.

Between these poles, Mr. Bullins positions his protagonist, Monty, a black poet shaped by white writers, a black who is drawn to whites. There is a crucial difference between his attitude and Janie's, and it is the hinge of the play. By her choice, the two have a continuing relationship, not an affair; consummation, many years later, is a case of rape. The author means the title of the play literally. All symbolism is intentional. Miss Janie, we are told, is Miss White America.

Approaching allegory, Mr. Bullins is trading in stereotypes, but he never loses sight of the truth that informs the cliché. Only Janie and the militant are really exaggerations (Monty and his quiet roommate are life studies), and in both cases the heightening is for comic purposes.

A willowy new actress, Hilary Jean Beane, and a sharp seasoned professional, Kirk Kirksey, are so amusing in those roles that they almost run away with *Miss Janie*. The audience laughs at her and cheers him. Janie's character verges on caricature; played broadly she would be unbearable. Instead the actress is unabashed and matter-of-fact. How else could you deliver a line such as "Monty's friends are so interesting and colorful" and make it funny?

The play is a sequel to *The Pig Pen*, which was presented in 1970 at the American Place Theater. Like that work, *Miss Janie* takes place at a party, but its structure is far more complex. The play weaves in and out of the party, forward and backward until we have a complete picture of a society in limbo. The play is, like *Moonchildren*, a time capsule of the sixties, with something pertinent to say about what made the seventies.

The production is directed by Gilbert Moses (with whom the author had a publicized disagreement over his staging of Mr. Bullins's *The Duplex* at Lincoln

Center). The play would benefit from a fuller production. At times the stage seems crowded, the scenes clustered. Actually, *Miss Janie* might be better served as *The Duplex* was on an open stage.

This time, author and director work harmoniously. They have chosen their cast carefully and Mr. Moses directs them with enormous assurance, stressing the comedy but not at the drama's expense.

Besides Mr. Kirksey and Miss Beane, there are excellent performances from Darryl Croxton, Lin Shaye, Robbie McCauley and Adeyemi Lythcott, as the poet confused about his identity.

CATHERINE BUTTERFIELD

JOINED AT THE HEAD: NOVEMBER 16, 1992

As *Joined at the Head* begins, Maggie Mulroney is in Boston on a book tour for her new best-selling novel when she gets a telephone call from her old high school boyfriend. But what happens next in Catherine Butterfield's play is not the standard *Peggy Sue* look back at the 1960's. *Joined at the Head*, which opened yesterday at the Manhattan Theater Club, is a jaunt into the writer's mind, a vibrant reflection on life, art and friendship.

In this, her first full-length play to be presented in New York, Ms. Butterfield is revealed as a playwright with a refreshing talent for probing the reality of relationships. The play is filled with inner voices and second thoughts. In a manner related to that of Tom Stoppard and John Guare, the work deals enticingly with truth and fiction. Whenever things threaten to become too literary, the playwright quickly edits herself.

Although the play is episodic, it is free flowing, ducking in and out of the protective theatrical framework. The playwright nimbly shifts her course until no artificial wall is left unbroken. For the audience, there is a pleasurable sense of engagement in the creative act and in the author's unmasking of her characters.

When the novelist visits her old boyfriend and his wife (who not so coincidentally is also named Maggy), she interrupts the apparent domestic harmony to offer shrewd comments directly to the audience. Maggie the novelist (Ellen Parker) always has something smart to say, sometimes to her own disadvantage. But there comes a point when she begins to sound like A Writer, and it is exactly at that juncture that the other Maggy steps forward to lighten things up by telling us her divergent side of the story.

As Donald Margulies did in *Sight Unseen* last season on this same stage, an artist looks at the present through a prism of the past. In Ms. Butterfield's play,

Maggie prepares to write the novel that is the play we are seeing. She keeps insisting she is only the narrator and the backdrop, that it is the other Maggy who is the protagonist. Although they were absolute opposites in high school, they prove to have a symbiosis, which has to do with more than the man both of them have loved.

The play achieves an extra spark because the married Maggy is played by Ms. Butterfield. A charming actress, she tosses off her lines as if she had written them herself (and of course she has). Both she and Ms. Parker offer lovely performances in roles that deal tellingly with questions of identity and mortality. Despite the fact that she has a serious illness, Ms. Butterfield's Maggy remains pragmatic, with a constantly replenishing personality. Ms. Parker's Maggie is edgier and relentlessly self-analytical.

As the three former schoolmates reminisce about not so happy old times, memories collide with facts, and the dialogue retains its pithiness. We hear about Gina Laszlo, the golden girl who peaked in her senior year. Gina was last seen in a parade on a float advertising her husband's Pontiac dealership, providing the trio - and the audience - with a lingering laugh about false values of high school days.

The play's problem area is the husband (Kevin O'Rourke), who is more an observer than an active participant, although eventually he confesses his feelings in a Socratic dialogue with himself. A watchful Maggie might have made him into a more expressive character, and she might also have reduced an extended sequence in which a landlady serves sentimentally as a substitute mother. There is still room for self-editing.

The central story line is enhanced with amusing overheard conversations that could act as journal notes for future books by the novelist. In a series of sardonic set pieces, the playwright also mocks pushy television interviewers and heartless hospital attendants, among others. That television interview is a slap at armchair academics, as the fusty host overanalyzes and misreads Maggie's novel (same title as the play we are seeing). He concludes that it is "a searing indictment of the father-daughter relationship." The novelist intended it as a funny book and prefers one of her earlier more serious works.

Joined at the Head wins both ways, as a comedy and as a play about the process of art and the discovery of kinship. It asks how such seemingly disparate women could have so much in common. In a short span of time, they become more than friends; they are the incarnation of the title of the play.

Pamela Berlin has directed the work as an adagio movement, with James Noone's scenery gliding on wheels and a troupe of agile supporting actors (the true backdrop of this story) playing a panoply of characters. At the curtain call after a recent performance, a theatergoer called out, "Author, author." *Joined at the Head* is a striking accomplishment for Ms. Butterfield as author, actress.

PING CHONG

A.M./A.M. - THE ARTICULATED MAN: FEBRUARY 4, 1982

Ping Chong turns dreams into visions and creates a theater of illusion. In his new work, *A.M./A.M. - The Articulated Man*, at La Mama Annex, he welcomes us to the atrium of his phantasmagoric imagination. Intellectually, the new piece is difficult to penetrate, at least without the help of exegesis from the author-director, but the images - visual, aural, choreographic, photographic and cinematic - are as ineluctable as they are beautiful. In its stunning procession of stage pictures, the play reminds one somewhat of the work of Robert Wilson, but Mr. Chong has his own distinctive touch.

Some other members of the American experimental-theater movement seem to take pride in the randomness of their efforts, but Mr. Chong's work is marked by its precision and its professionalism. There is no stray element, but the presence of an artist who knows exactly where he wants to go and how much he is willing to communicate. Even when we are confused by the direction, we are not disoriented; Mr. Chong makes the audience try harder.

The evening begins on a large screen, with still photographs seen in negative, starting with a view of a garden that an off-camera voice identifies as Gethsemane. This is followed by a film in slow motion of people at leisure in a park. Because of the slowness of the motion, the reversal of the film and the raga like background music by Meredith Monk, we feel as if we are entering a trance.

Without warning, the film spins into quick motion. The camera pulls back and we see that we are in Central Park, a long-distance view of people scurrying back and forth as if they are insects skating on a pond. Then the screen rolls down to the floor and we find ourselves facing a large, bright white box, a hospital room with a single patient (Ishmael Houston-Jones).

Completing the Magritte-like scene, there is a glass of red wine on the floor, a single dash of color on a white canvas. A woman enters, sips the wine, and then is followed by a trio of nurses each carrying a birthday cake with flaming candles, which they alternately offer to the young man and take away from his grasp. This theme of reward and removal is repeated throughout the evening.

A shift in the lighting causes the box to be bathed in op-art plaid. Then the brightness returns and the hospital room has been transformed into a bedroom. The centerpiece is a bed with white satin sheets, and Mr. Houston-Jones and one of the nurses mime a meeting of lovers. Suddenly a man emerges from behind the bed, provoking a laugh from the audience. Then with a faunlike grace he seduces the nurse.

In another striking sequence, a young pregnant woman conveys her uncertainty about her condition, then raises a knife and stabs herself. In stylized, balletic motion, she reaches under her dress and extracts a long black ribbon of mourning, which she unrolls until it almost covers the stage. In moments such as this, one realizes that Mr. Chong is as indebted to classical Oriental techniques as he is to the theatrical avant-garde.

The performance builds to a filmed sequence in which a man sits at a table before a potted plant, a small mound of earth (in black and white, it looks like caviar) and an apple. Just as he is about to bite into the apple, a hand moves on camera and takes it away. The action is repeated, as the man is manipulated by an unknown force. The notion of man as mechanical device is intentional; later we are told that the figure on screen has been "terminated."

Moving between live action and film, with a laserlike line of light occasionally drawing our attention to particular objects, Mr. Chong arranges compositions to be "photographed" by our figurative iris lens. On one level, his play illustrates various methods of repression, the way people are depersonalized and reprogrammed. On the other hand, one could also say that the play is simply about its images. No matter how one approaches *A.M./A.M. - The Articulated Man*, it is a spellbinding experience to somnambulate with Ping Chong.

KINDNESS: MAY 7, 1986

Six friends, seniors facing graduation, are at a school prom. The mirrored ball is spinning, and memories are in the making. Two boys are dressed in tuxedos, three girls are in gowns. The sixth, Buzz, is decidedly out of costume, though he is dressed in basic black. His classmates treat him like one of their number, perhaps as a foreign exchange student, but his difference is as plain as the fur on his face. Buzz is a gorilla.

The play is *Kindness* (at La Mama Annex), a case of Ping Chong in an antic New Vaudeville mood, complete with running gags and routines, but with a bittersweet aftertaste. The title, in typical Ping Chong fashion, is intended as a pun. *Kindness* means sympathy, friend to friend, and it also refers to species, as the author-director suggests, splitting the word in two, "kind-ness." The world is populated by humankind and gorilla-kind.

Kindness is an investigation, both literate and ingenuous, of what it means to be an outsider, a theme that has fascinated Mr. Chong (in *A Race* and last season's *Nosferatu*). In the new work he approaches the study on several simultaneous levels. The show is linguistic, psychological and, inevitably, metaphorical.

Mixing film with theater and dance, *Kindness* begins as an illustrated lecture. On a screen are projected a sequence of like and unlike words and objects. Playfully, Mr. Chong arranges them as building blocks until they form a superstructure of harmony and discord.

From there, he moves into live action and the tale of Buzz, a gorilla with soul and a limited future. What gives the comedy its impetus is the matter-of-fact style. No big deal is made about the gorilla; his schoolmates do not acknowledge his species and they intuitively understand his grunting form of communication. Idly, they all chatter about adolescent pursuits.

In a sense, this is a Ping Chong variation on the boy with green hair, the Elephant Man, the Ugly Duckling or, more aptly, the world according to Peanuts, with Snoopy cast in the role of a gorilla. Though not as cute as Snoopy, Buzz (played by John Fleming) is ingratiating, the kind of primate anyone would want as a friend. But would you want your sister to marry him? Romance is on the horizon, followed by tragedy.

In the background is a tuneful assemblage of eclectic music (from Jelly Roll Morton to Puccini), a pristine set design by Angus Moss and a directorial concept that is coordinated with light and sound effects. Most of the actors are from Mr. Chong's Fiji Company; all operate on the author-director's channel.

Repeatedly, in the course of the show, an actor walks across the stage carrying a large rock; it becomes a comic motif. Finally, he puts the rock down, then surrounds it with other rocks, slowly creating a habitat for Buzz: gorilla at large returns to the zoo. After this jolting reminder of civilization, Mr. Chong still has a twist up his magician's sleeve. *Kindness* is more accessible than many of his earlier pieces, but it retains its own sense of mystery.

CARYL CHURCHILL

SERIOUS MONEY: FEBRUARY 10, 1988

In its transfer to Broadway's Royale Theater, Caryl Churchill's *Serious Money* retains its vituperative sense of humor. This is a neo-Restoration comedy crossed with a Jacobean revenger's tale. As the author indicates, with all malice intended, there is no end to greed.

The shenanigans of *Serious Money* center on the City, London's financial domain, but, as the play circumnavigates the global theater, it appears to have a universal applicability. Wherever there is a distinction made between money and serious money, it should remain timely and impertinent.

However, with its overlapping dialogue, stock market slang and singsong verse, the comedy tends to confuse and can even alienate a theatergoer. The first 10 minutes, in particular, are cacophonous as the characters shout and outshout one another on the trading floor, a scene that is paralleled in Oliver Stone's movie *Wall Street*, an altogether less provocative descent into the money maelstrom.

By the second, or, in my case, the third time, that one sees the play, the devious plot begins to achieve a focus, although it never becomes entirely straightforward. As a tip, keep your eye on Jake Todd, who will soon be dead, although alive again in flashback, and on his sleuthing sister Scilla. With *Serious Money*, ours is not to reason why but to watch - and enjoy - the wherefore, to see how the rich become even richer while vying for green power.

Even in its London original, the play was always partly mid-Atlantic, swinging between stock exchanges and featuring two major characters from our side. There is the crafty Marylou Baines, an arbitrager who is, we are told, second only to Ivan Boesky. In the epilogue, it is announced that Marylou runs for President in 1996 (what's her platform?). Telling the story of *Serious Money* is the American wheeler-banker, Zackerman. One advantage of the Broadway production, as redirected by Max Stafford-Clark, is that there is now an American Zackerman, John Pankow. His English predecessor, though a good actor, seemed as American as Crocodile Dundee. Mr. Pankow, who is one of our more versatile young character actors, zealously incarnates this engaging opportunist.

On Broadway, Kate Nelligan assumes the role of Marylou Baines and two others previously played by Linda Bassett and equals her fierce intensity. Ms. Nelligan, who is Canadian and therefore bilingual (American and English) has a comic zest that has hitherto been under wraps in her dramatic career, except for the dinner party scene in *Plenty*. This time Ms. Nelligan savors her own wickedness - and we do, too - and, as another character, is also a clownish sight with a big plaid bow in her hair. A third asset is Allan Corduner, the sole holdover from the English cast, and an actor adroit at playing cabinet ministers as well as stockjobbers and backstabbers. He has been in the play since it first opened at the Royal Court Theater and is totally in accord with the author's attitude of cold, calculating sincerity.

In other roles, the new cast lacks the precision of the earlier company. The accents of the American actors are on a par with those of their English cousins, but Alec Baldwin and Michael Wincott, for two, miss the Churchillian malevolence. Mr. Baldwin plays Billy Corman, the takeover pirate, with a growl that is no substitute for the character's original roar. Mr. Wincott's Jake Todd courts blandness. At this stage, Mr. Stafford-Clark's production is not as taut as the version at the Public Theater.

There have been several minor alterations in the text. The white knight (now played by Melinda Mullins) has moved from the North of England to the American Southwest, with no appreciable change in sentiment. And a reference to the Wall Street crash that was written for, but never inserted in, the Public Theater production makes it to Broadway.

For those who have not seen *Serious Money* before, the new production may prove to be an eye-opener, entreating one to share in the author's mirthful condemnation of those dedicated to their own self-interest.

MAD FOREST: JULY 25, 1990

LONDON - In the 1970's, during the heyday of the Joint Stock Company and other politically inclined theatrical organizations, English playwrights like Caryl Churchill, David Hare and Howard Brenton often reacted immediately to public issues. Faced with urgent political questions, the writers reached for their quill cudgels.

Except for the agitprop days of the Living Newspaper in the 1930's, playwrights in the United States have traditionally left such quick commentary in the hands of stand-up comics and monologuists. Although in the 1980's this kind of political theater was on the wane in London - possibly because theaters were worried about losing financial support - there has been a reawakening of interest this summer in what could be called Theater of the Moment.

As in previous years, the playwrights are led by Ms. Churchill, whose new play, *Mad Forest*, is an insightful investigation of the revolution in Romania last December that toppled the regime of Nicolae Ceausescu and led to the execution of the Communist dictator and his wife. Simultaneously, the Royal Court Theater sponsored a six-week season of 15 issue-oriented dialogues, under the title *May Days*.

Max Stafford-Clark, the company's artistic director, has explained the impetus for the dialogues: "The swift course of events in Eastern Europe at the end of 1989 and the end of a decade of Thatcherism here in Britain prompted a wish for a kind of 'Royal Court Instant Response Unit,' able to give a theatrical platform to the immediate debate of political issues."

The immediacy of the playwrights' response does not necessarily insure wide public attention. The Churchill play is performed on a small stage in the Embassy Theater in North London by students at the Central School of Speech and Drama - a long way from the customary venues of the author of such trans-Atlantic successes as *Cloud Nine*, *Top Girls* and *Fen*. The show is scheduled to conclude its run this weekend. The May Days series, which ended this month, played to embarrassingly small audiences, a fact that was variously attributed to a dearth of publicity, mixed notices and public apathy.

Nevertheless, the plays - in particular, *Mad Forest* and Doug Lucie's Royal Court one-act, *Doing the Business* - are provocative in the extreme.

Ms. Churchill's play, commissioned by the Central School, is an incendiary piece of theater, which moves beyond reportage into a kind of historical analysis.

As a play, it still has rough edges. Some scenes are either underdeveloped or overextended. But it has a visceral sense of events happening as the audience watches and a feeling of first-hand truthfulness.

Together with her director, Mark Wing-Davey, Ms. Churchill visited Bucharest in March, amassing information and images. Two months later, the playwright had finished writing the play and it was in production, without the delays found in the commercial and even the institutional theater.

Sitting on hard concrete blocks, theatergoers are uncomfortable witnesses to the Romanian revolution, as it detonates and then is eventually surrounded by questions. In the first act there are glimpses of the repressiveness of the Ceausescu regime and the economic and political deprivations suffered by Romanian citizens. The view is through the eyes of two families, one working class, one representing the intelligentsia - about to be united through marriage.

The second act offers a collage of snapshot reactions to the revolution. As in a mystery play, people with limited knowledge try to piece together what actually happened. In the third and most amorphous act, the playwright describes the seismic tremors that continue after the initial revolution. Especially in this final section, there are indications of Ms. Churchill's more imaginative side, as she creates a sardonic encounter between a dapper Transylvanian vampire and a fleabitten dog, a stand-in for the bedeviled common man. Wisely, the playwright has refrained from sealing her play with a conclusion. Like the revolution itself, the play remains in progress.

The confused nature of the uprising, as Ms. Churchill sees it, is reflected in the title. *Mad Forest* refers to the name of a forest outside Bucharest, considered to be "impenetrable for the foreigner who did not know the paths." In other words, Ms. Churchill believes one would have to be Romanian to understand the intricacies of the events of the last year, and even then the view might be obstructed. Guided by the playwright, we begin to understand the political and moral complexity. In one of many bitterly comic interludes, the play's Ceausescu explains why he is mightier than God. God created the sun, the moon, the stars and mankind "out of chaos"; Ceausescu boasts, "I created the chaos."

The student actors are a closely allied ensemble, offering indications of their nascent theatrical talent. Similarly, there is a feeling of potential in the play - incomplete but far more evocative than the author's last effort (*Ice Cream*, produced last season at the Public Theater in New York). With work, *Mad Forest* could become the Eastern European political equivalent of Ms. Churchill's *Fen*, a play that far transcended its journalistic origins.

CHRISTOPHER DURANG

A HISTORY OF THE AMERICAN FILM: MAY 23, 1977

WASHINGTON - America, as seen in Christopher Durang's play, *A History of the American Film*, is not just movie-mad, it is movie-made. Sexism, militarism and sentimentality inhabit the delirious film palace of Mr. Durang's mind. And the House Un-American Activities Committee has Ma Joad executed for saying "We're the People."

It would be easy to regard *American Film* as a diversion - and it certainly is a grand popular entertainment. But, seeing it for the second time in an all-new production at the Arena Stage - the play has already been presented at the Hartford Stage Company and the Mark Taper Forum in Los Angeles - it is clear to me that this comedy is also a significant act of film criticism as well as wise social commentary. Mr. Durang has the waggishness of four Marxes and the malice of Jonathan Swift.

In Hollywood's archives, the author has discovered archetypal characters: Jimmy, the tough guy; Loretta, the sweetheart; Bette, the bad girl; aw-shucks Hank and Eve the wisecracker.

American Film is a cavalcade of the movies from the early silent *Broken Blossoms* through *Earthquake*. The heroine, Loretta, keeps waiting for the end title to come down so that she can be frozen, happily, behind it. The sign saying "The End" - in this production, it is as big as a billboard - does descend, and then goes right back up again. By the close of *American Film*, with *The Exorcist* wagging a lascivious tongue and everyone worshiping "molten images," Loretta is pleading tearfully for a return to a lost code of morality in which her husband, getting into bed, will "always keep one foot on the floor."

Through the history of the American film, we see a history of America - the turn from patriotism to cynicism, from optimism to sensationalism. Battered by Sensurround, the audience sits stupefied, waiting for the last picture show.

In the play's premiere at the Hartford Stage, there was a certain shakiness; play as well as production seemed to need more rehearsal. Since then, Mr. Durang has honed and tightened his script - and made a few necessary substitutions (a droll western has replaced a stuffy costume romance). At the Arena, director David Chambers wheels his cast smoothly - and gleefully - from era to era.

The clown-sharp company of comic actors strikes precisely the correct stance - total conviction and no camp. It is as if they have stepped right out of the silver screen, or we have stepped into it. All we need is popcorn in the lobby.

As Loretta and Bette, April Shawhan and Swoosie Kurtz are, quite simply, adorable - movie memories in the flesh. Miss Shawhan has that look of dewy innocence that carried celluloid virgins through countless, even Kong-ly courtships.

Ms. Kurtz's resemblance to Bette Davis enriches her lovely tart-tongued characterizations.

Gary Bayer, who looks a bit like Cagney, plays Jimmy with a light varnish of mimicry, and through his versatile performance we realize that all these screen tough guys had a certain nasality of speech. Terry O'Quinn is as dry as sagebrush as the "insufferably monosyllabic" Hank and Joan Pape gives a smartly tailored performance as Eve.

Guided by Mr. Durang, Chuck Patterson offers his own concise history of the American film Negro - leaping, with the panache of a Richard Pryor, from a back-talking maid to a Japanese house boy to a sitting bull of an Indian to a soft-soaping "Piano Man" in *Casablanca*.

In the first act, everything is in black and white, even the orange juice on William Powell's breakfast table and Carmen Miranda's bananas - until the Japanese bomb Pearl Harbor and the stage-screen explodes into Technicolor. Tony Straiges's scenery and Marjorie Slaiman's costumes are worthy of M-G-M. Mel Marvin's music, played by an on-stage pianist, is a tuneful setting for Mr. Durang's insouciant lyrics.

A History of the American Film is an A-movie, a glorious montage of myth-America. It deserves an Oscar, or, at least, the Jean Hersholt Humanitarian Award.

HARVEY FIERSTEIN

TORCH SONG TRILOGY: NOVEMBER 1, 1981

Arnold Beckoff, the lonely but far-from-forlorn hero of Harvey Fierstein's *Torch Song Trilogy*, is a die-hard romantic who takes his heart, soul and fatalism from the 1920's ballads that give the work its title and its tone. At the end of a long, infinitely rewarding evening in the company of Arnold and his family and friends, he confesses with a sigh that he has always wanted exactly the life that his mother has had - "with certain minor alterations."

Those alterations - Arnold is a homosexual and a professional "drag queen" - are the substance but not the sum of Mr. Fierstein's work, three plays that give us a progressively dramatic and illuminating portrait of a man who laughs, and makes us laugh, to keep from collapsing. The evening is a double tour de force for Mr. Fierstein, who, with his throaty Tallulah voice and manner, stars in his own touching triptych.

We first met Arnold in *The International Stud*, produced Off Broadway in 1978. At the time, I felt it was a sincere but sentimentalized view of a transvestite in extremis. Seeing the play again, in a carefully abridged version in a vastly superior staging by Peter Pope, I found myself enjoying Arnold's wit at the same time that I was moved by his dilemma. He is a man of principle who compulsively plays the fool.

As presented by the Glines company at the Richard Allen Center, *The International Stud* becomes the first chapter in a cycle of tales about Arnold, each originally produced at La Mama. The current evening, running more than four hours, is designed as a trilogy of related plays, but it turns out to be one cohesive three-act play.

Each succeeding "act" adds to our understanding and fully justifies what has gone before. Instead of reiterating positions, Arnold's story becomes richer as it unfolds. There are still flashes of sentimentality in Mr. Fierstein's performance as well as in the text. The author is so accomplished at playing Arnold that he cannot resist an extra flourish or an easy wisecrack, and the ending is too neatly symbolic. But the cumulative event is one to be experienced and savored.

Among other things, it deals fairly - without any attempt at exploiting the situation or manipulating our emotions - with varieties of sexual orientation. For example, Arnold's lover (Joel Crothers) is a bisexual who is caught between two magnets: what he thinks he needs and what he feels. The evening studies self-love and self-hate, headstrong passion and heartfelt compassion.

In the first part, the two men meet - to a counterpoint of torch songs, sung pensively by Diane Tarleton - and after a sequence of on-again, off-again encounters, many of them humorous, they separate. In the second part, *Fugue in a Nursery*, Arnold and his new lover, a male model, visit Arnold's "ex" and his new girlfriend (Ms. Tarleton) at their farmhouse. The tinseled cynicism of the first play sweetens as the quartet conducts a roundelay that is both fanciful and immensely civilized. The four switch partners, conversationally as well as romantically, with the irrepressibly sympathetic Arnold trying, but not succeeding, in turning a deaf ear to the problems of others.

In the third and best play, *Widows and Children First!*, we meet Arnold's past and present family. First there is his Jewish mother (Estelle Getty), fresh from Miami with an archetypal self-salute, "I'm the mother," and an unextinguishable hope that her son may yet blossom into heterosexuality. The final addition is a troubled teen-ager whom Arnold has rescued from the streets and wants to adopt. The sociological implications are complex and the author treats them with equanimity, demonstrating that the flamboyant Arnold is truly a reflection of his assertive mother, which is why they are destined to spend their lives at loggerheads.

Mr. Pope has given "Torch Song" an excellent production, which gains in intimacy from the open stage and from Bert Clephne's imaginative scenic design - three entirely different settings for the contrasting modes of the evening.

The cast is a closely meshed ensemble. Mr. Crothers is a stalwart presence as a man trying to sort his letters of identity. Paul Joynt manages to express the model's confidence while avoiding the path of narcissism. Ms. Tarleton is amusing as a woman with a fatal weakness for ineligible men, and the tiny Ms. Getty is perfect as a mastodon of a mother. Matthew Broderick brings a naturalness and a spontaneity to the role of the teenager.

All of the characters are of course subsidiary to Arnold's dominant personality. He is his own torch song, and the role is inseparable from the actor-author. I cannot - and do not want to - imagine anyone else playing Arnold. Mr. Fierstein's self-incarnation is an act of compelling virtuosity.

DARIO FO

WE WON'T PAY! WE WON'T PAY!: DECEMBER 18, 1980

If you are deflated by thoughts of inflation, if you have ever looked at the price of food in the supermarket or glanced at as a menu in as a restaurant and decided that we had suddenly moved to a different, less rewarding monetary system, then Dario Fo's *We Won't Pay! We Won't Pay!* should fill you with laughs of recognition. This comedy about consumerism was first produced in Milan, Italy, in 1974. In its New York premiere at the Chelsea Theater Center, as adapted and directed by R.G. Davis, it is as timely as the wage-price index and as saucy as spaghetti à la bolognese. Mr. Fo's manic farce should be obligatory viewing for anyone battling, i.e., succumbing to, the high cost of living.

For the purposes of his incautious cautionary tale, Mr. Fo, who is Italy's most celebrated and most controversial contemporary playwright, takes a typical Italian family, typical, that is, from Vittorio de Sica movies. Giovanni works, Antonia scrimps. He shouts, she slaves. She lives to cook his dinner and he carries chauvinism as a tattoo on his heart.

One day Antonia and her sister housewives, fed up with rising prices, stage an impromptu strike in a supermarket, and when the manager cold-shoulders their protest, they walk out with bundles without paying for the merchandise. At the same time, factory workers rebel against the inedible food in their cafeteria , and commuters block their railroad. Milan is at a standstill.

The last bastion of conservatism, the defender of the law, is Giovanni. Knowing that he will scold her for stealing food, Antonia appeals to his stomach. All she can scrape together on his slim salary, she says, is dog, cat and bird food. Would you like some canary birdseed soup?

What ensues is a madcap travesty of kitchen-sink comedies, which also manages to shoot satiric darts at the police, government bureaucracy, unions, the welfare state and masculine domestic privilege. *We Won't Pay! We Won't Pay!* has the outrage of that moment in the movie "Network" when Peter Finch shouted, "I'm mad as hell, and I'm not going to take this anymore."

Such is the impact of Mr. Fo's humor that he seduces an audience into responding to the most indelicate comic situations. Try to keep from smiling when Giovanni tells the crazy tragic story of a dog with an electronic hearing aid. The performance I attended was filled with older matinee ladies. Many of them seemed about to capsize with laughter, with only the merest squirm of embarrassment at Mr. Fo's occasional spiciness. The fact is that he tickled them in their pocketbooks.

In his freewheeling adaptation, Mr. Davis has inserted an occasional American joke without dislodging the play from Milan. The spontaneous approach can trace its genealogy back to commedia dell'arte and forward to the San Francisco Mime Troupe. The actors never forget that they are giving a performance, which allows them to step in and out of character. W.T. Martin, for example, plays five roles, including several policemen and an undertaker, without unduly altering his disguise. The other characters eye his phony mustache and his wavering accent with a certain suspicion, finally agreeing that the only reason for Martin's multiplicity is that this is an Off Broadway show with a tight budget.

The actors know their Fo, and each has a fusillade of lunacy. Karen Shallo and Bonnie Braelow are Antonia and her best friend, frantically trying to stuff their booty under the bed and under their clothes while convincing their spouses of their propriety. Robert DeFrank plays Ms. Braelow's husband with an air of ingenuousness, reaching an absurd apogee as he unknowingly eats dog food and savors the taste as if it were exquisite caviar.

Mr. Martin manages to keep a straight face - more than I was able to do - as a policeman in an open coffin in a closet with a door that never stays shut. Funniest of all is Harris Laskawy as the duped Giovanni, fulminating like a stick of dynamite. Watch him glow as it finally dawns on him that his wife is right, that the natural response to corporate thievery is a little household larceny. Or, as one character says, "Expropriation is the only defense against robbery."

In common with Mr. Fo's *Accidental Death of an Anarchist*, a long-running London comedy hit about the violence that government can inflict on concerned citizens, *We Won't Pay!* is the work of a social reformer with a fractured funnybone.

RICHARD FOREMAN

PANDERING TO THE MASSES: A MISREPRESENTATION: JANUARY 16, 1975

Richard Foreman's new play is called *Pandering to the Masses*, which, as he indicates in the subtitle, is *A Misrepresentation*. Though he is neither a panderer nor a popularizer, Mr. Foreman clearly wants to - and does - shatter the myth that his work is inaccessible. For this latest emanation from his Ontological-Hysteric Theater, he provides in the program a detailed plot synopsis, advising the audience to read it before or after, but not during the performance.

Just to be sure that we know exactly where he is at any given moment -actually he is sitting on the edge of the stage operating an electronic keyboard, flipping whirrs and buzzes along with music and speech - he narrates the entire event. In his deepest "Shadow-knows" voice, Mr. Foreman offers guideposts, interpolations and interpretations. Occasionally he recapitulates.

Back again are our old friends Max (the artist), Rhoda (his love) and Sophia (Goddess of Wisdom). The subject is that Foreman perennial - the search for knowledge. As usual, it is the search more than the knowledge that is the point of the play. This is an outlandish investigation of inner space (the mind of the author), a dream-like exploration of the associative method. Mr. Foreman puts one word-picture after another.

I can think of no other American experimental-theater artist, with the exception of Robert Wilson, who is so completely responsible for, and inextricable from, every single aspect of his art. Mr. Foreman is the author of the script, designer of the production, director and conductor (in several senses of the word). He leads the performers and also acts as our sardonic tour guide.

Very little of the dialogue is delivered, live, by the actors. Sentences and even syllables are electronically interspersed with mesages from the manipulative author. He is the prime ingredient in his play. Max is his alter ego, just as Ben is Max's alter ego. There are characters within characters just as there are plays within this play. The only play individually identified is *Fear*; the title character "enters left of center."

In the past, Mr. Foreman has occasionally led us down the path of boredom - ennui followed. This time the trip is tantalizing and enthralling. It completely commands our attention. *Pandering to the Masses: A Misrepresentation* is a playful and as self-mocking as its title.

Mr. Foreman challenges our equilibrium. His play is an unbalancing act. The stage, is long, narrow and steeply ramped, with a tiny doll's house on the horizon. The landscape is spliced with string defining distance and focus. Croquet balls roll down the ramp and turn into apples. Out dance five actresses sideways, like paper dolls or ducks in a shooting gallery. A young man furiously pedals a toy tricycle. There is a "snake dance fight" and peep-show nudity. Finally Max climbs on a high horse. This is, after all, an intellectual excursion.

"He's putting everything he knows into this play," says a voice helplessly. Mr. Foreman intones: "He always puts everything he knows into every play he writes."

The evening is idiosyncratic. The experience is unique.

RHODA IN POTATOLAND (HER FALL-STARTS): DECEMBER 24, 1975

In *Rhoda in Potatoland (Her Fall-Starts)*, the latest exploration of Richard Foreman and his Ontological-Hysteric Theater, potatoes are larger than life. These mammoth creatures have pinhole eyes and people feet. One of them wears a mirror over its forehead as if it were a tuberous Dr. Kronkheit. I think these vegetables also have a libido. Although Mr. Foreman says, "Potatoes have no specific feeling about proximity to other potatoes," two of them - one at the door, one at the window - seem to ogle the beautiful (often nude) Kate Manheim.

Rhoda (Ms. Manheim), the heroine of countless Foreman sagas, is having a vision, a nightmare, and we are her witnesses. At the electronic controls manipulating the buzzer and metronome, spinning gut-bucket jazz and other tapes, occasionally shouting "Cue!" and carrying on a nonstop, self-mocking dialogue with his own play, Mr. Foreman is the expressive tour guide.

"This text is, as it were, inside out," he intones, as if from the tomb. "At the end, you're at the beginning." Actually the work is nonsequential (or, as it were, consequential). In other words, it is all middle. The event is mostly experiential.

Sitting on bleachers, the audience is inside a shadow box. The walls are black and rigged with devices - picture frames without pictures, sliding platforms, a topsy-turvy bed. Intersticed string cat-cradles the stage space. A table is placed on a hill at a precarious tilt. On the horizon is a large shoe and a teeny boat. Clue! Each has something to do with travel. They take us there. Where?

The play is a picture puzzle of interlocking images. It tantalizes and confounds. Repeatedly it returns to the subject of potatoes, as in the author's observation: "Potatoes so far as we know have no art or literature of any kind." Easily, *Rhoda in Potatoland*, is first and best in its field, a walkaway winner in the potato-sack race (actually Rhoda and the other ladies run in one).

All this is not so confusing as it sounds, although we occasionally lose our place. Mr. Foreman's plays may seem like spontaneous bursts of surrealism, but they are all precisely charted and choreographed by their ingenious composer. Pay attention, relax, and collect keys to the mystery. This particular voyage is about comparisons - women and potatoes, Rhoda and Sophia (as we know from

Mr. Foreman's other work, Sophia is his Goddess of Wisdom), music and noise (what a cacophony the actresses concoct on three blaring saxophones and a trombone!) and life and theater.

At one point the usually sedentary Mr. Foreman is suddenly captured by his work. He is on stage and Rhoda is at the control board. He is seduced and transfixed. In the end, he is arrested. He holds up his hands in surrender - to a mirror. Simultaneously, a Damoclean sword dangles over his head. Is this punishment for his extolling Rhoda's search for fame and happiness?

Clearly what we have witnessed is Mr. Foreman's dream as well as Rhoda's - a combined trip, a tumble down the rabbit hole of the author's looking glass imagination.

FILM IS EVIL: RADIO IS GOOD: MAY 5, 1987

The title of Richard Foreman's quizzical new comedy, *Film is Evil: Radio is Good*, almost says it all. This is a cryptographic mystery about the encroachment of visual imagery into the world of sound. The heroic forces of broadcasting are represented by the proprietors of a small, unidentified radio station that suddenly finds itself besieged and undermined by a chorus of threatening cinéastes.

Because Mr. Forman is the author, director and designer, one can expect unpredictable displays of creative energy. In this eerie environment, film is evil, radio is good - and "theater" is enlivening, although elliptical. The show is produced by Mr. Foreman's Ontological-Hysteric Theater, in collaboration with the New York University Tisch School of the Arts drama department. The production artfully intermingles professionals with student actors.

For the occasion, Mr. Foreman has transformed the Tisch Mainstage 1 into a cavernous radio studio of the imagination - the Foreman equivalent of a Louise Nevelson environment lined with Joseph Cornell boxes. The stage is gewgawed with gargoyles and curios, including clocks and flashing signs indicating that the author's ego is active (the world "ego" lights up when the show is "on the air").

Coming after last season's show *The Cure*, the new play offers additional evidence that Mr. Foreman has recaptured the playfulness and spontaneity of his chamber pieces of the 1970's, after a more recent career staging operas and plays on a grand scale. Many of the earlier adventures traced the comic peregrinations of a woman named Rhoda, Mr. Foreman's archetypal heroine. As played by Kate Manheim, Rhoda was a damsel in and out of distress, often entrapped by extenuating circumstances involving the jaws of technology.

Portraying a new Foreman character, Estelle Merriweather, Ms. Manheim merrily weathers the storm of broadcasting inclemency. This time she acts as interlocutor and advance warning system, cuing her colleagues, David Patrick Kelly and Lola Pashalinski, when trouble is lurking on the silver screen. She is undeterred by the aggressive forces of cinemalice.

Movies, we are told, steal one's image and warp one's brain. Radio, on the other hand, is pure. It stimulates rather than suppresses the imagination. The baleful chorus, played by a dozen antic N.Y.U. undergraduates, attacks - and radio reacts. But before the battle can become too polemical or semiotic, Mr. Foreman interjects sight and sound gags. Cartoonlike creatures appear - a snowman and a duck that looks suspiciously like Howard, the grossest canard of the movie industry.

Though the play runs on a bit too long, it never loses its fervor, and it is sparked by the three central performances. Ms. Manheim, Mr. Kelly and Ms. Pashalinski are well-schooled in the Ontological-Hysteric approach. They are amusing while appearing to be in deadly earnest.

Midway through the exercise, a screen appears onstage and the play is interrupted by a short film, *Radio Rick in Heaven and Radio Richard in Hell*, written and directed by Mr. Foreman, who also - a first - stars opposite Ms. Manheim. Belying the title of the play itself, the film is good, wasting no words or pictures and serving as an acute annotation of themes raised by the live performance. As an actor on screen, Mr. Foreman has presence and a mobile, though dour, face and, as we already knew, a deeply sepulchral voice. Were Mr. Foreman not so pro-radio and anti-cinema, he might have a filmic future as actor and auteur.

WOYZECK: MARCH 6, 1990

HARTFORD - Though *Woyzeck* was written in the 1830's, it is a seminal play of the 20th century, the first to articulate the alienation of modern man driven to madness by forces far beyond his control. In a sequence of cumulative scenes, Büchner's play - based on a true story - follows the downward path of a barber who murders his mistress and suffers tragic consequences.

After Büchner came Kafka, Brecht, Camus and Beckett. In fragments, *Woyzeck* survived the playwright's death (at the age of 23) and has become a text to tantalize the imagination - a challenge to which Richard Foreman has responded. In his production at Hartford Stage, Mr. Foreman has unlocked a masterwork through the seemingly simple process of allowing the play to speak for itself. Running barely more than one hour, this is a stark embodiment of the original Büchner.

While staging plays of his own authorship, Mr. Foreman embellishes the text with directorial detail, with ear-piercing buzzers and hot lights. With *Woyzeck*, in direct contrast, he has been scrupulous about stressing the play, not the direction or the design (both of which are in fact to his credit). He has stripped the stage of all possible excess, and he has introduced no diversionary notes. Craning one's neck, a theatergoer can see, high overhead, Mr. Foreman's signature - string as long as a trapeze - but the director does not call it into action, and the audience is transfixed by what occurs onstage.

The setting is bleak and powerfully evocative, as barren as the exterior of a concentration camp (though without barbed wire). Around the stage runs a wooden track, and in the center is a raised floor padded like a cell. Entering the theater, one hears a throbbing heartbeat of a sound collage.

This could be Woyzeck's pulse as he is held in thrall by events around him, by what the doctor in the play diagnoses as an aberratio mentalis partialis, obsession with a general rational condition. Despite appearances, what happens is irrational. Beyond the fact of Woyzeck's momentary jealousy, there is no moral or even psychological explanation for his killing of his common-law wife, Marie, but in the context of Büchner's play it is unavoidable. As the author said in a letter to his parents, unconsciously revealing the theme of a play yet to be written, "It lies in no one's power not to become an idiot or a criminal ... because the circumstances lie outside ourselves."

There is something childlike about David Patrick Kelly's Woyzeck, as he converses with his friend Andres, as he moves through his daily drudgeries and as he tries to verbalize his inward feelings of imminent dread. At a distance, watching Marie's seductive behavior with the drum major (in this production, the drum major strides like a majestic lion), he is silent to the point of seeming abstracted. But everything that happens has a direct effect on him. As Woyzeck says, "Everyone is an abyss," and then, proving his point, he plunges on his vertiginous journey.

Again and again, one feels the character's foreboding as in the following exchange with Marie: "We have to go." "Where to?" "How do I know?" Like characters out of Beckett, the two are trapped in a continuum. They have no control of their future or even of their velocity. The carnival scene, barely indicated in the text, is like a brief flash of disequilibrium from the film *The Cabinet of Dr. Caligari.*

The murder is as vicious as anything in *Macbeth* but the murderer is also his own victim. Having been carried away by his aberrant act, he falls into a daze. He is remorseless but confused, covering the body with a cloth and pretending the death did not take place. Then, looking down at Marie, he asks, "Why is that red thread around your neck?" - a thread that has of course stained his own hands. The play (in Henry J. Schmidt's translation) resonates with such imagery, up to the moon, which is described as being so red that it is like "a bloody blade."

Instead of trying to visualize these images, Mr. Foreman counterpoints the words with the blacks and grays on stage, a landscape of the seemingly mundane and definitively impoverished. Woyzeck is as hapless a creature as one could imagine. Marie and their son are the only brightness in his dreary life, which makes the homicide even more horrendous.

Mr. Kelly's performance as the lonely Woyzeck is the linchpin of the production, with trenchant support from Gordana Rashovich (as Marie who, like Woyzeck, lacks will but not desire), Michael J. Hume (as the self-parodying doctor), William Verderber and Miguel Perez, among others. All of the actors are unified under Mr. Foreman's direction, as the play rushes pell-mell to its foregone, no less chilling conclusion.

CELEBRATING THE FALLEN WORLD: JAN. 17, 1994

As a playwright and director with a philosophical bent, Richard Foreman is a practicing metaphysician in the experimental theater. During the last 25 years, his plays - 40 of them since he originated his Ontological-Hysteric Theater - have repeatedly analyzed the imbalances between art and life. Even while he has branched out to become director of opera and plays by others, his contribution remains instantly identifiable. Whatever he does, he leaves sight and sound tracks as his signature, and his art has always had a deeply intellectual foundation.

In rehearsal at St. Mark's Theater with his new play, *My Head Was a Sledgehammer*, Mr. Foreman is at the electronic controls, interjecting suggestions to his actors and orchestrating the mechanics of the enterprise. With a mournful mien that extends from his eyes to his mustache, he is a younger, avant- garde doppelganger of Broadway's David Merrick. As the author fine-tunes the performance, a spiderlike chandelier revolves like a fan in a Singapore hotel; string - a Foreman trademark - crisscrosses and stratifies the stage, and Oriental carpets cushion the walls. Actors in black dunce caps rush by as a professor prepares to lecture at a blackboard.

The source of *My Head Was a Sledgehammer* is Friedrich Holderlin's fragments for a play about Empedocles, the Greek philosopher "who was destroyed because he tried to bring down to people a kind of truth not meant for humans." Mr. Foreman's version is, he says, "a gloss" on the original, and deals with a professor who "through silliness and weirdness tries to introduce his students to his poetic method."

Coincidentally, Eric Bogosian, who is a friend of Mr. Foreman's, will soon open his new one-man show, *Pounding Nails in the Floor with My Forehead*. Mr. Foreman jokes, "I thought we might have a Jack Benny-Fred Allen feud about who stole the title."

In his unwavering career, Mr. Foreman has been converting "clouds of language and impulse" into alchemic theater, from his early plays in which his muse-like heroine, Rhoda (played by Kate Manheim), undertook serendipitous adventures, to last season's *Samuel's Major Problems*, in which his authorial surrogate was hounded by questions of mortality. Beneath the surface somberness is a comedic disposition. The plays owe as much to vaudeville as they do to existentialism.

Bizarre humor remains endemic to his work, although these days Mr. Foreman is, for personal reasons, more dour. His father died last year and Ms. Manheim, who is the playwright's wife, is very ill and doctors have been unable to discover the cause of her malady. Some time ago, she stopped acting. At 56, he is feeling more contemplative.

Asked to comment on his plays, he apologizes for risking pretension, and says: "If you were going to ask Heidegger what his next book was going to be about, he would say, 'About Being.' Well, all of my plays are about that." He might have added that the subject is also about being Richard Foreman.

The plays, which are continuing chapters in the serial of his mind, start with half-page scenes in his voluminous notebooks. Periodically, he harvests his entries for material that is thematically related. During an intensive eight-week rehearsal period, he processes these excerpts through his directorial imagination, and searches for a scenic environment "in which those lines of dialogue can have some reverberation." He continues: "People might be amazed if they saw how carefully we worked, how much material is thrown out and how much we change. Usually my cast is in agony because they think I'm throwing out all the best parts."

In any traditional sense, his art lacks narrative. Things happen and then happen again. Scenes can be switched, without disturbing the work's intention. He is "much more interested in juggling ideas than in telling a story." To illustrate the approach, he recalls a statement made by John Gassner, who was his playwriting teacher at the Yale School of drama: "Richard, you have talent, but you have one problem, which is that you get a strong dramatic effect and you just want to repeat it and repeat it and repeat." Eventually, the playwright took that criticism as a compliment. That was exactly what he was trying to do, to find an effect worth repeating, "the one effect you never tire of."

Before going to Yale, Mr. Foreman graduated magna cum laude from Brown University. He has always had a scholarly streak, but only gradually was he able to accommodate it in his theater. At first, he wrote plays in a Murray Schisgal vein, one of which was considered for Broadway as a vehicle for Alec Guinness. The English actor declined the offer, saying that he liked the play but felt that he was the wrong actor to portray an overweight, middle-class Jewish man from the Bronx. In retrospect, Mr. Foreman says, "With his great chameleon quality, I suppose he could have played the part."

The author's career charged in the opposite direction. Taking inspiration from the independence of underground film makers of the 1960's, he asked himself what he wanted to see onstage. He had an image of a nonsequential, idiographic theater in which "people faced each other across a space and said a few abrupt things, then moved and said a few more abrupt things."

Beneath the apparent anarchy was a sense of order and mystery, even an Aristotelian logic. From the outset, his theater has had a strong literary base, drawing on works of philosophers, with whom he has one-way dialogues. Oddly, he has always had an ambivalence about his profession. Given a choice, he might prefer to be home writing or reading Eric Vogelin on the history of consciousness. "I've always been a rather withdrawn fellow who is occasionally dragged out into society to put on a play," he says. "I'd be a hermit if it wasn't for theater." Compensating for his shyness, he is an integral part of the performance, with his tape-recorded, sepulchral voice offering wry asides on the drama.

For Mr. Foreman, as a poet-philosopher, the plays are meant to be instructive. He explains: "Art is trying to redeem, to learn how to dance with the problematic aspects of the world. It's easy enough to imagine a beautiful world, and to celebrate it, but I would rather learn how to celebrate the fallen world we live in. People have looked at me awry when I say that I think my plays are pictures of paradise. There are obviously plenty of very aggressive, unpleasant elements in them, but I would like to think they are subjected to a kind of esthetic massage."

His distinctive brand of performance art communicates with a seismic, prop-dominated theatricality. From the beginning, he has tried "to build the potential for unexpected collisions into the physical materials on stage." The design - aural as well as visual - is fraught with peril, especially for the actors. "If a table has a fat leg or wobbles in a funny way, that automatically suggests trouble," and breakaway furniture results in breakaway comedy.

Despite his devotion to a theater of ideas, the playwright has an active interest in more popular aspects of culture. As an admirer of Jule Styne, he harbors a dream of directing a production of *Gentlemen Prefer Blondes*, his favorite musical. But he has no interest in reviving his own plays (although *Dr. Selavy's Magic Theater*, a musical collaboration with Stanley Silverman, was brought back some years ago). The works exist in the moment for the audience that is watching.

Reflecting on his theater, he says, "To me, art is really 99 percent courage, the courage to follow your vision, and to remember what your particular vision is. It's a struggle not to let your mastery take you down the easy road, and in spite of what some people think, I have a mastery in certain areas. I have to cast that off so that I'm back in a naked condition confronting the material of my life."

Serving as his own producer, he uses income earned from his outside directing assignments as well as foundation support, and loses money on his shows. "I don't make a living from the theater, but that's fine," he says philosophically, adding, "There's something missing from my life, in spite of the fact that I've been very lucky in many ways and I've lived with the same lady who I love very much for almost 30 years now." His theater is his relief. "I only do it to feed myself," he says, "and I hope that someone else needs the same food."

ATHOL FUGARD

A LESSON FROM ALOES: APRIL 1, 1980

NEW HAVEN - Athol Fugard's *A Lesson From Aloes* is a play about a country's violation of its people. It is a cry of anguish for a lost nation and a failed cause. Mr. Fugard, who is, in the theater, South Africa's conscience as well as a brilliant playwright, has moved past the point of indictment. The view from his new drama, now having its American premiere at the Yale Repertory Theater in a production directed by the author, is unrelenting, but it is also marked by the quiet nobility of its hero, an Afrikaner who endures a mountain of shame and suffering.

It is 1963 and the revolutionary spirit has been spent. Despite all of their efforts, the Afrikaner, Piet (Harris Yulin), who is a former bus driver, and his closest comrade, an inspiring radical leader, Steve Daniels (James Earl Jones), have been vanquished. The Government continues its acts of repression, and rebels of all colors are outcasts.

Piet has turned his attention from politics to plants. He is collecting and naming species of aloes, a rugged cactus-like South African plant. The aloe is a perfect metaphor for man's indomitability in the face of adversity. Looking at the gnarled plant, Piet's wife (Maria Tucci) wonders: "Is that the price of survival in this country? Thorns and bitterness." With a nod, Piet agrees. "We need survival mechanisms as well."

In *A Lesson From Aloes*, the tragedy of a nation is played out in intimate, human terms. Marriages, families and friendships have crumbled along with ideals. Released from prison, preparing to leave Port Elizabeth for an unknown future in London, Steve destroys a treasured photograph of his father. The last thing he wants to take with him in his exile is a memory of good times. He and his friend's wife have each banished all sentimentality - and the past itself. But one phrase of his father's lingers in Steve's mind: "Only ourselves to blame." The abusive system is manmade - and it can be man-saved. As Steve leaves, Piet continues his solitary vigil, and his hope for renewal.

In common with his central character, the author has achieved a kind of heroic stature - in his work and in his life. With his own aloelike stubbornness and his profound sense of morality, he offers a lesson to his audience. This is not only a play about South Africa and the lost South African, it is also a powerful statement about the urgent need for individual responsibility - and trust.

Yale is fortunate to have the playwright in residence as director. He knows how to communicate the heartbeat of his play. Under Mr. Fugard's unwavering direction, the actors are a superb ensemble trio. They seem to radiate the stress of emotional turmoil.

In the pivotal role, Mr. Yulin is a pillar of rectitude and patience. He exemplifies equilibrium, a man completely at one with his environment, who finds a certain solace - and dignity - by quoting poetry. As a man who is outwardly effusive, but guards his inmost struggles, Mr. Yulin offers a beautifully modulated, contemplative performance.

The first act of the play is a dialogue between husband and wife, awaiting their dinner guest. As they transmit a full, sad portrait of a marriage devastated by politics, they also convey the importance of Steve in their lives and in the revolution. When he arrives in the second act, we are not disappointed. As acted by Mr. Jones, Steve is a commanding presence, a man who could lead armies as well as boycotts. As he and Piet try to rekindle their friendship, we see the strain beneath the bonhomie. Just as the wife has been subjected to a kind of emotional rape by Government agents, in prison Steve has been unmanned by an insidious mockery.

In the difficult role of the wife, a woman drowning in disillusionment, Ms. Tucci is the essence of fragility. The actress has never been more moving. As she sits silently, to a background of her husband's botanical ruminations, we can feel the pulse of her neuroses. A woman without center, she sees her world diminishing. Having gone far past the point of politeness, she becomes the catalyst for confrontation. The final moments of *A Lesson From Aloes* are bruising; nothing will ever be the same again, except, of course, for Piet ministering to his plants. *A Lesson From Aloes* may be Mr. Fugard's wisest and most mature work in theater.

MASTER HAROLD ... AND THE BOYS: MARCH 21, 1982

NEW HAVEN - In *A Lesson From Aloes*, a soul-searing drama about guilt, suspicion and the need for individual responsibility, Athol Fugard used the hardy, cactus-like plant as a symbol of survival in a hostile environment. His new play, *Master Harold ... and the Boys*, in its world premiere at the Yale Repertory Theater, is equally brilliant, but it represents the author in a reflective mood.

The three characters in this sublime memory play are marked by their youthful ardor, and the appropriate central metaphor is ballroom dancing. This is an Astaire-ized vision of a ballroom where dancers smoothly glide, an ideal world "in which accidents don't happen ... a world without collisions."

The playwright is speaking, first of all, about the bond between a lonely white teen-age boy and an adult black man who becomes his best friend and surrogate father. The youngster is the master, the man is the servant. But which one is really the teacher? In the course of a rainy, revelatory afternoon, the man - one of two waiters in a tearoom run by the boy's mother - instructs the teen-ager in the "steps" of life, a lesson that echoes far beyond the cafe-classroom. He offers him a curriculum in the meaning of compassion, and the boy, who may or may not understand the message, is, we surmise, an awakening artist as well as prodigal son.

Master Harold is about a family - the boy and his offstage parents, his dominant mother and crippled father - and about friendship. The family is strained by self-interest and the friendship is buffeted by incipient racism. The play is the story of a boy's will and a man's way, a boy's loss of illusions and a man's quest for a renewal of innocence. The evening begins and ends with a dance, and it is very much a dance of life - lyrical, hopeful and radiant with possibilities.

In contrast to other recent plays by the author, *Master Harold* is, for all its seriousness of purpose, something of a celebration. It is suffused with warmth and flavored with engaging comedy, a lightness of spirit that we have not seen in the author's work since *People Are Living There*. As written and directed by Mr. Fugard and as impeccably acted by a three-man cast, the evening moves inexorably from light to shade and from vitality to despair, followed by a coda of attempted amelioration.

The play begins in the St. Georges Park Tea Room, as two black men, Sam (Zakes Mokae) and Willie (Danny Glover) ritualistically clean the room while exchanging thoughts about their favorite pastime, ballroom dancing, and about the challenge of an upcoming competition. For the two of them, dancing is both a joy and a release, but Willie, the less articulate of the two, is still self-conscous about the activity. Practicing with a towel as partner, he never stops looking down at his feet. Sam shows him how to look up, to move with the music; since neither can afford money for the jukebox, the music is in their minds. In a figurative sense, Sam has also tried to lead Master Harold to lift his eyes.

The Sam-Willie idyll, much of it in a comic vein, is interrupted by the entrance of the young master (Zeljko Ivanek), who is an adolescent blend of the eager and the officious. He treats Sam as a fellow schoolmate, then adds pompously, "Tolstoy educated his peasants and I educated you." Subtly and in close harmony, Mr. Fugard and his actors show us the depth of the friendship.

Then, without missing a beat, the characters play a contrasting melody. Embarrassed by his father's incapacity and fearful of the demands that will be made on him when the parent returns home from the hospital, Harold lets himself be swept away by self-pity. He asserts himself at everyone else's expense. The principal object of his suddenly rising resentment is Sam, whom he humiliates in a scene of harrowing cruelty.

As Sam calmly states, Harold's assault has hurt himself - and the wound may be irreparable. With mature restraint, Sam tries to reach out before the boy steps away into an invulnerable adulthood. The author suggests that if a man such as Sam fails with his single pupil the idea of true racial equality is unattainable.

In this initial production - a fact that brings honor to the Yale Repertory

Theater - there are a few moments that need brushstrokes of the author's artistry. The play has an occasional tendency to tell us what we have already learned, as in the lyrics of the song that closes the evening. However, under Mr. Fugard's knowing direction, the three actors are orchestrated into a flawless ensemble.

Mr. Ivanek, seen last season in a bizarre double role in *Cloud Nine*, is touching as young Harold. As he sits at a table, pretending to immerse himself in his homework, we can feel him responding to the congeniality of the waiters. He would love to emulate their expansiveness, but is unable to free himself from the role that he feels forced to play - as benevolent despot. When he thinks that he has been slighted, Mr. Ivanek responds with the snappishness of a terrier, immediately reducing friends to servants.

As the boy reacts, Sam watches, and we can read on Mr. Mokae's troubled face a landscape of sympathy and of sorrow. He asks for understanding, or at least equilibrium, but knows that through boyish petulance bonds will be broken. Mr. Mokae, who has had a long association with Mr. Fugard's work in America as well as in his native South Africa, has never been more deeply penetrating. He enobles Sam with an inner dignity and a quiet sense of proportion. As Willie, Mr. Glover is perfect, conveying both the character's simplicity and his charm. Unquestionably, *Master Harold* will have a long future in the theater. It speaks about a life-changing experience with universality as well as eloquence.

THE BLOOD KNOT: SEPTEMBER 24, 1985

NEW HAVEN - In 1961, *The Blood Knot* was introduced at a single, Sunday night performance in a private theater club in Johannesburg, a production that co-starred the playwright, Athol Fugard, and a former saxophonist, Zakes Mokae. The play went on to become an international triumph and the foundation of Mr. Fugard's career as a dramatist.

Almost 25 years later, a revival of the play begins the season at the Yale Repertory Theater - a theater that has become a home away from South Africa for the playwright. Reuniting the original two-man cast, and with Mr. Fugard again acting as director, the new production is a major theatrical event.

First of all, the revival certifies the play's position as a contemporary classic. As both a deeply human experience and a symbolic statement on the anguish of apartheid, *The Blood Knot* is undiminished in its power. In the light of recent and continuing outbreaks of violence in South Africa, it is, if anything, more pertinent.

An artfully executed theatrical dialogue, it is not the work of a novice but of a fully formed, though, at the time, youthful playwright. Both actors share an identification with their roles, as well as a vivid memory of how those roles are meant to be played. Returning to *The Blood Knot* after 10 other subsequent Fugard works, one can discover the seeds of the author's art. Themes, motifs, images and the author's own impassioned conscience are all there in organic form.

In the play, we see two brothers - one dark-skinned, one light enough to have passed as white. They are inextricably bound in a relationship that is as intimate as it is wounding. After his attempt to live as a white man, Morris (Fugard) has moved in with his black sibling, Zach, and is trying to atone for what he regards as his betrayal of his brother.

Though the roles are equal, Morris is the catalyst, stirring his brother and, later, himself, into self awareness. Morris is emotionally repressed, in contrast to the outgoing Zach. In previous productions, through force of personality, Zach has tended to dominate the drama, as was the case in the New York premiere starring James Earl Jones. One distinct difference in this authorized version is that, as intended, the play is seen from Morris's point of view.

As envisioned and enacted by the playwright, Morris is, to some degree, an adult version of the adolescent Hally, his autobiographical stand-in in *Master Harold ... and the Boys*, just as Zach could be considered a precursor of Sam, Hally's father image in the same play. Always instructive, Morris tries to educate and to elevate his disadvantaged companion, superintending his daily life as if that were his divine right.

Even as Zach goes through his nightly rituals, soaking his tired feet in a basin of bath salts, we are aware of his brother's watchful, supervisory attitude. Morris's obsessive concern is attempted compensation for his own inadequacy and his overwhelming sense of guilt.

In South Africa, the playwright acted in this play and others out of necessity - someone had to play the roles. He has developed into a fine actor, as evidenced on screen in roles as varied as that of Gen. Jan Christiaan Smuts in *Gandhi*, and, harrowingly, as the drug addicted naturalist, Eugène Marais in his own film, *The Guest*.

He is also, as we see in *The Blood Knot*, an articulate stage performer, not only capturing the tragic element of his character but revealing a latent talent for comedy. Trying on a dress suit at the instigation of his brother, he ambles into a clownish walk, beaming his brief pride.

Mr. Mokae, who originated the role of Sam in *Master Harold*, plays Zach with a brooding intensity, rising from quiescence to contempt and turning a moment of playacting into a moving recapitulation of the plight of the black man in South Africa. The two men are carried away by their game, forced into inevitable roles as antagonists. Together, they try to bridge the abyss. Even without a future to look forward to, the brothers cling to hope - as have characters in every other Fugard play.

For the current production, the author has trimmed the work and, in so doing, has distilled it to essentials. The evening moves ineluctably to its conclusion. The set by Rusty Smith is an appropriately seedy, crudely furnished shack. The two actors inhabit the environment and their characters, offering a double performance that is itself as close as a fraternal bond. The anniversary production of *The Blood Knot* is a celebratory occasion.

THE ROAD TO MECCA: APRIL 24, 1988

The title character in *Dimetos*, one of the few Athol Fugard plays that has not yet been performed in the United States, lives on a stark landscape, unidentified by name but a clear approximation of New Bethesda in South Africa. At one point, Dimetos describes a workman in the local quarries as a man who "assaulted" rock "as if nothing short of total obliteration would satisfy him." He adds: "Without that dour tenacity of purpose, survival here wouldn't be possible." That tenacity is pervasive in Mr. Fugard's work, from the earliest plays through his most recent, *A Place With the Pigs*. It defines Helen Martins, the iconoclastic heroine of *The Road to Mecca*, which has arrived in New York four years after its world premiere at the Yale Repertory Theater.

During the play's journey to Off Broadway, the playwright has worked on it as if it were a piece of sculpture, shaping and polishing it in different productions at Yale, London's National Theater, the Spoleto Festival, U.S.A. and, currently, at the Promenade Theater. Though the script has not markedly changed, through the casting, direction and performance, the tone has altered and relationships have been clarified. As a result, one can hear the heartbeat of the play.

After the death of her husband, Miss Helen, who is based on a real person, forges her own private identity in art. Populating her New Bethesda backyard with brooding, sculptural figures who become inhabitants of her *Mecca*, Miss Helen is considered by her neighbors to be an eccentric and even an outcast. *The Road to Mecca* is Mr. Fugard's attempt to understand the root of Miss Helen's resilience and the reason for her isolation within her community. The result is one of the author's most thought-provoking plays, a penetrating study of the friendship between two women, faith and the creative impulse.

Along with *Dimetos* and other Fugard plays, *The Road to Mecca* draws inspiration from Albert Camus, who, together with Samuel Beckett, is one of the two most important literary and philosophical influences on his life. Camus, Beckett and Mr. Fugard all have a kind of nondespairing pessimism. *Dimetos* itself is based on a paragraph in Camus's diaries, about a man's unnnatural love for his niece, who kills herself. The South African author reports in his notebooks that on first reading *The Rebel* he felt illuminated by a passage which declares that freedom "consists of the inward submission to a value which defies history and its successes."

In *The Road to Mecca*, Miss Helen's friend, Elsa Barlow (speaking for the playwright), quotes Camus's observation that "rebellion starts with just one person standing up and saying no," a statement that is exemplified by the life of Miss Helen. Defiant and rebellious, she confronts the blindness of her community. As the play begins, she is undergoing her own fearful crisis. Growing old and enfeebled, and still living alone, she is threatened with dispossession. Marius Byleveld, the rigid pastor of the village, wants her to move to a home for the aged. Seeking to withstand all external pressure, she looks to Elsa for support. But as Elsa knows, rebellion must be self-supporting.

Before the play is finished, we have learned not only about Miss Helen's indomitability and her triumph over darkness, but also about the warring ambivalencies within the other two characters - Marius's unacknowledged love for Miss Helen and Elsa's own enforced loneliness. To reach the dramatic heights of the play's second act, one must experience a discursive first act in which the two women prepare the ground for embattlement. As in *A Lesson From Aloes*, it is the delayed entrance of a play's third, catalytic character that detonates the drama. With Marius in Miss Helen's house, war is declared, and one's attention is riveted until the ennobling conclusion. The fact that the real Helen Martins committed suicide - not mentioned in the program for the Off Broadway production - does not negate the lyrical outcome of the play. The woman, as we see her on stage, is not about to settle for a semblance of a half-life.

On route to New York, *The Road to Mecca* has undergone a steady improvement. At Yale it was imprecisely cast and, as a result, the actors - all of them American - lacked a sustained identity with the characters. The London production was headed by Yvonne Bryceland, the author's first choice for the role of Miss Helen, and an actress who has been closely associated with his work. At the National Theater, at least late in the run, the actress overplayed Miss Helen's childlike innocence and the South African actor portraying Marius was stern and unyielding. In welcome relief, Charlotte Cornwell invigorated the role of Elsa. Both of these productions made the first act seem far longer than was necessary. Last year at the Spoleto Festival in Charleston, S.C., Mr. Fugard assumed the role of Marius, humanizing that character and restoring a balance in the play. Though Miss Helen is the pivotal figure, the characters in the play carry the same approximate weight and density. Working with Mr. Fugard as actor, Ms. Bryceland gave a more suitably restrained performance.

Since Charleston, both Mr. Fugard and Ms. Bryceland have deepened their performances and intensified the undercurrents. John Lee Beatty's new set design is also a considerable advancement over the more elaborate scenery used in the prior productions. The equilibrium is additionally enhanced by the presence of Amy Irving, now playing the role of Elsa. She energizes the voluble first act and she carries the second act to the brink of catharsis, as she confesses the emptiness in her life and empathizes with the nomadic black mother she passes on the road (a tragic figure who is the equivalent of a Lena without a Boesman).

Having frequently acted together on stage (and in the film of *Boesman and Lena*), Mr. Fugard and Ms. Bryceland share an authorial authenticity. This is how the playwright views the relationship of the characters. Marius is not, as he seemed in earlier productions, self-protective so much as paternal. He is sincerely concerned about the woman's welfare. At the same time, he is challenged - and finally terrified - by her commitment to her art. It has become her faith, and for him that is an act of blasphemy.

Watching Mr. Fugard in performance, one is reminded of his alter ego, Hally, in *Master Harold ... and the Boys*, a young man with a highly instructive air. Just as Hally tries to educate the waiter in his mother's restaurant and becomes pedantic in the process, Marius sermonizes to Miss Helen. He professes his liberal views while trying to force her to submit to his will. One might conjecture that Marius is a Hally who has grown old without discovering his own gift for creativity.

Mr. Fugard's art is one of the great personalized statements of the contemporary theater, whether he is dealing with autobiography (*Master Harold*), dramatizing the evils of apartheid (*The Island*) or speaking about psychological traumas at a symbolic remove (*Dimetos*). *The Road to Mecca* has a special relevance for the playwright as a story about stoic survival in a barren environment and about the perpetuation of art against all obstacles. In common with Miss Helen, the playwright has pursued his own creative path with an undiminishing tenacity of purpose.

PERCY GRANGER

SCHEHERAZADE: MAY 19, 1992

In *Scheherazade*, it is the playwright Percy Granger who is the tale spinner, with a lunatic comedy about life as soap opera and soap opera as it mirrors life. Pirandelloesque permutations brighten this journey in which the characters keep losing their place in the story line, and the audience shares the comic confusion. As airy as ether, *Scheherazade* is a high-flying one-act in Series B of the Ensemble Studio Theater's Marathon of short plays.

Tantrums flare as a television producer and his aide (she heatedly denies that job description) confront a new head writer for their show. He may be an imposter or even a spy. As played by John Pankow, the writer has the scruples of a housebreaker, which puts him in good company, as the other characters try to corner one another in a cul de sac. When the producer (John Rothman) says to the writer, "You think you can scare me with dialogue," full fright is intended.

The principal question here and in the unseen soap concerns a mysterious room. The last head writer arbitrarily anchored all scripts in that locale, and left the characters hanging when he departed from the show. Lost in the lurch, the remaining personnel grope for plot devices. For a moment, the doyenne of the soap (Lucille Patton) becomes Mr. Pankow's loyal supporter, but minds change freely in this vaporous environment.

Operating on several frequencies at once, *Scheherazade* crosscuts with a dizzying abandon while lampooning literary pretentiousness and plumbing various levels of artificial reality. In the background is the voice of doom, the piped-in sound of Standards and Practices, which occasionally breaks out of its robotic rigidity to ask for the punch line of jokes.

Mr. Pankow has all the limberness of a natural con man (though the character may be the real thing) and Mr. Rothman self-mockingly repeats trendy jargon. Ms. Patton and Kristin Griffith (as the aide) also add to the delirium. Under Matthew Penn's direction, invention never flags. When the writing is as clever as this, it makes the creation of one-act plays look easy.

RICHARD GREENBERG

THE AUTHOR'S VOICE: MAY 14, 1987

Earlier this season in *The Maderati*, Richard Greenberg spoofed the pretensins of the publishing world, and revealed himself as a deft social satirist. In his new literary comedy, *The Author's Voice*, the high point of Evening A in the Ensemble Studio Theater's annual marathon of one-act plays, he scores an ace: game, set and match to Mr. Greenberg.

This comic gem deals with the ambiguous relationship between the writer and his muse, while also commenting on *Beauty and the Beast* and *The Hunchback of Notre Dame*, among other literary precedents. *The Author's Voice* is a shaggy yarn about the headlong pursuit of 15-minute fame.

A pretty editor (Patricia Clarkson) accompanies her latest young writing protégé (Kevin Bacon) back to his apartment to see the author's lair and to toast their new creative partnership. Though she adores the handsome Mr. Bacon and his cool, low-key manner, she wonders aloud at the emptiness of his conversation; he is boring except when he is quoting poetic passages from his novel in progress.

Soon we learn the reason for his vacuity. The "reason" is played by David Pierce with a maniacal sense of absurdity. This three-character colloquy tumbles with twists and turns, including a conclusion in which everyone gets exactly what he deserves. Under the agile direction of Evan Yionoulis, each of the three actors is wedded to his character. Ms. Clarkson has a neat way of tossing off prolix platitudes, Mr. Bacon is an engaging cipher and Mr. Pierce is perfection as the uncloseted Quasimodo.

Leaving the first round in the three-round marathon, one is still smiling at the memory of *The Author's Voice*, Mr. Greenberg's diabolical assault on the hypocrisies of artists and their admirers.

JOHN GUARE

THE HOUSE OF BLUE LEAVES: APRIL 6, 1986

"For my dreams, I need a passport and shots. I travel the whole world." So says Artie Shaughnessy, the optimistic hero of *The House of Blue Leaves*. This was John Guare's breakthrough play (in 1971) and, as we see in Jerry Zaks's splendid revival at Lincoln Center (starring John Mahoney, Stockard Channing and Swoosie Kurtz), it is still his most euphoric work. "Optimistic" and "euphoric" would seem to be curious adjectives to use in reference to a play in which a young man plots to assassinate the Pope; in which one of the principal characters is out of her mind; and in which the hero himself is driven to a violent act of desperation. Yet, for all the mania and mayhem, *Blue Leaves* remains a joyful affirmation of life - and of Mr. Guare's artistry.

Though some of the odd events in the play may not seem so distant from Joe Orton's *Loot*, another recent comedy that has received an exemplary revival, *Loot* is a black farce. With its generosity of spirit, *Blue Leaves* is acutally a closer kin - and an equal - to such plays as William Saroyan's *Time of Your Life* and the Kaufman-Hart *You Can't Take It With You*. Each believes in the durability of dreams and the ultimate ascendancy of individualism. All three plays encourage one to follow one's heart, no matter how quixotic the journey.

Like Joe in *The Time of Your Life* and Grandpa in *You Can't Take It With You*, Artie Shaughnessy is an adult dropout, a man who has settled for far less than his potential and in so doing has found a kind of emotional fulfilment. Artie (Mr. Mahoney) is an animal keeper in the Central Park Zoo, married to a gently mad woman named Bananas (Ms. Kurtz) and unable to fly away with the fetching Bunny Flingus (Ms. Channing). He is forever writing and playing pop tunes at the El Dorado, a bar and grill of broken daydreams. As we know - and as he surely must know - his amiable songs are more than derivative. Tinkling his favorite composition, "I Keep Dreaming," on his piano, he falls into a rapture. Then

Bananas suggests, "Now play `White Christmas.'" Blithely he moves into that melody, without realizing that either he or Irving Berlin stole the music from the other.

That wifely request is one of a half-dozen moments in *Blue Leaves* that are among the most genuinely amusing in the contemporary theater. Each of them rises directly out of a situation. Occasionally, Mr. Guare ventures a joke, but more often he is building a pyramid of character and atmosphere. While never losing its spontaneity, the play is constructed on a firm dramatic foundation.

At the center is Artie the homebody, never organizing his household or his life, incapable of making a move that might bring him a respite from his everyday misery. The fact is that he does not know he is miserable. For one thing, he loves both his wife and his mistress - and he could probably even forgive his son for trying to blow up the Pope (the Pope's visit to New York in 1965 is the catalyst for the play's cataclysmic occurrences). Just as Artie reserves a corner of himself for himself - his songwriting, which is sacrosanct and not really for sale - Bunny has her own order of priorities. Though she and Artie are longtime lovers, she refuses to cook for him until they are married. He salivates at the thought of her eggplant meringue. Like a rebuffed suitor, he pleads for a sampling, but, as a cook, she remains virgo intacta.

When we first meet Bananas, wandering out of her bedroom, she might be confused with a bag lady or a stray puppy. As we soon realize she is an angel (with an occasionally tart tongue in the presence of her rival). One look at her and Artie can recall the romance of their youth. Through all the trauma of growing up, getting older, going crazy, Bananas has not lost her innocence. The Artie-Bunny-Bananas triangle is an inspired entanglement and the three actors add their own vibrancy.

Simultaneously avuncular and childlike, Mr. Mahoney disarms his character of all malice. Clearly something went awry between husband and wife, between parents and child (the would-be Pope's assassin), but, as Artie's role is written and performed, he is the essence of sincerity. As personified by Mr. Mahoney, Artie is a sweetheart of a zookeeper-songwriter. Even panthers eat out of his hands. The cuddlesome Ms. Channing is a portrait in fluffy pink. The actress now owns the role of Bunny, a wise dumb blonde who knows what she wants but remains a true romantic. Ms. Kurtz perfectly completes the triumvirate as the daffy "best dressed woman of 1954," frozen in time and in memory and affecting all others with her pensiveness.

With characteristic munificence, Mr. Guare has surrounded the three with a covey of flamboyant characters - three assertive nuns who crash Artie's party; Artie's son, who, before turning to terrorism, dreamed about playing Huckleberry Finn on the screen; and a beautiful starlet (Julie Hagerty) struck deaf on a movie location and beatifically misinterpreting everything that is said to her. Late in the play, Artie's oldest friend, Billy Einhorn, a golden-touch Hollywood movie director, enters in the person of Christopher Walken, the evening's final rara avis. As performed by this ensemble, the play is even funnier and more poignant than one remembered.

Mr. Guare has written seven plays since *Blue Leaves*, including three in his *Lydie Breeze* cycle (*Lydie Breeze*, *Gardenia* and *Women and Water*, which was presented earlier this season at the Arena Stage in Washington, D.C.). In his subsequent plays the author has let his imagination embrace the historical (the *Lydie Breeze* cycle as well as the apocalyptical *Marco Polo Sings a Solo*). He has been in search of a grand theme, but sometimes, as in the cycle, his ambition has overwhelmed his creativity. However, each of the plays has moments that catch one off guard and that move us to laughter and compassion. He is best when he is most down to earth, as in the musical version he and Mel Shapiro wrote of *Two Gentlemen of Verona*; in the Louis Malle movie, *Atlantic City*, and in *The House of Blue Leaves*. Among his other work, *Gardenia* (the second *Lydie* play) and *Landscape of the Body* are the most satisfying. Often the plays seem to improve in a subsequent production. This was the case both with *Landscape of the Body* and *Bosoms and Neglect* in the Yale Repertory Theater revivals. In a new production, *Bosoms and Neglect* will open Tuesday Off Broadway.

More than many of his comtemporaries, Mr. Guare has a definable style and perspective. No matter how grim the circumstances, the author never loses his sense of humor. For sheer congeniality, he is in a class by himself. At the same time, he veers away from sentimentality; there is always an edge of irony in his madcap humor. I can think of only one of his plays, *Rich and Famous*, in which he was caught up by his own antipathy, a bitterness apparently drawn from the author's experience trying to survive as a playwright. Curiously, it was the theater more than politics or society that made him seem momentarily misanthropic. In all other respects, he is a theatrical benefactor.

From the earliest one-acts, he has had a romance with lyrical language. It is no surprise that he is an accomplished songwriter, as he demonstrated in *Two Gentlemen of Verona*, with a far greater musical talent than he has given Artie Shaughnessy. The poetry is expressed by all the principal characters in *Blue Leaves*, each in a reverie. In the case of Artie, one of his dreams is to move his mad wife to a sanitarium on Long Island. Taking her by the hand, he tries to evoke the magic of the place, describing "a tree with blue leaves in the rain." He tells her that, as he stood under the tree, "all the leaves flew away." The "leaves" were birds, and they flew to another tree "and that bare tree blossomed" - a haunting central image.

Irrepressible optimism in the face of impending doom brightens Mr. Guare's plays. Though the people are beset by externals far beyond their control, they come through. Where Sam Shepard deals with prodigals on a mythic landscape, Mr. Guare is concerned with everyday eccentrics, each of whom is the soul of the earth. As Bunny says in *Blue Leaves*, "When famous people go to sleep at night, it's us they dream of." The very fact of celebrity removes people from their nurturing roots, one reason why the Hollywood director, Billy Einhorn, clings to his past. He makes his movies for his friend Artie. Before every take he asks himself, "Would this make Artie laugh? Would this make Artie cry?" Artie eagerly volunteers to come on the set and give him an immediate response, but that of course is not Billy's desire. He wants to think of Artie and Bananas safe in Sunnyside, Queens, where they remain his "touch with reality."

The success of the revival of *The House of Blue Leaves* in the downstairs Mitzi E. Newhouse has encouraged Gregory Mosher, the director of Lincoln Center Theater, to plan a move upstairs to the larger Vivian Beaumont stage at the end of this month. This will formally inaugurate the new constituency's residency in the Beaumont - with a play that becomes even better with time. It is a happy event for Lincoln Center and for theatergoers.

VACLAV HAVEL

A PRIVATE VIEW: NOVEMBER 21, 1983

The dehumanizing effects of totalitarianism are demonstrated with wounding honesty and irony in Vaclav Havel's *Private View*. This triptych of interrelated short plays, opening last night at the Public Theater, is an event of artistic and political urgency.

Convicted of subversion for his defense of human rights, the dissident playwright was twice imprisoned in Czechoslovakia. The plays, written in 1975 and 1978, are banned from public performance in his native country, along with other works by Havel. However, the author has played as his own protagonist in a private performance, and in a production on BBC radio in England the role was played by Harold Pinter.

Arriving in America in Vera Blackwell's translation, the plays - and Lee Grant's production - are providential. *A Private View* reminds us of the importance of the artist as provocateur. Despite his victimization, Havel has retained his comic balance and his sense of injustice. Confronted by public and private absurdities, the artist clings to first principles and respect and an unquenchable morality.

In Samuel Beckett's *Catastrophe*, a play that is dedicated to Havel, we see a Havel-like hostage silently willing his audience into an awareness of his - and their - predicament. Something similar occurs in Havel's three plays, with the addition of the fact that these are first-hand experiences.

The author's alter ego is a playwright named Vanek, who is an alien in his own homeland. In each of the plays we see how others react to him and to his martyrdom, how each wears his guilt as a badge of identity; the price of prosperity is the loss of humanity. Vanek has become a public conscience and his very presence is a "living reproach" to those who are compromisers and cowards. People play up to him, trying to win his absolution with favors. As sensitively played by Stephen Keep, he is a man who has weathered the tempest and is determined to weather the aftermath.

In the first of the plays, Vanek is working as a laborer in a Czechoslovak brewery - as Havel himself did - and is called in for an interview with the head maltster. Feigning conviviality, the boorish employer, a die-hard bureaucrat, plies Vanek with the house brew while tempting him with the possibility of a less arduous office job. In return, he would like Vanek to furnish him with reports of his own political activity. Astonished, Vanek explains that he cannot inform on himself. Such a dilemma reminds us that Havel's national and artistic antecedent is Kafka. Strange are the labyrinthine intrigues of a society trying to repress its people.

The play is a comedy, with the employer played with increasing agitation by Barton Heymann. He is a self-styled "brewery mug," and that description can be taken as a pun. In common with his own product, he foams to overflowing as he tries to win the dissident as confidant.

The second play, which gives the evening its title, finds Vanek in the bourgeois household of a married couple (Concetta Tomei and Nicholas Hormann) who have survived in high style. Their lavishly decorated apartment and their lounge clothes would be leisurely at home in an affluent American suburb. Vanek, on the other hand, looks frayed.

With a farcical fury that rises to surrealism, the couple attempt to entertain their "best" friend. The guest is eager to be pleased and is resistant only when personal questions are raised. He allows himself one moment of introspection: "I sometimes have a feeling of futility." That futility is endemic to his existence. There is nothing he can do except endure and try to play the game of social engagement.

In the third and most moving play, *Protest*, Vanek visits a former friend, a novelist who has sacrificed his art as well as his honor. With a convoluted logic, the novelist (Richard Jordan) turns every positive into a negative as he assures himself of the rectitude of moral abdication.

Havel's analysis of the novelist's self-induced quandary is richly detailed and Mr. Jordan creates an authoritative portrait of a scoundrel nervously seeking a regard from his erstwhile colleague that he is unable to find within himself. At the center of this and the other plays is Mr. Keep, who finds the resonance behind Vanek's reserve. With his basset eyes and world weariness, he adds immeasurable poignance to his character's bewilderment.

While the plays lack the linguistic complexity of Havel's earlier full-length works such as *The Memorandum*, each is a finely wrought cameo, and the political subject matter does not lead the author into didacticism. The plays are highly theatrical, an aspect that is embellished in performance. Making an auspicious debut as a director on the New York stage, Ms. Grant infuses the evening with spontaneity. All of the actors are adept, with especially articulate contributions from Mr. Keep, Mr. Jordan and Ms. Tomei.

Watching Mr. Keep move from menial labor to strained sociability with his superfluous friends to a reunion - and a memory of a time of freedom - one necessarily thinks of Havel, an artist who lost his liberty but not his creativity.

ISRAEL HOROVITZ

NORTH SHORE FISH: JANUARY 12, 1987

In his new play, *North Shore Fish*, Israel Horovitz focuses on the workers in a frozen-fish processing plant that is about to go out of business. Although the portrayal of a way of life through shared work activity is a familiar dramatic device, Mr. Horovitz is artful in his delineation of a dying economy and in his small but sensitive group portrait of people allied by geography, their Roman Catholic upbringing and their limited aspirations.

Mr. Horovitz originally wrote the play for and about Gloucester, Mass., where he is the artistic director of the Gloucester Stage Company. In its New York premiere at the WPA Theater last night, *North Shore Fish* resonates with local color, essential in a play such as this. The atmosphere begins with the fish factory itself, another strikingly detailed set design by Edward T. Gianfrancesco, who is an expert at transforming a compact stage into a richly inhabited environment.

"It's only work, it ain't life," insists John Pankow as a factory assistant who remains cheerful even as he is forced to be everyone's subordinate. But this is his life, and, as with his female co-workers, there is little he is able to do about it.

Generations of the same family have worked in this plant - or one like it -and even as the work ethic collapses, the oldest employee (Mary Klug) says, "We are fish people doing what we were born to do." The others can barely suppress their amusement at her remark, and when Ms. Klug begins one of her long-winded reminiscences about bygone days in Gloucester, they join in as a chorus, as if reciting a prayer.

Once there was a fish industry in town. The first downward turn came with the switch from fresh to frozen, and from there it is one short step to rewrapping "product" processed at distant plants. Without pressing the point, the author makes a provocative statement about the state of the American economy. This could be an automobile factory in Michigan or a steel mill in Pennsylvania instead of a small, home-grown Massachusetts business, soon to be replaced by a fitness center.

Individualism is at an ebb, and profits, when they exist, go far away from the source. At the same time, there is a grudging admiration for the new, unseen entrepreneurs. The Japanese, one worker says, have "a true respect for fish," a line that is especially amusing in context, because the "fish" we see on stage looks like - and probably tastes like - a frozen brick.

Mr. Horovitz is more concerned with establishing character than with imposing a narrative. Although some of the workers are less interestingly developed than others, the play offers a sympathetic understanding of its people and their tribal-like habits - and it is given a skillful production by Stephen Zuckerman. Accents stray from Massachusetts, but, in other respects, the actors are ingrained in their characters.

The plant foreman (Thomas G. Waites) is a petty tyrant who has superimposed his will over his employees, particularly the women, but he is the only one who appears to give serious thought to the future. The women, mostly working mothers, simply punch a time clock and then chatter, as if they are at a club meeting, while looking forward to idle off hours.

Christine Estabrook, in one of the play's pivotal roles, is the house cynic, quick with an earthy wisecrack. She has been bruised by life and is wary of further injury. Along with Mr. Pankow, she gives one of the evening's most persuasive performances. Mr. Pankow makes his put-upon character extremely likeable, whether he is trying to calm the tempers of others or crooning "Strangers in the Night" with his mop as microphone.

In addition, there is Elizabeth Kemp as a stay-at-home who puts notes in boxes of fish fingers as if they are bottles to be thrown into the ocean. She dreams about taking a vacation in Connecticut - the farthest reach of her imagination. Other roles are ably filled by Michelle M. Faith, Laura San Giacomo, Cordelia Richards and Wendie Malick.

It is Ms. Malick's character, a government inspector, who provides one of several unclear aspects of the evening. Considering her own need for employment, it seems precipitous for the inspector to condemn all of the plant's product. There are also some melodramatic passages in the text. But none of this seriously detracts from Mr. Horovitz's vivid microcosm of a society confronting the facts of obsolescence.

ALBERT INNAURATO

THE TRANSFIGURATION OF BENNO BLIMPIE: MAY 8, 1976

An immense, blubbery fat boy sits on a chair. He is so fat we can hardly see the chair. He looks like an inflated rubber toy, a Thanksgiving Day parade float, the figure on the marquee of the Fat Boy hero shops. He is a blimp, and is nicknamed Benno Blimpie. He never stops grinning, even as he jams potato chips into his mouth. He greets the audience. "I am Benno," he says, "and I am eating myself to death."

The play is Albert Innaurato's *The Transfiguration of Benno Blimpie* (at the Direct Theater), directed by Peter Mark Schifter. Several seasons ago when he was a student at the Yale University Drama School, Mr. Innaurato collaborated with Christopher Durang on a wicked literary insurrection, *The Idiots Karamazov*. Mr. Innaurato is still out there wrestling with the titans. Visions of Ionesco, and especially of Kafka, go through our minds as we watch this pitch-black comedy. In a sense, *Benno* is Mr. Innaurato's *Metamorphosis* - man into bug: everyone is trying to squash Benno.

He is the butt of all insults. He tells - and is - the story. But what the play is really about is the decay of the American family. In comparison, Edward Albee's *The American Dream* and Bruce Jay Friedman's *A Mother's Kisses* seem almost wistful. *Benno* is a nightmare, dreamed by Lenny Bruce.

Benno introduces us to his broad Italian cartoon family. The undershirted father is a loud sloth. The mother is a mean-mouthed termagant, making rotten remarks about their "monster kid." Around the kitchen table, they trade epithets, while ancient Pop-pop, the grandfather, chases a teasing nymphet (who knows more about sex than any dirty old man). These people are horrid, but they are also maliciously funny.

As the caricatures pass, Benno watches, wolfing ice cream cones, as if eating might distract him from the indecencies. He is treated as an object, a slave, forced to observe the defilement of civilization. He is in torment, teetering out of existence. He will explode. Life can not contain him.

Beneath the fat, he is a saintly spirit. The only real human on stage, he is treated inhumanely. The playwright is serious about the "transfiguration." What if Christ were fat and ugly?

Not everyone should see this play. Many will be offended, even insulted, but it has a dramatic and a comic power. Perhaps it could be more amusing - if all the acting were as outlandish as that of Jon Polito (who becomes Benno) and Kathy McKenna as the tease. She whisks through her perverse role like a nutty girl on roller skates. In contrast, the mother-father battles, ballasted in stereotype, have a tendency to be ax-heavy. At times, Mr. Innaurato's humor is itself a blunt instrument, but this is not a play one will easily forget.

GEMINI: DECEMBER 17, 1976

The comic vision of Albert Innaurato is fiendishly demonstrated in *Gemini*, at Playwrights Horizons, as it was in the author's earlier *The Transfiguration of Benno Blimpie*. Mr. Innaurato's instrument is not a needle, but a cleaver. There is a savagery in his humor that is, in a strange way, refreshing at the same time that it is terrifying.

Gemini is a longer, more comprehensive indictment than *Benno Blimpie*, but the target remains the same: Humanity, in particular the American family, slapped over the head with a pig's bladder. Mr. Innaurato is a caricaturist - closer to Mad magazine than to George Grosz - whose plays are like operas. *Benno* is an extended aria by an incredibly fat boy. *Gemini* is a grand soap opera. Everything is larger than life: laughter, tears, shouting, screaming. *Mary Hartman, Mary Hartman* fans might recognize the territory, but they will never see *Gemini* on television.

The scene is a backyard in South Philadelphia - an evocatively seedy set by Christopher Nowak. Clean laundry hangs high above a fence and dirty linen is out for airing. By far the dirtiest belongs to Bunny Lowenstein, fork-tongued and blowzy, a Phyllis Diller gone awry - whose vulgar speech might make Belle Barth blush. Swilling beer by the quart, shaggily boasting of her sexual exploits, she never stops complaining about her life's tragedy - her bloated, Benno Blimpie-like son.

Although Bunny (Jessica James) almost overwhelms the play, the protagonist is Francis Geminiani - from his name comes the play's title - the bookish son of a boisterous blue-collar father. Daily, Francis curses the day that he was born - exactly 21 years ago - in this pressure cooker environment.

To his embarrassment, Francis is paid a surprise visit by two friends from Harvard, a brother and sister (gemini?), two rich, beautiful people (and Sigourney Weaver, who plays the sister, is certainly one of the more beautiful actresses on the American stage). The guests pitch a tent in the backyard and join the neighborhood festivities, which in their case includes a sexual roundelay.

In a program note, the playwright takes his cue from Dante: "And I, who was looking out, saw a group of people running around crazily, who were unworthy of any kind of respect." These people are unworthy - even the over-achievers are losers - and Mr. Innaurato is disrespectful, but their behavior is so outrageous as to be blackly comic. There are moments that border on inspired lunacy.

Much of the groteque humor derives from interruptions and sudden changes of mood. Mr. Innaurato repeatedly shifts gears - high to low to reverse, pathos to buffoonery, tears to laughs. He sends the characters careening in one direction, then slams on the brakes. An argument ascends to caterwauling proportions and is stopped cold by the entrance of a crowd of people carrying a candlelit cake, wearing funny party hats and singing "Happy Birthday, dear Francis." A scene of quiet tenderness is interrupted by the off-stage sound of Bunny throwing a piano at her fat son.

Except for the ending, which seems appended and a bit too poetic, this is a swift, exuberant cartoon. Peter Mark Schifter as director would seem to be the author's alter ego. The play demands a directness of performance and there are spirited characterizations by Ms. Weaver, Ms. James and Jonathan Hadary as the mother and fat son, and Jon Polito - who last season played the title role in *Benno Blimpie* - as the agitated hero.

In common with David Mamet and Christopher Durang, the author is an original, an iconoclastic rebel in the American theater.

DAVID IVES

SURE THING: FEBRUARY 17, 1988

In David Ives's *Sure Thing*, a young man sees an attractive young woman sitting by herself in a cafe. Planning his maneuvers, he wonders if he should be cool, forward or flattering. She is reading *The Sound and the Fury*, and, furrowing his brow, he tries to remember what he knows about Faulkner. Later, Woody Allen is mentioned; his spirit already pervades the play.

In this delightful little one-act (in Manhattan Punch Line's Festival of One-Act Comedies), the man (Robert Stanton) uses every possible approach and the woman (Nancy Opel) offers every possible response. After each exchange, an off-stage buzzer sounds and the couple stop and start again, editing and revising as they speak. As the comedy proceeds, the conversation becomes shaggier while always retaining a base not too far off center from reality.

This is, in fact, a quintessential small-talk dialogue, and it is charmingly performed by Mr. Stanton and Ms. Opel under the carefully timed direction of Jason Buzas. The play lasts only 15 minutes. It is, therefore, a curtain-raiser, although the Punch Line has placed it second in the evening. One wishes that comedies of this caliber entirely filled the bill.

PHILIP GLASS BUYS A LOAF OF BREAD: FEBRUARY 4, 1990

A bakery is alive and atonal in David Ives's *Philip Glass Buys a Loaf of Bread* as two women, Philip Glass and a baker rap their way through a devastating send-up of this idiosyncratic composer. The play is the first of four in the Manhattan Punch Line's sixth annual festival of one-act comedies.

In imitation of Mr. Glass's lyrics, the linguistic patter is as intricate as it is meaningless. Monosyllables ("you I need," "loaf of bread") become the equivalent of solfege symbols while deadpan actors spoof the self-importance of postmodernist performance art.

Just when the quartet seems on the verge of running repetition into the ground (that in itself is intended as a parody), the actors dance. The tilted, robotic choreography merrily needles Lucinda Childs as well as Mr. Glass's author-director alter ego, Robert Wilson.

There is affection beneath the malice (and the mock-Wilsonian title), as well as an understanding of the art that is being lampooned. A familiarity with Wilson-Glass Einsteinian operas will double a theatergoer's enjoyment, but such is the precision of the sketch that even without prior knowledge, one will laugh along with the spoken music.

JOHN JESURUN

DEEP SLEEP: FEBRUARY 7, 1986

In Woody Allen's *Purple Rose of Cairo*, the leading man in a movie steps off the screen and into life and, conversely, the leading lady in life is magnetically attracted to the glamorous world on screen. John Jesurun's new play, *Deep Sleep* (at La Mama Annex), takes an alternative look at the crosscurrents of truth and cinematic illusion. His devious - and exceedingly clever - play considers the nature of the reel thing.

Mr. Jesurun, who is an experimental film maker as well as playwright, wonders if people are not the auteurs of their own imaginary movie of life, and if, on the other hand, movie characters cannot achieve a greater reality in fiction.

As a play, *Deep Sleep* is at least half on film, but such is the artfulness of the exercise that the two forms merge in mid-screen. Characters, live and on film, answer one another, interrupt action and, in several cases, change places, as the cinematic figures try to convince their rivals on stage that "up is better than down."

For the purposes of Mr. Jesurun's movie-play, the tennis court size Annex stage has been "twinned." At either end of the theater is a movie screen. The audience sits on the sidelines as at a sporting event and watches both screens as well as live actors stationed at separate tables on the broad, ground-level stage.

There is much audience head-swiveling as it tracks the concurrent images. In time, one picks up the jump-cut rhythm. We can sense when one cinematic figure will respond to another on the opposite screen, but it is usually something of a surprise when a live character issues his own pre-emptory challenge. To a great extent, the people on screen assume authority: the other actors become smaller than life. Theatergoers act as film editors, splicing images they catch on the wing.

The play begins with badinage on film, a dialogue that is more influenced by vaudeville than by Pirandello. The play's protagonist, a man named Whitey, tries to determine - and keeps losing - his identity. He confuses himself with a young boy named Sparky, who is on stage looking up. Before reaching a point of satiation with the amusing who's-on-first style comedy routine, Mr. Jesurun spins his play into its own split-screen orbit. The author is not one to be tied down to a sequential plot, but *Deep Sleep* is less elliptical than his previous *Red House*.

Though the show is shorter than *Purple Rose of Cairo*, it runs on a bit too long and after a menacing moment on film, the ending on stage is pallid. However, this does not substantially detract from the ingenuity of the evening. On a technical level, the production is to be admired, a credit to Mr. Jesurun's direction and to his lighting, sound and film crew, which manage to synchronize all disparate elements.

For the live actors, the play is a mine field as they play to, and with, those images on screen. If cues are missed, it is not evident to the audience. Steve Buscemi and Michael Tighe play leading roles with an appropriate feeling of disorientation, while, locked into celluloid, Black-Eyed Susan and John Hagan are prominent among those who eye the events on stage with baleful condescension.

In Mr. Jesurun's case, form is content, but there is sense within the apparent nonsense, and there is always room for commentary. Playfully he suggests that while life will end, films will go on forever - or at least as long as there is someone to operate the projector.

BLACK MARIA: APRIL 14, 1987

Entering La Mama Annex, rearranged to accomodate John Jesurun's *Black Maria*, one immediately wonders where the stage is. The seats are facing in all directions and fill the floor space. The fact is that there is no stage. With *Black Maria*, Mr. Jesurun has moved a step beyond *Deep Sleep* and *White Water*, the previous plays in his theater-movies-television cycle. This time, the audience is surrounded by movie screens, four of them as walls and one as ceiling. There are no live actors; the "play" is entirely on film.

Soon the screens are overflowing with vivid images - of actors and landscapes, both interior and exterior. As in the earlier plays, the actors speak to one another across the heads of theatergoers. We are thrown into the middle of a mystery, a threatening story that has something to do with a lonely house in the country, a leper colony, an escaped convict and a missing, perhaps dead horse. *Black Maria* could be called a case of habeas equus.

Clues fly as quickly as the crosscut images, but we never completely decipher the solution. This, however, should not stop one from enjoying the intricacy of the journey. Perhaps the key to the show is in the title. *Black Maria* refers doubly to a police van carrying away culprits and to Thomas Edison's movie studio.

Outdistancing Christopher Isherwood, Mr. Jesurun is apparently saying, "I am a projector as well as a camera." There are frequent photographic and cinematic references, including the suggestion by one of the characters that what we see is "my own private idea," with the pun on the last word intended.

Our eyes are transfixed by the waves of pictures passing back and forth and above our heads. Quite casually, without drawing attention to his action, one actor on film steps from one screen to another. At another point, characters on all four screens sit down to an elegant dinner. They address one another across the table, giving a theatergoer the strange sensation of feeling like the centerpiece.

The view from ground level, looking up at the screens, is the equivalent of sitting in the front row of a movie theater - or, rather, four front rows simultaneously. Swiveling our heads to keep track of the images and the voices, sometimes we seem to choose the wrong screen. A voice is coming from the other side of the theater. Actually, no screen is "wrong." Even when there is no one speaking, there is a field, the sky, perhaps a distant moon - or a mysterious pinprick of light. Occasionally there are pictures of paintings and painters (such as Picasso). Discussing art, one character says, "You never know what happens in the next moment of the picture" - after the painter has put down his brush. A painting is, in effect, time standing still.

As a theater artist, Mr. Jesurun forms a graphic composition, and it stands, enigmatically, by itself. We have no idea what his next move will be. Sometimes the fast-moving dialogue adds to the conundrum. Other times it is absurdly humorous, as in Black-Eyed Susan's announcement that an Indian woman is in prison for "killing and scalping my mother and father - who could blame her?"

On the technical side, Mr. Jesurun - author, director and designer - is ingenious, shifting from long shot to extreme close-up, panning vistas so that we seem to be in a moving vehicle and, with his multi-dimensional sound system, planting voice throughout the environment. At one crucial point in his drama, he suddenly appears to burn his film. Though one might question the substance of Mr.

Jesurun's work, the style and the mastery of form stamp him as innovative. The principal unanswered question is how to define his medium.

EVERYTHING THAT RISES MUST CONVERGE: MARCH 16, 1990

On one level, John Jesurun's *Everything That Rises Must Converge* is an incoherent play on the subject of language. That fact alone says something about the difficulty of communication, which is at the root of Mr. Jesurun's new work, a deeply layered multi-media theater piece that will leave audiences alternately fascinated and exhausted. Fascination wins by a millimeter, because of the playwright's originality and his command of theatrical and electronic techniques.

For the purposes of his play, theatergoers are seated on bleachers facing a white wall and a bank of five television monitors. As the show starts, actors on stage address one another as well as other actors who appear on the screens above their heads. In characteristic Jesurun fashion, words tumble fast and without apparent logic. With his plays, one often has the feeling of being thrown headlong into a labyrinth from which there is no exit - and no exegesis. The author uses the word "slashback," a neologism denoting the razor-sharp quickness of the images, as the play moves backward, forward and sideways.

Theatergoers naturally will try to find their equilibrium, or, at least, to locate a story. Mr. Jesurun is not interested. Instead of narrative, he offers a kinetic array of kaleidoscopic pictures and journal jottings, principally concerned with people who may be in the "control room of a capital city." The characters are interpreters translating information from one language to another, information that deals with, among other things, espionage, execution by poisoned glove and a fire that reduces a disco to ashes. Many of these are visions of violence, although they are communicated in a highly civil manner.

The actors, some familiar from past plays written and directed by Mr. Jesurun, are experts at the author's parrotlike style of performance. Most notable are Larry Tighe, Phyllis Young (who also sings) and Oscar de la Fe Colon. Mr. Colon figures prominently in a plot thread concerning the explorer Cabeza de Vaca and the King of Spain. Much of his dialogue is in Spanish (other lines are in German). To an English-speaking audience, even the English may need explanation.

None of this is made easy for the audience, whose best approach is to hold on tight as Mr. Jesurun's roller-coaster swerves to what seems to be no conclusion. This is a more demanding ride than previous Jesurun works like *Deep Sleep* and *Black Maria*, other plays in his movies-television-theater cycle that took greater advantage of the author's playful sense of humor.

What holds the audience's attention is the ingenious style of presentation. While we are still trying to correlate the barrage of words and of live and video figures, some of whom appear to be talking to themselves, the rear wall suddenly swings to a perpendicular, revealing an entirely different audience sitting on bleachers on the opposite side of the stage. In a mirror reversal, they have been watching our actors on monitors and our monitor-actors on stage.

Later, the wall turns to a diagonal, and oscillates like the blades of a propeller, bisecting our vision and leading to increasing disorientation. In a final coup de théâtre, the wall-as-propeller rotates on fast forward, circulating the play, aerating the theater with a cool breeze and threatening to levitate the actors. Simultaneously the video images are speeded up until voice and picture spin out of control, as in a massive computer glitch. While putting audiences through a stress test, the play demonstrates that with this theater artist everything that rises converges on the cutting edge of experimentation.

JOHN KELLY

PASS THE BLUTWURST, BITTE (THE EGON SCHIELE STORY): NOV. 8, 1986

Through his art, using himself as his model, Egon Schiele painted a lacerating self-portrait, which John Kelly re-creates with fierce intensity in his performance piece, *Pass the Blutwurst, Bitte*. Mr. Kelly's play, which opened last night at Dance Theater Workshop, captures both the narcissism and the masochism that made Schiele such an extravagant figure in the Viennese art scene in the early years of the 20th century.

As conceived, directed, choreographed and performed by Mr. Kelly, this is as much an expression of art as an impression of the artist. First presented in a shorter version in 1982, it could be approached as a biographical prelude to Martha Clarke's more comprehensive *Vienna: Lusthaus*.

With his cadaverous body, haunted eyes, flaring eyebrows and short, spiky hair, Mr. Kelly looks demoniacally like Schiele's self-image. That feeling is intensified when we see the actor behind glass on which is reproduced the artist's sketches of himself. Animated into action, Mr. Kelly's Schiele leads us through his brief biography. In a humorous scene we see him encounter the woman who became both his mistress and his model and, later, in quick cuts, we see her posing in his studio. Life impinges on art as he is imprisoned for pornography. Released, he is married, and then, at age 28, overcome in an influenza epidemic.

Both mistress and wife appear in the play, the first personified by Marleen

Menard, the second by the sylph-like presence of Vivian Trimble. Ms. Menard returns as the symbolic figure of Influenza, in her robe and gilded makeup looking somewhat like the portrait of Pallas Athena by Schiele's mentor, Gustav Klimt.

This is not, of course, a documentary, but a free-form series of vignettes combining dance, film and a lush musical background (including Strauss and Beethoven, among others). Although Mr. Kelly sings several arias, there is no dialogue. In a performance art world attuned to high technology, *Pass the Blutwurst, Bitte* is so modest that it sometimes seems like a shoestring silent movie on stage. That, in itself, is disarming. We are not bombarded by sonar and graphic effects. This is not art by computer but a highly individualized interpretation.

We see Schiele as still life, as if posing for his crucifixion. Then he moves in stop action; portraits accumulate, coalescing into multifaceted images of an artist in extremis. Clearly, Mr. Kelly has studied his source, but facts have not impeded his own theatrical imagination.

Schiele is shadowed by two apparitions of himself, identified as Alter Egons. They become his doppelgängers, dancing a pas de trois. Later, they move Schiele about the stage as if he were a bunraku puppet. Although there is this tinge of Orientalism in the performance, the style is basically Viennese, black and white, boldly designed by a team that includes Huck Snyder (scenery) and Trine Walther (costumes). Occasionally, there is a stray image (an actor dancing across the stage carrying a small pumpkin, as if he is, one supposes, riding in a coach), but, more often, the play has the tautness of Schiele's own work. It is a sharply etched vision of a cometic life in art.

ODE TO A CUBE: OCTOBER 27, 1988

Sitting at his dressing table on stage, John Kelly bears a fleeting resemblance to Jean-Louis Barrault. One would certainly not want to carry the comparison too far - for one thing, Mr. Kelly is primarily a comic performer - but there is something in his gaunt look that suggests the French master. In his new one-man show, *Ode to a Cube* (at La Mama), he is playing an actor, an American enfant du SoHo, lost in his own illusionary world.

This is a world in which the actor prepares himself to play a role and then repeatedly alters his persona, choosing from a selection of gowns and wigs. Opulently attired, but wearing cartoon glasses, Mr. Kelly faces the footlights and sings the Habanera from *Carmen* in his own signature falsetto. Later, he also lip-syncs to the voices of others. The theater piece is cubistic in that it deals with black boxes of various sizes, which the actor improvises into action.

The most prominent box stands in for a television set. As the actor looks at the unseen screen, we overhear a cacophony of scrambled sounds, clarifying into the melodramatic musical soundtrack from *King Kong*, followed by an excerpt from the narration in the movie *The Red Badge of Courage*. Then, in a channel switch, we hear an Italian artist speaking as if he were the title character in a television program dealing with the life of Leonardo da Vinci. Mr. Kelly's Leonardo tells us about his latest painting - of a woman with a secret smile.

Before you can say La Gioconda, Mr. Kelly has put on a silky black wig and black dress and has transformed himself into Mona Lisa. Considering the actor's gender, nationality and personality, the resemblance is uncanny. He strikes an enigmatic Mona Lisa pose, holds it and then smiles - revealing a blackened middle tooth, a sight gag of mirthful proportions. Speaking with a dialect accent, Mona Lisa complains about the painter, "He make-a me change my hair," and, most demanding of all, she adds, he took four years to complete the portrait.

Mr. Kelly's Mona Lisa is the centerpiece in this brief concert of Kelly songs and scenes, the second chapter in a projected three-part semi-autobiographical series, but it is only one of several auspicious moments, poignant as well as comic, including a solo ballet.

There is a strong esthetic element in his performing - even when he is lampooning Leonardo. As an appropriate background for the actor, Huck Snyder's setting and Howard Thies's lighting are pristine. Mr. Kelly can be more imaginative alone on stage for 50 minutes than some of his performance-art colleagues in one of their epic evenings.

LARRY KRAMER

THE NORMAL HEART: APRIL 28, 1985

Ibsen described Dr. Thomas Stockmann in *An Enemy of the People* as "muddleheaded," and he is, in the sense that he never learns, he cannot learn, the positive uses of pragmatism. In his headstrong pursuit of truth he consistently ignores political, economic and personal realities. Blunt, outspoken and adversarial, he is an innocent in a land where, in his words, people chase after expediency. He further weakens his own case by proclaiming that the majority is never right, thereby alienating those who could provide a measure, if not a maximum, of support. Although Stockmann's position may seem like moral elitism, there is a certitude in the purity of his vision. At the end of *An Enemy of the People*, stripped of his medical practice and treated as a pariah by the community he is trying to save from disease, he quixotically clings to his self-respect. It is his conviction that "the strongest man in the world is the man who stands alone."

With certain alterations, one could be discussing not only Stockmann but also Ned Weeks, the hero of Larry Kramer's *The Normal Heart*, a new play that speaks with passion about a contemporary problem that is not so far removed from the poisoned water of *An Enemy of the People*. The principal problem in *The Normal Heart* is not Acquired Immune Deficiency Syndrome (a subject that is not mentioned by name in the course of the play), or even the broader question of a bias against homosexuals. As Ned affirms, "This is not a civil rights issue. This is a contagion issue." In common with Stockmann, he is trying to staunch an epidemic. He is a whistle-blower and he is surrounded by people who are worried about their careers, their images and their sex lives. Life itself is at stake.

Both Ned and Stockmann realize that the prime power base in a community is public opinion, and each sees two obstacle-ridden routes to that source: the mayor and the press. In each case, the hero ascertains and assails recalcitrance, but where Ibsen attacks the mayor and the press with satiric humor, Mr. Kramer uses insult. In most cases there is no one there to reply to the charge. The approach vitiates the effectiveness of his argument on his targets.

The Normal Heart freely mixes fact, fiction and dramatization, somewhat in the manner of a Costa-Gavras movie. The author names names when it suits his thesis. But, as with the best of Costa-Gavras, *The Normal Heart* is a moral j'accuse, and it is an indictment with wide dimensions. At one point, Ned tells the fellow members of a health crisis center that is trying to make people aware of the plague-like proportions of the disease, that in their cause they "will never have enough friends." He makes it clear that, depending on the depth of commitment, his colleagues have the ability to become their own enemies.

The play follows a three-year period from 1981 to 1984, a time of consciousness-raising when the community at large was confronted with the horrific effect of AIDS, a disease for which there is no attributable cause or cure: diagnosis is tantamount to a death sentence, and deaths become like a battlefield body count. *The Normal Heart* is the second persuasive AIDS play of the season. The first, William A. Hoffman's *As Is* is a movingly personal consideration of the disease, focusing on two men, one of whom contracts AIDS, while the other becomes his sympathetic watchman and nurse. Both works are that rarity, plays that take an immediate, responsive stand on issues of great timeliness and consequence.

Though English dramatists from John Osborne to David Hare and Caryl Churchill have been concerned - and in some cases, obsessed - with questions of public portent, American dramatists have generally tended to neglect this area while contemplating questions of a more psychological and behavioral nature. When they have explored politics, it is often through a smokescreen of symbolism.

Both *The Normal Heart* and *As Is* confront their shared crisis directly and graphically. Though both plays share a milieu and a sensitivity, they differ in temperament. *As Is* is filled with rage, *The Normal Heart* with outrage. In addition, Mr. Kramer's play has a historical perspective both in its treatment of homosexuality and in its attitude toward public apathy. It also has a polemic purpose, one of several reasons why a comparison to *An Enemy of the People* is in order. Coincidentally the torpidity of the current theater season has been challenged by a revival of *An Enemy of the People* as well as by *The Normal Heart* and *As Is.* Unfortunately, the Ibsen play is less well produced.

In *An Enemy of the People*, Ibsen masterfully arranges his canvas in the opening minutes, introduces his rival factions, beginning with the idealistic Dr. Stockmann and his pompous brother, the mayor, and then sends them spinning on a disaster course. Seeing the play in revival at the Roundabout Theater, one realizes that it is a complex model of its political kind. Melodrama never gets in the way of message as the play builds to a momentous and ironic conclusion.

In contrast, *The Normal Heart* is episodic and overlaid with facts and statistics. It is, however, a deeply felt document and Michael Lindsay-Hogg's production is striking in its aptness and its austerity. The audience sits on two sides of the stage at the Public Theater, looking down as in an operating room. Scenery is functional and to a purpose and there is fine ensemble acting.

At the center is Brad Davis as Ned Weeks. With an unrelenting intensity, he conveys his character's compulsiveness.   Trapped between a reluctant Establishment and a frightened homosexual community, he never stops challenging - and taunting - the status quo. Mr. Davis's portrait is novelist-as-streetfighter: he keeps jabbing, even as body blows fall wide of the mark. Though the character is apparently the playwright's alter ego - events recounted on stage parallel Mr. Kramer's own campaign to arouse public concern for AIDS victims - the perspective is broadened to include other, divergent points of view. Contrasting personalities are given vibrant dramatic life by D.W. Moffett, Robert Dorfman, David Allen Brooks, William DeAcutis, Philip Richard Allen and Concetta Tomei.

Ms. Tomei, the only woman in the cast, plays a doctor, crippled by polio, who takes on AIDS as a crusade. Where Ibsen's Stockmann stands alone in his quest, Ms. Tomei's character becomes Ned Weeks's comrade-in-arms. In one of the evening's most incendiary moments she attacks public health officials for their neglectful attitude toward what she considers a national emergency. Her impassive antagonist is a contemporary American equivalent of those in *An Enemy of the People* who choose to disregard Stockmann's warning. They are, in Ibsen's phrase, people who "didn't dare do otherwise."

FRANZ XAVER KROETZ

REQUEST CONCERT: MARCH 17, 1981

Franz Xaver Kroetz's *Request Concert*, staged by JoAnne Akalaitis at the Interart Theater, is a strange, unsettling monodrama, a kind of voiceless equivalent of Jean Cocteau's *The Human Voice*. A middle-aged woman comes home to her apartment and goes through her nightly ritual. She hangs up her coat, prepares a dinner for one and immediately cleans up after herself. In this tidy studio apartment and in this equally tidy single life, there is a place for everything. She has sanitized, deodorized and compartmentalized herself into an ordered, empty existence.

After she leaves a room, she always turns out the light, conserving utilities as she conserves her emotions. Looking for distraction, she turns on the television set and then turns it off. She settles down with the radio, and when a telephone rings, she jumps. But it is not her phone; it is part of the broadcast. She is absolutely alone, and she never speaks, not even to herself.

For 70 minutes, without intermission, we watch the woman, played by Joan MacIntosh, a mouse in a maze, realistically going about her measured routines. At first we feel like voyeurs, but then we realize that we are both witnesses and invisible companions, matching her silence with ours, waiting out the limits of the woman's life. Some theatergoers may have an understandable recalcitrance about sitting in a theater and watching a silent scene from everyday life. *Request Concert* would be easy to parody. But such is the clear-sighted dramatic vision of Mr. Kroetz that the mundane is transformed into something close to hypmotic. *Request Concert* is a fascinating play about a commonplace subject.

For the playwright, it begins as a kind of found object, a story that one might encounter in life or described in fiction, but not, without words, in the theater. Despite the absence of dialogue, this is indeed a play, with a rhythm, a certain amount of dramatic tension and an exacting solo performance.

There is an apparently spontaneous side to the work that gives the evening a vicarious appeal. When Ms. MacIntosh turns on the radio, it is playing that night's programs. Or is it? In a taxicab after the theater, I heard the same night's news repeated, but the character had also tuned in to a question-and-answer show in which a listener recounted her own sparse life: "I sit in an apartment alone. I wait for a knock on the door." This could have been a recapitulation of the scene on stage.

By the end of the play, the apparently passionless character, a woman without biography, has communicated to us a feeling of ineffable loneliness. There is no solace or interruption in her regimen - no friends, phone calls or even soliciters or burglars. She does not have the grace of music, literature or self-indulgence. Through an accumulation of details and objects, we arrive at a point of complete empathy with the woman as she heads toward her inevitable conclusion.

Mr. Kroetz, a controversial young West German experimentalist, seeks to shatter theatrical convention, beginning with the reliance on the word. He is disturbed by what he calls the "garrulity" of theater. It should be explained that, at least in this play, he is not a visualist, like Robert Wilson or Ms. Akalaitis in her own work as a playwright. *Request Concert* is not a procession of images, but a life situation dramatized without sentimentality or artifice. What the character does is what we see.

In her staging, Ms. Akalaitis becomes the author's emissary. This looks like a real apartment. One could move in, but who would want to live in such a plasticized environment? Manuel Lutgenhorst and Douglas E. Ball have furnished the flat carefully with the accoutrements of middle-class urban living. Every inch of space is accounted for - from the utilitarian kitchen alcove to the convertible sofa. The sound, supplied by L.B. Dallas, is a lingering reminder that a world exists outside of the character. At intervals, Ms. Macintosh stops her routine and stares in our direction, as if straining to hear a voice or a murmur through the hush.

THE NEST: MARCH 2, 1989

Marriage for Kurt and Martha is the sheerest bliss, despite the fact that Kurt's income as a truckdriver is limited. In *The Nest* by Franz Xaver Kroetz, the two go through their daily routine. When Kurt comes home from work, his wife automatically gives him a bottle of beer. They have dinner and settle down with television, then convert their couch into a bed and go to sleep. The scene is West Germany but it could be any small town in the United States.

Martha is about to have her first baby. Sitting at their dining table, they tick off an endless list of expenses, refrained by Kurt's confident response to every financial request, "You got it." In the play, as directed by Bartlett Sher for the New York Theater Workshop, Kurt and Martha are a portrait of contentment, but with a gentle edge of self-parody. Significantly, they begin the play by watching a situation comedy on television, which is, in fact, a mirror image of their own story. Television reflects life, or vice versa.

It is easy to enjoy the mock banalities of these early scenes and the deft performance of Alma Cuervo and Matt Craven. Having seen the play before, in 1986, at the Bush Theater in London, my amusement was tempered by the fact that I knew what was coming - the sudden swerve of fate that would turn a situation comedy into an ecological nightmare. At that point, humor flees the stage.

To make extra money, Kurt does a special job for his boss, which entails disposing of toxic wastes. That disposal leads directly to the illness of the couple's new baby - and the happy world of Kurt and Martha spins awry. The change is total, and deleterious to the marriage as well as to the environment. Mr. Kroetz chronicles the decline with deliberation, as life's cruelty destroys an idyll.

Though understated, the commentary on industrial recklessness is embittered. *The Nest* attacks an urgent contemporary problem and identifies a cause, the casualness with which a faceless technocracy can poison a community, and the blindness with which people accept the status quo, whatever it may be.

At her most aggrieved, Martha accuses her husband of being nothing more than "a trained ape." As he realizes, there is a certain truth to the charge. He has followed his boss's suggestion - not even an order - without challenging its effect. It does not take much imagination to look behind the theme of the play and to uncover deeper parallels, including the rise of Nazism itself. The question posed is one of inaction in the face of evil.

Kurt, the ultimate blue-collar drone, eventually raises his voice, beginning with a mea culpa but ending with a charge of complicity. In this brief but compelling play, Mr. Kroetz strikes a vengeful blow against civilization's power to self-destruct. In contrast to Sarah Pia Anderson's starkly minimal London production, Mr. Sher's version at the Perry Street Theater averts some of the terror of the story; the first half is almost too funny. There is no need to make the nest quite so cozy.

At the same time, the staging is as crisp as Rob Murphy's setting. Mr. Craven subtly moves his inarticulate truckdriver from amiability to anger to overwhelming guilt, and Ms. Cuervo is a portrait of shocked awareness as she watches her household disintegrate.

Using Roger Downey's conversational translation, Mr. Sher makes one useful addition in the New York production. The baby, played in London by inanimate bunting, is portrayed here by a real infant. Michael Pryor, who alternates in that role with Justin Musumeci, is a real charmer. He meets every cue and is never at a loss for silence. Years from now, one may look back on his auspicious stage debut at 8 months in Mr. Kroetz's horrific domestic tragedy.

HUGH LEONARD

DA: MAY 2, 1978

Hugh Leonard's *Da* is a beguiling play about a son's need to come to terms with his father - and with himself. Warmly but unsentimentally, it concerns itself with paternity, adolescence, the varieties of familial love and the tricks and distortions of memory. In a class with the best of Sean O'Casey, it is steeped in Irish language, laughter and atmosphere, but it rises far above ethnicity. *Da* opened last night at the Morosco Theater after a successful run earlier this season at the Hudson Guild Theater.

The character of Charlie, a stand-in for the author in this admittedly autobiographical comedy-drama, returns home to Dublin to attend the funeral of his father, whom he calls Da. Sitting at the kitchen table in his parents' empty cottage, he begins sorting the old man's papers - destroying much more than he saves, which is true of memories as well as of mementoes. Anticipating an end to the past, he finds instead a flesh-and-blood ghost of his father who tenaciously inhabits the room and the son's mind.

The play moves seamlessly from present to past, from reality to reminiscence to imagined conversations. We see the traumatic moments in the characters' lives - Charlie confronts himself as a young man and the young man talks back to his middle-aged self - and we see the illusions that have been collected as a safeguard for survival.

Charlie tries but is unable to give up the ghost. For all of his derision of his father as a "malignant, lop-sided old liar," Charlie is irrevocably attached to the delightful codger, and, despite all the colorful exchange of bluster and blarney, he has a growing admiration for him. Da has lived a full and happy life, whereas the son is burdened with pessimism. With filial understanding comes an insight: as Charlie realizes in bemusement, "Love turned upside down is love for all that." By the end of the evening, we feel that we know these people, especially father and son, as deeply as we should know our own family.

With its many levels of consciousness, the sudden changes in time, the play must be extremely difficult to direct and to act. At one point, for example, the middle-aged Charlie is called upon to play himself at 7, embraced by his father in an idyllic stroll around town. Led by the astute, scrupulous staging of Melvin Bernhardt, the actors never falter.

Over the years, Barnard Hughes has given us considerable pleasure in a diversity of roles from Dogberry to television's *Doc*, but his portrayal of Da must be considered a high point in his career. In this play he takes a most ordinary man - who, issuing platitudes, blithely accepts the limits of his life - and makes him lovable to his sardonic son and to the audience. Mr. Hughes's success is complete: his Da is endearing.

Charlie is our surrogate on stage, our conductor in the journey to the center of Da, and much of the play has to be read in his reactions. Brian Murray is wonderfully expressive, his face a frieze of seemingly contradictory impulses. He is charmed by his father's ingenuousness at the same time that he is horrified by his placidity. As played by Mr. Murray, he is a man of impudence and wit.

In contrast, Charlie as a youth (acted by Richard Seer) stumbles through adolescence under the strict supervision of a rigid mother and an acquiescent father. In the pained expressions and perpetual embarrassment of the character - tellingly communicated by the actor - we can forecast Charlie's march to cynicism.

There is one other major character - Charlie's employer (Lester Rawlins), an educated and demanding master. His problem is that he has standards, and he suffers for them. He is sour and acerbic until late in life when he takes a cue from the contented Da, and learns to compromise. In common with Mr. Hughes and Mr. Murray, Mr. Rawlins is unerring.

Sylvia O'Brien is a bulwark of sanctimony as the mother. Mia Dillon is saucy as a young woman: a seduction scene with the young Charlie, interrupted by the effusive Da, is one of the most touching, personal moments in the play. Lois de Banzie has the proper air of self-importance as Da's stingy employer.

In the transfer from the Hudson Guild to the larger Morosco stage, the play has lost a bit of its intimacy. However, in all important respects - writing, direction, performance, design - the production is unaltered. This is one of those rare instances of a play that has not been artificially enlarged for Broadway. *Da* is a humane and honest memory play in which, with great affection and humor, we are invited to share the life of a family.

ROMULUS LINNEY

LAUGHING STOCK: APRIL 14, 1984

Romulus Linney is a playwright with a rich, Faulknerian sense of humor. In the best tradition, he is a local colorist, taking regional characters and showing us how their lives are inextricably bound up with land, family and ancestral roots.

The Manhattan Punch Line is fulfilling a valuable purpose by presenting three of Mr. Linney's one-act plays, grouped under the title *Laughing Stock*. Two of the plays, *Goodbye, Howard* and *Tennessee*, were highlights of past one-act marathons at the Ensemble Studio Theater. The third, *F.M.*, is new to New York. All three are vintage proof of the playwright's mastery of the short theatrical form.

Each deals with favorite Linney themes - death and departure, and the tricks that trip those who are unprepared for the inevitable. While sharing in lyrical, homespun language, they also demonstrate the breadth of the author's comic vision. The evening is beautifully acted by a cast headed by Frances Sternhagen and Jane Connell.

In *Goodbye, Howard*, three elderly sisters are in a North Carolina hospital "practicing repose" while keeping a death watch over their celebrated brother, Howard. The relationship is filled with sibling friction. Helen Harrelson is the quarrelsome one, given to casual cursing. Ms. Sternhagen maintains her even temper, while the endearing Ms. Connell, in the play's most amusing performance, remains childlike.

Howard is approaching 85, and his sisters are mostly worried how their absent mother will react to his imminent demise. One hesitates to think how old the old lady is. With a forward young man (Timothy Wilson) acting as buffer, Mr. Linney sends his three sisters spinning on eccentric byways of rambunctious comedy.

F.M. moves to an Alabama college for an adult course in writing fiction, led by Ms. Sternhagen as a novelist forced to teach for a living. Two of her students (Ms. Connell and Peggity Price) are dilettantes. The third (Leon Russom) is a scurvy outsider in club-lady company.

Passionately reading aloud from his thick, whisky-stained manuscript, Mr. Russom is clearly an offense to his classmates' decorum. He is also an artist on the hoof, in his own writing a kin to Faulkner himself. This is not parody, but serious comedy, with a heartwarming conclusion. As in the other plays, the predictability of the plot does not detract from the vividness of the dialogue and characters. All the actors are admirable; Mr. Russom is faultless as the rough diamond.

It is Ms. Sternhagen's turn to shine in *Tennessee*, a bucolic tale about the indomitability of the land and of the pioneer spirit. The actress plays an aged mountain woman, who wanders backward to tell the saga of her childhood, courtship and marriage. At 90 as at 19, Ms. Sternhagen is equally spunky; one of the author's achievements is to show the effervescence of the elderly.

In flashback, the heroine succumbs to the wooing of an undiscourageable swain (Harold Guskin), who then takes her on a roundabout journey to marital bliss. The path is strewn with folk wisdom, sights and aromas, as characters travel through forests of sourwood to return to "places of powerful remembrance." That phrase sums up the locus of Mr. Linney's plangent provincial comedies.

Laughing Stock is given an authoritative staging by Ed Howard, taking advantage of Paul Bryan Eads's set design, especially his wood-hewn Appalachian homestead. As a writer, Mr. Linney is himself a homesteader, staking his claim to a bountiful slice of Americana.

AMBROSIO: APRIL 28, 1992

In *Ambrosio*, Romulus Linney probes deeply into the nature of heresy and the power of love, both spiritual and temporal. Always a rapt student of history, he uses a seismic event in the past, the Spanish Inquisition, as a sounding board for his provocative thoughts on what drives people to irrational acts and crimes of passion. At the same time, the playwright never ignores his role as storyteller.

Ambrosio, the final production in the first season of the Signature Theater

Company, validates the premise behind the formation of the troupe. In the course of a single year, this enterprising company has devoted itself entirely to plays by Mr. Linney: revivals, revisions, the New York premiere of *A Woman Without a Name* and now a new play that ranks with the author's most challenging dramatic works.

In a taut 90 minutes, Mr. Linney demonstrates the crushing weight of the Inquisition, as it destroys dissent and raises hypocrisy to lofty heights. Abhorrent actions are followed by the prayerful words "with God, with God." From the author's critical perspective, it is not God but the Devil that is the primary force in Spain in 1500, but the answers to questions of diabolism are wisely left to a theatergoer's imagination.

The play is written with the utmost economy. As with the author's earlier historical efforts, beginning with *The Sorrows of Frederick*, the new work is the antithesis of self-important epics that subordinate meaning to panoply and melodrama. *Ambrosio* is a quietly intense chamber piece that keeps a sharp focus on its central subject at the same time that it widens its lens to include the background of a demoralizing society.

Throughout the play, there are alternating currents of rapture and retribution, as a charismatic priest, Father Ambrosio (Peter Ashton Wise), is overcome by temptations. The sanctity of his cloistered life in an abbey is suddenly invaded by a longing for two people: a lovely young woman (Marin Hinkle), for whom he acts as confessor, and a mysterious monk (Craig Duncan).

The characters are clearly individualized and also represent divergent attitudes toward conflicts between church and state. The Inquisitor turns out to be a surprisingly judicious man, insisting on differentiating among sins, declaring that certain acts demonstrate "vanity, lunacy and lust, but not heresy."

To provide additional historical perspective, the author makes a passing reference to Martin Luther as a rising young man of the church. While remaining scrupulously within its period, *Ambrosio* also raises relevant arguments about other more modern times of non-enlightenment.

As directed by Mr. Linney and James Houghton, the actors evoke their characters in appearance as well as sensibility. Playing the seductive monk, Mr. Duncan has the look and the innocence of the boy in Picasso's portrait *Boy Leading a Horse*. Similarly, T. Ryder Smith, through his invidious manner, underscores the diabolic nature of his character.

Moving from abject admiration for the priest to sudden moments of passion, Ms. Hinkle turns her confessional into a dream of lustful abandon. In his New York debut, Mr. Wise takes an understated approach to his role. While not soliciting sympathy, he elicits curiosity, entreating the audience into his nightmare and the contradictions of a man enthralled. The set design by E. David Cosier makes harmonious use of sparse scenery and slide projections, and Teresa Snider-Stein's costumes add authenticity.

With its intelligence and acuity about crises of faith, *Ambrosio* is a play that would honor any of our major theaters. That it happens to have its first production in the unpretentious surroundings of the Signature Company reinforces Mr. Linney's commitment to theater as an arena for the exploration of ideas.

CHARLES LUDLAM AND THE RIDICULOUS

BLUEBEARD: MAY 5, 1970

Charles Ludlam has apparently seen, adored, laughed at, been scared to death by and memorized every mad-doctor movie ever made. *Bluebeard*, which he wrote, directed and starred in, is a distillation of that ghoulish genre, and serves successfully as both a loving paean and a lunatic parody.

The root of this *Bluebeard* is that old 1935 Charles Laughton movie, *Island of Lost Souls* - with infinite revisions and elaborations by the devious Ludlam. There are intimations, for example, of *Faust*, and Bartók's *Bluebeard's Castle* is playing as the entertainment begins.

Ludlam's hero-villain is the Baron Khanazar von Bluebeard, and that K in Khanazar is as hard as a pile-driver. In one of Ludlam's consistently amusing linguistic conceits, characters occasionally rasp K's where there are no K's, just as, occasionally, they intentionally drop their Transylvanian accents for New Yorkese. Ludlam khids himself as well as Khanazar.

Bluebeard is trying to manufacture a new sex, specifically, a third genital. Any innocent female, such as the mad doctor's nubile niece Sybil, who visits Bluebeard's island, is almost immediately wooed, then wedded to a laboratory table for experimentation. The plot is complicated and digressionary, and great fun to follow - from boudoir (a blatantly lewd, hilarious seduction of Sybil's billowy guardian by the irrepressibly lascivious Bluebeard) to laboratory. No corny burbling decanters there, just a tinny chair that looks like an exploded box spring - placed on stage simply so that Ludlam can maniacally heave it off stage.

Ludlam's performance is deliciously rococo, and obviously he has infected everyone in his Ridiculous Theatrical Company. The masklike make-up, which is credited to the entire company, is near-miraculous (a knobby-faced slavey, a gilt-skinned angel).

Led by Ludlam, a truly terrible actor like Mario Montez (as Lamia the Leopard Woman) seems exactly right and the good actors seem perfect. I particularly liked Black-Eyed Susan as Sybil (she merits some sort of citation for the self-confidence with which she wears that third genital) and John Brockmeyer as the Karloffian servant Sheemish.

On the tiny raised stage, Brockmeyer looks about 12 feet tall, with a humpy stoop that totally obscures his head when he turns his back. Although a demi-monster, he is easily frightened out of his half-wits. Any threat of detention in the House of Pain, and he clutches his groin in anticipated anguish. At one point, he cringes, then hops right into Bluebeard's arms, totally obscuring his master from view.

In a beard that looks like blue Brillo, his eyes blazing with mad menace, Ludlam is a monstrous, but oddly ingratiating fiend. "When I am good," he boasts, "I am very good. When I am bad..." He pauses, considers his catalogue of turpitude, and concludes, "I'm not bad." As a villain, he is not only not bad, he is terrific.

CAMILLE: MAY 4, 1973

Charles Ludlam has brazenly cast himself on Garboed waters, playing Marguerite Gautier, La Dame aux Camelias, herself, in his own free adaptation of the Dumas work.

This is no facile female impersonation, but a real performance. Ludlam never forgets his gender, and neither do we. He makes his entrance lavishly gowned, his black wig rolled into ringlets, his features appliquéd with make-up. He looks womanly and vulnerable - except for the fact that over his bodice his hairy chest is clearly visible.

Unlike transvestite actors who play females as if to the manner born, Ludlam in drag remains a clown. Carefully he skirts camp, varying his pose from a tremulous fragility to a Tallulah assertiveness to a Ludlam textual commentary. Armand Duval tearfully confesses his undying passion for Camille. After listening indulgently, Ludlam (as Ludlam) quips, "So it's as bad as that, huh?"

The limitations of the Dumas play form the limitations of Ludlam's rerun. As a playwright and director, he is inspired by the grotesque. The monsters, demons and fools who usually populate his fantastical works expand his comic imagination. In contrast, *Camille* serves largely as an excuse for a lighthearted spoof of a sentimental classic.

The production has the Ridiculous Theatrical Company's usual ingenious theatricality. The sets by Bobjack Callejo are paragons of pseudo splendor, and the costumes by Mary Brecht seem like relics from a Dumas trunk. The regular members of Ludlam's comedy troupe offer their customary expert performances - Lola Pashalinski as a friendly voluptuary, Black-Eyed Susan as a jealous tart, Bill Vehr as an absurdly acquiescent Armand and John D. Brockmeyer as the lecherous Baron de Varville.

As with all "Camilles," this one builds toward the death scene. Zigzagging his eyebrows, feinting swoons, gingerly coughing (each cough is a sly comment), Ludlam mocks himself until - prostrate under a pink sheet - he turns his profile skyward and with a smile of momentary joy, suddenly collapses. Once again, poor Camille dies, but this time we laugh.

STAGE BLOOD: DECEMBER 9, 1974

Charles Ludlam's *Stage Blood* is *Hamlet* with a happy ending, which is of course, ridiculous - as in Ridiculous Theatrical Company. In Mr. Ludlam's latest comic invention (he is the director, author, and also Hamlet), a seedy troupe of actors is in Mudville, U.S.A., preparing to open *Hamlet* without an Ophelia.

Grumbling is interrupted by Lola Pashalinski (Hamlet's mother on and off stage) who says, "We don't need beauty and truth. We need an ingénue." On cue, down the aisle comes Black-Eyed Susan, a hopeful local, batting her wide eyes, proclaiming her ingenueness, and then delivering the mad scene, from memory, with an imaginary bundle of rue and rosemary for the flabbergasted company.

She wins the role and the show goes on. As Mr. Ludlam's revolving stage merrily spins, we see *Hamlet* between the scenes, which includes hanky-panky in the dressing room, a death by hatchet-in-the-neck (could it possibly be a suicide?) and two ghosts of Hamlet's father vying for the spotlight.

Laughs are freefalling, but the play is less wild and untidy than usual Ludlam. There is a slight loss in madness and nonsense but a gain in structure and discipline. This is a crisply wrapped comic package, with a clear plot and smart staging. Chiefly it is a showcase for the variegated performing skills of the company, which has been in existence for seven years. The six founding members form the entire cast, bouncing trick daggers and silly soliloquies off one another with the abandon of circus clowns.

John D. Brockmeyer, who is so long from head to foot that he walks through doorways at a stoop, is the embittered stage manager, Jenkins, forced to swab out toilets while privately crafting epic plays, such as *Fossil Fuel*, which he hugs to his chest like a fat bundle of old telephone books.

Ms. Susan is cheery and chipper, as the pert Ophelia, nee Elfie Fey, even while Hamlet is assailing her dignity and her décolletage. Ms. Pashalinski and Bill Vehr are mother and lover, she forthright, he a practical joker, their wild eyes and occasionally their hands stripping the other bare. Jack Mallory is a ghostly apparition - alive as well as dead.

Mr. Ludlam is a boyish Hamlet, not a buffoon. To play the role, he doffs his dashing leather suit in favor of doublet and hose - and a blond wig that looks as if it might have been used by Carol Channing. He is no happier with his hirsuteness than we are, but his mother insists that all Hamlets are blond.

The pun in the title is apt. *Stage Blood* is The Theater that gets into an actor's veins and also bottled paint slapped on fake wounds. The Ridiculous performers are irrepressibly stagestruck and their show is a fanciful entertainment. It is seasoned with Mr. Ludlam's comments on the art of artifice (for him, acting is "seeming not being") and valuable theatrical information. Did you know that the plays of Shakespeare were not written by Shakespeare but by another playwright of the same name?

DER RING GOTT FARBLONJET: APRIL 29, 1977

Charles Ludlam usually recycles old tales, such as *Bluebeard* and *Camille*. For his latest opus, he has tuned his demonic antennae to one of the oldest and hoariest stories of all, *The Ring of the Nibelungen*. Mr. Ludlam's Wagner's Ring - almost as irresistible a subject as Lincoln's Doctor's Dog - is called *Der Ring Gott Farblonjet*, which immediately indicates that this is Ridiculous Theatrical Company territory.

Give Mr. Ludlam points not only for nerve, but for ambition. This is unquestionably his most massive undertaking, a comic grand opera - with a score by Jim McElwaine that ranges from Wagnerian arias to the Rheingold beer commercial (played by a tiny, versatile orchestra). The plot is as thick as a briar patch, the characters are comprehensive (Rhine maidens, Valkyries and a talking bear), and the canvas sweeping from Valhalla to the nether regions of the Nihilumpen.

The author has set his madcap to tell the entire story of the Ring, in his own time and in his own patented fashion. The epic is three-and-one-half hours, which is much longeur than it should be. The story - spectacular, heroic, sexual - is a natural for the Ridiculous Theatrical treatment. There are moments when one feels that for Mr. Ludlam to have played Wagner straight might have been spoof enough.

The style is not a betrayal of its source so much as an elaboration and a commentary. Camp elements are kept to a minimum as the author (who is also the dirctor and designer) circumnavigates the Nihilumpen, a toadlike race of "uglische dwarfs." Too much of the dialogue is in fractured German (sprinkled with Yiddish). It wears out the actors' jaws and our tolerance, though occasionally it is used to make an effective point, as in the proclamation, "Today, the Nihilumpen, tomorrow, the world."

For Ludlamites and perhaps for Wagnerians as well, the evening has its delectations. First of all, there is Lola Pashalinski, who was born to be Brunhilde. With her zesty Mae West presence, her ample body, her golden tresses (topped by a twin-tipped tin horn), crying "Ho-yo-to-ho!" over the copulating forms of Siegmund and Sieglinda.

The adorable, doll-like Black-Eyed Susan undertakes three choice roles -the naked Sieglinda, the Saran-wrapped Earth Mother, and the leather-bound Gutruna. Our hero, Siegfried, is the stalwart John D. Brockmeyer, wearing fluffy cuffs, so that he looks like a tall, thin, plucked poodle. Mr. Brockmeyer, who has graduated from playing viperish villains to playing manly martyrs, has his grandest moment slaying a swashbuckling dragon.

Inevitably, with a cast so large, some of the chorus is simply ridiculous. But the three stars are inimitable, and there are effective performances by, among others, Richard Currie and Bill Vehr as creepy dastards, Adam Macadam as a one-eyed god and Beverly Brown (the most operatic voice on the premises) as a flighty forest bird. Absent on stage and definitely missed is Mr. Ludlam himself. This time he makes his primary contribution as a designer, a capacity in which he echoes his writing by cleverly recycling old material.

The scenery, costumes and makeup are a marvel of ingenuity. Dripping with paint-daubed plastic strips, the adaptable set is weird and unearthly. That dragon is a huffing, smoke-breathing monster - a runaway from a Chinese New Year. There are pin-thin giants, pointed helmets made to measure for pointed heads, and an army of loathsome Nihilumpen dressed in large green garbage bags. Mr. Ludlam's extravagant opera teeters as it passes through the doldrums, but it never capsizes.

THE VENTRILOQUIST'S WIFE: DECEMBER 28, 1977

If Charles Ludlam had lived 50 years ago, he might have been a vaudeville headliner, but he would have never lost his sense of the Ridiculous. Fascinated by ventriloquism, he has created a diabolical comedy coup de théâtre entitled *The Ventriloquist's Wife*.

As director, playwright, actor and founder of the Ridiculous Theatrical Company, Mr. Ludlam recycles the detritus of our culture. Just as his *Bluebeard* was influenced by the movie *The Island of Lost Souls* and his *Camille* by Garbo, *The Ventriloquist's Wife* draws wattage from that 1945 Michael Redgrave horror movie, *Dead of Night*. As you may remember, that was the movie in which a ventriloquist's life was taken over by a wooden dummy.

With the éclat and the raised eyebrows of a silent-film star, Mr. Ludlam plays "Charles," an actor down on his luck who buys a wooden dummy in a pawn shop, names him Walter Ego, and becomes his straight man. Walter - cute, cuddlesome, and as nasty as W.C. Fields was to Charlie McCarthy - artfully upstages his master and covets his wife. Walter is both the child in the house and the fiendish rival for the lady.

Mr. Ludlam's manipulation of the dummy - physically and vocally - is masterful. Goggling his eyes and bobbing his neck, Walter is not only a versatile piece of wood, he is also a marvelously animated actor. When Mr. Ludlam, furious at Walter's repeated mischief, crams the dummy back into his cardboard suitcase, Walter's whimpers of protest, muffled by his enclosure, are breathtakingly expressive. Later, when Walter responds to the abuse by refusing to speak, the figure suddenly loses its spryness and vitality. He is as limp as a beanbag; it is as if he had died. Then, just as suddenly, shot through with adrenalin, he springs back to life.

The title role is played by that fetching Ridiculous leading lady, Black- Eyed Susan. Having previously delighted us as besieged ingenues and battered orphans of the storm in a cycle of Ludlam epics, Susan is now cast as a cheerful, well-scrubbed housewife, the kind who might sell soapsuds on television. It is her misfortune to be married to a lunatic. Periodically, master and dummy take their act to a crowded, rather uncomfortable nightclub where they unveil a monumental supply of vaudeville jokes that grow woolier and weirder in the course of the evening.

Expanding his act, Mr. Ludlam dresses himself and his partner in matching tuxedos (Walter is the one in the turban) for a session with "Swami Ego." Mr. Ludlam hypnotizes the dummy, blindfolds him, then takes him on a jaunty mind-reading trip around the club.

Susan cannot stand it. "Oh, Charles," she cries. "Give up your ventriloquism. Stop throwing your voice!" In response, he decides to saw her in half, a scene made doubly amusing by the fact that the actress - who is as petite as a doll - is too short for the sawing box. Keening the saw so that it makes monster movie music - before he puts it to more practical use - Mr. Ludlam quips, "The last woman I sawed in half is alive and well and living in Paris and London."

Because the show has evolved in rehearsal and in performance, it still needs some polishing, particularly toward the trick Pirandello ending. But the script is one of Mr. Ludlam's most inspired creations, and the actors - all three of them - are mesmerizing. *The Ventriloquist's Wife* raises ventriloquism to a high comic art.

THE ENCHANTED PIG: APRIL 24, 1979

Imagine if you can a cross between *King Lear* and *The Frog Prince*, with a slipper-from *Cinderella* and a twist of *The Three Sisters*, and you have an approximation of *The Enchanted Pig*, Charles Ludlam's delirious new merriment. This comedy is clean and camp-free. It should appeal to both wide-eyed adults and sophisticated children.

King Gorgeous III is Mr. Ludlam's version of Lear, an arrogant monarch played by the spindly, skinny John D. Brockmeyer, his face so lined with makeup that he looks like a stained glass window. Marching off to still another battle, handsome Gorgeous tells his three nubile daughters that in his absence they can have the run of the castle, except they are not to venture into one particular room, referred to with dungeon intonations as "that room!"

Of course, this is the first place they go. In "That Room!" they discover a book of prophecies. The eldest daughter will marry a prince from the East; she glows with pleasure. The middle daughter will marry a prince from the West; she glows in anticipation. The youngest and prettiest daughter, played by the price-less Black-Eyed Susan, awaits her fate with trepidation. Then comes the prophecy: She will marry...a pig from the North.

Shortly after, the suitors arrive, and the marriages take place, Ms. Susan and her family holding their noses against the stench during her ceremony. From here on, it is a Ridiculous free-for-all, a giddy sendup of fairy tales and picaresque odes. The journey sends Mr. Brockmeyer's Lear shouting madly onto the heath - after he has been spanked by his nasty daughters. The heroine, Ms. Susan, tra-verses his kingdom in search of a miracle cure for her husband's snout.

Abetting her are three mythological mothers. Foiling her is a wicked witch, played by Lola Pashalinski with a nose like a parsnip and a look that could shrivel a dragon. Actually there is a dragon thrashing his tail in a prologue, and there is an army of oinking porkers.

The cast, veterans of the Ridiculous, is an animated cartoon, masters and mis-tresses of a style that is as emphatic as it is amusing: the sneaky Ms. Pashalinski, Bill Vehr as a cringing prince, Everett Quinton as an assertive pig, and, of course, the mighty Mr. Brockmeyer, who even gets to orate an occasional line from Shakespeare.

Center stage is given to Ms. Susan, who conducts herself with comic elegance even as she is subjected to a demeaning pig's marriage. Carrying a bouquet of car-rots, forced to wallow in a trough with her porcine in-laws, waiting on her mate "hoof and mouth," weathering the storm of outrageous sight and sound gags, she is an enchantress. She even gets to throw her voice, a trick she learned while play-ing in Mr. Ludlam's *The Ventiloquist's Wife*, and used here to dub her alternately squawling and laughing babe in arms.

Quite a measure of the evening's success must be attributed to the collabora-tive hands of Mr. Ludlam's designers - the children's-storybook set by Bobjack Callejo and the flouncy costumes by Gabriel Berry; when the sisters curtsy, their hoop skirts look like hassocks. Adam McAdam and John Cunningham, who are actors in the show, have contributed puppet paraphernalia, masks and apparitions that are a comic variation on Bunraku.

This time, Mr. Ludlam limits himself to writing and directing. He does not act on stage and, surprisingly, his presence is not unduly missed. His play is a pun-filled romantic adventure that cribs from a diversity of sources, spoofing but not debasing material. *The Enchanted Pig* has that spontaneity that we associate with Mr. Ludlam at his most effervescent.

THE MYSTERY OF IRMA VEP: OCTOBER 4, 1984

Charles Ludlam's latest Ridiculous Theatrical Company escapade, *The Mystery of Irma Vep*, begins at Mandacrest on the moors, in the manner of *Rebecca*, then, after wuthering heights of hilarity, it slinks off to Egypt for scenes spliced from *The Mummy's Curse*. The evening winds up with a howler, courtesy of *The Wolf Man*. Naturally, the entire collage is filtered through the eclectic memory and perfervid imagination of Mr. Ludlam as author, dirctor and star.

Even if this were the usual Ludlam yarn as performed by his resident troupe of zanies, *Irma Vep* would be a romp. What makes it singular is that every one of the myriad characters - men and women, more than 6, less than 12 - is played by Mr. Ludlam and Everett Quinton.

The two actors quick-change costumes, characters and genders, diving in and out of disguises and doors with lightning-flash dexterity. Each actor often barely misses meeting himself on stage, although sometimes offstage voices collide. Behind the scenery, the cast and crew may be in a frenzy, but what we see looks effortless. Between them, in performance, Mr. Ludlam and Mr. Quinton turn this self-styled "penny dreadful" into a double tour de force.

Blink your eyes, and the Boy Scoutish bravado of Mr. Quinton's master of the manse has been replaced by his Agnes Moorehead maidservant hiding her jealousy - and biding her time - behind a mask of self-sacrifice. The actor demonstrates here as he has in other Ridiculous jaunts that he has a genuine comic talent for pretending to be female.

As for Mr. Ludlam, he shifts from an ominous, one-legged haunter of the heath to the new mistress of Mandacrest. In one slightly offstage, extremely off-center scene, he simultaneously plays both the heroine and her assailant, changing profiles and voices like a hermaphroditic ventriloquist.

Despite all the dastardy, the playwright has an underlying affection for all his characters, even for the misunderstood vampire. That poor fellow simply cannot help himself and always seems to be on the lookout for a rising full moon. In the Egyptian crypt, the atmosphere turns frighteningly funny. That journey to archeological depths is led by Mr. Ludlam as a guide-guru outfitted with a Peter Sellers accent. Together with Mr. Quinton as an ace Egyptologist, Mr. Ludlam ransacks the past for missing tombs, pronounced "tombas." The imaginary descent of the grave robbers into the tombas is itself a stunt worthy of a fakir.

While the two actors are the entire Ridiculous foreground, the background - scenery artfully designed by Mr. Ludlam - is triggered for trickery, including an animated portrait of the first Lady Hillcrest (the former Irma Vep), a Sphinx, a false-bottomed sarcophagus and not so cryptic hieroglyphics. To keep everything equal, Mr. Quinton designed the ornate costumes, cleverly fashioned for split-second doffing. In all respects, this is a highly polished production.

In common with the play itself, Peter Golub's musical score is a Gothic movie patchwork. At one point, the actors - for the fun of it - take time out from the skullduggery to sit before the hearth like twinned club ladies and strum a sweet duet for dulcimers.

The script veers crazily from Brontë, borrows a bit of du Maurier and recycles Shakespeare while remaining firmly resident in the land of Ludlamania. Even a bouquet of wolfsbane could not keep laughter from this door.

THE MAN WHO MADE THEATER RIDICULOUS: JUNE 7, 1987

For 20 years, Charles Ludlam made a marvelous career out of being Ridiculous. As the comic genius behind the Ridiculous Theatrical Company, he was a grand recycler of popular culture, an entertainment ecologist, taking old tales and old movies and recharging them with his own extravagant imagination. His art continued unabated, from *Bluebeard* to this past season, *The Artificial Jungle*. Ludlam died on May 28, at the age of 44, ending a career and a brilliant, one-man way of theater.

For all his apparent iconoclasm, he was very much in the classical tradition of the actor-manager. He wrote all of his company's plays - more than 20 of them - directed them and played one or more of the leading roles in almost every production. He also designed many of his shows. More than anything, he gave his theater its unique character, which was larger and far funnier than life. Inventing himself and his troupe, he created a performance genre.

To be Ridiculous is to be a step beyond the Absurd. Ludlam defined his form of theater as an ensemble synthesis of "wit, parody, vaudeville farce, melodrama and satire," which, in combination, gives "reckless immediacy to classical stagecraft." That recklessness led some people to misinterpret his work as anarchic. It was spontaneous, but it was also highly structured - and always to specific comic effect. Though Mr. Ludlam was a titanic Fool, he was not foolish. He knew exactly what he was doing, whether the object of his satire was Dumas, du Maurier, the Brontës, Molière, Shakespeare, soap opera or grandiose opera - or himself.

I first encountered him in performance 17 years ago when he was playing *Bluebeard* far Off Broadway - with a beard like blue Brillo and a diabolical glare in his eye. This was a distillation of every mad-doctor movie ever made. In his role as Bluebeard, he said, "When I am good, I am very good. When I am bad...," and he paused to consider his history of turpitude. Then he concluded, "I'm not bad." As hilarious as *Bluebeard* was, it gave no indication of the body of work that was to follow it. Almost every year, sometimes twice a year, there was another Ludlam lunacy on stage. As a critic who reviewed almost all of his plays, I must say that Ludlam was always fun to watch and fun to write about. His flights of fancy could inspire a kind of critical daredevilry, as one tried to capture in words the ephemeral essence of Ridiculous theater.

Looking back on our debt to him, one remembers his rhapsodic, hairy-chested *Camille*; the Grand Guignol vaudeville of *The Ventriloquist's Wife*, in which he spoke both for himself and for his back-talking dummy, Walter Ego; *The Enchanted Pig*, a helium-high hybrid of *King Lear* and *Cinderella*; *Le Bourgeois Avant-Garde*, a Molièresque send-up of minimalism; *Galas*, with Mr. Ludlam as the title diva. The range ran from *Corn*, a hillbilly musical, to *Der Ring Gott Farblonjet*, a three-Ring Wagner circus. There were also sideshows - a Punch and Judy puppet theater in which he played all 22 characters, and *Anti-Galaxie Nebulae*, a science fiction serialette.

The Mystery of Irma Vep (in 1984) was a tour de force, a horror-comedy in which he and his comic partner, Everett Quinton, quick-changed roles in a scintillating send-up of "Wuthering" and other Gothic "Heights." For Ludlam, *Irma Vep* became a breakthrough of a kind. The first of his plays to demonstrate a broader, popular appeal, it has been staged by other companies, in other countries as well as in America's regional theaters. Not all of Ludlam was equal, but his batting average was extraordinarily high - as author, director and actor.

His acting was, of course, his most noticeable talent. As a performer, he unfailingly enriched his own work, as he charted a chameleonesque course, specializing in satyrs, caliphs and fakirs - as well as playing the occasional damsel. He was also an expert teacher of theater, as I discovered some years ago when, over a period of several months, I took an acting workshop with him. In these intensive sessions, we studied and practiced physical, visual and verbal comedy. He was most informative about what he did on stage. For example, he thought of his body as a puppet; through his imagination, he pulled his own strings.

Even with success, he stayed in his own stream, a tiny Off Broadway theater, with his familiar company (a few actors left and a few new ones arrived), making theater on a shoestring. Late in his career, he occasionally directed opera - and plays by others - but, for the most part, he kept doing what he alone did so well. As demonstrated by *Irma Vep* and *The Artificial Jungle*, he never stopped growing. Next in line, while directing *Titus Andronicus* for Joseph Papp, he was scheduled to present his new play about Houdini in his theater at One Sheridan Square.

One could easily envision him locked in a box at the bottom of the sea - and breaking out in a phantasmagorical display of theater magic.

Mr. Ludlam was an original theater artist, and, as such, his art will survive - in his plays, in our memories of performances and also in the actors whom he trained and who became his comic co-stars: Black-Eyed Susan, Lola Pashalinski, Everett Quinton, John D. Brockmeyer, Bill Vehr, Georg Osterman and others. Under his inimitable tutelage, they learned how to be Ridiculous in the land of Ludlamania.

At Mr. Ludlam's funeral, a Catholic service at St. Joseph's Church, the playwright Leon Katz delivered the euology. Recounting great moments in Ludlam theater, he concluded by describing the climax of *Camille*. Mr. Ludlam's tragicomic heroine had coughed a last cough. Passionately, Armand pledged his eternal love, and then he added, "Toodle-oo, Marguerite." As Mr. Katz remembered those last words, the mourners in the church broke into a cascade of laughter. In a wave, they rose and offered Mr. Ludlam his final standing ovation - and a salute of "Toodle-oo, Charles."

THE BELLS: FEBRUARY 21, 1992

The Bells was one of Henry Irving's greatest theatrical successes, a melodrama that the Victorian actor seemed doomed to perform forever. He played Mathias, a rich Alsatian innkeeper tormented by a guilty secret. In the Everett Quinton version of *The Bells*, Mr. Quinton outlaughs Irving by playing all the characters - male, female, heroic and villainous - as well as sight and sound effects. His ringing adaptation of this vintage thriller sweeps the stage at the Charles Ludlam Theater.

The Ridiculous Theatrical approach is akin to that of Mr. Ludlam and Mr. Quinton in the two-man tour de force *The Mystery of Irma Vep*. In that Gothic horror comedy, the actors darted in and out of a lonely cottage, each time emerging in a strange new guise. With *The Bells*, Mr. Quinton never leaves the stage or changes his costume. He simply swings with heightening flair from one role to another.

He is headstrong as the handsome young quartermaster engaged to Mathias's beautiful daughter. As the quartermaster eyes his fiancée, Mr. Quinton turns the other profile and smiles engagingly at her lover. Quick switch and he is a barfly, a barmaid, a barrister and a mysterious mesmerist with a hypnotic stare. The stage is soon crowded with Quintons. A watchful theatergoer should have no difficulty distinguishing them, though one may lose count of the number.

In a flashback, we see "the Polish Jew" (as in the title of the Emile Erckmann-Alexandre Chatrian novel that inspired the original play). Many years ago, this wanderer entered the town and never made it past an ominous bridge, where he was murdered by Mathias for his money. Now, as the mayor and the father of the bride to be, Mathias is swelling with pride but haunted by his dastardly deed. He is also haunted by the sound of belllllls, belllllls, belllllls, gonging through his mind (and our ears). Every time he hears them, he becomes more and more crazed, ending up the hapless victim of his tortured conscience.

Accompanying the actor's gestures with silent-movie background music is Mark Bennett at the piano. Eureka is the director, but Mr. Quinton is the show's centrifugal force. *The Bells* is not as devious or as complex as *Irma Vep*. Lasting 50 minutes, it is a curtain-raiser without a follower. But it is a deadly, diabolical showcase for the chameleonesque Mr. Quinton.

ETHYL EICHELBERGER AND HIS INTERIOR SPOTLIGHT: AUG. 26, 1990

With equal zest Ethyl Eichelberger played men and women. Sometimes portraying a dozen characters in a single show, he leaped from fright-wigged mad doctors to pompadourable courtesans. In *The Tempest of Chim-Lee*, he represented an entire gallery of Oriental characters (with no protest from Actors' Equity). There was something about his female roles - his towering height, the absurd wigs atop his bald head, his toes teetering on point - that made these impersonations unique, especially when he did cartwheels and splits in full drag.

Even as he drastically altered his appearance, his voice remained identifiably his own. Theatergoers could never forget that it was Ethyl behind the disguise. His specialty was mockery without malice. He had a gift for the exaggerated gesture as well as a sense of playfulness, and his passion for writing matched his passion for acting. In both domains he was not one to withhold energy.

Behind the flamboyant facade was a very private individual who refrained from burdening others with his problems. Debilitated by AIDS, and feeling unable to fulfill a commitment to act in *The Caucasian Chalk Circle* at the Arena Stage in Washington, he took his own life two weeks ago. With his death - at the age of 45 - the theater lost a rare and idiosyncratic comic spirit.

His impact on experimental theater was indisputable and, one assumes, he made his most sizable contribution by limiting his ambition and remaining true to his chamber-sized art. As an actor and playwright, he diminished sexual barriers and punctured pretension. Above all, he always retained his sense of the ridiculous. In performance, he seemed surprised to find himself on stage facing an audience, when, of course, that was the most natural place for Mr. Eichelberger to be. He had a kind of interior spotlight, and within his world he was a star.

Stagestruck since his childhood in Pekin, Ill., he studied theater at the American Academy of Dramatic Arts in New York. Then, for seven years, he was a member of the Trinity Repertory Company in Providence, R.I. Returning to New York, he began working in downtown performance theater. Later he apprenticed as a hairdresser to learn wigmaking, and perfected that craft as a fallback profession. In other respects he was the ultimate autodidact - actor, clown, playwright, singer, director, composer, accordionist, tumbler and fire-eater.

As he worked his way up in the theater, he broadened his audience while never diminishing his experimental base. Even as he entered the mainstream (appearing in *The Comedy of Errors* at Lincoln Center), there seemed to be nothing he could not do, or would not dare to do in performance. He had an excess of nerve, and the talent to match it.

Charles Ludlam, as the maestro of the Ridiculous school of comedy, was one of his mentors. In Mr. Ludlam's last play, *The Artificial Jungle*, Mr. Eichelberger portrayed the star's mother, maternally tending the ravenous reptiles in her son's pet shop. When the mother uncovered a murderous plot against Mr. Ludlam, she was struck dumb. Mama was paralyzed except for his accusing eyes, which continued rolling like loose marbles for the rest of the show - a sight gag that induced helpless laughter from the audience.

It was a natural step from acting to writing. Mr. Eichelberger created more than 30 plays in his lifetime, giving himself roles like Medea, Medusa and, in the same play, Abraham and Mary Todd Lincoln. He regarded himself as a storyteller who retold classics. Often his variations were so divergent as to be unrecognizable relatives of the original.

Treating Shakespeare as his own private Holinshed's Chronicles, he wrote *Leer*, a 32-minute "opera/comique" distillation of Shakespeare, which he performed on a double bill with his *Casanova*. In *Leer* he played the King, the Fool and Cordelia, while singing and playing country-western tunes on a concertina. During a respite in the show, he cracked a thundersheet. *Hamlette* was his female version of *Hamlet*. To Black-Eyed Susan's Hamlette, he played Gertrude, Claudius and the Ghost of Hamlette's father. This meant a series of very fast maneuvers during the closet scene.

He was often a one-man circus, but when he acted with others, he would encourage them to steal scenes. During a show he was a most watchful observer. Once, when the voluminous Katy Dierlam began to kneel on stage, Mr. Eichelberger issued a friendly warning, not so sotto voce, "Don't do it, Katy. You'll never get up."

His plays have not been published, and it is questionable how well they would communicate in print. So much of their humor was engendered by watching him improvise in performance. There was no dilemma that defeated him, beginning with the rising summer temperature at Performance Space 122, one of his favorite venues. A wilting audience was a particular challenge. During "Fiasco," two theatergoers exited in the middle of the performance. Stepping out of the scene, Mr. Eichelberger said, "Lock the door!" and, miscounting, added: "One of them is getting away."

Sometimes he had an off night, as a clever idea went askew. More often the plays simply seemed unfinished. Looking back one can see that the casualness was itself a source of his humor - a kind of spontaneous combustion in performance. A final draft might have rubbed out the surprises along with the rough edges.

In many of his plays he acted as critic. His last produced work, *Das Vedanya Mama*, was a spoof of Chekhov, Stanislavsky and the Bolshoi Ballet. This was a comedy in which Mr. Eichelberger played Olga to Black-Eyed Susan's "three sisters" (Masha, Irina and Maude). Rashly, he allowed his character to die before the show had reached its end, which meant that, following his own script, he had to remain motionless on the floor while his colleagues continued to act. He did not stay still for long. Suddenly Ethyl-Olga offered a posthumous accordion solo. Time permitting, he might have eaten fire and cartwheeled across the stage.

In his breathless career, Ethyl Eichelberger never could resist the impulse to perform.

DENNIS MCINTYRE

SPLIT SECOND: FEBRUARY 26, 1984

On a lonely West Side street a black policeman arrests a car thief, handcuffs him and waits for his backup patrol to arrive. The thief, who is white, tries to cajole the officer into releasing him, and after that approach fails he showers him with a torrent of racial insults. Silently, the policeman listens, and we can feel him bristling with years of suppressed rage. Finally, pushed past the breaking point, he takes out his revolver and shoots the man through the heart, turning off the stream of abuse.

So begins Dennis McIntyre's *Split Second*, an explosive new play dealing with primal dramatic issues, using - and lifting - the familiar police genre to tell a story about an individual facing a crisis of conscience. Mr. McIntyre is the author of *Modigliani*, a study of artistic desperation, and *Split Second* is as different from that as one could imagine, except that both are clearly the work of a gifted playwright. In addition, Mr. McIntyre, who is white, is able to write perceptively about blacks in urban society.

The opening scene is stunning, and it is followed by a tautly connected series of scenes in which the policeman faces an investigating officer, a friend on the force, his wife and his father. At first he invents a cover story, and then gradually confronts his guilt and tries to comprehend the reasons for, and the implications of, his inexcusable act. He is torn between the polarities of truth and pragmatism, self-justification and a desire for absolution.

We learn about his boyhood trauma, growing up in the shadow of a proud father, a policeman of unflinching probity. Woundingly, he reminds his father how, from an early age, he was indoctrinated with police lore and honor. "At 11," he says, "I was arresting every other kid on the block." A decade later, he was a soldier in Vietnam. Skillfully, Mr. McIntyre gives us a compassionate portrait of a man unable to live up to expectations of others. Two by two - son and father, husband and wife, comrades in action - we hear about the stresses and demands on the firing line, how an intelligent man has twisted himself into knots and why he finally detonates.

As he did in *Modigliani*, the author has clearly made an exhaustive study of his chosen environment and of the popular mythology that surrounds it. With pungency and humor, he compares life in the station house with images of that life on television. Much of the evening deals with role-playing, especially as it refers to black men within a white infrastructure. Despite that opening gunshot, the play never descends into melodrama, as it accelerates to its conclusion with a *Wozzeck*-like inevitability.

Under the astute direction of Samuel P. Barton, the actors have a uniform sense of identification with their characters. In the central role, John Danelle maintains his good-soldier facade even as he is assailed by doubt and by a compulsion to confess; his is a subtle performance.

Each of the other characters sheds a different light on the central predicament. As the demanding father, Norman Matlock has the authority of a saddle-sore veteran. Stiff-backed and unyielding in retirement, he is unable to accept an divergence from the letter of the law. Peter Jay Fernandez and Helmar Augustus Cooper bring conviction to their roles as policemen, and Michele Shay as the protagonist's wife rises to her moment as she challenges the equity of supposed justice. In order to accept what ensues, one must believe that the thief provoked his own death, and in his single scene Bill Cwikowski is perfect, offering a scathing portrait of a low-life punk.

The production has a workshop simplicity, using a few interchangeable chairs and tables. A detailed scenic design would add a firmer naturalistic base. *Split Second* already has emotional depth. One of the evening's several surprises is how a work of such excellence managed to elude all of our major institutional theaters.

A LOSS FOR THE THEATER: FEBRUARY 18, 1990

When Dennis McIntyre died on Feb. 1 (of cancer, at the age of 47), obituaries were brief and, for many, his name was unfamiliar. Sadly, his death will not inspire Broadway eulogies, but his life says something revealing about the plight of the playwright. He was a fine playwright with the potential to be a major one, but more than many of his peers he had difficulty getting his work produced.

Producers were hesitant and actors equivocated, balancing questions of their careers. Productions of his plays were promised and then postponed. Every year was supposed to be his year. While New York waited, his plays were done in Rochester, Philadelphia and New Haven. If his work had been staged with greater frequency, especially in New York, he would have been encouraged to write more plays. As is true with the majority of playwrights, he had to support himself through other activities like teaching.

The first time I saw one of his plays was in 1978, in a tiny Off Off Broadway theater. The play was *Modigliani*, a deeply sensitive study of the struggle of the creative spirit, as represented by Modigliani, a classic case of the neglected artist. When Modigliani cried, in the play, "I need a sale. Any sale. I need recognition," you could hear the playwright's own plea. McIntyre said later in an interview that it had taken him 12 years to get the play produced.

After its initial run, *Modigliani* transferred Off Broadway and became a modest success. One would have thought that, next time, producers would be more responsive to his work. Instead, the next play followed the same pattern. *Split Second*, a bruising contemporary drama about a black police officer's crisis of conscience, was rejected by almost 60 theaters and producers. It was presented only when a director, Samuel Barton, came across a script in the files of the Negro Ensemble Company. The play was given a showcase production by the director's own company.

In reviewing *Split Second*, I again expressed enthusiasm for the work of McIntyre and regretted that the play had been overlooked by institutional theaters. Rare for a work by a white playwright, *Split Second* was written from a black point of view with astonishing authenticity. For the second time, a play of his transferred for an extended run Off Broadway. Although the door opened slightly in terms of his future, McIntyre remained one of our theater's best kept secrets.

With his next two plays, he moved to regional theater. *National Anthems*, an excoriating examination of American values, received its premiere at the Geva Theater in Rochester, where it was acclaimed by this critic and others. While *National Anthems* moved on, with success, to a new production at the Long Wharf Theater in New Haven, another play *Established Price*, opened at the Philadelphia Festival Theater for New Plays. In this, his last work, he studied the dehumanizing aspects of a corporate buyout. Repeating the route of *National Anthems*, *Established Price* was restaged at Long Wharf (in a production starring Jason

Robards). Both plays were optioned for Broadway, but neither was seen in New York in McIntyre's lifetime.

Rejection, of course, can be endemic to the life of the playwright. It can come so quickly that the playwright may wonder if the mailman is not also the play reader. More often, the wait is interminable, as scripts grow old on the desks of producers. Every playwright has a horror story.

One special problem for McIntyre - it should have been an advantage - was that each of his plays was so different. Producers did not know what to expect. Thinking about his work, I was reminded of a novelist friend who was criticized by her editor because he could not categorize her books. Her response: did he want her to write the same novel over and over again? One might ask the same thing of producers in reference to McIntyre's plays.

If these producers had been truly perceptive, they would have realized that his plays have common themes, beginning with the author's profound concern with individualism, with people striving for achievement and being blocked by the traumatizing effects of society. All of his plays are also elevated by his gift for characterization and dialogue - conversational but poetic and scrupulously in character whether he was dealing with denizens of the Left Bank or New York streets. He had an uncanny ear and a compassion for the downtrodden in all areas of life.

Last weekend, McIntyre's friends gathered to pay tribute in the Astor Place Theater, once the setting for *Modigliani*. From lifelong friends, one received a picture of a troubled child and an imaginative man who found his purpose as a playwright. Following in the footsteps of Arthur Miller, he wrote plays at the University of Michigan and won the prestigious Hopwood Prize. Then, entering the theater, he began facing obstacles.

Arvin Brown, who directed McIntyre's last two plays at Long Wharf, expressed his anger at the neglect of this underappreciated artist. Mr. Brown added that McIntyre was a "true collaborator," a playwright who was nurtured by working with actors on a production. While looking forward to New York productions of his plays, one can also regret the plays that remained unwritten because more theaters - and foundations - did not take advantage of him as an artistic resource in residence. Although I knew McIntyre only from his plays, I share with his friends a sense of personal loss.

TERRENCE MCNALLY

THE LISBON TRAVIATA: JUNE 7, 1989

In *The Lisbon Traviata*, Terrence McNally has written the theatrical equivalent of an operatic double bill - an opéra bouffe followed by a tragic denouement. The first act, in the play's newly revised version, is a savagely amusing and empathetic study of two men whose lives have been lost in opera. The second act is discordant, as it was in the play's earlier showcase production in 1985.

Since the play was first presented, it has gone through alterations, all of which are improvements and help to bridge the difference between the two acts. John Tillinger's new production, which opened last night at the Manhattan Theater Club, is even sharper than his original at Theater Off Park. The performances by Anthony Heald and, in particular, by Nathan Lane, are among the finest offered by these estimable actors. But the author has not solved the play's structural problems.

In the first act, we are sequestered in a richly baroque apartment - itself a kind of red plush opera box - with the host, Mendy (Mr. Lane), and his guest, Stephen (Mr. Heald). Both are addicted to the genius and the memory of Maria Callas, almost to the point of exclusion of all other singers, whom they dismiss with the most excoriating remarks. One does not have to be a music critic to appreciate Mr. McNally's wit and his encyclopedic knowledge of the art form under scrutiny.

When Mr. Heald mentions an obscure pirated recording of a Callas "Traviata" performed in Lisbon, Mr. Lane is swept away in anticipation. That recording, still unheard by him, becomes a kind of Holy Grail.

In the first version of the play, the dialogue between the two men was almost too funny. Though Mr. McNally still cannot resist ridiculing his artistic peers (past and present), the act has been reshaped so that laughter is underscored with portent. As the two reveal themselves through their references to opera and to their own relationship, we can sense the abject loneliness and the desperation of both characters. The first act is tragedy in the guise of comedy.

Mr. Lane, formerly married and the father of a son (as he says, "Callas was named in my divorce for alienation of affections") is, for all his campiness, filled with feelings of immense insecurity. He is, one might say, all show and no follow-through. In contrast, Mr. Heald's character is as obsessed by love as he is by opera, to the point of confusing the two.

The play is an ambitious attempt to confront demons absent or suppressed in the playwright's other, engaging work. Mr. McNally is taking himself and his subject with the utmost seriousness. For a long time, we are held by his acuity -and by the intensity of Mr. Tillinger's direction. The audience's anticipation at the end of the first act almost equals that of Mr. Lane awaiting the recording of *The Lisbon Traviata*.

The second act moves to the apartment Mr. Heald shares with Dan Butler, an apartment that is the absolute opposite of Mr. Lane's - cleanly and stylishly modern (two splendid set designs by Philipp Jung). As is soon evident, the two halves of the play are as disparate as the settings.

In his home, Mr. Heald is unable to come to terms with what he considers to be Mr. Butler's betrayal. The latter is involved in a new liaison, which Mr. Heald, with carefully orchestrated malevolence, tries to torpedo. Though the confrontation retains the play's earlier vituperativeness, it swims into banal dramatic waters, as the homosexual characters echo clichés from fiction about heterosexual couples. Mr. Heald becomes the spurned "wife" deserted for a younger love and crazed in a pursuit of retribution. While the violent conclusion may seem inevitable in the context of opera, it is not convincing in this domestic drama.

The two minor roles, though deftly played by Mr. Butler and John Slattery, are undeveloped. Mr. Heald's character is, in the new version of the play, a book editor rather than a struggling playwright, but he still courts self-pity. Despite his supposed revelations, emotionally we learn little more about him than we knew in the first act.

At the same time, Mendy (Mr. Lane) does not appear after the first act. Mendy, the ultimate opera lover, the man who by his own admission is "too much for most people," becomes a supporting player in a drama in which he has earned a starring role. In a difficult assignment, Mr. Heald artfully avoids overstatement. But it is Mr. Lane who deserves the highest praise for a brilliant performance as a man doomed to live an ordinary life while aspiring to the ecstasy of opera.

DAVID MAMET

SEXUAL PERVERSITY IN CHICAGO AND DUCK VARIATIONS: NOVEMBER 1, 1975

From Chicago comes a talented new playwright, David Mamet, in an auspicious New York debut at St. Clement's. His two oddly matched one acts are fresh and pungent comedies about the rivalry within friendship and man's natural propensity for role playing.

The first play is tantalizingly entitled *Sexual Perversity in Chicago*, but expect no perversity or pornography (more like anthropology) although the language is salty. The four-character comedy deals with the mating habits of young people today - which seem not so different from the mating habits of young people any day.

Two Chicago chums, office-mates, Danny and Bernard, are on the constant prowl for women. Bernard is a swaggerer with delusions of machismo. He never gets to first base, while the modest Danny easily scores a home run. The play is not just about the tightrope romance of Danny and Deborah (a cheerful liberated woman) but about male and female bondings. Romance puts a strain on friendship. Bernard masks his envy with derision and Deborah's schoolteacher roommate is above the battle but not above being abusive. They know the affair is going to end badly - and they can hardly wait.

As directed by Albert Takazauckas, the play is a multi-paneled comic strip, with the action merrily hopping from bar to bedroom and finally to the seashore, where the boys are beached in their true avocation: ogling. Inevitably, a few of the panels miss, but on the whole Mr. Mamet's satiric aim is deadly. His cast, all new faces, seem to have a clear identification with the material. The work on all counts is unforced and spontaneous, with particularly ingratiating performances by Robert Picardo and Jane Anderson as Danny and Deborah.

In the second play, *Duck Variations*, we are suddenly in the world of the elderly, which is not to say that sex is a dead issue. Mr. Mamet's two loquacious oldsters, friends who chat over a park bench, are scandalous liars, each impressing himself more than his rival.

Their freewheeling conversation is basically about the natural world - ducks vs. the blue heron, the barnyard rules of order, animal misbehavior. Like vaudeville clowns, they swap tall tales and trade pseudo-sagacities (One says, "No man is an island unto himself"; the other answers, "Or anyone else either").

This play has some of the sound and flavor of the best Second City skits (such as Alan Arkin's classic portrait of an aged pretzel vendor). Even the wildest statements are dryly understated. The play goes on a bit too long - it is surprising how many things can be said about ducks - but the author never loses our attention or his sense of humor.

Paul Sparer, whose reputation has been built on Ibsen and Chekhov, proves eminently engaging in Mamet, adopting an accent you couldn't cut with chicken fat. Alone, he is a funny dialect comedian. Together with Michael Egan (equally amusing as the self-proclaimed expert on the blue heron) he is a comedy sketch. They are a pair of radiant sunshine boys, and Mr. Mamet's plays are a welcome gust of laughter from Chicago.

THE WATER ENGINE: MAY 14, 1977

CHICAGO - Charles Lang, the fictional hero of David Mamet's new play, *The Water Engine*, is a lowly punch-press operator and amateur tinkerer. In his home workshop he manages to remove the H from H_2O and - eureka! - he invents an engine that uses plain distilled water as fuel. The effects could have been revolutionary were it not for a small matter of Big Business.

Mr. Mamet's play (at the St. Nicholas Theater), is about the greed of corporations and the strangulation of individual enterprise. In other words, this "American fable" is about the failure of the American dream.

As we know from *Sexual Perversity in Chicago*, *American Buffalo* and *A Life in the Theater*, Mr. Mamet is an inventive playwright as well as Chicago's foremost young man of the theater. Mamet plays have their own idiomatic identity - a language that in another context in *The Water Engine* is referred to as "concrete poetry."

The playwright's weakness is usually in the area of plot. In contrast to his other plays, *The Water Engine* is talk and action - with a plot so intricate that it could serve as a subject for a Hollywood epic. It is the reverse of *Alexander Graham Bell* and *Young Tom Edison*. Lang becomes not a legend, but an enemy of the people. He is an American cousin of Alec Guinness in *The Man in the White Suit*. In this work, Mr. Mamet is moving into Kafka country. Lang, trapped in a labyrinth of avarice, does not know what's happening to him.

The Water Engine began its life as a radio play, and the author had not attempted to disguise its origins. He uses radio as a framework for social commentary. Actors sit at microphones and pretend to be a network of news broadcasters and spot announcers. The drama is punctuated by sound effects - the cacophony of Chicago in 1934. One of the evening's definite assets is John Carey's crackling sound design.

This is the time of the Century of Progress Exposition. The show, part radio play, part illustrated lecture, is presented as if it were a stop on a guided tour of the Hall of Science. This is a provocative platform for a play, but *The Water Engine*, as a theatrical invention, seems to be still in blueprint. It is sketchy and schematic.

The work might benefit from a fuller production. When *The Water Engine* shifts from the broadcast table into the life of the inventor, the actors work with a minimum of props and scenery. Lang's elaborate workshop is described, rather than observed, except for the water engine itself, which looks like a coffee filter with a pinwheel attached. Despite the physical limitations of Steven Schachter's production, the play moves with reasonable effectiveness from factory to street to exposition grounds, largely through the efforts of the active cast's doubling and tripling in roles. The only actor who really has a character to play is W.H. Macy. Wearing a cardigan, with stubble on his chin and a perpetual frown, Mr. Macy is intense as the incorruptible inventor - a man obsessed by an impractical vision.

The St. Nicholas, a small regional theater and one of the leaders in a burgeoning Chicago Off Broadway-type movement, was founded three years ago by Mr. Mamet, Mr. Schachter, Mr. Macy and Patricia Cox. Having presented a number of Mamet premieres, it has become known as the author's home base. The theater, a former bakery, is snug. The company is industrious. The playwright continues to be a theatrical explorer. *The Water Engine* is his sardonic, though still tentative, expedition into the halls of science, commerce and conscience.

A LIFE IN THE THEATER: OCTOBER 21, 1977

David Mamet is a playwright who loves the theater - the mystery, the illusions, the code of behavior. His glorious new comedy, *A Life in the Theater*, which opened last night at the Theater de Lys, is a short play written with humor, affection and sophistication. It is an evening of pure theater.

When the play had its premiere last winter at the Goodman Theater in Chicago, I described it as a comedy about the artifice of acting. Seeing it again in Gerald Gutierrez's Off Broadway production, featuring an exhilarating performance by Ellis Rabb as the older of two actors, it is clear that it is also about the artifice of living.

Mr. Mamet's approach is deceptively simple. In a series of scenes we see two actors - a seasoned professional (Mr. Rabb) and a novice (Peter Evans) - backstage and onstage going through a cycle of roles and an entire wardrobe of costumes. With a sigh that could sink a ship, Mr. Rabb says, "Ephemera! Ephemera!", summing up his livelihood. Acting is for the moment, and Mr. Mamet has captured moments that add up to a lifetime. The play is like that beautiful Zero Mostel sketch, *An Actor Prepares*, extended into Marcel Marceau's seven ages of man.

The comedy deals not only with two actors, but with teacher and pupil, mentor and disciple, and the rites of passage. In the beginning, Mr. Rabb leads - dogmatically and deliciously - and Mr. Evans follows as if he were a pet on a leash. He is so eager to please that it is as if he had no opinion. Gradually, the roles begin to change; in the end, it is Mr. Rabb who lights the younger man's cigarette, who becomes his shadow. At times they are as antic as vaudevillians, using each other as targets. A master of stage lore and etiquette, the older actor knows, and has played, all the tricks. Even in a wheelchair he can upstage the younger man. Egos are rampant. Each always seems to be inspecting himself in a mirror.

On stage, in malicious Mamet spoofs of everything from Chekhov to romantic melodrama, the two suffer a compendium of acting accidents. Lines are blown, properties collapse, wigs fly off, cues are askew. In one uproarious sequence, Mr. Rabb is forced to play a scene with his zipper undone - an actor's nightmare - and in characteristic fashion, the graceful actor performs with utmost delicacy (and swift movements) to conceal his embarrassment from the audience.

Off stage, in a dressing room as tiny and as cluttered as a cupboard, they exchange close-quartered camaraderie and an occasional elbow in each other's ribs.

Later, they sit at makeup tables littered with the detritus of the profession, practice at the barre, and wait impatiently in the wings.

Though the work has serious undertones, it is, first of all, a comedy - and Mr. Mamet's language glistens. His writing is a cross between the elegant and the vernacular, an ironic combination that is uniquely his own. Much of the buoyant humor also occurs between the lines - in daggered looks, portentous pauses and incisive silences. The playwright's timing is as exact as Accutron.

Since the Chicago premiere, Mr. Mamet has slightly expanded his play - it now runs 90 minutes - and added a third, silent character, who changes the scenery. The original production had a free-flowing spontaneity and there was a balance between the performers, who played it as if it were Story Theater. Mr. Gutierrez's staging is more structured and the play is now more of a performance piece.

Ellis Rabb wears his role as if it were a tailor-made theatrical cape of many colors. He gives a grand performance, with a panache and glamour of a Barrymore, crisply slicing his syllables, extracting the comic essence from every innuendo. He is so much in character that, when called for, he can even play a bad ham actor convincingly. In a far less flamboyant role, Mr. Evans is an intelligent and agile buffer; much of his performance is reacting to his fellow actor.

Another change - and improvement - from Chicago to New York is John Lee Beatty's ingenious set. The actors face two audiences - those of us in the theater and the imaginary audience on the other side of the stage, represented by the designer's clever twist of stage perspective (a backdrop that recedes to minuscule exit signs).

The actors play to that imaginary audience, while we, behind the scenes, see and hear the artifice - the asides, whispers and blunders. In a poignant pair of scenes, each acts to an empty house and the other, not so silently, watches. We eavesdrop on the eavesdroppers - a triple Pirandello for this acrobatic playwright.

Mr. Mamet proves in this play, as he has in other works, that he is an eloquent master of two-part harmony. An abundantly gifted playwright, he brings new life to the theater.

AMERICAN BUFFALO: OCTOBER 26, 1980

NEW HAVEN - David Mamet's *American Buffalo* becomes richer with every viewing. One sign of its quality is its malleability. I have seen four interpretations of the play - the latest, Arvin Brown's vivid production at the Long Wharf Theater, starring Al Pacino as Teach, a role that seems made-to-measure for his talent - and each is distinct. The play takes on different colorations, depending on the director, the shape of the stage and the cast, especially the actor playing Teach, the edgy agitated catalyst of the drama. To a certain extent, as Teach goes, so goes *American Buffalo.*

In Gregory Mosher's Off Off Broadway production at St. Clement's in 1976, Teach was Mike Kellin, a character actor who is adept at playing homespun antiheroes. His woeful countenance is a canvas for comic pathos. Even at his angriest, Mr. Kellin's Teach seemed hapless, a habitual offender magnetically drawn into petty crime. The production itself stressed the seedy authenticity of the locale, a jumbled Chicago junk shop, a way station for Mr. Mamet's trio of lesser lives - the good-natured proprietor, Donny Dubrow; his eager young disciple, Bobby; and the aggressive Teach.

In Ulu Grosbard's excellent Broadway version the following year, the play became larger and more dramatic. It was charged with intensity, and a primary reason was the casting of Robert Duvall as Teach. Mr. Duvall can assume diverse personalities - from Sherlock Holmes's Dr. Watson to the daredevil officer in *Apocalypse Now*. In *American Buffalo*, he exuded menace; he was tough and mean. The director stressed the tautness of the situation. The evening was pregnant with portent and when Mr. Duvall struck Bobby (John Savage) across the head with an iron, it was a sudden, but not unexpected, outbreak of violence and it sent a shudder through the audience.

The British production at the National Theater was, in all respects, a transplant. Three English actors managed to approximate urban American accents, but they lacked the proper American sensibility. Bobby, for example, was portrayed as a kind of punk rocker. This was the broadest of the four productions, even to uncovering a line of latent homosexuality between Donny and Bobby. Jack Shepherd's Teach was a flashy East End hoodlum, and the production was brisk, almost breakneck. While vitiating many of the values of the play, the National Theater made one aware of the work's comic nature.

The Long Wharf production restores the humor, but, unlike the London version, it is genuinely funny, easily the most amusing *American Buffalo* I have seen. At the same time, it does not sacrifice the sense of imminent danger. First of all, the open, three-sided stage, with an appropriately detailed but not cluttered setting by Marjorie Kellogg, offers a most intimate environment. It pulls us into the play. *American Buffalo* was not an ideal candidate for a big Broadway stage. It led the audience to have certain dramatic expectations, and as anyone who has seen the play knows, there is not much physical action in the course of the evening. The movement is interior and verbal.

The play begins with Donny, a role that seems reserved for overweight actors - Clifton James at Long Wharf. That heaviness is endemic to Donny's sedentary life. One thinks of him in a swivel chair, making deals by telephone or sitting at a card table eating coffee cake from the nearby Riverside diner. Unseen on stage, another play appears to be taking place at the Riverside; perhaps it could be a companion piece to *American Buffalo*. Mr. James's portrait is of an archetypal junk shop owner, and the same thing could be said about the two other actors who played the role in New York; they could have exchanged productions. At Long Wharf, Thomas Waites's Bobby is drawn along the lines of his Broadway predecessor, John Savage, with an added note of head-bobbing nervousness. To date, Mr. Savage has offered the most authoritative rendering of this flighty character.

When Mr. Pacino makes his entrance on the Long Wharf stage, the play accelerates in a fresh direction . It is not that he is better than Mr. Duvall; he is different, as different as they were in *The Godfather*. In Mr. Pacino's hands, the character becomes street-smart, cocksure and self-mocking. He knows what he wants - he wants to steal a coin collection in a late-night raid on a neighbor's home - but his characterization is of a man in distress. He looks disheveled, a man who has been lying awake nights dreaming about scores and scams.

Mr. Pacino could have approached the character somewhat in the style of his two early New York stage successes, *The Indian Wants the Bronx* and *Does a Tiger Wear a Necktie?*, emphasizing Teach's retributive sense of malice. Instead, he chooses to look for the comic insecurity. He is always on the move, restlessly skittering through the junk shop as if it were a cage. His hands entwine a rubber band; he himself is a cat's cradle of anxieties. He rummages through the merchandise, leftovers from other lives, studying every object quizzically, searching for an identification.

Of all the characters Mr. Pacino has played in films and on stage, his Teach is perhaps closest to his disturbed and disoriented bank robber in *Dog Day Afternoon*. In common, each gets carried away. When Teach realizes that the burglary plan is swerving out of control, we can feel his desperation. Without losing the character's willfulness, Mr. Pacino makes him seem perplexed; his reactions are intuitive rather than conceptualized. Fueled by frustration, he is unpredictable, and his act of violence against Bobby seems almost accidental. More than his predecessors, Mr. Pacino seems to relate to his fellow cast members. We feel a real alliance among them. Working in close harmony, the trio of actors communicates the play's tension as well as its playfulness.

That playfulness is primarily in the dialogue - a shower of vulgarities that still disturbs some theatergoers. Mr. Mamet has been criticized for the limits of his vocabulary. Actually, within his chosen lexicon, he is extremely inventive. In fact, not since Michael McClure's controversial play *The Beard* has a playwright used the vernacular to such specific and valuable artistic purpose.

On one level, *American Buffalo* is a play about language - the repetitions, contradictions and elisions that make up daily speech and that often disguise feelings. What we omit is often more important than what we reveal, and meaning can be implied from intonation. Just as any word can become an epithet - the most obvious example is any reference to the deity - the most seemingly insulting statement can become a kind of compliment or it can be used to humorous effect. Mr. Mamet gets a hammerlock on clichés, twisting them into new images and malaprops. His characters alternate monosyllables with ornate phrasings, as people do in life. He diagrams the sudden stops and starts of conversation, perfectly capturing the shorthand of human communication.

Here is Mr. Mamet at work (and at play): Donny, on the phone: "If I could get ahold of some of the stuff you were interested in, would you be interested in some of it?" Or Teach, explaining why he is carrying a gun, "God forbid, something inevitable occurs."

More than anything, this is a play about business against friendship. In business people take care of their own interests. In friendship, they take care of one another. Problems arise when friends do business together and are confronted by a conflict of self-interest and loyalty. Donny wants to send Bobby on the burglary, as an act of faith and as part of the young man's training. Teach fears the boy's ineptitude, and he also wants to do the job himself - for profit and as a demonstration of his own virility. The job can be his comeback.

By extension, this could be a play about men in battle. They are about to begin an operation, but first they question each other's right to command. The three enact a ritual of challenge and response, of retreat and advance, always measuring each other's vulnerabilities.

This is the second modern American play that Mr. Pacino has revived soon after its original production. The first was David Rabe's *The Basic Training of Pavlo Hummel*. The actor has chosen wisely. In each case he has confirmed a play's position in our dramatic literature and he has staked out an impressive claim to a challenging contemporary role.

LAKEBOAT: FEBRUARY 17, 1982

NEW HAVEN - Sailing through the season's slough is David Mamet's *Lakeboat*, a small gem at Long Wharf Theater's Stage Two. *Lakeboat* is Mr. Mamet's *Life on the Mississippi* - the artist as young river pilot, or, in Mr. Mamet's case, lakeboat steward. Through his eyes, we see a cross-section of flavorful characters, imparting lore, both landlocked and seaworthy.

The play, apparently the first by Mr. Mamet. was originally staged by John Dillon at the Milwaukee Repertory Company. In a revised version, it is briskly redirected by Mr. Dillon at Long Wharf. The work is close in spirit to the author's other early short plays, combining the counterpointed style of *Sexual Perversity in Chicago* with the shaggy tale-telling of *Duck Variations*. Whatever the provenance of *Lakeboat*. the writing is effortless and intuitive. It is a composition on "My Summer Vacation," and easily the best paper in class.

The author's spokesman, a young college student (David Marshall Grant), ships aboard the lakeboat T. Harrison on the Great Lakes. The play is his dramatized logbook and also his rite of passage, as old salts - and a few young ones - fill his ears with the wonder of their stories of seduction and their recurrent dreams.

John Spencer, as a down-to-earth seaman with the looks but not the laconic manner of Steve McQueen in *The Sand Pebbles*, unravels the yarn of his first sexual conquest, a hilarious Rabelaisian tale of four-star male chauvinism. In contrast, there is Larry Shue as a taciturn malingerer, who seems less like a sailor than a stowaway. In a moment of reflection, he confesses that he once wanted to be a ballet dancer, and his eyes light up at the memory. What makes the scene so amusing is that Mr. Shue is the last person one could imagine lifting a swan on stage.

Mr. Mamet's crew repeatedly reveals sudden turns of personality, delivered with such sincerity that we come to be believers - and some of the tales are as tall as Twain. One of the saltiest seamen is played by Clarence Felder. His job, he insists in a loud voice, is watching, not doing. He is all brawn and bluster and always seems on the verge of exploding, but occasionally he interjects an insight, as in his statement, "This boat's becoming a bureaucracy."

Highest in the hierarchy is the captain, called Skippy, and played with comic dispatch by Dominic Chianese. He introduces Mr. Grant to his duty by demanding to know what his F-and-E number is. The boyish Mr. Grant stares blankly even after the captain explains that the initials stand for fire and evacuation.

In this journey, there is neither fire nor evacuation, and not even a hint of adventure. Mr. Grant's most demanding assignment is to make a constant supply of egg sandwiches for the men on watch. Even the slapdash sandwiches are a source of amusement; the food disappears into a bottomless maw, and there is none for the captain.

Time stands still on the boat - a suitably seedy design by Laura Maurer - a fact that often catches characters off-guard. A seaman rushes on deck to announce breathlessly that one of the men "lost two fingers in the main winch." Asked when the accident occurred, he answers matter of factly, "A couple - four, five years ago." The plot, what there is of it, occurs off stage on land and deals with the man that Mr. Grant has replaced. No one seems to know exactly why he failed to report for duty, although for some inexplicable reason everyone assumes that he has been mugged by a whore in Chicago.

Watching the play, one is reminded not only of *Life on the Mississippi*, but also of *Mister Roberts*, as the craft plies its path from Tedium to Apathy. But there is no war to look forward to, and no tyrannical captain to rebel against. *Lakeboat* is like life, slightly askew. Wide-eyed and receptive, Mr. Grant is marking time between semesters and having the time of his life. The play is short - 80 minutes without intermission - but it is substantial, and it is as zestful as a breeze over Lake Michigan.

EDMOND: JUNE 17, 1982

CHICAGO - In David Mamet's new play, *Edmond*, the portrait of a man swept away by a wave of events beyond his control is as bleak and relentless as that in Buechner's *Woyzeck*, a play with which it shares common ground. The title character of Mr. Mamet's drama, in its premiere at the Goodman Theater, swirls from rejection to desperation to a homicide that seems almost involuntary. Woyzeck is the essential uneducated common man; Edmond is a middle-class contemporary suburbanite, but Mr. Mamet clearly sees him as a representative of an abused underclass.

The landscape in *Edmond* is New York-by-nightmare, a misguided tour of a netherworld. Walking out on his wife, the protagonist (Colin Stinton) searches for sexual release and finds himself victimized in a series of entrapments - by pimps, whores and street con men. Early in his career, the author wrote *Sexual Perversity in Chicago*, a jaunty comedy about young men looking for romance. *Edmond* is that play's dark opposite - a Walpurgis vortex about a man's uncontrollable panic in a threatening environment.

While I prefer the earlier Mamet - the openness and youthful euphoria of *Lakeboat*, his boy's life on Lake Michigan, and his menacing comedy of friendship, *American Buffalo* - there is no denying the dramatic impact of his latest work. It is not an easy play to like, but it will be a difficult one to forget.

The play begins on a note of mysticism. Edmond (his last name is Burke, for reasons undisclosed by the author) visits a fortune teller who projects him on a fatalistic course - dozens of short, sharp scenes that move from naiveté to mordancy. At first, his journey deals with sexual economics. He bargains for favors and is repeatedly cheated. Frustration turns him into an urban vigilante. Before he realizes it, he is speaking and acting like a redneck racist and male chauvinist. He cannot prevent his descent into madness. Later, when he is asked if he has killed someone, he replies, apathetically, "I don't care."

Prison becomes a kind of final domicile for the annihilation of self. In the last and most striking sequence in the play he and his domineering cellmate sit, spotlighted on their bunks, and speak about man's inability to control his destiny. Condemned to their fate, they try to comprehend it. They suggest that they are animals (a final evocation of *Woyzeck*) - and that animals are their superiors, perhaps even intelligent creatures from outer space. By their measure, life for humans is hell on earth.

The cellmate, played by Paul Butler, is the only character other than Edmond who achieves an individuality, and he does that largely with his strong silent presence. The other 25 characters, played by nine actors, are voices in limbo.

The writing is terse, the scenes staccato; by comparison, Mr. Mamet's other work seems verbose. The play is short and intermissionless. Mr. Mamet has squeezed it almost dry of humor and color, and what little comedy remains seems accidental. At times the work seems like a skeleton for a play still to be fleshed out.

Coordinately, Gregory Mosher's production is often as spare as that of a workshop. A few tables, chairs and counters serve interchangeably although the locale shifts from bars to peep shows to prison. One could imagine a more extensive production, including a background of music, and also a more emotional performance than the one given by Mr. Stinton. But elaboration in writing and performance might act against the starkness of Mr. Mamet's vision. *Edmond* is a brutish, unsparing, sleepless night of a play.

SPEED-THE-PLOW: MAY 18, 1988

In an essay entitled, *A Playwright in Hollywood*, David Mamet said that he was not asking for altruism on the part of movie producers, "just a little creative venality." His uproarious new play, *Speed-the-Plow*, makes it clear that hypocrisy and greed are no assurance of profit and that art is less than a by-product in Hollywood. Even as he himself has mastered the medum (as the screenwriter of *The Untouchables* and as the auteur of *House of Games*), he has never forgotten that the people in the movie business are "interested solely in making a buck on the buck they put out." Assailing Hollywood, Mr. Mamet speaks with authority, and in *Speed-the-Plow* he spites the hand that needs him. Hollywood can and will take it. He is too valuable to ignore.

For years, critics have talked about Mamet's Ear. Let us now speak about his Nose. He can sniff out a fishmonger no matter what his profession, be it real estate (as in *Glengarry Glen Ross*) or the movies. Bobby Gould (Joe Mantegna) and Charlie Fox (Ron Silver), scheming sidekicks and rivals since they worked in the mail room, will do anything to sit at the Hollywood "Big Table", while pretending to have an intuition about the medium. As Mr. Silver says, "There are films that, whaddyacallit, make it worthwhile." Actually he is not talking about the possible adaptation of *The Bridge*, the end-of-the-world, anti-radiation novel by an "Eastern sissy writer," but about a jailhouse buddy movie starring Doug Brown, the mythical box-office king in *Speed-the-Plow*.

As the self-impaling lines fly back and forth between the two, the author pinions the characters for their egocentricity and their complete lack of taste. One recalls an earlier Mamet writing about other media, namely the theater and radio. In both cases, his attitude was one of great affection. *A Life in the Theater* was a celebration of actors and of the art of acting. In his many radio plays, including, most notably, *The Water Engine*, the author showed a deep appreciation of the broadcasting medium, where he learned to create scenery with words. Radio plays threw him back on his first love - language.

Mr. Mamet's feeling about stage and radio is akin to his memories of working on a boat in the Great Lakes, a part of his life that inspires *Lakeboat*, one of his gentlest comedies and one of the few longer Mamet plays that has not yet been done in New York. In *Lakeboat*, there was an atmosphere of youthful adventure reminiscent of Mark Twain. In common, these plays are romances of a kind.

In direct contrast are *American Buffalo*, *Glengarry Glen Ross* and *Speed-the-Plow* - plays that explore a harsher, even a sinister side of life. The three share that Mamet theme of "doing business," of "business as usual," in which personal feelings are not allowed to intrude on what passes for professionalism. At the same time, each of the works raises the matter of the limits of loyalty, which in a dog-eat-dog world is always superseded by self- interest and the survival instinct. One can only carry friendships so far - and not as far as the bank.

Mr. Mantegna is glad that Mr. Silver has brought him the Doug Brown movie package, that he has "stuck with the Old Firm" instead of going "Across the Street" to the other studio. In a showdown, everyone can be sacrificed. None of the three plays could be remotely regarded as a celebration. However, they are filled with laughter, and none more than *Speed-the-Plow*, a play that is as sharp as a buzz saw.

The role-players may look different but Hollywood has not really changed since the days of studio moguls. The principle, as always, is to try to imitate success, to "make the thing everyone made last year." Though producers are fond of calling the movies "a people business," money talks and power listens. It is power, not money, that is at the root of the process, having and using the ability to, in Mr. Mantegna's words, "decide, decide, decide." Whoever has the power for a millisecond can determine what the public can choose to see. The audience is the last to have its say, although, if given the choice of the Doug Brown buddy movie or the radiation epic, many of us would stay home and watch a favorite film on the VCR.

Several questions arise from *Speed-the-Plow*, beginning with the meaning of the title. Supposedly it is a farming expression meaning good luck, but, in context, it is filled with innuendo. One could regard it literally, as a commentary on Hollywood business-as-usual, as in "speed the plow through the same old furrow." Another question concerns the author's attitude toward the anti-radiation novel. Certainly there is no satiric edge to the excerpts quoted in the play. The obvious conclusion is that Mr. Mamet is equally cynical about those who want to save our lives and those who want to wreck our lives.

The final question concerns the third member of the cast, Madonna, playing the demure office temporary. In her Broadway debut, she has the challenge of acting opposite Mr. Mantegna and Mr. Silver, who, under Gregory Mosher's dynamic direction, are shewd, fast and immensely funny - experts at playing Mamet. Although Madonna is overshadowed by her colleagues, that would seem to be at least partly intentional. She is playing the character as conceived by the author. In the purest sense, she is an ingenue - unknowing in Hollywood - not a crafty Eve Harrington plotting her way to stardom or studio chiefdom. She is sincere, self-effacing and tightly controlled. To further her goals, in this case the filming of the anti-radiation book, she is prepared to be manipulative.

As with other Mamet heroines (the few that there are), the character has an other-worldliness. In that sense, she is related to the protagonist of the movie *House of Games*, played by Lindsay Crouse, and to the character that Ms. Crouse portrayed in an earlier Mamet play, *The Shawl*. In both of those cases, a woman is drawn into a confidence game. With Madonna, it is the confidence game of Hollywood.

From *Sexual Perversity in Chicago* through *Speed-the-Plow*, Mr. Mamet's plays have been male-dominated. Each takes place in a man's world, and women remain on the periphery (except in *The Woods*). One waits until they enter the center ring. Meanwhile, Broadway nights are brightened by *Speed-the-Plow*, the wittiest and most fiendish comedy about American business since Mr. Mamet's own *Glengarry Glen Ross*.

"You ruined my life," says Mr. Silver, the suddenly spurned producer. His heart not touched, his rhino hide intact, Mr. Mantegna reflexively responds, "Be that as it may," and gets on with his uncreative venality.

EMILY MANN

EXECUTION OF JUSTICE: MARCH 14, 1986

In Emily Mann's *Execution of Justice*, the case of the People vs. Dan White is on trial in the court of theater and is found guilty of a miscarriage of justice. That conclusion is reached after a thought-provoking evening that is scrupulous in its quest for objectivity. With the playwright acting as investigative reporter, the play is not a polemic but a judicious assessment of a turbulent episode in recent American political history.

Written and directed by Ms. Mann, the play opened last night at the Virginia Theater after previous productions at a number of America's regional theaters. During the work's journey to Broadway, Ms. Mann has carefully distilled the text, eliminating testimony that might be considered extraneous or hortatory.

The basic facts of the case are: In a double-barreled act of violence in November 1978, Dan White killed George Moscone, the Mayor of San

Francisco, and Harvey Milk, a city Supervisor and the first avowed homosexual to hold high public office in that city. After a trial that polarized San Francisco the following year, the accused was convicted on the lesser charge of voluntary manslaughter and sentenced to seven years and eight months in prison. He was released in January 1984 after serving a little more than five years, and last fall he took his own life.

The trial had political reverberations and more than the usual set of court-room contradictions. The killer, himself a former Supervisor and Army veteran, had been a policeman and a fireman. As a spokesman for law and order, he is heard saying, in one of the play's many telling lines, "This city isn't safe," ignoring the fact that he himself was a threat.

Mr. White was vigorously supported by members of the police department. Ironically, the chief inspector of homicide was an old friend of the accused and became his chief character witness. Because the prosecutor was apparently wary of the caloric temper of the community, similar testimony was not solicited to vouch for the moral character of the deceased. The victims were further victimized by the public perception of them as outsiders. One watches the play -and this is the third time I have seen it in different productions - with a sense of outrage, not only at the miscarriage but at what the play suggests about a public and legal mind-set that allows criminals to avoid just punishment.

The White case could have been a subject for fictionalization or for a documentary (as it was in the Academy Award-winning *The Life and Times of Harvey Milk*, excerpts from which appear in the play). Ms. Mann has chosen the more difficult middle ground of documentary drama. In an approach that she labels "theater of testimony," the text is drawn entirely from the trial and other records, supplemented by interviews. Nothing, presumably, is invented, and the facts speak for themselves.

While the author is notably more successful in this approach than was the case in other recent related plays (*In the Belly of the Beast, Dennis*), she pays a price for her method. By restricting herself to the record, she necessarily limits her authorial imagination. Some of the testimony is banal, as it evidently was in real life. The legal case was not brilliantly argued, though the advantage goes to the defense. Whether through neglect or complacency, the prosecution refrains from challenging jurors and overlooks important witnesses.

In an artful insertion, Ms. Mann partly compensates by letting us hear from "uncalled witnesses." A policeman who acted as White's guard makes it clear that the accused showed absolutely no remorse. The district attorney, whose political career was ended by the trial, declares, after the fact, that Mr. White was motivated by malice.

As director, the playwright has not always abetted her own script. In the Broadway production, the prosecutor (Gerry Bamman) fusses and fidgets - and is condescending in his cross-examination. This stage portrait of a prosecutor's incompetence could be an attempt to record accurately the attorney's manner in court, or it could be a case of an actor trying to embellish a role with character details - in other words, to make his man more dramatically interesting. In any case, the characterization is distracting - and several other actors are led into unnecessary histrionics. This was not true in Douglas C. Wager's production at the Arena Stage in Washington.

Ms. Mann utilizes some of Mr. Wager's hi-tech television techniques - as in an effective depiction of a candlelit parade - and a proscenium adaptation of Ming Cho Lee's set design. She has drawn excellent performances from a number of actors - Peter Friedman as the defense attorney; Isabell Monk, Earle Hyman, Donal Donnelly and Jon DeVries in a variety of roles; and, especially, from John Spencer as Dan White. Mr. Spencer holds firmly - and convincingly - to the conception of the accused as a man who believes in himself as a responsible public servant even as he commits his horrendous act.

Because of the need for exposition, the first act is discursive, but the second act brings the seemingly diffuse elements into focus. In a collage technique, testimony overlaps and counterpoint is created. The defense's argument, absurd but apparently conclusive, that Mr. White had "diminished capacity" due to an excessive ingestion of junk food, is supported by the testimony of psychiatric experts - in the play a self-satiric colloquy.

Perhaps the most bizarre testimony comes from the doctor who suggests that a gun be regarded as a "transitional object," clung to in situations of "anxiety and insecurity." In other words, an adult's version of a teddy bear. Such statements chill the theatergoer into understanding the climate of opinion and fear that produced the verdict. The play is a bold attempt to explore not just one crime but contemporary moral values and the criminal justice system.

JANE MARTIN

TALKING WITH: APRIL 4, 1982

LOUISVILLE, Ky. - The hit of last year's Festival of New American Plays was a 17-minute , one-woman play called *Twirler*. The author was anonymous. Since then, she has become pseudonymous, adopting the alias Jane Martin and writing 10 more short plays. Jon Jory put them all together under the title *Talking With*, and they represent a dramatist with an original voice and a talent for writing quintessential cameos. Ms. Martin is clearly a cousin to Flannery O'Connor and also to Carson McCullers, with a gift for Southern Gothic and flavorful local language, but with her own vision.

Twirler and its successors are theme-mates. They are tales about enthusiasms that become obsessions, eccentric confessionals that levitate with religious symbolism and gladsome humor. The best are stamped by a single image - the baton (or 'ton) that soars like a celestial rocket, the 20-odd lamps that an elderly woman keeps in her loft and treats as a high-wattage glass menagerie and, most touching of all, the 30 "Clear Glass Marbles" that represent the final month of a dying woman's life.

Two of the monologues are hilarious, and, coincidentally, both deal with the theater. In the first, an actress, about to go on stage, muses about the "unilateral" experience of appearing in the light before spectators in the dark. The second is the ultimate audition, with an actress - superbly controlled hysteria provided by Ellen Tobie - describing her bizarre choice of classic and modern pieces and proving that she will do anything to secure a role.

The 11 characters are played by individual actresses, but one could imagine one mercurial performer, such as Meryl Streep or Louisville's Susan Kingsley, spinning the cycle into a singular act of virtuosity, ending as a tattooed lady with Charybdis and Scylla on her chest.

Ms. Martin is apparently without ambition or excessive ego. Echoing the actress in her play *15 Minutes*, she would also seem to be worrying about "lacerating self-exposure." The playwright's anonymity is, of course, her own business, but the theater needs her creativity. Next step: two characters in a dialogue.

KEELY AND DU

MARCH 24, 1993

Louisville, Ky. - With violent protest erupting into murder, abortion has become a most explosive and exploitable political issue. The pseudonymous Jane Martin has stepped into this crisis and written a play that is compelling in its sense of urgency. As directed by Jon Jory, *Keely and Du* features superb performances by Julie Boyd and Anne Pitoniak in the title roles as a pregnant rape victim and a nurse who is firmly opposed to abortion.

This is a play that is bound to stir vigorous discussion wherever it is presented. In that regard, Ms. Martin has done for abortion what David Mamet did for sexual harassment in *Oleanna*. In her play, Ms. Martin imagines the horrifying possibility of a militant Christian organization in "our Lord's underground" kidnapping pregnant women at abortion clinics and forcing them to have their babies. The victim, Keely, who has been raped by her abusive former husband, awakens to find herself handcuffed to a hospital bed in a basement cell. As written by Ms. Martin and as fiercely portrayed by Ms. Boyd, the character is observed in all her rage and panic.

In a sequence of taut scenes, the playwright reveals her understanding of the intensity and the complexity of the arguments. To her astonishment, Keely even comes to respect the fact that her kidnappers are willing to go to the limit to defend their position. The play builds to the moment when the former husband, now a born-again Christian, visits the prisoner and begs forgiveness. Silently Ms. Boyd exudes the deepest hostility: his violation of her can never be forgiven, or forgotten.

With her first play, *Talking With*, a dozen years ago, Ms. Martin revealed her gift for depicting obsessive women in monologues of self-revelation. With *Keely and Du*, she moves forthrightly into a more challenging and dramatic arena. While dealing with irreconcilable conflicts, she reinforces the humanity at the heart of life and death decisions.

MARLANE MEYER

ETTA JENKS: APRIL 14, 1988

Etta Jenks arrives in Los Angeles hopeful, homeless and eager to become a movie star. Discouraged by a lack of opportunity, she is soon acting in pornographic films and her Hollywood ambitions fade into memory. Marlane Meyer, a California playwright, has taken this ancient story and turned it into a sardonic, eye-opening plunge into a contemporary netherworld. Ms. Meyer's play, *Etta Jenks* may chill theatergoers with its amoral air, but as a slice of seamy life, it has the hard-edged intensity of a Martin Scorsese film.

Studying male oppression and violence - an increasingly prevalent theatrical theme - the author leaves us with a cautionary message. The play's sinister male characters regard themselves as entrepreneurs, unconcerned with questions of morality. As Etta undergoes her own metamorphosis, they begin to wonder what would happen to them if women decided to "get even." On one level, *Etta Jenks* deals with retribution, as the heroine realizes the complete invidiousness of those who exploit her. By the end of the play, she has mastered the manly art of manipulation.

Etta (Deirdre O'Connell) and her sisters do not seek empathy. They know exactly what they are doing. Etta, herself, was born out of incest; all innocence was abandoned in childhood. Her pride is in her vanity, what she considers to be her professionalism, the ability to fake pleasure as she participates in pornography.

In other words, this is no stereotypical runaway waif seduced by casting-couch promises, but a young woman possessing a certain kind of mentality that allows her to be desensitized and to subject herself to physical and emotional abuse. Etta begins, we are told, as a tabula rasa, a blank surface to be filled in with graffiti. In the course of the play, she becomes sly if not wise. In a series of terse episodes (with scenes cleverly differentiated by the set designer, Rosario Provenza), we follow Etta's apparent descent into the maelstrom. However, as she sinks, she also begins to take charge of her life and to assume a dominant role in the lives of others.

As performed under the astute direction of Roberta Levitow, the play has an instinctive humor. Amusement arises less from specific lines than from attitude, the way urbanity is conveyed in the sleaziest of circumstances. The portraits of pornographers and those on their fringe are diabolical. One of the oddities of the play is that, among the women, only Etta achieves an individuality, while each of the male characters is clearcut. There are incisive portrayals by Ebbe Roe Smith, doubling as Etta's protector and a hit man; Abdul Salaam el Razzac as a high-toned pimp-pornographer; and John Nesci as a coolly imperturbable maker of snuff films.

At the center is Etta, in Ms. O'Connell's knowing performance, a self-victimizer who gradually becomes an avenger. It is her acceptance of a pornographer's version of Darwinism - outfitting herself for survival in the urban jungle - that gives the play its momentum. Occasionally, the dialogue settles for familiarity, as in Etta's explanation that acting in pornographic films "makes me feel like I'm really here." More often the play has a pungency, and it ends in a bitter aftertaste. *Etta Jenks* is a compelling introduction to a playwright with an uncompromising voice.

PETER NICHOLS

JOE EGG: JANUARY 20, 1985

"Every cloud has a jet black lining," says Bri, the protagonist of Peter Nichols's *Joe Egg*, and the line echoes throughout the author's body of work. In *The National Health*. an injured motorcyclist, released from the hospital, suffers another accident and becomes a basket case, just as in *Joe Egg* a married couple have a brain-damaged daughter. Nichols writes comedies of desperation. The emphasis is not on despair but on the lengths people have to go in order to maintain their sanity.

One of his principal subjects is what he calls the "genetic trap" - the circumstance of family. As his alter ego says in *Forget-me-not Lane*, one of several undisguised theatrical accountings of his own life, "However highly we regard ourselves, we owe our being to some unlikely people we meet at Christmas." "Dependence," he says, "dies hard." In other words, we are not only permanently affected by our progenitors, we become what they are, inheriting distinctive traits, tics and limitations, and carrying them into adulthood.

In play after play, unfulfilled sons and husbands are forced to respond to domestic crises. Bri, the husband in *Joe Egg* (revived by the Roundabout Theater) ends the evening by walking out on his wife, their marriage and the burden of their daughter's incapacity. But one suspects that in art as in life there will be, if not a rush of conscience, at least a reassertion of the familial connection.

Other contemporary British playwrights have also dealt perceptively with aspects of family life. It is, in fact, the second favorite British theatrical theme -after the decline of the Empire. David Storey has reflected ruefully on the chasm between working-class parents and upwardly mobile offspring. Both Harold Pinter and Tom Stoppard have probed infidelity in and out of marriage, and, in *Ashes*, David Rudkin studied the question of infertility. Among these peers, Nichols is the most concerned with family as formative influence and with the varying ways that one keeps trying to come to terms with one's ties. As stated in *Forget-me-not Lane*, the question is, "Is the family inevitable?" The answer, from this author, is always, sometimes regretfully, in the affirmative. When there is not a biological family on stage, Nichols creates one of convenience - a family of patients linked in a hospital word (*The National Health*), a family of soldiers (*Privates on Parade*) bound together to amuse themselves and entertain the troops.

After many years as an author of television drama, Nichols wrote the stage play *Joe Egg*, opening in England in 1967, playing the following year on Broadway and beginning a theatrical career that is a kind of public self-analysis. It is interesting to read Nichols's autobiography, *Feeling You're Behind* (published last year in England but not yet available in the United States) and to realize that we already know so much about the man from his plays. In some areas, we know more about him from his plays than we do from his memoir. In his prose there is a reticence, while his plays reveal an abundance of privileged information.

In *Forget-me-not Lane*, he tells us in vivid detail about his youth, through post-adolescence and into marriage, and especially about his ambiguous relationship with his demanding father - a far more complex and ingratiating figure in the play than in the book. In *Privates on Parade*, the author goes to war and deals with matters of sexual identity, and in *The National Health*, he is inspired to art by his depressing experiences as a hospital patient. His most recent comedy, *Passion*, deals with middle-aged marital ennui. Parenthetically, in its abbreviated Broadway engagement, *Passion* suffered from a crucial miscasting in a pivotal role. Seen in London last year with an English cast, the play was an altogether more rewarding evening. With justification, this season it has become one of the most frequently performed plays in American regional theaters.

In each of these plays, as in *Joe Egg*, the narrative is interrupted by a second line of comic attack, often comedy sketches - asides from the author. At first glance, they may seem to be digressions. Actually, they are extensions of the characters. The author refuses to be limited by naturalism. As a result, his plays are vibrantly theatrical, one reason they are so difficult to transplant onto film. The most personal and the most disturbing of his works is *Joe Egg*, which directly derives from a crisis in the playwright's life. He and his wife were the parents of a daughter (now deceased), afflicted as the child is in the play. When Nichols decided to tell his story on stage, he was surrounded by discouragement from friends and agents who wondered how he could possibly transform such a trauma into a theatrical comedy. Watching the first act for the first time at a runthrough in Glasgow, the playwright broke into tears. Theatergoers were to have a similar reaction wherever the play was done.

To Nichols's dismay, *Joe Egg* was to be followed by a wave of other plays from other authors dealing with physical disabilities, but none of them proved to be as moving. While many of these plays deal specifically with a malady or a disfigurement or reached for a metaphor, *Joe Egg* deals with a marriage under duress. The subject is not Joe Egg, herself, but the effect of the maimed child on her parents - how they cauterize their pain.

For the mother, the daughter is an obsession; for the father she is the sum of their separation within marriage. To cope, he plays the fool, creating a clown show in which the parents and the child serve as objects of comedy. In Nichols fashion, Bri steps in and out of the play, breaking the proscenium in order to address the audience. With jokes, games and songs, he undertakes sardonic subterfuges. They become his illusions as well as his technique for survival.

In the Broadway production, an on-stage jazz band helped to distinguish the two modes of performance, to signal the audience that the play was shifting from domestic reality to music-hall commentary. In his Roundabout revival, Arvin Brown, as director, aims for a more matter-of-fact approach. Except for an opening confrontation with the audience as school class, the vaudeville interludes are somewhat toned down. Pursuing seamlessness, the production sacrifices some of the play's double-edged oxymoronic flavor.

Jim Dale, who was hilarious as the flamboyant officer in the Long Wharf Theater production of *Privates on Parade*, has a more challenging task in *Joe Egg*. He is deft at impersonation, at conjuring up characters who include a German-accented pediatrician and a platitudinous minister. Mr. Dale is a natural comedian but he pays a price for his comic virtuosity. When it comes to the sobering side of the evening - Bri's heartbreak - he seems to lose dimension. As a husband in turmoil, Mr. Dale is more lightly shaded than Albert Finney was in the role on Broadway. As a result, Bri becomes less sympathetic.

On the other hand, Stockard Channing, as the wife, delivers a performance of deeply felt persuasiveness. The result is to turn the play slightly in the direction of the wife. We become more conscious of, and more touched by, her helplessness. As she joins her husband in clowning, we see that for her the games have a greater immediacy. Together, Mr. Dale and Ms. Channing communicate a closeness even as their loyalty is under siege.

Joe Egg and *Forget-me-not Lane* (one of Nichols's finest plays and still not produced in New York) are allied as brilliant acts of self-exposure. As the playwright says in his autobiography, "To make an audience cry or laugh is easy - they want to. In reviews of *Joe Egg*, it became a critical truism to speak of its capacity to do both at the same time, yet this is only worth doing if one thereby catches a whiff of life, a true tang of the bitter mixture we all have to drink." Watching the parents in *Joe Egg*, dedicating themselves to the perpetuation of a myth of parenthood, drowning their marriage in recrimination, we realize that in their case they are laughing to keep from dying.

MARSHA NORMAN

'NIGHT, MOTHER: MAY 1, 1983

In Marsha Norman's *'Night, Mother*, an aging woman lives with her adult daughter in an ordinary house on a lonely country road. Minutes after the play begins, the daughter announces that she is planning to kill herself. *'Night, Mother* becomes the heart-rending battle for the daughter's life. The horrified mother tries every possible method of dissuasion while the daughter calmly puts their house in order. By the end of the evening - 90 minutes without intermission - the audience has shared a catharsis of grief and pain.

For Ms. Norman, a 35-year-old native of Louisville, Ky., *'Night, Mother*, winner of the 1983 Pulitzer Prize for Drama, represents a confirmation of a remarkable talent first encountered in her excoriating *Getting Out*, an Off Broadway success in 1979. This is the second time in three years that the Pulitzer has gone to a woman dramatist. Beth Henley won it in 1981 for *Crimes of the Heart*.

A spare but lyrical dialogue, *'Night, Mother* probes deeply into the mother-daughter relationship while making a disturbing statement about responsibility and courage. It is as artfully designed as a sonata, rising in each dramatic movement until it arrives at its inevitable destination, a conclusion that asserts one's right to control one's life even to the point of suicide. In common with *Getting Out*, which dealt with a young woman on her release from prison, *'Night, Mother* is as tough-minded as it is sensitive. The play stands out as one of the season's major dramatic events.

This dark view of life comes not from a Samuel Beckett but from an affable, determined and petite young woman who looks more like a graduate student than a serious playwright wrestling with profound emotions. Referring to Susan

Kingsley, the Louisville actress who created one of the two leading roles in *Getting Out*, Ms. Norman says, "Susan told me I should shave my head and smoke a cigar, and then people would believe I had written *Getting Out.*"

A powerful dramatist, Marsha Norman is at the crest of a wave of adventurous young women playwrights - a proliferation that is the most encouraging and auspicious aspect of the current American theater.

JOE ORTON

LOOT: FEBRUARY 23, 1986

At first, Joe Orton labeled *Loot* a farce. Seeing the play again in John Tillinger's mirthful new production at the Manhattan Theater Club, one fully accepts the author's initial evaluation - as well as such alternate designations as a satire and a comedy of bad manners. If farce, as defined in the Oxford Companion to the Theater, is "an extreme form of comedy in which laughter is raised at the expense of probability, particularly by horseplay and bodily assault," then *Loot* is a priceless contemporary example of the genre. Horseplay rides high, and bodily assault refers not only to the body English of the actors but also to the attack on the audience's collective funnybone.

As Orton explained, "*Loot* takes a farcical view of things normally treated as tragic," thereby differentiating it from lesser categories of comedy. *Loot* deals humorously with funereal matters, while also offering scathing commentary on the church, the police and the legal and medical professions, all of which, in the author's jaundiced view, are avaricious institutions.

In Orton's lifetime, his plays were considered scandalous; *Loot*, written in 1964, has in it something to offend almost everyone. One finds it, in revival, no less iconoclastic, but with an irrepressible joie de mort that allows the author to get away with murder. *Loot* is all in Grand Guignol fun, a farce about a corpse and loot from a burglary, which becomes confused in mid-casket. They interchange places in full view of the audience, but with officialdom (Inspector Truscott) none the wiser. Non sequiturs snap as the dialogue cloaks the characters in misunderstanding. Each is tuned to his own insane wavelength. As Orton knew and as Mr. Tillinger remembers, the key to farce (and to comedy) is to underplay the extremism. Nothing is done for the sake of laughs, yet the play is consistently amusing. To camp Orton would be to defeat him. Wisely, Mr. Tillinger and his fine company of farceurs keep cool heads and reflexes as quick as those of a racing car driver.

Truscott of the Yard, as hilariously personified by Joseph Maher, is the quintessential English gumshoe, the rule-bound sleuth who is always outfoxed by a Holmes or a Marple. He thinks he knows everything, but, by our measure, he is a bumbler of huge proportions. Posing as a fact finder for the Metropolitan Water Board, he fools no one except himself. He is, as we eventually see, egregiously on the take. Accepting a bribe - and recognizing the theatricality of his circumstances - he confides that the exchange "had better go no farther than these three walls."

As a comic actor, Mr. Maher is a master of the fast burn. Consider his delivery of the line, "The things you say are quite ludicrous, lad," words, which, according to the stage directions, are spoken "with contempt" and followed by the character's mirthless laughter. The actor adds anger, exploding in generational rage on the word, "lad," and provoking a triple somersault of laughter from the audience. Mr. Maher and his fellow actors are expert at such sudden shifts of tone - a tea-cozy tepidity interrupted by a roar that startles the roarer.

Just as Mr. Maher's Truscott is a showoff, swaggering into the scene of the crime and then missing all the obvious clues, Zoë Wanamaker's nurse is the most artful dodger of her just deserts. As the inspector reveals, in a rare statement of fact, the nurse has slain a series of husbands - and eluded punishment by slipping through loopholes in the law. It takes little inspection to realize that she has added her late mistress, the corpse in question, to her list of victims - and is staking out the widower as her next conquest.

Ms. Wanamaker, who has made her reputation on stage in England (principally with the Royal Shakespeare Company), is adorable as the kittenish coquette. While flirting with every man in the play, she maintains an air of fluttery decorum. "Shhh!," she warns the disrespectful. "This is a house of mourning." With the help of Miss Wanamaker, this is also a house of laughter. Physically as well as verbally, she is a delight. Watch, for example, how she opens a bureau drawer with her hand and then, casually, closes it with a pert twist of a hip.

As the deceased's husband, Charles Keating is hangdog even as he weighs the financial and sexual opportunities of widowerhood. His dour face is the ideal canvas for mock bereavement. When Ms. Wanamaker asks him, "Have you ever seen Paradise?," he answers glumly, "Only in photographs." Kevin Bacon and Zeljko Ivanek are a jaunty pair of young adventurers, Mr. Bacon as a young funeral director and Mr. Ivanek as his sidekick, the son of the deceased. Each is out for a lark with the loot, and readily adaptable to every absurd turnabout of plot. Both make a mockery out of the macabre, while keeping an eye on the swag. Add Nic Ullett in a walk-on and also a sewing dummy mummy and you have a droll, Ortonized landscape. Even as we renew our appreciation of the author, one cannot underestimate the contribution of the director. Clearly, Mr. Tillinger (who is also an actor) has found his forte. Several seasons ago he directed Orton's *Entertaining Mr. Sloane* (with Mr. Maher). On the basis of the two Orton revivals, his recent production of Terrence McNally's *It's Only a Play*, and other productions, he has earned a position as one of our sharpest directors of comedy, especially of the kind of black comedy honed by Joe Orton.

ERIC OVERMYER

ON THE VERGE OR THE GEOGRAPHY OF YEARNING: FEBRUARY 10, 1985

BALTIMORE - Cross the wordplay of S.J. Perelman with the world-in-a-time-warp vision of Caryl Churchill and you might approximate the special flavor of *On the Verge or the Geography of Yearning*. In Eric Overmyer's chimerical new comedy at Center Stage, three Victorian lady explorers set out on an adventure that takes them to darkest Africa, highest Himalaya and Terra Incognita.

Equipped for every eventuality, they encounter a jungle of Wild Things, beginning with a cannibal. As one of the women observes, there are two kinds of people, "cannibals and lunch." Everything occurs in a rain forest of rhetoric. The author is aggressively alliterative and recklessly in love with the sound of words, so much so that one wishes he would slice the underbrush of the script with an occasional thwack of his machete.

Inspired by true tales of Victorian adventurers, each of the three heroines represents a different attitude toward her expeditionary mission and her awakening consciousness. Marek Johnson is an impressionable innocent abroad; she speaks words as if she coined them. Mary Layne believes in bringing back specimens; one should not trust memory. Brenda Wehle is tradition-bound, dreaming about her husband back home in Terre Haute. A bit more character delineation would be desirable; some of the comic palaver seems interchangeable.

Before the trek can evolve into "Around the Word in 80 Ways," Mr. Overmyer zooms into another, more dramatic sphere. Following their figuratively cracked compass, the women step anachronistically through the uncharted territory of the 20th century. Just as they were once puzzled by ancient artifacts, they are now perplexed by the purpose of relics of the future. In both cases they try to analyze a civilization through its objects. Just what do you do with an eggbeater? They use it as a kind of divining rod.

Cultures collide as a palanquin pulls up at an Esso station (one fully expects Groucho to alight, and his spirit seems to affect much of the humor). Two of the women decide that the year 1955 is paradise, while Ms. Layne strikes out on her own, heading toward the indeterminate future (our present) with a syncopated soliloquy of brand names and buzz words. On one plane the play is about language

- and about the debasement of language by slogans and neologisms. As one of the women says, "I have seen the future and it is slang."

Taking a clue from the playwright, the director, Jackson Phippin, views the characters as "prisoners in a kaleidoscope." Aided by his set designer, Tony Straiges, he imaginatively mixes live performance, projections (on a kaleidoscopic screen) and a larger-than-wildlife cardboard menagerie. Hedge-hopping across decades, the Victorian ladies look up and see a constellation of marketable utensils - hard, soft and medium ware - hanging overhead like an exploded celestial supermarket.

The three actresses are marked by their vivacity and by their ability to skip, double-Dutch, over the words without stumbling on their diction. Quick- changing costumes, James McDonnell demonstrates his versatility in eight guises, man and beast, including that of a yeti so cute he could be an Adorable Snowman.

A frolicsome jaunt through a continuum of space, time, history, geography, feminism and fashion, Mr. Overmyer's cavalcade is on the verge of becoming a thoroughly serendipitous theatrical journey.

IN PERPETUITY THROUGHOUT THE UNIVERSE: JUNE 20, 1988

As he amply demonstrated in *On the Verge*, Eric Overmyer is a playwright with a linguistic limberness to rival that of Tom Stoppard. Punster and anagrammarian, he is infatuated with language and with word games. His new play, *In Perpetuity Throughout the Universe*, at the Hudson Guild Theater, is filled with the author's verbal felicity and intelligence, but, in contrast to *On the Verge*, it has no inner momentum. It is less a play than a thesaurus. Though there are enough ideas and funny lines for a dozen comedies, it adds up to less than one. *In Perpetuity* is a literary exercise that might be more alive in the reading than in performance.

The two principal subjects are chain letters and ghost writers. On one side of the stage, Arthur Hanket, as a character named Lyle Vial, reads us his daily chain mail. Alternately, Carolyn McCormick and Tzi Ma, playing co-ghosts in the Montage agency, pursue their subliterary profession.

The letters, threatening doom for those who break the chain, end with the receipt of the world's oldest example, written 900 years ago during the Norman Conquest. Perhaps one can blame subsequent wars and disasters on the slowness of the postal delivery. Meanwhile, the spectral scribes are preoccupied with turning neo-Nazi propaganda into massive tomes of "reality/fiction."

Mr. Overmyer takes the opportunity to ridicule publishing, professional conspiracy theorists and illiteracy in all its forms. His acronymic attack is inclusive - from C.I.A. to VCR , both of which he would like to see R.I.P. There are also indications that he has something deeply seriocomic in mind, such as the state of the world, in, as he would say, the "prelapsarian sense of the word."

In their off moments, Ms. McCormick and Mr. Ma indulge their appetite for irony, often with risible results. Mr. Ma tells one long joke in Chinese and Ms. McCormick greets the punchline deadpan, announcing that she heard the joke told better before. Then, without missing a beat, she tells it in Chinese, complete with gestures, apostrophes and imitations, all of which remain delightfully undecipherable to those who do not speak the language.

Periodically, the two play their favorite party game, writing the names of their antipathies on slips of paper and then incinerating them in a glass bowl. First come "people to kill after the revolution," then B movies. If I could find a fireproof salad bowl, I might try this game with names of plays, exempting, of course, the work of Mr. Overmyer. *In Perpetuity* may be self-indulgent but it is salvageable.

Though most of the actors appeared in the work's premiere at Baltimore's Center Stage (both productions were directed by Stan Wojewodski Jr.), several of them seem daunted by the intricacy of the language. Mr. Overmyer's plays need actors who are verbal gymnasts. One such is Mr. Hanket, who played a chameleonesque variety of characters in several productions of *On the Verge*. Unfortunately in *In Perpetuity*, he is confined to that small role as the receiver of chain mail.

Among the others, the most adept is Laura Innes who moves from her role as a ghost-agency assistant to several richly accented incarnations, including one as a "joculatrix," an old vaudevillian translating for us from the ancient Norman. Ms. McCormick is most appealing as a new-fledged ghost writer and teller of jokes in Chinese.

Along the path of *In Perpetuity*, Mr. Overmyer raises tantalizing questions, such as the notion that everyone is an alien, not least of all those who arrive from outer space. He is also clever at purposeful misquotation, as in his suggestion that Josef Stalin said, "Love knows no frontier." Perhaps Stalin wrote that line during his apprenticeship in a Manchurian fortune cookie factory. Mr. Overmyer remains a cosmically inclined theatrical court jester, but in *In Perpetuity* the whole is less than some of its parts.

NATIVE SPEECH: APRIL 17, 1991

Hunkered in his acoustically controlled basement bunker, Hungry Mother is the self-crowned king of the nighthawks, turning dead air into delirium. From his one-man studio, he broadcasts to an audience of insomniacs. Spinning disks and offering advice to "the rubble," he imparts doom and gloom in a nonstop socio-cultural effusion. Hungry Mother is the demonic center of Eric Overmyer's *Native Speech*, a vertiginous black comedy that, with Hungry Mother's radio station, operates on its own renegade frequency.

After several regional productions, *Native Speech* is running its sizzling course at SoHo Rep. The play is early Overmyer, written before his *On the Verge* and before Eric Bogosian's *Talk Radio*, and sharing with that latter work a nerve-twitching intensity. Alone at his console, the talk showman bedevils his midnight callers and is besieged by invaders in the dark, some of whom he waylays into speaking unknowingly over a wide-open microphone.

Karlo Salem, who has played Hungry Mother in previous productions, has stamped the role with his wit and ferocity. With his glaring eyes and corona of curly hair, he looks a bit like Mr. Bogosian, but with his own idiosyncratic rhythm and command of verbal and physical comedy. In his bravura performance, he rappels his way down the linguistic peaks of the dialogue. As usual, Mr. Overmyer is omnivorous in his appetite for onomatopoeia - and unable to eschew eschatology.

Although the play is overlong and it ends in a predictable, studio-leveling apocalypse, it is a live-wire experience. Tune in and hold on tight for a manic riff of language, metaphor and zounds of the Zeitgeist.

The evening is additionally enlivened by the outcasts who cruise through Hungry Mother's orbit. They include endangered species like an American Indian trio of "patho-rockers." The hero's nemesis is a pimp named the Mook, who also happens to be the icy impresario of the twilight station. Sámi Chester plays this role with guile and bite; his scenes with Mr. Salem are menacingly mano a mano. As a battlefront report on urban guerilla warfare, *Native Speech* is, to borrow a word from the playwright's lexicon, radioactive.

SUZAN-LORI PARKS

IMPERCEPTIBLE MUTABILITIES IN THE THIRD KINGDOM: SEPTEMBER 20, 1989

Behind the imposing title *Imperceptible Mutabilities in the Third Kingdom*, there is the voice of a thoughtful young playwright, Suzan-Lori Parks. In a quartet of thematically related scenes (at BACA Downtown in Brooklyn), the author demonstrates a historical perspective and a theatrical versatility. The title of this piece is entirely applicable. In this study of the black experience from slavery to the present, the changes are almost invisible - like geological shifts in the earth.

Ms. Parks's heightened, dreamlike approach is occasionally reminiscent of the work of Adrienne Kennedy and Ntozake Shange (the evening begins with a young woman considering suicide). But there is substantial evidence of the playwright's originality; ironically this occurs in a play that deals partly with the loss of identity. Ms. Parks's identity as an artist is clear. In her four *Mutabilities*, she is earnest about making political points but has a playful sense of language and a self-effacing humor that leavens the work whenever it threatens to become pretentious.

In the opening scene, "Snails," three contemporary black women have their privacy invaded by a nosy naturalist masquerading as an exterminator. Insinuating himself into their habitat, he spies on them with the help of a camera hidden inside a mechanical mock-up of a giant cockroach. Too large to step on, the bug lurks like a killer mutant. Despite the invasion, the women continue to converse, in dialogue that achieves an unconscious urban lyricism.

"Snails" is concerned with such vital matters as education, literacy, domestic violence and tangentially, the preservation of wildlife. One of the characters habitually watches the television show *Wild Kingdom*, and is astonished when she sees the peaceful Marlin Perkins carrying a gun on camera. The world, as we soon see, is falling apart, or, in the words of the pompous exterminator, "the great cake of civilization is beginning to crumble."

Open House is a symbolic case of open-heart surgery, an exploration into the life and mind of a former slave who is dying. In a collage of nightmarish images, she relives events from her plantation past, including her disparagement at the hands of the white girls whom she raised for her master.

In the climactic piece, *Greeks*, a black marine sergeant plays the role of good soldier far beyond the call of duty. He is all starch and polish, mimicking the white man and debasing himself as he waits for his unknown and perhaps irrelevant "distinction" to arrive. His family at home extols him in his absence, maintaining a happy facade while falling into blindness (literally, in the case of the sergeant's wife).

This is a double-edged comedy, mocking stereotypes while leaving us with a bitter message about the pitfalls of assimilation. As in the other scenes, the work is shadowed by myth and metaphor, in this instance, Icarus, whose story is woven into the narrative.

There are occasional rough patches in the writing and some of the projected photographs (by Phil Perkis) impede the flow of the play. One scene, "The Third Kingdom," about the rocky passage of slave ships, is as brief as an interlude. But *Imperceptible Mutabilities* is filled with surprising turns that demonstrate the playwright's ingenuity and humanity.

Within the somewhat austere confines of the BACA stage, Liz Diamond, the director, has given the work a striking production, drawing on the talents of a fine cast and taking advantage of the imaginations of the set designer, Alan Glovsky, and the costume designer, Laura Drawbaugh.

The five actors (Jasper McGruder, Pamala Tyson, Kenya Scott, Shona Tucker and Peter Schmitz) inhabit the various worlds of Ms. Parks's play with sensitivity. Mr. McGruder and Ms. Tyson are especially moving - Mr. McGruder as the sergeant who calmly embraces self-sacrifice, Ms. Tyson as the soldier's dutiful wife and as the former slave. On her deathbed, haunted by ancient memories, she embodies the anguish of a life in subjugation.

MIGUEL PIÑERO

SHORT EYES: JANUARY 8, 1974

Miguel Piñero is a 27-year-old playwright and poet who has spent seven years in prison. The first time I saw his work was in 1972 during a visit to Sing Sing (the Ossining Correctional Facility), where a number of his short skits and street plays were performed by him and other inmates. Mr. Piñero's work was remarkable for its humor, perception and theatricality.

After his release from Sing Sing, Mr. Piñero became director of *Third World Projects* for Theater of the Riverside Church, where his first full-length play, *Short Eyes*, recently had its world premiere. *Short Eyes* proves that Mr. Piñero's prison sketches were no fluke. He is an original writer for the theater, whose plays we should be seeing in the future.

In this production, his director, Marvin Felix Camillo, also reveals a rare talent for taking raw material (the cast as well as the play) and, without distorting its essential nature, giving it dramatic stage life. If the team of Mr. Piñero and Mr. Camillo could be utilized in America's prisons, they would probably work wonders of rehabilitation. This production is significant, not only as a theatrical event but also as an act of social redemption.

Only one actor in the cast is a member of Actors Equity. Half of the others have acted with "The Family," Mr. Camillo's company of former inmates and former addicts. Most members of the cast have served time in prison, which explains their authenticity, but not their talent for expression. Because of the cast's performing inexperience (and also the theater's acoustics), occasionally the dialogue is inaudible, but the actors are not self-conscious - and they are playing characters, ranging from street-wise criminals to a religious fanatic. Several of them, particularly Bimbo as a reluctant jailhouse confessor, clearly are actors in the making.

The play is, as the subtitle indicates, about *The Killing of a Sex Offender by the Inmates of the House of Detention Awaiting Trial*. That offender - "short eyes" in prison slang - is white. All but one of the other inmates are black or Puerto Rican (the actual killer is the other white prisoner, the psychotic Charlie "Longshoe"

Murphy). Despite their own records, they think of the sex offender as the true criminal - an object of disgust.

Except for the murder, there is little physical brutality in the play, but there is a sense of emotional deprivation. These are stunted lives, and prison as well as society bears the responsibility. The prison becomes a microcosm of that hostile society, and the inmates retreat into cells within their cells. The demarcation among races is rigid, the prison codes inflexible - a source of comedy as well as of conflict.

Short Eyes is not a perfect play. At moments its plotting is too tricky. But in it we learn the intricacies and the rituals of the prison system as it is practiced by the prisoners as well as by the jailers. This personal statement - from inside - is instructive and provocative.

FROM THE CITY STREETS, A POET OF THE STAGE: JULY 3, 1988

In 1972 I visited the Ossining Correctional Facility (Sing Sing) in order to write about theater in prisons. While I was there, the inmates presented an anthology of their own short plays, monologues and poems. Twelve of the 20 pieces were written by - and some of them were performed by - one inmate, Miguel Piñero.

It was immediately evident that he had a striking, raw talent, as he demonstrated in a poem he entitled *Gospel.* In it, he brought God down to earth, announcing, "In the beginning God created the ghettos and slums/ And God saw this was good/ So God said let there be more." By the seventh day, his God was so tired he "called in sick" and collected overtime. This and other pieces by Mr. Piñero were marked by a bitter humor and a lilting kind of street poetry.

After the show, I spoke with the author. He said that he had started stealing when he was 8 in order to provide food for his siblings, and that he had spent 7 of his 25 years in prison. Sentenced most recently on a charge of second-degree robbery, he had written poetry in his cell and kept his artistic interest to himself. Then he joined Clay Stevenson's prison workshop where he was encouraged by, among others, Marvin Felix Camillo, an actor and director with the workshop. Mr. Piñero said that when he was released, he planned to go into the theater rather than back on the street.

After reading my subsequent article, Arthur Bartow, director of the Theater at the Riverside Church, contacted Mr. Piñero in prison and asked him if he were writing a full-length play. This began a cycle of events that led after the inmate's release, to the Riverside production of his play, *Short Eyes*, as directed by Mr. Camillo. Wrenched from the author's own experience, *Short Eyes*, a harrowing slice of prison life, was like a message from a combat zone. In my initial review, I commented on Mr. Piñero's originality and his potential. The prediction proved only partly correct. The playwright died (of cirrhosis of the liver) on June 21 at the age of 41.

In 1974, *Short Eyes* went from Riverside to the Public Theater to the Vivian Beaumont Theater in Lincoln Center. It deservedly won the New York Drama Critics Circle prize as best American play of the year and was subsequently made into a film. The success of the play transformed the playwright's life. He became famous while never losing his notoriety. Miguel - or Mikey as he was known to his friends - seemed to cherish his role as an outcast, playing it in real life as well as in movies and on television. As an actor, he appeared on such shows as *Miami Vice*, often cast as a drug addict or pusher.

Even as he continued to win acclaim for his plays and his performances, he still had trouble with the law. I was in court the day that a judge dropped a charge against him for using obscene language to a subway attendant. The judge suggested that if he were abusive he should apologize because, as an artist, "other avenues of expression" were open to him, and added, "We're proud of you. You're a talented man."

Outside the courthouse, the Transit Authority officer who had made the arrest shook his hand and praised *Short Eyes* - one of many favorable reviews he was to receive in his lifetime. In a further twist of irony, while Robert Young was directing the film of *Short Eyes* on location in the Tombs, the playwright was being indicted in that same building on charges of grand larceny and possession of heroin.

As Mr. Piñero increasingly became a public personality, he seemed to divert his energies further away from playwriting, spending much of his time helping younger writers. But periodically he returned to the theater. Though none of his other plays measured up to *Short Eyes*, several demonstrated the vibrancy of his talent. *Eulogy for a Small-Time Thief, The Sun Always Shines for the Cool, A Midnight Moon at the Greasy Spoon* - his titles as well as his plays were redolent with authenticity. The most provocative was *A Midnight Moon*, which treated the author's favorite subject, the under-class, with a lingering sense of hopefulness.

His life and work were recently celebrated in a memorial at the Public Theater, with relatives and fellow actors and writers paying homage. Joseph Papp, who presented *Short Eyes* at two of his theaters, said that Piñero was a man of a thousand faces - and before he died, he was wearing his writing face. He was working on a new play called *Every Form of Refuge Has Its Price*. The producer added that Mr. Piñero's effect on other playwrights was not to be underestimated.

Short Eyes was a breakthrough, not only in personal terms, but as a harbinger of the art that is coming from the Hispanic-American community. In that sense, it served a purpose not unlike that of John Osborne's *Look Back in Anger*, challenging theatrical tradition and conceptions. *Short Eyes* opened the door to urban reality, and among those who entered was Reinaldo Povod, one of a number of emerging young artists who studied with Mr. Piñero.

The playwright never made a secret about his own problems. As he freely confessed in a poem, "A thief, a junkie I've been/ committed every known sin." But that poem also demonstrated a lingering idealism. It began:

"Just once before I die

I want to climb up on a tenement sky

to dream my lungs out till

I cry

then scatter my ashes out thru

the lower East Side"

Sadly, Mr. Piñero's death comes soon after the death of Marvin Felix Camillo. If Mikey was, by his own admission, "bad" (in the Michael Jackson sense), "Pancho" Camillo was good, even saintly, a man whose theater group, The Family, is an invaluable resource as a human reclamation project. As playwright and as director, each man went his individual way. The partnership that produced *Short Eyes* was dissolved. But each remained active within the community and both were devoted to former inmates and potential offenders who found that, through theater, they could make a creative contribution to society.

Thinking about Mikey, I remember the enthusiasm with which he greeted my review of *Short Eyes*. It was the first indication that his voice was reaching the outside world, that his message was being received. He telephoned me and vowed an oath of eternal friendship. With the authority of someone who had grown up on the streets, he added that if I ever needed protection, he would see that it was provided. More compassionate words were never said to a critic.

Miguel Piñero's death cuts short what could have been - what should have been - a remarkable career.

HAROLD PINTER

THE LOVER: APRIL 25, 1990

NEW HAVEN - Though both Joe Orton and Harold Pinter are playwrights with original, distinct voices, they have similarities as well as disparities. Arriving first, Mr. Pinter became something of a model to Mr. Orton. Just as Pinter plays have a metaphorical weasel lurking under the cocktail table, Mr. Orton's plays are inhabited by carpenter ants insidiously attacking the roofbeams and floorboards.

For both playwrights, nothing is as it seems to be as they investigate dualities in everyday life.

The director John Tillinger has had the ingenious idea of pairing two early one-acts by the writers, *The Ruffian on the Stair* by Mr. Orton and *The Lover* by Mr. Pinter. This double bill fills Long Wharf Theater's Stage II with sinister comedy and also offers an arena for versatility to the production's leading actors, Nicholas Woodeson and Joanne Camp.

The Ruffian was Mr. Orton's first play (in 1963), broadcast on British radio and subsequently adapted to the stage. Clearly it was influenced by Mr. Pinter, even to Mr. Orton's imitating some of the lines in *The Birthday Party* in the first version of the play. Menace stalks interior rooms as well as the unseen stairwell as a working-class couple's apparent tranquility barely conceals a predilection for casual mayhem.

A young man of ambiguous sexuality (Tate Donovan) - a forerunner of the author's Mr. Sloane - insinuates himself into the placid household and moves from victimizer to victim. The man of the house (Mr. Woodeson) is a truck driver of vengeful instinct, and his common-law wife (Ms. Camp) has submerged her own shady past in her housewifely present.

On the surface, the two are the most guileless of company as the woman invites the intruder in for a cup of tea. Humor arises from the fact that the characters affect the airs of their so-called betters. The play becomes a reverse comedy of manners.

With an insouciance that was to grow to maturity in his full-length plays, Orton keeps everything matter-of-fact and tongue-in-cheek. As the author wrote about *The Ruffian*, "Everything the characters say is true" - no matter how bizarre it may seem. Mr. Tillinger has closely followed the playwright's prescription, right through the doubly murderous conclusion.

In *The Lover*, originally written for television, a couple from the professional class belie their social status. As a dapper businessman goes to work, he asks his wife if her lover is expected that day, posing the question as calmly as if he were asking her what they were having for dinner. Later, when the lover arrives, he turns out to be the husband, who is supposedly having a tryst with his favorite prostitute.

Conducting this duplicitous charade, the husband and wife awaken each other's libido. Underlying the comedy is a feeling of displacement and sadness, in contrast to *The Ruffian*, which manages, despite the malevolence, to seem oddly cheerful. *The Lover* is the more seriously inclined play, but each makes acidulous points at the expense of domestic discord.

Between the plays, the actors are transformed. Mr. Woodeson is amiable as the plebeian truck driver (in the Orton) and suave as the executive (in the Pinter). These are only two sides to this diversely talented actor, who several seasons ago was a Napoleonic King John at Stratford-on-Avon and was most recently seen in New York as Henry Fielding in *The Art of Success*.

In *The Ruffian*, Ms. Camp remains convivial as the dowdy housewife (she stops short of being slatternly), padded out to fill the physical dimensions of the role. Then she persuasively becomes the seductress in *The Lover*, crossing and uncrossing her legs with a confident sensuality. As demanded, Mr. Donovan is both affable and suspicious as the unfortunate ruffian.

Through a series of productions, Mr. Tillinger has become America's foremost directorial interpreter of Orton. With this double bill, he makes a nimble transition to Mr. Pinter, a playwright with whom he seems to feel an equal compatibility - and a taste for conspiratorial humor.

BETRAYAL: FEBRUARY 3, 1991

NEW HAVEN - Harold Pinter's *Betrayal* is a malicious comedy of manners about mutual deceit. In this 1978 play, the web is taut and the words are weighted with portent and humor. The playwright tells his story in nine pithy scenes, all he needs to capture the hermetic world of his three conspirators. The essence of this devious work is delineated with precision in John Tillinger's revival at the Long Wharf Theater.

In *Betrayal*, time moves backward, a method of storytelling that deepens the narrative. Answers are followed by questions, apparent contradictions by clues to behavior. Characters are revealed through a warp of memory, as time tricks the unwary.

The first scene takes place in a pub after an affair has ended between a woman and her husband's best friend, the best man at their wedding. Then, step by step, the play returns to the start of the romance, the flame that has been extinguished at the beginning of the play.

The primary question is not what drove the adulterous couple together, or, later in their lives, what separated them, but who knew what and when, and what anyone did about it. Did the husband, Robert, know of the affair before or after he and his wife, Emma, took a trip to Venice - and what did Robert do on his own solitary journey to Torcello? Is Jerry, the lover, the only one who thinks the years of afternoon trysts occurred in a vacuum?

There is less of a mystery here than the characters would like to believe. Surreptitiousness, it seems, is only in the eye of the secretive. In fact, in *Betrayal*, there are apparently no secrets, only closely guarded trains of thought and artificial walls of forgetfulness.

Betrayal, Mr. Pinter explains, need not be an act of infidelity. It can be the simplest of deceits or words not spoken - for example, Emma's not telling Jerry that her husband knows about their affair. The play is most intricately plotted and subplotted as other, unseen characters pass through the orbit and affect the people we see on stage.

Most of the characters, seen and unseen, are involved with literature. Robert is an editor with a distaste for books, and Jerry is an author's agent with his own ambiguous allegiance to his clients. Neither of these two should be confused with the seemingly related publishing figures who populate plays by Simon Gray (to whom *Betrayal* is dedicated). The professional life of Robert and Jerry is untapped territory. It is the play and counterplay of their friendship and rivalry - at home, about Emma and even on the squash court - that fascinates the playwright and the audience.

Betrayal was beautifully orchestrated in Peter Hall's original London production and in the subsequent film, less so in the Broadway version, in which an American cast obscured the work's Englishness. Although the American actors in Mr. Tillinger's production - Maureen Anderman as Emma; Michael Goodwin and Edmund Genest as the men in her life - assume only the slightest of English accents, they artfully communicate the Pinter landscape and language. The turntable setting by John Lee Beatty has its own pristine self-assurance.

As intended, each actor conceals facets of a character's personality. Ms. Anderman's Emma is more a willing accomplice than a temptress. She seems awakened by the idea of dalliance but is not transported by the actual romance. The actress retains an air of graceful reserve. As portrayed by Mr. Goodwin, Jerry emanates self-control and an odd sense of self-entrapment. Mr. Genest's Robert remains the coolest of the three. More than the others, he seems aware of what is going on, but he is manipulative about what he cares to reveal.

Under Mr. Tillinger's guidance, the actors are finely tuned to the indirect actions of their characters and to the dramatic currents beneath the terse dialogue. The many guises of betrayal are explored with eloquent dispassion in this tantalizing play.

JONATHAN REYNOLDS

GENIUSES: MAY 14, 1982

The director and his crew have spent three months in the Philippine jungle making *Parabola of Death*, which is variously described as a movie about the war in Angola and as the director's autobiography. They are 28 days behind schedule on this mega-buck epic and have shot only 10 tiny minutes of film. Sound familiar? Before you say, "play à clef," notice that the director is named Milo McGee McGarr and he is Irish.

In any case, a Francis Ford Coppola picture could not be nearly as much fun on location. Jonathan Reynolds's *Geniuses*, at Playwrights Horizons, is an apocalyptical laugh at the expense of the movies. This is the second time the author has spoofed a national pastime. Some years ago, he hit an inside-the-park home run with *Yanks 3 Detroit 0 Top of the Seventh*.

From Mr. Reynolds's point of view, Hollywood is a case of mistaken identity - neither art nor economics, but an ego-tripping shell game, which can accidentally arrive at entertainment. It is a sound stage for con men, madmen, dreamers and dupes who lash themselves to the mizzenmast of a sinking ship and smile as the typhoon strikes.

The author speaks with an authority to match his acerbity. Not since S.J. Perelman has anyone savaged Cloudland with such malice aforethought. Among other things, *Geniuses* is an insidious act of movie criticism. Make no mistake, beneath the japery, there is a warning: movies can be injurious to your health; keep them out of the reach of children-directors.

Wisely, the author has focused not on his auteur but on the "geniuses" in the background. For two of the comedy's three acts, Milo McGee McGarr is kept off stage whirling in his own copter while the supporting players bastion themselves against a torrential storm.

First we meet Jocko Pyle, the screenwriter, or, as Darryl F. Zanuck used to say, "the present writer," to distinguish him from all past and future scriveners who will follow a path into unemployment. As Jocko, Michael Gross reads aloud from his script, "Dissolve to the holocaust. The End." Then he rips the paper out of his typewriter and crumples it. Later he will tear a totally blank sheet from the machine and crumple that.

Though bereft of inspiration, he is an arch-cynic who can outdo Woody Allen in his hatred of California ("where the smog creeps in on little rat feet"). Mr. Gross attacks the wrong enemy, not his director but the director's quondam mistress, a luscious centerfold played by Joanne Camp. Ms. Camp is daffily amusing as this Billie Dawnish "sex subject," who has been flown in to do a "30-second naked walk-on," but is much smarter than she seems.   Should Mr. Reynolds ever consider writing a sequel to *Geniuses*, surely she will be ensconced as head of production at Paramount.

Kurt Knudson has the choicest lines - and the perfect delivery - as a makeup man who thinks he looks like Hemingway. Actually he thinks he is Hemingway, and after a tasty native dinner, he breaks into Hemingwayese: "Papa loved dog and dog was good." As Mr. Knudson tells us, when Hollywood wants "age," they go to Dick Smith, but for pillage and carnage, they come to him. He is proud of the fact that his nickname is "Mr. Wounds." Suggesting a new ending to the endless picture, he says that the hero should live, "but with a big wound."

Together with a sadomasochistic art director (David Rasche), who would just as soon blow up a set as build it, and a crafty Filipino bodyguard (Thomas Ikeda), the crew survives the storm with limericks, jokes and thrusts at the insanities of their industry. In the second act, the antics momentarily subside. The central conflict is a melodramatic mood-changer, and the conclusion is tentative, as if the author, not the characters, were trying to make up his mind which way to go. None of this seriously detracts from our mirth.

Much of the humor is bull's-eye parody, with the characters retaining a tinseled reality. Looking more like Spielberg than Coppola, McGarr (David Garrison) is the prototypical boy wonder fresh out of a film can. Studying the shambles of his creation, he observes, "Somehow it just got away from me." Actually, for him, movies are anticlimactic. "The only excitement," he says, with relish, "is the deal." "Geniuses" skewers dealmakers, agents and all satraps who overdose on self-importance.

Andrew Jackness's setting is a Malaysian vision in bamboo and rattan. Gerald Gutierrez's direction is as crisp as celluloid, and the special effects by Esquire Jauchem and Gregory Meeh bash the stage with enough wind and rain to drown Ranchipur. The actors are a deliriously supportive team, and Miss Camp is heavenly. There is comic genius afoot at Playwrights Horizon, and his name is Jonathan Reynolds.

DAVID RUDKIN

ASHES: DECEMBER 15, 1976

In *Ashes* (at the Manhattan Theater Club) by David Rudkin, a married couple are trying, with urgency and, finally, in desperation, to conceive a child. The play takes the couple from gynecologist to semenologist to bedroom and shows in vivid detail the humiliations - psychological as well as physical - that each is forced to suffer in the quest for parenthood. Each begins to long for the nights when sex meant love and not a feat of clockwork engineering.

"The things a silly sod will do for fatherhood," says the husband. Then he asks himself the crucial question, "Or is it fatherhood? Might it not be the myth of manliness?" Just as the husband begins to question his masculinity, his wife begins to question her femininity. Increasingly both feel that they need proof of their sexual nature - and identification of their roles in life.

Those who see *Ashes* only as a clinical dissection of the problems of conception - which on one level it certainly is (it is exceedingly graphic although never pornographic) - miss the major point of this marvelous play. It is a dissection, as moving as it is comic, of a marriage, of two people bound in a relationship that is under extreme stress. And it is a play not just about birth but about death.

In theme and tone, *Ashes* is a companion piece to Peter Nichols's *A Day in the Death of Joe Egg*. In each case a crisis that should reinforce a relationship - doesn't shared tragedy bring people closer together? - begins to wedge the characters apart.

Failing natural conception, Mr. Rudkin's couple apply to adopt a child and are peremptorily rejected - because of their honesty and frankness, he about his homosexual past, she about understanding that past. United in their needs and desires, they are a loving couple. But biology and society prove unresponsive.

Wedded in an impossible situation, they refuse to indulge in self-pity. Unfailingly they see the grotesque humor. Finally the husband contemplates the future: "From ashes, the fields are fertilized." Life at its most disappointing is life. Even without hope, the marriage endures.

The play deals fiercely with matters of birth and death. The husband returns to his native Ireland for the funeral of an uncle killed in an explosion, and he runs into the barricade of prejudice. To his family, he is a traitor. Not only is he childless, "the dead branch" of a fertile family, but he has also deserted his homeland for England. Piercingly, he sees the waste that is built into revolution, the cheapness of life (babies abandoned and killed) - juxtaposed next to the costliness of his own drive to bring about life.

Operating simultaneously on several levels, *Ashes* is never self-conscious about symbolism, and it never pleads for compassion. By holding its almost microscopic focus on one couple's plight, it reveals truth about other people, other bonds.

Ashes may make some theatergoers uncomfortable. In common with its protagonists' attitude toward adoption, it is unflinching in its honesty and frankness. It makes emotional demands on the audience and on the actors. Few tears are shed in *Ashes*, but hearts are exposed.

As the husband, Brian Murray creates a less romantic figure than Ian McKellen did in last year's London production, but he touches us with his helplessness. Roberta Maxwell keeps the wife single-minded without making her astringent. Together, in harmony with their author, they win our empathy. John Tillinger and Penelope Allen offer brisk support as various well-meaning and supercilious doctors, nurses and advisers.

There is a suitable starkness and coolness about Lynne Meadow's staging. John Lee Beatty, as designer, has given the stage a mechanical look, edging it with metal poles and using a long pull curtain to denote changes of scene. The drawing of that curtain - quick and precise - is icily impersonal, providing the perfect environment for this searingly personal, disturbing play.

WALLACE SHAWN

AUNT DAN AND LEMON: NOVEMBER 10, 1985

In his introduction to the published version of *My Dinner with Andre*, that tantalizing tête-à-tête between the playwright Wallace Shawn and the director Andre Gregory, Mr. Shawn briefly describes his life in the theater. He calls his plays "intense, extreme, even maniacal," and suggests, with tongue only partly in cheek, that he has "generously shown on stage my interior life as a raging beast." That raging beast has the oddest effect on audiences, driving them into paroxysms of dismay, anger and, as the author might say, "even disgust."

Seldom has sexuality been so graphically described on stage as in Mr. Shawn's *Our Late Night*. His *Marie and Bruce* was a clinical dissection of the emotional violence in a modern marriage. His new play, *Aunt Dan and Lemon* (at the Public Theater), deals with two immensely eccentric characters. Aunt Dan is an Oxford don who offers a ringing defense of Henry Kissinger's foreign policy, and Lemon, the protagonist, is a febrile young Englishwoman who finds a rationale for Nazi genocide. No wonder people have been know to storm out of Mr. Shawn's plays, an act made doubly difficult by the fact that they have no intermissions, whether they are brief like his cameo epic, *The Hotel Play*, or long, like *Aunt Dan and Lemon*. The playwright himself remains surprised that theatergoers think his work is outrageous. As he once said in an interview, "It's what I hear, after all."

One might add that what he hears is not on any standard wavelength, but originates on some private channel. He has his own simultaneous decoder, revealing secret thoughts beneath conventional conversation. How many times have we heard the most everyday chatter lapse into offhanded bigotry and then return to gossip? In his plays, characters speak the unthinkable in the most matter-of-fact fashion - as if they are ordering groceries from the market. For example, Lemon praises the Nazis for being "ruthless and thorough." Accepting without questioning, she has been indoctrinated into a placid acquiescence to evil.

It is the juxtaposition of manner and meaning that is at the root of Mr. Shawn's comedy - and it must be affirmed that he is primarily a comic playwright. Because he cuts close to the marrow, he is not one for the mainstream. He speaks with his own individual voice. In fact, he is a playwright of astonishing originality and veracity.

For most playwrights, it is easy to find antecedents, even if unintentional. But Mr. Shawn, more than his peers, including such contemporary stylists as Sam Shepard and David Mamet, creates his own idiosyncratic art. Any attempts to link that art with that of other writers will lead directly up a blind alley. One could say about *Our Late Night* that the elegant party guests crowded onto the playwright's sofa are émigrés from a Noel Coward comedy, but there is nothing Cowardly about the author's assault on the rude banter that constricts our private lives. Similarly, one could regard *Marie and Bruce* as an absurdist variation on Strindberg or Ingmar Bergman, as scenes from a mordant marriage. But those baleful Swedes are not as overtly misanthropic as Marie, who tells her timid husband that he is a "horrible piece of dead meat."

Even by the author's own standards, *Aunt Dan and Lemon* is bizarre and also unclassifiable. The closest one can come to a category is to say that there is a Lewis Carroll quality to the storytelling. Greeting us as "dear good people," Lemon seems as innocent as any Alice descending into Wonderland. However, one could never confuse the play with a nursery rhyme. It is a dire portrait of the kind of thinking that leads to a world in collapse.

One reason that Mr. Shawn's plays disturb theatergoers - and critics - is that the playwright steadfastly refuses to unveil his own partisanship. His characters are as outwardly reasonable as any guest in our house, yet their decadence would drive any decent host to open the door and usher them out. The playwright lets Lemon have her say, even as she compares the Holocaust with household roach extermination. It would be a mistake if theatergoers thought the playwright believes that equation. It is the judgment of the character, Lemon, and it is up to the audience to cast the accusation against her.

The author is showing us how perilously close we are to self-extermination. By extension, *Aunt Dan and Lemon* is not only anti-Nazi but also anti-nuclear armament. That conclusion, however, is far from obvious. The play takes no position, and, in fact, Lemon's only opposition is provided by her ineffectual mother. Coincidentally, David Hare's politically minded *A Map of the World* is also playing at the Public Theater. The Hare play presents diverse sides to the issues that it raises, whereas the Shawn play ostensibly presents only a single side. In common, neither playwright imposes his point of view on the theatergoer, preferring to allow everyone to make up his own mind. In that sense, each play is the opposite of a polemic though both are filled with ideas.

Mr. Shawn deepens the problem for his audience by his choice of style. In *Aunt Dan and Lemon*, long monologues loop around themselves like unspooled tapes. Sometimes they turn into dialogues or diatribes, but rarely do they become dramatic conflicts. Often they lapse into the thicket of repetition. Judicious pruning would bring the play down to a taut 90 minutes. However, there is something to be said in favor of the repetition: it wears down one's resistance and it underscores the nature of our entrapment. Two hours with *Aunt Dan and Lemon* and their weird friends is like being a guest at Luis Buñuel's apocalyptical party in *The Exterminating Angel*. Dramatically, there is no exit; in a positive sense, the play is disquieting.

There is, however, more to the play than is transmitted on stage at the Public Theater. One can envision a more imaginative, less naturalistic production that would convey the dreamlike side of the narrative. This is, after all, a tale told by an armchair analysand, a confidential confessional that draws us seductively into the rabbit hole of 20th-century politics. Max Stafford-Clark's production has a certain languidness.

The evening is enlivened by several of the actors - Larry Pine, a familiar figure in plays by Mr. Shawn, as a paradigm of everyday indecency; the playwright, himself, as Lemon's hysterical father whose simple guideline to success is how much the product sells. Kathryn Pogson has an eerie sincerity as Lemon; her political perversions are as natural to her as her organically grown health juices. The actress's almost anorexic appearance is an asset; we feel that Lemon is a blossom drying on the vine. Linda Hunt is more a questionable choice as Aunt Dan, an unforgettable character who would seem to be made to measure for the dynamism of an actress like Vanessa Redgrave. The role of Aunt Dan is cast too much against type.

That in itself - the casting against type - is characteristic of the art of Wallace Shawn. Seeing his plays, one never knows what to expect. In a theater wedded to predictability, he is marked by his rashness. He breaks rules, slays sacred cows and reinvents theater as it suits his purpose. Theatergoers should seek no sanctuary here, but if they unburden themselves of preconceptions, they will be challenged. *Aunt Dan and Lemon* is a play designed to provoke argument.

SAM SHEPARD

SUICIDE IN B FLAT: OCTOBER 25, 1976

NEW HAVEN - With the plays of Sam Shepard, it is the withheld information and the ellipsis as much as the revealed truths and the rambunctious humor that hold us. In *Suicide in B Flat*, which recently joined the fall repertory at the Yale Repertory Theater - it is one of four new Shepard plays scheduled for production at various theaters this season - the author is even more mysterious than usual. This is Mr. Shepard at his most tantalizing.

A jazzman named Niles has killed himself. Or has he? As Lawrence Wolf, at the piano, his back to the audience, sits on stage playing jazz of his own composition, the comedy begins.

Two bumbling detectives are investigating the "crime." They are as inept as Harpo and Groucho looking for purloined jewels. There is an outline of a dead man taped to the floor, and Joe Grifasi tries the outline on for size. Repeatedly he pratfalls, attempting to force his limbs to fit the ungainly posture. Meanwhile Clifford David, as the other government operative, cocks his hat with his thumb and then shuffles classified documents as if they were a deck of marked cards.

Soon the stage is filled with metaphorical marked cards - false leads and dead-end guesses. The jack-in-the-box laughter mounts; this is Sam Spade down the rabbit hole trying to find Alice. The conundrum of a story is never fully deciphered, but with Mr. Shepard, one learns not to worry about plot coherency. He deals not in linear movement but in moods and impressions. This is a jazz dreamworld, by the author's intention, a new dimension (actually two plays occupy the same place, Niles's apartment, at the same time). He gives us hints and clues to his caper. As William Hickey, playing a cadaverous saxophonist, warns, "It takes a while to attune your ears to the frequency we're playing in."

Mr. Shepard's plays have their own heartbeat, an idiosyncratic sensibility that is both primitive and sophisticated. Mr. Shepard is a playwright of the American West, the open spaces, whose plays often occur in locked, tight rooms. It is the collision of myth and reality that fascinate him. "You can't kill a myth," says one of the characters, but you can wound him with arrows and insults. In Shepard plays, myths are pummeled by civilization.

In his recent work, the author has become a critic of our culture, of the demands that it makes on the artist (whom he sees as a kind of natural hero). In *The Tooth of Crime*, Hoss, the rock singer, is forcibly replaced by the younger Crow; it is a commentary on the obsolescence of stars. In *Geography of a Horse Dreamer*, the cowboy, a free spirit who can predict horse races, is thought-controlled, robbed of his creativity by gangsters. In *Suicide*, Niles (who is playing dead just as he once "played alive") speaking for himself and the other mythological figures that populate Mr. Shepard's landscape, says, "We've all lost our calling."

Instead of giving us a pontificating poet or philosopher, Mr. Shepard spotlights the buffoon on the barroom floor. He buffaloes us with comic-strip comedy. The detectives are bogus Bogarts. Mr. Hickey is a lonesome fugitive from the Dorsey Brothers band. Twisting like a reed, he blows his sax - and no sound emerges. This is "visual music," he explains, and that label can act as an apt description of Mr. Shepard's art. He treats our eyes to visual music, our ears to a concatenation of word images.

Mr. Shepard's theater has its own inner orchestration. It needs and, in Walt Jones's production, it finds, the right jazz combo of actors tuned in to the author's rhythm. The play, though carefully arranged, has to seem like an improvisation. All the actors are authentic, and Mr. Grifasi is something more. His detective is the essence of the cheap hoodlum; the playwright sees a symbiosis between cops and robbers. In common with cowboys, rock stars and jazzmen, they are fallen heroes on Mr. Shepard's magical silver screen.

THE DEEPLY AMERICAN ROOTS OF SAM SHEPARD'S PLAYS: JANUARY 2, 1979

In Terrence Malick's movie *Days of Heaven*, Sam Shepard is first seen standing on the porch of his house - a lonely sentinel surrounded by a sweeping field of wheat. As a rich landowner, that tall, lanky Mr. Shepard embodies the American West. His presence on screen is so filled with authenticity that, if he chooses to do so, he might become a western movie star - a Gary Cooper for the late 1970's.

Acting in movies is only one, and up to now a minor, aspect of Mr. Shepard's career; most importantly, he is a significant American playwright. But the performance in *Days of Heaven* does indicate something about his role as an artist. Many of our best young dramatists, including David Rabe, Lanford Wilson and Thomas Babe, are endemically American, but among his peers Mr. Shepard probably has roots that are most deeply embedded in the bedrock of our environment and our national mythology.

Cowboys, rock stars, jazzmen, gangsters and gamblers populate his theatrical world as they did the movie screens of our collective childhood. As Patti Smith has written in a poetic reminiscence about Mr. Shepard, a friend and occasional collaborator, he is a "man playing cowboys." The theater of Sam Shepard is playful, comic and freewheeling - continuing chapters in a talking blues about the West - but it is also serious in its contemplation of lost values.

One of his favorite subjects is the shattering of the American family. As a surly old man says to his prodigal grandson in Mr. Shepard's new play, *Buried Child*. "You think just because people propagate, they have to love their offspring." For Mr. Shepard, love and friendship are ties that can be thicker than blood. Parents and children have to "prove" themselves, to earn their relationships, just as homesteaders have to earn - and defend - the land they inhabit.

Last year in *The Curse of the Starving Class* and this season with greater effectiveness and lucidity in *Buried Child*, Mr. Shepard writes his epitaph for the family as an institution. In *Buried Child*, after an absence of years the grandson returns to the family farm, bringing with him a young woman, played by a new and very attractive actress, Mary McDonnell. Precisely because of Ms. McDonnell's character, *Buried Child* is more accessible than many other Shepard plays. As an outsider, she is the audience's point of identity, bringing a measure of normality into an alien society. Mirroring our skepticism and surprise, she keeps the evening from becoming hermetic. Looking through a porch screen at her friend's family, she announces her expectation that the group will resemble a Norman Rockwell portrait.

Actually, the group is far closer to Erskine Caldwell. The clan is seedy, disreputable and perhaps even insane. "Stop calling me grandpa!" shouts the old man. He is the opposite of grandfatherly. Several times he seems on the verge of expiring, which might be met with relief by his equally uncharitable kinsmen. His two lumbering middle-aged sons are strange, half-crazed creatures; one keeps carrying in loads of fresh vegetables from a supposedly barren garden - one of many mysterious portents in this ominous and engrossing play.

The buried child of the title, though actual, reminds us of the imaginary child in *Who's Afraid of Virginia Woolf?* It is a dark secret, whose existence is never to be acknowledged in public. Although the play deals with a homecoming - one of several points in common with Harold Pinter - it is equally connected to the work of Edward Albee. This is an American nightmare in which an ingrown family bastions itself against invading reality. Mr. Shepard is a playwright of the American frontier, but his plays generally take place in confined, even claustrophobic, rooms.

These plays, representing the author's 14 years as a professional playwright, form an abundant body of work, one of the most sizable and tantalizing in the American theater. Although he has still not had a popular, long-running success in New York, Mr. Shepard has had his plays presented Off Broadway, Off Off Broadway, in regional theaters, at Lincoln Center and throughout Western Europe. In contrast to some of his contemporaries, he has demonstrated definite growth: A spokesman for the 1960's has become a voice of the 70's. Each play seems to reveal a new edge to an innovative talent.

As an incisive commentator on our native culture, Mr. Shepard sees the American hero as a dying species. In *Geography of a Horse Dreamer*, his hero was a mystical tout named Cody; inevitably he was kidnapped and forced to make his magical predictions for the profit of others. In *The Tooth of Crime*, a famous rock star was pushed off his pedestal by a quick-rising newcomer and a fickle public.

Suicide in B Flat turned to the world of jazz for an absurd caper comedy about misplaced identity. As the lead jazzman in the play said, speaking about himself and, presumably, other Shepard heroes, "We've all lost our calling." Jobs available; heroes need not apply. The author came close to autobiography in *Angel City*. As a screenwriter on Antonioni's *Zabriskie Point*, he observed the attraction of Hollywood as well as its ability to corrupt.

This theme of seduction and betrayal is the root of the next Shepard play to be seen in New York - *Seduced*. In this diabolical comedy, Mr. Shepard chronicles the self-destruction of the man that he sees as the ultimate American hero: Howard Hughes. Mr. Shepard's fictionalized billionaire is a visionary entrapped by his limitless wealth and by the pathology of his personal obsessions. Unable to face reality - or even the bright rays of the sun - he retreats to an antiseptic room, placing himself under temperature control, making outrageous demands on his employees and cultivating his outlandish daydreams.

In his own inimitable fashion, Mr. Shepard is a daydreamer, a tale-spinner, evoking a world of myths, legends and heroism, sending us on a chairborne flight into the outer space of his imagination.

BURIED CHILD: JANUARY 25, 1979

NEW HAVEN - One of the many themes in Sam Shepard's tantalizing play *Buried Child* (in a new production at the Yale Repertory Theater) is the question of recognition and identity. How do we know - who - or what - we are? In the, play which is also running Off Broadway, a prodigal grandson returns to the family homestead after an absence of six years, and no one knows him, or, perhaps, everyone pretends not to know him.

Finally, his father peers into his eyes and thinks that he recognizes "the face within the face." This phrase refers to the child within the man, the past behind the present, and also the father himself. For a moment, he thinks that in his son he sees his own image. Each of the strange characters in *Buried Child* is searching for his heritage, as if it were something that had been mislaid in the attic or under the derelict sofa. The grizzled old grandfather, Dodge, traces his roots back to the grave, and, as we watch him, he appears to be disintegrating into dust.

The symbol of this mordant clan - the American family gone to seed - is the buried child of the title, an infant who has mysteriously disappeared. In the play, we see three lost generations of one family. The grandfather has been replaced; he lingers without purpose, cauterizing himself with alcohol and television. His older son has misplaced his reason; he is unable to function in an adult society. The grandson is displaced; where does he belong? The tone of the play is almost surrealistic. Like a figure out of Ionesco, the father brings in armloads of fresh vegetables from a garden that has been barren for years. As Dodge waspishly comments, "Can you trust a man who keeps bringing in vegetables from out of nowhere?"

To those unfamiliar with the work of Mr. Shepard, the play itself may seem to be coming "from out of nowhere." Actually it has its roots firmly in America, and in our concept of the family as an ideal. *Buried Child* is one of Mr. Shepard's most accessible works, principally because we view this family through the eyes of an impressionable outsider, a young woman accompanying the grandson on a journey into his past. She expects to find "apple pie and turkey dinner." Instead, she discovers cynicism, infantilism and hints of brutality.

This may not sound like a comedy, but it is funny, particularly the second of the three acts, when the young woman is suddenly beset by a kitchen closet of family skeletons. Adrian Hall's Yale production is more overtly amusing than Robert Woodruff's current Off Broadway production of the play, but in the end it is no less serious. Off Broadway the scene is shabbily threadbare. At Yale, Adrianne Lobel's more evocative set is a solid, two-story, wood-shingled house, in which only the interior is in disrepair. Each production is precisely cast and staged.

In both productions the most skillful performances are in the roles of the grandfather and the female stranger. Ford Rainey's Dodge is a representation of that Walter Brennan-Gabby Hayes oldtimer so familiar from scores of cowboy movies. In Mr. Shepard's vision, as personified by Mr. Rainey, the oldtimer is not merely crusty, he is an enraged archetype, denying his paternity, excoriating his progeny and boasting about his misanthropy. As the visitor, Polly Draper, a student at the Yale School of Drama, has the necessary combination of tentativeness and boldness. She is alternatively repelled and amused by this unseemly household.

The father - and vegetable bearer - in the Yale production is a much more child-like creature than the character that we saw Off Broadway. John Seitz portrays him almost as if he were the backward Lennie in *Of Mice and Men* - with a gentleness that belies his hulking appearance. In contrast, the grandson (Tony Shalhoub) becomes a more defiant character.

Finally, the difference in the two productions is one of gradation rather than of interpretation. Despite somewhat different approaches, both end at the same destination - a dirge for the decline of traditional values, a wake for the American dream. *Buried Child*, a penetrating excavation into the essence of blood ties, is further proof that Mr. Shepard is, in several senses, one of our most prodigious dramatists.

THE UNSEEN HAND: JANUARY 6, 1982

The centerpiece of Sam Shepard's *The Unseen Hand*, in revival at La Mama, is a shell of a derelict 1951 Chevrolet convertible that appears to have taken root in the ground. Sitting in the car, and encrusted with age, is Beeson Carroll, recreating his original role as Blue Morphan, a 120-year-old relic of the Old West and a rambling wreck of a monologuist.

His opening conversation with the nonexistent driver of the car is a lowdown and lunatic reflection on the price of changing times. Blue and his long-dead brothers, Cisco and Sycamore, peers of the Jameses and the Daltons, were no menace like the hotrodders of today. Such is the confusion of the modern age, says Blue, that one can no longer tell riffraff from the gentry.

Soon Blue is aroused from his soliloquy by an intruder from Outer Space who wears the brand of the mysterious "unseen hand" on his shaved head and spouts jargon like a computer headed for the repair shop. The Space Freak calls forth the shades of Blue's brothers, makes Blue young again, and tries to enlist the three desperadoes in a revolution in far-out Nogo land. But all systems are "baffled," so the revolution never takes place.

The play is not really extraterrestrial. It is about the depressive state right here on earth, on the loss of innocence and individuality and other matters that have troubled Mr. Shepard since he first began his folklorist investigation of the decline of the American West (and East). The Morphan brothers are outlaws as heroes. For all their shooting and shouting, they are bonded together in a love of the pioneer spirit.

Returned to life, Cisco (Michael Brody), who is as leathery as an Indian scout, is mistaken for a hippie, and Sycamore (Walter Hadler), who is a black-clad evocation of Bat Masterson, is shrugged off as a sharpie. However, unlike their correlatives in today's society, they know what they stood for. Sycamore, for example is a great train robber, and when he is informed that there are no more trains to rob, his body quakes with a mournful tremor. The Morphans are out of time, place and sync - as disoriented as that space freak from the future.

The Unseen Hand, first staged at La Mama in 1969, is from the same period as the author's full-length *Operation Sidewinder*, seen at Lincoln Center. It lasts about one hour, and there is barely an ounce of ennui in this time warp. *The Unseen Hand* is a six-pack of vintage Shepard.

Tony Barsha's production is just the right blend of seediness and spontaneity. Dorian Vernacchio's set could have been transported, intact, from an automobile graveyard. Deirdre O'Connell and David Watkins, representing space-age future and punk present, are craftily in character. Mr. Brody and Mr. Hadler are so authentic that they look as if they hiked over the nearest butte. Mr. Carroll is inimitable. As the ancient incarnation of Blue, he is a figure of ambulatory decrepitude, a quintessential Shepard old man - a character later represented on stage by Henry Hackamore in *Seduced* and Dodge in *Buried Child*. When he is transformed back to his youthful self, it is as if he has suddenly swallowed a pill of rejuvenation. The dry crackle disappears from his voice, he sheds 90 years and stands tall - a living icon of the American frontier.

TRUE WEST: OCTOBER 18, 1982

The production of Sam Shepard's *True West* that opened last night at the Cherry Lane Theater is an act of theatrical restitution and restoration. Two seasons ago, the Public Theater presented the New York premiere of this comedy - a production that was disclaimed in absentia by the playwright - and this work seemed, for the freewheeling Mr. Shepard, uncharacteristically heavy-handed.

Seeing the play in revival, one realizes that it was the production not the play that was originally at fault. The new version - using the same script - is an exhilarating confluence of writing, acting and staging. As performed by John

Malkovich and Gary Sinise, two members of Chicago's Steppenwolf Theater Company making their New York debuts, and as directed by Mr. Sinise, this is the true *True West*. The compass needle is unwavering.

The play is a rambunctious and spontaneous tale about sibling rivalry and the cronyism of popular culture. It shares with an earlier Shepard, *Angel City*, a sardonic concern with the seductiveness of Hollywood and with the battle between art and business. The play's principal characters, Lee and Austin, are fraternal opposites. Lee is a scurvy desert rat, Austin a hot shot intellectual screenwriter. They are country and city mouse, or the old and the new West.

The main problem with the first New York production was that the actors cast as the brothers were too similar in type and temperament. As wittily played by Mr. Malkovich and Mr. Sinise, the brothers become idiosyncratic individuals. As Lee, Mr. Malkovich looks as if he had been sleeping under benches in bus terminals. He is the prototype of a seedy scrounger, and his very presence is an offense to his brother's dignity. As Austin, Mr. Sinise is sober and respectable - an insult to his brother's sense of freedom.

Beneath Lee's animalistic exterior, there is a brazen opportunist. Even when he is pretending to be a yes man - to sell himself to his brother's erstwhile producer - he remains a con man. At first he infiltrates his sibling's life, then he walks all over him and supersedes him as scenarist. Soon he is pecking at the typewriter while his dethroned partner, switching roles, assumes his antisocial attitudes, including door-to-door burglaries. In one of several uproarious interpolations, Mr. Malkovich becomes befuddled at the typewriter, unable even to insert a fresh piece of paper, finally jamming it in under the roller with the help of a kitchen knife.

Though the two actors are a symbiotic team, it is Mr. Malkovich, in the more flamboyant role, who ambles away with the evening's acting trophy. With his air of feigned confidentiality and affecting a slight lisp, he sounds a bit like Jack Nicholson at his wiliest, and in common with Robert Duvall, he offers a threat of imminent explosiveness. However, the performance is a comic original.

With perfect timing and inexhaustible expressiveness, he is amusing and menacing at the same instant - bumping into Mr. Sinise as if trying to bounce him across the room; opening a beer can so close to his brother's nose that the fizz clouds the other man's spectacles, and doing a flamenco on pieces of burnt toast. When he attacks his typewriter with a golf club, he is unrelenting in his hatred for the offending machine. The performance is an acting hole-in-one.

The quieter Mr. Sinise keeps his character from becoming a milque-toast; this worm has to be capable of turning violent. In a supporting role, Sam Schacht has the insincere smile and plumage of the crass producer. As director, Mr. Sinise is an ideal interpreter of Mr. Shepard; he is finely tuned to the special wavelength. He allows for pauses - at moments in the play, the author seems like an American cousin of Pinter - but never impedes the conversational progress of the dialogue. *True West* is acted for its reality even when the events are surreal.

No one forgets that the playwright means to be playful, and the stage business - including the transformation of a spotless kitchen into a trash bin of beer cans and plastic crockery - is made to seem organic (though not biodegradable). Credit should be given to the modular authenticity of the set design by Kevin Rigdon and Deb Gohr, resident designers with the Steppenwolf Theater, and to the nimbleness of the unseen stagehands.

True West, revivified, should now take its rightful place in the company of the best of Shepard - along with *The Tooth of Crime*, *The Curse of the Starving Class* and *Buried Child*.

THE TOOTH OF CRIME: MARCH 2, 1983

Sam Shepard's *Tooth of Crime* is his most savage vision, a diabolical duel between the fading king and the fast-rising challenger. Both men, Hoss and Crow, are rock stars, but on this multi-metaphorical landscape, they are also cowboys, auto racers, gangsters and starship commanders, in each guise vying for the supremacy of power and fame.

In his revival of the play at La Mama Annex, George Ferencz has given the work a slashing interpretation. The production is, as Crow would say, "very razor." At times, however, the evening becomes a war of two worlds, the director versus the playwright. Mr. Ferencz draws freely from his palette of Expressionistic devices, a palette he has used in the past in his Impossible Ragtime Theater versions of early O'Neill. The victor, finally, is Mr. Shepard's play.

This was not the case with the New York premiere of the play in 1972 at the Performing Garage. On that occasion, Richard Schechner gave the work an environmental treatment, awkwardly trying to involve the audience in the action. For greater effectiveness, *The Tooth of Crime* should be seen on a stage, preferably a proscenium, at a remove from the audience.

Mr. Ferencz has had the ingenious idea of staging the entire evening, not simply the showdown, as a rock concert. He took a somewhat similar approach last season with *Cowboy Mouth* by Mr. Shepard and Patti Smith, but that was, in all respects, a less ambitious venture. This time the director has cloistered a hard-driving rock band in a cage under a severely sloping platform. The play itself is enacted on that platform. The two-tiered effect simulates a juke box grown to gargantuan proportions.

On the stage we see Hoss (Ray Wise) at home, ensconced on a black leather couch as throne. In his lair, he does battle with his own insecurities and eventually confronts his fearsome younger antagonist (Stephen Mellor). The shifts between music and drama have the fluidity of a long-playing record, moving from cut to cut.

The design is a collaboration of Bill Stabile (scenery), Paul Mathiesen (lighting) and David Kobernuss (sound), with one source infiltrating the other. The evening begins in total darkness, suddenly pierced by flashing streaks of light and music. The show's colors are Brechtian black and white, with occasional strokes of blood red, as when Hoss exercises his animosity by attacking a fighter's dummy with an open blade.

The first act belongs to Mr. Wise's Hoss, played with feral ferocity, and to Hoss's mistress (the sensuous Jodi Long). Hoss prides himself on being a "Cold Killer," in the title of one of Mr. Shepard's muscular rock songs. As we watch, he becomes obsolescent. The second act turns to the challenger, Crow, in Mr. Mellor's version, an animated gargoyle. With vampire-like claws, he crouches on Hoss's couch in the manner of a Poe-tic raven bearing a message of nevermore.

While both principal actors project the proper edge of malice, each is lacking in a light touch. To alleviate the evening, the director occasionally attempts a bit of vaudeville business. For example, the referee is on roller skates, a dangerous maneuver on that sloping stage. But, for the most part, the evening takes itself too seriously, especially in the long second act. This is in direct contrast to the refreshing spontaneity of the production of Mr. Shepard's *True West*, across town at the Cherry Lane Theater. Renegade comedy is endemic to all of Mr. Shepard's plays, to the portentous *Tooth of Crime* as well as the rambunctious *True West*. However, Mr. Ferencz's concept is marked by its boldness, and it is justified by the relentless nature of the story.

Moving freely from gangster movies of the 40's to punk rock of the 70's, Mr. Shepard speaks in a language that is vividly idiomatic. The imagery is visceral and sexual, a necromantic view of a rapacious society where, for an achiever, there is no acceptable alternative to being on top of the charts.

BACK BOG BEAST BAIT: DECEMBER 16, 1984

Sam Shepard has written in excess of 40 plays, a body of work that for its richness of language and imagery is unmatched by that of any of his peers. Though he experiments and grows with every new play, one can already trace a clear line of artistic development. After an initial outpouring of brief, open-ended anecdotes and sketches, he has progressed through at least three full creative periods.

During the first phase, in the late 1960's and early 70's, he produced a series of mystical epics (on both a large and small scale), mixing figures from folklore with visitors from the outer space of fantasy fiction. These plays include *Mad Dog Blues*, *The Unseen Hand*, *Operation Sidewinder* and *Back Bog Beast Bait*, all four produced in a span of two years. Then, as the author became recognized as an artist and found himself courted by such unearthly powers as Hollywood, he went through a Faustian phase. The result was a series of plays about art and the seduction of the artist (variously represented by a screenwriter, a cowboy, a musician or a gambler or a combination thereof) - *Angel City*, *Geography of a Horse Dreamer*, *Suicide in B Flat* and *The Tooth of Crime*. Reflecting changes in his own life, he next wrote about marriage, the family and American roots. In this third phase has come, I think, his most mature work to date: *Curse of the Starving Class*, *Buried Child*, *True West* and *Fool for Love*.

These categories are, of course, somewhat arbitrary. The plays overlap and counterpoint one another. Themes and motifs appear and reappear - sibling rivalry, voodoo magic, the hero's lost calling, the artist's misplaced muse, the fall of the American dream. One could trace the origins of the couple in *Fool for Love* (1983) all the way back to *La Turista* (1967). Furthermore, any attempt at cataloguing his plays leaves no room for such oddities as *Seduced*, his droll spoof of Howard Hughes, or for the poetic catharsis of *Tongues* and *Savage/Love*, the monologues he wrote in collaboration with Joseph Chaikin.

Shepard is a diverse and unpredictable artist, impossible to contain within any traditional conception of playwriting. He offers theatergoers constant surprises, as he writes new plays and as directors reconsider plays from his past, especially from his mystical phase. Several seasons ago, *The Unseen Hand* returned, with its tale of a confrontation between a desperado of the Old West and an intergalactic space traveler. The latest newfound Shepard is *Back Bog Beast Bait*, revived by George Ferencz as the third in a festival of "jazz plays," three previously produced works by Shepard, given new musical scores by Max Roach. The three, *Angel City*, *Suicide in B Flat* and *Back Bog Beast Bait*, have been running in repertory. The first two have been revived with a certain frequency, but *Back Bog Beast Bait* is one of the author's neglected pieces. First presented in 1971 at the American Place Theater, it was never opened for review. Several years later it briefly surfaced Off Off Broadway. Mr. Ferencz's version is an authentic discovery.

In *Back Bog Beast Bait*, a two-headed "pig beast" is ravaging the Louisiana countryside. Its objective is to annihilate the human species. A terrorized pregnant bayou mother - she has already lost one daughter to the monster - has summoned help. To the rescue ride Slim and his sidekick, Shadow, hired guns come to slay the Beast. As theatrical characters, the two are as old as the James Brothers, all the dauntless cowboys who have populated American movies and mythology. They have also become, under various names, archetypal Sam Shepard heroes, remnants of the Old West, rummaging around for battles to fight, for scores to settle.

The hero in *Angel City* is a cowboy who rides to California in a buckboard and has a head-on collision with Hollywood; the play is the author's pre-*True West* assault on the power brokers who are gassed by the smog in and out of the studio. *Suicide in B Flat* is a mock mystery about the suicide - or disappearance - of a jazzman, who, in search of a new artistic identity, has tried to obliterate his past. Slim and Shadow in *Back Bog* are paradigmatic riders of the purple sage. But heroism has fallen on hard times, and Slim, saddlesore and battle-weary, has lost the old "power." In common with Hoss, the washed-up rock star in *The Tooth of Crime*, he knows that one day soon some hot-shot dude is going to gun him down. No longer so quick on the draw, Slim is spending his declining years walking "all over tarnation" - tarnation being a Shepard synonym for America - "lookin' fer people with enemies." His clients include "bankers and financiers and loan sharks - men who make the country run." The arc is complete - the cowboy hero has moved from myth to mercenary.

Does the arch-fiend really exist or is he a figment of a tormented psyche? As we soon discover, the creature is as visceral as he is metaphorical. He is the apocalypse beating at the door. On one level, *Back Bog* is about "what the wind blows in" - noxious fumes, toxic waste, carcinogens in our food. The Beast's arrival is heralded by Gris Gris, a derelict swamp witch and conjur woman who is bedecked with spells, potions and a bag of mad mushrooms, "beast bait" to trap the careless and the overconfident. Alone among the characters in the play, Gris Gris has a philosophical attitude towards death and pollution. As she says, "Poison's in the air, Jack. Some people take it. Some leave it." By the end of the evening, mimicking the Beast, the human characters have been transmogrified into animals - alligators, bulls and wildcats. Our hero, Slim, is a coyote yelping at the moon. The world has become a miasma in which everything is a mutation.

Because the author is Sam Shepard, the play is a comedy - as grotesque and as amusing as they come. In Mr. Ferencz's production, it has a pulsating kinetic energy that sweeps us through the exclamatory monologues and sudden transformations and brings out the best - and the beast - in the acting company.

Reversing Shepard's physical descriptions, Mr. Ferencz has chosen a short Slim (Raul Aranas) and a tall Shadow (Jim Abele) without denaturing the relationship. Both are swaggeringly in character, Mr. Aranas all strut for the shoot-out, Mr. Abele with the nerve to munch those toadstools as if they are peanuts. Surrounding them is a totemic gallery of gargoyles. Akin Babatunde is an eerie Elijah who crashes through the door spouting deranged sermons, Deirdre O'Connell conveys the borderline insanity of the grieving mother and Sheila Dabney is a virago of a voodoo woman. Dreamily drifting through the play is Zivia Flomenhaft as a specter of the bayou woman's daughter. In looks and in voice, she is also the ghost of Janis Joplin.

Mr. Roach has composed a vibrant jazz score, including new music for the play's three original songs (one with lyrics by Shepard). Sometimes the instrumentation is almost subliminal (from a keyboard comes the quiet wail of a harmonica). As played by a four-piece pit band, the music underscores the rising tension on stage. When the Beast nears the door, the music scrapes and squeals

-on stage, Ms. Dabney herself fiddles fiercely - into an ear-bending cacophony that could frighten a Wookie.

The single regret of the evening is that Mr. Ferencz has been unable to match the acting, conception and music with a visual climax. Bill Stabile's set is rock-solid Shepard - a spare house with a single door and two windows (watch those windows). But when the Beast finally arrives, a creature that is vividly described in the script, he falls short of our fearful expectation. Perhaps it is asking for too much on stage - the phantasmagoric inventiveness of a George Lucas.

Except for the Beast, this is a dynamic production, and one that should consolidate Mr. Ferencz's position - shared with the author himself - as one of the foremost directorial interpreters of Shepard. Mr. Ferencz first came to our attention as a director at the Impossible Ragtime Theater with highly charged productions of early O'Neill (*The Hairy Ape, Dynamo*). Perhaps influenced by those Expressionistic experiments with O'Neill, he has had a tendency when dealing with Shepard to underscore the mystical elements and to slight the author's spontaneous humor. Such is not the case with *Back Bog Beast Bait*, a Doomsday comedy that is as spirited as it is prophetic. Encouraged by *Back Bog*, this may be the time to reconsider Shepard's most spectacular apocalyptic vision, *Operation Sidewinder*, a densely layered "fantasy" about computer technology gone haywire. That play, the subject of controversy when it was presented at the Vivian Beaumont Theater in 1970, is the closest that Shepard has come to Broadway.

CURSE OF THE STARVING CLASS: MAY 24, 1985

Toward the end of Sam Shepard's *Curse of the Starving Class*, a father offers his insight into the family. It is, he tells us, not "just a social thing," but "a reason of nature that we were all together under one roof." Elemental and animalistic roots keep Shepard's embattled clan - mother, father, son and daughter - locked in a lacerating embrace. The family is, in the author's final, terrifying image, like a cat and an eagle tearing each other apart in the sky, but unable to release their hold on one another.

Curse of the Starving Class is, at the same time, Shepard's most comic and most excoriating study of the indomesticity of the American household, where isolated individuals spend hours staring at the bare inside of a refrigerator - the hearth of the contemporary home - and where everyone is plotting an escape. With all the apparent selfishness, these people feed off one another; they are immutably entwined, and no amount of violence can eradicate the blood tie.

Robin Lynn Smith's revival of *Starving Class* captures the full dimension of Shepard's play. Led by the impeccable performances of Kathy Bates as the mother and Bill Pullman as the son, the production etches the shifting shadings of the text, the sudden reversals in temperament as well as the mythical implications of a sweet and sour world gone awry.

Ms. Bates has become one of our finest character actresses, a fact that is demonstrated in her portrayal of the mother in *Starving Class*. Though the role is substantial, in other productions it has tended to be subordinated to those of the son and the father, allied as personifications of "liquid dynamite." Here the mother is given a drily comic presence, as a smart country woman whose head can be turned by the flattery of a shifty lawyer.

One has only to watch Ms. Bates in hair curlers and bathrobe, frying bacon for her own breakfast, to feel that she is indigenous to this chicken-shack house on a forlorn stretch of Southern California land. In common with the rest of the family, she has a fantasy, and when she glamorizes herself to receive a gentleman caller, she is about to become a fool for love - like so many other Shepard characters. When Ms. Bates announces, "Nothing surprises me anymore," she makes the line sound like folk wisdom, even as the house is bombarded with unpredictable events.

As her son, Mr. Pullman begins in a laconic manner - a bit like Mr. Shepard himself, when he acts - making quietly sardonic remarks about the insularity of others. As we soon realize, he is a firm defender of family honor. In a performance that is increasingly incendiary, Mr. Pullman is called upon to perform several of the more outrageous actions to be seen on stage, and he does them all with aplomb. Both he and Ms. Bates move effortlessly from the comic to the pitiable as each tries to make self-liberating moves.

In contrast, the father (Eddie Jones) begins in a derelict rage - Mr. Jones overdoes the storm cloud - and then undergoes a rebirth, a cyclical reversal of his son's rite of passage. Reformed, he restores order to the household, but he will soon be a man in flight. As his wife notices, "Everybody runs away."

As the daughter with hopes of becoming a mechanic (or perhaps a novelist like B. Traven), Karen Tull has the right edge of tomboy willfulness. Playing disparate swindlers, one businesslike, the other boisterous, James Gleason and Jude Ciccolella are icily matched in their guile. In addition, there is a live lamb on stage that deserves a baa for adding its spontaneity to the evening. Brian Martin's appropriately seedy set design looks as if it had been constructed from leftover lumber and laundry washboards.

For all its earthiness, the play has a strong lyrical line, as in the solo reveries of the father and son, as each dreams about unattainable idylls. Since its American premiere in 1978, *Curse of the Starving Class* has deepened with every viewing. Ms. Smith's revival is a realization of the author's vision.

R.A. SHIOMI

YELLOW FEVER: DECEMBER 2, 1982

Standing in a back alley, with his hat shadowing his face, the raincoated figure lights a cigarette, and, in carefully clipped dialogue, he begins to tell us about his latest and toughest crime caper. This man is not Sam Spade, but Sam Shikaze, private eye, and the story is not *The Maltese Falcon* but R.A. Shiomi's *Yellow Fever*.

Mr. Shiomi's new play scores both as parody and as comedy mystery. It is as smart as the snap brim of Sam's hat, and in all senses - writing, acting, directing and design - it is one of the most polished productions of Tisa Chang's Pan Asian Repertory Theater.

Sam (Donald Li) is a Japanese American Bogart, a worldly wise detective who has seen it all, drinks whiskey for breakfast and has sworn off women (don't bet on it). He works from dusk to dawn for little reward, except the pleasure of helping the underdog and of uprooting villainy wherever he finds it. His lair, Vancouver's Powell Street, is a Canadian equivalent of the downtown strip in the movie *Chinatown*. Like Jack Nicholson in that film, Sam is often the luckless victim. With his face plastered with Band-Aids, he says, "I feel like a bruised banana."

The author has memorized the collected cases of Philip Marlowe and Sam Spade, among others, and the dialogue is faithfully lodged in its genre. But for all its passing salutes, it has a flavorful, contemporary Pan Asian air and its own pungent brand of comedy. Sam's private-eye life is complicated by the disappearance of the local Cherry Blossom Queen. Hired to find her, he soon falls into a maelstrom of deception, racism and political intrigue, all of which may have something to do with the diabolical Hong Kong tong connection.

As a playwright, Mr. Shiomi is his own crafty private investigator, making his points through indirection and with droll humor. Underneath a nail-hard exterior, Sam has a redeeming social consciousness. After a foe suggests that he go on a holiday, he says, with nisei bitterness, "The last time I took a vacation, we all went to summer camp - in the winter."

Mr. Li is charming as the crusty hero. He easily makes us believe that he is, in Mr. Shiomi's words, the Sam Shikaze; there can be no other. When he is on a case, everything takes second place. To remind us of that fact, whenever the gumshoe turns on his office radio, he hears "Body and Soul." His sidekick in sleuthing is an amiable, ambitious lawyer named Chuck Chan, played with stylish authority by Henry Yuk. He cuts an exceedingly sporty figure, twirling his umbrella as if it were a nightstick. Freda Foh Shen is seductive as the love interest, a reporter with a gift for karate and an eye for a deadline. Heading the local precinct is Captain Kadota, a former friend of Sam's. Kadota has risen on the force by kowtowing, in contrast to the uncompromising hero washed out in his own early efforts to be a police officer. As played with great conviction by Ernest Abuba, the captain is a man almost doubled-up with anxiety.

Raul Aranas's crisp staging blends the melodramatic story with Sam's diarylike narration. The setting by Christopher Stapleton compactly nestles Sam's seedy office next door to an Oriental safe, and Dawn Chiang's lighting beams atmosphere. In the course of the evening, there are a few excisable jokes, and the climax could be tightened, but these are small reservations. Mr. Shiomi's *Yellow Fever* is so captivating that it makes one eager for further adventures of the inimitable Sam Shikaze.

TOM STOPPARD

UNDISCOVERED COUNTRY: JULY 15, 1979

LONDON - In its search for plays to fill the monumental Olivier stage, Britain's National Theater has turned its sights towards Middle Europe. Several seasons ago the National rediscovered Odon von Horvath and *Tales from the Vienna Woods*, an epic about Austria before World War II, in a new adaptation by Christopher Hampton. This season the National has pushed the clock back to pre-World War I Vienna, with a production of Arthur Schnitzler's *Undiscovered Country* (*Das Weite Land*), in a new version by Tom Stoppard. If anything, the Stoppard-Schnitzler hyphenate is an even more fruitful cross-century collaboration than Hampton-Horvath.

The prolific Schnitzler is, of course, best known in America as the author of *La Ronde* and *Anatol*. *Undiscovered Country* was first produced in 1911 and is only now receiving its English premiere, but through the efforts of Mr. Stoppard and the National Theater it earns a place in the international repertory. However, enterprising companies should be warned that they will need the facilities - and the money - of the National in order to realize the full dimensions of this tragicomedy.

Undiscovered Country is a massive, critical study of a wealthy segment of Vienna, a society that manages to be both self-indulgent and unfulfilled. The symbol of that shallow society is Friedrich Hofreiter (John Wood), a rich industrialist whose primary business seems to be lovemaking. He is a middle-aged Austrian Don Juan, a man who compulsively has an affair with almost every young woman within flirting distance. His mission is a pursuit of youth, and when a woman of his own generation marks him as being too old for youthful follies," Mr. Wood twists his head in amazement. Too old? The pity is that he was "young too soon." One could imagine that in an Austrian production Hofreiter might be played stolidly and plutocratically, perhaps even with a monocle. That is not the way of Mr. Wood. He makes the man's romantic obsession palpable, charging the character with energy, passion and velocity. He rushes across the stage to embrace a new-found love object with his eyes if not quite yet with his arms. Like a child, he wants immediate gratification, and is sometimes surprised by the quickness of his success. As we realize, the character is cold-blooded, but he is also immensely human - and a fleshly contrast to the actor's famous larger-than-life performances in *Sherlock Holmes* and *Travesties*. Similarly, Mr. Stoppard has harnessed himself to his collaborative purposes. His adaptation avoids the Scylla of German por-tentousness and the Charybdis of Stoppardian frivolity. Without neglecting his source, he views Vienna from a contemporary advantage. *Undiscovered Country* seems newly written, a shrewd and caustic look at a declining civilization and a world that retains its relevance.

Infidelity is at the core of the evening. Hofreiter's wife, a proper, somewhat languid woman (Dorothy Tutin), rejects the love of an admirer, who happens to be one of her husband's best friends. The rejection causes the man to commit sui-cide. Instead of extolling his wife's virtue, he reproves her for driving a good man to his grave. At the same time, he is callous about the death itself. What he can-not comprehend is the "foolish vanity of defending a travestied honor," meaning his own honor. Had he been faithful to his wife or were she not attracted to her admirer, Hofreiter might have reacted in sympathy - or so he says. Because of the circumstances he strikes a stance that might be described as amoral outrage. Actually he is a performer, playing the game of love with a triple standard. When the wife undertakes a subsequent liaison with a young officer, her husband is fu-rious. He is a man totally committed to his own self-regard and the jaded world in which he thrives deserves him. It is a society in which an occasional adventurer may "climb the scenery" (a witty description for mountain climbing), but, more often, people remain at garden parties or in the boudoir. Psychoanalysis is treated as a "light hobby" and art is of no consequence. There is a single conversation about the theater, which probably owes more to Mr. Stoppard than to Mr. Schnitzler. Asked to identify a play that he has seen, a superficial young man an-swers blandly, "I never really noticed...Lots of Frenchmen in wigs. I think it rhymed." A poet comments: "One pours out one's life's blood for people like that."

The landscape is panoramic, sweeping from a sumptuous summerhouse to an elegant mountaintop hotel. As interludes there are mimed entre acts - a white suited chorus of tennis players, climbers emerging from the mist to a snowcap. The play is equipped for the long climb - nearly three hours - with a Grand Hotel of characters, who include gossipmongers, idlers and opportunists. The volumi-nous cast, moving on and off stage in twos and threes, gradually grows in individ-uality. At times, the group portrait seems Gorkyesque, as in *Summerfolk*, but the tone is cynical rather than rueful. We do not feel compassion for these people, but we understand them, particularly as we see that the protagonist's self-regard is actually a mask for self-defeat.

Mr. Wood gives a dynamic performance. He is unafraid of the grand gesture, leaping into his role as if demons were driving him as well as the character. The rest of the exemplary cast also conveys the sometimes frantic quality with which these people attempt to avoid ennui. There is incisive acting by, among others, Emma Piper as an available young woman, Joyce Redman as an aging actress, Ms. Tutin as the dutiful wife and Greg Hicks as her successful suitor.

Central to the play is the minor figure of a philosophical hotelkeeper (Michael Bryant) who is an older semblance of Mr. Wood. Living at the peak of a mountain, Mr. Bryant exudes haughtiness as if it were ether; the air seems thin around him. "What a strange uncharged country is human behavior," he tells Mr. Wood, delivering the message. In this country there is room for "love and deceit, loyalty and betrayal." Should Mr. Wood outlive his usefulness, he may become like Mr. Bryant, an aging, dapper philanderer in a velvet suit. But Mr. Wood is plunging into an abyss, courting disaster as calmly as he courts romance.

The National has spared no expense - or expanse - in outfitting *Undiscovered Country*. Using the entire breadth of the open stage, Peter Wood's production is opulent, with furniture that might set records at Sotheby's and clothes that seem to come from a manor-house wardrobe rather than a costume shop. Where else, except perhaps in the movies, can one see such a lavish, authentic recapitulation of a time, place and sensibility?

ROSENCRANTZ AND GUILDENSTERN ARE DEAD: JANUARY 31, 1990

Rosencrantz and Guildenstern Are Dead, Tom Stoppard's virtuosic play on *Hamlet*, vaults a time and language barrier in the Gesher Theater Company production, performed in Russian at the Brooklyn Academy of Music. While retaining its essence as an existential comedy about a pair of classic outsiders caught up in the confusion at Elsinore, the play gains new relevance in this production and in the light of recent political turmoil in the former Soviet Union.

This refreshing, swift-paced version of Mr. Stoppard's youthful travesty is directed by Yevgeny Arye, leading an Israeli company of émigré Russian actors. Simultaneous translation back into English is provided over headsets, adding a further Stoppardian twist to the multi-cultural experience.

The production, using an adaptation by Joseph Brodsky that abbreviates the text, retains the author's linguistic limberness at the same time that it adds sprightly physical comedy. The Gesher actors are adept as clowns and mimes.

The result is considerably livelier than the recent film version directed by the playwright.

Mr. Arye places the characters on a narrow runway, a precarious strip of stage between sections of the audience. While Rosencrantz and Guildenstern struggle for their equilibrium in the mysterious story that engulfs them, there are glimpses of that other play in progress. Hamlet chases Ophelia, or is she chasing him? Uprooted from their source, the words fly up. Hamlet's "to be" is not to be. Claudius and a particularly lusty Gertrude are rough and tumble in their randiness. Carrying a diplomatic pouch, Polonius looks as imperious as a sommelier brandishing a wine list. Without clarification by Shakespeare, the rest is chaos, and it is an antic antidote to the intense chamber *Hamlet* presented on this stage last week by the Cameri Theater of Tel Aviv.

Even as Rosencrantz and Guildenstern lose their footing, they retain their sense of foolishness. Mark Ivanir's impish Rosencrantz had the wider mood swings while Yevgeny Terletsky's Guildenstern is the more eupeptic and philosophical. The two move a step closer to Estragon and Vladimir, their models in this game of waiting. At the same time, one is more keenly aware of their roles as hired henchmen of the king, dupes enlisted in the Danish equivalent of the K.G.B. Over everyone's shoulders is the specter of contemporary politics.

Along with the title characters, the leading player (here called the Actor) is at the center of the charade. He brings his motley troupe into the castle's pandemonium. With his natural hauteur. Boris Achanov could offer histrionic instruction to Macready and Forrest in *Two Shakespearean Actors*. His underlings, jumping in and out of roles and costumes, are a gymnastically inclined ensemble. This is especially so in the case of Alexander Demidov as Alfred, the actor who specializes in female roles and is prepared to play the one-woman version of *The Rape of the Sabine Women*.

The play within the play becomes a quick flurry of blackouts and tableaux: at one point a pitcher of poison is poured into the ear of the player king. There is a brief let-up in the third act, but not enough to becalm the comedy. Repeatedly, the director stresses the overheard nature of the story. Things are witnessed at odd angles and, on the run, through doors at either end of the platform. In the scene aboard ship, the stage itself suddenly rocks as if struck by a tempest.

In the background is heard the hurdy-gurdy of Felliniesque music, emphasizing the carnival aspect of the show. Galina Lioly's modern-dress costumes provide their own amusing commentary in an invigorating reinterpretation of the original Stoppard. The production is inventive without obscuring the author's ideas. Man is at the mercy of history. In life as in the play, it is impossible to know exactly what is happening, even if one is at the vortex of the event.

☙

THE REAL INSPECTOR HOUND: AUGUST 14, 1992

Before Tom Stoppard became a playwright, he did a stint as a theater critic. In *The Real Inspector Hound,* he gets even with his former colleagues and with the hazards of the profession. With this devious theatrical comedy, nimbly revived by the Roundabout Theater Company, he kills two critical birds, or in Stoppard parlance, one Birdboot and one Moon. For a playwright, this is a case of character assassination. Clearly Mr. Stoppard had fun writing the play, a pleasure that is shared by his audience. In its time, 1971 Off Broadway, it seemed an amusing trifle. It has ripened into an amusing truffle.

At its root, it is a play on criticism. Moon is a second-string drama critic, an eternal stand-in, always a backup and never a lead singer, a role that he describes in an irate stream of resentment that identifies with all the understudies in life. Whenever Moon goes to the theater, he is affronted by the question, "Where's Higgs?" The absent Higgs is his newspaper's first-stringer, and the object of Moon's wrath. Birdboot, in contrast, represents critical complacency. A smug sybarite, he is a blurbster, reveling in the fact that one of his reviews has been reproduced in its entirety in neon at the Theater Royal. For him, no favoritism is strong enough to be labeled a conflict of interest.

As we watch Moon and Birdboot at work at play, they watch the unfolding of a creaky Agatha Christie-like whodunit in which there is a madman loose on the moors. Or is he already inside Lady Cynthia Muldoon's manor house? In rude critical fashion, Moon and Birdboot begin to compose their reviews before they see the show, each finding within the text what he chooses to find.

For Moon, who can spot high art in a flyspeck, the potboiler is "sort of a thriller," but with undercurrents: "The play, if we can call it that, and I think on balance we can, aligns itself uncompromisingly on the side of life." Birdboot is more interested in the acting, or rather, in the actresses. As a freelance philanderer, he has already had a fling with the actress playing the ingénue Felicity and now has his eye on Lady Cynthia.

During a lull in the mystery, the telephone rings on stage, and when it keeps ringing, Moon rises from his seat in the theater and answers it, thereby shattering the fourth wall. To Moon's amazement, the call is for Birdboot. Soon both critics are onstage and enmeshed in the mystery. Bodies fall, the plot spirals and three characters vie for the role of the real inspector, who is a hound but not much of a sleuth. The play wins laughs every which way and disarms all criticism. Repeatedly Mr. Stoppard writes his own review. It is Hound who observes that the show "lacks pace," that it is a "complete ragbag."

As a point of fact, *The Real Inspector Hound* is an exceedingly clever lampoon, sharply in focus and at least double-barreled in its own critical assault. But Gloria Muzio's production at the Roundabout could use more pace. The non- mysterious part moves too slowly, and not all of the actors have mastered the art of Stoppardian spontaneity.

Simon Jones, who can be a devilish comic actor, is a shade too dour as Moon; more linguistic enthusiasm would spark even more humor. David Healy has greater vim as the smarmy Birdboot. J. Smith-Cameron and Anthony Fusco are stylish poseurs as the juveniles, and Jeff Weiss dives diabolically into his role as the "wheelchair-ridden half-brother" of her ladyship's husband, "who 10 years ago went out for a walk on the cliffs and was never seen again," at least not until the last scene of the comedy. John Lee Beatty's set, which puts the audience backstage looking at the actors and the critical contingent, has its own drollness.

Along the way to the cliffhanging conclusion, Mr. Stoppard takes time to twit the twaddle that critics encounter on stage and to mock the ennui of the English gentry as well as the game of bridge, which is confused with chess and bingo. Critics are the primary target. They are, in the author's words, pillified and viloried.

Real critics, of course, are impervious to criticism and always maintain their objectivity, except when they are being subjective. They are not a whit like the fictive Birdboot and Moon. This review, if we can call it that, and I think on balance we can, aligns itself uncompromisingly on the side of *The Real Inspector Hound*.

To expand the audience's amusement and also the length of the evening, the play is preceded by Mr. Stoppard's *15-Minute Hamlet*, an extract from his play *Dogg's Hamlet*. In this curtain-raiser, an acting troupe does a fast forward through the high points of *Hamlet*. Shakespeare (Mr. Weiss) offers a pauseless prologue that segues from "Something is rotten in the state of Denmark" to "To be or not to be" and Hamlet's own "To be" rushes into "Get thee to a nunnery."

Excising Rosencrantz and Guildenstern (amply provided for in another Stoppard opus), the sketch scampers from battlements to bedchamber, inventing new and tricky transitions. Mr. Jones is a dizzy Hamlet, and Mr. Weiss switches so suddenly from Claudius to Polonius that he almost collides with himself behind the arras. *The 15-Minute Hamlet* is followed by a two-minute tongue-tripping abridgement. It is just long enough to catch the conscience of the king and the short attention span of critics like Birdboot and Moon.

DAVID STOREY

THE MARCH ON RUSSIA: NOVEMBER 15, 1990

In David Storey's novel *Pasmore*, the title character is troubled by a recurrent dream. Running in a race, he finds himself overtaken by everyone, even the "idlers and dullards." Suddenly awakening, he feels an "undiminished sense of terror." That fear - that life itself has passed one by - shadows Mr. Storey's new play, *The March on Russia*, a seemingly becalmed but quietly turbulent drama about Colin Pasmore, a university lecturer and author, and his family. For the Pasmores, fulfillment is no longer even a wishful fantasy. All that the characters can see on the horizon is more of the same, followed by "fullstop."

The play was first presented last year at the Royal National Theater in London, in a production reuniting the playwright with his symbiotic director, Lindsay Anderson. In May, Josephine Abady staged it with an American company at the Cleveland Playhouse, and that production opened this week at Chelsea Stage.

Though one would never suggest that the American actors could duplicate the authenticity, especially the Yorkshire accents, of their English predecessors, Ms. Abady's production is exactingly shaded and subtle in its delineation of these regional characters. Led by John Carpenter and Bethel Leslie as the father and mother, the actors capture the underlying humor as well as the sadness. Each of the three younger actors, Carol Locatell and Susan Browning as the daughters and Sean Griffin as Colin, is sensitive to the disparities as well as the similarities of these siblings. Together the five actors evoke a moving family portrait.

In more hopeful times, there were happier dreams. The father recalls, with poignancy, his youthful military service invading the Crimea around the time of the Russian Revolution (his march on Russia). It was a moment of adventure, followed immediately by marriage and 45 years of work in a Yorkshire coal mine. The father's life has been more forcefully circumscribed than the lives of his wife and children, but each one has been trapped within a self-limiting world.

Family rivalries become family rituals. Which child was loved most? To the audience, it should be clear that each was equally unloved, despite signs of occasional favoritism, and that the elder Pasmores have moved past their own despair to a kind of barely controlled disharmony.

At least for the first act, the story may seem deceptively light as the three adult offspring arrive separately at the parents' retirement cottage to help them celebrate their 60th wedding anniversary. There are no character revelations, as in Mr. Storey's *In Celebration*, which deals with a related family situation 20 years earlier. But *The March on Russia* is suffused with sorrow and understanding as the characters find themselves unable to achieve a sense of kinship or of mutual support.

The play becomes elegiac, a longing for lost times that never were, except perhaps for the father's "march on Russia," and even that story seems to be disappearing from his memory. At the end of the play, his wife has to prod him to remember the facts (and perhaps the fiction) of his tale, the thought of which has become as important to her as it is for him.

In his plays and novels, Mr. Storey has tellingly explored the nature of families, especially those with working-class backgrounds, in which the offspring are educated and elevated to a higher social and economic level. The generational chasm between a father who has worked with his hands as a collier and a son who works with his mind cannot be bridged. People in Storey plays may embrace, but they are unable to touch one another emotionally. Instead, they either repress their feelings (like the mother) or suffer breakdowns (like Colin).

For Mr. Storey, *The March on Russia* is a return to an earlier mode. After *In Celebration*, he moved on to the poetic symbolism of *The Contractor* and *Home*, and in more recent years he has concentrated on fiction. Some may regard the new work as overly traditional, but family plays are always viable when they are as deeply felt as this one and when they are written with such lyrical understatement. Though the Pasmores are definably from Yorkshire, they are recognizable wherever sons and daughters are encouraged to excel and then do not realize their own ambitions and the expectations of their parents.

WENDY WASSERSTEIN

ISN'T IT ROMANTIC: DECEMBER 16, 1983

In her new, improved version of *Isn't It Romantic*, Wendy Wasserstein has added a sweet humanity to her comic cautionary tale about a young woman's ascent to adulthood. When the play was first presented two years ago at the Phoenix Theater, it overflowed with amusing lines about such protean subjects as indulgent parents, rebellious offspring and food as a substitute for love. With careful rewriting, the playwright has turned the tables on her own play. Opening last night at Playwrights Horizons, it is now a nouvelle cuisine comedy.

While the heroine, Janie Blumberg, waits for romance, she is bedeviled by parents who telephone her at 7 A.M. to sing "Sunrise, Sunset," and to find out if an eligible man has entered her life - and if not, why not? Resisting dependency is no small feat, but she does it by dint of her own doughtiness.

As charmingly personified by Cristine Rose, Janie has the heart of a waif and sometimes the demeanor of a clown. Some of the character's jibes are still inner-directed, but the author has cut back on self-mockery and has even sacrificed a few of her funniest lines. She allows us to see the character as a trusting woman who wants "it all" - marriage, family, a job writing for the "large bird" on *Sesame Street*, and loving parents who respect her distance.

At its core, the play is about mothers and daughters and friends as "family," paralleling the lives of Ms. Rose and her best friend, Lisa Banes, a lithe WASP who is upwardly mobile on Madison Avenue and who is a stylish role model for the down-to-earth heroine. Each is guarded by the guiding hand of a mother. Ms. Rose's parent, gracefully portrayed by Betty Comden (in a rare nonmusical performance), is her own free spirit, an ardent student of the dance who belongs to no company and is, in her daughter's apt word, an "independent." The other mother (an elegant Jo Henderson) is a self-willed tycoon and a feminist before it was acceptable. Each daughter has too much to live up to.

Approaching 30, they are slightly older versions of the *Uncommon Women* who graduated from Mount Holyoke in Ms. Wasserstein's first play. As she follows them through the rites of career and courtship, we see their different reactions to encumbering alliances with men. Ms. Rose is taken with her mother's dream figure of a son-in-law, a prosperous Jewish doctor (Chip Zien). He is the scion of a long line of assimilators: His father is the Frank Perdue of popovers. Ms. Banes is enamored of her boss's boss (Jerry Lanning) who is sincere about his male chauvinism.

Watch Ms. Rose, an incompetent in the kitchen, when the doctor comes to call and brings a chicken for dinner. Frantically she phones her friend and whispers, "Howdja, howdja, cook a chicken?" - repeating the line as if she were the straight man in a vaudeville sketch. Breezy, fresh and unaffected, *Isn't It Romantic* skips its mother-daughter showdown, becomes belatedly tearful, but is immediately redeemed by a touching conclusion in which everyone agrees that "It's just too painful not to grow up."

Gerald Gutierrez's production is less cluttered than its predecessor, although there are still too many scene changes, a fact that is partly disguised by having stagehands pose as moving men and waiters. Another added comic touch arrives on the heroine's telephone answering machine, which is filled with breathless messages, including many from a former classmate who is a one-woman disaster when it comes to romance. That taped role is played with a gleeful insanity by Meryl Streep. The visible cast is entirely ingratiating. In the central role, Ms. Rose is the witty embodiment of an endearing sprite who finally arrives at a point where she can unpack her belongings and move into her life.

THE HEIDI CHRONICLES: DECEMBER 12, 1988

Deep into *The Heidi Chronicles,* Wendy Wasserstein's enlightening portrait of her generation, the title character makes a speech to her high school alumnae at a "Women, Where Are We Going?" luncheon. In the speech, a tour de force for the author, Heidi vividly describes an aerobics class that proved to be an epiphany. While exercising, she was surrounded by an inferno of "power women" both young and old. With sudden intuition, she realized that as a child of the 1960's -

as a woman subjected to judgment by men and as a humanist trying to position herself among feminists - she is stranded, and no one is about to rescue her.

She simply wants to be Heidi, but the closest she can come to self-definition is ambivalence, empathizing with the Heffalump in *Winnie-the-Pooh*. As chronicled by Ms. Wasserstein (and as acted by Joan Allen), Heidi's search for self is both mirthful and touching.

In *The Heidi Chronicles*, at Playwrights Horizons, the author looks beyond feminism and yuppie-ism to individualism and one's need to have pride of accomplishment. We are what we make of ourselves, but we keep looking for systems of support. As Heidi learns, her friends are her family.

Ms. Allen plays the title role with an almost tangible vulnerability and a sweetness that is never saccharine. In her hands, Heidi always remains sympathetic even when she forgets to be self-protective. The role calls for the actress to seem happy (a smile, as for the camera) when she is really contemplative. Ms. Allen fills the role with a quiet gentility, while also conveying Heidi's natural wit.

In *Uncommon Women and Others* Ms. Wasserstein offered a collage of Seven Sisters school graduates. In *Isn't It Romantic?* she sharpened her focus on a single woman (and her best friend) trying to be grown-up. With her ambitious new play, she both broadens and intensifies her beam, to give us a group picture over decades, a picture of women who want it all - motherhood, sisterhood, love and boardroom respect.

The play opens with Heidi as art historian, delivering a lecture on the neglect of female painters from "the dawn of history to the present," and uses that neglect as an artful motif to depict man's exclusionist attitude toward women. During a series of pithy flashbacks, we see Heidi on her own rock-strewn path to liberation. As she moves from high school intellectual to awakening feminist, in the background we hear about political and cultural events. Heidi and her group are emblematic of their time, but the historical references never become intrusive. They form a time line on which Heidi teeters like a tightrope walker.

Around her, women take advantage of opportunity, and one man, Scoop Rosenbaum, takes advantage of Heidi. Scoop is an arrogant idealist. Even as he offers Heidi no choice but subjugation to his will, he is becoming a prime mover of his generation, through his high-flying magazine, Boomer, the beacon of the baby-boomer crowd. In one of the play's few minor weaknesses, neither the character nor the actor (Peter Friedman) is as charming as he is supposed to be. One necessarily wonders why Heidi has such a diehard affection for him. Far more believable is Peter Patrone (Boyd Gaines), a hugely successful pediatrician, who is gay. In all matters except sexuality, he is Heidi's soulmate.

Ms. Wasserstein has always been a clever writer of comedy. This time she has been exceedingly watchful about not settling for easy laughter, and the result is a more penetrating play. This is not to suggest, however, that *The Heidi Chronicles* is ever lacking in humor. Several of the episodes are paradigmatic comic set pieces

- a consciousness raising session, the aerobics speech and a hilarious television program in which Heidi, Scoop and Peter are brought together as representative spokespersons. The colloquy is misguided by an airhead talk-show hostess (delightfully played by Joanne Camp). When Scoop becomes characteristically self-serving, the pediatrician steals the spotlight, as is often the case - a credit both to the character and to Mr. Gaines's sensitive performance.

As Heidi's childhood friend, Ellen Parker transforms herself from "sister shepherdess" on the front lines of feminism to queenpin of the movie and television industry, trying and failing to convince the heroine to become a sitcom consultant. Ms. Camp, Sarah Jessica Parker and Anne Lange amusingly play all the Jills, Debbies, Betsys and Beckys who complicate Heidi's life.

Subtly the play parallels aspects of the original *Heidi* novel. As we are reminded, in the first two chapters the heroine travels and then "understands what she knows." At the beginning of her journey, Ms. Wasserstein's Heidi is adamant that she will never be submissive, especially to men. To our pleasure, the character finally finds selfless fulfillment. Following the chronicles of Heidi, theatergoers are left with tantalizing questions about women today and tomorrow.

MICHAEL WELLER

LOOSE ENDS: FEBRUARY 14, 1979

WASHINGTON - Michael Weller's *Moonchildren*, first presented in the United States at the Arena Stage in 1971, became a pivotal play of its period. It caught, as if for a time capsule, young people of the 1960's escaping from the demands of their lives by "putting on" their friends and spoofing strangers.

In his new play, *Loose Ends* - once again Mr. Weller is at the Arena Stage and directed by Alan Schneider - the author looks at his moonchildren passing into adulthood in the 1970's, moving from restlessness to rootlessness. Faced with a choice of freedoms, they sample everything and find little sustenance. *Loose Ends* is at the same time a wise and funny play, not only a worthy successor to *Moonchildren*, but also one of the more pertinent plays of this season.

It firmly demonstrates that Mr. Weller is a perceptive, humane playwright who has something important to say about his contemporaries, a generation that is not lost or silent, but shifting - dropping in and dropping out, making and unmaking its lives.

Just as *Moonchildren* was a play of the 60's, *Loose Ends* speaks about the '70's, and manages to do it without being either topical or political. Although the play reaches from 1970 to 1979, through Vietnam and Watergate, neither event is discussed. The closest that the author comes to politics is a mention of the Peace Corps, which starts the play on a note of regret for failed ideals.

In Mr. Weller's approach, there is a reminder of Chekhov. Offstage there are cataclysmic social upheavals, but the playwright is concerned with the behavior of his representative people, their mutually wounding personal relationships. Mr. Weller speaks with his own, indelibly contemporary voice. He knows the jargon and patter of his peers and has the artist's ability to transform them into revealing theatrical dialogue.

The play begins in Bali, with a young couple (Kevin Kline and Roxanne Hart) falling in love. For a brief moment, Bali is paradise enough, but as the two of them return to civilization, undertake a relationship, and begin to go through changes, we see the widening chasm between them. We grow to like this couple so much that we hope for their happiness even as they head toward their inevitable separation.

For most of the evening, the play is a refreshing exercise in loose ends -with deceptive casualness giving us a complete group portrait of people in flux. However, toward the end of the play, searching for a conclusion, the author grasps the wrong strands, suddenly revealing that what divides his couple is not only a lack of trust, but the husband's obsessive desire to have a child. We are not convinced either by the motivation or the resolution. The scene is damaging, but not fatal. Then the playwright pulls the strands together with a wistful epilogue as the principals look to their past to find their future. In keeping with its title, *Loose Ends* becomes a play of searching rather than of solutions.

Loose Ends derives from Mr. Weller's one-act *Split*, presented last season at the Ensemble Studio Theater. The far more ambitious full-length play uses the same theme - splitting couples - but not the characters or dialogue. *Split* was like a short story. *Loose Ends* is like a novel, resonant with atmosphere, humor, character and conflict.

To a certain extent, the supporting players are even more evocative than the central couple. Mr. Weller introduces us to a young woman (Robin Bartlett) who is as impressionable as clay. One second she is a rapt follower of a complacent guru (Stephen Mendillo), another she is the contented wife of a city planner. Dealing with such targets, Mr. Weller has a satiric prowess as sharp as that of Mike Nichols and Elaine May. Similarly, he comments on the source of fraternal and "sisterly" competition - in scenes between Mr. Kline and his showboating brother (Jordan Charney) and between Ms. Hart and her own friendly rival (Jodi Long). One of the author's most incisive characterizations is of a frequently pregnant young woman (Celia Weston) and her aggressively unsophisticated lover (Jay O. Sanders). As was the case with *Moonchildren*, a large cast seems to live rather than to play, its characters.

The most impressive performance is given by Mr. Kline, who manages to keep the hero ingratiating even as he wanders through different states of mind.

Mr. Kline combines the good looks of a leading man with an exuberant sense of comedy. As his character becomes, in society's sense, a success, he never forgets that inside his Madison Avenue disguise he is still a moonchild.

Because of the play's extensive geography, it is not entirely at home on the Arena's open stage. For example, the beach at Bali in the moonlight cannot be convincingly conveyed in this cold, bare space. Despite the physical limitations, Mr. Schneider creates a harmonious ambience for Mr. Weller's exhilarating new play.

MAC WELLMAN

BAD PENNY: JUNE 20, 1989

Moving environmentally through the streets and buildings of Manhattan, En Garde Arts is an invigorating urban presence. With its current *Plays in The Park* trilogy, Anne Hamburger's nomadic troupe takes a venturesome stride forward. Mac Wellman's *Bad Penny*, the centerpiece of the company's current experiment in site-specific theater, encapsulates the lunacy of Central Park and the city that surrounds it.

Bad Penny is a sharply satiric comedy as well as an on-location performance event, a play that earns its setting on and around Bow Bridge on The Lake. Sitting on a lakeside rock, two strangers (Jan Leslie Harding and Stephen Mellor) have a conversation that reveals their obsessive personalities. Ms. Harding is playing an outer-borough New Yorker with an ardent belief in the power of myth, while Mr. Mellor, as a visitor from Big Ugly, Mont., is a "freelance memory fabulist." He has been trudging through the park with a flat tire, heading west to find someone to fix it. As the audience eavesdrops on the dialogue, strange things happen.

In the middle of the Lake, a man sits on a tiny island and shouts rude remarks through a megaphone. A woman on Bow Bridge adds her own vocal challenge and, across the water, Reg E. Cathey, who may be a homeless person, orates in company with a 12-member chorus carrying umbrellas. In oblique fashion, the conversation accrues a stereophonic richness.

Ms. Harding warns Mr. Mellor about the "hideous Boatman of Bow Bridge." But in true New York spirit, he remains complacent, even as the masked Boatman appears, rowing a boat that is shrouded as if it had just come from a five-alarm pyre. The Boatman could be Charon himself crossing our local Styx. Mr. Mellor calmly disregards his danger as he is beckoned to the play's diabolical conclusion.

As ingeniously directed by Jim Simpson, *Bad Penny* is nurtured by its outdoor landscape, but it is good enough that it could also be staged indoors (if a theater could float the Boatman across a stage). Alternatively, the play could be portaged from park to pool.

As the unabashed actors went through their public, highly emotive artistic endeavors at a twilight performance on Saturday, a few passersby (on foot and in boats) stared. But most seemed oblivious or at least unmindful of the theater happening around them, as if this were just another average evening in Central Park. This is, of course, one of the salient points of En Garde Arts, and, in particular, *Bad Penny*.

TERMINAL HIP: JANUARY 12, 1990

Terminal Hip, Mac Wellman's *Spiritual History of America Through the Medium of Bad Language*, is a post-Joycean Jabberwocky. Expect no exegesis. Just sit back and enjoy the torrent of language, as Mr. Wellman zigzags through time, space and participle.

This riff (at Performance Space 122) is a crazy quilt of slang and circumlocutions, double negatives and oxymorons gathered under a baldachin, or ornamental canopy of the mind. Listening to it, one repeatedly reaches for a mixed metaphor as steering wheel. *Terminal Hip* is a word processor gone awry garbling "grammatical shibboleth" on a scrambled screen.

Occasionally, the playwright strikes a note of clarity, trashing beachfront condos, assailing United States foreign policy in Central America (presidents who "jubilate with successive Somozas") and parading the component parts of the panda. For fun, there is a replay of Abbott and Costello's "who's on first" routine. If all this sounds illogical, that's for a reason. Think too hard about meaning, or listen for "chtonic murmurs," or primitive sounds, and one might be overcome by vertigo.

Amazingly, the actor Stephen Mellor tones and tames the monologue so that it seems to have an organic flow. Mr. Wellman and Mr. Mellor, who have often worked together, are quite a team, especially as evidenced in this play and in last summer's *Bad Penny*. *Bad Penny* made a certain sense, as Mr. Mellor's character summed up a mad tourist's underview of New York. In contrast, *Terminal Hip* whirligigs its way without a thought about destination while taking theatergoers for a wild word-busting ride.

With all its convolutions and neologisms, the text must be impossible to memorize, but then who, except for Mr. Wellman, could tell if Mr. Mellor missed a word - or made up a word? The dream-of-consciousness principle is the thing, and the actor gives *Terminal Hip* a kick of kinetic energy. He seems to know what he is saying even when the audience is left musing in the dark. His acting provides punctuation, as when he exclaims, "Why Russia? Why Brooklyn? Why lard?" and punches his fist into the air.

Mr. Mellor's expressions are those of a political candidate who believes everything he is told to say. Expostulating and extrapolating, he is sometimes like a hipster version of Prof. Irwin Corey, delivering a doubletalk lecture as the world's greatest authority. If the play is a "maniacal hubbub," it is a literate, amusing hubbub. It may be true, as the author says, that "any airhead can play an air guitar," But only Mr. Wellman could have written this play and only Mr. Mellor could have imbued it with such histrionic variety.

CROWBAR: FEBRUARY 20, 1990

Crowbar, the newest site-specific project of Anne Hamburger's En Garde Arts company, is an act of reclamation and renewal. On Sunday, the Mac Wellman play reopened the Victory Theater on West 42d Street as a home for legitimate theater.

Built by Oscar Hammerstein in 1899, the theater was originally a grand Broadway palace, a home for stars as well as theatrical spectacles. In recent years, it has been a porno movie house. *Crowbar* is part ghost play, part sound-and-light show such as one might see at a chateau in France, echoing with memories of the Victory's illustrious past.

The audience sits on and near the stage while the play takes place throughout the theater - itself a novel event. The exit signs themselves look like a hundred points of light. As we watch, aisles, balconies and boxes come alive with actors playing out Mr. Wellman's thesis that "all theaters are haunted." A spotlight strikes the building's dome, with sculptured cherubs that could have flown over from a Boucher painting. Then, with a thud, a sandbag falls to the stage, and Mr. Wellman sails into his archival recreation. *Crowbar* supposedly takes place during the intermission of the play that opened the theater, James A. Hearn's bucolic *Sag Harbor*. The narrative revolves circuitously around a father's search for his missing daughter and various factual deaths of the period, including that of a workman who died in an onstage accident.

The tales are wrapped in the author's elliptical, rhapsodic language, aerated by quirky humor. An actress playing a patient theatergoer awaits the end of this "longest intermission" in order to go backstage and ask for an autograph from Lionel Barrymore, "a fine young actor."

For a 90-minute play, there are perhaps too many tangents, with the playwright reaching out to be inclusive of time, place and metaphor ("America is an empty theater"). The show is most intriguing when it holds to the building itself and to the story of Hammerstein and David Belasco, who operated it in the first decade of this century. From accompanying slide projections, arranged by James Sanders, one receives a photographic representation of what the theater was like in its heyday, when it housed everything from Houdini to *Abie's Irish Rose*.

At the same time, the play reveals information about the secret apartment that Belasco kept for his mistress above the dome; the roof garden with a Dutch village and a working mill, and the artificial lake beneath the stage. Even when the narrative becomes convoluted, our senses are stimulated by the environmental aspects of the evening, a credit both to Mr. Wellman and to the director, Richard Caliban.

In the spirit of En Garde Arts, the two are restlessly inventive in using the vast space, even the great height over the heads of theatergoers on stage. As an actress speaks her lines, three specters parrot her words on three levels of the theater - in the orchestra and the two balconies - and at other moments 20 specters snake through the house. Suddenly, a character appears in a box, followed by a laugh reverberating from the last row of the second balcony. Seated on stage, the audience sees the theater and the theatrical event from the viewpoint of the actor, except, in this case, the theater becomes the protagonist of the play.

Throughout the show is filtered a musical score, written by David Van Tieghem and played by him on various timpanic instruments. The score eerily conveys an air of mystery and Kyle Chepulis's sets and properties and Brian Aldous's lighting effects are additional atmospheric assets. Bearded and in period costume, Omar Shapli exudes turn-of-the-century theatricality in the leading role of the father of the lost daughter. Reg E. Cathey, Yusef Bulos and Elzbieta Czyzewska evoke the feeling of characters recently released from a state of suspended animation.

Interest is so stimulated in the lost architectural splendor that a second-act tour of the Victory would have seemed most appropriate - from the sky-high dome to the depths of the artificial lake, which, if it still exists, might be a byway for a phantom of 42d Street. Such musings are immediately forgotten when theatergoers exit back into the tawdry street, but for the duration of *Crowbar*, our imaginations are heightened along with those of Mr. Wellman and his collaborators.

SINCERITY FOREVER: DECEMBER 8, 1990

In *Sincerity Forever*, Mac Wellman's savage comedy about everyday lunacies in America, two adolescent girls in a dirt-poor Southern town calmly accept the order of the universe. God must have a plan, says one, or why else would He keep both of them "ignorant forever in absolute sincerity."

Like everyone else in Hillsbottom, the two are wearing Ku Klux Klan costumes. They are blissful in their brainlessness, confessing they cannot tell good art from bad art and do not know why junk bonds are junky. The conversation dwells on important matters like boyfriends rather than on child abuse or the plutonium-poisoned water that is killing their community. Mr. Wellman's view of contemporary society is dire but not doleful. In his headlong search for social and political commentary, he never neglects his comic instincts, starting with the fact that the play is dedicated to Jesse Helms. Though not mentioned in the text, Senator Helms is as omnipresent as air; the characters exist in an age of "infinite regress."

Sincerity is the key to that infinitude. The message is that one can do anything and say anything as long as it is said with conviction. This goes equally for questions of racism, religion and art, and, of course, confuses sincerity with truth. While pursuing polemics, the author retains his role as a theatrical conjurer. *Sincerity Forever* (at BACA Downtown) is very much a heightened act of the imagination, the success of which is shared by Mr. Wellman's director, Jim Simpson, and by their droll, cone-headed cast.

The framework of the play is fantasy. A "mystic furball" has infected Hillsbottom. What, you may ask, are furballs? They are foul-mouthed aliens that look like partly plucked chickens. The two who have landed (or have emerged from Hell) are played in full comic plumage by Stephen Mellor and Jan Leslie Harding. The grand furball design is to glitch Hillsbottom. Those two teen-agers (Amy Brenneman and Leslie Nipkow) are succeeded on stage by two crude dudes, and as the furball effect occurs, their dialogues are cross-pollinated. Deviously, Mr. Wellman churns the worlds into a Babel, so that the teen-age girls talk like beer-bellied rednecks, and vice versa.

Sincerity Forever does not follow a straight narrative path, but is brambled with digressions and allusions to Wotan and other figures from legend and mythology. A theatergoer may be mystified, especially by the sudden appearance of a character identified as Jesus H. Christ (who is black and female), carrying a suitcase that may contain the secrets of the universe. Behind the seeming blasphemy is a deeper sense of morality and a knowledge that a Messiah would be greeted with cynicism by these natives. What connects the scenes is the evocative power of Mr. Wellman as word-spinner. As in his other plays (*Bad Penny, Terminal Hip*), he writes a kind of rapturous rap - street language mixed with metaphorical flights of fancy.

An atmospheric dread hangs over the evening. As David Van Tieghem's score curls around the dialogue, one realizes that those furballs could be fugitives from a David Lynch dream. But *Sincerity Forever* is very much its own thing, just as it is becoming increasingly clear that, as a playwright, Mr. Wellman is sui generis.

In all respects, he is abetted by his company, beginning with Mr. Simpson, who keeps everything both eerie and matter of fact, a combination that enhances the menace - in the performance and in Kyle Chepulis's setting. The lighting is dim; the acting is bright. No one dashes for laughs. Instead, all the actors play with sincerity, absolutely necessary under the mysterious circumstances. Ms. Brenneman and Ms. Nipkow are twinned in their charm, blending innocence with insouciance, Zach Grenier is properly bullheaded as a redneck and, as the furballs, Mr. Mellor and Ms. Harding are a delirious double act.

Because of the play's graphic language and its approach to piety, some theatergoers may find *Sincerity Forever* offensive, a fact that should please the playwright. Mr. Wellman does not play anything safe as he does his danse macabre far out on the cutting edge.

Mr. Wellman, who received a grant from the National Endowment for the Arts in 1990, had initially acknowledged the endowment along with other foundations as providers of support in the creation of his new play, but he removed the credit at the request of endowment officials. For the record, *Sincerity Forever* is the Wellman play that "was not made possible by the generous assistance of the N.E.A."

A MURDER OF CROWS: MAY 1, 1992

In Mac Wellman's apocalyptic vision, civilization is facing a Love Canal of the mind and body. The view is as urgent as it is fearful. It is an ecological nightmare, as weather reports from past centuries become auguries of approaching climatic catastrophe. No matter where we are, "we are downwind of something peculiar." Mr. Wellman's scathing new comedy, *A Murder of Crows* (at Primary Stages), is a red alert, to be ignored at one's peril. Acid rain is coming, and the playwright is our caustic commentator and meteorologist.

The medium for his warning is a Middle-American mire. The people in this anonymous small town have moved past hard times to desperate days. As one character says, with full symbolism intended, "It's lucky the shallow end is near the beach." Otherwise everyone would drown in sludge.

In free-flowing Wellman fashion, there is a sense of surrealism afoot, which to cynics among us may seem scandalously close to reality. A prophet of misfortune, the author pinpoints the poisons in everyday life, describing how mankind is polluting the planet. He is also out to smash that other American dream, of getting something for nothing, and, with devilish glee, he mocks our hypocrisy about true and false heroics. A survivor of the war in the Persian Gulf comes home and literally turns into a public monument. He is gold-leafed and frozen on a pedestal.

Watching the grotesqueries unfold, one may ask why the play is so amusing. The answer is easy. Mr. Wellman has a gymnast's sense of equilibrium and a clownish sense of comedy. In virtuosic form in this new play, he never allows his danse macabre to become a dirge. There are hints of early Sam Shepard and of the socially conscious side of Franz Xaver Kroetz, but with the author's original voice.

Characters exorcise their anxieties, sometimes in direct address to the audience. Confessionals become riffs: from mother, daughter, crusty Uncle Howard and his Klan-leaning wife (who could be a fugitive from Mr. Wellman's redneck romp, *Sincerity Forever*). Even the statuesque war hero finally takes the opportunity to talk back. And a father who seemed to be dead magically returns to life, looking as encrusted as if he had been weekending in a Dumpster. In the background are three scavenger crows, mocking and baiting what is left of humanity.

As director, Jim Simpson animates a devious text into a dexterous performance. Many of the actors are experienced Wellman interpreters. The cast knows that in this comic territory overstatement would be damaging. The bizarre becomes matter-of-fact and the matter-of-fact seems bizarre.

Annie O'Sullivan and Jan Leslie Harding are distorted mirror images as embattled mother and daughter. William Mesnik is dryly bemused as Uncle Howard, even as his wife (Lauren Hamilton) waxes prejudiciously. That essential Wellman spokesman, Stephen Mellor, expounds with a customary loop-the-loop circumlocution. In the hands of the actors, words fly fast.

Among the crows is David Van Tieghem, who is also responsible for the music and sound, a synchronized tapestry that ranges from sitcom strains to a pulsating beat that would be equally at home in Hitchcock. The designer, Kyle Chepulis, outdoes his previous Wellman efforts with an imaginative setting that poses its own danger.

The stage is seeping, as water drains ominously toward the front row of the audience. The dripping is incessant. This play needs a plumber! At one point, there is a sudden shower. Actors raise umbrellas, but, like the characters they are playing, they are unable to duck for cover. In Mr. Wellman's ringing incitement, the world ends not with another big bang, but with a chorus of crows mischievously tapping and singing their way through the metaphorical landscape.

THREE AMERICANISMS: JUNE 5, 1993

Mac Wellman's theatrical riffs liquefy language into rapturous conundrums of onomatopoetry and unsprocketed metaphor. Imagine James Joyce as a rap artist, and you might have an inkling of the effect in performance of the playwright's monologues: brief blank-verse adjuncts to his lexiconically liberated plays like *A Murder of Crows* and *Sincerity Forever*.

In *Three Americanisms*, at the SoHo Repertory, he has written a trio of etherized soliloquies circling the subject of justifiable paranoia. Just as it is difficult to comprehend the precise meaning of the rodomontade stream of subconsciousness, one cannot easily identify individuals, although one or more of the three speakers may be a homeless person. All three, in the author's word, have "hadituptohere," and they want to do something about it.

The monologues are peppered with puns and salted with neologisms and mythicisms. Listen closely and catch a particle of plot dealing with such unseen personalities as "our wide one, Chubby." He would seem to be the master of some nameless intrigue, perhaps in concert with that fellow named Ralph. Everyone is high on what Mr. Wellman calls glimmergas, which is infectious rather than toxic. And watch out for those "wigglies." In and out of this circumnavigatory flight, there are brief returns to everyday urban life, with newspaper headlines like "Robber Shoots Robber as Victim Ducks." As always with this masterly wordsmith, a theatergoer is invited to sit back and go with the show even as the words seem one step from Jabberwocky.

These torrents demand performers with exceptional verbal fluency, people who can make the audience believe that they believe what they are saying, no matter how outlandish it sounds. That is exactly what Mr. Wellman receives with the first two of the *Three Americanisms*, as delivered by Mark Margolis and Ron Faber.

An earlier paradigm of Wellman interpretation is represented by Stephen Mellor's self-defining performance of the political bramble patch of *Terminal Hip*, revived in repertory with the new monologues. In the first *Americanism*, Mr. Margolis unleashes his mind without benefit of filter. He is playing the most overtly homeless of the trio, a man protecting his turf from invaders. "My stuff is worthless," he insists as if those words would act as guard dog. The words, of course, are as effective as those "No Radio" signs posted in parked cars. Funeral-parlor music underscores the diabolical dirge, in which Mr. Margolis uncovers a cache of black comedy.

Next on the firing line is Mr. Faber, as dapperly dressed as someone only recently ejected from long-term employment. He is trying to find his center in a world without gravity. I have always admired how actors can memorize Mr. Wellman's loop-the-loop linguistics while avoiding the steeplechase of tongue-twisters. On opening night, I admired an actor who went up on his lines. Although Mr. Faber faltered and became silent, his actor's intensity never abated. Wordless, he remained viscerally in character.

After an offstage prompt, Jim Simpson, Mr. Wellman's symbiotic director, came forward. Like a baseball manager, he took his ace actor aside in lieu of waving to the bullpen. With the director's encouragement, the actor worked his way back into the monologue and rode it to its moonstruck conclusion. Jan Leslie Harding, third on deck, could not keep up with the obsessiveness of her predecessors, but the word-spinning continued as Mr. Wellman leaped into the stratosphere without a net. *Three Americanisms* is, in his words, beyond broccoli. It is vertiginous.

TIMBERLAKE WERTENBAKER

OUR COUNTRY'S GOOD: OCTOBER 21, 1990

HARTFORD - Timberlake Wertenbaker's *Our Country's Good* is an enlightening exploration of the inhumanity of the penal system in New South Wales, the British colony that became Australia. Ms. Wertenbaker's drama is now running at Hartford Stage in a perceptive production directed by Mark Lamos.

In this free-handed adaptation of Thomas Keneally's novel *The Playmaker*, the author uses inventive stage devices to bring a distant world to life and to view it in historical perspective. By extension, the play is prescient about the founding of Australia itself. First presented in London at the Royal Court Theater, *Our Country's Good* received an Olivier Award as best play of 1988.

Both the novel and the play deal with events in the late 1780's in the ultimate penal colony, a final station for the dregs and outcasts of British society. For the most minor crimes, convicts, some of them adolescents, are made to pay disproportionate consequences. Arriving by prison ship, the convicts continue to be brutalized in their new encampment.

Suddenly there is a ray of hope with the announcement by the settlement's Governor that a play will be presented with the convicts as actors. A stage-struck lieutenant in the Royal Marines is named the director, and he chooses George

Farquhar's Restoration comedy *The Recruiting Officer* for the simple reason that he has two copies of the play. This much of the story is true - the play turned out to be the first ever presented in Australia - and many of the characters are based on real people. From here, the playwright lets her imagination expand. *Our Country's Good* becomes a backstage play with a social conscience, demonstrating the redemptive power of theater and of education. While making political points, Ms. Wertenbaker underlines the humanity of her characters and the grotesque humor that is so endemic to their daily existence.

The thought of being onstage energizes the convicts. As Mr. Keneally wrote in his novel, they sensed "that their best chance out of hunger and lovelessness and a bad name was to capture the first primitive stage of this new earth." The lieutenant finds himself besieged by competitive candidates, at least one of them insane, and beset by the rigid structures of the military community. As he tries to put together a production with this motley troupe of misfits, many of them illiterate, art is repeatedly imperiled by life.

In Christopher Barreca's haunting scenic design, the roof of the Hartford Stage sprouts a field of nooses waiting to ensnare the convicts, who go about their acting as their sole escape. Eventually they become actors, with temperaments as well as talent, and the lieutenant begins to play the role of actor-manager. At one point, he becomes the audience's guide, admonishing that "people who can't pay attention should not go to the theater."

Several factors elevate the play: the use of *The Recruiting Officer* as reflective subtext confronting convicts with roles seemingly contradictory to those they play in life, and Ms. Wertenbaker's artfulness in moving among the various stages of reality. In her adaptation, she wisely underplays the native symbolism and focuses on the play within the play. The lieutenant's faith in his actors is confirmed. Acquiring a sense of self worth, they begin to see a path through the wilderness.

As director, Mr. Lamos meets the challenge with a theatricality matching that of the playwright. Because of the elements of role-playing, this is one play that can support the concept of cross-casting. Ten actors double in roles, playing officers as well as convicts, men and women, blacks and whites.

Only Michael Cumpsty portrays a single character, the stalwart director of *The Recruiting Officer*, a man who marches on his own interior journey in the course of the narrative. In particular, one prisoner (Tracey Ellis) makes him realize the iniquities within the penal colony as well as the moralistic limits the officer has imposed on his own life.

At times, Mr. Cumpsty overplays the pietism, but he grows with his character, as does Ms. Ellis. Both are movingly at the center of the drama, and there are also penetrating performances by Sam Tsoutsouvas (as the convict who in real life subsequently founded Australia's first theater), Stephen Rowe, Amelia Campbell, and, especially, Helen Carey as a woman rescued by theater from her own desperation.

It is left to Richard Poe, portraying the potential playwright of the troupe, to articulate the meaning behind the title of the play. In his character's invented prologue to Farquhar, he says the convicts have left England "for our country's good," not as exiles but as patriots. The irony in that declaration resonates throughout Ms. Wertenbaker's compelling drama, even as the new prologue is censored for being too provocative. The play ends, as it should, with the audience eager to see an actual performance of these actor-convicts in *The Recruiting Officer.* At the Royal Court, both plays were performed in repertory.

RICHARD WESLEY

THE LAST STREET PLAY: MAY 25, 1977

Off stage, voices sing in hearty, foot-stomping unison, "We're the Mighty Gents!", a martial air of memory to the roughest, meanest gang in Newark. On stage, Frankie, the leader of the Gents, now descended into mediocrity, takes a drink and confides in us. He talks about his failed dreams, thwarted pride and rising sense of desperation. The play is Richard Wesley's *The Last Street Play* (at the Manhattan Theater Club), an eloquent threnody to lost, spent youth.

Ten years have passed since the Gents ruled the Central Ward, and in that time the gang has stagnated. At 30, the members have become "surplus people," hanging around street-corners, drinking from pint bottles, searching for "chump change," and swapping old tales of terror about the time they drew "first blood against the Zombies." Mr. Wesley's Gents are the black American equivalent of Fellini's *Vitelloni*, overgrown boys who exist as artifacts of their own adolescence. But they were once proud warriors, "barbarians," according to their boast. Another modern movie classic comes to mind: Kurosawa's *Seven Samurai*.

Streetfighting was their only trade. With no wars and no weapons, they are like retired samurai, helpless and impotent - and they don't know what has happened to them. Frankie still lives with his woman - she was his watchdog in battle - but the relationship has eroded into inertia. "These days," says Frankie, "people are into surviving." But is survival - without purpose - enough? And what is the alternative - to be smalltime crooks like the haughty ex-Zombie who lords it over them? The playwright sends the Gents into one last street play, with disastrous and unexpected results.

The play is short and deceptively modest - soliloquies interspersed with street scenes - but it is tautly constructed and filled with the grittiness and lyricism of the urban landscape. As we know from *The Sirens, The Past is the Past, Black Terror*, and his other plays, Mr. Wesley is a natural playwright, with a great gift for creating character, evoking atmosphere and using dialogue and gestures as motifs.

In *The Last Street Play*, there is one Gent named Eldridge - always argumentative and alienating - who rises to every challenge by removing a handkerchief from around his neck and wrapping it around his fist. This is a sign - as funny as it is touching - that Eldridge, the fierce pretender, is edging into action. Jostling one another, yearning for renewal, these characters are beautifully observed by the author and they are acted by an uncommon cast with an empathy that approaches symbiosis. Play and performance have a single identity.

As Frankie, Roscoe Orman strikes exactly the right balance between lingering bravado and complete loss of confidence. He is on a wire and unable to put one foot ahead of the other. Mr. Orman, Richard E. Gant, J. Herbert Kerr and Brent Jennings form an ensemble of accomplices. There are also exemplary characterizations by Yvette Hawkins, Maurice Woods, and, especially, Morgan Freeman as a burdensome, overbearing derelict - the ultimate wino - who assails the Gents and also attacks our privacy in the audience.

Under the meticulous direction of Thomas Bullard, each actor is totally authoritative. This is an Upstage presentation at the Manhattan Theater Club, which means that it is staged with a minimum of scenery and production detail. But it would be difficult to envision a more satisfying and authentic performance of Mr. Wesley's poignant, truthful play.

PETER WHELAN

THE HERBAL BED: JULY 23, 1996

STRATFORD-ON-AVON, England - Writers from Virginia Woolf to Edward Bond have made fictional conjectures about Shakespeare's life. It was Woolf, of course, in *A Room of One's Own*, who suggested that if Shakespeare had had "a wonderfully gifted sister" named Judith, she would never have been allowed to fulfill her genius. In his play *Bingo*, Mr. Bond considered Shakespeare in retirement as a disgruntled landowner and eventual suicide.

In his new play, *The Herbal Bed* (in the Other Place theater at Stratford), Peter Whelan muses about a sidelong event in the life of Shakespeare's family and creates a finely textured tapestry of love and lies in early-17th-century Stratford. In contrast to Mr. Bond, Mr. Whelan circumspectly keeps Shakespeare just offstage. Yet his presence is deeply felt. Through the eyes of his older daughter, Susanna Hall, we have a telling glimpse of the playwright's mortality, and also of his impact on his tightly knit Elizabethan community.

The Herbal Bed begins with a known fact. In 1613, Susanna, the wife of a doctor, was publicly accused of committing adultery with a Stratford neighbor. She sued for slander and won her case. Inspired by the actual events and by the doctor's own journal, Mr. Whelan makes a bold leap of the imagination.

The play deals with everything from homeopathic medicine to Puritanism, while focusing on Susanna's dilemma. Subjected to what she calls "love's alchemy," she is torn between her heart and her duty. She has been unfaithful in her mind, and almost with her body (one night in her garden with a family friend). In one of the play's most visceral moments, she denies the charge in an ecclesiastical court in order to save her husband's medical practice. To what extent is her deception justified? The suggestion is that she who makes her herbal bed must lie in it.

In this and other plays, Mr. Whelan is a speculative playwright with a keen sense of history. Several years ago, in *The School of Night*, he investigated political questions behind the mystery of Christopher Marlowe's death in 1593. In *Divine Right* (presented earlier this year at the Birmingham Repertory Theater), he projected himself forward into the year 2000 and predicted the end of the monarchy in England. The Prince of Wales renounces his right to succession, and his 18-year-old son takes a *Henry V*-like anonymous walk among the people and then makes his own highly principled case for graceful withdrawal from the crown.

Along with Alan Bennett and Richard Nelson, Mr. Whelan takes a long view of historical precedent, wondering what motivates people to try to change their times. It is with regret that he has watched "the tides of old certainties recede in the world." While his characters are rooted in their various periods, they are viewed from the perspective of a contemporary author with a pronounced social conscience, someone with an affection for those old certainties and an ability to reflect on the moral complexity of a decisive moment.

For Arthur Miller, the story of *The Herbal Bed* might have borne a message, but with Mr. Whelan the interest is principally on a personal level, as an independent woman is forced to come to terms with what might be regarded as justifiable hypocrisy. Although this is not a play about Shakespeare, it is a play about his times, and as such it has authenticity and humanity. It is enriched by the splendid performances of Teresa Banham as Susanna and Joseph Fiennes (Ralph Fiennes's younger brother) as her putative lover. The confidently low-key production is staged by Michael Attenborough.

In his characteristically explorative manner, Mr. Whelan raises the possibility that the real Susanna might have been Shakespeare's model for Helena, the potion procurer and self-appointed physician in *All's Well That Ends Well*. Then he takes his premise a step further by proposing that the Countess in *All's Well* was actually a fictional approximation of Susanna's mother, Anne Hathaway, another offstage character in *The Herbal Bed*.

In Mr. Whelan's play, Susanna is a herbologist and her husband's collaborator in prescribing curative remedies, a notion that is itself met with criticism by the community. As the author says, Susanna's Stratford epitaph records that she was "witty above her sexe, but that's not all." Reinvented by Mr. Whelan, she becomes a pragmatic Shakespearean heroine.

As a resident playwright with the Royal Shakespeare Company, Mr. Whelan has had a continuing connection with Stratford, which also furnished him the context for another recent play, *Shakespeare Country*, a festival-style pageant. It was simultaneously performed in 1993 by 48 little theater companies in Britain.

In this "comedy of reconciliations," he fantasizes that Shakespeare had an illegitimate son who emigrated to America and became the forefather of a line that leads to a contemporary country singer named Billy Shakes. Twang in cheek, Billy makes a pilgrimage to his ancestral Avon, now a "Shakespeare theme park," where he becomes enmeshed in activities that parallel those in *A Midsummer Night's Dream*. In all these plays, Mr. Whelan maintains his equanimity and his humor; he is not swept away by thoughts of political correctness.

Born in 1931, he has had a long career but has been an overlooked playwright of his generation. One reason for his relative obscurity is that most of his plays have been presented away from the West End, in one of the Royal Shakespeare's smaller theaters or by regional or fringe companies. With the success of *The Herbal Bed*, and its inevitable move to London, he is at last receiving the recognition he deserves.

THORNTON WILDER

OUR TOWN: DECEMBER 11, 1988

In 1956, on a ship crossing the Atlantic to meet Samuel Beckett for the first time, Alan Schneider found himself sitting at the captain's table with Thornton Wilder. As Mr. Schneider recalled in his autobiography, Wilder had seen both the French and German productions of *Waiting for Godot*, felt he knew exactly what the play was about and proceeded to give Mr. Schneider a line-by-line analysis. At Wilder's recommendation, Mr. Schneider had just been hired to direct the first American production of *Godot*, and he listened intently, as Wilder told him that the play was an existential work about "the nullity of experience in relation to the search for an absolute."

The director eventually realized that Wilder, acting as irrepressible scholar, was in effect rewriting *Godot* and re-envisioning it as if it were a work of his own. But there was no denying Wilder's affinity for Beckett - also expressed on other occasions - nor his understanding of the play, at a time when others were confused by it. Something similar certainly could be said about Wilder's response to James Joyce and *Finnegan's Wake*, the source of his play *The Skin of Our Teeth*. Perhaps part of Wilder's enthusiasm for *Godot* was a reflection of the dark undercurrents in *Our Town*, an aspect of the play that has long been neglected.

Our Town could be approached as an American expression of Beckett's observation that man is born astride the grave. This is precisely the path that Gregory Mosher has taken in his revival of the play at the Lyceum Theater, the first presentation in Lincoln Center Theater's season on Broadway. *Our Town* is seen through a Beckett prism.

The comparison between Wilder and Beckett should not be overstated. For one thing, Wilder was a quintessential American writer, just as Beckett is a quintessential Irish writer. Though Wilder's theatrical body of work was small - two full-length plays, several adaptations and a number of one-acts - he was a more cynical and less whimsical dramatist than is generally acknowledged. The serious side of Wilder is best exemplified by *Our Town* and by the one-acts, including *The Happy Journey to Trenton and Camden*, *Pullman Car Hiawatha* and, later, *Plays for Bleecker Street*, all of which could stand the scrutiny of revival. *The Skin of Our Teeth*, venturesome in its day, has not aged as well, though an imaginative revival might alter that assessment. (*The Matchmaker*, his adaptation of Johann Nestroy, retains its antic quality, even without Jerry Herman's music.)

As a stylist, especially in the one-acts, Wilder prefigured American absurdism, as later developed by Edward Albee and Christopher Durang, among others. Similarly, in his emphasis in *Our Town* on finding "a value above all price for the smallest events in our daily life," he affected the work of writers like Lanford Wilson and Romulus Linney.

In his lifetime, Wilder was considered an optimist and a traditionalist, especially as *Our Town* was done across the country in high schools and community theaters. In the theater, he occupied a position akin to that of Robert Frost in poetry. Both estimations are less than accurate. Behind Wilder's exuberance - what Harold Clurman identified as his "avuncular celebration of the commonplace" - was a suppressed pessimism. *Our Town*, commonly accepted as a play about love and marriage (as in the title of the song from the television musical adaptation), is actually a play about life and, particularly, death.

Without textual changes, but with a shifting in mood and emphasis, Mr. Mosher has managed to eliminate decades of gauzy sentimentalism. As Simon Stimson, the choirmaster who dies of alcoholism, indicates, it is not necessarily a wonderful life. For him and others, life can be brief, ordinary and brutish.

In his revival of the play last year at the Long Wharf Theater in New Haven, Arvin Brown took a step in this direction. His treatment de-emphasized the idealized moments in the play.

The Long Wharf production was anchored and defined by the choice of Hal Holbrook as the Stage Manager. Mr. Holbrook was fine on his own terms, and his identification with Mark Twain gave the character an extra archtypal quality. But the actor was in the mode of traditional Stage Managers. As with others who preceded Mr. Holbrook (from Frank Craven in the original to Henry Fonda), his portrayal of the Stage Manager was folksy and benign, a cracker-barrel philosopher, who seemingly accepts the verities of Grover's Corners.

Mr. Mosher moves further into re-evaluation, beginning with his bold stroke of casting Spalding Gray in the role of the Stage Manager. Mr. Mosher has taken away the Stage Manager's pipe, and with it goes the character's twinkle. The Stage Manager in this *Our Town* looks, dresses and acts like Spalding Gray. The actor carefully avoids anything that might be misinterpreted as charm. At the same time, he is not dispassionate. He is, instead, realistic, as he explores the small pleasures and defeats in *Our Town*.

Introducing Doc Gibbs, he immediately tells us of the doctor's death; as Mr. Gray delivers the line and others, it is not with regret but as a simple statement of fact. Though Wilder was almost Brechtian in his insistence on removing all suspense from his play, Mr. Gray makes it even clearer that not for a moment should we think the characters are going to lead long and happy lives. Death, in *Our Town*, can come suddenly and quixotically.

This sobering approach is also carried out by the other actors in a production that has been precisely cast from major to supporting roles, from Peter Maloney as the self-involved editor Webb and Frances Conroy as Mrs. Gibbs to Bill Alton as Professor Willard and Jeff Weiss as the choirmaster.

At the heart of any production of *Our Town*, of course, are Emily Webb and George Gibbs, those timeless emblems of teen-age romance who find first love over strawberry sodas at Mr. Morgan's fountain. In an extraordinarily tender double performance, Penelope Ann Miller and Eric Stoltz play this scene - and the characters - as if for the first time, and, astonishingly, for many theatergoers, it will be for the first time. Despite the acknowledged familiarity of the play, many in the audience do not know from the instant of Emily's entrance that she will have died within two hours of stage time.

When I first saw the play in a high school production, I was 14 and the actors playing Emily and George were the age of the characters. Emily's death in childbirth gave me and my classmates a jolt, one that occurs every time that Emily, the prettiest and smartest girl in town, dies. The character's story is unfailingly moving, but never more than in the current production.

Seeing the play again, one realizes that her marriage was not intended as an idyll. To marry George and to take up the role of farmer's wife, Emily has abandoned her desire for independence and self-fulfillment. Similarly, even before George has decided not to attend agricultural college, he has forfeited his chance to become a professional baseball player. At least covertly, the playwright is suggesting that if the young couple had not fallen in love and married so young, life would have been different and probably more rewarding. In performance, Ms.

Miller conveys the struggles within the character, as hope is outweighed by expectancy.

In his original conception in 1938, Wilder stripped the stage to essentials -a few tables and chairs, and with the actors miming details of the action. He attempted something similar in his one-acts, in which kitchen chairs became trains and automobiles; those works have a purity as well as an austerity. Denying a role as an innovator, Wilder called himself "a rediscoverer of forgotten goods and I hope a remover of obtrusive bric-a-brac." It was as a kind of theatrical house-cleaner that he made his primary contribution to American playwriting.

As Wilder said, "Our claim, our hope, our despair are in the mind - not in things, not in 'scenery.'" He added about *Our Town* that the climax "needs only five square feet of boarding and a passion to know what life means to us." The current revival fully demonstrates that the play - and the staging - benefits from terseness. When Emily returns from the dead for one final look at her life, Ms. Miller omits the sobs suggested in the author's stage directions and in so doing provokes the audience to greater emotion. Her question to the Stage Manager, "Do any human beings ever realize life while they live it? - every every minute?" resounds with plangency through the play. Emily's unwillingness to re-experience the quickness is itself like a vision from Samuel Beckett, reminding one of the old woman in *Rockaby*, rocking herself into memory and out of life.

Mr. Mosher, Mr. Gray, Ms. Miller and company invite us to see an *Our Town* untarnished by nostalgia. The result is heartrending rather than heartwarming.

TENNESSEE WILLIAMS

SUMMER AND SMOKE: JULY 31, 1986

WILLIAMSTOWN - Though less often seen on the stage than either Amanda Wingfield or Blanche DuBois, Alma Winemiller is one of Tennessee Williams's most moving heroines, a woman who is possessed by that classic Williams conflict between the soulful and the sensual. Aptly described as "a flame, mistaken for ice," in the course of *Summer and Smoke*, Alma takes a step toward becoming Blanche.

In his *Memoirs*, the author allowed himself a rare observation about a character when he said, "Miss Alma Winemiller may very well be the best female portrait I have drawn in a play. She simply seemed to exist somewhere in my being and it was no effort to put her on paper." He added that Alma's love, Johnny Buchanan, "never seemed real to me."

In a revival of the play at the Williamstown Theater Festival, Laila Robins gives a dazzling performance as Alma. Many theatergoers may have vivid memories of Margaret Phillips, who created the role on Broadway, and Geraldine Page, who presided at the play's Off Broadway rebirth in 1952 (Ms. Page was the first Alma I saw), but it would be difficult to imagine a more fully realized performance than the one Ms. Robins is offering at Williamstown under the direction of James Simpson.

From her first fluttery entrance, she is a woman gasping for air - and for life. Straitlaced by her role as minister's daughter and self-styled sharer of her father's cross (her emotionally disturbed mother), the actress never forgets that Alma has a split personality. She has, as Johnny Buchanan says, another person inside her. Even as she withdraws from Johnny's touch, as she surrounds herself with protective affectations, Miss Robins projects an underlying passion. Watch her, for example, as she tries to discuss sex with Johnny's understanding father. With delicacy, she admits, "Naturally, marriage leads to ... contact," and, as she speaks the last word, beneath the fear we can feel the longing.

The suppressed Alma emerges in a scene in which she reads aloud *Love's Secret* by William Blake. What makes the actress's achievement all the more admirable - and this is something that can be said about her eminent predecessors as Alma - is that in *Summer and Smoke*, Williams was not able to create a dramatically satisfying opposition. Blanche has Stanley but Alma has only Johnny, a schematic portrait of a man who traverses Alma's journey in reverse. As she finally embraces the sensual, he finds his "true nature" as a doctor with moral principles. In each aspect, both characters border on fanaticism. Changing personalities, they pass in the night; the two can never synchronize their passion. It is Alma's transformation that is, by far, the more persuasive.

At Williamstown, the role of Johnny is undertaken by Christopher Reeve, and, as intended, he is a dissolute without a "sign of depravity" showing in his face. Despite his reckless life, Johnny is supposed to emerge unmarked, which Mr. Reeve does with some of the same equipoise that he brought to his role in the film *The Bostonians*. It is the dissolution, itself, that appears to put a strain on the actor's talent. Drowning himself in alcohol, lusting after the local temptress (Ann Reinking), Mr. Reeve seems less decadent than persistent.

On one level, this period play depicts the repressive atmosphere in the ironically entitled town of Glorious Hill, Miss., a community that is circumscribed by its own narrowness. Gossips abound, eager to record every real or imaginary fall from propriety. This is not a town where an Alma (or a Blanche) can find sustenance, and it takes a long summer of despair for Alma to come to that realization.

Using a two-tiered set by Santo Loquasto, Mr. Simpson has encompassed most of the play's emotional elements on stage. Though a few of the supporting actors sacrifice character for caricature, there is an incisive performance by William Swetland as the town's dedicated doctor. At the heart of the story, of course, is Alma, and Ms. Robins recreates the role with extraordinary subtlety. She exudes the very essence of Alma.

THE NIGHT OF THE IGUANA: AUGUST 11, 1987

WILLIAMSTOWN - In its earliest form in 1948, *The Night of the Iguana* was a short story about Hannah Jelkes (at this point her first name was Edith), a spinster temporarily sequestered in the Costa Verde, a bohemian hotel in Mexico. Years later, when Tennessee Williams re-created the story as a play, Miss Jelkes was joined at the Costa Verde by the characters of Shannon, the defrocked preacher; Maxine Faulk, the earthy hotel owner, and Nonno, the spinster's aged poet-grandfather.

On Broadway and in John Huston's film, the story was dominated by Shannon and Maxine. At the Williamstown Theater Festival, where *The Night of the Iguana* has been revived, the play takes a decided turn toward Miss Jelkes. The reason can be attributed to the drama itself - the role is almost as long and certainly as consequential as that of Shannon - and to the performance by Maria Tucci.

Ms. Tucci, who in play after play has demonstrated that she is one of our finest actresses, fills the role to the brim with tragic self-awareness. Miss Jelkes is not, one must add, the saintly spinster portrayed by Deborah Kerr in the film but a real woman with extraordinary resilience. Even as the character expresses in purest form the Williams theme - in Harold Clurman's words, of someone "yearning to transcend the senses," she exists on terra firma - and much of that terra forces her to make an uphill climb.

Of all the characters in the play, she alone has discovered a method of survival. She hustles her quick character sketches, but she is no hypocrite. Rather, she is a stoic who has defined the limits of her life. Similarly, her grandfather, reading his poetry for a pittance, is a bit of a showman, but his verse comes, as he acknowledges, from "the frightened heart."

As Ms. Tucci and Emery Battis (as the grandfather) illuminate their roles, they also tilt the play. This kind of shift in emphasis has itself long been a fact of performance in the work of Tennessee Williams. An actor or actress can make his character take command of a play. For example, it is generally assumed that Marlon Brando left his indelible imprint on the role of Stanley. It could also be said that after Brando, *A Streetcar Named Desire* has become - as it should be - a play about Blanche.

Ms. Tucci does not overwhelm and certainly does not distort *Iguana*, but, in her soulful performance, one can feel the full strength of the character, who is a perdurable version of Blanche, one in whom, for all appearances, the tiger outweighs the moth. Unlike Blanche, Hannah Jelkes can endure the flame.

Though James Naughton (as Shannon) and Joan Van Ark (as Maxine) also play their roles for the reality, in performance their characters become somewhat less than the author probably imagined. Shannon, for example, tells Maxine, "You're bigger than life and twice as unnatural," which could of course be said about Bette Davis in the Broadway premiere. Ms. Van Ark is as large as life and quite natural in her lustfulness, but she misses the character's unbridled possessiveness. Similarly, Mr. Naughton's touching portrait is more pathetic than that of his predecessors (Patrick O'Neal was right on the mark on Broadway, while Richard Burton went over the precipice in the film).

These and other performances might have been improved if there had been a single, purposeful director at the helm. Plays at Williamstown are placed on stage after a brief rehearsal period. In the case of *Iguana*, that problem was deepened by the fact that a new director, Margaret Booker, replaced Walton Jones during the final week of rehearsal. There is also a credited assist from John Malkovich. One assumes that with time, any one of these directors could have marshaled the production into a cohesive whole. In single file, no such success seems possible.

Led by Ms. Tucci, Mr. Battis and an atmospheric set design by Christopher Barreca, the Williamstown *Iguana* has the seeds of a first-quality revival. It is, in any case, rewarding to see the play again, as it deals perceptively with such Williams subjects as a test of religious faith and the battle between man and his doppelgänger. Both Shannon and Miss Jelkes are shadowed by their personal demons. Each is or has been trapped (or self-victimized) like that iguana that is tied under the porch at the Costa Verde.

The symbolism of the play remains overstated, just as the German guests in the hotel are unnecessary cargo from a World War II ship of fools (this production wisely reduced the roles of the Germans). But the principal characters themselves are vibrant and the dialogue is filled with Williams's pungency and lyricism. As in the best of Williams, the play's conclusion has an inevitability that emerges directly from the desperate lives of the characters, each of whom is "one of God's creatures at the end of the rope."

THE GLASS MENAGERIE: JANUARY 21, 1991

PRINCETON, N.J. - Emily Mann opened her first season tonight as the artistic director of the McCarter Theater with a production of *The Glass Menagerie* that demonstrates the director's fidelity to Tennessee Williams and the play's eloquence, undiminished after 46 years. *The Glass Menagerie* remains Williams's most deeply personal work, a play that expresses both his rite of passage and a coming to terms with family ghosts.

Williams's memories in *The Glass Menagerie* were burnished by regrets about the limits of love, especially as represented by Amanda Wingfield, a transposed portrait of the playwright's mother. Defeated in her dreams, she strives for a kind of romantic fulfillment through the image of her crippled daughter.

Having called his public self "that artifice of mirrors," Williams looked for reality in *The Glass Menagerie* and found a searing truth. In the play he tells us how his surrogate, the prodigal son, Tom, could begin to seek his own vision only by abandoning his mother and sister, leaving his sister adrift in an illusory world. The guilt for that action was something the playwright was to confront throughout his life and work.

In Ms. Mann's production, Shirley Knight is a radiant Amanda. She is a grand Southern belle who one afternoon in her youth received 17 gentleman callers and is also a self-martyring matriarch desperately trying to hold on to the remains of her hopes. As called for by the role, Ms. Knight is demanding to the point of being overbearing, but always with a grasp of Amanda's gracefulness.

Within this story there are deceptions, a word that is heard almost as frequently in *The Glass Menagerie* as the word mendacity is heard in *Cat on a Hot Tin Roof*. Amanda is fearful of facing facts. From her perspective, her long absent husband, a telephone man "who fell in love with long distance," is simply traveling on the road and her daughter, Laura, is not crippled.

In lesser hands than those of Ms. Knight, Amanda can seem like a termagant. But she should never be less than charming, or, on her own terms, well-intentioned. This is a woman "bewildered by life," but still "obsessed with jonquils," those remembrances of her girlhood. Ms. Knight has had a long affinity with the works of Williams, as exemplified by her soulful Blanche in *A Streetcar Named Desire* at the McCarter, and her subsequent appearance in *A Lovely Sunday for Creve Coeur*. She fills the role of Amanda with compassion.

This is especially evident when she prepares herself for the visit from Laura's gentleman caller, a friend of Tom's at the shoe factory. Dressed in her cotillion gown, Amanda is girlish but not foolish. When the caller expresses his admiration, it is with believable sincerity. Even at her most anxious, Ms. Knight carries with her intimations of a faded glamor.

As Laura, Judy Kuhn exudes fragility, in direct contrast with Amanda's vivacity. Timid to the point of being tremulous, she seems to wilt when anyone looks in her direction. Ms. Kuhn conveys Laura's longing as a woman unable to free herself from the private dimensions of her menagerie of glass objects. The scene in which Laura meets her caller (Jeff Weatherford) and is led to reawaken her schoolgirl crush on him is played gently and with freshness. Mr. Weatherford's caller is, as the playwright described him, "a nice, ordinary young man." He is a high school star who has never measured up to the potential that others saw in him. Mr. Weatherford finds the lost boy behind the bravado. He is kindly even as he momentarily deceives Laura as to his intentions.

With an assurance that partly derives from the fact she has staged the play before at the Guthrie Theater in Minneapolis), Ms. Mann lets *The Glass Menagerie* unfold with a quiet resonance. A playwright and a director, she shares with Williams a concern for people trapped by their lives.

There is a single problem in this production and that is in aspects of Dylan McDermott's performance as Tom. Irritated by his mother's solicitous manner, he overdoes Tom's anger, and he blurs several soliloquies. But he and Ms. Kuhn delineate the intimacy that exists between siblings. He also underlines Tom's insularity, as in his confession to Amanda. "There is so much in my heart that I can't describe to you." That line is made even more meaningful by the fact that Williams himself was eventually able to communicate his inmost feelings to strangers in a theater.

The staging is enhanced by Ming Cho Lee's impressionistic setting, which removes the walls from the Wingfield home, and in so doing adds a fluidity. The action remains interior; unlike other productions of *The Glass Menagerie* there is no representation of the bright, tempting lights of the Paradise Dance Hall across the alley. The Wingfields are seen in a world by themselves, shimmering with the beauty of a fond but rueful look back at an artist's formative experience.

LANFORD WILSON

THE HOT L BALTIMORE: FEBRUARY 8, 1973

In his new play, *The Hot L Baltimore*, Lanford Wilson writes with understanding and sensitivity about unwanted people. His characters are locked in interior worlds, clinging to solitary, futile dreams - and stubborn about not being defeated.

The play is filled with runaways - a brother and sister pair of urchins with a fantasy about organic farming in Utah, a young wanderer seeking a grandfather he has never met, a waif who can individually identify the far-off whistle of trains. These characters and many more - from adolescence to senility, sit in, and pass through, the lobby of the condemned Hotel Baltimore, a hotel so derelict that the "e" has dropped out of its marquee (giving the play its title). Like the hotel itself, the characters belong to an immutable past where trains were on time and where playwrights could afford to be sentimental and unfashionable.

There are moments in this play (and in his others) when Wilson - with his passion for idiosyncratic characters, atmospheric details and invented homilies - reminds me of William Saroyan and Thornton Wilder. The comparison is not at all to his disadvantage. He, too, is a very American playwright, with a nostalgic longing for a lost sensibility.

TALLEY'S FOLLY: MAY 4, 1979

Lanford Wilson's eloquent new play, *Talley's Folly*, is, as the playwright promises in the opening scene, "a waltz... a no-holds barred romantic story." It deals with two particular people in a special time and place - beautifully played by Judd Hirsch and Trish Hawkins. In addition, through indirection, humor and stage poetry, Mr. Wilson has made them stand as paragons of truth and self-fulfillment.

Talley's Folly, which opened last night at the Circle Repertory, is a play about those decisive moments in all of our lives when choice can lead to a destination. It is a play about the romantic sensibility, the need for lyricism and imagination to sustain us on our voyage past the shoals of reality.

The action of the play predates that of Mr. Wilson's last work, *The Fifth of July*, taking place in 1944, 33 years earlier, on the same family homestead in Lebanon, Mo., which also happens to be the birthplace of the author. The title refers to an ornate Victorian boathouse built by a Talley ancestor, a dreamer who decorated the countryside with gewgaws and gazebos. The town laughed at this romantic, but his grand vision endured.

The boathouse is the private hideaway for Sally Talley, the enchanting misfit of her family. In her, we see the essence of all Lanford Wilson womanly strays, repressing her longings behind a curtain of discretion, denying herself until she meets Matt Friedman. Matt, played with encompassing wit and tenderness by Mr. Hirsch, is a Jewish accountant from St. Louis - bookish, erudite, a man who has, as he says, "a reading vocabulary, not a speaking vocabulary." He uses big words voluminously - and hilariously.

On the night of the play, at sundown, Matt has come to claim Sally for a marriage that their families will look upon with disdain, a marriage that will prove indomitable - as we know from *The Fifth of July*. In that later play, it is Matt's ashes that an aging Sally touchingly carries back to Lebanon. Like the stage manager in *Our Town*, Mr. Hirsch affectionately and theatrically welcomes us to the boathouse, one of John Lee Beatty's most atmospheric settings. Matt is a rare character who is as charming as he is meant to be. Gradually, he opens his life to his love, telling her of the tragedy and the mystery of his youth, moving us with his story of escape and exile.

With even greater reluctance, the shy Sally described her estrangement from her family and her community. Despite the apparent differences between them, the two are emotionally in tune with each other - the opposite of star-crossed lovers. Matt has come to awaken Sally to the possibilities of a life together. With the sun down and the faraway sound of dogs barking, *Talley's Folly* becomes a final chance to catch a dream in flight.

This romance is also a play with a mind. Writing with lucidity and certainty and without wasting any words, Mr. Wilson always remembers the time and the place. *Talley's Folly* deals intelligently with such important issues as prejudice, labor organizing, women's rights and a nation emerging from war and facing a radical change in economy.

There are only two characters on stage, and we come to know them intimately. Never are we bored by their presence - and the dialogue brings to life numerous interesting people who are offstage. The scale of *Talley's Folly* is deceptively small. Actually it is one of Mr. Wilson's most expansive works, wise with a knowledge of humanity.

Marshall W. Mason, who over the years has been Mr. Wilson's principal directorial interpreter, has given this play an inspired production, with symbiotic performances by Mr. Hirsch and Ms. Hawkins. With a closely cropped beard and a manner that is alternately tentative and forward - he leaps impulsively into a story - Mr. Hirsch creates a quintessential portrait of an outsider. He is part bookkeeper, part clown, an irrepressible romantic who dramatizes himself with jokes, games and imitations. It is a role of considerable size and depth, one that seems made to measure for the actor. In it, he gives his finest performance.

Ms. Hawkins's Sally is slight and wispy, in spirit as well as in looks. She fights to keep from being capsized by Matt's vigorous personality. We see her in small glimpses and gestures, the way she avoids coming to terms with her suitor and with her future. In this quietly consequential role, the actress is subtle, unmannered and lovely.

It is clear to me - from following his work from his earliest plays - that Mr. Wilson is one of our most gifted playwrights, a dramatist who deals perceptively with definably American themes. Not only has he created a large, cohesive body of work, he has also steadily grown and explored his art. In *Talley's Folly*, he introduces us to two wonderful people, humanizing and warming them with the radiance of his abundant talent. *Talley's Folly* is a play to savor and to cheer.

THE MOUND BUILDERS: FEBRUARY 9, 1986

"Vanished without a trace" - those words echo through *The Mound Builders*, Lanford Wilson's dramatic exploration of the world of archeology and its relevance to contemporary life. In the course of this probing drama (currently being revived by the Circle Repertory Company), the author contemplates the varying ways in which we can learn about the past; he asks what constitutes "a trace" - artifacts or collective memory? The play also deals with the environmental battle between conservationists and land developers. At the heart is the question of signs of life - what we know about our ancestors and what our descendants will learn about us. *The Mound Builders* is a moving, richly charactered play about people united in, and separated by, a shared activity.

As societies - and, by inference, species - become extinct, we search for our inheritance. What we know is what we read in history or in myth. If there is tangible evidence of antiquity, one must be able to assess its validity in order to determine the nature of the mind behind the dead civilization. At one point in *The Mound Builders*, an archeologist describes a bone awl that survived from the time of the Indian chief, Cochise. It is, he says, "one of the finest crafted utilitarian tools discovered in North America," and proof that "Cochise did not disappear without a trace." His older colleague comments, "We have no clear idea what the bone awl was used for, but it was undoubtedly used for something." A third character, a burnt-out novelist, says, in a line that is reminiscent of E.E. Cummings's cynical observation about Buffalo Bill, "Well, that's a real keen bone awl, Cochise, but what have you done recently?"

In the play, a team of archeologists is encamped for a summer in a dig in southern Illinois, excavating a series of "mounds" left by ancient tribes. A deadline hangs over their heads. A nearby lake is about to flood the valley and the site will be taken over by a real estate entrepreneur. Mr. Wilson is fair-minded in his assessment. The archeologists are as dismissive of the needs of local citizens as they are protective of the prerogatives of their profession. The developer is a descendant of Lopakhin in *The Cherry Orchard*. He craves the respect of the more educated outsiders, but for him, land development means progress as well as income.

Reflecting its subject matter, the play has an archeological texture. By the end of the evening, we have learned about the substrata impulses of the diggers and also have at least a theoretical history of the mound builders themselves. To some extent, the author wears his symbolism on his sleeve, as exemplified by his character names. The head of the expedition is August Howe. An academic, he is devoted to the mechanics of exploration. His sister, the disillusioned novelist, is D.K. Eriksen, and her initials are a sign of her psychological erosion. The land developer is Chad Jasker, whose name is as harsh as all the upstart Jukes and Snopes of fiction. The labels are not intrusive; the play comfortably wears the cloak of metaphor. Mr. Wilson has always dealt, at least glancingly, with ethical and social matters, but never more so than in *The Mound Builders*. In this play, a family of characters arms itself against the encroachment of philistines, who, from an alternate point of view, could be seen as social progressives. Serious doubts are raised about the methods of preservationists; one could regard them as plunderers - as grave-robbers.

The author has made minor revisions in his play since it was first done in 1975, eliminating the inessential role of Dr. Howe's teen-age daughter and giving the work a double frame. Dr. Howe sits in his office and tells the story in flashback as he screens slides of the expedition. In the background, we occasionally hear the voice of his novelist-sister putting the summer in imaginative perspective. The text is sharper - and so are the performances. Emphasizing the ensemble nature of the company, the Circle Repertory has double-cast *The Mound Builders*. The actors in the performance I attended were persuasively in character - Jake Dengel as Dr. Howe, Stephanie Gordon as his wife, Ken Marshall and Sharon Schlarth as a younger couple and Bruce McCarty a volatile presence as the land developer. Repeating her original role (and appearing in both casts) is Tanya Berezin. She plays the novelist as someone who is overdrawn on her artistic and emotional bank accounts and who is fearful of the return of inspiration. Miss Berezin is the sensitive center of a mutually responsive acting team.

As directed by Marshall W. Mason, the play seems more at home on the Triplex Stage at Manhattan Community College than it was in the first production at the Circle Repertory's own theater. As designer, John Lee Beatty anchors the house at the side of the lake. Slides add to the enrichment of the atmosphere. *The Mound Builders* thoughtfully plays with ideas while never sacrificing the identity of its individual characters. A play to ponder, it is one of Mr. Wilson's most deeply speculative ventures. Coming after the revised version of *Talley & Son* and recent revivals of *Serenading Louie*, *Balm in Gilead* and *Lemon Sky*, it further reminds us of the visionary breadth of the playwright's body of work.

THE LONELY WORLD OF DISPLACED PERSONS: OCTOBER 25, 1987

From his earliest plays to his latest, *Burn This*, Lanford Wilson has been firmly committed to the free expression of the individual spirit, no matter how nonconformist or even prodigal that spirit may seem to be. Outcasts populate his work - the young man in *Lemon Sky* who is desperately trying to find his place in his estranged father's new family; the waif in *The Hot l Baltimore*, who yearns for the far-off sounds of trains calling her to the road, Sally Talley in *Talley's Folly*, who upsets WASP family traditions and runs away with a Jewish man.

In the sense that it deals with lonely and displaced characters, *Burn This* is in the Wilson tradition. Where it breaks dramatic ground for the author is in its passion. The playwright has specialized in characters with a certain reserve and in situations not generally marked by their explosiveness. In other Wilson plays, we have heard about fervent love affairs, acts of violence, criminality, even about war itself but, for the most part, such events have been kept off stage. The play *Serenading Louie*, with its homicidal conclusion, is a distinct exception, and *Balm in Gilead*, as a raw slice of urban life, is a possible one.

In *Burn This*, however, Mr. Wilson exposes deep, uncauterized emotional wounds - and offers no salve. His unlikely romantic couple come together at the end of the play, but it would be precipitous to think of that as a happy ending.

There is no guarantee of durability in this relationship (in contrast to the foreseeable permanence of Sally Talley and her husband). The affair is a daring - and even questionable - step for the characters, Anna, a dancer-choreographer, and Pale, a wild man and certifiable outsider.

Pale is the most incendiary character in Mr. Wilson's extensive portrait gallery - a highly volatile figure incarnated on stage by John Malkovich. Beneath his long, Cochise-like hair (a disconcerting visual choice), he is a beast in a jungle of his own devising, and, intuitively, he is on the attack. Pale is not, as it turns out, the principal character in *Burn This*. In common with Tennessee Williams's Stanley Kowalski, Pale takes over the play through the force of his muscular personality. He is a catalyst who energizes others at the same time that he alienates them, carrying with him a threat of imminent danger.

The central role is that of the dancer (Joan Allen); the play is about the effect of Pale on her insulated life. Before he arrives, she has had two apparently total commitments - to her career and to her close friendship with Robby, who was her dancing partner and roommate as well as Pale's younger brother. But her creativity has been unproductive and the extent of her intimacy with Robby has been limited by the fact of his homosexuality. With Robby's sudden accidental death, Anna is forced to come to terms with the paradoxes of their relationship. How truly close were they? With his family, she plays the uncomfortable role of bereaved widow. After the funeral, Pale forcibly enters her loft - and her life. He apparently bears a passing physical resemblance to the dead brother, but in other crucial respects he is his opposite.

The twinning of opposites proves to be a fascinating subject for Mr. Wilson's scrutiny. Anna is initially drawn to Pale as his brother's surrogate, and because of the possibility of heterosexual fulfillment. Oddly, when she succumbs to his savage charm, she responds maternally, as if to soothe the wild beast. But their mutual attraction is visceral. Further complicating the sexuality of the liaison is a third character, Anna's other homosexual roommate (Lou Liberatore). He begins as a witty, disengaged observer, but is caught up by the passion of Pale and Anna and becomes instrumental in furthering their relationship. We are led to believe that the intensity of their bond is something beyond the roommate's emotional capacity. Finally, he sends a letter to Pale urging the two of them to resolve their differences. "Why should life always be tragic?" he says, insisting that this is life and not opera. He ends the letter by asking the recipient to "burn this."

The title of the play is meant to be taken literally as well as symbolically. It refers to any revelation or confession (in a letter or, by inference, in a work of art such as a play) that is so fiercely personal that it frightens the writer. The "secret" in the case of *Burn This* is that Mr. Liberatore's character is destined to be a watcher on the sidelines, at most a voyeur, but not someone who can realize his own passions. In a sense, that charge becomes self-descriptive of the plight of the objective artist, the playwright, who is condemned to be an observer and not a participant. Interestingly, Anna's ardor for Pale not only allows her to release her emotions, it also enables her to create a dance about their passion.

Of course, were it not for the brother's death, Anna and Pale would never have met. The situation is contrived, but, at the same time, the relationship is as classic as that of *Beauty and the Beast*. It represents a need in both parties to seek out opposites to fill a void in themselves. Anna must understand that Pale's rage emerges from outrage. Although it is not clear enough in the text, beneath the animalistic exterior there is a poetic sensibility. Pale must see that, for all Anna's seeming composure, she is burdened with frustations.

Because this is a play by Mr. Wilson, one is always aware of the comic absurdities of daily strife. Mr. Liberatore, in particular, lightens the evening with social commentary and gallows humor. But it is Pale who is the author's most original character. So much of his larger-than-life comedy is in the jarring juxtaposition of attitudes. Thundering into the dancer's loft, he shouts his hostility and bashes furniture and then, in a wry moment, reveals a tenderness for a well-prepared pot of tea. Pale is a ripe, colorful character and Mr. Malkovich plays him in full fever. Under Marshall W. Mason's symbiotic direction, Ms. Allen, Mr. Liberatore and Jonathan Hogan (in the play's most schematic role, as a successful screenwriter) hold fast to their characters as they are buffeted by the wind of Mr. Malkovich's performance.

The play should be approached as a change of pace for the author, as a search for dramatic elbow room. If it is not as humane as *Talley's Folly* or as resonant of time and family as *Fifth of July*, it has its own Wilson heartbeat, and there are moments - title in mind - when it has a searing immediacy. Mr. Wilson has many artistic appointments to keep, including his promised play about old Whistler Talley, the eccentric who designed the gewgawed family boathouse in the Talley cycle of plays. *Burn This* may represent a transitional phase in an extraordinary career, as the playwright continues his exploration of our need to connect with one another.

4

MODERN MASTERS

SAMUEL BECKETT IS DEAD AT 83; HIS "GODOT" CHANGED THEATER: DECEMBER 27, 1989

Samuel Beckett, a towering figure in drama and fiction who altered the course of contemporary theater, died in Paris on Friday at the age of 83. He died of respiratory problems in a Paris hospital, where he had been moved from a nursing home. He was buried yesterday at the Montparnasse cemetery after a private funeral.

Explaining the secrecy surrounding his illness, hospitalization and death, Iréne Lindon, representing the author's Paris publisher, Éditions de Minuit, said it was "what he would have wanted."

Beckett's plays became the cornerstone of 20th-century theater beginning with *Waiting for Godot*, which was first produced in 1953. As the play's two tramps wait for a salvation that never comes, they exchange vaudeville routines and metaphysical musings - and comedy rises to tragedy.

Before Beckett there was a naturalistic tradition. After him, scores of playwrights were encouraged to experiment with the underlying meaning of their work as well as with an absurdist style. As the Beckett scholar Ruby Cohn wrote: "After *Godot*, plots could be minimal; exposition, expendable; characters, contradictory; settings, unlocalized, and dialogue, unpredictable. Blatant farce could jostle tragedy."

At the same time, his novels, in particular his trilogy, *Molloy*, *Malone Dies* and *The Unnamable*, inspired by James Joyce, move subliminally into the minds of the characters. The novels are among the most experimental and most profound in Western literature.

For his accomplishments in both drama and fiction, the Irish author, who wrote first in English and later in French, received the Nobel Prize in Literature in 1969.

At the root of his art was a philosophy of the deepest yet most courageous pessimism, exploring man's relationship with his God. With Beckett, one searched for hope amid despair and continued living with a kind of stoicism, as illustrated by the final words of his novel, *The Unnamable*: "You must go on. I can't go on. I'll go on." Or as he wrote in one of his later works of fiction: "Try again. Fail again. Fail better."

Though his name in the adjectival form, Beckettian, entered the English language as a synonym for bleakness, he was a man of great humor and compassion, in his life as in his work. He was a tragicomic playwright whose art was consistently instilled with mordant wit. As scholars and critics scrutinized his writing for metaphor and ulterior meaning, he refrained from all analysis or even explanation. As he wrote to his favorite director, Alan Schneider: "If people want to have headaches among the overtones, let them. And provide their own aspirin." When Mr. Schneider rashly asked Beckett who Godot was, the playwright answered, "If I knew, I would have said so in the play."

His greatest successes were in his middle years, in the 1950's, with *Waiting for Godot* and *Endgame*, and with his trilogy of novels. It was suggested that for an artist of his stature, he had a relatively small body of work - but only if one measures the size by number of words. Distilling art to its essence, he produced scores of eloquent plays and stories, many of those in his later years not strictly defined as full length. But in terms of the intensity of the imagery, plays like *Not I, Footfalls* and *Rockaby* were complete visions.

He wrote six novels, four long plays and dozens of shorter ones, volumes of stories and narrative fragments, some of which were short novels. He wrote poetry and essays on the arts, including an essay about Marcel Proust (one of his particular favorites), radio and television plays, and prose pieces he called residua and disjecta.

In his 80's, he became an icon of survival. Even as he vowed that he had nothing more to say, he continued to be tormented and sustained by midnight thoughts and nightmarish images. Having discovered what was for him the non-meaning of life and its brevity (man is, he observed in *Waiting for Godot*, "born astride the grave"), he never stopped looking for ways to express himself. Once in writing about painting, he said, "There is nothing to express, no desire to express, together with the obligation to express." For him that obligation was ineluctable.

Despite his artistic reputation, his ascension was slow and for many years discouraging. He labored in his own darkness and disillusionment, the equivalent of one of the isolated metaphorical worlds inhabited by his characters. When his work began to be published and produced, he was plagued by philistinism, especially with *Waiting for Godot*, which puzzled and outraged many theatergoers and critics, some of whom regarded it as a travesty if not a hoax.

From the first he had his ardent supporters, who included, notably, Jean Anouilh, the bellwether of French theatrical tradition. He greeted *Godot* at its premiere in Paris as "a masterpiece that will cause despair for men in general and for playwrights in particular." In both respects, Anouilh proved prescient.

Today *Godot* is generally accepted as a cornerstone of modern theater. It is performed worldwide in schools and prisons as well as on public stages and, in its Grove Press edition, is a perennial bestseller. With *Godot* and his other plays, Beckett influenced countless playwrights who followed him, including Edward Albee, Harold Pinter, Tom Stoppard and David Mamet.

The name *Godot*, along with that of the author, is part of international mythology. Godot, who may or may not be a savior, never arrives, but man keeps waiting for his possible arrival. Waiting, in Beckett's sense, is not a vacuum but an alternate activity that can be as visceral - or as mindless - as one makes it. For Beckett himself, waiting became a way of living - waiting for inspiration, recognition, understanding or death.

For more than 50 years the writer lived in his adopted city of Paris, for much of that time in a working-class district in Montparnasse - a move that was to have the greatest effect on his life. Though he wrote most of his work in French, he remained definably Irish in his voice, manner and humor. Even in his final years, when he lived in a nursing home in Paris, he joined friends in a sip of Irish whiskey, which seemed to warm his bones and open him to greater conviviality. Throughout his life he was as craggy and as erect as a Giacometti sculpture. When he was healthy, he took long, loping walks on Paris streets.

In no way could he ever be considered an optimist. In an often repeated story, on a glorious sunny day he walked jauntily through a London park with an old friend and exuded a feeling of joy. The friend said it was the kind of day that made one glad to be alive. Beckett responded, "I wouldn't go that far."

Samuel Barclay Beckett was born in Foxrock, a suburb of Dublin, on Good Friday, April 13, 1906 (that date is sometimes disputed; it is said that on his birth certificate the date is May 13). His father, William Beckett Jr., was a surveyor. His mother, Mary Roe Beckett (known as May), was a nurse before her marriage. Samuel and his older brother, Frank, were brought up as Protestants. They went to Earlsfort House School in Dublin. Samuel Beckett then continued his education at Portora Royal School in Enniskillen, County Fermanagh, and at Trinity College, Dublin, where he majored in French and Italian. At school he excelled both in his studies and in sports, playing cricket and rugby. He received his Bachelor of Arts degree in 1927 and his Master of Arts degree in 1931.

In the intervening time, he spent two years in Paris in an exchange program, lecturing on English at the École Normale Supérieure. In Paris, he met James Joyce and other members of the literary and artistic set. He was not, as is commonly thought, Joyce's secretary, but he became a close friend and aide, reading to him when Joyce's eyes began to fail. Beckett's first published work was an essay on Joyce that appeared in the collection *Our Exagmination Round his Factification for Incamination of Work in Progress*, the work in progress being Joyce's *Finnegans Wake*. His first poem, "Whoroscope," was printed in 1930, followed one year by his essay on Proust.

Returning to Ireland, he taught Romance languages at Trinity. He thought briefly about remaining in the academic profession but decided otherwise. He resigned abruptly in 1932 and left Ireland, returning only for annual visits to his mother. (His father died in 1933, his mother in 1950.) He wandered from England to France to Germany before moving to Paris permanently in 1937. By that time he had published *More Pricks Than Kicks*, a collection of short stories; *Echo's Bones*, a volume of poetry, and *Murphy*, his first novel. Written in English, as were all his works at the time, *Murphy* was about an Irishman in London who tries to remove himself gradually from the visible world.

Settling down in Paris, Beckett became a familiar figure at Left Bank cafes, continuing his alliance with Joyce while also becoming friends with artists like Marcel Duchamp (with whom he played chess) and Alberto Giacometti. At this time he became involved with Peggy Guggenheim, who nicknamed him Oblomov after the title character in the Ivan Goncharov novel, a man who Ms. Guggenheim said was so overcome by apathy that he "finally did not even have the willpower to get out of bed."

In 1938, while walking with friends on a Paris street, he was stabbed with a knife by a panhandler. He was immediately taken to a hospital. One of his lungs was perforated and the knife narrowly missed his heart. Beckett fully recovered from the wound but it left psychological scars. After he recovered, he visited his assailant in prison and asked him the reason for the assault. The man replied, "Je ne sais pas, monsieur." More than ever, Beckett became aware of the randomness of life. Before the episode, he had met a young piano student named Suzanne Deschevaux-Dumesnil. She did not rescue him from the knifing - as was sometimes thought - but she did visit him in the hospital. They began a lifelong relationship and were married in Folkestone, England, in 1961.

With her, he chose to remain in France during World War II rather than return to the safety of Ireland. Both became active in The French Resistance. Forced to flee Paris, the couple went to Roussillon in the south of France. While working as a farm laborer and running messages for the Resistance, Beckett wrote the novel *Watt*. It was often said that his experiences in hiding during the war were an inspiration for *Waiting for Godot* and for the novel *Mercier and Camier*. At the end of the war he worked at the Irish Red Cross field hospital in St.-Lo. For his heroic services he was later awarded the Croix de Guerre and the Médaille de Résistance.

After *Watt*, he began writing in French, which allowed him, as the Joyce biographer Richard Ellmann observed, "a private liberation from the English tradition." The five years starting in 1947 were his most intense creative period, producing most of his major work. That year he wrote his first play, *Eleutheria*, and began the novel *Molloy*. They were followed by *Waiting for Godot*, which he wrote in longhand in a composition book. It took him four months. In a little more than a year, he had finished his greatest play as well as the first two parts of his trilogy of novels (*Molloy* and *Malone Dies*).

Though he found a publisher for the trilogy (Jerome Lindon at Éditions de Minuit, who remained his French publisher for the rest of his life), the plays were more difficult to place. Ms. Deschevaux-Dumesnil took them from producer to producer, a thankless route that the playwright once compared to giving the plays to a concierge. Then Roger Blin, the French actor and director, agreed to present one. He chose *Godot* over *Eleutheria* partly because it had fewer characters. At Beckett's behest, *Eleutheria* was never produced in his lifetime. It was only when

Waiting For Godot was in rehearsal, with Beckett in attendance, that Blin fully realized the excitement of his discovery.

En Attendant Godot, as the play was titled, opened on January 5, 1953, at the Théâtre de Babylone, and beginning a lifetime practice, the author did not attend. The first review, written by Sylvain Zégel in La Libération, said Beckett was "one of today's best playwrights," a fact that was not universally acknowledged. The first London production, using the playwright's English translation and directed by Peter Hall, received generally dismissive daily reviews. It was rescued by Harold Hobson, then the drama critic of The Sunday Times in London, who said the play might "securely lodge in a corner of your mind as long as you live."

In January 1956, Michael Myerberg opened the first United States production at the Coconut Grove Playhouse in Miami, with Bert Lahr and Tom Ewell cast in the leading roles as those Beckett tramps, Estragon and Vladimir. Expecting a Bert Lahr comedy, the audience was mystified. As Lahr said, doing *Godot* in Miami was like dancing *Giselle* at Roseland. With both the director Alan Schneider and Mr. Ewell replaced, the play moved to Broadway in April. With the exception of Eric Bentley and a few others, the critics were confounded. Several were abusive. Despite the producer's vainglorious advertising campaign to draw intellectuals into the theater, the play closed after 59 performances.

That *Waiting for Godot* became a contemporary classic can be attributed to the enthusiasm of its champions and to the profundity of the work itself, which became more apparent with subsequent productions. *Godot* came to be regarded not only as a clown comedy with tragic dimensions but as a play about man coping with the nature of his existence in a world that appeared to be hurtling toward a self-induced apocalypse.

Before *Godot* was produced in London, Beckett completed a second play, *Fin de Partie*, or *Endgame*, as the title was translated. In this dramatic equivalent of chess, Hamm the master oppresses Clov the servant in a bunker looking out on the void of the world. *Endgame* was followed by the radio play *All That Fall* and by the monodrama *Krapp's Last Tape*, written for the actor Patrick Magee. In 1961, he finished *Happy Days*, about a long and not always happy marriage, in which a woman eventually is buried up to her neck in earth. In 1964, he made his only trip to the United States for the filming of *Film*, the short Beckett movie that Mr. Schneider made with Buster Keaton. Uncomfortable in the hot July weather in New York, he was eager to return to Paris.

About the same time, he wrote a number of stage, television and radio plays, including *Play* (in which three characters are encased in urns), *Cascando* and *Eh Joe*, as well as the narrative fragment *Imagination Dead Imagine*.

In 1969 he was awarded the Nobel Prize in literature for a body of work that "has transformed the destitution of man into his exaltation." Karl Ragnar Gierow, secretary of the Swedish Academy, said his writing "rises like a Miserere from all mankind, its muffled minor key sounding liberation to the oppressed and comfort to those in need." He was on holiday in Tunisia at the time of the Nobel announcement and in characteristic fashion offered no public statement and refused to attend the ceremony. He sent his publisher in his stead. Reportedly he gave his prize money of $72,800 to needy artists.

As undeterred by the acclaim as he had been by his years of obscurity, he continued to write and to maintain his privacy. His plays and prose became shorter and even terser, as in *Not I*, in which the play's principal character is a woman's heavily lipsticked mouth; *That Time*, in which a spotlight shines on a man's head and his corona of white hair, and *Rockaby*, in which an old woman rocks herself to death. In these plays he chose to deal with what he called "the battle of the soliloquy," sifting the past and enduring the continuum of life. Two of his prose pieces, *Company* and *Worstward Ho*, were published as short novels. On occasion, he would visit London to supervise a production or Germany, where he frequently worked on television plays and where he staged a definitive German-language version of *Waiting for Godot*.

During Beckett's lifetime he had many close collaborations with actors (Jack MacGowran, Patrick Magee, Billie Whitelaw, David Warrilow) and with several directors, especially Mr. Schneider, who staged most of the American premieres of his plays. When Mr. Schneider was killed in a London traffic accident in 1984, it was a blow to the playwright.

In the same year, the New York Drama Critics Circle awarded him a special citation in recognition of his body of work and in particular for two evenings of Beckett short plays produced that season in New York. One of those plays was *Catastrophe*, written for Václav Havel. It was for Beckett a rare political work about the interrogation of a dissident.

In Beckett's later years, directors staged his radio plays or adapted his prose to the stage. Mabou Mines offered dramatizations of *The Lost Ones, Mercier and Camier* and *Company*. Though Beckett was liberal about allowing adaptations of his prose, he was scrupulous in demanding absolute fidelity to the stage directions as well as to the dialogue in his plays. In 1985, JoAnne Akalaitis, a director with Mabou Mines, changed the setting of *Endgame* from a bare interior to an abandoned subway station. Through representatives, Beckett issued a formal complaint against the production at the American Repertory Theater in Cambridge, Mass., and his objection appeared in the play's program.

On his 80th birthday in 1986, Beckett was celebrated in several cities. In Paris, there was a citywide festival of plays and symposiums, and in New York there was a week of panels and lectures analyzing his art.

As usual, he kept his silence, as in the characteristic note he sent to those who approached him about writing his biography. He said that his life was "devoid of interest."

He steadfastly maintained his routine through his later years. He lived on the Boulevard St. Jacques in an apartment adjoining that of his wife and overlooking the exercise yard of the Santé prison. Regularly he visited his country house, some 60 miles outside Paris. He made daily trips to a neighborhood cafe where he met friends, had a double espresso and smoked several thin dark cigars. Periodically he wrote brief plays and small prose pieces.

Around him and without his encouragement, his reputation grew unbounded. The Mike Nichols revival of *Waiting for Godot* at Lincoln Center in 1988 was an event of magnitude, drawing together the diverse talents of Steve Martin, Robin Williams and Bill Irwin and selling out for its entire engagement. This year there was a festival of Beckett radio plays on National Public Radio, reminding his audience that this was still another form that he had mastered.

About a year ago, after falling in his apartment, he moved to a nearby nursing home, where he continued to receive visitors. He lived his last year in a small, barely furnished room. He had a television set on which he continued to watch major tennis and soccer events, and several books, including his boyhood copy of Dante's *Divine Comedy* in Italian.

On July 17 this year, his wife died and he left the nursing home to attend the funeral. Late this year, after he became ill, he was moved to a hospital. There are no immediate survivors.

His last work to be printed in his lifetime was *Stirrings Still*, a short prose piece published in a limited edition on his 83rd birthday. In it, a character who resembles the author sits alone in a cell-like room until he sees his double appear - and then disappear. Accompanied by "time and grief and self so-called," he finds himself "stirring still" to the end.

JEAN GENET: APRIL 16, 1986

Jean Genet - playwright, novelist, poet and one of the revolutionary artists of the 20th century - died yesterday morning in the Paris hotel where he lived. He was 75 years old.

According to a representative of Genet's publisher, Librairie Gallimard, the author had been suffering from throat cancer and had been undergoing renewed radiation treatment.

A short, bald man with a compact, muscular body, Genet was an exceedingly private person, despite his notorious personal life. The Paris hotel room in which he died had been his home for several years, but even his publisher did not know how to reach him. Reportedly the room was pristine and cell-like, and all of his possessions fit into one small suitcase. His mail was delivered to his publisher's office; even the address on his passport was Gallimard's.

A self-confessed criminal and an ex-convict, Genet was a poète maudit in the

classic French tradition, a pioneering author of confessional novels and a dramatist of the first magnitude. Along with Samuel Beckett, he was a towering figure
in the experimental theater of the mid-century. Genet's plays, *The Maids*,
Deathwatch, *The Balcony*, *The Blacks* and *The Screens*, each a raging subject of controversy - as was the author throughout his lifetime - are among the most influential and consequential in the international repertory.

"Jean Genet has left us," said Jack Lang, former Minister of Culture in
France, "and with him, a black sun that enlightened the seamy side of things. Jean
Genet was liberty itself, and those who hated and fought him were hypocrites."

Attacked and even vilified, imprisoned as a thief, prostitute and pimp, Genet
was an outlaw in life and in art. But from his life he created an art of the blackest
blasphemy, a distorted mirror image of the society that bred him. As surprising as
it still seems to those unfamiliar with his work, he was, at heart, a moralist, albeit
one of a fiendish variety.

Reviewing *The Screens*, Genet's play condemning the French role in Algeria,
Harold Clurman said that the author had earned the right to his "epic nihilism."
Genet, he said, "is one of the few creative dramatists of our epoch. From the holo-
causts of the day he lights his own flaming torch. It illuminates what we are, what
we have wrought, what we must renounce."

Genet was also an actor in the play of his life, putting on masks, rearranging
facts to suit his purpose and clouding himself in mystique. In 1952 Jean-Paul
Sartre published *Saint Genet: Actor and Martyr*, a massive volume that sanctified
Genet and apparently, for a time, provoked the author into a severe case of writer's
block. All his life, Genet resisted categorization and, one might say, canonization.

The first question, as yet unanswered, is whether he was born, or made, a
criminal (and an artist). He was born, illegitimate, in Paris on Dec. 19, 1910, and
his mother abandoned him. Until the age of 7, he was a foundling; at 21 he saw
his birth certificate and discovered that his mother was Gabrielle Genet. He never
learned the name of his father.

As a youth living with foster parents in the country, he was an altar boy. When
he stole some money from his foster mother's purse, she called him a "little thief"
and, as Genet told the story, from then on he lived out that role and whatever role
that was imposed on him. As he said, "Abandoned by my family, I found it natural
to aggravate this fact by the love of males, and that love by stealing, and stealing
by crime, or complicity with crime. Thus I decisively repudiated a world that had
repudiated me."

His adolescent delinquency led him to a reformatory, where he was confined
for a number of years. According to his account, when he was 21 he escaped from
the reformatory and joined the French Foreign Legion, which he subsequently
deserted. For the next 10 years he led a nomadic and often criminal life in Europe,
often expelled from countries or expelling himself, as was the case in Nazi

Germany. In that "nation of thieves," he said, he saw "no special act" in being a thief.

Back in France, he spent much of the Occupation in jail - and it was there that he began to write. His first work was a poem, *Under Sentence of Death*, memorializing a fellow prisoner who was executed for murder. The poem came to the attention of Jean Cocteau, who became the first of Genet's many artistic mentors and one of his strongest champions. Soon after, he began writing a book in pencil on brown paper. When the manuscript was confiscated, he started anew. As *Our Lady of the Flowers*, it was published in a limited edition in French in 1943, and in English in 1949. That novel was the genesis of his extraordinary career.

At first, that career was restricted to fiction - or fantasies based on reality, his self-inventions - but in the late 1940's he began writing plays, beginning with *Deathwatch*. In his first play, as in his books, Genet turned evil on its head, treating it as if it were sainthood. The most sainted figure in *Deathwatch*, not seen on stage, is Snowball, a king of crime.

Genet's next play, *The Maids*, was based on the true story of two sisters who murdered their employer. In Genet's version, the roles were to be played by actors, although in the original Paris production, in a concession to the celebrated actor-director Louis Jouvet, the roles were played by women. As in his subsequent plays, the characters assumed guises, enacting rituals of domination and violence.

The Maids, his first play to be staged in Paris (in 1947), brought him artistic credibility and even respectability, but the following year, after still another conviction for theft, he was faced with the prospect of a sentence of life imprisonment. Artists rushed to his defense with a petition - signed by Sartre, Cocteau, André Gide and Paul Claudel, among others. Genet was pardoned, which is not to say that he subsequently avoided crime. It was later reported that, for a time, he ran a bookstall by the Seine that was stocked with stolen volumes.

Deathwatch and *The Maids* had only brief runs Off Broadway, but his next two plays, *The Balcony* and *The Blacks* (as translated by Bernard Frechtman), were critical and public successes in America and elsewhere. Opening at Circle in the Square in 1960, in a production directed by Jose Quintero, *The Balcony* ran for 672 performances. The following year *The Blacks*, directed by Gene Frankel, began a run of 1,408 performances and became a home for scores of talented black actors.

The Balcony, which takes place in Madame Irma's House of Illusion, reverses the civilized order. In this phantasmagorical brothel, ordinary citizens act out elaborate sexual, religious and political fantasies. Outside, a revolution is in progress, and in Genet's turnabout, the mock figures assume real-life roles. The result is a bizarre hall of mirrors, refracting a state of national and psychic emergency.

The Blacks was his "clownerie," or clown show, in which black actors put on white masks to play - and to mock - their white aggressors, as represented by a colonial society. The central ritual enacted is the murder of a white woman. As with *The Balcony*, *The Blacks* is a comedy, one of the most diabolical variety.

Genet's last play, *The Screens*, was his longest and most ambitious, lasting more than five hours and calling for a cast of 40. An epic accusation against his native country for its role in North Africa, it was published in 1960 but not staged in France until 1966, in a production directed by Roger Blin (who staged the original production of "Waiting for Godot"). *The Screens* reached America in 1973 in a monumental production presented by the Chelsea Theater Company.

Genet's theater could be regarded as a natural outgrowth of his confinement - and his isolation - in prison. As Richard N. Coe wrote in his book *The Vision of Jean Genet*: "Solitude, then, with all its complexities, its rewards and its terrors, is Genet's main theme." For him, Genet was "the poet of solitude."

Influenced by Verlaine, Rimbaud, Pirandello, Sartre and, perhaps most of all, Antonin Artaud (and his Theater of Cruelty), Genet, in turn, had affected playwrights of his time and later.

In addition to *Our Lady of the Flowers*, Genet wrote the books *The Miracle of the Rose, Funeral Rites, The Thief's Journal* and *Querelle*. Reviewing *Funeral Rites*, V.S. Pritchett said, "In the most literal sense of the phrase, Genet is a writer who has the courage of his convictions. Out of the lives of criminals, and following a tradition in French literature, he has built an erotic mystique, even a kind of metaphysic." He was, said Pritchett, "the autodidact of the jails."

Genet was also responsible for several screenplays, one filmed in 1966 under the title *Mademoiselle*, directed by Tony Richardson and starring Jeanne Moreau, and a number of essays, which Grove Press, his New York publisher, plans to bring out in a collection. On two crucial political occasions he visited the United States: in 1968 to write about the Democratic National Convention for Esquire, and in 1970 when he activated a friendship with members of the Black Panthers.

In the last decade, so far as is known, he did no writing, but his plays continued to be produced with regularity. *The Balcony* was staged this winter both by JoAnne Akalaitis at the American Repertory Theater in Cambridge and by the Comédie Française in Paris - earning the ultimate imprimatur of respectability for an artist who luxuriated in his iconoclasm.

EUGÈNE IONESCO: MARCH 29, 1994

Eugène Ionesco, whose wildly innovative plays, among them *Rhinoceros, The Bald Soprano* and *The Chairs*, overturned conventions of contemporary theater and had a profound effect on a new generation of playwrights, died yesterday in Paris, where he lived. He was 84.

Mr. Ionesco's "anti-plays" satirized modern society while discovering new uses of language and theatrical techniques. Inspired by silent film clowns and vaudeville, he was a playful playwright, clownish in his own personality as well as in his work onstage. With outrageous comedy, he attacked the most serious subjects: blind conformity and totalitarianism, despair and death. Repeatedly he challenged - and accosted - the audience and his critics. As he said, "The human drama is as absurd as it is painful."

Along with Samuel Beckett and Jean Genet, he was one of a trinity of pioneering experimental playwrights who lived and worked in Paris. Although there were thematic bridges among the three, Mr. Ionesco's distinction was in his fanciful surrealism and sense of Dada. Among the playwrights he influenced were Tom Stoppard, Fernando Arrabal, Edward Albee, Tina Howe and Christopher Durang. Mr. Ionesco was among the playwrights often grouped as practitioners of the Theater of the Absurd. He objected to the label, preferring, he said, the Theater of Derision.

In his work, he turned drawing-room comedy on its head (*The Bald Soprano*), had a stage filled with empty chairs (*The Chairs*) and transformed man into beast (*Rhinoceros*). Although his playwriting career did not begin until he was 40, he wrote 28 plays as well as several books of memoirs. The plays have been performed around the world in various languages, although in recent years his work has been neglected in the United States. Throughout his career, he was an imaginative iconoclast who could create the most bizarre imagery.

Rhinoceros, in its 1961 Broadway production, proved to be his breakthrough play, enriched by Zero Mostel's virtuosic performance, in which he transmogrified himself from man to rhinoceros without altering his makeup or costume. Roaring, bellowing, hilarious Mostel put the playwright on the international theatrical map, and *Rhinoceros* ran for 241 performances. But the play was only one of many that insured Mr. Ionesco's stature.

Despite his reputation for controversy, he saw himself as a preserver of theater, a classicist and "a supreme realist." He insisted that he wrote archetypes, not stereotypes. As he said in 1958, "I believe that the aim of the avant-garde should be to rediscover - not invent - in their purest state, the permanent forms and forgotten ideals of the theater." He added: "I make no claim to have succeeded in this. But others will succeed, and show that all truth and reality is classical and eternal."

He was "the Molière of the 20th century," said Rosette C. Lamont, the author of "Ionesco's Imperatives: The Politics of Culture" (University of Michigan Press, 1993) and an acknowledged authority on Ionesco's work. "Like Molière in his late plays," she continued, "in Ionesco's plays, there is a seamless amalgam of the comic and tragic." In her eyes, he was a master of the "metaphysical farce," an oxymoron that the playwright accepted as accurate.

Eugène Ionesco was born in Slatina, Romania, on Nov. 26, 1909, although he took three years off his age and claimed 1912 as his birth year, presumably because he wanted to have made his name before the age of 40. His father was Romanian, his mother French.

As a child, he lived in Paris. In an article titled "Experience in the Theater," he remembered his introduction to a world that would preoccupy him for a lifetime. The Punch and Judy show in the Luxembourg Gardens fascinated him as the puppets "talked, moved, clubbed each other." It was, he said, "the spectacle of the world itself...presented itself to me in an infinitely simplified and caricatured form, as if to underline its grotesque and brutal truth."

In 1922, he returned to Romania, where he went to high school and later studied at Bucharest University. At first he wrote poetry, not plays (except for a historical drama he wrote at 13). He married Rodica Burileanu in 1936; eight years later, their daughter, Marie-France, was born. Both his wife and daughter survive.

In 1939, Mr. Ionesco moved back to France and worked for a publisher. He became a French citizen and remained there for the rest of his life. During World War II, he and his wife were in hiding in the south of France.

The Bald Soprano (*La Cantatrice Chauve*) was inspired by his own attempts to learn English by using an English-French conversational manual. Copying out phrases, he realized he was relearning obvious truths, that there are seven days in a week and that the ceiling is above, the floor below. Carrying that premise to the ridiculous, word-spinning heights, he wrote his first play - and no bald soprano appeared onstage. An actor improvised those words, and Mr. Ionesco seized upon them and changed the play's title from *English Made Easy*.

The play was intended, he said, as "a parody of human behavior and therefore a parody of theater, too." Presented in 1950 at the tiny Théâtre des Noctambules in Paris, it received some initially hostile reviews but became the catapult for his career. More than 40 years later, the play is still running in another theater in Paris.

The Bald Soprano was quickly followed by *The Lesson* (1951), *Jack, or the Submission* and *The Chairs* (1952) and *Victims of Duty* (1953), all of which certified his avant-garde credentials. In *Amédée, or How to Get Rid of It* (1954), a corpse grows larger and larger until it takes over the stage, and in *The New Tenant* (1956), a man rents a new apartment and the furniture takes over the stage. These and other works are filled with sight gags and silent comedy as well as intricate plays on words.

Rhinoceros brought him his widest public. Jean-Louis Barrault starred in the play in Paris and Laurence Olivier in London. But it was the Broadway production, directed by Joseph Anthony and starring Zero Mostel and Eli Wallach, that brought him his greatest celebrity. Mostel later starred in an unsuccessful film version of the play, directed by Tom O'Horgan. *Rhinoceros* and other plays charted the progress of Mr. Ionesco's Everyman, a character named Berenger.

In 1960, *The Killer*, a comedy about a serial killer in "the radiant city," had a brief run Off Broadway, and in 1968 Ellis Rabb directed *Exit the King* on Broadway. From then on, Mr. Ionesco was often absent from the New York theater. Some of his plays were presented in regional theater, with the United States premiere of *Macbett* at the Yale Repertory Theater in 1973. Taking off from Shakespeare, he regarded *Macbeth* as a grotesque joke. How else could he explain mass murder, a favorite subject for his dark comic contemplation?

Throughout his life, he said he was apolitical, a fact he often disproved in his plays, especially those in his later period, like *A Stroll in the Air*, (a cosmic walk with reference to World War II and the Holocaust) and *Man With Bags*, a play about exile, in which a traveler is adrift in a world without place names. (Is there life without geography?) His last play, *Journeys Among the Dead* was scheduled to be performed at the Guggenheim Museum in 1980 but never opened. In his own life, the playwright often took strong stands on public issues, speaking out about the rights of dissidents.

Mr. Ionesco also wrote a novel (*The Hermit*) and short stories, dramatic theory (*Notes and Counter Notes*), memoirs (*Fragments of a Journal, Present Past Past Present* and *The Intermittent Quest*) and fairy tales for children. He also painted and made lithographs; in the 1980's he stopped writing plays, and devoted much of his time to painting and exhibiting his artwork.

In 1970, he was elected a member of the French Academy. In his address to the Academy, he spoke of his faith in illogicality, the confusion of rules and the impotence of intelligence.

On a number of occasions, he visited the United States, in 1988 for the first New York International Festival of the Arts. He delivered a lecture titled "Who Needs Theater Anymore?" His pithy answer: "Tout le monde." Looking back at *The Bald Soprano*, he said that at the time "it was a pleasure to destroy language." Now, he said, he found "the disintegration of language tragic."

In his early 20's, he wrote about his reasons for wanting to be a writer: "To allow others to share in the astonishment of being, the dazzlement of existence, and to shout to God and other human beings our anguish, letting it be known that we were there."

5

ONE PERSON SHOWS

EILEEN ATKINS

A ROOM OF ONE'S OWN: MARCH 5, 1991

In *A Room of One's Own,* Virginia Woolf used her discerning wit and intellectual acumen to assail the bastion of male prejudice against women as artists. Her two historic lectures and the book that grew out of them are a cornerstone of feminist doctrine and free thinking criticism. Although the essay was written to be delivered in public (at Cambridge University in 1928), it was not regarded as a dramatic piece - until Eileen Atkins gave it life on stage.

In her performance at the Lamb's Theater, Ms. Atkins offers a virtuosic feat of acting and a luminous portrait of the artist. She brings to the role a great assurance, humor and resonance.

The reinvention of Virginia Woolf is in spite of the fact that Ms. Atkins does not really look like her, though her hairstyle and tailored clothes are in the Woolfian mode. Emotionally, she has plunged to the heart of her character, as a wise and demanding woman of feverish intensity who was unequivocal in matters of art and ethics. Though the brilliance of the performance might seem to contradict the public image of this private artist, it is clearly a reflection of how the writer must have seemed to those who were close to her.

Ms. Atkins instills the performance with a conversational flow, the feeling that the words are being spoken for the first time, that theatergoers are, in fact, in the audience at Cambridge with the young women whose artistic hopes are destined to be dashed by the realities of a patriarchal society. In performance, Ms. Atkins becomes the woman whose self-knowledge allowed her to admit to her own "remorseless severity." Behind that severity is a scathing humor, which she directs against all those who believed that women were capable only of child-bearing and husband-pleasing. With controlled fury, she lashes out at the diffidence felt toward women by the ruling class of men, the economic, political and artistic repression practiced through history.

Picking up a copy of Trevelyan's *History of England,* a contemporary book, she reads, "Wife beating was a recognized right of man," and continues that a woman who rejected her parents' choice of a husband was "liable to be locked up, beaten and flung about the room." That last phrase, "flung about the room," is repeated with increased mockery. It is unthinkable that anyone would ever have the nerve to try to fling Woolf or Ms. Atkins about the room, and the very idea provokes laughter from the audience.

There is a steeliness but never a stridency in this characterization, which burnishes word, inflection and gesture. Disallowing herself acting mannerisms (a pitfall in any such one-woman performance), Ms. Atkins delights in the nuances of the author's graceful language.

Though her anger is self-evident, she does not become exasperated, but maintains a gentility that makes her indictment more devastating. Striking the paradox at the core of her argument, she indicates that at the same time that women were treated as chattel in real life, their heroic and romantic qualities were celebrated in fiction and drama. Ms. Atkins describes Shakespeare's women with artfully understated irony.

High in her pantheon are Jane Austen, Emily Brontë, Aphra Behn - and Judith Shakespeare. The last is, of course, a Woolf invention, Shakespeare's imaginary, gifted sister, who, forbidden to be creative, was driven to suicide. Her tragedy and that of those who came after her could be avoided, she says, if a woman had an annual income of £500 and a room of one's own.

The challenge echoes to today, down to the fiery conclusion that the spirit of Judith Shakespeare lives on in the potential of all her sister artists. Were Ms. Atkins to have delivered the original lectures, the audience of women might have marched on Parliament, or at least on Cambridge.

A shorter version of the performance was recently presented on *Masterpiece Theater* on television. The play benefits from being seen in its longer form and from the responsiveness between audience and actress.

In his adaptation, Patrick Garland (who is also the director) has somewhat compressed the original text and interwoven it with commentary from the author, heard on tape. The taped segments allow Ms. Atkins breathing space in a demanding evening but they are questionable additions, and also threaten the performance with the quirks of electronics. That choice aside, this is an event of theatrical magnitude.

With her Virginia Woolf, Ms. Atkins joins Hal Holbrook (for *Mark Twain Tonight!*) and Alec McCowen (for *St. Mark's Gospel*) at the pinnacle of the monodramatic art. Each is a perfect meeting of actor and subject.

FRED CURCHACK

STUFF AS DREAMS ARE MADE ON: NOVEMBER 2, 1989

In Fred Curchack's *Stuff as Dreams Are Made On*, a one-man show becomes a stage-filling phantasmagoria. This freehand reinvention of *The Tempest*, in which Mr. Curchack plays all the roles and assumes all directorial and scenic responsibility, opened Tuesday at the Brooklyn Academy of Music as part of the Next Wave festival.

With lightning dexterity and to the sound of his own thundersheet, he quick-changes from Prospero to Ariel to Caliban, sometimes managing to keep several characters on stage at once. When he is playing Caliban, his Prospero mask and his Miranda doll (acting as ventriloquist's dummy) are watching and commenting. One of his feats is in changing and throwing his voice.

Diverging from *The Tempest*, he conducts conversations among the characters on such subjects as Shakespeare, the pretensions of performance art and the fact that after touring the world, he has finally - sigh of relief - arrived in Brooklyn. Miranda warns him to watch his step or he may lose his audience.

Mr. Curchack is a clown as well as a commentator. On one level, his play is an act of criticism - of the artist himself as well as his source. Repeatedly he inter-rupts his own performance with a comic aside in an attempt to demystify the event. His art is created as we watch it. Apparently he is opposed to atavism - and he is also not happy about late-comers to his show and people unfamiliar with the plot of *The Tempest*.

While remaining faithful to his text in principle, he omits characters and in-serts occasional contemporary dialogue. For all his apparent informality, he comes up with evocative interpretations of a Curchack kind, like his investigation of the relationship between Caliban and Miranda. They may have been closer than one suspected, despite the fact that Miranda can dismiss Caliban as an illiterate repre-sentative of the third world. This Caliban refuses to cringe; in his monstrous mask, he could frighten Freddy from *Nightmare on Elm Street*.

The masks are themselves a chimerical gallery of distorted faces, often caught as in stop-action photography. As for Prospero, he is a top-hatted, white-masked Mephisto, an actor conducting a backstage tour of his magical island. There are different voices for each of the characters, including a singing voice for the an-drogynous Ariel and an amusingly broad Neapolitan accent for Ferdinand. Miranda is smitten by this preening "biceptual" pinhead but retains her self-par-odying intellectualism, as in her description of her world as a "deconstructed Jungian paradise."

In response to Mr. Curchack's diverse talents, one is most captivated by his role as designer in motion. Wielding a battery of handheld lights (flashlight, cig-arette lighter, floor lamp), he uses himself as a shadow puppet. In giant silhouette, he becomes fearsome specters and demons, populating a Rorschach landscape of images. At one climactic point, his shadow looms larger and more menacing and then levitates into space. At such moments, it is clear that when Mr. Curchack is on stage, imagination knows no limitations.

His art is firmly rooted in technique, ranging from Noh to kathakali, from classic mime to Method acting (his Caliban has elements of Brando). The fact that he has condensed *The Tempest* into 80 minutes, while adding extras, should come as no surprise to anyone who has seen his previous shows, such as *Fred Breaks*

Bread with the Dead, which was a collage of *Hamlet* with music, *The Hairy Ape*, *Ulysses* and other literary works.

Mr. Curchack is so polymorphous in performance that at the end of the show, one might expect to see a dozen participating artists take a bow instead of one unmasked, seraphic-looking theatrical virtuouso.

KAREN FINLEY

WE KEEP OUR VICTIMS READY: AUGUST 1, 1990

The rejection of Karen Finley and three other experimentalists for grants from the National Endowment for the Arts has made the term "performance artist" the subject of considerable debate and wide attention. People who have no conception of the range or purpose of the form now use the words with alacrity, as a synonym for anything outrageous. The fact is that performance art is one of the most inclusive - and misunderstood - of theatrical arts.

The crowds and critical enthusiasm that greeted Ms. Finley's one-woman show, *We Keep Our Victims Ready*, at Alice Tully Hall last week bear witness to this performance artist's suddenly increased popularity and to her newly won role as public victim.

Being denied a grant by the National Endowment for the Arts has transformed a fringe artist into a star. Despite her celebrity, Ms. Finley has not altered her confrontational politics. She still speaks with boldness about the issues that concern her, all of which center on restrictions to personal and civil liberties.

Though she can be amusing, especially in her off-handed, self-deprecating remarks, Ms. Finley is not essentially a comic. She is a polemicist, and acting would seem to be the least of her skills. It is as a writer and as a conduit of ideas that she has made her primary contribution. Her talent is in her ability to use (and even abuse) herself on stage.

As a performance artist, she becomes a work of performance art, even to the extent of treating herself as a sculptural object, covering her partly nude body with chocolate to simulate excrement and symbolize the debasement of women. On stage, she is like a medium, through whom societal anxieties are transmitted and acted out. The medium (Ms. Finley) is the message.

That McLuhanesque statement could be regarded as a step toward a definition of performance art. It has long been true that almost anyone can claim to be a performance artist. Under this vast creative umbrella are stand-up comics and sit-down monologuists, and conceptual directors, as well as Ms. Finley and the three other artists (John Fleck, Holly Hughes and Tim Miller) who were denied endowment grants.

Ms. Finley's theatrical polemics, Bill Irwin's clowning, Michael Moschen's balletic juggling, Eric Bogosian's urban backlash and Spalding Gray's continuing memoir in progress share stage space with Stuart Sherman's postcard-size impressions of great authors, Lily Tomlin's gallery of eccentrics and Fred Curchack's one-man version of *The Tempest*. Mr. Curchack was among 14 performance artists who were awarded grants by the endowment this year.

What these creators have in common is their interest in melding arts and in annotating their thoughts in theatrical form. Each is a self-starter. It is difficult to imagine their work engendered or reproduced by anyone else. Whether the result is a monologue or a multi-media epic, in the purest form, each performance artist is sui generis.

Although some of these artists have gone on to appear in works by others, or to write plays in a more recognizable tradition, they are identifiable as members of the experimental theater movement, as it has become allied with dance, music and the graphic arts. On stage, the creators exhibit their art, which is often themselves. They are their own installations.

Had the term existed in the 1950's, Lenny Bruce would have been considered a performance artist, and had the National Endowment existed then, he very likely would have been denied a grant. More recent humorists like Richard Pryor and Robin Williams could claim membership; there is nothing removed and impersonal about their comedy, and they can be as outrageous as anyone in the avant-garde.

Though the term "performance artist" was first popularized in the United States in the 1970's, the form is at least as old as Russian constructivism of the 1920's, an early attempt at coalescing diverse arts in synergistic unity. Stanislavsky and Mayakovsky are pivotal figures. Richard Schechner, founder of the Performance Group, one of the earliest American progenitors of the form, has written that Stanislavsky's exercises led to actors "building whole shows around the expression of their personal lives." Tracing this approach through popular entertainment, rock, poetry and fiction, Mr. Schechner continues: "The performance of self in theater has also been strongly influenced by the movement from visual art to environments to happenings. The confluence of these tendencies has created a new genre: Performance Art."

Ms. Finley is herself a throwback to happenings, Beat poetry and the Living Theater, all from an earlier era. Her play *The Theory of Total Blame* with its graphic and realistic portrait of a kind of family life (with both anger and ennui) is reminiscent of the apparently unprocessed, live-in plays of the 1960's avant-garde and of films by Andy Warhol.

Jerzy Grotowski, influential in the development of performance art - along with such fellow directors as Peter Brook, Andrei Serban and Andre Gregory -

stepped beyond Stanislavsky in opening up the performer as creator, rather than as a more passive interpreter. In his manifesto, "Towards a Poor Theater," he proclaimed, "We consider the personal and scenic techniques of the actor as the core of theater art." On the other hand, there are more recent innovators like John Jesurun who subordinate the role of the actor to that of the scenic and cinematic conceptualist, as in his *Everything That Rises Must Converge*, a collage of visceral imagery (at one point a wall of the set spins around the stage like a giant propeller).

Performance art has spread throughout the world - in the work of Tadeusz Kantor of Poland and Giorgio Strehler of Italy. In New York, Ellen Stewart's La Mama is one of several international centers for such theater. Despite the success of individual artists, performance art has until recently been a significant dramatic form that operated outside of the mainstream.

As it proliferated, the term became an honorific. On one level, it was a way for night club comedians to change their calling cards and upgrade their images - to transform show business into art. Even Jackie Mason could represent himself as a performance artist. Eventually, the line between old and new vaudeville became blurred. The profession, though still nebulous, was legitimized.

What Senator Jesse Helms and others equally censorious have done is to give performance art a new and decidedly unwarranted pejorative cast. There is an unknowing public at large that now thinks of it as the devil's art, conjured in dark alleys and derelict warehouses. Fearful about risking guilt by association - and rejection - candidates for endowment grants might think twice about putting "performance artist" on their applications.

The reverse could also be true. The attacks could give the label a cachet, increasing the public awareness of the expansiveness of the form, which by being boundless in its receptivity allows for congeniality (the Flying Karamazov Brothers) as well as controversy (Ms. Finley). Performance art, as the indeterminate art, welcomes anyone exploring new dimensions in theatrical self-expression.

THE OTHER LIFE OF KAREN FINLEY: SEPTEMBER 22, 1997

NYACK, N.Y. - Just off the main street of this small Hudson River town is a large, rambling house, a converted barn built in 1886. In the garden, a gray-haired woman is puttering and pruning. Inside the house is a catacomb of rooms filled with old and antique furniture. It is a jumble of work and play, the play area belonging to a 4-year-old named Violet, who attends school nearby. The homey environment and the three generations of occupants - grandmother, mother and daughter - are like an image of Victoriana thrust suddenly into the modern age.

With her long hair and her blouse and long skirt, the 41-year-old lady of the house looks as if she might have been posing for a portrait by Sargent. She is, however, Karen Finley, the performance artist whose name is synonymous with controversy, the "chocolate-smeared woman" of Senator Jesse Helms's nightmares.

But this is the other Karen Finley, a single mother since she and her husband separated, a socially committed artist surviving through her talent and her persistence, and managing a household with the help of her mother, the woman in the garden. For several years, Ms. Finley's mother, Mary Finley, has lived with her daughter and taken care of her granddaughter when Ms. Finley is on tour (from Boston to São Paolo, Brazil).

In her highly visceral, startling monologues, Ms. Finley forthrightly confronts urgent issues: prejudice, censorship and, most of all, the abuse of women. *The American Chestnut*, her current show (running through Sunday at P.S. 122) takes its title and metaphor from the trees that were struck by blight at the turn of the century. Recently, a chestnut tree in the garden next door to the Finley house bloomed for the first time in more than 75 years. The show is about women's survival, although should Ms. Finley's Congressional critics see it, they might focus on other subjects, beginning with obscenity.

Outspoken language and nudity are essential to Ms. Finley's art, but, she emphasizes, everything is for a specific political purpose. She is a performance artist as provocateur, a role she also fulfills as a visual artist and author. In her sitting room, surrounded by her paintings and sketches (and the thick fall fashion issue of Vogue), she talked about some of the misconceptions that have plagued her during her intertwined careers. First of all, there is the charge that her approach is negative. "I think I'm positive," she said. "I would say I'm a healthy neurotic. I try to fix things with my art. But I'm not a Pollyanna. I can see the limitations and restrictions."

Contradicting another criticism, she said, "People think I'm hysterical and out of control. They expect that I'll just be taking my clothes off and using foul language, and that I would do this in my kitchen. Many times when people, journalists, meet me, they're afraid of me. They think I'm going to embarrass them. I don't know what they're afraid of. Is it like an archetype or an image, a vagina with teeth?"

Asked to describe herself, she said, "I think I'm a dreamer. I like to laugh. I like to poke fun at things, and I'm also crying in these throes and bemoans, like in the last scene of *American Chestnut*," in which a woman tells about being chased and raped by two men, a scene based on an episode in Ms. Finley's own life. "That scene disturbs me," she said. "It offends me. I'm sure that some people hearing me have to close their ears."

For her, the monologues are "physical, carthartic experiences," and earlier in her career she would be sick before and after a performance. She traces her pain back to the trauma of her father's suicide. She was 21, the oldest of six children. Her monologues remain extremely personal, which is why she cannot imagine anyone else performing them: "it would be like someone else doing my painting."

After receiving a grant from the National Endowment for the Arts in the early 1980's, Ms. Finley moved to New York from Chicago and began building her reputation Off Off Broadway. Later, as one of the so-called N.E.A. Four (the others were Holly Hughes, Tim Miller and John Fleck), she was to be the recipient of another small endowment grant, which was denied after a Congressional protest led by Senator Helms, Republican of North Carolina. That action became a cause celebre.

Since then, she has been the center of a lawsuit challenging the standards of decency imposed on publicly financed art. Her lawyers won the first two rounds, and, in a follow-up appeal, the Clinton Administration filed a petition on Aug. 29 asking the United States Supreme Court to hear the case. David Cole, a lawyer for the N.E.A. Four, said the case raised broader issues about Federal financing in other areas, including public education, libraries and television.

When the suit began, Ms. Finley taped a deposition, in which she was quizzed in what she called nitpicking detail about the sexual and scatological nature of her performances. "At one point," she said, "I stopped and said, 'I feel like you're Roy Cohn at the McCarthy hearings.' " The details that came out in the deposition dealt with, among other things, Ms. Finley's use of chocolate and yams in connection with her naked body. She said that the smearing of chocolate was a direct reference to the Tawana Brawley case, in which a young black woman was found covered with feces, and that the yams were a reference to the abuse of old women. These symbolic moments were taken out of context and, to some people, made Ms. Finley a figure of fun. Asserting that "ridicule is important," she is the first to mock herself.

In the name of parody, she thinks almost anything can be spoofed, especially sacred cows. Her most recent book, *Living It Up: Humorous Adventures in Hyperdomesticity*, mocks Martha Stewart so directly that the original publisher (one of Ms. Stewart's publishers) rejected the manuscript. It was published last year by Doubleday.

Ms. Finley's current sacred cow is a teddy bear. Reading *Winnie-the-Pooh* to her daughter, she realized that the characters are all male, except for Kanga, and then she began fantasizing about trouble at Pooh Corner, wondering if Pooh had an eating disorder and if Eeyore was terminally depressed. Nimbly mimicking the original illustrations, she drew her own outrageous version. The real Pooh, albeit male, remains a favorite of her daughter.

In various museums and galleries, Ms. Finley has had frequent exhibitions of her artwork, ranging from her Pooh drawings to her still lifes (lush bouquets of flowers with pithy messages as captions) to *Memento Mori*, her compassionate walk-through environment about AIDS. Next December she will have an installation at the Whitney Museum of American Art. Each day brings a new idea, like Dial an Artist. She is planning to set up a 900 number. Dial, and she will answer with a recorded message.

"Art has become taboo in our culture," she said. 'Like sex, or even astrology. It's fringe. There's a deviant element to it. With the people who call those numbers, there is usually an emptiness in their lives," an emptiness she would fill with words about art. "Sports are mandated in order for someone to graduate, but art isn't," she said. "I think that's vulgar."

Suddenly she asked, "Did you hear about Rauschenburg, the Tie Collection?" She mentioned that Robert Rauschenburg's current retrospective at the Guggenheim Museum has Hugo Boss as a co-sponsor and said there was talk about Mr. Rauschenburg's doing a tie collection. As a great admirer of the artist, she is unofficially volunteering a portfolio of sample ties, as well as Perfume Bob. (" A special gift, a new fragrance, smell like a real artist: Rauschenburg.") Then she remembered: "Someone once called me and asked: 'Could we make some yam bookends? Could we bronze them?"

She is tempted by the notion of creating a performance art kit, though she is adamant about not capitalizing on her controversies. She turned down an offer from the Gap to appear in an advertisement, she said, because she felt that her censorship problems would be highlighted. Similarly, she rejected offers to pose nude for men's magazines because that would " further the misinterpretation of what I do in my work," her attempt to desexualize the female body.

As performer and artist, Ms. Finley is a freelance, and spends her afternoons making "cold calls" on the telephone trying to book herself. Looking in the Art in America catalogue, she will choose museums and galleries and say, "Hi, this is Karen Finley. Would you like me to do a performance?"

Usually people know who she is. If not, she may list her credits. Recently she called the City Gallery of Contemporary Art in Raleigh, N.C., and was astonished to discover that it had closed because it had lost its financing. "I'm concerned about Raleigh, that there are young artists there and they don't have a stepping stone."

Nothing seems to cool her cheerful demeanor, not even the fact that as a self-employed fringe artist she makes little money. (A Guggenheim fellowship helped to finance her current show.) There are always calls to be made and work to be done around the house, "scrubbing the tub, vacuuming, mowing the lawn." In her free time, she straps her daughter into a car seat and takes her for a drive in her Ford Explorer, "like any other suburban mother."

After a tour of the house (individual rooms for writing, painting and career development), Ms. Finley turned the stage over to her mother. Karen's Mom, who looks as neat and prim as Dave's Mom, said her daughter had always been involved in the creation of art. As a child growing up in Evanston, Ill., she began drawing at the age of 2 and was performing by 12. Mrs. Finley sees all her daughter's shows. "It took me a while to see what she was trying to do, to show what's going on underneath the garden," she said. "I guess the only way you can do that is to rake it up."

Asked if anyone else in the family was an artist, Mrs. Finley said one of her sons was a poet and another was a lawyer, and added, "And who isn't a performance artist?" Is she? "I think raising six children was quite a performance." She expressed sympathy for her daughter's "juggling motherhood, daughterhood, sisterhood, neighborhood, everything at one time," adding, "I wish she had more time for her creativity."

Then Mrs. Finley defended the integrity of her daughter's art. I've seen so much obscenity in my life," she said. "It's all around us. This child of the world is not obscene. One of the things I admire about Karen is that she is open to the world, and that's hard to be. You get a lot of slaps in the face. She just has courage to stick to her belief system, and, I want to tell you, she has the kindest heart." Perhaps Karen's Mom could sway the Supreme Court.

WHOOPI GOLDBERG

THE SPOOK SHOW: FEBRUARY 3, 1984

In her brief, late-night *Spook Show* at the Dance Theater Workshop, Whoopi Goldberg is revealed as a fresh and very funny character comedian with a distinctive point of view and rich comic potential. In one-woman sketches of her own creation, this slight, unassuming actress plays misfits and social outcasts, beginning with a doddering young dope fiend on his first trip abroad.

For an urban American womanchild, it is like a journey into outer space, and she spoofs everything from the haughty stewardess to the so-called food in flight. Remembering the contents of the dinner dish, she says, "I didn't see nothing I recognized." Then she does a dead-on imitation of airline stringbeans. After the streetwise character arrives in Amsterdam the monologue takes a serious turn as he visits the home of Anne Frank and muses caustically on various kinds of inhumanity. Quickly we realize that Ms. Goldberg is not simply a stand-up comedian but a satirist with a cutting edge and an actress with a wry attitude toward life and public performance. Despite the outrageous quality of much of her commentary, she averts bad taste and retains her winning personality.

At various points, she humanizes characters who, on first glance, might seem grotesque. There is a crippled young woman whose head lolls precariously on one of her shoulders. Without self-consciousness, she confesses, "This is not a disco body," and adds, "Normal is in the eye of the beholder." Then she proves that she is as normal as the other figures in Ms. Goldberg's gallery. In dealing with such a delicate subject, the actress is never patronizing, and, finally, in a transformation, she straightens her gnarled body and dances, communicating the young woman's inner grace.

She closes with a black child's dream of blondness. Covering her hair with a white skirt, smoothing it in place as if it were a wimple, she then tosses her head so that the cloth becomes a symbolic mane. Sweetly she fantasizes her way into a dance-with-words that is both clownish and touching.

It would not be inaccurate to suggest that her comedy is a cross between Lily Tomlin and Richard Pryor, but, given the wide audience she deserves - and with more material - it may not be long before people will try to compare future comics to the inimitable Whoopi Goldberg.

WHOOPI AS ACTRESS, CLOWN AND SOCIAL CRITIC: OCTOBER 28, 1984

Whoopi Goldberg is a slight, sprite-like comic actress whose mind and body are inhabited by some of the drollest and most touching characters one is ever likely to encounter in a Broadway theater or on a city street. She has the face and personality of a wise child - with ingenuous eyes and a puckish smile. As she tells her tales of misfits and outcasts, and even as she offers wry satiric comments, she is consistently disarming. Bantering mischievously with the audience, she warms up a Broadway theater, winning us as her confederates.

She has artistic antecedents, but her own comic sensibility. In common with Lily Tomlin, she is a monologuist who offers character sketches of her own devising about men and women who reside in individual dream worlds. In common with Richard Pryor, she is also a realist, in touch with deadbeats, derelicts and dope addicts. There is a hard cutting edge to her comedy. It is no surprise that Mike Nichols is one of her greatest admirers and one of the presenters of her show on Broadway. As with Mr. Nichols and Elaine May, she has an ability to take a premise and run with it to its furthest destination, so that an everyday moment can achieve absurdist dimensions.

Her monologues are not anecdotes but complete short plays with a twist or two at the ending. In that sense, they are an urban kin to Jane Martin's Southern Gothic one-act comedies. These plays, collected under the title *Talking With*, were performed by 11 different actresses. Ms. Goldberg does it all by herself. She is, simultaneously, an actress, dramatist, clown and social critic - a detonation of comic virtuosity.

In performance, she improvises, diverges in tangential directions but never loses her focus. Looking down at us from the stage of the Lyceum, she says, "There ain't no third wall." When she is talking, there is no wall at all.

Last winter she made her New York concert debut in a series of late-night shows at Dance Theater Workshop, that valuable company that has been a haven for such performance artists as Ms. Goldberg, Bill Irwin and the "Foolsfire" trio. Ms. Goldberg's Broadway venture is an expanded and polished version of her Dance Theater Workshop show. The material may vary from performance to performance, but one supposes that the carryover material is a constant. The new monologues, two at the preview performance I attended, have their priceless moments, but are evidently still in process. The four original ones, on the other hand, are vintage examples of her wit.

Daringly, she does her boldest number first, entering as Fontaine, a male hipster and self-styled "dope fiend." With a riff of language and considerable body English, Fontaine takes us on a personal fact-finding mission to Europe. It is his first flight and he is abashed by the airline's apathy, beginning with an overbooked plane ("seats for 100, sold tickets for 3,000") and the abject anonymity of airline food. ("I didn't see nothing I recognized"). Fontaine lands in Amsterdam, and, wide-eyed in "Am'dam," he walks through incredibly narrow streets, sidling as though passing through the eye of a needle. Finding a drug store that sells hard drugs, the character is in hashish heaven until he notices that one of the customers is a Dutch policeman. Fontaine concludes if drugs were legalized in America not only would "we" have them but "they" would have them, too. With that perverse thought, he does a hilarious impersonation of a dreamily drugged policeman trying to arrest a speeder.

The journey leads to Anne Frank's house, through a museum decorated with artifacts including the Oscar that Shelley Winters won for her performance in the movie of *The Diary of Anne Frank*. In the girl's attic hideout, the street-smart hustler suddenly finds himself overcome with grief at the thought of Anne Frank's lost life. Then Fontaine reads her saintly testimony emblazoned on a wall, "In spite of everything, I still believe that people are really good at heart," and shakes his head in disbelief. Trying to comprehend the selflessness of the statement, he realizes that because he is a black man, pessimism is ingrained in his nature, but that Anne Frank was a child and "kids can be forgiving."

In this and other sketches, Ms. Goldberg is adamant about giving us the child's-eye view of adult behavior, rediscovering the innocence in unlikely circumstances. The language can be quite graphic, but her aim is ameliorative. She wants theatergoers to see the humanity in the strange characters she creates on stage. She is so convincingly in character as Fontaine that one might tend to think of the two of them as synonymous. To contradict that image, in her next scene she plays Fontaine's absolute opposite, a lily white "valley girl," a surfer who bubbles with buzz words and wants nothing more than to have a good time. But as with Fontaine and with all of her people, there is an underlying sense of tragedy.

Quick change, and the actress is transformed into a young black woman with

a grotesquely deformed body; her head lolling on one shoulder. Without bitterness, she tells us that she had been placed in a home for the elderly so that old
folks wouldn't "feel so bad about dying." Her story is a fairy tale, Cinderella complete with Prince Charming, but with an urban grittiness. In one of the evening's
several magical moments, the young woman dreams about wholeness. She
straightens her body and does a dance, projecting her inner beauty. Finally comes
a cautionary reminder that resounds throughout the evening: "Normal is in the
eye of the beholder."

Ms. Goldberg is capable of astute observations, as in her aside on the political nature of punk, "It came from London to America and ended up in Bergdorf
Goodman." At one point, she plays a derelict, a one-time tapdancer who remembers Bill (Bojangles) Robinson. He observes scathingly that Robinson's little
girl partner was nothing without him and adds, "They ain't never made a Bill
Robinson doll."

First of all, Ms. Goldberg is an actress, and one could envision her playing
roles in works by others; she could have stepped off the pages of Alice Walker's
Color Purple and Toni Morrison's *Bluest Eye*. However, there is something exhilarating about seeing her in the theater in the works of her own invention, as in her
intimate story about a 9-year-old black girl who longs to be white. Covering her
tight braids with a white skirt, she wears it on her head as a wimple, which in her
imagination becomes flowing blonde tresses. Tossing her "mane," she dances - a
kind of homespun *Swan Lake*. Finally, she puts down the cloth as if to banish it.
Then, tentatively, she takes it up again, reserving it as a security blanket against
injustice. In this wistful scene and others, the actress is, quite simply, lovable.

Reviewing her show at Dance Theater Workshop last winter, I suggested that,
before long, people would try to compare future comics to the inimitable Whoopi
Goldberg. One should add that her time has arrived.

SPALDING GRAY

SWIMMING TO CAMBODIA: NOVEMBER 16, 1984

Were it not for the absolute simplicity of the presentation, one might be tempted
to say that Spalding Gray has invented a performance art form. Sitting at a card
table and talking to the audience, he offers a virtuosic evening of autobiographic
storytelling. With the perspicacity of a master travel writer, he acts as reporter,
comic and playwright of his own life.

His latest and best work is called *Swimming to Cambodia*, presented in two
parts, in repertory, at the Performing Garage. The double-barreled dose of

Spalding Gray was inspired by his experiences as an actor in the movie *The Killing Fields*. The film is a screen adaptation of a magazine article by Sydney H. Schanberg, the New York Times correspondent, concerning his friendship with his assistant Dith Pran while covering the war in Cambodia. Mr. Gray played the small role of an assistant to the American ambassador, and from that vantage point was able to see the movie, whole, and - using his own reading and research - also to comprehend the military and political complexity of our Cambodian involvement.

On the one hand, *Swimming to Cambodia* is an informative supplement to the heat and fire of *The Killing Fields*. On the other hand, it is a close-up, on-location analysis of the monumental absurdities of movie-making, of people and places in Thailand (where the movie was shot) and of the interpersonal relationships of men and women in film combat. One of Mr. Gray's several provocative theories is his concept of "war therapy." He suggests that every country should work out its militaristic aggressions by making "a major war film once a year." He also believes in "displacement of anxiety" - a small worry substituting for a great pain.

Mr. Gray's stream of experience has the zestful, first-hand quality of a letter home from the front. One could enjoy his narrative in print, but it gains enormously from the fact that he is recounting it in person, acting it out and commenting - with a quizzical look as he tells us about a particularly grotesque Asian sexual practice. In performance, Mr. Gray is a one-man theatrical equivalent of the movie, *My Dinner with Andre*.

Most of his previous monologues have been drawn directly from his personal life. With "Swimming to Cambodia," he expands his world view. He observes a panoply of others as well as himself, bringing back pithy commentary on his producer, his director (a combination of "Zorro, Jesus and Rasputin"), his fellow actors (Haing S. Ngor, John Malkovich) and the lesser known people on the project, who walk around, at least in Mr. Gray's mind's-eye, wearing T-shirts that say, "Skip the dialogue, let's blow something up."

He weaves his observations with aspects of his inner life - as an insecure actor with a "very confrontational" girlfriend and as a man who has two desperate, equally important wishes. He wants to get an agent and to experience a perfect moment. In the second part of the monologue, Mr. Gray embraces the mystical; he is a Holden Caulfield seeking nirvana on a Thai beach, while never losing his self-mocking sense of humor or his gift for telling a shaggy story.

Some of the reportage is so bizarre, it must be fantasy - or is it? In any case, acting in a war movie was clearly a mind-expanding time for this impressionable actor. Completing his brief role in "The Killing Fields," Mr. Gray remains landlocked on location - in contrast to his colleagues who fly home at the first opportunity. He feels like a poor relation who has stayed too long as a house guest, but he cannot help himself. He is obsessed by the filming, and he transmits his fascination to the audience.

TERRORS OF PLEASURE: MAY 15, 1986

Having defined the performance art form of the autobiographcial monologue, Spalding Gray has moved deeper into theatrical creativity. *Swimming to Cambodia*, his two-part rumination on his role in the film *The Killing Fields*, was an insider's report on the battle between illusion and reality. His new monologue, *Terrors of Pleasure*, is a hilarious tale of his harrowing quest for home ownership, a milestone on the perilous road to becoming a grown-up.

Opening last night at the Mitzi E. Newhouse in Lincoln Center, *Terrors of Pleasure* represents Mr. Gray's first step into the New York cultural mainstream, from which he emerges undaunted and ego intacta. The mainstream has joined him. The Newhouse, more comfortable for the audience than his usual habitat at the Performing Garage, turns out to be an ideal setting for his expository revelations.

For the occasion, Mr. Gray has slightly spruced up his act. There is carpeting under his card table and he uses a microphone and a few more visuals (books, pictures) than usual, but, essentially, this is the identical Spalding Gray who transformed solo conversation into a performance phenomenon.

Terrors of Pleasure begins in Krummville, a tiny town in the Catskill Mountains, where the actor-author has decided to set up housekeeping. First he must find a house to keep and, as his tale unfolds, it is a *Candide* comedy about a city dweller who becomes a self-made rube.

All he wants is to be landlocked on Shady Valley Road in what appears to be an idyllic red bungalow, but, as he discovers, dreaming is merely the tentative prelude to home owning. Visiting the chosen homestead with his girlfriend, Renee Shafransky (judging from Mr. Gray's monologues, she is a wise and patient counselor), he learns that the building appears to have no foundation all the way down the line. In addition, the furnace is in the attic, which he decides, is "an analogue for my psyche."

For our edification, he plays a taped telephone message from the man who is trying to sell him the house. Listening to the self-defensive salesmanship, Mr. Gray smiles sardonically - after the fact. "Would you buy a house from this man? he asks, and before the audience can shout back in unison, "Not on your life!" he confesses, "So I bought the house."

From here, the dream becomes a nightmare. He is plagued by powder-post beetles, a sinking substructure, a sievelike roof and local carpenters, plumbers and odd-job men whose role in life seems to be to relieve him of his bank account and his porch while making no dent on his desperate living conditions.

Suddenly, from the depths of comic despair comes an artist's realization. His eyes light up as he wonders, "Did I buy this house in order to make a monologue?" Watching Mr. Gray turn his trauma into comedy, one considers the following fact: If Job had been a poet, it might have helped him to cope.

To pay for the renovation of his home, Mr. Gray takes the only possible recourse known to actors. He flies to Hollywood to seek a fortune and the monologue merrily loops off on a satiric account of the idiocies in lotus land and the search for "spiritual materialism."

Because of his newly acquired celebrity, he is now a candidate for leading roles on sitcoms and in made-for-television movies, opposite actresses such as Patty Duke and Farrah Fawcett. Naturally he is rejected for everything, including an appearance on the Johnny Carson show. When he fails to win the Farrah Fawcett opportunity, he is confronted with his principal problem. In performance, he is told, he projects a "quality of thinking."

That very quality, of course, enriches his stage monologues. Through a look or a comment, he offers intelligent analysis. Though the narrative is entirely centered around Mr. Gray himself, it never suffers from self-pity or self-indulgence. He remains the antihero in his own fascinating life story, the never ending tale of EverySpalding.

In his earlier one-man shows such as *Sex and Death to the Age 14* and *A Personal History of the American Theater*, Mr. Gray amusingly strung together anecdotes on such subjects as theater, romance and travel. But in *Terrors of Pleasure*, as in *Swimming to Cambodia*, he has a single roller coaster of a story to tell. The narrative has dramatic cohesiveness as well as comic insight, building to a climax that would have been appreciated by Don Quixote. For Mr. Gray, the whole world is his windmill and his siege, his terrors, become our pleasure.

EVAN HANDLER

TIME ON FIRE: MAY 14, 1993

Hypocrisy fights the Hippocratic oath in Evan Handler's *Time on Fire*, a laceratingly funny and self-revealing one-man show about the actor's survival of a medical ordeal. Afflicted with acute myeloid leukemia and told that the chances of reversal were slim, Mr. Handler finds surprising solace in a hospital visit from a rabbi. The rabbi tells him an ancient story. By changing their names, he says, people can make it more difficult for the Angel of Death to find them. Years later, recovered from his illness, Mr. Handler realizes that he has in fact "fooled the Angel of Death." It is a moment of euphoria that is shared by theatergoers at Second Stage, where Mr. Handler is performing his monodrama.

Although he was cured through a bone-marrow transplant, his healing is also one of self-recovery. As he makes clear in this memoir onstage, he has come through with a surer sense of his own identity and a greater feeling of time escaping. From now on, for Mr. Handler time is on fire.

It was eight years ago, at the age of 24, that he received his diagnosis. Resigning his role in the Broadway production of *Biloxi Blues*, he checked into a clinic to begin treatment at the Memorial Sloane-Kettering Cancer Center in Manhattan. What follows is an all too imaginable, terrifying case history, as vividly detailed as an "Annals of Medicine" article in The New Yorker. Mr. Handler indicts a health-care system that subjects a patient to mortification, ignorance and human error while keeping him in the total dark. Going through the process, he discovers that the "truly horrible and the terribly funny" not only coexist, they are the same thing.

His stories about medical maltreatment should send a shiver down the spines of theatergoers even as they laugh. It is not so much the negligence as the sheer impersonality. With the eye of an intelligent actor watching everything and storing observations for future use in his art, he captures the characters on his case: the doctor whose role in the movie version of Mr. Handler's life should be played by Richard Nixon; the doom-saying nurse who is "Florence Nightingale from hell." Around them are crowds of the infirmed and the maimed waiting for tests and looking like extras from *The Snake Pit*. In charge of the patient's personal bedlam is a physician who wants Mr. Handler to feel sorry for him because he has been charged with medical malpractice in the deaths of several of his other patients.

Euphemisms become endemic and a macabre note arrives from a friend: "We will always remember you." Doctors warn patients against having false hope, which Mr. Handler regards as an oxymoron. Hope is, by definition, subject to cancellation. Because he is an actor, he repeatedly puts his experience in a theatrical and cinematic context. After a particularly demeaning day in the hospital, he ponders the thought that "John Wayne had cancer. Did he put up with this?"

One of the most humiliating and also hilarious episodes is his trip to the Madison Avenue sperm bank where he is supposed to make a deposit against the probability that the treatment of his illness will make him sterile. Kafka would laugh if he followed the actor into a chilly closet-size room where he is supplied with pornography and strict rules of order. Then he has to stand in line while his sperm is publicly weighed for storage purposes. He fully expected applause from the other depositors, as at a weigh-in for a boxing match. Touchingly, he muses about how he will describe this grotesque scene to his future children.

His family and his girlfriend are constant sources of support, and he wonders how they can endure his black moods, his sudden tears and his solipsistic worries about his career. In the second act he goes to the Johns Hopkins Medical Center in Baltimore, for which he can offer only the highest praise, not just for the miraculous bone-marrow transplant but also for the humanity he finds in at least this one aspect of the medical profession.

After recovery, he resumes his career. At an audition, he is greeted with astonishment by a rival actor who thought that he had died. Telling that story onstage leads Mr. Handler to a highly personalized coup de théâtre, which would be an accurate characterization of the monodrama itself. As unobtrusively directed by Marcia Jean Kurtz, it begins as a confidence between actor and audience and becomes a moving contemplation of the years he has lost and the time he has gained.

Having seen him in plays in numerous New York theaters, one wants to say, Evan, we hardly knew you. He is a fine actor, an equally fine writer and a consummate re-enactor of his own experience. One wishes - and no false hope here - that between performing his life-embracing show, he will write another play.

ROBERT LEPAGE

NEEDLES AND OPIUM: DECEMBER 10, 1992

Robert Lepage's magical *Needles and Opium* begins in a Left Bank hotel in a room formerly occupied by celebrated French artists. Playing himself as a visitor to Paris, Mr. Lepage is facing a long sleepless night when his thoughts are invaded by the spirits of Jean Cocteau and Miles Davis. From here the play embarks on a journey that is filled with indelible imagery and observations about Surrealism, existentialism and jazz.

The show, which is part of the Next Wave Festival at the Brooklyn Academy of Music, is a tour de force for Mr. Lepage as playwright, director, designer and solo performer. It is the opposite of his recent, aberrant version of *A Midsummer Night's Dream*, staged in a sea of mud at Britain's National Theater. In contrast to that sprawling Shakespearean oddity, "Needles and Opium" is a chamber work marked by its absolute precision.

In some sense, it could be regarded as a movie on stage, artfully merging cinematic and theatrical techniques. Although this is an exceedingly complex production, filled with intricate mechanical devices, it shifts from one form to another without a glitch. In contrast to lesser performance artists, Mr. Lepage veers clear of pretension, lightening the trip with wry humor. As a performer, he moves with an acrobatic agility on a revolving platform that acts as stage, movie screen and trampoline. He disappears and then reappears in a new guise, all in the quickest of crosscuts.

At the root of the narrative is the fact that in 1949 Cocteau and Davis, each a major artist in his field, reversed paths. Cocteau, the archetypal French Surrealist, was in New York, and Davis, a maestro of modern jazz, was discovering Paris. He was also discovering Juliette Greco, herself an icon of French existentialists.

The playwright weaves together the stories of the two men, including the bouts each had with drugs. Simultaneously he creates an impressionistic collage of their art and their cities. Filtered through the play are Cocteau's poetic words about his love affair with New York and also Davis's music, the coolest and most limpid of underscorings. The music is one of the show's most essential elements.

Cocteau, portrayed by Mr. Lepage, is headed home. Onstage he is strapped into a harness that suddenly flies free of his plane. He becomes his own flying machine circling New York. In one of a number of transporting sequences, Cocteau seems to plunge down the caverns between skyscrapers. While Cocteau soars, Davis travels by sea; on a screen we see his trumpet merrily bobbing beneath the waves.

Repeatedly Mr. Lepage alters and expands the audience's perspective, swinging back and forth among live performance, film and shadow puppetry. When Davis and Miss Greco meet in a cafe and drink wine, we view the scene from above. On the screen are objects, cleverly manipulated to give a picture of a relationship that will prove to be far more than a flirtation.

Mr. Lepage's own character is the autobiographical conduit between Cocteau and Davis; the play is his search as well as theirs. Often we return to that Paris hotel room for incidents ostensibly from his life. In the middle of the night, the telephone rings and the caller demands to speak to Jean-Paul Sartre. Mr. Lepage explains that he has been dead for many years. But the caller persists. Finally, Mr. Lepage sheepishly confesses, "I took the message."

In the course of his performance piece, the playwright uses the word "super-vision" and, I think, the pun is intentional. *Needles and Opium* is a super-visionary work. In common with the character of Cocteau, it flies.

PATRICK STEWART

A CHRISTMAS CAROL: DECEMBER 20, 1991

A Christmas Carol has been so musicalized and cinematized that it may be difficult to remember the beautiful simplicity of the original Dickens story, an ode to Christmas past, present and future and a moral fable of heartwarming intensity.

Patrick Stewart's one-man dramatic version at the O'Neill Theater is restorative, revealing the work's full narrative splendor, its humor as well as its humanity.

The show could be considered a coda to the Royal Shakespeare Company's *Life and Adventures of Nicholas Nickleby*. The actor offers his solo equivalent of that expansive ensemble act of the imagination, making an audience believe it has entered a magical world dense with character, atmospere and action.

For those who think of Mr. Stewart principally as Jean-Luc Picard on television's *Star Trek: The Next Generation*, it must be said that before he captained the starship Enterprise he was a stellar member of the Royal Shakespeare Company. He was brilliant in roles as varied as Enobarbus in Peter Brook's production of *Antony and Cleopatra* and Shylock at Stratford-on-Avon.

His supple look and voice enable him to portray the widest range of Dickens characters without altering his costume or makeup. Classically trained, he has the verbal dexterity of Ian McKellen. All this is combined with his own delectation in performance. In this show, that performance is both Dickensian and Shakespearean, with the actor savoring each role as well as the lush descriptive language and, whenever possible, re-creating dramatic encounters.

The large stage is bare except for several pieces of utilitarian furniture. Informally dressed, Mr. Stewart makes a casual entrance and holds a book - presumably the text of his performance - over his head like a beacon. Then he runs with *A Christmas Carol*, in his own careful two-hour distillation of the story. Although the reading would be even more congenial in a smaller theater, he easily fills a Broadway stage.

All of the essentials are in place, with the accent on the juxtaposition of despair and joyfulness. At the center, of course, is that "squeezing, wrenching, gasping, scraping, clutching, covetous old sinner," Ebenezer Scrooge. Mr. Stewart allows for no softening around the edges, in either the character or the story, yet he does not make Scrooge into a caricatured villain.

From his initial appearance in the frigid offices of Scrooge & Marley, there is a feeling that his self-containment is also an evasion, that he has buried a side of his personality. Acting as narrator, Mr. Stewart says, "Darkness is cheap - and Scrooge liked it," and he shows us how the man's emotional life was as dim as the embers in his hearth.

As Scrooge is returned to his past and then recalled to life, Mr. Stewart plays all the roles (including a merry crowd of dancing Fezziwigs) as well as imitating sounds like chiming clocks and bells. He mimes the props and the scenic effects, simulating the wind on the streets and the echoes in Scrooge's solitary chamber. As called for, he is cheerful, sepulchral, childlike and feminine, as well as stouthearted when it comes to Bob Cratchit.

The Cratchit Christmas dinner, in which the actor portrays the entire family, Scrooge and the Ghost of Christmas Present, and is also on the verge of impersonating the goose on the table and the Christmas pudding with holly stuck into its top, is a tour de force. It reminds us not only of what an inventive actor he is, but also of Dickens's own great theatricality.

Seeing the actor in this show is the closest we can come to Dickens in his public performances, in which he also dominated a bare stage with his talent and his zest for his subject. At the end of Mr. Stewart's eloquent *Christmas Carol*, one wishes he would move on to *The Cricket on the Hearth* and other Dickensian treasures.

CALVIN TRILLIN

CALVIN TRILLIN'S UNCLE SAM: SEPTEMBER 27, 1988

If humorists thrive in adversity, Calvin Trillin is an anomaly. As he describes himself in his one-man show, *Calvin Trillin's Uncle Sam* (at the American Place Theater), he is a happy husband, father and author. But he is not complacent, and it is from that fact that he draws his telling comic arsenal.

Whether he is writing or talking, he is a commentator, wryly demonstrating the free range of his wit, which is sometimes self-mocking but never solipsistic. As a son of middle America (once removed from a suburb of Kiev), he moved to Yale, where he waspishly observed his three-name often doltish classmates waiting until they were put "in charge of things" - like the State Department.

America, he explains, is divided in two, those few states that had major league baseball before World War II and the rest of the country, the "expansion teams." This is the sector where he first seasoned his comic perspective on worldly dilemmas. Despite his small-city childhood, he speaks for all of us when he complains.

Among his complaints are chicken á la king (that once ubiquitous food is now stored, he thinks, in silos in the Dakotas); lawyers (if law school is so hard to get through, how come there are so many lawyers?) and, most of all, anyone who goes too far. He remembers a woman who posted rules of order on her refrigerator as guidelines for her son. She stressed Rule 6: "Enough is enough."

On Sunday afternoon, the day of the first Presidential debate, Mr. Trillin illustrated the principle. When George Bush visited a flag factory, the humorist expected the Vice President's mother to telephone her son and say, "George, remember Rule 6."

Though many of Mr. Trillin's sharpest sallies are sociological, cultural and culinary, politics is never too distant from his uncivil libertarian mind. He talks about having a feeling of nostalgia for whatever happens to be the previous administration. Already he has fond memories of the Reagans, for "not inflicting their family on us - or on themselves."

He is somewhat abashed to find himself on a stage in a spotlight. For security, he has a podium, several chairs and a number of maps, including one of O'Hare airport, where he "lived" when writing his "U.S. Journal" series for The New Yorker. He also discusses his starving-journalist days as a columnist for The Nation, for which he was paid in the "high two figures." Success through syndication has not muffled his quiet cynicism.

His voice - even when electronically amplified - could not be heard in a subway. But his delivery is dry and his timing is precise, having been honed by the printed pause. In his usual deadpan fashion, he starts telling a story about his daughter's first taste of spinach and repeats her comment, "It's better than a carrot." Then he uses the carrot as a stick with which to measure other experiences. Coming out of a movie, he will say to his wife, "It was better than a carrot," or "It was not as good as a carrot." In performance, Mr. Trillin is better than a bunch of carrots.

Another catchall phrase he favors is the universal noncommitment, "Too soon to tell." Could Mr. Trillin challenge Jackie Mason as a stand-up comic? Too soon to tell. One keystone of his humor is his apparent nonchalance, the conversational ease with which he approaches urgent (often urban) anxieties. His admirers should recognize stories. Obeisant to the ecology of the freelance writer, he does not waste anything and has gathered previously published Trillin material. But it is a pleasure to hear the words delivered by the source.

Over the years, the American Place Theater's American Humorists' Series has specialized in plays and revues about humorists or drawn from their work. But recently the theater has encouraged the humorist to stand up for himself. When the droll, sensible Mr. Trillin is on stage, there is never a need for Rule 6.

PAUL ZALOOM

MY CIVILIZATION: JANUARY 10, 1991

To create his theater, all that Paul Zaloom needs is a stage, himself as actor - and enough trash to fill a month's quota at a recycling center. In Mr. Zaloom's dextrous hands, the detritus of consumerism is converted into artful subjects for satire. One can imagine him wheeling a cart through a supermarket, shopping for visual puns and metaphors. The result, as demonstrated in his new show, *My Civilization* (at Dance Theater Workshop), is puppetry of a high political priority.

The title piece, the first of three monologues, is nothing less than a solipsistic history of the world, from protoplasm through the Garden of Eden and on to the life of Mr. Zaloom, all in 30 minutes. Using an overhead slide projector and an assortment of liquids and solids, both syrupy and spidery, which he sloshes and manipulates on transparent surfaces, he takes us on a jaunty tour back to the beginning of time.

As these various items are orchestrated into mysterious and comic patterns on screen, he delivers a demented, nonstop play-by-play description of civilization and his insecure place in it. The Zaloom of *My Civilization* is besieged by forces beyond his, or our, ken. Wherever he turns, something is testing his mettle, whether it is a self-corruptive society or unpredictable natural occurrences (a fork suddenly jumps on screen to simulate a bolt of lightning).

The monologue is a kind of satiric acid rain, insidious and damaging to the accepted order of things. His attitude as author and director is one of abashment, as in his suggestion that either he is going through an early midlife crisis or, as usual, he is indulging in cheap special effects. These effects may be cheap in price, but they are very special. I know of no other performance artist who is working in this idiosyncratic mode.

In his second sketch, "Phood," he attacks foolishness and faddishness in food, a favorite target of this consumer advocate who is ever ready to warn us not to eat before analyzing content. Employing photographs and other promotional material, he hangs the food industry by its own labels while he pretends to lecture a conference of like-minded individuals who care less about nutrition than about profits.

At the top of his indictment is the use of artificial ingredients - the reconstituted made to look like the real thing; additives that preserve a product to perpetuity, unless they happen to explode. There is no short shelf life in this world. Everything lasts forever, or at least until it kills us.

Having disarmed his audience with laughter, Mr. Zaloom then unveils his finale, a sketch entitled "Meanwhile," a shorter version of which was seen earlier this season in the Dangerous Ideas marathon. Somehow he mixes foreign policy with the savings and loan scandal and the controversy over public support of the arts. Dashing from cluttered table to table like a crazed table tennis player, he animates a tag sale of objects and becomes a quick-change puppetmaster.

Naturally, some of the remarks are too off-the-cuff, just as some of the assault moves from wryness to a lesser plane of whimsy, but enough of the humor is derisively on target. Mr. Zaloom's mind and funnybone are synchronized, especially when he is dealing with questions of endangerment to the arts.

Here comes the National Endowment for the Arts, as represented by a football with a pipe in its mouth, equivocating about awarding grants to performance artists (the grants are frugally distributed from a family-size tin of peanuts - and are then reclaimed). Private patronage is a tall, thin brand name cigarette and the Internal Revenue Service by two giant screws, marching alongside a large can of squiggly worms. That Senator from North Carolina is personified by a big prop foot and the artists themselves are small tomatoes, easily squishable.

In Mr. Zaloom's performance, there is a quality of child's play, but it is most inventive gamesmanship. In the years since he began performing, he has grown as a clown and as a social commentator. He has become an ecological antidote to the poisons and pollutants in everyday life.

6

CLOWNS, NEW VAUDEVILLE, CIRCUS, COMEDY, PUPPETRY

BILL IRWIN

NEW MIME II: RENEWED INVESTIGATIONS IN A THEATER OF MOVEMENT, SEPTEMBER 24, 1981

Traditional variety skills such as clowning, juggling and tapdancing are becoming more and more popular among young entertainers, as exemplified by Bill Irwin, who recently completed a too-brief engagement at the Dance Theater Workshop. Remember his name and look forward to his return. Mr. Irwin is an extraordinary clown and dancer who has been working largely in California, which seems to nurture talents like his. Also from the West Coast are the puppeteers Winston Tong and Bruce D. Schwartz, who appeared last year at the Dance Theater Workshop.

Mr. Irwin cannot be categorized easily, even as a comedian. He calls his current show *New Mime II: Renewed Investigations in a Theater of Movement*, and movement is the key to his act. In the purest sense, he is a quick-change artist, altering his facial expressions as if caught in stop-action photography, and doing sudden turnabouts on stage, defying gravity in the manner of a cantilevered terrace. The "investigations" are both a renewal and a redefinition, uniting vaudeville with silent movie comedy, commedia dell'arte, modern dance and mime.

He begins his show modestly - a handsome young man alone in a rehearsal studio with an electronic console and a theatrical trunk. As the actor pushes buttons on the console, the trunk becomes a Pandora's Box of disguises and contraptions, and the studio is invaded by a series of alter egos who can seemingly do everything better than he can. Sheepishly, he tries to compete with Michael Moschen as a juggler, smiling helplessly as he is outclassed at every turn. Even a ball becomes his enemy; it bounces in the wrong direction. Doug Skinner, Charles Moulton and Tommy Sellars issue a variety of challenges. Mr. Sellars's singular talent is to play an accordion while cavorting on roller skates. Without skates or musical instrument, Mr. Irwin copies and competes.

If he is not beaten by someone else, he is tripping himself up, falling over an imaginary bump in the floor that magically seems to follow him around the stage. When he does something with deftness, or when he mischievously hoodwinks the competition, he shyly dismisses audience appreciation, then changes his mind and silently gives his assent for just a little bit of applause - and then just a little bit more. The show is filled with running jokes that build like a pyramid of gymnastic jesters; there is always one teetering topper.

In the second half, with Mr. Skinner offering Victor Borge-style accompaniment on the piano, Mr. Irwin doubles as a querulous Pantalone and an antic Harlequin, darting between the characters and in and out of a false-bottom trunk. Along the way, he skewers the ballet, modern dance and eating (an uproarious piece about pasta that has the elasticity of Silly Putty). For an encore, Mr. Irwin joins Mr. Skinner in strumming twin ukeleles while doing a two-man comedy routine, adding the spoken word to a bag of brilliant tricks.

THE REGARD OF FLIGHT: MAY 25, 1982

Bill Irwin, a brilliant clown, mime, dancer and prankster, defies gravity - in both senses of the word. As he tells us in his uproarious entertainment *The Regard of Flight*, at the American Place Theater, he does not do tricks. He does "moves." Then he shows us a typical "hat move." Placing his squashed cabbage of a derby upside down on the floor, he dives into it headfirst, and comes up standing with the hat so firmly in place that it is pulled down over his eyes and ears.

At that moment, Mr. Irwin resembles Red Skelton. When he trips over imaginary bumps that seem to follow him around the stage, he is Jacques Tati. Standing at a 45-degree tilt - his partner, Doug Skinner, tells us that he is wearing special "lean shoes" for a "lean effect," but we know that it is the actor who is cantilevered - he is Buster Keaton on the deck of a sinking ship.

Mr. Irwin is the inheritor of a grand comic tradition that stretches back past burlesque and silent-film comedies to commedia dell'arte, but he is also very contemporary - and unique. His new show, written by and starring Mr. Irwin, is more verbal than his last late-night cavalcade at the Dance Theater Workshop - and equally funny. In addition to pratfalls, pantomime and a zany chase, it offers tongue-in-cheek commentary on the pretensions of the so-called "new theater," of which he is a primary exponent.

This is a theater in which performance takes precedence over the written word, which celebrates "the decline of the playwright and the rise of the actor as poet." At the basis of performance art is "a profound mistrust of the proscenium." Along with a pesky interviewer, played by Michael O'Connor, the proscenium is Mr. Irwin's greatest nemesis.

The vaudeville begins with the clown in bed, wearing a fool's cap and trying to figure out why the bed is on stage. Mr. Irwin spends most of the rest of the evening in a state of bewilderment. Holding a hat and a cane, he struts out of the spotlight, but as he approaches the curtain at the edge of the proscenium, he is suddenly captured by an imaginary suction. Feet first, he is whisked offstage. Soon, all that remains is his hat and his cane. Whenever he comes near that curtain, he is swept away. He becomes suspicious, but never seems to learn his lesson.

His face is animated and his body is elastic. Threatened by a bully - the same Mr. O'Connor - he shrinks into his skin, losing about a foot of height. Wearing a voluminous cloak, he waddles across the stage as a portly midget. Standing inside a steamer trunk, he pretends to walk down a circular staircase, round and round, until his body is out of sight.

While Mr. Irwin is turning the American Place Theater into a circus, Mr. Skinner offers musical encouragement at the piano. With the glistening-eye look of an eager floorwalker, he plays pep tunes of his own invention and, like an academician writing a dissertation on the striptease, he tries to analyze the essence of Mr. Irwin's art. For variety, the pianist does a brief stand as a ventriloquist, and with a sheepishness that could cow a shepherd, returns to what he does best - plinking the keys.

The term "running gag" is meant to be taken literally. The ubiquitous and cranky Mr. O'Connor is often in pursuit of the star, chasing him through swinging doors, into the audience, and onto a trampoline conveniently placed to catapult clowns up to the stage. Mr. Irwin almost flies from a lofty promontory, but peering down at the audience, he has qualms. There is just so much blind faith that one can have in "lean shoes."

As a fillip, Mr. Irwin concludes the show with a quick cycle of "clown bagatelles," many of them reprised from his last New York engagement. He plays a man plugged into and possessed by the demon of his transistor; he joins Mr. Skinner in a two-ukelele skittish send-up of minstrel shows and performs his inimitable stint as a waiter trying to serve an impossibly knotty tangle of pasta. Soaring high and low, *The Regard of Flight* is an evening of priceless comedy.

THE REGARD OF FLIGHT AND THE CLOWN BAGATELLES: APRIL 13, 1987

As Bill Irwin demonstrates in *The Regard of Flight* at the Vivian Beaumont, it is not the size of the theater that matters but the size of the talent. Mr. Irwin has performed versions of this signature show in the studio space at the Dance Theater Workshop, on the compact open stage at the American Place Theater and on *Great Performances* on public television. *The Regard of Flight*, which returned to New York last night, is blissfully at home at the Broadway-size Beaumont, which, for Mr. Irwin's special spring engagement, echoes with the sound of bountiful laughter.

To those who have managed to miss his previous appearances, it should be said that Mr. Irwin is a contemporary American performance artist whose name belongs alongside those of Buster Keaton and Marcel Marceau. One difference is that he is a New Vaudevillian, a member of that amorphous band of variety artists who take a postmodernist approach to classic comedic techniques. One of the most refreshing things about Mr. Irwin is his sense of self-mockery. At its most seriously comic, *The Regard of Flight* spoofs itself and other examples of the so-called New Theater, in which, as we are told, there is no playwright or director but "only the actor and the mythic text."

In the case of *The Regard of Flight,* Mr. Irwin is his own playwright and director, and in both roles - as in his clowning - he is virtuosic. On one plane, the show is a dazzling display of physicalized wit, as the star offers doubletakes, pratfalls, hat moves and feats of gestural wizardry (such as walking down inside a trunk, as if descending a steep staircase). With his extraordinarily elastic body, he can sink his head into his chest and appear to lose half a foot of height, or, under a tentlike robe, he can scoot around the stage at a Toulouse-Lautrec level.

His facial expressions - bemusement, innocence, surprise, rapture - are an exhibition by themselves. Watch him, for example, combine daring with trepidation as he tempts fate on the proscenium. For some reason, perhaps metaphysical, he is always threatened by the proscenium arch. Whenever he approaches the wings of the stage - the Beaumont has been artfully converted into a proscenium theater for the occasion - he is vacuumed offstage by an unseen force. Feet first, he is hysterical, and, inevitably, this gives him a fear of flailing.

Being funny in the spotlight, cavorting with his colleagues (Doug Skinner, his alert ally on the piano, and M.C. O'Connor, a skeptic in the house), he is hilarious. As a running gag, there is the chase, as Mr. O'Connor ardently pursues the star on and around the stage and through the audience. Trying to elude the pursuer, Mr. Irwin craftily assumes alternative guises, at one point emerging from his apparently bottomless trunk wearing a big nose and glasses. With a smile, he lets us know that behind the deceptive facade, "It's me!"

There is, of course, no mistaking Mr. Irwin. He is one of a kind, and in the revived *Regard of Flight* he is in glorious comic fettle. The new production offers minor variations, the recognition, for example, that the performance is in a larger theater. This means that he demonstrates the gravity-defying effect of "lean shoes" from the topmost aerie of the Beaumont - a moment of cantilevered comedy. At Lincoln Center, the show has not lost a bit of its edge or its artistry.

A swift 60 minutes of *The Regard of Flight,* proper, is followed by a postscript of *The Clown Bagatelles,* including a transformation from a Shakespeare-spouting Pierrot to a marionette Harlequin, an eloquent mime in which Mr. Irwin appears to operate his own invisible strings.

In a time when musicals have become top-heavy with technology, it is a pleasure to return to the pristine simplicity of *The Regard of Flight.* Once again, we see that one artist (with two talented helpers), precise staging and a total lack of pretension can unite in a magical evening of theater.

⌒

LARGELY/NEW YORK (THE FURTHER ADVENTURES OF A POST-MODERN HOOFER): MAY 16, 1988

As usual, Bill Irwin's show - in this case, *Largely/New York* at City Center Theater - begins with no overture or fanfare. The clown is by himself on stage. Holding a remote control, he points it up at the curtain and slowly the curtain rises, revealing another curtain. Abashed, he pushes the button again. The second curtain rises and behind it is ... another curtain. Two (or was it three?) curtains later, with a look of perplexed bemusement, he is standing alone on an empty stage.

From here on, for 70 mirthful minutes, Mr. Irwin takes us on a jaunty tour of mock post-modern dance. Caught up by rivalry, he finds himself dancing with several choreographic species, starting with Meg Eginton, whose supersynchronized steps are in stunning contrast to Mr. Irwin's own antic New Vaudevillism.

Dazzled by Ms. Eginton's beauty, he falls in love. To woo her, he imitates her steps, and soon the two are performing a pas de deux. Whenever he glances in the opposite direction, she falls - and he turns just in time to catch her in his arms. He lifts; she soars. Later the two of them and a video camera dance a hilarious pas de trois. With his limbs entangled with the camera's tripod, Mr. Irwin moves in an instant from would-be Baryshnikov to bungling Bolger.

At other moments, the clown may remind one of Gene Kelly while still maintaining his own indisputable individuality. As Mr. Kelly did on film, Mr. Irwin does on stage, shifting from Ms. Eginton's arch modernism to the street smarts of two breakers and poppers, Leon Chesney and John Christian. Ever the outsider eager to join the fun, he watches in amazement as the two breakers electrify their limbs. Then, with feigned confidence, he joins them, and, despite their skepticisim, he quickly becomes an adjunct to their choreographic tics and twitches.

In *The Regard of Flight*, the show that brought him his first wide acclaim, Mr. Irwin spoofed experimental theater. This time, in *The Further Adventures of a Post-Modern Hoofer*, he extends his lampoon to the dance. Mischievously he sends up his subject with the help of a 21-person supporting cast and ensemble choreography by Kimi Okada. Mr. Irwin's fellow performers play dancers as well as academics in caps and gowns - a gaggle of graduates who, en masse, look like a pack of penguins. The academics are both chorus and silent commentators, and, occasionally, trip headfirst into pratfalls.

For a theater audience, some of the specific dance references may be elusive, but there is no mistaking the generic tomfoolery. The show is iconoclastic in the extreme, even to making fun of Mr. Irwin himself. Whenever he is doubtful about his next move, he dashes to his theatrical trunk, a kind of security trunk filled with sure-fire devices.

That remote control is an almost constant companion, as is a handy book of misleading instructions. Lost in an abstract world, he is an innocent searching for equilibrium. His droll misadventures are additionally complicated by the presence on stage of a television crew, trying to multi-mediate the confusion. The clown's curiosity about the sophisticated electronic equipment eventually leads him - or rather, his image - to be trapped inside a television monitor, which could be described as a coup de video.

Largely/New York opened Saturday and is in residence at City Center for only three more performances. Despite the brevity of the engagement, this is no casual concert of work in progress. As conceived, directed and performed by Mr. Irwin, it is a sustained flight of comic inspiration.

TEXTS FOR NOTHING: NOVEMBER 2, 1992

Rising from a crouching position, the tramp surveys his surroundings, a mysterious environment of overlapping planks, and wonders where he is. As Samuel Beckett's *Texts for Nothing* unfolds, we can sense that the man is trapped in limbo. Perhaps the last man on earth, he is hanging on for life while waiting for a "desinence," a Beckettian word meaning an end, as in the end of a sentence. He has no idea when it will come. But until it comes, he is "a prisoner, frantic with corporeality." As he says: "I can't stay. I can't go," and adds with curiosity, "Let's see what happens next."

This prose piece, 13 terse chapters of a fiction, followed onstage by a coda extracted from the novel *How It Is*, is a distillation of the author's art and philosophy. Therefore it is fitting that the dramatization of *Texts for Nothing* is given an astonishing performance by Bill Irwin, a clown in an intense tragicomic mode.

With Mr. Irwin alone with Beckett's words and thoughts, the play is an eloquent 65 minutes, saying more about man's misfortunes than many plays do in double or triple the time. The performance offers an acting lesson in how Beckett's prose can be transformed into theater.

When the piece was first staged in 1981, the actor was Joseph Chaikin. (The adaptation is by Mr. Chaikin and Steven Kent.) The new production is scrupulously directed by Mr. Chaikin. Beckett's primal themes are all in place: his cogitation of the brief abyss between birth and death, his reflections on man's inability to ascertain his place in the cosmos. Mr. Irwin's character seeks to name what is unnamable, using a blanket of precise words to prove that words are useless.

On the page this is a haunting interior monologue. Onstage, it is both internalized and externalized, moving deeply within the meaning of the prose and also contemplating the subtext, including the kinship between the writer and his character. Shifting from perplexity to wonderment to despair, the actor breathes a visceral actuality into the nightmare. Led by Mr. Irwin, the audience enters that nightmare, as he feels his way around the "inextricable place" searching for a foothold and a mind hold.

A word about the setting: Christine Jones has artfully detailed the wooden landscape (like the interior of a hull of a Viking ship) with hidden crevasses in which Mr. Irwin can amusingly lose himself, or his hat. When he finds that hat, he flips it onto his head and smiles with satisfaction, one of the few moments in which he allows himself a clownish gesture.

Along with other Beckett actors like Bert Lahr and Buster Keaton (in the short *Film*), Mr. Irwin is a masterly clown and mime. He punctuates his words with expressive looks and animates his nimble limbs with a dancer's agility. With him, the visual and performance elements assume equal weight with the text.

With wide-ranging resourcefulness, the actor illuminates the complex narrative, whether he is using his hands to measure the length of an hour or a century (arms stretching elastically across the stage) or miming the ages of man, playing a feeble "Old Tot" reaching high into the air to grasp his nanny's arm for support. When the character talks to his body, the actor becomes his own puppeteer, activating his arms and legs. Searching for a resting position on this unyielding landscape, he sits, lies down, discovers the alternative of kneeling and finds no comfort. Called upon to conjure other characters, he achieves a kaleidoscopic diversity: the scene of a father telling his son a ghoulish bedtime story turns into a small two-character comedy.

In his original performance in the role, Mr. Chaikin assumed a childlike air, retaining his boyishness even as he aged. Maintaining a related aura of innocence, Mr. Irwin pitches his voice in the range of Mr. Chaikin's. When he is briefly heard on tape, acting as his subconscious, the tone is deeper. The seedy figure, wearing vest and spats to denote his once dapper existence, is marked by his world-weariness and his word-weariness. Has not everything been said, he scolds his author. Through his approach, Mr. Irwin brings the character closer to other Beckett tramps, like Didi and Gogo. In his somber introspection about his "old wander years," about what he has lost in his life, there are also aspects of *Krapp's Last Tape*.

Hugh Kenner has summarized the events in *Texts for Nothing* as "fantasies of nonbeing." Mr. Irwin makes the fantasies corporeal without losing any of their fanciful context. Although he does not have the richly timbered voice of a Jack MacGowran, he is in total command of Beckett's "pell-mell Babel of silence and words." In performance he offers stunning still pictures as well as tragicomedy in motion.

In Mike Nichols's Lincoln Center production of *Waiting for Godot*, Mr. Irwin delivered Lucky's monologue with staccato brilliance. With *Texts for Nothing*, he spurs a theatergoer's anticipation for more of the actor's explorations into the world of Beckett.

ᏋᎧ

AVNER EISENBERG

AVNER THE ECCENTRIC: SEPTEMBER 24, 1984

Avner Eisenberg, or "Avner the Eccentric," as he bills himself, is a lovable fool with an expressively funny face and a streak of innocent vulgarity - a mischievous child in an adult's body. No wonder he was once arrested in Paris on the charge of buffoonery in public.

In his one-man show at the Lamb's Theater - an equally spontaneous version of the evening he offered a year ago at the first New York Festival of Clown-Theater - he begins as if he were a member of the audience. Tall, bearded, with a bulbous red nose and baggy pants, he is sitting on stage impatiently waiting for the show to start.

While popping popcorn into his mouth with hook-shot dexterity, he discovers himself in performance. Quickly he pinpoints the more pliable members of the audience, especially the children. They become his straight men. He appears to let them do much of his comic footwork, but he never stops being an inventive comedian.

When a latecomer enters the theater, he taps a clock face, tsk-tsks his annoyance, and then, without encouragement, repeats the entire show to that point in quick-march time. He can bring a napkin doll so resoundingly to life that when, at a preview performance, he pretended that the doll had "died," a small boy cried, "Oh, no." In response, Avner resuscitated the napkin.

He never says a word - he makes some sounds, mostly on a kazoo - but we read his face as if it were a cartoon balloon. Balancing a chair on his chin, he hears the applause and "says," "If you think this is hard, let me do something bigger," and replaces the chair with a teetering 10-foot ladder.

Like a circus clown, he intentionally fumbles tricks, dropping his hat while picking up a baseball bat, dropping a bat while picking up the hat, kicking the hat out of his reach - and then pulling his right arm with his left until it appears to grow a foot longer. With the newly extended arm, he picks up the vagrant hat and realizes, to his chagrin, that he now has two limbs of different lengths.

Actually Avner is an accomplished juggler, mime, magician and slack-rope walker. The slack-rope walking - a reprise of a scene he performed in Chicago in the Flying Karamazov Brothers' version of *The Comedy of Errors* - ends the first act on a note of manic tomfoolery. On the current bill, it swaps places with Avner's other virtuosic stunt, eating a pancake stack of paper napkins with the delicacy of Chaplin savoring his boot in *The Gold Rush*.

Though the clown is often deadpan, he is a connoisseur of laughter. Hear a giggle and he can spot the culprit, and may even chase him down from the balcony. Hear a strange chortle and he will stare the perpetrator into a paroxysm, and then offer a glass of water as a cure for hiccups. At first, laughter pleases him, then it stimulates him to top himself, and finally, with a scowl, he pretends that he is exasperated. In that imaginary cartoon balloon, we read, "Will they never stop laughing?" With Avner, the fun is contagious. Bring a child and ignore your inhibitions.

THE FLYING KARAMAZOV BROTHERS

THE FLYING KARAMAZOV BROTHERS: OCTOBER 19, 1982

The Flying Karamazov Brothers, four unrelated American lunatics, have been bounding across the country with their *Juggling and Cheap Theatrics*, a perfectly descriptive title for their unrestrained entertainment. The result is an evening of airborne hilarity.

If you think juggling is a limited art form, remember what Harpo did with harp-playing or what Groucho did with his cigar. It's not what you do, but what you do with it, or, to borrow a line from the American Karamazovs, "It doesn't matter how you get there - if you don't know where you're going." These California clowns know exactly where they are going - to the moon and beyond.

Everything flies - tenpins, swords, flaming torches, apples and jokes - in sweeping, gravity-defying arcs. In one particularly suicidal number, the brothers challenge the audience to supply objects to be juggled. Diehard Karamazovians plan ahead and arrive at the theater bearing blocks of ice, pepperoni pizza and blunt instruments.

On opening night at the Brooklyn Academy of Music, the relatively unprepared audience offered a portable baby carrier (the baby removed for safekeeping), a boot and a cold cut identified as brisket. Did you ever try to twirl brisket? Even an expert deli waiter would consider this an indelicate task. But the sticky-fingered Karamazovs have a daring to match their mania.

On one level, the show demonstrates the surprising variety of juggling. Anything that can be thrown can be caught, although the clowns are cowardly enough not to throw caution into the air. They offer this motto: "There is only one edge of a sickle one can catch - more than once."

One of their cleverest notions is to juggle music, bouncing tenpins on cymbals, drums and xylophone and playing a syncopated tune. Occasionally, a brother drops a club or more sinister object and then eyes a comrade or a theatergoer as if it were his fault. Sometimes they issue a futile promise - or threat. They do not really juggle those two trusting pussycats that travel with them as entourage, although one tabby appears to be catapulted out of a cannon.

What makes the evening more than a sideshow or a one-trick pony is that while juggling, the Karamazovs never stop talking. They are as longwinded and as literate as Dostoyevsky, and they have nothing else in common with their Russian master.

Enter cheap theatrics. Like strays from Tom Stoppard country - they pay passing homage to the playwright - they have a passion for punning, wisenheimer remarks and the gymnastic properties of the English language. Some of their lines deserve, and receive, groans. As Russophiles, they confide, "You ain't seen nothing nyet." But they are as quick-tongued as they are light-fingered.

In long hair, beards and ballooning pantaloons, Howard Jay Patterson, Paul David Magid, Samuel Ross Williams and Timothy Daniel Furst look like Tartars or Cossacks. As the Flying Karamazov Brothers, they are part of a West Coast wave of new vaudevillians - clowns, mimes, jugglers, puppeteers and aerialists - who are expert in traditional variety skills and are also experimental performance artists. For the sake of laughter, theatergoers are advised to book passage to Brooklyn.

THE COMEDY OF ERRORS: FEBRUARY 13, 1983

CHICAGO - As virtuosi of the New Vaudeville, the Flying Karamazov Brothers - a team of unrelated young American zanies - juggle everything from tenpins to telephones. At the Goodman Theater, they are proving that they can also juggle Shakespeare. Gregory Mosher, the artistic director of the Goodman, has had the inspiration to match the Karamazovs' breakaway clowning with a classic text, and the result is an irreverent, unbridled assault on *The Comedy of Errors*.

At times, the anything-goes approach threatens to undermine rather than enliven the Bard. Robert Woodruff's production seems to suffer from an excess of lunacy, but one could say the same thing about the Marx Brothers, who are the natural antecedents of the Karamazov Brothers. As actors, the Karamazovs are not about to challenge the Royal Shakespeare Company. But can Ian McKellen juggle?

Earlier this season, at the Brooklyn Academy of Music, four Karamazovs offered an evening of *Juggling and Cheap Theatrics*. Now there are five in the troupe, with the return from paternity leave of Randy Nelson. To those unfamiliar with their antics or their individual personalities it may look as if there are dozens of them on stage at the Goodman. The Karamazovian spirit is effervescent.

The evening begins with Avner Eisenberg, billed as Avner the Eccentric, a sad-faced circus clown and not a Karamazov. He sweeps the stage and lifts a trapdoor to dispose of the litter. Then the trapdoor reopens and out pops an agitated William Shakespeare (Timothy Daniel Furst, the silent Karamazov): One might say that Shakespeare has just been trashed. And so it goes. Later, all trapdoors flip open and a chorus of Señor Wences voices echoes, "Right? All right!"

The other Karamazovs play the twins, masters and servants, and it is difficult to tell one Antipholus from the other. Howard Jay Patterson and Paul Magid are both long-whiskered Cossacks quick with a retort. Their Dromios (Samuel Ross Williams and Randy Nelson) look different but their comedy is equally demented. More than his partners, Mr. Nelson has a linguistic ability that is within the reach of Shakespeare.

They toss the plot up in the air as if it were a dish and then keep it spinning. Jokes wander as far afield as Broadway (*West Side Story*) and Chicago politics (Mayor Jane Byrne). However, whenever possible, the company takes its cue for comedy from Shakespeare. A Dromio reference to football, which is in the text, is followed by a huddle, a game of touch and a cheer for old Notre Dame.

Verbal and visual puns tumble as fast as one can say Syracuse, although the name Epidamnum trips over every tongue. Pratfalls alternate with custard pies in the eye. When Shakespeare said that the setting was a town "full of cozenage" and promised "a thousand idle pranks," he didn't know the possibilities within *Comedy of Errors*. On stage are belly dancers, stilt walkers, unicyclists, two-tiered rope jumpers (a case of Double Dutch?) and a statuesque trapeze artist, Wendy Parkman - and almost all of them juggle.

As a wife of an Antipholus, Sophie Schwab is herself a bonanza. Remembered as the high-tossing twirler in *Barnum*, she uses her baton as a lethal comic weapon. When she squabbles with her sister, the equally appealing Gina Leishman, she accompanies her accusations with dangerous circles of her baton. This is one of the production's most successful attempts at enlisting vaudeville in the service of Shakespeare. Avner the Eccentric also offers a consistent current of merriment, with a puppet theater version of a quack doctor and as a teetering "loose rope" walker trying to hang out his laundry.

The adaptation is uncredited and, presumably, it was improvised in rehearsal by the actors and director. There are moments when one fully expects Mr. Woodruff to step on stage and blow the traffic whistle like a Keystone Kop. To his credit, he avoids gridlock; accidents are intentional. David Gropman's setting is a flamboyant street bazaar of trick props and cuckoo devices. Douglas Wieselman's score, played by the Karamazovs and others, might serve alternately at a bar mitzvah or in a harem.

Necessarily there are errors along with the comedy. The first act could be speeded up and some of the running gags - for example, the goldsmith played as a hermaphrodite - wound down. On the other hand, beneath the anarchy there is synchronization, as typified by ensemble juggling, the show's equivalent of musical production numbers. In the finale, following the happy ending, the Karamazovs perform their patented brand of music juggling. They tunefully bounce clubs off xylophones, marimbas and drums - a Spike Jonesian symphony that could set Shakespeare's bones dancing.

FOOLSFIRE

FOOLSFIRE: APRIL 6, 1983

The last time that those comic marvels Bob Berky, Fred Garbo and Michael Moschen were in residence with a clown show at the Dance Theater Workshop's late-night Economy Tires Theater, they posed the title question, *Is 60 Minutes Enough?* It certainly wasn't. In response, the trio has returned with the full-length *Foolsfire*, reprising a few of the choice numbers from the earlier show and adding new airborne material. The result is helium-light and hilarious.

The three are clowns, mimes, dancers and jugglers, often at the same time and never at rest. *Foolsfire*, with a repertory that rushes from circus tomfoolery to twirling with fire, shows each performer to his best advantage.

Mr. Berky is a contemporary equivalent of a top banana burlesque clown, occasionally ribald and always anarchic, whether pretending to take a shower with a piece of soap the size of a cookie crumb or, at his most spontaneous, engaging in the death-defying feat of audience participation.

In bulbous nose and jackanapes costume, he draws two volunteers from the audience, enticing them into a syncopated song and dance for left feet and twin kazoos. It is a dangerous exercise to depend on the buffoonery of strangers, but Mr. Berky has blind faith in his ability to make someone else seem funny. At the performance I attended, he won his loudest laugh with the simple act of peeking at one volunteer's ankles and discovering that the man's socks did not match. Speechless in this number, he communicates with a kazoo, which he uses as a versatile voice box.

While Mr. Berky clowns on a broad vaudeville scale, Mr. Garbo is a solitary sketch artist in a scene about a timid soul, outfitting himself for daredeviltry. The instrument of his adventure is a newly purchased unicycle. Carefully, he reads and follows the detailed instructions, and then mounts his vehicle only to discover that he has made one disastrous mistake. He has forgotten to put the cycle in a standing position. To his extreme embarrassment, he realizes it is impossible to ride when one is lying on the ground. After repeated defeats, he finally conquers the obstinate vehicle, then sweeps away on a confident but teetering turn around the stage, which ends with his crashing headlong into a wall.

Though Mr. Moschen joins his partners in eliciting laughter, his primary talent is for juggling, which in his hands becomes a balletic art. In the current show, he approaches his acme as the animator of four crystal balls, rolling them over his palms, around his fingers and then across his body until they seem to have a life of their own. His hands ripple like waves, and the balls float on air. As usual, the extraordinary beauty of Mr. Moschen's singular performance draws a sigh of admiration from the audience.

Mr. Moschen joins his madcap companions in their trademark mime extravaganza, *Nightflight*, in which they become a squad of flying aces. Holding large inflated model rubber planes, they gracefully dip and dive, in and out of formation, while one of them, in costume, momentarily portrays a billowy puff of cumulus - a definite cloud pleaser.

MICHAEL MOSCHEN IN MOTION: NOVEMBER 17, 1988

Michael Moschen is a juggler by profession, but there should be a more chimerical way to characterize what he does in performance. He is a movement artist, a manipulator of geometric forms, a sculptor in motion. To borrow the title of the two-man show he performed with Bob Berky, he is an alchemedian, transforming ordinary objects into objects of esthetic value.

In his new show, suitably entitled *Michael Moschen in Motion* (in the Next Wave Festival at the Brooklyn Academy of Music), he is the only person on stage, but he is surrounded by balls, rings, pyramids and spheres that achieve a life of their own. While Chinese jugglers at the Big Apple Circus twirl a dozen hoops, Mr. Moschen works wonders with two. They become appendages of his own lithe body.

He can also do more with a single crystal ball, rolling it on his palm until it seems to fly across the stage. With Mr. Moschen, metallic objects appear to bend and flex; solids flow. He conjures an image in performance of those Gjon Mili stop-action photographs of dancing light.

For a number of years, by himself and in the company of others (including Bill Irwin as well as Mr. Berky), he has tantalized theatergoers with his feats of balance and timing. With his new show, he moves to a new creative plane.

Imagine, if you will, that Mr. Moschen has wandered into a gallery where he interacts with the sculpture. He sets the sculpture spinning until the environment becomes a kinetic field of Brancusi, Calder and Miró. Something along this order occurs in an extended scene in the second act as he animates objects and then moves among them, enveloping himself in their world - artist merging with art. As the objects seem to hum with David Van Tieghem's score, the effect is eerie and fantastical.

During the 80-minute show, he reprises, with variations, a few of his signature routines, with white balls, crystal balls and fiery batons, and adds to them other signs of his juggling ingenuity. He caroms balls on the inside of a wooden triangle, sending off rhythmic resonant sounds like those of "drummologie" - African talking drums.

Several of his moves, at least on opening night, were slightly miscalculated, including those that deal with a giant hoop, but he never lost his equipoise. In his performance, Mr. Moschen elevates a minor theatrical art to visionary heights.

PENN AND TELLER

THE REFRIGERATOR TOUR: APRIL 4, 1991

A chandelier drops to the stage in *Phantom of the Opera*. A helicopter lands in *Miss Saigon*. And in *Penn and Teller: The Refrigerator Tour*, a refrigerator crashes down on the show's two stars. Where the Broadway competition delays a big theatrical moment in order to increase anticipation, Penn and Teller brazenly use it to begin their show. Should something go awry, it would, of course, end the show. Fearful theatergoers need not worry about the squashing of Penn and Teller. They survive the refrigerator, laugh at the audience's gasp and move into two hours of iconoclastic assault on the temple of magic.

Searching for a category in which to pigeonhole the partners, one might come up with new-wave magicians or comic illusionists. They are also - to use their own word - charlatans. As debunkers, they seek to remove the mystique from magic, to demonstrate the digitation behind the presti. In that sense, they are cogent critics of their own profession. Practicing the art of show and tell, first they do it, then they explain how they did it, while still leaving ample subterfuge in the air.

Because they are evidently so pleased with the title trick, they perform a variation of it later in the show, with an anvil substituting for the refrigerator and a duck standing in for Penn and Teller. In other words, one duck equals two quacks.

To those who may have missed their previous New York performances, their television appearances, or their movie, *Penn and Teller Get Killed* (everyone missed their movie), it should be said that Penn Jillette is big and burly and has long hair, though he has combed away the Daliesque curl on his forehead. Teller (who goes by no other name) is short and seemingly timid, but leonine in his daring, especially when he is on a stage yawning with animal traps.

In their return to New York, in a show that opened last night at the Eugene O'Neill Theater, Penn and Teller have added a number of new routines to twists and variations on ones from past performances. Card tricks still share the stage with large-scale Houdini-style disappearing acts. As usual, not everything is intended to amuse, although almost everything is intended to confound.

Even if they were available for hire, they would not be magicians of choice for a child's birthday party. In at least one routine, the show leaps over the edge into grotesquerie, as Penn and a female assistant, Carol Perkins, engage in a mock-sexual challenge match of prandial pyromania - or fire-eating. Though the show may not be to everyone's taste, one cannot deny the originality of the performance.

In a switch on sawing a woman in half, Penn does a trick in which he appears to shuffle Teller's disembodied head and limbs in a variety of boxes. Then he repeats the moves with transparent boxes and we see Teller slither from place to place, poking his head, waving an arm and flexing a foot. For all the candidness about magic trickery, they reveal only as much as they want to. We never do find out how they manage to float a volunteer in the air while her head rests on the back of a chair.

Watching the show, I was reminded of Alfred Hitchcock (not just in the malicious humor). With Penn and Teller, magic gains a MacGuffin: a hook, sometimes farfetched, on which to hang invention. Some of the tricks are so complicated as to make one lose sight of the original purpose. The fun is in the playing out of the exercise. It becomes shaggier and more labyrinthine, as in an audience-involving game show entitled *Mofo, the Psychic Gorilla.*

In this routine, Teller speaks, though he pretends not to. For most of the show he is mum. This is certainly not the case with Penn, who is unable to stop talking. Like a sideshow barker, he gabs his way through a rodomontade spiel in which he needles his fellow magicians, fools the audience and foils his partner. Teller is no easy mark. Even wordless he may be the wittier half. Together, Penn and Teller are a matchless team of self-mocking sorcerers.

CIRQUE DU SOLEIL

JUNE 5, 1988

The Cirque du Soleil is not only a captivating entertainment, it also provides a cautionary lesson in a theatrical time when musicals are becoming more elaborate and more expensive. With Cirque du Soleil, the French-Canadian one-ring circus at Battery Park City, less is, legitimately, more.

Take, for example, the climactic sequence, *Tower on Wheels.* In related circumstances in a three-ring circus, this might be an extravaganza with gymnasts jumping back and forth on motorcycles or on the backs of prancing horses while high flyers switch trapezes in mid-air. Here the act is performed with one bicycle, whose rider is joined by three friends, then by three more, and so on, until, before we know it, 13 people are perched on a bicycle built for one. The cycle is so layered with passengers that it is almost invisible as it glides smoothly round the ring. To emphasize the fact that a single cyclist can be the equivalent of a one-man band, Luc Tremblay rides a bicycle into the arena and takes no passengers. He flips, turns, spins on one wheel, rides backwards and treats the vehicle as an extension of his own anatomy.

At such moments as this the Cirque du Soleil is imaginative to the extreme (and certainly indebted to Chinese acrobats, some of whom act as trainers). Not only has the company banished all animals from its acts, it offers no large-scale production numbers and has severely limited its use of mechanical equipment. Though we are sitting in a big tent, with, at capacity, some 1,700 other patrons, this is an intimate backyard circus, the lower-case garden variety, and its considerable pleasures are enhanced by being so close to the action. We do not have to strain our eyes or our necks to catch a distant flip in the sky.

Despite all the pre-opening fanfare that made it sound as if the Cirque du Soleil were unique, the troupe has to be considered within a context. This is not the first small circus to make a large impression. One-ring circuses tour throughout Europe. The Big Apple Circus is a New York favorite and the Pickle Family Circus is an equally admired company in San Francisco. Among other migrant troupes, there has also been Le Cirque Imaginaire, the fanciful, two-man, toy circus, invented by Victoria Chaplin and her husband, Jean Baptiste Thierrée, and in several locations in New York it has been possible to see Huck Snyder's vest-pocket play entitled *Circus*, in which actors portray animals. Though it is on a grander scale, in common with Ms. Chaplin's and Mr. Snyder's companies, the Cirque du Soleil is an adjunct to performance art.

The Cirque du Soleil is a cirque with a difference. It offers a cohesive theater piece - conceptual art in perpetual motion. The individual acts flow into one another, unified by music, movement and point of view. The principal idea, which sounds simpler than it actually is, is that anybody can do anything, that the most ordinary person can be transformed into an equilibrist - with, of course, a maximum of practice and determination. One does not have to train with a flying fraternity of Wallendas of Gaonas in order to win circus wings. In fact, many of the members of the resourceful company have a double or triple expertise and all are marked by their youthful vitality.

As Agatha Olivier and Antoine Rigot dance and change places on a low wire, sometimes to the tune of Mr. Rigot's oboe, the two are like incarnations of Bo Widerberg's Elvira Madigan, practicing in a secluded country garden. They are experts in slow motion. On the other hand, there are Jacqueline Williams and Andrew Watson, spinning each other at a high speed on a high trapeze (without benefit of a safety net). They twirl so quickly they become a blur.

Slow or fast, these performers are perfectionists, including Angela Laurier who, using her body as her instrument, raises contortionism to an art. Twisting her apparently boneless frame into awesomely intricate positions, she seems to have grown additional limbs - whose legs are those around her head? As is also true of her fellow performers, she makes the effortful look easy.

Although there is humor in some of the acts, such as the teeterboard ensemble, whose shower-capped members look like refugees from Woody Allen's futuristic *Sleeper*, the Cirque du Soleil is weakest in the clown department (a weakness shared by the Big Apple Circus, whose funniest performers are elephants). Denis Lacombe's slapstick stunts, especially his conducting of an imaginary orchestra while his feet are strapped in "lean shoes" on a trampoline, has a manic fervor. But Mr. Lacombe is not to humor what the artful Eric Varelas and Amélie Demay are to balancing acts (each takes a turn in balancing the other upside down on his head). Also, there were too many forced attempts at involving reluctant members of the audience in routines.

Watching these clowns go through their moves, one wishes for one of the Olympian gymnasts of New Vaudeville comedy to enter the ring. Many of them polished their techniques with the Pickle Family and other circuses, and are throwbacks to the clowns of silent movies. One might suggest that the Cirque du Soleil performing artists are themselves throwbacks to the saltimbanques, the circus performers recorded in paintings by Picasso. The Cirque du Soleil shares that saltimbanque feeling of spontaneity, of theater being created as we watch it. As such, the company is in stunning contrast to the computerized, overamplified world of Broadway show business.

LE CIRQUE IMAGINAIRE

NOVEMBER 20, 1986

The circus comes in three guises - three-ring, one-ring and *Le Cirque Imaginaire*, the fanciful creation of Victoria Chaplin and her husband, Jean Baptiste Thierrée. In this show, at the Triplex Theater, Ms. Chaplin, the third of Charlie Chaplin's daughters, stands in for an entire troupe of aerialists, equilibrists and wire-walkers. She also plays tame and wild animals, which she evokes through the chimerical use of costumes and masks. Singly, Mr. Thierée represents all the clowns. Together, they are a complete, portable toy circus.

Lithe, with a dancer's body, Ms. Chaplin is a finely trained circus performer. When she walks a low wire, she does a split and dances a jig. Later, when she swings and spins on a rope over the heads of theatergoers, she displays the athleticism and grace of a high flier. Clearly she has the talent to headline a major circus, but has chosen to remain within her imaginary family kingdom.

Less is more as she performs, a kinship she shares with America's New Vaudevillians. With bells like baubles studding her costume, she is a mirthful one-woman band. On stilts, towering over the stage in gaudy disguise, she is a mythical beast - and, as a comic fillip, she toots a tin horn.

As a mime in mask, she transforms herself into a menagerie of bizarre creatures - a king-size crab, a large, winged kite bird and, with the limberness of a contortionist, she plays a pair of limbs that has misplaced its torso. All this happens, quick change, in full view of the audience, as the actress enfolds herself and unfolds intricate designs; she becomes animated origami. For a finale, she does a number with fans and parasols that would make Busby Berkeley glow with envy.

It is Mr. Thierée's primary role to entertain between her acts, which he does with juggling, puppetry and magic tricks. His routines often involve gadgets and, in particular, suitcases. Like a French Paul Zaloom, he places a suitcase on a podium and then takes out odd items. In one of his more amusing gambits, he arrives on stage in a vividly patterned coat with matching trousers, shirt, shoes and suitcase. Then he reaches inside the case to extract a banana - and the peel is color coordinated to match his outfit.

Sometimes he goes to a great deal of effort to win a tiny laugh, as exemplified by an attentuated sketch about paper fish. As a clown, he has a tendency toward coyness. But, in his favor, he is quite ready to spoof himself, as in a scene in which he imitates his wife and falls flat on his face.

Ms. Chaplin remains silent throughout the evening. Mr. Thierée occasionally speaks in French, encouraging the audience to be his accomplice. There is no communciation barrier for adults or for children. The two are assisted by their son, several stagehands and a covey of small animals, which appear and disappear on cue. Everything else is left to the actors' - and to our - imagination. In performance, Ms. Chaplin is very much her father's daughter. When she smiles, she radiates innocence and charm, reminding one of the tramp clutching a flower in *City Lights*. The feeling is beyond Chaplinesque.

COMEDY

BILL COSBY

RADIO CITY MUSIC HALL: MARCH 17, 1987

In his show last year at Radio City Music Hall, Bill Cosby talked about the pleasures of being 48 years old. He is far less sure about 49. In his new show, he fixes his gaze on those of his age in the audience and says that once his body had "definition." Now he has to remember to breathe in and to stand tall. Recently, he said, he stepped out of the shower and accidentally walked past a mirror without preparing his body for the reflection. Seeing his once athletic form in its present, middle-aged shape, he wondered who the stranger was who had invaded his bathroom.

Age is only one of the many issues on Mr. Cosby's current comic agenda. He also talks about his children, especially his 13-year-old daughter; his marriage, and adult offspring who continue to live with their parents. Sooner and later, however, he returns to his most pressing concern, himself. Bill Cosby, in what he is beginning to regard as the twilight of his life.

Those who watch him regularly on his top-rated series, *The Cosby Show*, who smile as Dr. Cliff Huxtable acts as the wise and patient husband and father of one of the most engaging families on television, only know the half of it. The Cosby concert reminds us that there is far more to this humorist than meets the electronic eye.

In his live performances, free from restraints, he reveals more of his psyche and gives hints of irony and pessimism, leading in this new monologue to a vivid discussion of a comprehensive physical examination he had at the Mayo Clinic. The younger members of his audience may find the description overly graphic, but it was clear from the laughter Saturday night that, for many of his admirers, he provoked a sharp shock of recognition.

During the examination, reality repeatedly collides with illusion as he tries, with increasing urgency, to save face (and body), worrying that he might lose health points for every huff and puff. Subjected to bodily probes by a team of prying doctors, he declares, "Whatever it is you're looking for can't be as painful as what you're doing to me now."

Confronted with doubt about his cholesterol count, he is urged to alter his diet - and this sends him off on a typical Cosbyian tirade on "health food," words that wither on his lips (along with "skim milk"). He tells us about his love of pasta, adding that one does not just eat pasta, one has to have "sauce." Repeating the word "sauce," he seems to salivate in anticipation, followed by the immediate letdown of his next - and possibly last - meal: everything boiled and bland. In his show last year, he attacked broccoli. This year he adds cauliflower to his enemies list. When he eats cauliflower, he imagines his mouth asking him why he put it in there. His definition of nutrition: "eating to move things along."

In his 20's, in his first New York appearances, he told tales out of Temple University. Soon he was regaling us with reminiscences of Philadelphia life with Fat Albert and the other kids of movie matinee days. The transition to paterfamilias was swift - and apparently never-ending. In those early coffeehouse performances, he could be funny without having anything to say. Now he has a great deal to say, and almost everything is funny.

For a full two hours, he treats the Music Hall as his living room - and politicians should learn the power of such informatlity. Like Spalding Gray, Mr. Cosby is a performance artist of a kind, threading his life through his art, and vice versa. Years ago, he occasionally heightened reality into absurdity. Heightening no longer is necessary. The absurdity of everyday living is his primary subject, and he communicates his comic self-awareness by staging imaginary conversations among various Cosby components, his inimitable brand of body language.

When he returns in concert next year, Mr. Cosby will be 50. Presumably he will be healthy (if only he eats his cauliflower) and filled with fresh material from his new perspective. To his contemporaries, he offers a single bit of encouragement: "When you become senile, you won't know it."

GROUCHO MARX

JUNE 21, 1971

While waiting for a limousine to whisk him to a reception held by Angier Biddle Duke - perhaps for a repeat of Mrs. Rittenhouse's house party in *Animal Crackers* - Groucho Marx rambled conversationally the other night.

Groucho had come to New York to promote the rerelease of *Animal Crackers*, when it opens Sunday at the Sutton Theater, and also to promote Groucho watches and T-shirts. He was wearing both. The T-shirt was hidden by his overshirt and stylish jacket. The watch was in full view. He looked at it. "Twenty minutes past Groucho," he said, as the Groucho eyes darted back and forth on the watchface.

Asked how he liked *Animal Crackers* after all these years, he said: "I was in it, and I thought it was pretty funny. How did you like *Animal Crackers?*" His manager-companion, Erin Fleming, smiled. She had seen the movie 15 times recently and been bold enough to indicate that she was getting a little tired of it.

"I liked *Night at the Opera*," Groucho continued. "It had a sensible story. None of the others had a sensible story. I liked *Duck Soup* too. I don't drink it, but I like it."

"I'm 83 now," he said. Groucho was on a salt-free diet, and has been forced to give up cigars and alcohol. "I don't do anything any more."

The party in Mr. Duke's apartment at the River House was for the Democratic party, a fund-raising event with each guest paying $1,000. The figure fascinated Groucho, who wondered what everyone did and how much they made.

Robert S. Strauss, Democratic National Chairman, squeezed Groucho's hand and smiled heartily. Groucho said to him, "I didn't know that Democrats were millionaires." One man was introduced as a New York City commissioner.

"Commissioner of what?" asked Groucho. "I have no idea," he answered. "And what do you do?" he asked another dignitary. "As little as possible," he said, and then clarified, "I'm still in the Foreign Service."

Only one man seemed to have a specific occupation. "I manufacture trimmings," he said. "What do you trim?" asked Groucho. "Whoever I can."

Leaving the party, Groucho and friends proceeded to "21," where - to his annoyance - he was obliged to put on a house tie.

Looking up at the waiter, he said, "Have you got frogs legs?" The waiter said, yes and they could be cooked salt free. Groucho interrupted. "Do you have frogs legs?" Catching the joke, the waiter lifted his trousers and raised a foot. Almost every waiter who passed the table was subjected to the same inquisition, "Do you have frogs legs?" Soon "21" was filled with tuxedoed servers lifting a foot.

"Braised celery and coffee," ordered Groucho, and then changed the order to a more expansive scallops. Ms. Fleming tasted the dish to see if it were salt-free. "Taster for the king," said Groucho with an affectionate smile.

At the end of the dinner, he decided to commit an act of civil disobedience. He removed his necktie. Then he walked around the room and asked all the men to remove their neckties. Some laughed, some grinned. One man loosened his tie, and, as soon as Groucho's back was turned, he quickly tightened it up again. "Anyone who doesn't take his tie off is chicken," said Groucho.

He asked the waiters to remove their ties, and they smiled guiltily. Finally, he stopped at a table that appeared to be filled with dignified African diplomats. He asked them to remove their ties. They said nothing. The request was repeated. They were oblivious. "Groucho," said Ms. Fleming, "they don't know who you are."

He gave his tie back to the manager, and walked to the door past two prosperous-looking men. "What do you do?" Groucho asked one. "I breathe deeply and enjoy myself," he answered.

"You mean you're rich!" said Captain Spaulding, walking toward his waiting palanquin.

RICHARD PRYOR

AUGUST 17, 1983

If there is one thing funnier than Richard Pryor's concert films, such as *Richard Pryor Live on the Sunset Strip*, it is Mr. Pryor live in performance. This week he is offering a series of midnight shows at Radio City Music Hall, and his peerless talent as a comic, mimic and commentator makes this a comedy evening of the first magnitude.

On film, Mr. Pryor's monologue is shaped from more than one performance. Through editing and cinematography, one receives a comprehensive picture of the comedian in action. In contrast, his Music Hall show is not entirely structured - at moments he seems to be feeling his way with his material and his audience - but that only adds to the evening's excitement. As we watch, we wonder which way he will go and how far he will go. With Mr. Pryor, of course, there are no boundaries.

At Monday's opening, the capacity audience was urged on by the lateness of the hour, a high-decibel musical act by Julia McGirt and the rarity of Mr. Pryor's appearance on this stage. He was greeted with an ovation and with the popping of flash cameras (despite the announcement that no electronic equipment was allowed in the house).

With theatergoers milling in the aisles in order to stare at the comedian's friends (Eddie Murphy, Robin Williams and Christopher Reeve) in the audience and also to shake the hand of the evening's star, the show seemed threatened with further delay. However, Mr. Pryor - dressed in a white suit and grasping a hand microphone - dove unflinchingly into his performance. Though this is a cavernous theater instead of a cabaret, he worked the audience beautifully, creating his own intimate ambience.

In the course of 60 minutes, he moved from politics to sex to race. While reintroducing us to a few of his favorite characters, he never strayed from the central subject of Richard Pryor. Politically, he revealed himself as something of a seer. He had been to the White House (in the company of Superman) and he had firsthand impressions to deliver. On the nuclear question, he said that the building of home fallout shelters was a good idea. Then, looking around the hall as if he expected an imminent attack, he added, "But you're here." In case of nuclear emergency, he said, he wants more than a half-hour warning, "I want nine months," he said, and then detailed exactly how he would spend the remaining time of his life.

As usual, sex was uppermost in his mind. He told us about his loves and his losses, his exploits and the times he has been exploited, how he has failed in marriage but not in alimony. Conversing candidly with himself and with various parts of his anatomy, which respond on cue, he liberates the language (as Lenny Bruce did before him) and he expands the highways of humor.

Even as we laugh, we cannot ignore the underlying pain of much of what he says. When he speaks about his former reliance on drugs and about the natural high - and the nervousness - that he now feels in facing reality without an artificial support, the evening takes on the air of a confessional. What we know of Mr. Pryor, of a life lived on the edge of anger, nurtures our appreciation of him as an extraordinary comic actor. His show is not so much a routine as autobiographical performance art.

FORBIDDEN BROADWAY

THE BEST OF FORBIDDEN BROADWAY: APRIL 9, 1992

Isn't it *Grim Hotel* and not *Grand Hotel* that moved from the Martin Beck to the Gershwin? People come, people go, people move chairs, and *Forbidden Broadway* may be eternal. This is the gleeful message of *The Best of Forbidden Broadway*, a retrospective look at the last 10 years of Gerard Alessandrini's cabaret revue.

Pretension, pomposity and sheer star power are always ready for a comeuppance, as demonstrated by a vintage crop of spoofs in this anniversary anthology. Whenever possible, Mr. Alessandrini has added a veneer of timeliness to his recycled songs. There are also rude topical remarks, such as the suggestion that Tony Randall's repertory company is "proof that art should not be subsidized."

As usual, almost all the targets are musicals, and the key to the malice is in the stars, who define themselve through their roles and then live on in those who imitate them. The current cast of five is one of the revue's sharpest ensembles. Not only are the actors expert clowns and mimics, they could also play many of their roles straight in the original shows (at least if that were still possible after their devastating impersonations).

Although his characters have been performed by others in *Forbidden Broadway*. Patrick Quinn seems inimitable. A tall leading man with a diabolical sense of humor, he is funniest at playing the big guys. A broad-shouldered Topol lumbers onto the tiny stage to milk applause by singing... as... slowly...as...he...can. Jean Valjean wails in pain as he sings "This Song's Too High" in the show that is making him more miserable. Jonathan Pryce is still insisting against all ethnic evidence that he is an Asian too. In the revue's chef d'oeuvre, "Into the Words," Mr. Quinn becomes Stephen Sondheim mischievously entrapping unwary actors in a tongue-twisting thicket.

Patti LuPone spans the decade from "Don't Cry for Me, Barbra Streisand" to "Anything Goes" in which she seems to blot and blur every lyric. As Leah Hocking raises her arms in Evita's salute, there is a blackout, and she is replaced in exactly the same pose by Alix Korey's *Annie*, that former tyke who sings: "I'm 30 years old, tomorrow. And I haven't worked since I did *Annie*." Actually *Annie* is only 15 years old, though she may seem like "Forever!"

Michael McGrath ranges from scenery eaters like Mandy Patinkin to scenery like Richard Harris. In that "quasi Nazi musical," Mr. McGrath seems to be playing all the parts, except for Ms. Hocking, who makes a leggy arrival as Cyd Charisse. It is left to the impish Ms. Korey to impersonate a Julie Andrews who has been too long away from her songbook.

Trying to be up to the second, Mr. Alessandrini gives us a whiff of future *Forbiddens*. In his version of *Crazy for You*, the co-stars share the dimmest wattage. Then there is Mr. Quinn striding on stage to announce "I am I, Raul Julia, the new Don Quixote." He may be the first Hispanic star of this show, but he is not the first singer to be crushed by the weight of singing an impossible song. At his side is Ms. Korey delivering a valley-girl impersonation of Sheena Easton's Aldonza.

Any *Forbidden Broadway* is allowed a misstep or two. In this case it's two: one old (a mindless Madonna mimicking Mamet) and one new (a wrongfooted sendup of *The Most Happy Fella*). Otherwise, the show is felicitous, without a single song about Cameron Mackintosh and with only passing reference to Andrew Lloyd Webber. *Cats* calls, but there is no Phantom in the shadows. Despite the doldrums of the decade, *Forbidden Broadway* manages to raise its satirical banner and continues to delight a theatergoing public.

SAN FRANCISCO MIME TROUPE

AMERICANS OR LAST TANGO IN HUAHUATENANGO: NOVEMBER 27, 1982

"No resemblance between the personages and events of this play and actual persons and events is entirely coincidental." That reverse disclaimer, tucked into the program for the San Francisco Mime Troupe's new show, *Americans, or Last Tango in Huahuatenang*, exactly summarizes the topicality and the relevance of this fearless political assault. With the Mime Troupe, everything is intentional.

Back in New York for a too-brief Thanksgiving-weekend run at the Washington Square Church, the company savages American "intervention" in Central America, bureaucratic jargon, double-think-do-gooders and the business-as-usual philosophy that puts profits before questions of humanity.

The show is a kind of musical-comedy equivalent of Costa-Gavras's *Missing*. If that sounds like a dubious idea for theater, you may underestimate the collective imagination of this agit-propelled band of clowns and satirists. For almost a quarter of a century, the Mime Troupe has been an ensemble provocateur. The new musical is a considerable improvement over last season's *Factwino Meets the Moral Majority* and a return to the sardonic heights of *The Dragon Lady's Revenge*, itself a merciless attack on American involvement in Southeast Asia.

On this trip we visit the mythical banana republic of San Martin, a cockeyed country near El Salvador, where there is a weekly uprising. Governments are marked by their liquidity. Before you can "piña colada," a new presidente has been exiled or assassinated.

It is impossible for the dunderhead of an American ambassador to accomplish his mission of "steering the ship of state through the stormy seas of democracy," or even to determine which dictator is coming to bat. In San Martin, lying is the national sport, closely followed by killing. Truth turns on its heels as if it were a tango.

The labyrinthine plot charts a course of mistaken identity. A blissfully unaware photojournalist is on assignment from Experience magazine, seeking an upbeat story in a strife-torn country. On arrival, she is immediately mistaken for a loudmouth, right-wing troubleshooter from Washington, and, in the other woman's stead, she is captured and held for ransom by the rebels. The confusion of identities is eased by the fact that both characters are played with dizzying comic abandon by Sharon Lockwood.

No one knows whom to trust. The worst manipulator is the most congenial, a friendly American mercenary (Gus Johnson) who is also an undercover agent for the Central Intelligence Agency; he sells shells to the rebels while secretly setting them up for slaughter. Along the way, we also meet the inspiring commandante guerrillera (a vivid performance by Audrey Smith) and a warmongering general (Ruben Garfias) who blithely declares, "Let the domino fall!"

Even as events become increasingly dire, the Mime Troupe never loses its sense of absurdity. But for all the playfulness, the purpose of *Americans* is basically serious. The company is outraged by a cynicism that it sees as a kind of international conspiracy: the middle of the road has been co-opted by the right and the left. Sanity has lost its elbow room.

The show was conceived and written by Joan Holden after she visited Nicaragua - and the subject, in common with the show, is a composite. As with all Mime Troupe projects, this is a collaborative venture. Using the company's broad style of performing, the actors leap between roles as dupes and deceivers and also take time to join the on-stage band, playing infectious Latin-flavored songs. Curtains are used as backdrops, including one striking landscape by Larry Montgomery that recalls the horror of Guernica.

Everything is as timely as tomorrow's headlines. Anyone concerned about the state of global politics - and about the state of political humor - should listen to the Mime Troupe's message.

⌘

SECOND CITY

COMPASS AND THE SECOND CITY IMPROVISE REUNION IN CHICAGO: OCTOBER 21, 1976

CHICAGO - At class reunions old graduates often idealize the past, disguise the present and take the measure of one another's success and failure. In contrast, when the graduates of the Compass and the Second City gathered last weekend at the University of Chicago (where the improvisational movement began 21 years ago), the reunion was primarily a celebration and a re-creation.

In performance - one night for the Compass players, one for Second City, each a part of a two-week *Festival of Chicago Comedy* - these actors proved that memories have played no tricks. To this observer, who has been following Second City since its arrival in New York 15 years ago, the performers seemed sharper and funnier than ever. They are still fast on their feet and quick with their tongues. They have lost none of their agility in improvising or their zany humor. The comedy sketches have ripened into classics.

The 14 returning graduates, many of them members of the original Compass company, the brief predecessor of the long-run Second City, felt a little odd, even embarrassed, at finding themselves at a reunion.

With a nod to her friends and partners in comedy sitting on stage, Barbara Harris told the audience that it was "like old Trotskyites getting together and trying to remember the good old days." Roger Bowen said, "It's good to have an old-timers' night to give people a chance to see our obsolete satire."

In the show, Severn Darden brought back his Prof. Walter von der Voegelweide, a nitpicking pedant who talks like this: "Which poses the question: Who are we? Are we just a bunch of me or shall I include them?"

Anthony Holland played one of his favorite characters, a perpetual student who has lingered at the university for 20 years - seeing *Alexander Nevsky* 437 times, filing foreign periodals in the library - while his best friend has gone on to become a rich, stuffy investment broker.

The peak of hilarity was reached in a scene in which Eugene Troobnick played a scrofulous, flea-ridden bum, sitting on a park bench, and Paul Sand played a clean-cut dog. With a woof and a look of puppy vulnerability, Mr. Sand - on all twos - walked over to the bum, nuzzled his shoulder, and eyed him with a look so endearing and dogly that Snoopy would have yapped in envy.

The shows were a breeze, but rehearsal was a free-for-all exercise in reconditioning reflexes. As Mr. Troobnick explained: "We're not rehearsing. We're trying to remember." Although a few improvisations have been immortalized on records and in movie shorts made by Alan Arkin, Mike Nichols and Elaine May (three of the more famous alumni who were unable to come to Chicago), for the most part the scenes exist only in memory.

The actors have drifted apart. The most recent appearance, in company, of some of the graduates was on Broadway six years ago in Paul Sills's *Story Theater*. Each has followed his own career. Ms. Harris has become a star on Broadway and in Hollywood. Bill Alton produces television commercials. Mr. Troobnick has turned to regional theater. Mr. Sills operates a theater in Milwaukee.

What unites all the performers, besides shared roots, techniques and sketches, is their allegiance to Mr. Sills (who, along with David Shepherd, founded the movement). The fact that Mr. Sills was coming to the reunion was enough to insure the presence of many of his actors.

At rehearsal, he was clearly the center of attention, listening to all suggestions, trying to give a structure to the performance. "It's a very nice feeling being together," he said, "but it's a little desperate trying to concoct a show. No one's done this madness in 20 years."

Whenever improvisers get together, they swap taglines and catch phrases. Old envies and conflicts often collide in midair. One basic company difference has always been about humor: Is it at the basis of improvisation, or is it merely a byproduct?

Somewhere between the polarities of jokes and commentary falls the main line of the movement - in timeless social satire and the humorous contemplation of the absurdities of human behavior. The humor is physical, verbal and gestural - from the Harpoesque, silent comedy of Mr. Sand to Mr. Darden's dazzlingly convoluted geyser of words.

Mr. Darden, who is a folk hero in Chicago, occasionally uses visual aids. Hovering over the rehearsal was the actor's elephant. For a special afternoon with Professor von Voegelweide, he had asked the university to supply him with a live elephant. Despite their admiration for the actor, officials hesitated at spending $1,000, the current rental price for elephants in Chicago. Instead, students built a life-size mock elephant out of paper, paste and gray paint.

What was Mr. Darden going to do with the elephant? No one, perhaps not even Mr. Darden, knew. Said one actor, "Severn did say he might tell the audience there was a real elephant wrapped up inside - and some lucky person would win it."

For all the banter and spasms of laughter, rehearsal was hard work. As Mr. Bowen said, succinctly, "One thing I've learned in improvisation - never leave anything to chance."

On the afternoon between the two evening shows, there was a reunion luncheon to stimulate the feeling of community. Mr. Holland got the affair under way by announcing about the previous evening's Compass entertainment, in which he did not participate, "The actors were so spry."

His luncheon companions nearly "spried" Mr. Holland out of the window. Soon the table began to resemble a Friars Club roast. As the insults and rodomontade observations flew through the air, Mr. Sills commented that "language" was at the core of improvisation.

When the group began, as Mr. Shepherd has described it, "it was the brainiest theater in America." The Compass and Second City grew out of the intellectual ferment at the University of Chicago. As the Festival of Chicago Comedy tried to demonstrate, these actors were not alone. At a related time in history, Chicago also gave birth to Dick Gregory, Dave Garroway and Kukla, Fran and Ollie, and others.

As improvisation proliferated, it also began to fragment. But no matter how far individual members have gone, artistically as well as commercially, graduates still look to the Compass and Second City as a home, as a source for creative survival. Those who came together in Chicago seemed to instill in each other adrenalin and comic inspiration.

When the second and last show ended with the audience eagerly asking for more, Mr. Alton, speaking for the company, said: "Thank you very much. See you in 20 years." Twenty years? How about this season in New York?

TONY 'N' TINA'S WEDDING: FEBRUARY 23, 1988

As well-wishers stood on the sidewalk outside the Washington Square Church, throwing rice at Tony and Tina Nunzio, an elderly passer-by inquired what was going on. Told that it was a show about a wedding, she stared in disbelief and said flatly, "No, it couldn't be." Noticing that the bride and groom were smoking while posing for pictures, another observer said, "It must be a cigarette commercial." Neighbors across the street must have been wondering why this same couple was marrying every Saturday and Sunday afternoon for the last three weeks. Beginning this week, they will also marry on Thursday and Friday evenings.

Later, at the wedding reception (at Carmelita's hall, one flight up from Disco Donuts), I danced with Sister Albert Maria and asked her exactly how many times this marriage had taken place. Keeping in sisterly character, she responded, "Just this once, I hope."

The show is *Tony 'n' Tina's Wedding*, and, as the tongue-in-cheek creation of the Artificial Intelligence comedy troupe, it is a live-in cartoon, a walk-around wedding in which the audience helps the actors do their work.

A cast of more than 20 is involved in the nuptials, although one cannot always tell the actors from the theatergoers - the actors are more formally attired. At the center of the bridal party are Tony (Mark Nassar) and Tina (Nancy Cassaro) and Tina's gum-chewing bridesmaids. The maid of honor is pregnant, which is the first of many complications.

The ceremony itself is conducted by Father Mark, an amiably sanctimonious young priest, who acts as master of ceremonies, introducing the guests to Sister Albert Maria, who is, of course, a singing nun; the decrepit Grandma Nunzio (a triumph of make-up) and the groom's slick, womanizing father. After Father Mark unites the couple, they are whisked off to Carmelita's, on 14th Street, in a car with New Jersey plates. After a honeymoon in the Poconos, the couple will set up housekeeping in Queens. But first they have to survive the reception.

Having attended weddings of the Corleone and Prizzi families, one is prepared for this tacky version of those more excessive festivities. There is dancing to the tune of Donny Dulce and Fusion, a congenially mediocre combo specializing in theme music (from *Rocky* and *Starlight Express*).

At *Oil City Symphony*, theatergoers are invited to do the hokeypokey. Here, for the $40 admission price, they can do the alley cat and join hands for "Hava Nagilah." The music may be ecumenical, but this is, by definition, an Italian-American affair, with all stereotypes reinforced. As we watch la famiglia, drama erupts at odd moments. Elderly relatives suddenly pass out, the priest drinks too much, one of the bridesmaids begins to do a striptease and the bride and groom have an argument that can be heard all the way to the Poconos.

Depending on the acting ability of the audience, the story may vary from performance to performance. At Saturday's matinee, a number of young female theatergoers seemed to have a crush on Tony, who responded with artfully arched eyebrows. Mr. Nassar and Ms. Cassaro are convincing as Tony and Tina and they and others in the company could conceivably move on to potentially more dramatic situations, such as "Tony 'n' Tina's Divorce."

One's enjoyment of the show will be based on what might be called the participatory factor. Eagerness equals entertainment. If you want to have a good time, you will. On the other hand, the entire event lasts three and one half hours, and, as in any wedding and in many shows, there are doldrums. Audiences may leave the reception feeling theatrically undernourished. Food, however, is provided - baked ziti from the steam table. After that, one can move uptown and have supper at *Tamara*, completing a full day of theater-dinner.

PUPPETRY

THE BREAD AND PUPPET THEATER

AH! OR THE FIRST WASHERWOMAN CANTATA: JANUARY 21, 1980

Peter Schumann's Bread and Puppet Theater celebrates the underdog, the outcast and the rebel in society. Its new play, *Ah! or The First Washerwoman Cantata*, now running as a Dodger Theater presentation at the Brooklyn Academy of Music, takes an heroic view of a homely subject. By "washerwoman," Mr. Schumann means not just servants but all women who are devoted to domestic chores. The show honors their efforts and ennobles their fortitude in original Bread and Puppet fashion, which is part spectacle, part protest drama.

As usual, the company plays with the audience's perspective, populating the stage with mites and giants. *Washerwoman* uses tiny cutout figures the size of toy soldiers - pulled across the stage on strings - and tall, tottering puppets the height of telephone poles. In the middle, at eye-level, are the toiling washerwomen, themselves, actresses and actors wearing calico dresses, aprons, kerchiefs and huge gourd-like masks as heads.

In some of the company's past work, such as *The Grey Lady Cantata*, the puppet people have been as somber and as sorrowful as whalers' widows. In contrast, all of these women have at least the faintest trace of a smile on their faces. They exude a note of contentment and confidence even as they are accosted by fire-breathing, tail-thrashing dragons and demons, monsters that would dominate any Chinese New Year parade.

As outlined in a cartoon strip in the program - a kind of storyboard - the evening begins with the "joys and plights of the members of the International Union of Washerwomen." The joy seems mostly instinctive and familial - at-home portraits in a pastoral, floral environment. The backdrops, painted in primary colors, are as crisp as a child's picture book. On one side of the curtain is a portrait of a cherubic angel, on the other a nasty devil. Center stage is a battle between good and evil. The play is determinedly pro-feminist and pro-union; it is opposed to a repressive Establishment.

In the second half, the washerwoman grows up and faces personal as well as public tragedy. Language remains sparse and simple. The pleasures are mostly visual and musical. Two musicians play a battery of instruments, including penny-whistle and electric violin, and are accompanied by an all-washerwomen band - experts on the frying pan, washtub and washbasin. The result is clangorous but pleasantly rhythmic and martial.

Emotion is communicated by the presence of the puppets. Even motionless, in tableau, they can express bereavement and also exaltation. There are moments of gentle, often whimsical humor. Bright paper stars fall from heaven as an actor simultaneously drops pins -plink! - into a bucket.

The cast is filled with domestic and wild animals, played by actors in costume. A cow is imitated by an actor bent double at the waist. On cue, he delivers cartons of milk. The company is unselfconsciously childlike in its directness. This is a theater that even the smallest child should be able to relate to, although its general audience is intended to be adult. For all of its international success, the troupe has never lost its sense of wonder.

The artistry of the theater has been perfected over two decades - the group was founded in the early 60's - and it is still committed to first principles. For one thing, authorship, design and performance are not individually credited. As an activist organization, Bread and Puppet seeks change, which is why it performs in streets as well as in theaters. The new cantata is inspired by the civil protest of the author, Grace Paley. By linking her anti-armament stand with the stoicism of the symbolic washerwomen, the company creates an alliance of womanhood. With placards raised, the pot-and-pan brigade is on the march.

At intermission, the company sells posters. After the show, it distributes bread to the audience. In performance, it offers theater for entertainment and for social progress. Just as the Japanese elevate their most esteemed actors to a higher status, the Bread and Puppet Theater could be considered an American "national living treasure."

BRUCE D. SCHWARTZ

THE STAGE THAT WALKS: SEPTEMBER 23, 1982

By profession, Bruce D. Schwartz is a puppeteer. By extension, he is also a mimic, storyteller and clown. In his aptly entitled show *The Stage That Walks*, which began last night this season's American Humorist Series in the American Place Theater's Subplot Cabaret, he enters encased within a boxlike puppet stage. He is a puppet theater, surrounding himself with a jaunty array of animated characters.

He begins the evening with the cascading comedy of a competitive recorder duet introducing his principal characters - his leading lady, Eleanor L'Amor, and her put-upon spouse. She is a preening queen, a Judy with all the punch lines.

The centerpiece of the show is a thickly plotted saga called *The Rat of Huge Proportions*, a knockabout feral tale about mistaken identity, jealousy, adultery and cheese - a heady Gorgonzola of an Elizabethan romp. As the star of the escapade, Ms. L'Amor is ridiculed by her husband and wooed by a rat of huge proportions and French accent.

Between purple phrases, the star murmurs cynical asides to the audience, which she regards as a personal claque. When the adventure is ended, Mr. Schwartz, still hidden in the walking stage, twirls like a top, and every time the puppet proscenium faces us, the prima donna takes another hammy bow.

Later, she returns to star as *The Farmer's Cursed Wife*, an absurdly shrewish crone who not only henpecks her husband, but also bedevils the devil. Abducted to hell, she is assailed by a gaggle of monsters, including a hungry crocodile, who opens wide, takes one taste of her and cries, "Yecht, pooey."

The sketches are mirthful examples of a performing art that Mr. Schwartz, a young Californian, has polished to perfection. *The Stage That Walks* is an improved version of a show that he first presented two years ago at the Dance Theater Workshop.

We are so caught up by the myriad characters on the walking and talking stage and by the battery of voices and sound effects that emerge from behind the curtain that we lose sight of their creator. His dexterity is such that we begin to believe that he must be assisted by an undercover army of small assistants. Actually, he works entirely by himself, with two hands doing the work of four. Beneath his canopy-cape, he switches puppets and quick-changes puppet costumes, never gets tangled in his own yarns and is relaxed enough to banter with the audience. He also designs the puppets and writes the scripts.

For variety - and for a breath of air - he periodically emerges from his walking stage, faces the audience and operates Victorian rod puppets. With enormous verisimilitude, he flexes the limbs and appears to alter the expressions of a mother singing a lullaby to her baby, a ritualistic Japanese dancer and a Pierrot brought back to life by the sight of a fluttering butterfly. These gracefully executed vignettes demonstrate that Mr. Schwartz has a serious side - he also has a good singing voice - adding lyrical pantomimes to comic pandemonium.

THEODORA SKIPITARES

DEFENDERS OF THE CODE: FEBRUARY 19, 1987

As a science fact musical, Theodora Skipitares's *Defenders of the Code* is an innovative advancement for this puppeteer and theatrical conceptualist. In her previous work, Ms. Skipitares has been concerned with such subjects as the Revolutionary War and the Age of Invention. Now she expands her canvas in order to probe and to test everything from creation myths to theories of eugenics.

Defenders of the Code, presented by Ms. Skipitares at the Apple Corps Theater, is that rare show that is both educational and entertaining. It dramatizes and musicalizes unlikely texts, including Plato's *Republic*, Darwin's *Origin of the Species* and James Watson's *Double Helix*, and consolidates them into a collage with historical dimension.

As any high school science student might testify, there probably is nothing as boring as memorizing the periodic table - unless, of course, it is accompanied by music. Here, we sing a song of krypton, xenon and helium and dance to a merry tune (syncopated music by Virgil Moorefield, clever lyrics by Andrea Balis).

Phrenology, physiognomy and craniometry also receive a tongue-twisting workout, as Darwin's analysis of noses - how noses shape one's character - becomes a singing and dancing chorus line. One should not get the impression that Ms. Skipitares is making light of serious matters. Rather, she is using her sense of humor and her vivid imagination to make scientific discoveries accessible to a wider public.

At the root of the evening is Ms. Skipitares's puppetry. With the help of her collaborators, she has created life-size replicas of Madame Curie, Darwin, Mendel and others. Manipulated Bunraku-style, they move their facial features as well as their limbs, and achieve such a degree of reality that one fully expects actors to emerge from behind the puppets.

In the performance, the puppets are the equivalent of mimes, while, standing at a podium, actors (in particular, Tom Costello) narrate and read the dialogue. Simultaneously, the composer leads an on-stage band, with singing by Victoria Klamp. The scenic design, by a variety of contributors, is an animated panorama from the worlds of chemistry and biology.

With what appears to be greater resources, Ms. Skipitares, previously a practitioner of theater on a shoestring, takes a step into higher theatrical technology. Without losing her childlike playfulness - toys still take part in her show - she has conceived a more elaborate visual environment. Despite the intricacy, *Defenders of the Code* proceeds without a noticeable glitch.

Some of the most evocative touches arise from the director's straightfaced skepticism. She lets scientists satirize themselves, as in her consideration of the racist side of eugenics. At the same time, she stresses the suspenseful nature of the discovery of DNA' s structure - as she sees it, a pursuit of knowledge and a race for a Nobel Prize.

The show is highly collaborative. The choreographer, Gail Conrad, has to set the oddest things dancing - noses, brains and a quartet of genetically improved cows. Mr. Moorefield, a regular member of the Skipitares team, this time takes center stage as composer, and acts, engagingly, as musical synthesizer. The music ranges from rap songs to melodic commentaries on "earth, fire, heat and flames." Ms. Balis's lyrics provide linguistic inventiveness.

As narrator, Mr. Costello varies his voice to simulate everyone from Socrates to Darwin (one would not dare question the accuracy of the imitations). The black-garbed puppeteers are, as intended, unobtrusive. *Defenders of the Code* is one of the most unconventional theatrical events of the season, an illuminating exploration into the laboratories of life.

WINSTON TONG

THREE SOLO PIECES: MAY 10, 1978

Winston Tong's *Three Solo Pieces* at La Mama is a one-man show only in the strictest definition of the term. Using dolls as puppets, voices on tapes, slides and illuminations, the most exact words, settings and costumes - and himself as actor, puppeteer and presence - Mr. Tong creates a multidimensional world. Mr. Tong's pieces are related to Bunraku puppetry, mime and environmental theater, but they coalesce into a startlingly original art. Performed before an enraptured audience, *Three Solo Pieces* is a fantastical evening of theater.

At the root of this theater are three-foot puppets, which Mr. Tong, a San Francisco actor, manipulates with extreme delicacy and precision. Under Mr. Tong's control, the puppets assume a life of their own. They become silent, dramatic figures on an eerie, pristine landscape. In contrast, Mr. Tong as overseer seems larger than life and even godlike. But although he creates life, he himself continues to act.

The central piece in this three-part tapestry is entitled *Bound Feet*, a play about the Chinese custom of binding the feet of young maidens. Dressed in a black robe, his face whitened, the actor introduces the story by commenting that it will show the torturous extent to which people will go in the name of love.

Wordlessly, he bathes one of his own feet, covers it with powder, binds it tightly with a long ribbon, then modestly places a low screen between himself and the audience, and, in private, continues his ablutions and the ceremony. In the background we hear the voices of a woman and child (text by Mr. Tong), speaking in Chinese. A mother is apparently indoctrinating her fearful daughter in the ancient "art." As her feet are forced to become deformed, the child whimpers in anguish.

Then Mr. Tong tips his own bound feet into minuscule red slippers and limps forward. To music by Satie, he enacts a play with two puppets: a beautiful young woman and a handsome young man. The woman, her feet encased in the tiniest of red slippers lies down. The man falls to his knees next to her as if in worship and, with great tenderness, he leans forward and kisses her foot. He lies with her and they begin an act of love.

The manipulation of the puppets is so astonishingly realistic, subtle and intimate that we feel like voyeurs. The scene becomes increasingly erotic. Suddenly - in an act of discretion - Mr. Tong covers the figures with a cloth, banishing them from view. A sorrowing Jove, he stares down at his handiwork with a look of ineffable sadness. The piece, exquisitely detailed, is distilled poetry, telling us all we need to know about the ancient and barbarous binding ritual.

In his final piece, *A Rimbaud*, Mr. Tong reads one of Rimbaud's *Illuminations*, articulating the words with an actor's dispassionate coolness. Then he places seven small candles as stagelights. For this erotic fable, he uses four puppets - a sultry mermaid, a skeletal death-as-woman, an elegant young man, who looks like a small copy of Mr. Tong, and a mysterious catlike female predator.

Under Mr. Tong's sensitive fingers, moving a leg, crooking an arm, turning a head, each comes throbbingly alive - while that death figure, when stripped of its dress, seems to disintegrate. The cat throws herself at the mermaid, catching her in a death grip and the victim clasps a hand to her throat. We can almost feel her shudder of pain.

The opening piece, an adaptation of William Burroughs's *The Wild Boys*, is a direct antithesis. It is brutally and harshly contemporary, a stage equivalent of punk rock. On a stage cluttered with the detritus of a rebellious youth living alone, Mr. Tong prepares for battle. He strips, nestles a pistol in his jockstrap, dons a helmet and shoulder guards and ambles off to fight a war in Katmandu.

What elevates this weird scene is Mr. Tong's imaginative staging and his use of projections and silhouettes on a brightly lighted screen. Standing behind the screen so that his face is outlined and enlarged, he becomes a huge animated sculptural bust - and tells the tale of himself as wild boy.

With its jagged discordancies, this first piece may disturb theatergoers, enough perhaps to impel them to leave the theater. Certainly it does not prepare us for the wonders that follow. Reconsidering *The Wild Boys* at the end of the evening, we realize that its existence demonstrates the range and intensity - as actor as well as director and author - of this singular theater artist.

7

MUSICALS

CHRISTOPHER DURANG AND ALBERT INNAURATO

THE IDIOTS KARAMAZOV: NOVEMBER 11, 1974

NEW HAVEN - *The Idiots Karamazov*, which opened last night at the Yale Repertory Theater, is, more or less, a musical comedy based on *The Brothers Karamazov*, which is enough to make Dostoyevsky turn over in his grave. Actually there is nothing grave about this antic undertaking. A travesty by Christopher Durang and Albert F. Innaurato, two recent graduates of the Yale School of Drama, it is as precocious as it sounds - but it also has moments of comic inspiration.

The authors are Yale's response to Tom Stoppard and Vladimir Nabokov. The script is riddled with literary allusions and intellectual jokes. This is a lampoon not only of Dostoyevsky, but also of all Western literature.

The star role is the translator, Constance Garnett. As portrayed by Meryl Streep, she is a daft old witch (the play is daft, too) in a wheel chair, attended by a butler named Ernest, who eventually blows his brains out. Absentmindedly, Miss Garnett leads us through the Karamazov saga, offering absurd footnotes and marginalia (such as the conjugation of the verb Karamazov).

The brothers' mother is named Mary Tyrone Karamazov. She wanders in from another play, shooting dope and confusing the saintly Alyosha with the sickly Edmund Tyrone. Linda Atkinson's performance is delirious, briefly and maniacally lapsing into an exact imitation of Katharine Hepburn as Mary Tyrone. The brothers are more Marx than Karamazov, four pratfalling mad Russians (Charles Levin, R. Nersesian, Stephen Rowe and Christopher Durang as Alyosha). There appear to be more students in this cast than in other Yale productions - with the noticeable exception of Jeremy Geidt, who doubles as a pederastic priest and a samovar. (He is a very effective samovar.)

Textually the play occasionally smarts from its own archness, but musically it is right on its satiric target. If the authors are really as clever as they seem to be, they - in collaboration with their talented composer Jack Feldman - will add songs and make it even more of a musical.

Dostoyevsky's Karamazov brothers enter like Chekhov's sisters, singing, "We gotta get to Moscow," and Grushenka (a rousing performance by Franchelle Stewart Dorn) musically describes her romantic predicament, "Fathers and sons. I'm in love with fathers and sons." Eventually Alyosha is transformed into a pop star and plays the Palace, accompanied by a chorus of crazy ladies, Constance

Garnett, Grushenka, Anais Pnin and Djuna Burnes. Later there is a send-up of L. Frank Baum, "Totem and Taboo and Toto Too," and Miss Garnett gets to yodel, solo.

Everything is twitted, even the Yale Theater itself, with scenery removed by a black-shrouded stagehand, a creepy leftover from the company's last production, Andrzej Wajda's version of *The Possessed*. One might say that *The Idiots Karamazov* is the flip side of Dostoyevsky.

I liked the all-nonsense attitude, but some of the humor seemed too facile. The evening needs refining and William Peter's direction needs tightening. Instead of building to a zany climax, the show dribbles off into a recitation by Miss Garnett of famous first lines (from Joyce to Melville) as if the playwrights felt a need to impress us. I was already impressed - with their wit as well as with their scholarship.

FRANK LOESSER

GUYS AND DOLLS: AUGUST 1, 1976

One comes out of the new all-black version of *Guys and Dolls* singing the songs and singing the praises of Frank Loesser. Is there a richer, more harmonious and more American score in the modern musical theater? Was there a composer-lyricist more adept at integrating words, music and character? Songs not only flow out of the Abe Burrows-Jo Swerling book but they flow into one another. For example, in *Marry the Man Today*, the long-engaged Adelaide and Salvation Army Sarah weave their individual romantic laments into a universal tapestry about the plight of women at the hands of men.

The success of this *Guys and Dolls* (a success despite the fact that the sets are flimsy, the choreography sparse, the production seemingly geared to quick out-of-town travel) makes one wonder about the impact of race on a show.

Perhaps the most surprising conclusion about Loesser's score, as performed at the Broadway Theater, is that it has a definite line of black sensibility and rhythm. When Ken Page, in his smashing Broadway debut as Nicely-Nicely Johnson, sings "Sit Down, You're Rockin' the Boat," the number becomes a hand-clapping tambourine-slapping gospel song. What once was a showstopper is now a soul-stopper (two deserved encores on opening night) that almost obliterates the memory of the seemingly unforgettable Stubby Kaye in the original 1950 Broadway production.

"Sit Down" is the clearest, although not the only example of the blackness that has been discovered within *Guys and Dolls* - largely, one assumes, by director-choreographer Billy Wilson. "If I Were a Bell," sung by Ernestine Jackson (as Sarah) is given a funky beat. "My Time of Day," as crooned by James Randolph (as Sky Masterson) could have been written by Duke Ellington.

The book, however, presents something of a problem: Damon Runyon wrote in definably white Broadwayese; yet, with only a few minor - and interesting - alterations, the story turns black. Mindy's cheesecake is now apple pie and ice cream. Adelaide retains her nasality, but, being black, loses her New York accent. The new tone is accentuated in performance - in the dancing, walking, singing and talking (greeters slap hands). Certainly, the milieu - compulsive bettors, sidewalk sharpies, storefront salvation centers - is as endemic to blacks as it is to whites.

Nathan Detroit, that charming rascal first personified on stage by Sam Levene (and later by the very different Frank Sinatra in the movie version), is now enacted by Robert Guillaume, deadpan and offhanded, somewhat in the manner of Bill Cosby. In fact, there were moments as I watched the dryly amusing Mr. Guillaume and the tall, stalwart Mr. Randolph out-play the gamblers from Chicago that I was reminded of those Cosby-Sidney Poitier movie comedies. This *Guys and Dolls* is a musical *Let's Do It Again Uptown Saturday Night*.

As in those movies, the Cosby character steals the show. The seemingly secondary comedy leads, Mr. Guillaume and Norma Donaldson, are really the stars. She finds the intelligence behind Adelaide's gullibility; she makes this lady's ingenuousness endearing. And Mr. Guillaume's casual con-man is a perfect match. Unavoidably, the romantic leads, Mr. Randolph and Ms. Jackson, finish second. In their cases, it is their singing more than the characters that we may remember, which of course, has always been true of *Guys and Dolls*.

The crucial question is whether a play should be cast entirely with black performers or with a mixed company. The former can seem racist if there is no artistic validity for the switch in color. Then its only justification is to give minority actors employment. The mixed company makes far more sense, but there are those special cases, such as *Guys and Dolls*, and there are other, possibly adaptable candidates, such as *Pal Joey* and *How to Succeed in Business Without Really Trying*. There's no need to limit such productions to musicals with urban backgrounds. One could imagine, for example, a black *Carousel* with a Southern background. Sometimes a black company can itself act as a re-interpretation of a show.

There are, of course, many musicals that would be distorted if played by all-black companies - for example, *My Fair Lady* and *Oklahoma!* In each case, the atmosphere is essential to the show. Musicals embedded in a specific ethnic or national landscape are difficult, if not impossible, to translate. Some shows are simply more indigenous than others -and that is as true of black shows as it is of white shows. What would be the point of doing a white *Raisin* or *Ain't Supposed to Die a Natural Death*?

In the Circle in the Square production of *Death of a Salesman*, the fact that the neighbors of Willy Loman were black was sociologically jolting, considering the time and place of the play. On the other hand, several seasons ago, Center Stage in Baltimore presented an all-black *Death of a Salesman*, which proved that Willy could be black, that his drive to be liked could be viewed from a black perspective, as a quest for acceptance and assimilation. *Salesman*, like *Guys and Dolls*, is relevant to the black experience, whereas *The Cherry Orchard*, which was given an all-black production at the Public Theater, seemed irrelevant.

In almost all cases, the healthiest approach is the integrated company. Pearl Bailey's *Hello, Dolly* would have made much more sense if the production had not been all black. We kept wondering what all those blacks were doing in Yonkers at that time. Yet a black Dolly Levi is imaginable, if she has the force of personality of a Pearl Bailey. *Hello, Dolly* is about its star's force of personality, whether that star is Ms. Bailey or Carol Channing. If the King of Siam could be played by Yul Brynner, why could the role not also be played by a black man? Some years ago I saw Godfrey Cambridge do the Zero Mostel role in an otherwise white production of *A Funny Thing Happened on the Way to the Forum*. Having one black slave added an edge of irony to the musical. Actually, the further a show is from contemporary society, the easier it is to make a switch in color. Were Frank Loesser alive and writing today, one assumes that his musicals would be cast without regard to color. But black or white - or black and white - it is a tremendous pleasure to have *Guys and Dolls* back on Broadway.

ELIZABETH SWADOS

RUNAWAYS: MARCH 10, 1978

Elizabeth Swados's *Runaways*, which opened last night at Joseph Papp's Public Theater Cabaret, is an inspired musical collage about the hopes, dreams, fears, frustrations, loneliness, humor and, perhaps most of all, the anger, of young people who are estranged from their families and are searching for themselves. There are moments of joyfulness and youthful exuberance, but basically this is a serious contemplative musical with something important to say about society today.

This is a rare case in which a show was organically created. Ten months ago, Ms. Swados decided to write a musical about runaways and to do research for the project at the same time that she was gathering a cast. As composer, lyricist and author, Ms. Swados has transformed the material. As director, she has transformed her cast. Some of the youths were actual runaways, a few were experienced professionals; now they are all actors. One of the pleasures of *Runaways* is that the company retains its rough edges and its freshness.

The structure of the show seems simple. On a playground, a functional de-

sign by Douglas W. Schmidt and Woods Mackintosh, the company gathers together and, in a mosaic of songs, monologues, scenes, poems and dances, gives us
a complete portrait of urban children on the run. We see what prods youngsters
to leave home and what disturbs - and nurtures - them in their escapes. The musical takes a harsh and uncompromising look at the world of runaways, but it is
written and performed with great compassion.

Up to now, Ms. Swados has been known chiefly for her classical collaborations with Andrei Serban and for her lighthearted vaudeville, *Nightclub Cantata*.
With *Runaways*, she steps right into the front line of popular American theatrical
composers. This is the first musical since *Hair* to unite, successfully, contemporary popular music and the legitimate theater. The cabaret rocks with the pulsating sound of disco, salsa, country-and-western and blues.

A pivotal song - an absolute showstopper and one of a dozen or so exciting
numbers - is "Where Are Those People Who Did Hair," a lowdown travesty of
punk rock. On one level, *Runaways* poses the question: What happened after the
Age of Aquarius? With the death of Woodstock and the wilting of the flower children, America was faced with nuclear dropout. Confused and undirected, adolescents unmounted their *Easy Rider* motorcycles and looked for methods of survival.
In the words of one of the more infectious songs, in order to survive, you've got
to "enterprise."

The kids in *Runaways* find their center in sports (a basketball, twirled on the
tip of a finger, becomes a planet of possibilities), graffiti, ("I paint multi-colored
curses late at night"), sex, small crime and street con. Actually, the Papp show that
Runaways is closest to in spirit is Ntozake Shange's nonmusical *For Colored Girls
Who Have Considered Suicide/When the Rainbow is Enuf*. In common with Ms.
Shange, Ms. Swados creates art with her nerve ends.

Not just the songs, but the soliloquies and poems - some of them contributed
by members of the cast - are also deeply personal. With gathering speed and emotion, a young man delivers a school current-events report, awesomely burdened
by the bitter news of the day - and events in his own home. Is this what he faces
in the outside world, a world that we are later told is "an orphanage for grown-
ups"?

Runaways is a concerned citizen of a musical, but it is also a buoyant entertainment, filled with the bright colors, language and vivacity of the street. The authenticity extends to the costumes - sneakers, leg warmers and Levis - and to the
vibrant ensemble performance.

WONDERLAND IN CONCERT: DECEMBER 29, 1978

The tale of Elizabeth Swados's musical version of *Alice in Wonderland* grows curiouser and curiouser. Originally scheduled to begin public previews this week, the production was suddenly postponed by its producer, Joseph Papp. Then it was decided to offer three concert performances of the musical portion of the projected evening. *Wonderland in Concert.*

Although this has to be an interim report on a work still in progress, there is such an abundance of rich material in Ms. Swados's new show that it is apparent that *Wonderland* should be allowed to achieve artistic fruition. This *Alice* has two primary assets - the composer's musical kinship with Lewis Carroll, and Meryl Streep as Alice.

In the concert there are 29 songs, 20 patterned after sequences in *Alice in Wonderland* and a short second-act song cycle entitled "Pieces of the Looking Glass." In the second half there are no misses, and a few of the numbers - a Humpty Dumpty hymn, a raga played on a tiny accordion, and "The Sister's Song (What is a Letter?)" - are soaringly melodic.

In the *Alice* act, some songs are better than others. What is most impressive is Ms. Swados's symbiosis with Carroll. His freefalling absurdities and dazzling wordplays are intact, as filtered through the composer-lyricist's antic imagination. Many of her musical choices are surprising, and offer a refreshingly contemporary note without undercutting the spirit of the original.

Alice's descent into the rabbit hole is sung as a ballad. Her incredible spurt of growth, "Good-by Feet," is given a calypso beat. The Mad Tea Party becomes a country western hoedown. The show also includes a barber-shop quartet, a Swados version of "Pig and Pepper" with the Carrollian title "Wow wow wow," and more nonsense songs than anything this side of Edward Lear (who provides an alphabet lyric) and Carroll himself.

Just as it is sometimes difficult to determine where Carroll ends and Ms. Swados begins, Ms. Streep metamorphoses into Alice. Wearing cheerful lavender overalls, she sits on the stage in front of her eight-person supporting cast and merrily dreams her way into the fantasy. This is a mature actress who has reinvented herself as a magical, ageless child. By the end of the concert we are convinced that Alice is tall, blond and lovely - just like Meryl Streep.

Ms. Streep has a small voice, but a pure one, and she uses it to its best advantage, alternately singing and talking. Her speech has the lilt of song, as she rambles through the thicket of puns, allusions and lunatic repartee. She is hilarious as she describes how to play croquet with a flamingo as a mallet, as she swats an annoying fiddle as if it were a mosquito, and, best of all, as she leads us through the mystery of "Who Stole the Tarts." Assuming all the voices, from King to Queen, from Hatter to Dormouse, Ms. Streep is a one-woman cavalcade of zany personalities.

The other actors play the other characters, but few attain an individual identity. Joan MacIntosh functions nicely as a kind of alter ego to Alice. Paul Kreppel sings "The Walrus and the Carpenter" with the blind comic confidence that Bert Lahr brought to his woodman recitation. Rodney Hudson, the outstanding member of the supporting cast, suavely turns himself into the tardy rabbit and the unique unicorn, among other creatures. Mr. Hudson's singing voice is as stylish and as versatile as his acting.

Accompanying the actors is a seven-man band led by Ms. Swados on the guitar (she also contributes one flamingo cry), playing a pride of musical instruments, including tinkling bells, a conch shell, a mouth harp and a loud crash of falling objects to signify the end of Humpty.

A concert is an informal, convivial way to encounter Ms. Swados's musical - it is a little like a backers' audition - but there are moments that demand to be acted and staged. "Jabberwocky," for example, would be better if the sedentary actors were allowed to dance as well as sing.

Wonderland should come up from the rabbit hole. Ms. Swados's frabjous score and Ms. Streep's enchanting performance deserve a full resplendent production.

∽

THE MARX BROTHERS

A DAY IN HOLLYWOOD/A NIGHT IN THE UKRAINE: MAY 2, 1980

Do you remember the scene in *The Wizard of Oz* when Judy Garland clicked her heels twice in order to frighten Bela Lugosi, and the scene in Chekhov's *The Bear* - or was it *The Seagull?* - when Nina and Konstantin sang a love song while Chico Marx tinkled the ivories? You will remember them if you see *A Day in Hollywood/A Night in the Ukraine*, the zany new musical review that opened last night at the Golden Theater.

Hollywood/Ukraine, which could be called "The 1930's Movie Hour," is a double-barreled pastiche of the golden days of the silver screen. The show is of British origin, the creation of Dick Vosburgh (book and lyrics) and Frank Lazarus (music), who is also one of the more antic members of the cast. However, the evening's top billing unquestionably should go to Tommy Tune as director and choreographer. Mr. Tune is the toe-tapping Broadway heir to Busby Berkeley. What his predecessor did with 50 dancing girls and a sound stage, he can do, in cameo, with four feet.

In several senses, the high spot of the evening is a number called "Famous Feet." Far above the footlights on a ribbon-tin catwalk we see only the dancing feet of Niki Harris and Albert Stephenson. Clattering their heels, the dancers merrily impersonate a cavalcade of stars: Judy, Charlie, Fred, Marlene, and even Mickey and Minnie. They all seem to dance on air; it is as if they are lightfooted puppets on strings. For Mr. Tune the idea is a small miracle of theatrical inventiveness, and it provides a perfect comic counterpoint to the reel life on the main stage below.

The first half of the show is devoted to Hollywood musicals. As a formidably tonsilled Jeanette MacDonald, Peggy Hewett sings to a cardboard Nelson Eddy - in this show he really is a piece of cardboard. To the tune of "Sleepy Time Gal," Priscilla Lopez spins like a dervish, deftly spoofing all those Hollywood ladies who spend their lifetime being serenaded by Hollywood gentlemen. The eclectic score ranges from three new upbeat Hollywood numbers by Jerry Herman to a nostalgic "Thanks for the Memory," sung winsomely by Stephen James and Kate Draper.

The background of this potpourri of songs and sketches is Grauman's Chinese Theater, a candy-box version of that movie palace designed by Tony Walton. Everything is kept appropriately within its chamber scale, as the act quicksteps to its finale, a small production number about the Hollywood production code.

In the second half we move to Russia to spend *A Night in the Ukraine*, which is the screenplay that Anton Chekhov did not write for the Marx Brothers. The source of the script is Chekhov's *The Bear*, that short vaudeville that made Tolstoy laugh. If he had seen *A Night in the Ukraine*, Tolstoy might have grinned all the way home to Yasnaya Polyana.

As written by Mr. Vosburgh, this is a crackling compendium of Marx Brothers comedies, packed with all the obligatory gambits, routines and running gags. Instead of playing Captain Spaulding, the African explorer, this Groucho is Samovar the Lawyer, which also happens to be the title of a clever Gilbert and Sullivan-like patter song. Chico is a faithful footman who can be bought for any price and Harpo is a maid-chasing, horn-beeping gardener. The lady of the house is, of course, a Margaret Dumont act-alike, and there is even a Zeppo-ish coachman who wins the girl. He croons a lovesick ballad entitled "Again," which is an endless reprise of the title. Just when things seem to be winding down, he winds up and delivers still another impassioned "again."

In performance, the second act is not quite as amusing as it should be. I could imagine a funnier Groucho than David Garrison. He has the appearance and even a reasonable approximation of the voice, but he misses that devil-may-care quality of the original. Groucho tossed off his lines as casually as ashes from his cigar. Mr. Garrison has the tendency to savor the jokes while contorting himself into Grouchoesque positions - although he does leap agilely onto a chaise longue.

Ms. Lopez as Harpo (heresy! a lady Harpo) and Mr. Lazarus, repeating his London role as Chico, are more comfortable and more madcap, each managing to comment on his or her character in the course of the performance. Ms. Lopez is a doll as Harpo, an incessant flirt always offering a leg up instead of a handshake, drinking ink, and delivering a rapturous harp solo on an upside-down bicycle - low notes on the back tire. Mr. Lazarus is a cheeky Chico, playing him with an Italian-Jewish-English accent - an easy fall guy for all of Groucho's duplicities and also a long-playing pianist. Ms. Hewett is a suitably imposing Margaret Dumont.

In his design for *A Night in the Ukraine*, Mr. Walton is an expert miniaturist, with a plush, long-corridored Russian estate that has the detail of a Pollock's toy theater. The presiding maestro of the evening is Mr. Tune. For him, the show is a marvelous directorial feat.

BROADWAY FOLLIES: MARCH 16, 1981

P.T. Barnum would have blushed at the flimflammery of *Broadway Follies*, a small brash vaudeville show that opened last night at the Nederlander Theater. The title tune labels the evening an "extravaganzicle," which elasticizes the English language and leaves the show open to charges from a Bureau of Standards and Practices. The producers have searched the globe for top-flight variety talent and have come up with, as headliners, the Ken and Barbie dolls of pantomimists and a supporting cast that features six boxer dogs chasing balloons and wrestling with a roly-poly woman.

This is not a show with a theme or a concept, but an unconnected series of seven vaudeville acts: one stellar attraction, another that can be greeted with nostalgic affection and five that, with extreme politeness, one could call limited. In the high-powered, top dollar ticket, spotlight of Broadway, one and one half out of seven won't wash, which is regrettable since Michael Davis, making his Broadway debut, deserves to be seen.

Mr. Davis is a comic juggler. He appears on stage with the disarming timidity of a Charles Grodin and kids about his craft. In juggling, it is not what you do but how you do it, he says, as he calmly tosses one ball up and down in one hand. By the end of the evening, he has juggled three vicious-looking weapons - a machete, an axe and a meat cleaver - and if you wonder why the act is going on so long, he will tell you: it is a very difficult one to finish.

With cutting humor, he also demonstrates that a bowling ball is sharper than a knife and then he tosses the bowling ball, an apple and a raw egg into the air. As he juggles them, he takes a bite out of the apple - narrowly missing the bowling ball - and ends, hilariously, with egg on his face. Whether he is juggling nine balls (there is a trick to that one) or juggling water (anyone can do it), Mr. Davis is a deadpan comedian. I was as close as I have ever been to rolling in an aisle with laughter. Very wisely, the director, Donald Driver, has given him the closing spot.

Nothing could top him, certainly not the show's putative stars, Robert Shields and Lorene Yarnell.

Shields and Yarnell, to give the team its aggregate name, are street performers turned television celebrities. On stage in Broadway Follies," they begin by effectively simulating the stiff-jointed, expressionless movements of toy soldiers. This is, as it turns out, their major talent. Later, Mr. Shields does a solo pantomime as a frog prince that will not give Marcel Marceau or Kermit cause for insomnia. Ms. Yarnell does a tap dance and manages to recede into the chorus.

Easily the most extraneous act is entitled Los Malambos. Three young men in gaucho costumes play three tall drums and then race around the stage on their knees while keeping their long hair in motion. Their real talent, it seems, is for twirling the bola, the Argentine version of the lasso. Each takes turns twirling the bola; it is not only how you do it, but what you do. Los Malambos twirl very well, but it is about as exciting as watching six boxers battling balloons.

Tessie O'Shea sings a few of her so-called "silly" songs, makes faces at the audience and leads willing theatergoers in crumpling paper bags (enclosed in the program) and "playing" them as if they were banjos. This is one of many non-musical sounds in the evening. Ms. O'Shea does her final number in a chicken suit that could clothe an ostrich. Backed by a chorus of dancers dressed in feathered shells, she sits on a nest and pretends to lay an egg. No comment.

There is also a man and horse act. In looks and attitude, the man resembles Bruce Forsyth, the English vaudevillian who unpacked the Winter Garden two seasons ago. The horse can walk on his knees. With a little practice, perhaps he can become Un Malambo.

Brightening the doldrums, along with Mr. Davis, is a team of magicians, Milo & Roger. They do ancient tricks, but they do them expertly and with an appealingly offhanded manner. They look something like Stan Laurel and the movie producer Joseph E. Levine. The Levine half of the team wears a large satin pillow as hat and it seems to bounce in time with his eyes.

As the self-appointed census taker of animals employed on Broadway, I must note that in *Broadway Follies* there are six boxers, a fox terrier, a horse and a disappearing duck named Spiro. The duck is imported from France. Presumably a star of international magnitude, he must be here through a special dispensation from Animal Actors Equity. Hermione, the acclaimed American duck in *Scrambled Feet*, need not be a-quack with envy.

ALAN MENKEN AND HOWARD ASHMAN

LITTLE SHOP OF HORRORS: MAY 30, 1982

Little Shop of Horrors, at the WPA Theater, drawn from a low-budget 1960 horror movie by Roger Corman, is a Faustian musical about a timid clerk who sells his soul to a man-eating cactus. Admittedly this is rather a rarefied idea for a musical comedy, but the evening is as entertaining as it is exotic. It is a show for horticulturists, horror-cultists, sci-fi fans and anyone with a taste for the outrageous.

The evening, with score by Alan Menken and book and lyrics by Howard Ashman, begins as a kind of New York slum version of *The Little Shop Around the Corner*, but before it has gone halfway round that sentimental corner, it has turned into *The Invasion of the Body Snatchers*.

The show's hero (Lee Wilkof) shyly pines for a waif (Ellen Greene), his fellow flower seller at a Skid Row flower shop (a nice floral design by Edward T. Gianfrancesco). He finds a way to her heart and to success with the discovery of a bizarre new plant. The plant is green and toothy - a cross between an avocado and a shark. Placed in the window, it quickly becomes a tourist attraction, which proves that the world will beat a path to your door if you invent a better flytrap.

Existing on a diet of human blood - in a pinch it tries rare roast beef from the deli - the plant grows larger and larger until it is a monstrous mutant. This is a singing Thing, a pistil-packing vampire. It is also a scene-stealer, finally hogging the entire stage and threatening the audience.

As the gardener of the supertuber, Mr. Wilkof has an affable, offhanded manner that allows him to get away with grotesque activities such as homicide, and Ms. Greene is sweetly guileless as his self-sacrificing love. Franc Luz plays a villainous dentist with a swaggering air of self-mockery. There are engaging performances by Michael Vale as the well-meaning proprietor of the shop, and by a backup trio of urchins (Leilani Jones, Jennifer Leigh Warren and Sheila Kay Davis), who view the strange events with more amusement than alarm.

The score, played by a small combo led by the composer as pianist, is a spicy blend of rock, pop and Latin. The lyrics, a step down from the music, have an appropriate simplicity. Mr. Menken and Mr. Ashman collaborated on the musical version of Kurt Vonnegut's *God Bless You Mr. Rosewater* (also at the WPA), and their new show shares some of the same cynical sensibility.

In *Little Shop of Horrors* there is even a late-blooming attempt at a message - or Flowergram - in the finale entitled "Don't Feed the Plants." One could approach the evening as a hothouse version of *Dr. Strangelove* or *How I Learned to*

Stop Worrying and Love the Plant, but that would be taking it much too seriously. As intended, this is a fiendish musical creature feature.

POLLY PEN

GOBLIN MARKET: OCTOBER 25, 1985

Whether or not one regards Christina Rossetti's poem *Goblin Market* as a fairy tale for children or a psychosexual plunge into the repressed Victorian heart, there is no denying the forbidden-fruit fascination that it continues to have for the reader - of whatever age, or whichever sex.

The new musical version of the poem, as adapted by Peggy Harmon and Polly Pen, runs a brief 70 minutes, but it is no small accomplishment. With the collaboration of the director, Andre Ernotte, and a two-woman cast, Terri Klausner and Ann Morrison, they have created a Rossetti offering. The musical, *Goblin Market*, at the Vineyard Theater, is heady in its atmosphere and has an almost tactile emotional strength.

The adapters have framed the poem as a flashback. Rossetti's closely bonded sisters remember and re-enact their childhood journey to a "haunted glen" where goblins - tiny men with animal heads - seduce them with their luscious treats. Soon the women transport us back and we are sampling the "bloom-down-cheeked peaches" and other savories in the goblins' onomatopoeic orchard.

Wisely, there is no attempt at animation or anthropomorphism of the creatures. We feel their presence through the wise eyes and incantatory memories of the sisters. By turn, each is overcome, first, Laura (Ms. Klausner), then Lizzie (Ms. Morrison), who, confronted with her sister's enchantment, returns to the goblins and is ravaged by them.

The two actresses speak lines from the poem and then launch into a seamless flow of song. The words are by Rossetti, the music by Ms. Pen, with, in each case, certain complementary additions. Two of the most ethereal songs borrow from Brahms (music for "The Sisters") and John Gay (lyrics for "Some There Are Who Never Venture").

The sisters do not know what is happening to them. Tripping arm in arm through the woods, they could - in contemporary terms - be regarded as "stoned" siblings, wafted away by an elixir of wormwood. There is, however, no attempt at updating or altering the original. In the interpretation, we are given a direct musical emanation of Rossetti, and can draw our own judgment about post-Freudian applicability.

Ms. Klausner makes us feel the "leaping flames" of the excitable Laura; she is bold, eager to undertake experience. Ms. Morrison catches Lizzie's contrasting timidity. In the sanctity of their home, Lizzie can lose her reserve, but, outside, she is more given to qualms, all of which she abandons in her climactic descent into the world of the demonic goblins.

They sing separately and in duet, accompanied by a harmonious chamber quartet under the direction of Lawrence Yurman. In accord with the instrumentalists' piano, violin, cello and percussion, the actresses are like twinned flutes. With her striking looks and voice, Ms. Klausner is a particular pleasure. Mr. Ernotte's direction and William Barclay's design subtly evoke the mystery of the popular Arthur Rackham edition of the poem.

Admittedly, there is something rarefied about the musical *Goblin Market*, as there is about the poem itself. It is, however, an entrancing expedition to "Those pleasant days long gone/Of not-returning time."

MICHAEL JOHN LA CHIUSA

BELLA, BELLE OF BYELORUSSIA: JANUARY 20, 1992

Bella, Belle of Byelorussia at the WPA Theater, a delirious new comedy with music about neogeopolitics, might have been conceived by the Marx Brothers (Groucho, Harpo, Chico and Karl). The play was written by Jeffrey Essmann, the music by Michael John La Chiusa. Although the show is brief, it is packed with shaggy commentary about everything from gulags to glasnost.

The title character is a young woman out of step with her time. She is as wide-eyed as Judy Garland in an M-G-M backstage musical. The year is 1989 and the Soviet Union is on the verge of collapse, but the backward-looking Bella, a tractor-factory worker in Minsk, wants nothing more than to be enrolled as a member of the Communist Party. In contrast, her pragmatic family and friends are scrambling aboard the leaky ship of capitalism.

The humor that aerates the book and music also extends to Christopher Ashley's production, which never drops its deadpan approach. Led by Claire Beckman, who is a winning Bella, the cast remains dry even as the vodka flows and the jokes spin into the land of the ridiculous.

Ms. Beckman's Bella is one of three women on a mini-assembly line. They are united nonworkers idling in a factory left over from a Stalinist propaganda film. At Bella's side are Harriet Harris, who confides that she is a princess from pre-revolutionary days (she has czars in her eyes), and Becca Lish, who is so peppy that she might have been a cheerleader in her homeland of Uzbekistan.

The characters are soon caught in an intricate web of blackmail and black-market icons. Some of these shenanigans could stand clarification, but to their credit Mr. Essmann and his collaborators maintain their uninsistent attitude, throwing away the more disposable jokes.

In the playwright's conception, Minsk might be mistaken for a city in any country fighting a recession. The accents are intentionally American, with occasional infusions of da and nyet and a final burst of Uzbek to remind one of the territory. Despite their school courses in subjects like the decline of Western civilization, these young people have an affection for all things American, beginning with Hollywood movies.

Representing the old line of politics is Joe Grifasi, as an apparatchik with a top-heavy chest of medals and the gray-faced look of a Leonid Brezhnev. Even this grave image has an antic side; he breaks into a song and dance. Love interest is provided by Willis Sparks, whose double agentry is as broad as his smile.

Everyone sings, beginning with Ann Mantel as Bella's mother, who opens the show with a mock Brecht-Weill salute to misery. In the words of another song, "We'll keep on building tomorrow if we can just get through today." Comedy derives from such futile stoicism. The score is a clever pastiche, including Red anthems, a rap song and a Mongol lullaby, with some of the music played on a balalaika.

The scenic designer, James Youmans, makes his own amusing contribution. Tilted at crazy angles, the factory set looks like a caricature of Constructivism. The costumes by Anne C. Patterson add a note of impertinence, as in Ms. Lish's party dress, a wedding cake of tiers and frills.

As brisk as it is subversive, *Bella, Belle of Byelorussia* takes a Gogolian glee in its spoof of Soviet disunion. In its originality, the show compensates for recent WPA musical missteps (like *20 Fingers, 20 Toes*) and reminds one that this is the company that first gave a stage to *Little Shop of Horrors*.

STEPHEN SONDHEIM

COMPANY: JANUARY 3, 1996

LONDON - Side by side in London this season are two inventive revivals of Stephen Sondheim musicals from the early 1970's, *Company* at the Donmar Warehouse and *A Little Night Music* at the Royal National Theater. Both are major critical and popular successes.

Seeing the shows in close succession, one is made doubly aware that Mr. Sondheim always had a flair for writing songs that are both self-sustaining and integral to a narrative. The purest example is "Send in the Clowns" (in *Night Music*), a complete story song that is even more moving in context as the climax of a musical about the absurdities of missed opportunities. In spirit, the song echoes "Sorry-Grateful," a sign of profound regret in *Company*. Both shows evoke feelings of love and lovelessness.

Mr. Sondheim's musicals seem to be in permanent repertory in England, especially at institutional theaters. Annually, his work is rediscovered: in recent years, *Follies*, *Sweeney Todd*, *Sunday in the Park With George* and *Assassins*, with *Passion* next in line.

With the possible exception of Arthur Miller, he is England's favorite American theater writer. Several years ago he was named the first Visiting Professor of Contemporary Theater at Oxford University, a revolving position later held by Mr. Miller, among others. In London there is a Stephen Sondheim Society, which publishes a quarterly newsletter. Little wonder that the composer is a professed Anglophile.

Both Sean Mathias's production of *A Little Night Music* and Sam Mendes's *Company* are adornments on the London stage, as they would be in New York. *Company* is the real surprise, especially after the recent Roundabout Theater Company revival on Broadway.

At the Royal Shakespeare Company and currently as the artistic director of the Warehouse, Mr. Mendes has demonstrated his assurance with an expanding range of material: Shakespeare, Brian Friel, Tennessee Williams and American musicals. With *Company* following *Assassins* at the Warehouse, Mr. Mendes demonstrates a special affinity for the work of Mr. Sondheim.

He has taken a fresh approach to *Company*, updating the show with minor topical references and enhancing the role of the protagonist, Robert. In a new exchange of dialogue, it is suggested that Robert has had homosexual encounters but has decided to find a woman with whom to share his life.

The director has excised the "Tick-Tock" number, danced in the original 1970 Broadway production by Donna McKechnie, saying that musically it was "out of character with the rest of the show." There is a minimum of scenery on the small stage. More than in previous versions, it is evident that the musical is taking place inside Robert's mind, as he muses about the demands made on him by the various couples in his life.

Mr. Mendes's boldest stroke is his casting. Robert is played by Adrian Lester, a charismatic black actor who had the romantic lead in the National Theater's *Sweeney Todd* and was Rosalind in Declan Donnellan's all-male *As You Like It*. Previously Robert had been a more passive observer, an approach that began with Harold Prince's original Broadway production. As portrayed by Mr. Lester, the character now has a virile presence, and it makes all the difference. Imagine a Denzel Washington who can sing and dance with zest and you would have an idea of the impact of Mr. Lester's performance.

One of the canards about the show is that Robert is a cipher. Yes, the role is underwritten, which means that it is waiting for an actor to fill it out. There has to be a reason why the other characters, male and female, are so eager to make him a perpetual third in their relationships.

Mr. Lester adds charm and even a certain seductiveness. He is active as well as reactive in pursuit of what he thinks of as his goal: marriage. Up close he sees marriages on the rocks. As part of the updating of the show, the couple in the first scene is interracial. In Robert's liaisons race is never an issue.

"Marry Me a Little," a song that has been reinstated (at the Warehouse as it was at the Roundabout), is pivotal to Robert's dilemma. He is reluctant to take more than half a step until the finale, "Being Alive," when he finally turns in the direction of commitment, the musical's principal theme.

The George Furth book seems more fully integrated, though of course it is the score that is the essence. Most of the songs are strikingly sung, as is the case with Sheila Gish, who brings a sensuality to the cynicism of the woman who sings "Ladies Who Lunch." The show and Mr. Lester reach their apotheosis in "Side by Side by Side," which now centers around Robert, singing and dancing with an almost manic intensity in an attempt to deny his loneliness. Paradoxically, the couples envy his independence.

A Little Night Music remains a more dramatically cohesive and substantial work than *Company*, a credit to Hugh Wheeler, who wrote the book for this musical as well as for *Sweeney Todd*, the Sondheim shows with the strongest narratives. Mr. Mathias, who staged *Indiscretions* on Broadway last season and is known for taking directorial liberties, does not tamper with Mr. Sondheim. He gives *A Little Night Music* a richly atmospheric production, conjuring images of Swedish city and country life and of *Smiles of a Summer Night*, the Ingmar Bergman film that inspired the musical.

Although intimacy is lost in the wide-screen environment of the Olivier stage, the show is engagingly performed. Through her singing as well as her acting, Judi Dench adds poignancy and humor to the role of the actress Desirée, and Laurence Guittard, who played the jealous count in the original production, moves effortlessly into the leading role of the lawyer Egerman.

The English favor American musicals, as demonstrated by the National Theater's success with *Carousel* and, before that, *Guys and Dolls*, but they are particularly drawn to Mr. Sondheim - for his English attributes. The composer admires the English for their love of language. They love his language and his urbanity, and the subtle manner in which he courts contradictions.

⮧

8

CLASSICS

SHAKESPEARE

HAMLET: MAY 29, 1986

In a lecture at Cambridge University, as recently reported in Plays and Players magazine, Tom Stoppard discussed various historical revisions of Shakespeare - attempts, he said, "to save Shakespeare from himself." By this he meant the odd twists and happy endings cavalierly appended to the tragedies: Nahum Tate's rewrite of *King Lear*, which closed with Cordelia marrying Edgar; Romeo and Juliet revived from the dead for a reconciliation scene; the Garrick version of *Hamlet*, in which Hamlet stabs Claudius after Claudius threatens to send him to England (anything to keep from going to England). Reading Mr. Stoppard's wry comments reminded me of more modern mischief perpetrated on Shakespeare, in particular on *Hamlet*.

Some 15 years ago there were, back to back, two exceedingly bizarre versions of the play. The first, at the Roundabout, was an all male cross-dressed diversion. This meant that, among others, Hamlet's father-mother was much offended. The second was a touring Oxbridge company directed by Jonathan Miller. In the latter production, the Ghost arrived late and sat on a park bench chatting with his heir about old times at Elsinore. A crew-cut Claudius concluded a soliloquy by whistling and Hamlet spoke directly into Yorick's skull as if it were a microphone. Everything led helter-skelter to the duel where Hamlet kicked Laertes in the groin. Both Claudius and Hamlet died offstage. The play died in full view of the audience.

I have seen three actresses in the title role, Judith Anderson, Diane Venora and Black-Eyed Susan (chef's choice). Dame Judith's depiction was a rare instance of a Gertrude (she played mother to John Gielgud's Hamlet) going on to play her son. It was not so much Dame Judith's gender that defeated her or even her age - though at 72 she was a bit old for bodkin and buskin. The principal problem was with her acting, which seemed to lack commitment except for those soliloquies that passingly caught her interest. Repeatedly she courted self-parody. One waited for her to say, "It is I, Hamlet the Dame." I remember having sympathy for the actress playing Dame Judith's Hamlet's Ophelia.

Ms. Venora headed a company at the Public Theater and Black-Eyed Susan starred in the Ethyl Eichelberger version, *Hamlette*. Mr. Eichelberger reserved the roles of Gertrude, Claudius and the Ghost of Hamlet's Father for himself - an especially difficult feat during the closet scene. The versatile Mr. Eichelberger also has a one-man *King Lear* in his repertory. He calls it *Leer*, and he plays both

King and Cordelia, an approach that finally eliminates the obstacle of Lear having to carry his daughter onstage. As for Black-Eyed Susan, she once played Ophelia to Charles Ludlam's Hamlet, in Mr. Ludlam's backstage spoof, *Stage Blood*.

When Christopher Walken attempted Hamlet at the American Shakespeare Festival, his rhyme was out of joint. "To be or not to be" was spoken directly to Ophelia, who naturally had no response, though on the word "contumely" Hamlet hugged her. Mr. Walken's delivery of the Yorick number might even make Nahum Tate rumble in his grave. Holding the skull up like a cue ball, he said, 'Alas poor Yorick! I knew him. Horatio, a man of infinite jest." Never would one regard Horatio as a man of jest, infinite or otherwise. However, in this aberrant production, the directorial handiwork of Peter Coe, Horatio was ridiculous. When Hamlet was not looking, Ophelia climbed on Horatio's back and pretended he was Macaroni.

Christopher Martin directed a *Hamlet* that was curiously credited as being "after Shakespeare." Were he alive, Shakespeare might have been after the director. In this shuffled script version, the play began and ended with Ophelia's funeral, which meant that the Gravediggers had the longest roles. They buried Ophelia along with Polonius, Rosencrantz, Guildenstern and Shakespeare. Hamlet entered by stepping up from the grave. Among the missing in action was Horatio; his lines were given to the First Gravedigger. One fully expected Hamlet to say, "Alas poor Yorick! I knew him. First Gravedigger, a man of infinite jest."

HAMLET: MARCH 10, 1986

If there is a young American more accomplished than Kevin Kline in playing major classical roles - in terms of imagination, intelligence, bearing and voice - he has yet to make an appearance on a New York stage. As he moved from *Richard III* to *Henry V*, while finding time for such lighter shaded heroic characters as the Pirate King in *The Pirates of Penzance* and, last season, Captain Bluntschli in *Arms and the Man*, Mr. Kline has displayed a dazzling virtuosity. His success in *Hamlet*, which opened yesterday at the New York Shakespeare Festival Public Theater, is all the more admirable because many of the actors in the company are not in his solar system.

As he did in his 1978 production at the Arena Stage in Washington, the director Liviu Ciulei, situates *Hamlet* in a time and place that could be regarded as Bismarckian - more German than Danish. The principal aim is to stress the internal machinations of the court and the life within Elsinore, a world that acts as an entrapment for Hamlet. Mr. Ciulei's new production, using an almost full-length version of the text, is filled with striking pictorial images and also has more than a few odd directorial interpolations.

In his architecturally inclined version at the Arena, Mr. Ciulei turned Elsinore into a castle city. At the Public, he lifts the roof off the castle and shows us, in greater detail, the life within, including a most tangible Ghost and extending to scenes of dining, dressing and affairs of state.

Characters wear smartly tailored uniforms and luxurious gowns. Laertes clicks his heels and salutes. When the courtiers meet with Claudius, they stand facing an imaginary camera with looks of smug satisfaction as suits their level of office. Pictorially, this *Hamlet* has the look of 19th-century etchings. Bob Shaw's handsomely designed settings are enriched by tall, burnished, bronzed columns and strong side lighting by Jennifer Tipton.

While the players don their costumes for the performance, on the other half of the stage the members of the court dress to play their roles in the theater of life. Anchoring both halves is Mr. Kline's mesmeric Hamlet. Instructing the players, he puts clown makeup on his face and then acts as interlocutor for "The Murder of Gonzago."

Mr. Kline has not settled for one face of Hamlet, but offers a variegated version - devoted son, avenging angel, devious actor. This is a player Prince who can manipulate others to his purpose. There is little doubt that he is feigning madness. Accenting the point, the director has chosen to end the first half of the performance with Claudius's observation, "Madness in great ones should not unwatched go."

The actor is as playful as he is unpredictable, with an extraordinary physical as well as verbal agility. Teasing Polonius, he rests his arm on a chair and, challenging gravity, pretends to sit on air. Describing Polonius's mortal remains, he worms his finger in double-jointed circles.

"To be or not to be" begins in a dreamy, contemplative mood, then rises in heat. Mr. Kline is artful at changing tone in mid-sentence, surprising us with his choices of cues for his passion. Wittily he crosses words with Rosencrantz and Guildenstern, but is no less commanding in dramatic contest with Gertrude and Claudius. As an actor in a company, however, Mr. Kline's path is uphill in Elsinore.

Harris Yulin's Claudius is stalwart and Priscilla Smith's Gertrude, though too young, has a sexual languor that is an asset in her scenes with her husband. Leonardo Cimino, who played Polonius for Mr. Ciulei at the Arena, is competent but predictable. Most of the other players are, in one way or another, insufficient to the demands of their roles - or they are misdirected.

David Pierce's Laertes is a petulant prep school boy in beret and velvet collar. In Harriet Harris's version, Ophelia's madness is unwisely preceded by nervous anxiety; she doesn't need Hamlet to drive her crazy. The Laertes-Ophelia relationship is too fond by half, and, in contrast, the Hamlet-Ophelia encounters are lacking in chemistry (in this instance, Mr. Kline shares the responsibility). In his customary fashion, Mr. Ciulei stages the mad scene at a banquet table laden with food and candelabra, adding distraction to an otherwise unconvincing tantrum.

Because of the inept acting of Marcellus, Bernardo and Fortinbras (not the only ones liable to that charge), the production has a dim prologue and conclusion. The ineffectuality of the ending is compounded by Mr. Ciulei's decision to set the duelling scene apparently al fresco before a long line-up of white wicker furniture. As the sport becomes a blood battle, the bored guests scurry for cover. Staging the duel in this manner ignites a tinder box of contradictions as in Hamlet's cry, "Let the door be locked."

Next to Mr. Kline, the most intriguing acting comes from Jeff Weiss, an idiosyncratic actor and playwright in the experimental theater. Mr. Weiss plays the Ghost, the Player King and Osric and, notably in the first and third roles, reveals a hitherto concealed talent for the classics.

Overriding the eccentricities and the limitations of the production, Mr. Kline reigns. Adding *Hamlet* to his other theatrical and cinematic laurels reinforces his position as a ranking American actor of his generation.

RICHARD III: FEBRUARY 11, 1973

BOSTON - It is rare that an actor of Al Pacino's stature, following such an enormous film success as *The Godfather*, returns immediately to the live theater. Obviously, Mr. Pacino wants to expand his talent, and his choice of roles shows his seriousness of purpose and also his courage. Last year he did *The Basic Training of Pavlo Hummel,* and last night he opened in *Richard III* - on both occasions with David Wheeler's admirable theater company of Boston.

Mr. Pacino is a surprising actor, not only in the way he avoids typecasting (his *The Indian Wants the Bronx* tough New York mug image was shattered by his smooth, suave son of the Godfather) but also in his performing. You never know what he is going to do, which is why he is exciting to watch.

In the opening scene of *Richard,* as the crowd mills around, Mr. Pacino suddenly edges his head into view over the side of a pulpit (the not entirely receptive setting for the production is the lofty Church of the Covenant). His face slightly distorted by a tic, his shoulder humped and one arm immobile, his voice nasal and his tone quietly confiding, he describes the winter of his discontent with reptilian malevolence and insinuating wit.

Visually and vocally, it is a stunning entrance, creating a level of performance that the actor does not - at this point - maintain (and to which the rest of the production - at this point - can only aspire). Mr. Pacino is still investigating his character, exploring the nature of the fiend and feeling his way toward discoveries.

Basically, this is a playful Richard, emphasizing the humor along with the malice. Mr. Pacino woos Lady Anne not with charm but with intellectual persistence. He vanquishes antagonists with language. His asides, his confessed hypocrisies are mordantly amusing - an actor relishing his own extraordinary performance. And we end up feeling that these people - many of them dissemblers too - deserve exactly what he gives them.

What is imprecise are the actor's wavering accent and some of his (and his director's) choices. For example, on the day of battle Mr. Pacino momentarily warms up like a boxer, using his good right hand to practice-punch an aide. The gesture is not entirely inappropriate - the deformed villain trying harder to achieve physical prowess - but it is not supported by anything else in Mr. Wheeler's production.

There are a number of discordant notes, including the haphazard use of costumes, props and scenery. This is a classic, but modern-dress *Richard*. The actors wear what suits them. One wears a suit and a vest and another wears a dashiki. This would not be so disconcerting were it consistent, but there are vague attempts at costuming. Soldiers use stockings - with eyeholes - as hoods. The effect is to dislodge *Richard* in time and place.

There is a vagueness about the entire production, a lack of point of view. For one thing the play has been hurt by cutting. It still runs three hours and seems long (partly because the church is huge, and much time is taken with actors running and shouting up the aisles). Lost in the cutting, among other important things, is old Queen Margaret, who most clearly represents the female forces against Richard. The women who remain, and the actresses who play them, are simply no match for Richard - with the possible exception of Harriet Rogers, who has a dignity as Richard's mother.

The best advice when seeing this production is to keep your eyes on Richard - which is very rewarding because of Al Pacino.

AN 'AUSPICIOUS' YEAR AT BRITAIN'S STRATFORD: JULY 16, 1978

STRATFORD-ON-AVON, ENGLAND - While the audience is still settling into its seats, a bearded, scruffy, obstreperous young man, clenching a bottle of whiskey, begins to shout and to create a disturbance in the aisle. A helpful female usher tries to break up the melee. The rascal shoves her aside, saying, "No bloody woman is going to talk to me like that," and then climbs on stage, gets into a fist-fight, and starts to destroy the elaborate scenery. This is the boisterous beginning of Michael Bogdanov's iconoclastic production of *The Taming of the Shrew*, the centerpiece of this summer's season at Stratford. Despite the theatricality of the staged altercation - and the fact that it has been well-reported in the London press - it is handled with such ease, spontaneity and conviction by Jonathan Pryce that it still takes some theatergoers by surprise. At the performance that I attended, two women in the front row were so unnerved by the disturbance that they scurried up the aisle to safety. A real usher led them back to their seats, hurriedly explaining that the performance was in progress.

The scene has no direct relevance to the play that we are about to see, except for the fact that Mr. Pryce's drunkard in the audience passes out on stage, awakens as Christopher Sly in the prologue to *The Taming of the Shrew*, and later turns into Petruchio. Indirectly, however, it encapsulates the outrageous, anything-goes attitude of the director. What Frank Dunlop and Jim Dale did to *Scapin* in *Scapino*, Mr. Bogdanov and Mr. Pryce do to the *Shrew*, even to stressing the contemporary Italianate atmosphere. A leather-coated Petruchio enters on a roaring motorcycle, wearing sunshades, Paul Brooke's Baptista uses an adding machine to tote up the assets of Bianca's suitors - acting like a mafioso contemplating an addition to the family. A carabinieri brass band marches saucily through the entertainment serenading Shakespeare with *Here Comes the Bride*, a tinge of *2001*, and random swatches from *Kiss Me Kate*. The director and his star, Mr. Pryce, have certainly brushed up their Shakespeare - with broad, sparkling Day-Glo colors.

First of all, it must be said that the production is great fun, second that it is a travesty that does not corrupt the original. Some of the accoutrements might be more at home in a pizza parlor or a penny arcade, but the shade of Shakespeare is unstirred. Furthermore, there is such élan and good humor in the performance that it sweeps away all reservations. Besides, a *Shrew* staged straight might seem annoyingly archaic and chauvinistic: Petruchio would be guillotined by today's sisters and a tamed Kate would deserve her own equal rights amendment.

Mr. Pryce, the demonic, black-souled comedian in Trevor Griffith's *Comedians*, is an actor transformed. Here he is bold and lusty, a super-salesman of himself. He has come to wive it wealthily, and Paola Dionisotti's Kate simply has no say in the matter. Such is the comic vigor of Mr. Pryce's performance that Kate is submerged. Actually she dwindles in comparison not only to Petruchio but also next to several manipulative servants. David Suchet, as Petruchio's back-up man (helmeted, he crouches behind his leader on his cycle) is a grand Grumio, and Ian Charleson is a triple-tongued Tranio. Initially Mr. Charleson has a Scottish burr as thick as a thistle, but drops it when he turns from servant into master, adopting a nasal English snootiness while still retaining just a touch of the old Scots to remind us of his place of origin.

This *Shrew* reveals the breadth of Mr. Pryce's comedic talent. Masterfully he articulates Shakespeare's verse, and with equal panache he plays the clown, performing with the nimbleness of a Groucho and a Harpo. A long-stemmed flower stuck like hayseed in his hair becomes a slapstick with which to whack his companions across the face. With a wince, he gets his own stomach ensnared in a clanging cymbal. Never overplaying, Mr. Pryce remains handsomely romantic while cavorting as Shakespeare's "madcap ruffian."

To move from Mr. Bogdanov's *Shrew* to Barry Kyle's *Measure for Measure*, from Mr. Pryce's extroverted Petruchio to his earnest Angelo, is a step from comic-strip vaudeville to moral parable. There are weaknesses in this *Measure*. As director, Mr. Kyle performs too many tricks in Christopher Morley's black box set. This set - there are as many doors as in a locker room - is the flexible core of the production, standing for court and prison, bordello and convent (the same actresses play both whores and nuns), and used as as a comment on the hypocrisy of Viennese society. Mr. Kyle further underscores the point by having the whores look down at the action from the top of the box set - as if they are watching wrestlers in a bear pit. Whimsically, the director dumps a huge pile of straw and a mound of soiled laundry in the middle of the stage (Ms. Dionisotti has to sit on the laundry). Ms. Dionisotti herself poses a problem. A strong actress somewhat in the manner of Maggie Smith, she is too determined and forthright for Isabella. It is difficult to believe in her vulnerability and her innocence. Marjorie Bland, who plays Angelo's betrothed, would have probably been more advantageous for this pietistic novice. With his hair combed back to reveal a receding forehead and with a harrowed, harassed look on his face, in *Measure for Measure* Mr. Pryce somewhat resembles the late American actor John Cazale - the last actor whom I saw play Angelo (for Joseph Papp in Central Park). The two performances have much in common - Angelo not conceived of as a villain, but as a tormented ascetic, shrinking from power, then embracing it as an act of will. As the Duke's deputy, he is compulsively forced to be stringent and unyielding. Irresistibly he is drawn to Isabella and to his own defeat. Mr. Pryce unerringly conveys Angelo's anguish and his helplessness.

The man who anchors this production is the duke, a character who in the past has often seemed misguided, if not an outright blunderer. In a beautifully conceived performance, Michael Pennington restores the duke to his role as master, in directing the evening's events, testing the citizens as if to prove their moral mettle, pushing them to the extreme even to playing a game with life and death. He is more of a machinator than Angelo but as Mr. Pennington makes clear, he is a man of excellent intentions - a public conscience. Very early the director indicates that there is an attraction, physical as well as moral, between the duke and Isabella, so that their match now seems inevitable rather than gratuitous.

The effectiveness of simplicity is evident in John Barton's *The Merchant of Venice*, presented arena-style in the Royal Shakespeare Company's small experimental stage, the Other Place. This is a *Merchant* shorn of weighty scenery and magnanimous manners - stripped to its characters. Patrick Stewart's Shylock is sour, bookish and short-tempered, a narrow man whose limits are defined by the discrimination of his society. "Hath not a Jew eyes" is delivered as quick tirade, an edgy man fighting to suppress his hysteria. James Griffiths's Antonio is a confident scion who wears his hauteur lightly. He and his companions are close-knit and clubby, meeting for cigars and brandy and sharing the same prejudices as if they are an old school tie. Attired neatly in smart suits, they form a community, one that Shylock is forbidden to enter. When Shylock and his friend Tubal meet, it is almost a parody of the Christian culture: a two-man club immersed in a cloud of cigar smoke.

In contemporary terms Shylock is as untenable as the tamed Kate. Wisely, the director and the actor keep him small. Without melodramatics, he earns our sympathy, if not our allegiance. The play turns naturally to Portia. She is the evening's engineer, magically changing herself and her maid into an attorney and his clerk, tying up the plot strands, and using Venetian justice to suit her needs. The quality of mercy is strained when it is applied to the outsider, Shylock. Portia is Marjorie Bland and she is captivating - as is Diana Berryman as her equally antic assistant. John Nettles is a dashing Bassanio. Hilton McRae's Launcelot Gobbo is a merrily Artful Dodger. Although the director does not ignore the play's message - in tandem with *Measure* it shows a preoccupation with the collision of law and justice - he is even more interested in its theatricality. This *Merchant* proves that Shakespeare does not need frills and flourishes - particularly when he is in the hands of good actors.

Good actors and good acting are endemic to the Royal Shakespeare Company. The company aspect of the R.S.C. is demonstrated in all of the productions, but perhaps most noticeably in its one current non-Shakespeare at Stratford, *Captain Swing*, a new play by Peter Whelan staged at the Other Place. This is a play about an agrarian rebellion in Sussex in 1830. Led by the legendary figure of *Captain Swing*, impoverished field workers rise up against low wages and encroaching mechanization - the proliferation of threshing machines - and are beaten down by a reigning tyranny. Though the details of the rebellion are specific, the play achieves a universality. The theme - individual liberty in conflict with unjust law - is applicable to everything from the grape-pickers strike in California to the French Revolution. The issues are somewhat simplistic, the action is discursive (there are as many scenes as in a movie), but the evening is engrossing and there are several scenes that prove that Mr. Whelan is definitely a playwright to watch. For example, in one encounter two militant dragoons suddenly find themselves outnumbered, facing off a silently hostile mob. Singing a song, they sidestep to their horses. The play shifts from irony to explosive dramatics. As is the case with *The Merchant of Venice*, *Captain Swing* - directed by Bill Alexander - uses the small open stage to full advantage. With a minimum of scenery and a maximum of ingenuity, the ensemble makes one feel the authenticity of the environment. Although the play is historical, Mr. Whelan's language seems as natural as that of David Storey. The actors, many of whom double in Shakespeare, are exemplary, particularly David Bradley as the gilt-edged hero, David Lyon as a dragoon and Zoe Wanamaker as a banner-waving trollope.

The season at Stratford is auspicious: a provocative new play, a Royal Shakespeare Company deep in talent and versatility, and a shrew'd team of originals - the expansive Jonathan Pryce and the insouciant director Michael Bogdanov.

TWELFTH NIGHT: JUNE 11, 1980

STRATFORD, Ontario - The 28th season of the Stratford Festival, Canada, the sixth under the artistic direction of Robin Phillips, opened last night with a resplendent production of *Twelfth Night*, one that articulates the work's melancholic humor as well as its beauty and sagacity. Primary among its numerous assets, Mr. Phillips's production features Brian Bedford as Malvolio, a performance of grand comic dimension.

It is Malvolio, Olivia's misanthropic steward, who gives us an ironic perspective on this fanciful world of shifting guises, an Illyria in which mistaken identity is carried to extremes of dissimulation. Malvolio is both an insufferable moralist and a harbinger of a society that would subordinate sentiment to reason. Unlike Tartuffe, whom he somewhat superficially resembles, he has a certain unquenchable integrity.

Mr. Bedford is not simply severe. He is exquisitely austere, a paradigm of priggishness. The voice that the actor assumes is akin to that of Noël Coward (Mr. Bedford is as expert in Coward as he is in Shakespeare), but with an added icing of imperiousness; one word can wither, an insult maim.

Quite early, Mr. Phillips, as director, and Mr. Bedford, as performer, let us see the petulance, the latent childishness, beneath the hauteur. Blustering on stage in his nightdress, as irate as Scrooge aroused by a ghost, he carries, half-concealed, a small stuffed animal. Do all Malvolios have such secret securities?

The bloated Sir Toby Belch and that sorry suitor Sir Andrew Aguecheek set their trap for Malvolio, a bogus love letter from his Lady Olivia. Enter Mr. Bedford, the perfect foil, plucking the petals from a daisy and murmuring she-love-me's and silently demanding a recount. Snatching a sealed envelope from the ground, he talks to it and cajoles it into surrendering its contents. With his line, "By your leave, wax," he literally addresses the envelope. Thus begins Malvolio's hilarious comeuppance.

Later, when Mr. Bedford reappears, absurdly gartered, he is a man unhinged. A pinched face unaccustomed to smiling is treated to a grin so broad and unseemly that it looks as if the man's cheeks will crack. Finally, when he is pushed to his fall, he is flabbergasted, for once at a loss for a comeback. Mr. Bedford, who also played Malvolio at Stratford in 1975, should be granted permanent tenure on the role.

In this production he is exceedingly well-matched by his blithefully deceitful

foes. Barry MacGregor's Sir Toby is a briny braggart, a tankard of genial disre-
pute. As Sir Andrew, Richard McMillan is a scarecrow teetering on toothpick legs.
A coward of "dormouse valor," he seems to be in a constant state of flight and agitation, his feet automatically leading him in a direction opposite to all potential
confrontation.

William Hutt plays Feste as an old fool, a semi-retired clown. He is the opposite of a jackanapes - a forlorn family retainer who exudes maturity and wisdom.
He is a cadger as well as a codger, always seeking to double his remuneration. The
performance, in common with the repeated solicitations for money, is irresistible.
In addition, Mr. Hutt, with a voice of Walter Huston warmth and venerability,
sings "O, Mistress Mine" and other lyrics.

In the center of the festival stage, the designer, Daphne Dare, has placed a
large open-meshed cage, a bower for hiding, eavesdropping and delivering asides.
As the men chauvinistically cavort, the bower is often filled with watchful women.
This *Twelfth Night* deals subtly with questions of male supremacy and female subjugation.

The evening is particularly fortunate in the choice of Patricia Conolly to play
Viola. In costume, she looks and acts with an appropriate boyishness, but she
never loses her spark of femininity. We readily understand why Orsino is smitten
- against his masculine will. When Ms. Conolly fluently executes her commission,
pleading Orsino's suit before Olivia, she has the passion of a Portia.

There are also helpful performances by Pat Galloway as Olivia, Kate Reid as
Maria, Jim McQueen as the lovesick Orsino and Lorne Kennedy as Viola's twin
brother. From the opening soliloquy to that conciliatory recognition scene, Mr.
Phillips's production proceeds with certitude and confidence - and in Mr. Bedford
it has a definitive Malvolio.

CYMBELINE: JANUARY 16, 1981

HARTFORD - Mark Lamos, the new artistic director of the Hartford Stage
Company, earned his reputation as the head of the California Shakespeare
Festival. For the third show of his first season in Connecticut, he has chosen to
direct that unwieldy epic *Cymbeline* and to put his credibility on the line in a single production.

That Mr. Lamos has staged a stirring *Cymbeline* is evidence of his ability and
his imagination as a director of Shakespeare and also of the extraordinary emotional power of Shakespeare in his final phase. *Cymbeline* is the second play of a
last quartet that includes *Pericles*, *The Winter's Tale* and *The Tempest*, works that are
usually linked as romances but might more accurately be called romantic adven-

tures. Each is a fanciful and even fantastic tale of exiles, lost children and the apparently dead returning to life.

Of the four, *Cymbeline* depends the most on coincidence and contrivance. Sudden, outlandish juxtapositions and scenes that could seem like travesties of other Shakespearean plays such as *Romeo and Juliet* all culminate in a climactic sequence of heartwarming reconciliation, a cascade of turnabouts that is unmatched even in other plays by Shakespeare.

Productions of this rarely revived play often emphasize the spectacle. A decade ago at the Stratford Festival, Ontario, in an otherwise excellent version, Jean Gascon prolonged the battle scenes; the play lasted almost four hours. A.J. Antoon's Central Park production was populated by "wild things" out of Maurice Sendak. At the outset of his production, Mr. Lamos has apparently made three clear-cut decisions: that the play is romantic, not tragic; that it must glide us swiftly to its embracing conclusion; and that the title might more justifiably be "Imogen," after old king Cymbeline's daughter, who is the heroine and the catalyst of the entire evening.

Led by the director, the audience keeps its eyes fixed on Imogen, as beautifully portrayed by Mary Layne, a vibrant new actress who has performed many major classical roles for Mr. Lamos at the California Shakespeare Festival. Ms. Layne is an ideal Imogen, a woman who can project innocence along with resilience - and can also articulate the Shakespearean language. As the character is overwhelmed by tumultuous events, the actress never loses her purity of vision. Even in that absurd scene in which Imogen awakens from a draught-induced sleep to discover a headless body, which she mistakes for her husband, Ms. Layne manages to be believable. Throughout, she is the essence of her adopted name, Fidele.

The company is large, and unevenly cast. Outstanding in small roles are Robert Cornthwaite as a faithful servant and William Wright as a banished lord. J.T. Walsh is stalwart as Imogen's mercurial husband, and Mark Capri delivers a playfully cavalier picture of Iachimo, a variation on Iago. Although Richard Mathews fades even further into the background than necessary as Cymbeline, and Barbara Bryne and Steven Ryan are one-dimensional villains, even the less-convincing actors are carried along in the tide of events.

Once the pieces of the plot are in place and the play is set on its course, the journey is inexorable, and the climax becomes a Shakespearean wellspring of joyful tears and laughter. Our pleasure comes from being several steps ahead of the characters. We watch the astonished reactions as revelation tumbles after revelation until Cymbeline awakens from his dotage to issue a pardon to everyone.

As designer, John Conklin has gracefully layered the large thrust stage with three enormous disks, plateaus as playing spaces, backed by silvered moon-shapes and silky tapestries. Décor and costumes, both by Mr. Conklin, glisten like medieval antiquities. They help us find our place in this tempestuous saga of reunion, forgiveness and universal redemption.

THE MERCHANT OF VENICE: AUGUST 2, 1981

LONDON - Reflecting the current English concern with royalty and history, this season the London theater has been reconsidering its own past - Shakespeare, his contemporaries and their immediate successors. In many ways this has been a celebratory time, with an abundance of classical poetry readings and a revival by the Royal Shakespeare Company of *The Hollow Crown*, its collage view of the monarchy. Not only Farquhar, but Ben Jonson, George Chapman, John Marston and Thomas Dekker have all been represented on various stages.

As for Shakespeare, this has not been an exceedingly auspicious period, and between the lines one can detect a certain boredom on the part of some English directors - a reaching for innovation at the expense of essence. In common, a number of current productions - of plays by Shakespeare and others - emphasize the role of the servant, of the lower classes; on local stages the aristocracy is being studied to its disadvantage.

One example of this trend is John Barton's version of *The Merchant of Venice* at the Royal Shakespeare Company, the most notable of the Shakespearean productions. Antonio and his cronies are a club of shallow snobs; they are also bad businessmen. It is only Shylock, played by David Suchet, who seems to know the basic rules of management. This is a strongly individualistic Shylock, who is in earnest about his contract with Antonio. When he wins, he really wants his pound of flesh. Mr. Suchet enters the Venetian courtroom carrying a scale and later sharpens a malevolent-looking butcher's knife - a compelling visual image. Shunned and abused by his society, which takes advantage of him in time of economic emergency but treats him as a lower species, he is an underdog who suddenly gains power. There is no appeal to this Shylock, not even on the grounds of mercy. Why should he be merciful to a Venice that has insulted him?

Mr. Suchet is a bold actor, one of the most promising of the younger members of the R.S.C., as he previously demonstrated at Stratford-on-Avon as a motorcycle-jacketed servant in *The Taming of the Shrew* and as a grotesque Caliban. He is unabashed in his belief in Shylock and unashamed by the stereotypical aspects of the character. He plays him neither for melodrama nor for sentimentality, but for his strength, as a man oppressed but not overcome. This is a pragmatic and resilient figure in a society that seems most concerned with living beyond one's means. In his confident approach, Mr. Suchet's Shylock reminds one of Laurence Olivier in the role.

Because the actor performs with such clear-eyed conviction, one wonders how he will react when Shylock is vanquished. He does not, in league with other Shylocks, bemoan his misfortune, but, with almost a twinkle in his eye, he accepts his fate. For all his earlier jubilation, as a realist he has remained a pessimist. In defeat he is "content," and we feel it as a matter of fact. Compared with a sentence of death, confiscation of property seems an endurable punishment. He will bide his time, and, we suspect, he will make his comeback.

For the present Shylock has met his match in Portia, played by Sinead Cusack as a woman bound by male propriety and prejudice. Ms. Cusack forcefully frees herself. She manipulates her suitors. When Bassanio appears in the person of handsome Jonathan Hyde, we can sense her trying to exude influence. When he chooses the correct casket, she is unleashed from arbitrary restraints. With a burst of passion, she picks up the caskets and the table they have rested on and actually flings them across the room. It is a symbolic gesture, like throwing open the windows in a stuffy drawing room or slamming a door on an unhappy marriage. Donning masculine disguise, the liberated Ms. Cusack becomes an authoritative person who is going to interpret the law to suit her sense of justice. Mr. Suchet and Ms. Cusack are the keystones of Mr. Barton's production, but there are also fine performances by Mr. Hyde, Corrina Seddon as Portia's servant and Rob Edwards as Launcelot Gobbo, who serves as a sardonic chorus.

Almost everything is right with Mr. Barton's *Merchant of Venice* and almost everything is wrong with Terry Hands's version of *Troilus and Cressida*. This complex and devious play has been camped up and broadened beyond all reason. Pandarus, trilling his r's as if he is singing Gilbert and Sullivan, becomes a merry old English auntie with a parasol. Agamemnon is a relentlessly pill-popping wreck of a general. Ajax demonstrates his strength by smashing orange crates as if he were Popeye's nemesis Bluto, an attitude that leaves the actor at sea when he has to behave with some intelligence. Paris and Helen are served by a mincing chorus of cupids and when Helen looks in a mirror, she cries (no wonder).

The relationship between Achilles and Patroclus has been underscored for blatant homosexuality and when Hector goes to Achilles's tent, there is no doubt about the erotic nature of the encounter. The role of Achilles is played by Mr. Suchet, often naked to the waist, his torso glistening as if he had been dipped in a vat of olive oil. Behind the preening, there is a glimmer of a characterization. Mr. Suchet and his fellow warriors are the dregs of dying civilizations, and none is as jaded as Achilles.

Troilus and Cressida is one of the most difficult Shakespeare plays to realize on stage -as exemplified by the Lincoln Center production some seasons ago in which a dead (stuffed) horse lay on stage as a symbol of the evening's ineptitude - but Mr. Hands has compounded the obstacles by overloading the system with gimmickry. The same director has taken a more reasonable approach to *As You Like It*, which has moved from Stratford to join *The Merchant of Venice* and *Troilus and Cressida* in repertory at the R.S.C. in London. *As You Like It* is twice blessed - with performances by Susan Fleetwood as Rosalind and Sinead Cusack as Celia.

KING LEAR: AUGUST 8, 1982

STRATFORD-ON-AVON - As a national center of theater, history and tourism, Britain's Stratford - the Royal Shakespeare Company's home away from London - crosses the bridge between tradition and experimentation. After several seasons, a Shakespeare play may be repeated but in a new and often inventive way, and the company is expanding its non-Shakespearean repertory continually to include other classics and, occasionally, modern plays. The troupe operates year-round in two theaters, one for large-scale productions, the other a small open space for intimate drama. This season *King Lear* and *Peer Gynt*, two Promethean masterpieces, are given bold dramatic treatment. Adrian Noble's production of *King Lear*, starring Michael Gambon on the Royal Shakespeare Company's mainstage, draws from a lavish palette of sights and sounds. Ron Daniels's *Peer Gynt*, starring Derek Jacobi on the company's Other Stage, is a chamber version of Ibsen's epic. Both achieve classic unities through an expenditure of imagination - on the part of directors and actors, and in the case of *Peer*, of the translator, the playwright David Rudkin.

Mr. Noble's *King Lear* begins with a tableau: the Fool and Cordelia sitting together on Lear's throne entwined in a cat's cradle of string, representing a child's game and perhaps a hangman's noose. As two sides of the King's conscience, they are metaphorically joined even unto death. The image is compelling, and it is followed by a *Lear* of remarkable expansiveness. There is far more to this version than Lear himself, with Mr. Noble accentuating the parallel story of Gloucester and his sons and placing extra emphasis on the role of the Fool. Mr. Gambon's Lear and Anthony Sher's Fool equally share, in Lear's words, "this great stage of fools," a line that is a hallmark of Mr. Noble's approach. Along with other characters such as Kent, Edgar and Edmund, the two are role-players who are carried away by their own performances. As the King, Lear can play the fool, and the fool is both coxcomb and wise man of the kingdom. Mr. Gambon is as willful as he is commanding, flexing his ego as he solicits testimony from his daughters, toying with Cordelia's suitors as he refers with almost incestuous envy to their "amorous sojourns." Abandoning responsibility while seeking to retain power, he calls for his Fool, who curtly puts him in his place.

Mr. Sher is a baggypants, bulb-nosed vaudeville clown and conjurer, who treats the King's court as his private circus. He enters to his own fanfare ("Da-dah!"), squeaking a toy violin. He remains much in evidence and the two cronies divide the spotlight (and even the curtain calls), with Mr. Gambon playing straight man - an eager diversion from his monarchical travail. Together they seek sanctuary in the wilderness, and the director places them high on a perch - like flagpole sitters - where they sit precariously as the world rushes by below them. It is an interesting variation on the scene in Peter Brook's *King Lear* where Paul Scofield sat on the ground like a lonely figure out of Beckett, surrounded by a hum of offstage activity. Mr. Gambon never sacrifices Lear's stature, and even as he succumbs to madness he has moments of blinding sanity.

It is Mr. Noble's provocative suggestion that in their last encounter, the Fool may have been accidentally wounded by Lear, as the King, in one frenzied spasm, unconsciously stabs him in the middle of an embrace. In the Fool's absence from the stage, we become even more conscious of Kent and Edgar (the latter, of course, with his father, Gloucester). All three of these roles are given performances of countervailing weight. When Malcolm Storry's Kent objects to Lear's cavalier banishment of Cordelia, it is with a patriot's cry of rage. When Jonathan Hyde's Edgar appears on the heath as Poor Tom, he explodes through the floor like a case of detonating dynamite. David Waller's Gloucester is a figure of nobility and passion. One measure of Mr. Noble's production is the persuasiveness of Kent and Edgar's charades. Each is unrecognizable in his assumed guise. Mr. Storry moves from military spit and polish to guerilla partisanship and Mr. Hyde becomes as grotesque as Caliban.

Although the drama is dominated by the men in the cast, Lear's daughters also stand out in bold, individual relief: Sara Kestelman's cold-blooded Goneril, Jenny Agutter's insidious Regan and a Cordelia by Alice Krige that exudes tenderness. In an otherwise uncluttered staging, the director falters once, with the intrusion of a stream on the apron of the stage, used for a variety of shallow dramatic devices (Edgar washes off Poor Tom's grime and later tries to drown his bastard brother).

Fresh from his triumph last season at the National Theater in the title role of Brecht's *Galileo*, Mr. Gambon now adds an eloquent Lear to his laurels.

In contrast, Derek Jacobi is an actor familiar to the American public, through his television appearances as *I, Claudius* and *Hamlet*. His *Peer Gynt* is a display of acting intelligence, ingenuity and self-effacement.

Along with Christopher Martin's longer two-part version of *Peer Gynt* at the CSC, Mr. Daniels's version is simple rather than spectacular. Stratford's gain is in the performance of Mr. Jacobi. He plays all divergent aspects of the multi-linear character, metamorphosing several times during the play's five acts. He begins the evening as a boyish upstart, a kind of Nordic Mickey Rooney with an English back country brogue. Next he becomes an outlaw initiated into the troll kingdom. By the fourth act, he is a robber baron, with Mr. Jacobi assuming the haughty manner of an imperialist.

The portrait is intentionally English; this *Peer* is a peer of the realm. Torn between conscience and self-preservation, he chooses a course of compromise, and the commentary, in Mr. Rudkin's version, is clearly intended to apply to England as well as Norway. In the final section of the play, as the hero returns to his native land and comes to terms with his "misused life," Mr Jacobi ages decades and becomes an Ibsen alter ego, in stovepipe hat and sideburns looking like a semblance of the playwright himself. Vocally, physically and emotionally, the role is demanding in the extreme, and the actor confidently rises to the challenge. He is helped enormously by Mr. Daniels and Mr. Rudkin, a collaborative team since Mr. Rudkin's *Ashes*. The director simplifies scene changes, but leaves no doubt about the locale, whether it is a rustic countryside or a shipwreck at sea. In fact, he does far more on a minimal budget than more elaborate ventures, such as the National Theater's opulent but empty approach to another picaresque tale, *Don Quixote*.

As for Mr. Rudkin, the alliance with Ibsen allows him to realize his own epic vision, advanced several seasons ago in his *Sons of Light*, an adventurous but inchoate attempt at a kind of fantastical folk theater. Unlike some of his contemporaries who work from literal translations and then try to superimpose their personality on a classic, Mr. Rudkin knows Norwegian and evidently feels a kinship with Ibsen. This tale of a global search for self shares some of the gnarled poetry of *Sons of Light*, as clarified by Ibsen's unwavering perception. Rudkin and Ibsen are a most compatible team and Mr. Jacobi is their astute interpreter. The other actors play diverse roles, with assiduous work from Brenda Peters, Derek Godfrey and Sinead Cusack as Peer's abandoned mistress and troll princess.

RICHARD III: AUGUST 12, 1984

STRATFORD-ON-AVON - The key to Antony Sher's daring performance as Richard III is a pair of crutches. Glistening like highly burnished ebony bones, they become an extension of Richard's maimed physique and perverted psyche. Mr. Sher's Richard becomes stronger because of his incapacity; the crutches are a compensation, and he uses them to their utmost advantage. They make him the equivalent of a bionic king. He is as quick with his crutches as he is with his wit. They are his sword and battering ram, prod, whipsaw and vaulting pole. He is a jet-propelled projectile, flying across the stage to pinion an opponent. Always in earnest, he can also be fiendishly playful, holding the crutches in front of his face and peering through them as if they form a fan. In every regard, they enlarge his opportunity for dastardy, and they serve as a twin scepter of office.

In performance, what could be considered simply an actor's choice - like a hat or a false nose - becomes a concept. Crutches define the character and the playwright. This is the most mobile and physically aggressive Richard within my memory; he is very much a man of action. In his hands, these supports are so integral to his performance that when Richard is unseated in battle, one almost expects him to cry not for a horse but for his crutches.

The Richard that Mr. Sher has created in collaboration with his director, Bill Alexander, is the centerpiece of a Stratford season that, for the most part - for better or for worse - buttresses theatrical tradition. The 1984 Henry V, Kenneth Branagh, is as heroic as Richard is villainous. As played by Ian McDiarmid, Shylock, in the weakest of the company's three Shakespearean productions, is an unsuccessful attempt at revivifying the stereotypical moneylender. On the company's second stage, the Other Place, Pam Gems offers the old coughing Camille. However, Louise Page's *Golden Girls* - along with *Richard III*, a work of persuasive merit - is a study of the changing and challenging role of women in sports.

Mr. Sher eschews any attempt to be charming. Savoring his own malice, he manipulates his way step by step to the top as if climbing a pyramid. For him, murder and marriage are equally justified political expediencies. In this unabashed attempt at incarnating evil, Mr. Sher is monstrously convincing, a Richard that is guaranteed to cause others to cringe. Skittering across stage he resembles various venomous creatures - from spiders to vipers. The physicalization leads to an emotional identification. When he and Lady Anne are seen briefly with bare shoulders, he seems to have retained his hump. His eyes are also of enormous aid in evoking the spirit of Richard, darting feverishly with a madman's glint. As for his voice, it is a carefully modulated instrument with a vibrato of range and depth.

Necessarily, Mr. Sher carries the production on his back. Except for Malcolm Storry who emphasizes Buckingham as a political animal of a smoother stripe, Brian Blessed and a few others, the actors are not contestants in Mr. Sher's court. The women, in particular, fade, and the dimmest is Penny Downie's Lady Anne. This limited support blurs the background but does not detract from Mr. Sher's brilliant impersonation.

Last year at Stratford, he played the Fool to Michael Gambon's Lear. They shared the stage and the play equally; Mr. Sher's Fool was a baggypants vaudeville clown and kind of shadow king, with Mr. Gambon as his straight man. For Mr. Sher, *Richard III* is a further Olympian leap.

As this season's ascendant star, Mr. Sher is one of several skillful new actors appearing to advantage on Stratford's two stages. The Royal Shakespeare Company seems to have a constant replenishment of talent. As actors move up in the company - or sidewards to the National Theater - other newcomers assume their positions. This is also the summer of Mr. Branagh, making his Royal Shakespeare debut as Henry V, a king of youthful exuberance, monarchically speaking the very opposite of Richard III.

Introduced to West End audiences several season ago in the role of a Cambridge University student in *Another Country*, he moves with assurance into the classic lineaments of the warrior king. As with *Richard*, the production is not seamless; it is strong in court, less secure in the tavern. But Mr. Branagh is well-outfitted to carry the kingly standard, whether it is spreading a little Harry in the night, thundering on the battlefield or wooing the discreet Princess of France. In a subtly unadorned production, Adrian Noble, the most consistently imaginative of the company's younger directors, has filled the stage with the white heat and fire of heroism.

TITUS ANDRONICUS: AUGUST 16, 1987

STRATFORD-ON-AVON, ENGLAND - Revenge abounds on Stratford stages this season, beginning in the Swan Theater with a visceral production of *Titus Andronicus*, Shakespeare's bloodiest tragedy, and extending to the mainstage where Antony Sher is performing *The Merchant of Venice* and *Twelfth Night* in repertory. Though the spotlight is on Mr. Sher after his inspired *Richard III*, the most notable production is *Titus Andronicus*, as directed by Deborah Warner and as acted by a cast headed by Brian Cox. With this production, Ms. Warner, founder of the small classical Kick Theater Company, makes an auspicious debut at the Royal Shakespeare Company, and Mr. Cox adds further certification to his position in the front ranks of English actors.

The Stratford *Titus* is a headlong plunge into the heart of a piercingly dramatic tale of savagery and vengeance, albeit one of the least performed of Shakespeare's plays. I first saw *Titus* many years ago in London in the legendary Peter Brook version, starring Laurence Olivier in the title role, Vivien Leigh as Titus's maimed daughter, Lavinia, and Anthony Quayle as the amoral Aaron the Moor. That particular performance was made additionally memorable by the fact that Winston Churchill was also in the audience, murmuring Titus's lines along with Olivier.

While one could not pretend that any production could match the Brook version, or, rather, what seems to be one's memory of it, the current Stratford production is close to that mark - and the Swan, as a reproduction of a Shakespearean theater, is its ideal setting. At the Swan, the audience is enveloped in the tragedy, rather than being distanced from it, as is sometimes the case on the main Stratford stage. With the barest of scenery and props, the play communicates so directly that theatergoers in the front rows occasionally flinch from all the stage blood and thunder. This is, of course, the play where half the characters lose their lives, or, at least, a limb. In the Grand Guignol conclusion, Titus, dressed in a butcher's apron and looking like a fugitive from an abattoir, serves the loathesome Tamora a pie whose ingredients include her jackal-like sons.

Though a director could emphasize the play's grotesqueries, Ms. Warner goes in the opposite direction, playing *Titus* for its heightened reality - and Mr. Cox is her powerful spokesman. His Titus is a peasant warrior, grizzled, plain-spoken and given to outrageous fits of temperament. He believes, wrongly, that his first obligation is to the head of the Roman state, and it is only after others have committed several murderous deeds that he becomes aware of a greater responsibility. Taking revenge, Mr. Cox becomes a tank on the warpath. Stocky, stolid, the actor looks like a huge blunt object, and when, at the play's conclusion, Derek Hutchinson, playing his sole surviving son, picks up the dead Titus in his arms, one marvels at the younger actor's strength. Mr. Cox is the opposite, in all senses, of a light Titus. The performance is, in fact, one step from *Lear*.

In addition to Mr. Hutchinson, others in the cast are equally striking, starting with Estelle Kohler's Tamora. The actress plays her character not as a wicked witch, but as a queenly bird of prey, at once sensual and manipulative. As her sons, Piers Ibbotson and Richard McCabe are as repulsive a pair of villains as could be imagined, and there are also resilient performances by Peter Polycarpou as Aaron, Donald Sumter as Titus's temperate brother and Sonia Ritter as the tragically abused Lavinia.

Without fanfare, Mr. Cox, follows up his Titus with a change of pace in Doug Lucie's *Fashion*, one of several contemporary plays alternating at Stratford's small studio theater, the Other Place. In this unrelenting indictment of political image-making and cut-throat business as usual, Mr. Cox plays a tough, career-minded advertising man, someone with no interior life. In the play's "hit and run culture" everyone is on his guard against backstabbing - although Mr. Cox's character seems to court danger.

Quite Mr. Cox's equal is Alun Armstrong as a once-celebrated film director (and socialist) emerging from a state of alcoholism to make a propaganda film for Mr. Cox in support of the conservative government. Mr. Armstrong warms to the promotional project to such a degree that Mr. Cox can say "You're not just selling out. You're having a grand closing-down sale." The play is filled with pithy satiric comments ("Advertising is the revenge of business on culture"), as one would expect from the author of *Progress*, a scathing play about social activism in Britain. In tandem with Caryl Churchill's *Serious Money*, *Fashion* reveals a harder line of cynicism among English playwrights.

For a lighter theatrical sport, one has to turn to a playwright from the past, James Shirley, a 17th-century author of comedies of manners, as well as revenge tragedies. One of his comedies, *Hyde Park*, has been resurrected at the Swan. According to the program, the last professional production of the play was in 1668 - and that is a serious oversight. This is a still lively, youthful play about romantic hunters and huntresses in London's dashing set, young people who seem to tumble in and out of love. Fiona Shaw and Alex Jennings are at the center of this romp as a kind of James Shirley version of Beatrice and Benedick. In his production, Barry Kyle has moved the play from the 17th-century to the Bloomsbury period, which would seem suitable to a world in which everyone was - or could pretend to be - a courtier. One wonders if the director might not have gone the whole distance and placed *Hyde Park* in modern dress as a tale about the trendy Sloane

Ranger crowd of today. *Hyde Park* was one of some 40 plays written by Shirley, who must be regarded as an authentic R.S.C. rediscovery.

THE WARS OF THE ROSES: JUNE 7, 1988

STAMFORD, Conn. - Deep into *Henry VI*, a soldier unknowingly slays his father and another soldier unknowingly slays his son. Sitting on the ground, watching in horror, Henry VI seems to mourn his life, his country and the way of the world. The moment - along with scores of others - illuminates Shakespeare's view of history endlessly repeating itself, a succession of wars, pitting countryman against countryman, nation against nation. Beseiged by broken promises and infinite cycles of revenge, the warriors never seem to learn from Shakespeare's words, "Ill blows the wind that profits nobody."

Watching the English Shakespeare Company's marathon performance of *The Wars of the Roses* - presented here this weekend under the auspices of the Stamford Center for the Arts - one is rewarded by a comprehensive overview of English history (as interpreted by England's greatest poet) and of Shakespeare's history plays.

In a marathon lasting more than 23 hours, seven unrelated plays were performed, *Richard II*, followed by *Henry IV, Parts I and II*, *Henry V* and the three *Henry VI* plays distilled to two, followed by *Richard III*. It was, in all senses, a prodigious undertaking, most of all for the indefatigable actors but also for those theatergoers who experienced the complete and indispensable Shakespearean event.

Taken together, the plays clarify both history and theater, with an arc that reaches from the effete Richard II to the diabolical Richard III, traversing an England that finds a hero in Henry V and then wanders under the aimless rule of his son Henry VI. From play to play, we see the gradual development of character, most indelibly with Henry V and Richard III.

Though Richard loses not one iota of his malevolence, meeting him first in *Henry VI* he is seen in context as a creature of his society. The people who surround him are almost as demonic as he is. Encountering Queen Margaret in her youth, one realizes the depths of her malice. Similarly, Richard's brother, Edward IV, assuming power, is marked by his own air of arrogance. While Richard III is seen (and understood) in his totality, other less familiar figures are introduced in the seldom performed but rousing *Henry VI* plays, including Henry VI himself, a decent man and an inept king, and Joan of Arc, who in Shakespeare's version is a victim of a tragic flaw.

Though the new company, under the co-artistic direction of Michael Bogdanov and Michael Pennington, thins out a bit in subsidiary roles, it has a resilience and, as is essential for repertory, it has a remarkable versatility. Mr. Pennington, who has been seen to great advantage with the Royal Shakespeare Company at Stratford-on-Avon, outshines his previous accomplishments, playing Richard II, Prince Hal and Henry V, as well as a variety of minor roles from a doddering ancient to a punk version of the rebel Jack Cade in *Henry VI*. His finest hour is at Agincourt as a bold Henry V, and it is no disparagement to suggest that his energy seemed somewhat depleted by the end of the marathon when he played Buckingham in *Richard III*. For Mr. Pennington, the marathon is a feat of artistry as well as of memory.

His performances are matched by those of Andrew Jarvis. Because of his striking appearance - he is a young bald actor - Mr. Jarvis is always distinguishable in the ensemble, as he works his way toward Richard III by playing assassins as well as the petulant Dauphin. In character as Richard, he steadily ascends in the role, until, with a vicious and triumphant smile, he commands center stage and the kingdom.

Among the other formidable performances are Barry Stanton's Falstaff (in his modernized costume, he is the beefiest Beefeater one has ever seen); John Castle, who moves from a severe Henry IV to a low-comic Pistol; Chris Hunter's volatile portrayal of Hotspur and other hotheads; Mary Rutherford's Joan of Arc, and Paul Brennen's appropriately weak-willed Henry VI, who keeps reminding us that he became King when he was but 9 months old.

Authoritative behind the scenes is Mr. Bogdanov, who directed all seven plays and filtered them through his own historical perspective. It is his intention to describe the universality of the events, and in so doing he cues the audience with anachronisms. From a mid-19th-century *Richard II*, he moves slowly - and sometimes jarringly - into the present. By *Richard III*, we are in modern times.

Frequently, the director interjects either a contemporary note or its reverse, a classical reminder. A knight in chain mail appears in the company of doughboys, and contemporary music often counterpoints the action. The approach is not as intrusive as it may sound. It acts to keep the audience - and the actors - on their toes, and, caught up by the method, theatergoers may discover their own references. When the Duchess of Gloucester goes to a soothsayer to foresee events, it is barely a leap to a contemporary parallel. In any case, the quality of the acting overcomes any doubts one may have about the directorial concept.

The Wars of the Roses is a monumental achievement in which the whole is even greater than its considerable parts. One's only regret is that the marathon was a one-time-only presentation in Stamford. Continuing its international tour, the company will play the York Festival in England. In New York, as in Stamford, it could have been its own festival.

When Charles Dale's Richmond unites the Houses of Lancaster and York at the end of *Richard III* - in Mr. Bogdanov's version he addresses a battery of television cameras - and says, "The day is ours," he could also be speaking for himself and his colleagues in the English Shakespeare Company. After an intensive week-end of non-stop Shakespeare, the days and nights are theirs.

KING LEAR: APRIL 4, 1990

Robert Sturua's extraordinary production of *King Lear* is so unyielding in its intensity that one can see why the Rustaveli Theater Company from Soviet Georgia might regard Shakespeare as its national playwright. This distinguished company began an all too brief one-week engagement on Monday at the Brooklyn Academy of Music's Majestic Theater.

In Mr. Sturua's version, the play begins with everyone waiting for Lear. The court assembles in what appears to be the remains of a once-elegant theater. Standing at attention, the characters become impatient at the interminable delay. The Duke of Albany faints. Finally Lear shuffles onstage, carrying a birdcage and totally oblivious to his court.

Like a dictator in his dotage, Lear publicly indulges his fancies, alternately favoring and badgering his daughter Cordelia. Finally, as he divides his kingdom, he becomes diabolical. He seems to act foolishly, but he is no fool, as the actor Ramaz Tchkhikvadze unveils an unpredictable and penetrating portrait of a king who will never really abdicate.

Though the language is Georgian, the actors are in modernized dress and the ending of the play has been altered. It is not an idiosyncratic interpretation like Lee Breuer's recent gender-switching version (situated in the American state of Georgia), but a splendidly acted production that reaches to the heart of the tragedy of self-deception and of suffering leading to self-knowledge.

Even while conveying the bleakness of *King Lear* (and any comparisons to the Soviet Union under Stalin are there for the audience to make), the actors unearth comedy. At moments, Mr. Tchkhikvadze is disarmingly funny, like the cartoon Little King or a despotic Hollywood tycoon who can and will humiliate anyone he pleases. Anger suddenly replacing affection, he strikes Cordelia as if she were an unruly pet, then he embraces her - and she reciprocates. Within his family, he remains an often inclement force of nature, and Goneril and Regan endure his shenanigans, at least until they assume control.

Once the daughters are in power, they mimic the old man and return his unkindness in full, driving him from court. In Mr. Sturua's interpretation, Goneril and Regan are not wicked witches. They are glamorous creatures, a match in beauty with the fair Cordelia. In their elegant plumage, they stand out against the monochromatic background of Mirian Mshvelidze's scenic design.

Without using elaborate devices, the director and designer are imaginative in their production detail and their imagery, creating storms without thundersheets, using lighting to impale characters and taking advantage of the theater-within-a-theater framework. In the starkness of the approach, the production is comparable to that of Peter Brook's *Lear.*

In the role of Gloucester, the actor Avtandil Makharadze, portly and bushy-bearded, looks fleetingly like the late Zero Mostel, and in his confusion over which of his two sons to favor one can see a semblance of that American actor at work. He finds comedy within paternal perplexity while not ignoring the man's blind despair. Naturally Gloucester makes the wrong choice, listening to the crafty Edmund (a jaunty figure in formal attire) rather than Edgar, who seems like a modern version of the young Prince Hal.

Eventually the Gloucester subplot is subordinated as Mr. Sturua focuses on the King and his retinue in exile: Edgar transformed into Poor Tom; the worthy Kent (as stalwart as in other productions) and Zhanri Lolashvili's Fool. With great tufts of hair covering each ear, Mr. Lolashvili looks like a clown in alarm. He is more active than pensive (as is the production itself), and not one who easily suffers Lear's abuses.

In this three-hour production there are questionable directorial choices, beginning with the background music, which sometimes seems like a 1950's movie soundtrack. The translation over headphones becomes more of an encumbrance than an aid. A voice selectively summarizes events and occasionally speaks a soliloquy, in the latter instance reminding us of the language we are missing.

For those who do not understand Georgian, this is, of course, a *King Lear* without Shakespeare's words. But as with Ingmar Bergman's *Hamlet* and Akira Kurosawa's film adaptations of Shakespeare, Mr. Sturua's *King Lear* transcends language barriers.

Mr. Bergman ended his *Hamlet* with Fortinbras's storm troopers taking over Elsinore. Mr. Sturua ends his *Lear* with Lear dragging out a dead Cordelia and sitting in the middle of a field of carnage. After his mournful howl, he remains the only man alive, forced to face his own self-victimization and the destruction of his kingdom. With a shudder, the setting - the theater as scenery - begins to fall apart. As expressed by Mr. Sturua, the conclusion of *King Lear* is a fearful vision of the apocalypse.

KING JOHN: AUGUST 7, 1988

STRATFORD-ON-AVON - Women directors are in the ascendancy at Stratford this season. Last year, Deborah Warner made her Royal Shakespeare Company debut with her stunning production of *Titus Andronicus* (starring Brian Cox). That production has since moved to the small Pit Theater in the company's London home, the Barbican. Ms. Warner has followed up that initial success with her Stratford production of *King John*, once again demonstrating her ability to vivify one of Shakespeare's lesser works. At the same time this season, Garry Hynes (an Irish director and a company-founder of the Druid Theater in Galway) has made her own Stratford debut with *The Man of Mode*, an acerbic Restoration comedy by George Etherege. Di Trevis, by comparison an R.S.C. veteran, offers as her seasonal contribution a mainstage production of *Much Ado About Nothing*. Ms. Trevis's exuberant revival of *The Revenger's Tragedy* recently completed its engagement in the Pit, where it ran along with Ms. Warner's *Titus Andronicus*.

The three are on the crest of a wave of women directors. Sarah Pia Anderson also directs for the R.S.C. and Janice Honeyman has just staged Athol Fugard's *Hello and Goodbye* in a special R.S.C. collaboration with the Almeida Theater. This season two first-rank British actresses, Judi Dench and Geraldine McEwan, directed Shakespeare plays for Kenneth Branagh's Renaissance Theater, and other women are represented at various Fringe Theaters.

Of all the English women, Ms. Warner is the one who has made the greatest impact. As demonstrated by both *Titus Andronicus* and *King John*, she has a visceral sense of theatricality. In her hands, plays draw an immediate responsiveness from the audience. With *Titus Andronicus* and *King John*, we share the heat and lightning of the performance (and on a summer evening we also share the warmth in Stratford's Other Place Theater).

"Zeal" is a prevalent word in Shakespeare's version of King John's reign (a history play that omits all mention of the Magna Carta). As played by Nicholas Woodeson, King John is zealous about improving his political advantage, even to having himself crowned twice, and the bastard Philip Faulconbridge, as played by David Morrissey, is hot-blooded and hot-headed. Usually considered a patriot, Faulconbridge becomes a zealot in this production, shifting his allegiance in order to remain on the firing line.

Mr. Woodeson's performance in the title role is the fulcrum of the production. Napoleonic in stature, garbed in an oversized great coat, he looks like Maurice Sendak's storybook Max in battle dress when he is crowned king of the Wild Things. Like Max, Mr. Woodeson's sometimes childlike John is surrounded by a rumpus, which he controls by the force of his personality. At the same time, the King still reflects the will of his formidable mother (Cherry Morris) and he is antagonistic to Constance (Susan Engel), mother to his nephew and rival, Arthur (Lyndon Davis, who played Michael Gambon as a young man in television's

Singing Detective). As movingly portrayed by Ms. Engel, Constance has a firm dedication to purpose (installing her son on the throne in place of John). Ms. Engel exudes conviction. If the son had had half the driving ambition of his mother, he might have been able to supplant the king.

In the background are two other women of authority, Faulconbridge's mother and a Spanish princess able to juggle loyalties to various warring soverigns. Led by Constance, *King John* has more important roles for women than most other, more popular Shakespearean plays. This may have been one of the attractions of the work for the director, but more than anything else she seems fascinated by the intricate political canvas. Instead of battle scenes there are repeated peace negotiations. At the brink of war, there is always someone to offer a conciliatory solution, marital or martial. In this sense, the play wears its relevance like a coat of mail. We can see in the stalemated confrontations between England and France, between church and state, a reflection of our own times.

Although nothing can completely disguise the contrivances of the play, the rough hewn *King John* remains captivating, and the actors throw themselves into the fray, igniting the unadorned atmostphere with panoply and fervor. Ms. Warner has seemingly collected all the ladders in Stratford and neighboring communities for the production. They become a barricade as well as ramparts and, in one case, a treaty table. The only other prominent scenery is an assortment of hard-backed chairs, which leads one to regard this as a chairs-and-ladders production. Ms. Warner emphasized the gamesmanship of the contest - *King John* as power play. She works so imaginatively in the tight confines of Stratford's Other Place and the Barbican's Pit that one wonders how she would approach a mainstage Shakespearean production. She would, one assumes, bring new energy to that environment.

Ms. Trevis's mainstage *Much Ado About Nothing* is standard fare. It was just a few years ago that the R.S.C. offered a version with Derek Jacobi as Benedick and Sinead Cusack as Beatrice, and there would not seem to be a need for a new Stratford *Much Ado* so soon. But the play is a consistent crowd-pleaser, and the audience seems pleased with the broad antics of Clive Merrison and Maggie Steed, the B&B of this season. Mr. Merrison is a sour-tempered Benedick. Ms. Steed is more animated than her partner, but her strength is more that of a compulsive comedienne than a witty Beatrice. There is little sexual chemistry between these two lovers. They and the production are overshadowed by the Kevin Kline-Blythe Danner version recently in Central Park. There are stalwart performances, however, by David Lyon and Ralph Fiennes as Don Pedro and Claudio, and a mirthful one by David Waller as Dogberry. Ms. Trevis has unconvincingly transported the play to 20th-century Italy, where militiamen of vaguely World War I variety drop out of the sky. This is one Shakespeare play that rarely benefits from transplantation.

For a clearer view of Ms. Trevis's directorial capabilities, there was Cyril Tourneur's *Revenger's Tragedy*, which moved to the Pit from Stratford.

Spearheaded by the galvanic performance of Antony Sher in the title role, counterpointed by Nicholas Farrell as his chief foe, *The Revenger's Tragedy* filled the small R.S.C. theaters with blind retribution and black humor.

Sharing the main stage with *Much Ado* are a revival of Adrian Noble's *Macbeth* and Nicholas Hytner's new production of *The Tempest*. Returning to England's classical theater after an absence of 10 years, John Wood is a commanding Prospero. Duncan Bell is a haunting Ariel. But the production lacks the requisite sense of magic. The play is precariously aligned on a steeply raked stage, and the minimal scenery and sudden shifts in lighting do little to enhance the mood. Deep within, there may be an attempt to reduce the play to essentials, to create a kind of Samuel Beckett *Endgame* out of Prospero's plight. If so, such a concept is unfulfilled. The production is marked by its lassitude.

The other noteworthy event at Stratford, in addition to *King John* is *The Man of Mode*, a malicious comedy about style and sexism. The play is a challenging choice for Ms. Hynes, but Etherege's theme does allow for commentary from all corners, and she has given the play an ecumenical reading, with each character receiving his or her comeuppance. The title character, Sir Fopling Flutter, does not appear until the play is well in progress, but his spirit - luxuriously exemplified by the actor Simon Russell Beale - is infectious. Sir Fopling, an oafish Englishman turned Paris dandy, makes a case for "mode" (what today might be called attitude), one that is expressed in alternative fashion by the play's anti-hero, Dorimant (Miles Anderson).

Dorimant is a duplicitous seducer devoted to the art of the chase and unchastened by the selfishness of his escapades. The character finally suffers his fate (marriage) at the hands of an heiress (Amanda Root) who will not settle for morality à la mode. In the role, Ms. Root is a clear-eyed and determined challenger, and Mr. Anderson's Dorimant is, to a great extent, her victim.

In Ms. Hynes's otherwise exemplary production, there is one instance of miscasting and there is a dubious scenic choice. Holes are torn in the walls, ostensibly to symbolize the fact that the society is so devoted to gossip and voyeurism. The result is that the set simply looks in need of refurbishing. Ms. Hynes's command of the comedy is stylish, and, like Ms. Warner's contribution, unaffected. There are no intrusive anachronisms, but there are contemporary parallels for us to draw.

HAMLET: AUGUST 20, 1989

LONDON - In Richard Eyre's production of *Hamlet* at the National Theater (starring Daniel Day-Lewis in the title role), Polonius (Michael Bryant) was giving instructions to his aide Reynaldo. Suddenly Mr. Bryant stopped speaking, then said, as if in a daze, "I was about to say something," and searched his mind for his place in the play. Finally, after an extended pause, he asked, "Where did I leave?" The actor playing Reynaldo reminded him, "At 'closes in the consequence,' at 'friends or so,' and 'gentlemen,'" and Mr. Bryant picked up the thread of the conversation.

The moment, of course, is direct from the text. I have heard many actors play this scene with believable absent-mindedness, but when Mr. Bryant did it, it was startling. The actor waited so long between the apparent memory loss and his request for help that there was an audible murmur in the audience. Was it Polonius or Mr. Bryant who had forgotten his lines? Actually Mr. Bryant was word perfect in his Shakespeare. Soon after the performance, I happened to see an English actress of my acquaintance and described the moment to her. She said, admiringly, "Michael does that every night!"

Something similar happened years ago when Laurence Olivier was playing in Strindberg's *Dance of Death*. At one point, the actor - in character - fell to the floor as if struck by lightning. The moment was so sudden and convincing that theatergoers thought the actor had suffered a stroke in mid-performance, a fact that, as I remember, was reported in the daily press. Lord Olivier was able to repeat that "stroke" night after night. Some years later, in Harold Pinter's *No Man's Land*, Ralph Richardson was also called upon to fall down and he stumbled with such verisimilitude that it seemed as if Sir Ralph, not the character, had toppled.

With all three actors, Lord Olivier, Sir Ralph and Mr. Bryant, life seemed to be imitating art when actually the reverse was true in the extreme. Each of the actors was swept away by his role onto a mysterious plane where theater could not be distinguished from reality. The result is a performance of intense identification.

Because of Mr. Bryant's impassioned portrayal of Polonius, we hear some lines as if for the first time, an unusual thing to say about Polonius, who is of course one of the most familiar figures in all of dramatic literature. No longer is Polonius a fussbudget; in Mr. Bryant's interpretation he is an immensely concerned parent in great distress about both of his offspring. One feels that concern not only in his admonition to Laertes but in his irate charge to Ophelia that she is being naïve in accepting Hamlet's "tenders of affection." It is possible, in Mr. Bryant's remarkable performance, to view the events at Elsinore through the eyes of Polonius.

In this production there is a second commanding performance - by Judi Dench as Gertrude. She is sensual with Claudius, maternal with Hamlet, confused about her identity and dazzled by her son's evident dementia. Although Mr. Day-Lewis has several striking moments as Hamlet, his performance does not have the riveting immediacy exemplified by his two older colleagues.

Both Mr. Bryant and Dame Judi are among a phalanx of experienced English actors who with an astonishing consistency seem to elevate whatever production they happen to be in - Mr. Bryant last year as Prospero at the National, Dame Judi the previous year as Cleopatra. It is heartening to realize in a season marked by the death of Lord Olivier that the great English acting tradition survives, as versatile actors continue to challenge themselves in classics on stage. This summer, one could see - and enjoy - Alan Bates and Felicity Kendal, Juliet Stevenson, Edward Petherbridge, Jim Broadbent and, in a modern play, Prunella Scales.

When such actors return for a single play or a seasonal repertory, the English are eager to receive them. On Broadway, actors of this stature would be more hesitant about making a commitment - a hesitancy shared by producers - and audiences would want to be sure that the production itself was a critical success.

In London, theatergoers are more willing to go along with proven favorites, especially, one might add, with actresses like Ms. Kendal and Ms. Scales who are television stars as well as theater artists. There is of course a reverse side - actors may choose a vehicle, spin-offs of television roles, stage sitcoms or creaky thrillers, all of which are staples in London. It was not so long ago that Donald Sinden triumphed on the West End as King Lear. This year he is appearing in *Over My Dead Body*, which, undiminished by disastrous notices, continues to cater to a nondiscriminating public.

Mr. Bates and Ms. Kendal shared star billing in a repertory pairing of *Much Ado About Nothing* and *Ivanov*," both staged by Elijah Mojinsky. For *Much Ado*, the director transposed the play to a sunny land that resembled the border between Mexico and Texas, with bare wood furniture that might have been at home at a taco stand.

In spite of the disconcerting décor and a vaguely modernized directorial approach, the two actors pitched themselves into their roles with gusto, even to playing upon the fact that each was a bit too old for Benedick and Beatrice, peering with feigned myopia at each other's love letters. After enduring performances by attitudinizing young actors in the title roles of *Hamlet* and *Romeo and Juliet* at Stratford-on-Avon, it was refreshing to be greeted by the assurance and articulation of Mr. Bates and Ms. Kendal.

At the National, Ms. Stevenson is playing a particularly headstrong *Hedda Gabler*, clearly the most charismatic person in her conservative community. Howard Davies's production is in the Olivier Theater, the largest of the company's three houses, and the director has unwisely filled the stage with a set that looks more like a public library reading room than the parlor of the Tesman home. In the middle of the stage is a towering - and teetering - staircase, which creaks every time Hedda goes upstairs. But Ms. Stevenson's performance overrides such distractions, and she is ably abetted by Suzanne Burden, who lends a vitality to the often colorless role of Thea Elvsted.

In his book, *Being an Actor*, Simon Callow expresses an actor's lament: the subjugation of the performer in a theater increasingly dominated by directors who place concept above all and regard themselves as the theatrical equivalent of auteurs on film. Mr. Callow refers to this as a rule by "directocracy."

One of the most delightful performances in London this season is given by Ms. Scales in *Single Spies*, Alan Bennett's double package of espionage stories. The two plays are staged by Mr. Bennett and Mr. Callow, each of whom are also actors. As directors, they disarm the directocracy; they are less superimposers than the actors' encouragers and accomplices. In the second play, Ms. Scales, best known for playing Sybil Fawlty on television's *Fawlty Towers*, transforms herself into Queen Elizabeth II. Marching through the Queen's picture gallery with that titled traitor, Sir Anthony Blunt (Mr. Bennett), she gives a performance that is both a spoof and a tribute. Impersonating Her Majesty with regal humor, she exemplifies the actor's art as well as acting at its most English.

THE NOBLE LOOK AT STRATFORD-ON-AVON: NOVEMBER, 1991

There is a sense of sorrowful self-awareness behind the heartiness of Robert Stephens's Falstaff. Roistering with Prince Hal and boasting about his imaginary exploits as a highwayman and military hero, he is a rogue for whom deceit is as natural as eating and drinking. For all his manipulativeness, he is not a self-deceiver. Hal's eventual rejection of him is of course the most crushing of weights, but in Stephens's double-edged performance, it does not come as a complete surprise. Falstaff has been the architect of his own defeat.

While not overlooking the goodly portliness of his character, Stephens never allows Falstaff to become a cheerful Father Christmas. Instead he charts an introspective course that leads him to locate and to define the concealed side of Falstaff. With his thickly padded girth, he does not look like himself, and his familiar fluty voice seems to be pitched at a lower level. Face, figure, manner and intonation unite in a portrait with a majestic grandeur. A true knight and not a bogus one, Falstaff even looks spiffy when attired in his military uniform. He is like a king trapped within the body of a clown, and he will suffer the consequences of a life of excess.

Stephens's astute portrait is the linchpin of Adrian Noble's ambitious paired productions of *Henry IV, Parts One and Two* at Stratford-on-Avon. He dominates the plays and Hal himself. The actor who is second to him in importance is, surprisingly, not Michael Maloney as Hal, but Julian Glover in the title role. Maloney previously played the gardening columnist accidently turned war correspondent in the television version of Evelyn Waugh's *Scoop*. Unfortunately, a measure of the Waughian wimpishness intrudes on Maloney's Hal. When he vows to his father that he will redeem himself and the family name, he does not persuade us of his latent gift for leadership.

In contrast, Glover remains a steely and commanding presence, even as he is overtaken by his illness. One feels that, given a magical turnabout in his health, Glover could once again assume the full authority of his regal office. This is not a weak-willed king, but forever Bolingbroke, the man who usurped the crown from Richard II and is ready to be the nemesis of any future usurper. As is seldom the case, the performance in the role of Henry IV justifies the title of the play, which in other hands could more accurately be called "Prince Hal, Parts One and Two."

Noble, the incoming artistic director of the Royal Shakespeare Company, has brought to the plays a visual ingenuity and a Shakespearean veracity, demonstrated in previous Stratford seasons in such plays as *King Lear* and *Antony and Cleopatra* (both starring Michael Gambon). In contrast to the New York Shakespeare Festival production of the two Henry plays last season, the English director grounds the work in finely detailed authenticity before expressing his own artistic personality. His Shakespeare has a Noble look - painterly, panoramic and, at moments, breathtaking.

In *Henry IV*, collaborating with Bob Crowley as scenic designer, he creates stage pictures that look like antique engravings of scenes from Shakespeare. This is especially true when Falstaff is cavorting in pubs and bawdy houses. At one point, the curtain parts to reveal a two-tiered cross-section of London lowlife, the rooms of a bordello crowded with boiterous activity. The effect is like an animated version of Hogarth's *Rake's Progress*. In terms of his environmental authority, Noble is the equal of Peter Stein, as demonstrated in Stein's production of Verdi's *Falstaff* for the Welsh National Opera. The landscape shifts dramatically in Noble's battle scenes. Swords clang and shouts ring out. One can feel the smoke and fire, as the clash of wills becomes visceral. Dueling with Owen Teale's arrogant Hotspur, Maloney rises above petulance to princely fervor.

After the rousing encounters in Part One, Part Two succumbs to a certain placidity. This is partly a result of the long expository scenes with Falstaff traveling the country as recruiting officer and the fact that Falstaff's accomplices in this endeavor are no match for Stephens. Furthermore, Maloney is unable to sustain the momentum in his role (as Alan Howard did at Stratford when he marched through a trilogy, from Prince Hal to Henry V). But Noble's own inventiveness continues in Part Two, especially in his use of a fluctuating depth of field. He draws the theatergoer's eye to both the background and the foreground, occasionally overlapping scenes so that one has a cumulative, cinematic sense of the breadth of Shakespearean life.

The Stratford schedule allowed me to see *The Two Gentlemen of Verona* at the Swan, in David Thacker's delightful quasimusical version. This is not a full musical comedy like *Kiss Me Kate*, but *Two Gentlemen* itself, staged in a modern mode with a dash of Cole Porter and his contemporaries (including George Gershwin and Irving Berlin) between the lines. An onstage band plays a prelude and continues during the interludes. As charmingly sung by Hilary Cromie, the numbers add a tuneful motif of musicalized romance as counterpoint to the escapades on stage. Neither aspect of the production intrudes on the other; they become complementary.

On an estate that could be in Bertie Wooster-country, guests loll on the lawn while their host, the Duke of Milan, suavely dabbles in gourmet cookery. Everyone continues to live the life that late he led, until couples find themselves at cross purposes. The spirit remains lighthearted even when it comes to Proteus's betrayal of his best friend, Valentine. Among the lovers, the most willing is Clare Holman as the justly admired Julia. There is a drollness in the air, captured by servants (Josette Bushell-Mingo and Richard Moore) as well as masters.

Moore, playing Launce, is, however, upstaged by a dog, cast in the role of Crab, Shakespeare's top dog. The Buster Keaton of hounds, the frizzy-haired animal performs with a dogged deadpan - or a deadpan doggedness. He yawns on cue, does double takes and looks as if he cannot wait to get to his dressing room. An expert at feigning disinterest, this character dog maintains a critical distance from the folly of the human characters. Theatergoers may go to Stratford to savor Stephens's Falstaff or to visit the new Other Place, but should they see *Two Gentlemen of Verona* they will leave town laughing at an uncanny Royal Shakespeare canine.

ACTORS PUT A NEW SPIN ON THE OLD BARD AT STRATFORD: NOVEMBER 1994

Is Shakespeare still a player? That was the headline this summer on an essay by classical scholar Colin Burrow in the Sunday Times of London. The answer was a qualified yes, the qualification being that it is precisely the quality of untimeliness - "the sense of perilously withheld topicality that Shakespeare himself tried to generate" - that makes our greatest of dramatists great. Substitute the word universality for untimeliness and the picture clarifies. The most relevant productions at Stratford-on-Avon in the recent past - and I am thinking of productions like Deborah Warner's *Titus Andronicus* and Sam Mendes's *Troilus and Cressida* - kept the work in period while looking at it through a contemporary prism.

The choice of actors can be the impetus for the directorial approach. Casting the very young and relatively inexperienced Toby Stephens as Coriolanus, as David Thacker did at Stratford this season, is itself a statement on the play. Evidently this was not going to be the heroic Coriolanus we have seen in the past (as in Charles Dance's performance of several seasons ago), the noble general brought down by his constitutional inability to compromise.

Stephens (son of Robert Stephens and Maggie Smith) makes the character very much the young man on the quick rise, someone who has vaulted so quickly up the military heirarchy that he has not had the time or inclination to understand the demands of leadership. He is as smug with his equals (who have helped him) as he is dismissive of the common people. When the Tribunes ask him to trust them, he responds, "Trust ye? Hang ye!" Stephens sounds as if he means it.

Harley Granville Barker observed that Coriolanus remains to the end "the incorrigible boy," and this has never been truer than in Stephens's performance. Placed on a pedestal by his mother, he cannot view himself with objectivity. When the people turn against him, he can only respond with petulance. A prodigal, he runs away from Rome. In this production, Coriolanus becomes less admirable than his rival Audfidius (Barry Lynch, with a slash of a scar on his face). Normally, *Coriolanus* fills one with regret at the loss of a potentially strong ruler, but Stephens's stress on the character's failings - of youth, of temperament - shows how they should disqualify him for leadership. Brilliant in battle, he would always be a misfit in public life.

Casting Simon Russell Beale as Ariel, as Sam Mendes did in his production of *The Tempest* (which moved from Stratford to the Barbican in London), is even more daring and automatically suggests a shift in weight. Russell Beale, who is indisputably one of the most emotionally penetrating of actors, is, to put it candidly, unprepossessing of appearance. Short and stocky, he does not project a heroic image. But his appearance has, if anything, nurtured his virtuosity in such widely divergent roles as Konstantin in *The Seagull*, the title role in Marlowe's *Edward II*, the son in *Ghosts* and, most startling of all, as Ariel.

Russell Beale's Ariel is the opposite of an airy sprite. One could hardly imagine him perching on Prospero's shoulder. Playing to the actor's strength, Mendes transforms him into a white-faced, deadpan mime who orchestrates an Arielized version of *The Tempest*. Stepping out of a wicker basket like a New Vaudevillian, he precipitates storms and performs magic tricks. Prospero is a sorcerer in exile, but it is Ariel who is the master illusionist. This heightens the conflict between the two. Physically, Prospero keeps his distance: an acerbic, professorial Alec McCowen is often seen atop a ladder looking down on his island. When he promises Ariel freedom and then delays it, he seems like a teacher holding back the grade on a student's term paper in order to keep the latter in his thrall. Finally set free, Ariel offers not an inch of gratitude. In the original Stratford production, Russell Beale spit at McCowen. That gesture was removed from the London production, but the spirit of rebellion remains in the air.

Twelfth Night may be foolproof. Unquestionably, it can withstand all sorts of transplantation. In his production at Stratford, Ian Judge simply asks us to sit back and enjoy the entertainment, as he did several seasons ago with his effervescent *Comedy of Errors*. Both productions starred Desmond Barrit, a rotund clown. In *Twelfth Night*, Barrit's Malvolio is as gullible as he is garishly gartered. The emphasis in his performance and in the staging is on the playfulness of the comedy - darker dimensions are unexplored, except in Derek Griffiths's Feste. This jester's melancholic air suggests that he wants to end the crazy shenanigans; his bitter-sweet singing adds a threnody of ruefulness.

Still, for all its pleasurable moments, and despite Emma Fielding's forthright Viola, this *Twelfth Night* seems staged by number. Far more evocative is *Peer Gynt*, as directed by that Shakespearean veteran John Barton, who, in approaching Ibsen, has achieved a model of Shakespearean staging. Almost everyone takes on double and triple roles: In one neat quick change, Haydn Gwynne plays both Peer's mother and his love Solveig. The linchpin of the production is Alex Jennings, one of the most sheerly ingratiating of young English actors. He fully commands the Swan stage with a boisterous performance as a pleasure-prone, prankish Peer. Unlike some Peers, we will forgive him anything.

As it turned out, the most exciting Shakespeare was not at Stratford or at the Barbican but at the Lyric Hammersmith, the final stop on a tour taken by the no-madic Cheek by Jowl company. Declan Donnellan's black-and-white *Measure for Measure*, enacted on an almost bare stage, pierces to the ethical heart of the mat-ter. Without updating the play (except for costumes), the director gives it a re-newed urgency. As played by Adam Kotz, Angelo is no wild-eyed wraith but a handsome, highly professional politician, calmly dispensing injustice as if it were largesse. In him, one can see the dangerous hypocrites of today's religious right. When Isabella (a passionate Anastasia Hille) presses her suit for her imprisoned brother Claudio, Angelo's interest quickens. Calculating his demands - favor for favor, measure for measure - he becomes an embodiment of sexual harassment.

This is a *Measure* of great moral strength, a visceral successor to Donnellan's all-male *As You Like It*, restaged this fall at the Brooklyn Academy of Music. As was also evident in his National Theater productions of *Angels in America*, *Fuente Ovejuna* and *Sweeney Todd*, Donellan is a director with an intelligence to equal his immense theatricality, a man who finds modernity in classics and classicism in the modern. In his hands, as in those of Deborah Warner and Sam Mendes, Shakespeare reasserts his position as our contemporary.

ANTON CHEKHOV

A SEAGULL: DECEMBER 17, 1985

WASHINGTON - At the climax of *A Seagull*, Peter Sellars's revamping of the play by Chekhov, Paul Winfield, as the doctor, goes offstage to investigate the sound of a gunshot - and the actors freeze in a tableau. Mr. Winfield is gone so long that one begins to wonder if the actor, fed up with the production's diminu-tion of its source, has gone home. Such is not the case, and the evening ends as in

Chekhov, but strange are the vagaries that have led the director into the never-never land of his *Seagull*.

The altered title, *A Seagull*, is a rare apt note in the production at the Kennedy Center for the Performing Arts. This evening of studious eccentricity is like no other version of *The Seagull* that one has seen - or hopes to see again. Along the way, it undermines Chekhov, as well as a number of otherwise capable actors. Colleen Dewhurst and Henderson Forsythe are among the few who survive. Others are apparently more readily subservient to directorial whim.

Entering the Eisenhower Theater, we see several dozen chairs of an identical wooden kind, aligned on stage as if for a private viewing. Seated with their backs to the audience are two actors, Priscilla Smith and Jan Triska. They are waiting for the play within the play to begin. After a long delay, Ms. Smith, as Masha, addresses us, as an audience within an audience: "The performance will start soon." There is a hint of annoyance in her voice.

An onstage pianist, ubiquitous but unnoticed by the actors, plays Scriabin (the play is interpolated with a Scriabin concert, a fact that adds at least 30 minutes to an already over-long production). Ms. Smith walks to the piano and takes a sniff of snuff. She answers her suitor's solicitation with "Your love moves me," and then is moved to sneeze.

Ms. Smith's sneeze is indicative of the director's aberrant approach - tricks, quirks and sight gags at Chekhov's expense. For example, Nina's performance in Konstantin's play is accompanied by a laser-beam light show that makes Kelly McGillis (the Nina of record) look like a cousin of Carrie Fisher in *Star Wars*.

Ms. McGillis makes her first entrance at a run; she is so out of breath that she is forced to gasp between her words. Repeatedly, she and others rush onstage, and then stop dead in their tracks as if playing a childhood game of statues. The sudden sweeps of movement are followed by stasis and silence, just as a darkened stage is suddenly struck by a blaze of light. Chekhov's play of inaction has become hyperkinetic.

Actors gratuitously climb on chairs to deliver speeches. Other chairs are kicked over. Konstantin in particular seems to regard the furniture as his enemy. Remembering the opening scene, one begins to think that the production has more to do with chairs than with Chekhov.

There are clues that Mr. Sellars wants to stress the theatricality of the text (Maria M. Markof-Belaeff's adaptation is no advancement over other versions). Konstantin's commentary on art is extruded, like academic footnotes, and delivered lecture-style. However, in common with much else in *A Seagull*, that motif is dropped. In search of directorial signatures, Mr. Sellars cannot seem to keep his mind on the play's values.

On one level, the evening is lacking in that sense of youthful ardor so essential to the personality of Nina. In Ms. McGillis's portrayal, she seems merely high-strung. Kevin Spacey's Konstantin, in contrast, is almost sinister in his surliness.

Though David Strathairn, as Trigorin looks Russian - or at least he looks like a Flying Karamazov Brother - he never convinces one that he is an eminent author or a remotely possible match for Ms. Dewhurst.

With a becoming serenity, Ms. Dewhurst goes about the business of being Arkadina. In antique gowns and cossack pants, she looks glamorous, and she acts like a grand lady of the theater (which both she and her character are). Mr. Forsythe persuasively assumes the mantle of decrepitude as the elderly Sorin and Mr. Winfield carries off the role of the doctor with dispatch, if not panache.

The production exists irrespective of the actors. They are figures on a Sellars landscape, the backdrop of which consists of enormous Rothko-like monochromatic planes. In the program, between the names of the American National Theater and the play, appear the words, "Search for New Forms," a reference to Konstantin's demands that "new forms are needed." In his own impetuous pursuit of newness, Mr. Sellars has relegated Chekhov to the role of apprentice playwright.

WILD HONEY: DECEMBER 28, 1986

Writing about Chekhov's first extant full-length play, Henri Troyat (in his biography, *Chekhov*) says, "For all its melodrama, chaos and verbosity, this immature work contains all the great Chekhovian themes in embryo." Acting as Chekhov's collaborator and editor, Michael Frayn has reduced the melodrama, trimmed the verbosity and made the chaos seem more comic. The result, *Wild Honey*, is one of those rare adaptations that is faithful to the spirit, if not the letter, of the original. The play draws strength from the dual authorship - the young Chekhov's ebullience and incipient sensibility, combined with Mr. Frayn's knowledge of dramaturgy. If Chekhov had had the time and the inclination to revise and polish his early play, it might have become *Wild Honey* - the comedy that Chekhov never wrote.

Wild Honey is not in a dramatic class with the author's four late masterpieces, but it is at least as stageworthy as *Ivanov*, and, revised, it is no longer a rough draft, as was the case with *The Wood Demon*, the first sketch for *Uncle Vanya*. In *Wild Honey* are the concerns that were to obsess Chekhov throughout his life's work. Women are starved for love and purpose (as in *The Three Sisters*). The hero, Mikhail Platonov, is trapped - trapping himself in the role of seducer. Platonov is the dramatic progenitor of Ivanov and, later, of Trigorin in *The Seagull*, and Astrov in *Uncle Vanya*, men who become the obsessive object of female desire. Though the characters have different professions and different perspectives on their predicament, they all share a lassitude even as others extol them for their charisma. In contrast, there is Sergey in *Wild Honey*, whom Platonov casually cuckolds, the first in a line of self-dramatizing Chekhovian failures, flailing themselves with their own ineptitude while idly dreaming of a life of poetry and commitment. From Sergey, it is but a step to Uncle Vanya himself.

In *Wild Honey*, an heiress, Anna Petrovna, has fallen on hard times and her family estate is threatened with foreclosure. Outside the gates is the rising middle class, as represented by the boorish merchant. By the time of *The Cherry Orchard*, Anna Petrovna, still glamorous, has aged into Madame Ranevskaya, and the merchant has become Lopakhin. As in all of Chekhov, a doctor drinks and ignores his patients, officers live on old memories and fall asleep in the middle of conversations and servants see far more than they are credited with seeing. Under a burdensome cloud of ennui, everyone is waiting for someone else to do something. In this case, everyone looks to Platonov for excitement.

As Chekhov matured, his characters refrained from histrionics. Farce was replaced by comedy emerging more from character, and people were less prone to philosophize at length, although they never stopped saying how bored they were. In his early plays, Chekhov was not yet fully aware that important things could be said without words, through indirection. In his adaptation, Mr. Frayn has the double obligation of keeping the youthful freshness of the work while removing the awkwardness of Chekhov's apprenticeship.

In order to understand the progression of the play from discarded manuscript in Chekhov's time, to the Michael Frayn adaptation on Broadway, I looked at three published scripts: David Magarshack's unabridged translation, entitled *Platonov;* Alex Szogyi's abbreviated translation, produced Off Broadway in 1960 as *A Country Scandal;* and *Wild Honey.* The first is impossibly long and discursive, a full four acts and five scenes. Mr. Szogyi brings the play down to manageable performance length while following the structure of the original. In his ending, Platonov is not shot (as in the original), but dies of fright. The version is broad to the point of being farcical. With boldness, Mr. Frayn has served both as translator and adapter, excising minor characters, shifting scenes and locations and rewriting both the beginning and ending. Almost all of the second act now takes place in Platonov's schoolroom home. The Frayn finale, neither homicide nor fright, is more dramatic as well as more symbolic. Platonov is less a manipulator than a victim of circumstance.

In contrast to previous translators, Mr. Frayn is himself an accomplished playwright as well as a Russian scholar. The language flows, as it does in Mr. Frayn's own plays - although the territory is far removed in style as well as content from that of *Noises Off* and *Benefactors.* Just as Tom Stoppard has demonstrated a kinship with the work of Arthur Schnitzler, Mr. Frayn has an affinity for the Russians - Tolstoy as well as Chekhov. The tone of *Wild Honey* is Chekhovian, with a Frayn comic twist. For this transformation, Mr. Frayn has had two close collaborators, the director Christopher Morahan and the actor Ian McKellen, both of whom were involved in the production at England's National Theater as they are in the current Broadway incarnation at the Virginia Theater. In the various translations, including Mr. Frayn's, there are no clues as to the look of Platonov and there is little indication of his behavior on stage. Mr. McKellen, with the help of his director, has had to fill in his own comic portrait.

Platonov is a great distance from the actor's other notable characters. Although in New York Mr. McKellen is known largely for his performance as Salieri in the Broadway *Amadeus*, in England he has played a galaxy of great Shakespearean roles (Hamlet, Macbeth, Coriolanus) as well as appearing in plays of related periods, such as *The Duchess of Malfi*. As diverse as his roles are, so many of them have a dignity and a sobriety; they are kings, princes, warriors and men of court. He has specialized in plays with a tragic consequence.

Many of his peers, fellow claimants to Lord Olivier's classical acting crown, have been more insistent about varying their choices. Derek Jacobi alternates *Cyrano de Bergerac* with *Much Ado About Nothing*, and then moves on to a modern play. Michael Gambon shifts effortlessly from Lear and Galileo to Simon Gray and Alan Ayckbourn. Alan Howard plays the king and then spoofs himself in comedies like *Wild Oats*. Mr. McKellen, however, is most often seen in period costume, doing battle with weighty classics - and, as he demonstrated in his one-man show, *Acting Shakespeare*, he is a most authoritative and articulate expert on the art of classical acting. When challenged, he readily reveals his versatility - as the anguished husband in David Rudkin's *Ashes*, as an oppressed homosexual in a Nazi prison camp in the London production of Martin Sherman's *Bent*. Some years ago, he played the title role in *The Wood Demon* (at the Brooklyn Academy of Music). It is in that absurdly comic performance as an idealistic poet and painter that we can find the genesis of his Platonov.

The first decision on the part of Mr. McKellen and Mr. Morahan was to play this romanticist as an unromantic figure. From his first hurried entrance, he looks as if he has moved too precipitously from sleepless night to sybaritic day. He scratches his head, yawns and slouches. Exuding irresponsibility along with seedy charm, Mr. McKellen's Platonov is a clown and an actor in life. He amuses himself by being anti-social - it is his means of survival - and no matter how badly he behaves, women adore him. He is the most dynamic man in town, a fact that testifies to the dreariness of the town itself. Like Lear's fool, he does not censor his opinions, issuing insults up front rather than behind one's back.

Mr. McKellen so splendidly captures Platonov's roguishness and his mocking self-criticism that he wins our allegiance; poor fellow besieged by so many beautiful women. Through his performance is revealed the character's deep malaise. The pleasures are evanescent and the appetite for excess is insatiable. Toward the end of the evening, the friend whom he has cuckolded bemoans his own misery, adding that, in contrast, Platonov has "everything." Aimed at Mr. McKellen, the word "everything" is a piercing lance. Wounded by the charge, he looks as woeful as a` pallbearer; the reaction provokes one of the play's heartiest laughs. His "everything" is in such total chaos. For the Broadway production, the play has been recast largely with American actors. The staging does not have the seamless unity of the National Theater original. Several of the older male characters blend into the background, but the women are vividly individualized by Kathryn Walker, Kate Burton and J. Smith-Cameron. Ms. Walker plays Anna Petrovna, an emancipated woman who stirs up all the women. In a romantic play, the two would flee the provinces together. Because this is a Chekhovian comedy, an entirely different fate awaits them, arrived at after an evening at once mirthful and melancholic.

THE CHERRY ORCHARD: JUNE 1, 1988

WASHINGTON - Some directors revive classics, others deconstruct them. A few such as Lucien Pintillie and Peter Brook are theatrical explorers reinventing classics. Coincidentally, Mr. Pintillie and Mr. Brook each recently applied his wizardry to *The Cherry Orchard*. Mr. Brook's version, produced earlier this season by the Brooklyn Academy of Music, stripped the play of its non-essential trappings, distilling it to its emotional core. Mr. Pintillie's version, currently at the Arena Stage, is equally fascinating but even more radical.

For some theatergoers, the embellishments of the Rumanian-born director may be too drastic. Among other things, he adds two silent characters to *The Cherry Orchard*, restores a scene that Chekhov cut at the suggestion of Stanislavsky and stresses the play's comic elements, even to having the guests in the party scene wear clown hats and false noses.

All the alterations are intended to serve a specific dramatic purpose - in direct contrast to Peter Sellars's arbitrary production of the Chekhov play he entitled *A Seagull*. For all its buoyant humor, Mr. Pintillie's *Cherry Orchard* is obsessed with mordancy - deaths in Mme. Ranevskaya's family and the end of an era in Russia. The characters are less victims than self-victimizers, provocateurs of their downfall.

Have you ever wondered about Mme. Ranevskaya's dead son, who is briefly mentioned in the text? Contemplating that subject, Mr. Pintillie has evidently decided that the boy's drowning was the single most important event in his mother's life. The director prefaces the play with the appearance of a young boy (a silent stand-in for the son). He emerges from an armoire, a representation of his mother's favorite bookcase - and as populated a piece of furniture as C.S. Lewis's wardrobe in *The Lion, the Witch and the Wardrobe*.

Later the child reappears as an unconscious memory of a lingering tragedy. The vision is not so bizarre when one remembers that, at one point, Mme. Ranevskaya imagines she sees the ghost of her own mother. In such a fashion, the production shifts seamlessly from realism to surrealism. To a great extent, the approach is cinematic, as the director imaginatively depicts the environment - geographic and behavioral - that surrounds the play.

Taking a cue from the text, he stresses the childlike side of Mme. Ranevskaya (Shirley Knight) and of her brother (Richard Bauer). At one point they look inside the armoire and, with fraternal abandon, play with toys of their youth. As in other instances, the moment establishes a motif, also true in the case of the brother's criticism of his sister. To him, in the words of Jean-Claude van Itallie's translation, she has been "weak" and "licentious." As we realize, Mme. Ranevskaya need not be the grande dame of tradition. In Ms. Knight's portrayal, she is fallible, vulnerable and even a bit ridiculous.

In this production, Firs is played by W. Benson Terry, a tall, dignified actor, who, in his stately interpretation, becomes an island of calm rationality in a sea of absurdity. In the scene that has been restored, Firs and Charlotta - the play's two outsiders - share a dialogue in which each reveals details of a personal life. Firs, we learn, served a brief time in prison on a minor charge - a past that indicates something about his willingness to endure his servitude.

That scene, at the end of the second act, should take place in a meadow with cherry trees in the distance. In Mr. Brook's production, the meadow was simulated by carpets. In Mr. Pintillie's version, the setting undergoes a stunning transformation. In the dark, without an intermission break, the first-act nursery is suddenly replaced by a vast field of wheat (perhaps foreshadowing the fate of the cherry orchard itself). In that field, we spy the characters and we also see the production's other new figure, a scarecrow, which becomes a tangible metaphor for the offstage throb of a Chekhovian heart-string. The sets and costumes, so bound up with the costume, are by Radu and Miruna Boruzescu, the director's long-time scenic collaborators.

As in Mr. Pintillie's *Tartuffe*, some of the directorial touches are overdrawn. There are a few too many pratfalls, and several actors court caricature. At the same time, however, the director sheds an unfailingly clear light on the motivations of the people, elucidated by, among others, Ms. Knight, Mr. Bauer, Mr. Terry, Tana Hicken (as Varya), and Henry Stram (as Trofimov).

In a final image, Firs emerges from the mysterious armoire and expresses a philosophy that acts as a bridge from Chekhov to Beckett: "Life is over before you've lived it." Then a single champagne glass on a side table undergoes its own spontaneous death rattle - a startling conclusion to a mesmerizing production.

HENRIK IBSEN

PEER GYNT: APRIL 11, 1989

HARTFORD - *Peer Gynt* represented, as Ibsen wrote, "a process of spiritual liberation and catharsis," for the title character as well as for the playwright. Though Ibsen himself regarded it as his play least likely to be understood outside of his country, it has become one of his most universal works. Along with *Brand*, *Peer Gynt* is a poetic masterpeice, fraught with dangers for theatrical mountaineers daring to climb its craggy peaks. For this reason, the play is seldom performed, rarer still in its entirety.

Mark Lamos's two-part, five-hour production, starring Richard Thomas, is monumental, both as risk and as achievement, drawing upon the artistic resources of the director and the Hartford Stage and inspiring Mr. Thomas to a feat of acting. Following his *Hamlet* last season at Hartford, his fearless performance further validates his position as one of America's leading classical actors.

The last two productions of the play that I have seen, both admirable, both spare, were at the CSC and at Stratford-on-Avon (with Derek Jacobi in the title role). In contrast, Mr. Lamos's more ambitious version has a visual richness that is itself transporting. It is, one might add, in direct antithesis to his recent, muted production of *Measure for Measure* at Lincoln Center.

Mr. Lamos has a clear-sighted view of *Peer Gynt* as both timeless and timely. As Peer undertakes his journey to find his innermost self, peeling an onion to its nonexistent core, one can find contemporary existential parallels. And in Peer's penchant for troll-ery can be read all the self-indulgences that deflect man from a truer purpose.

The sweep of *Peer Gynt* is cinematic, for which the director and his designer, John Conklin, have found imaginative theatrical equivalents. Peer's journey is visualised with a sequence of striking scenic alterations, using perspective-distorting panoramas; sculptural figures (a huge pig, a small Sphinx), landscapes in miniature; and stage-filling dropcloths of sharply varying color. In characteristic Lamos fashion, individual scenes conjure painterly images that run all the way from Bruegel to Manet (a picnic on the beach).

In one of several coups de théâtre, the director turns the stage into the deck of a ship during a storm, then instantly transforms it into the roiling sea itself (Peer fights a diabolical fellow passenger for posssssion of a toy-size lifeboat), and, finally, into the bleak Norwegian landscape. In such a fashion, the director repeatedly stimulates the audience's imagination.

This is not to suggest that the production (or the play) is flawless. There is a dramatic ebb toward the end of the first act of the second half, as Peer wanders through several continents, scenes that in other productions are often abridged. More in question is the translation by Gerry Bamman and Irene B. Berman.

Though it is in verse, it is not always poetic and there is often an awkward slanginess, as in the use of words like phooey and hunky-dory. At other times, however, the translation has a flow that overrides such eccentricities, and there are several interesting variations. For example, the symbolic Great Boyg becomes the Great Between.

Mr. Thomas's Peer is a kind of anti-Hamlet, a man of action who refuses to be introspective. A fantasizer and an improviser, he is not to be trusted, yet women repeatedly put their faith in him. Any actor playing Peer must capture both the recklessness and the charm. Mr. Thomas has both in abundance.

The production opens inside Peer's home rather than outdoors, as is customary. The room is decorated as a nursery, with Peer and his mother (Patricia Conolly) rummaging through the attic of memory. Then Peer begins to spin his story about his wild ride on the back of a reindeer. His mother - as well as the audience - is spellbound by the fabulous tale. It is, of course, a fiction, a fact that does not vitiate the storytelling.

In subsequent scenes, Mr. Thomas maintains that high level of excitement, as he seduces a bride on her wedding day; provokes a second woman, Solveig, to become his lifelong muse, and flees through the wilderness. His adventure in the kingdom of the trolls is, as it should be, vulgar, comic and threatening, and he escapes with his humanity barely intact. In the second half of the play, which theatergoers can see on alternate evenings or on marathon days after a dinner break, Peer circumnavigates the world.

In Mr. Thomas's older Peer, the weight of his worldliness is reflected in his stance and in his voice. Even as he becomes an international robber baron and sinks more deeply into cynicism, he retains his curious sense of honesty. He never fools himself, ultimately realizing that "life is too high a price to pay for birth," and persisting on a path to enlightenment.

Ms. Conolly finds endearing qualities in Peer's mother and there are also persuasive performances, in a variety of roles, by Stephen Rowe, Philip Goodwin, Wyman Pendleton, Leslie Geraci and Tara Hugo (as the saintly Solveig). For Mr. Lamos and Mr. Thomas, *Peer Gynt* is a significant accomplishment, precisely the kind of work institutional theaters should be attempting.

HEDDA GABLER: AUGUST 20, 1991

DUBLIN - The boldness that Deborah Warner brought to Shakespeare in her productions at the Swan Theater in Stratford-on-Avon was reasserted this summer with Ibsen at the Abbey Theater. As directed by Ms. Warner and as compellingly portrayed by Fiona Shaw, *Hedda Gabler* becomes an even more impassioned, psychologically prescient study of a woman totally out of step with her time and her society.

The fact that this striking production opened in Dublin rather than at Stratford or in London says something about the convocation of talent that is energizing the Irish theater. The revitalization comes not only from new Irish plays but also from a linkage with a world theatrical tradition. Clearly this is one reason Dublin was named the European City of Culture for 1991.

In the performing arts, theater has always been the city's primary strength, although Dublin has far fewer theaters than London. The audience is small but committed. The works themselved draw from a relatively limited pool of actors, directors and playwrights. This season, for example, that fine actor Donal McCann starred in revivals of both *The Faith Healer* by Brian Friel and *A Life* by Hugh Leonard.

In the case of *Hedda Gabler*, most of the talent happens to be female: Ms. Warner, who is English; Ms. Shaw, an Irish actress who has made her reputation in London, in her Irish theatrical debut, and Garry Hynes, who recently moved from the artistic direction of the experimental Druid Theater in Galway to the august Abbey, the Irish National Theater. In her choice of company-workers (like Ms. Warner and Sebastian Barry, a young playwright who is on the theater's board), Ms. Hynes seems determined to be forward-looking and to shatter stereotypes of what constitutes theater in Ireland.

Hedda Gabler has been an undisputed success, with Ms. Shaw filling the role with urgency. From the moment she appears onstage in a silent prelude devised by Ms. Warner, she is an explosive force. Before dawn she is prowling her household. Trapped in the cage of a meaningless life and obsessed by her pregnancy, she is on the brink of madness. This is a woman who can do damage to others as well as to herself. She is helplessly enthralled to her anger and frustrations.

Her home is as under-furnished as her life. In Hildegarde Bechtler's monochromatic design, there is cold comfort, only a bare dining table, wooden chairs and a small couch. Hedda's meddling aunt, a meaner figure in this production than is generally the case, keeps shifting the furniture, and Hedda compulsively rearranges it, as if in so doing she can instill her own idea of order in her life. Nervous, restless, she remains in incessant motion. When the Lovborg manuscript is left in her care, Ms. Shaw hides it in plain sight, putting it under the couch rather than in a drawer. We are always aware of the manuscript, even as Lovborg remains oblivious of its presence. After he leaves, Hedda takes the book and burns it. But instead of placing it a few pages at a time in the fireplace, as indicated in the text, she flings it whole into the flames. It is a shocking moment - as if she has tossed a child onto a funeral pyre - and it is one that encapsulates the entire production.

In less artistic hands, the largeness of the gesture in this scene and others might lead to self-indulgence; not with Ms. Shaw. With the help of her director, she keeps herself contained within the role. As a result, Hedda's suicide achieves the inevitability it deserves. When Judge Brack says, "People don't do that kind of thing," the unstated response is, not unless the name is Hedda Gabler.

Except for the few jarring Anglicisms in Una Ellis-Fermor's translation and the fact that Tesman is played in a familiar wimpish manner, the production exudes authority. Ms. Shaw is evenly matched by Hugh Ross's patrician Judge Brack and Robert O. Mahoney's Byronic approach to Lovborg. The actress locates the embittered laughter without diminishing the brooding Hedda flailing against the encroaching night.

GHOSTS: DECEMBER 1993

STRATFORD-ON-AVON - "An open drain," "unutterably offensive," "repulsive and degrading," "garbage and offal" - these were typical of the critics' comments on Ibsen's *Ghosts* when it opened in London in 1891. William Archer, one of the playwright's most fervent admirers (and his translator) collated the horrendous reviews and called them a "shriek of execration." In these more liberated times, it may be difficult to understand the outrage that greeted *Ghosts* then and in subsequent productions. Jesse Helms's attack on the American avant-garde is tepid in comparison.

As for those like Archer who thought of the play as a great moral drama, they were linked in the local press as "lovers of prurience" and "muck-ferreting dogs," a graphic way of saying pshaw to Shaw, among others. As Archer said about the Norwegian dramatist on a previous occasion, "Alas, poor Ibsen! It is well that he does not read English."

Misunderstanding of Ibsen came in the highest places. At a state dinner at which the playwright was the guest of honor, the king of Norway admonished him for writing *Ghosts* and instead praised one of his earlier minor plays. Ibsen could only respond, "I had to write *Ghosts*."

It would be gratifying to say that the play was now universally recognized as one of the author's most valuable works. Instead, some would argue that it is dated or that its residual power remains in the reading of the text. All such thoughts are banished by the current Royal Shakespeare Company production at Stratford-on-Avon, as staged by Katie Mitchell. At 28, she is one of a wave of talented young English directors (whose numbers also include Deborah Warner and Sam Mendes).

The necessity of *Ghosts* suffuses every aspect of Mitchell's version, which is as close to a perfect production as one could imagine. In her hands, the play is an emotionally shattering experience as relevant as any modern work about the ravages of AIDS. The subject is not unrelated, as young Oswald Alving is devastated by syphilis and other symbolic sins of his dissolute father. Above all, Ibsen explored the tragedy of the devotion to dead ideals and outmoded beliefs as represented by Oswald's mother, who is the reverse of Ibsen's Nora. Trapped in a poisonous domestic environment, she chooses hypocrisy over freedom. She slams no doors but stays on in order to preserve the facade of a debilitating marriage.

Mitchell's production skillfully focuses on Mrs. Alving's struggle to whitewash her husband's name. In so doing, she eventually realizes the damage she has caused to her husband as well as to her son and herself. Oswald and Pastor Manders, the well-intentioned but wrong-headed family advisor, are important as reflections of Mrs. Alving's self-deception. In reviewing the last Broadway mounting of *Ghosts*, starring Liv Ullman, I said that we rarely felt the intensity and the metaphorical mist of unforgiving memory that pervades this blighted Nordic household. That is precisely what Mitchell and her actors convey at Stratford's intimate Other Place.

A dozen years ago, this theater was the setting for Adrian Noble's production of *A Doll's House*, which achieved a rare equilibrium between the characters of Nora and her husband. He became a man defeated by his own sense of rectitude. Both directors approached Ibsen plays for their tangibility, avoiding histrionics and uncovering the humanity of all the characters.

In Mitchell's production, we hear sounds of sea and rain outside the Alving home. Inside, it is all tension and expectation. Jane Lapotaire gives a remarkably restrained and well-modulated performance as the mother, and Simon Russell Beale emphasizes Oswald's yearning for art and experience. John Carlisle lends credibility to the difficult role of the pietistic Pastor who has encouraged Mrs. Alving's hollow martyrdom. In a time when theatrical deconstruction is in vogue, Mitchell is scrupulous about holding to the text and refraining from anachronisms. The play reinterprets itself. Remaining in period and in atmosphere, it transcends its time, demonstrating once again that Ibsen is our contemporary.

Throughout, the production captures the dark ambiguities of the play, none more than in the climax when Oswald cries out to his mother, "Give me the sun." As Russell Beale delivers the line, it is an expression both of the character's "joy of life" and the cracking of his mind. The final ghost has come home to rest.

Despite his unprepossessing, portly appearance, Russell Beale is an actor of virtuosity. In several seasons with the Royal Shakespeare Company, he has moved from hilarious foppishness in *The Man of Mode* to the decadence of Thersites in *Troilus and Cressida* while also playing a Konstantin riddled by melancholy in *The Seagull* and the title roles of Marlowe's *Edward II* and Shakespeare's *Richard III*. His Oswald is a man grasping for life at the point of death.

FEDERICO GARCÍA LORCA

BLOOD WEDDING: MAY 15, 1992

The revolutionary legacy of Federico García Lorca endures in his poetry and in his three poetic tragedies. The first of the three plays, *Blood Wedding*, surges with passion and earth wisdom, both of which are captured in Melia Bensussen's vivid production at the Joseph Papp Public Theater.

Using a lyrical translation by Langston Hughes, Ms. Bensussen explores the heart of this tale of barrenness and blood lust. Beneath the surface calm, all is turbulence, as fate and the masterly hand of the playwright drive the characters to their shared catastrophe. Inspired by a true story, García Lorca wrote of acts of violence that destroyed several families. As in Ibsen's *Peer Gynt*, a man steals a bride on her wedding day, but with García Lorca the marriage thief pays the ultimate price.

From the opening scene, as a domineering mother (Gloria Foster) and her son (Al Roderigo) discuss the son's wedding plans, thoughts of death are omnipresent (and, later, death appears in the figure of a beggar woman). The mother has not recovered from the loss of her husband and her other son. "Grief stings my eyes," she says, and that grief quickly becomes a lamentation.

Swirls of passion engulf the characters, even as they go through the ritual formalities of the wedding ceremony. Glowering on the sidelines is Leonardo, the bride's former suitor, who is discontented in his own marriage. Selfishly pursuing his own interests, he will soon eradicate everyone else's chance for romantic fulfillment.

In 90 unabated minutes, Ms. Bensussen and her company clarify the overweaning love of the mother, the innocence of her son and the insidiousness of Leonardo: the warring elements that divide one character from the other and that activate this deadly dance.

As directed by Ms. Bensussen, and as choreographed by Donald Byrd, the production merges both the naturalistic and metaphorical elements of the drama. Movement rises to flamenco, as characters stomp staccato messages. In the background we hear Spanish strains with the flavor of jazz. At one point, three young women become entwined in a cat's cradle of red string as they sing about winding a symbolic skein of wool.

The Langston Hughes translation, in its first professional performance, is relatively close to the traditional one by Richard L. O'Connell and James Graham-Lujan, but with greater smoothness and poetic intensity. The imagery remains visceral: tears "burn like blood" and eyes are "as sharp as thorns."

Evidently encouraged by the heightened language, Ms. Foster initially overdramatizes her dialogue, but soon holds herself to García Lorca's pitch. His plays are a natural subject for her talent (in the late 1960's, she played the title role in

Yerma at Lincoln Center). Ultimately, her performance consolidates the mother's stoicism with her ferocity. She will stand for no questioning of her rights and motives, and when she is overcome she is devastated, and has no room for anyone else's remorse.

Mr. Roderigo and Elizabeth Peña (as the bride) are evenly matched, in his resolute self-confidence and in her wishfulness, as she is seduced into a romance outside of marriage. Joaquim de Almeida is a brooding Leonardo, Ivonne Coll strikes musical sparks as a voice of caution and Mike Hodge offers a portrait of dignified restraint as the father of the bride.

Derek McLane's set design is an active participant in the performance, with stuccoed walls and cycloramic strips of sky simulating the Spanish landscape. The setting extends into the area just offstage in Martinson Hall, where we glimpse the edge of a Spanish garden. Late in the play, with the characters embarked on their tragedy, the backdrop turns into a Miró-like landscape. As events accumulate, the color of the environment shifts from blue to red and finally to black, for the play's conclusion.

LUIGI PIRANDELLO

SIX CHARACTERS IN SEARCH OF AN AUTHOR: OCTOBER 29, 1988

WASHINGTON - The contradiction between truth and illusion is given striking theatrical life at the Arena Stage with the pairing of Luigi Pirandello's *Six Characters in Search of an Author* and Jean Anouilh's *Ring Round the Moon*. Though the Pirandello is a work of genius and the Anouilh a caprice, seeing the two in tandem reinforces the thematic bonds between the innovator and his follower.

By the playwright's own definition, *Six Characters* deals with organic chaos and "the inherent tragic conflict between life (which is always moving and changing) and form (which fixes it, immutable)." A production should convey all the warring elements - the brittleness of the histrionic life as well as the passion of the characters who suddenly challenge the actors' complacency.

As a widely accomplished man of the theater, Liviu Ciulei (acting as director and designer) puts his trust in Pirandello, in contrast to other conceptualists who seek to re-envision him in their own image. The alterations in Mr. Ciulei's production are minor - like the discovery of real stage blood at the end to underline the tragedy of a character's death.

In Robert Cornthwaite's translation, the actors are rehearsing Pirandello's *Rules of the Game* (as in the original text), a fact that acknowledges the playwright's self-criticism. The actors, led in flamboyant fashion by Richard Bauer as the

Director, are startled by the invasion of the homeless family of characters. But their suspicion soon turns to compulsive fascination as a tumultuous story unfolds.

Striving to become people in a play within a play, the characters are more real than the actors. The actors are imitators of life, as demonstrated by the ingénue who mimics the mannerisms of the Stepdaughter character. Mr. Ciulei's cast is more adept at delineating the actors than the characters, who, at least in the case of the Stepdaughter, bare outsize emotions. Roxann Biggs's performance in that role verges on stridency. As a stabilizing influence, however, there is Stanley Anderson's Father, the essence of bourgeois respectability even as he commits acts of psychological violence against his family.

In performance, the play shifts slightly in favor of the acting company - Halo Wines and Henry Strozier as the leading actors, Marissa Copeland as the ingénue and, especially, Mr. Bauer. This Arena Stage stalwart is a proven expert at playing highly theatricalized figures, and the Director is one of his more vital characterizations, capturing both the temperament and the intellectual curiosity of a man who is suffering his own crisis of faith.

As a commentary on theater as life and on life as theater, *Six Characters* has inspired generations of artists, from Jean Anouilh to Robert Zemeckis. In *Who Framed Roger Rabbit?*, Mr. Zemeckis frees the persecuted title character from his cinematic confines in search of an author to bring order to his Toontown chaos. In the case of Anouilh, the playwright was a confirmed Pirandellian, enchanted by the uses of artifice and by the way people play the game of reality.

With *Ring Round the Moon*, it is Isabelle, the Cinderella-like ballerina, who is most closely in touch with the truth and Hugo, the self-willed cynic, who is unable to perform a spontaneous act. In common with the Director in *Six Characters*, Hugo is dismayed by the intrusion of reality into his artfully constructed charade. Both would insist that art has a greater truth than life.

The play, in Christopher Fry's translation, remains frothy and, at moments, facile; it could be reduced in length without loss. But it would be difficult to deny the idyllic aura that pervades it like moonlight. Even Anouilh's ameliorative ending has, in this revival, a fairy-tale innocence. Douglas C. Wager has given *Ring Round the Moon* an appropriately lighthearted production, marred only by several overly playful performances and George Tsypin's inelegant modernistic setting.

Three performances are particularly engaging, two of them by Tom Hewitt (in the double role as the twins, Hugo and Frederic) and the other by Elizabeth McGovern as Isabelle. As demanded, Mr. Hewitt individualizes the lookalikes through body language as well as manner and voice. Hugo has a Nöel Coward imperiousness. Frederic is recessive and apologetic.

When Ms. McGovern confesses her love to Mr. Hewitt, the actor listens silently. He looks authoritative, like Hugo, but, the moment he speaks, he reveals himself as the self-effacing Frederic. The double performance deserves double applause and Ms. McGovern adds her own winning impulsiveness.

There are also antic contributions from Helen Carey and Tana Hicken as helpless meddlers, Ralph Cosham as the haughty butler and Patricia Conolly as a kind of angel ex machina. Mr. Wager's production approaches Anouilh on his terms as a fantasist with romantic inclinations, and, as a result, "Ring Round the Moon" seems renewable. In Mr. Ciulei's production, *Six Characters* remains a self-replenishing masterwork.

PIERRE CORNEILLE

THE ILLUSION: JUNE 18, 1990

HARTFORD - Pierre Corneille, France's first great tragic playwright, called *L'Illusion Comique* a strange and capricious "monster" of a play. Coming from the man who is best known as the author of the heroic *Le Cid*, it is certainly an oddity - a fanciful comedy on the subject of love, paternity and the art of theater itself.

As elegantly directed by Mark Lamos at Hartford Stage, *The Illusion* (as the play is titled in Tony Kushner's free adaptation) becomes a chimerical vision complete with hidden crannies and mysteries. Though it is presented in its period (the early 17th century, in France), it resonates with modernism, both in style and in commentary. Behind the poetic language and ornate costumes, *The Illusion* is a forerunner of plays by Luigi Pirandello and other masters of theatrical charades.

In it, a father regrets banishing his son and journeys to a magician to find out what befell the youth after he left home. On cue, the magician, Alcandre, conjures scenes from the son's life, which the father greets with increasing amazement.

In a play within the play, the son appears as a lovestruck swain, in and out of jeopardy (and in and out of jail). The play is concerned with the illusions of love, repeatedly putting the father - and the audience - on guard to distinguish the real from the feigned. Scenes are stage-managed by Alcandre, a man of wizardly and decidedly unpredictably ways.

One of the father's perplexities is that in the play within the play, the son and other characters keep changing their names and, at times, alter their relationships. Eventually, Alcandre clears up the confusion by revealing that the son is an actor. The scenes from life are scenes from theater, though apparently related to real events and sentiments.

The play operates both as a picaresque romance and as a comedy of love, or, to use Corneille's word, as a caprice. One's enjoyment derives from the father's attitude, the son's adventures and the interference of the diverse characters, especially the son's employer, Matamore, and his love's jealous maid.

Identified by the adapter as a lunatic, Matamore has designs on the woman the young man adores. When defeated in this pursuit, he reverts to cowardice, barricading himself in an attic until he thinks it is safe to emerge. Others do not behave so self-protectively. The scenes are filled with sword fights as well as incidents of witty verbal abuse, as the son marches merrily though all difficulties with a confidence bordering on arrogance. As he insists, "Obstacles are only obstacles until they are overcome."

In collaboration with the scenic desinger, John Conklin, Mr. Lamos has given the play a doubly ingenious production. The magician's cavern is a landscape to delight the eye, decked with sweeping transparent curtains, tilted mirrors, pillars and flying objects from a surrealistic dream. Merlin-like, the magician (Frederick Neumann) animates his lair and his mute manservant, who in moments of stress finds his tongue.

As the father, Marco St. John is alternately astounded and bemused, but he remains a magisterial figure defined by his curiosity. On occasion, he tries to enter the play within the play and has to be restrained by the magician. J. Grant Albrecht and Ashley Gardner are suitably impetuous as the romantic partners.

All the actors convey the suaveness of language, but two of them are especially diverting: Philip Goodwin as the enlightened lunatic and Bellina Logan as the maidservant. As a trickster, she could give that wizard a run for his magic. Ms. Logan is as guileful and as amusing as any maid in similar circumstances in plays by Shakespeare or Molière.

In his adaptation, Mr. Kushner has excised several characters while retaining the essence of the text. One of his alterations is worthy of special notice. The play no longer concludes with a Corneille salute to the glamour and the value of theater. In this more cynical and realistic version, the father is guarded in his attitude toward his son's choice of acting as a career. In the 17th century, even more than today, theater could provide only an illusion of security.

DENIS DIDEROT

RAMEAU'S NEPHEW: OCTOBER 20, 1988

As a protean man of ideas during the Enlightenment, Denis Diderot was a philosopher, encyclopedist, critic and playwright - and an influence on generations of thinkers and artists in each of his various fields. One of his most consequential works is *Rameau's Nephew*, an apparently fictive dialogue that was unpublished in Diderot's lifetime.

Though intended to be read rather than performed, the dialogue has been reinvented as a play by the director Andrei Belgrader and his co-adapter Shelley Barc. Their new version, as vibrantly acted by Tony Shalhoub and Nicholas Kepros at the CSC Repertory, turns out to be provocative theater and an 18th-century harbinger of absurdism. Impertinently, it ridicules greed, corruption and self-interest, subjects that remain as acute today as when Diderot first decried them.

The text has been streamlined and made colloquial while retaining the sardonic spirit of the original. The characters wear period costumes and behave as if they had just stopped by for a drink at the Café de la Régence. At the same time, what they say is seasoned with contemporary parallels. At its root, this is a collision between a philosopher (a stand-in for the author) and the title misanthrope, the nephew of a famous composer of the period.

The nephew, who is called Rameau like his uncle, is disreputable, but with a certain seedy charm. His frankness about his appetites and ambitions (he wants the highest reward without working for it) makes him a social pariah - and, were he alive today, the piquancy of his language would assure him a regular role on television talk shows.

"The rich and famous sleep better," he says as a simple fact and then offers such challenging questions as "Does anyone in this country need to know the subject he teaches?" While boasting of his own guile at bilking his patrons, he swears he is the soul of mediocrity. As a would-be artist, he is the Salieri to all Mozarts (beginning with his uncle). Scrutinizing the record, the philosopher says, "You have brought the art of debasement to its utmost heights," a line that should have a special aptness in a time of political handlers and spinners.

Mr. Belgrader and his two actors have given this dialogue a stage life by treating it as scathing satire. In their hands, Diderot time travels and joins the absurdist ranks of Ionesco and Arrabal. The roles are ideally cast for contrast. With his hangdog mien and foolscap air of bravado, Mr. Shalhoub proves to be a droll clown.

Pretending to be a fellow philosopher, he haughtily challenges his companion's moral complacency and, later, he turns into a vaudevillian, lampooning an orchestra of instruments, all of which he mimics with voice and gesture. Tossing off asides as he plays with the audience, the actor makes Diderot seem improvisatory, a scamp ad-libbing his way through the Enlightenment.

Listening to such knavery, Mr. Kepros is aghast. Sniffing imperiously, he looks as if he wants to hold the younger man at 10-foot pole distance, but his curiosity and his own amusement keep overcoming him. A kind of envy filters through their conversation, as if the astringent philosopher would prefer to be offensive.

To theatricalize the colloquy, Mr. Belgrader and Ms. Barc add their own interpolations, some of them linguistic (Donald Trump joins a line of geniuses that includes Caesar and Copernicus), some of them kinetic. In one delirious scene, Mr. Shalhoub drinks dozens of glasses of an indeterminate alcoholic beverage, with the glasses passing back and forth between the actors like bowler hats in a silent clown routine.

Though Mr. Shalhoub and Mr. Kepros are the entire cast, the audience becomes their accomplice, drawn into the dialogue as straight men. Stagehands also serve visible purposes that do not always have to do with scene-changing, and the scenery itself - designed by Anita Stewart - furnishes a few sight gags.

By inserting an intermission, the director has slightly overextended the dialogue. But the language is literate (as well as earthy) and the author's iconoclasm is all-inclusive. Commentary leads from politics and literature directly to the world of theater, which is labeled the "house of torment," although, we are told, plays can be instructive. From Molière, says Mr. Shalhoub, one can learn to be a miser or a hypocrite - if we keep our Tartuffication to ourselves. He ends the play with the incomplete assertion, "He who laughs last..." With *Rameau's Nephew*, one laughs first, last and later.

JAPANESE THEATER

MEDEA: SEPTEMBER 5, 1986

The Toho Company production of *Medea* is an interweaving of Eastern and Western performance techniques cohering in a cross-cultural version of a seminal work of Greek tragedy. Deeply influenced by Kabuki and Noh theater, the production acts to transform Euripides into a Japanese classic. As directed by Yukio Ninagawa, the work is related to the films that Akira Kurosawa has made from Shakespeare; it is true in spirit to the source and rich with its own demonic Oriental character.

Playing the title role, Mikijiro Hira is most decidedly the star of this all-male, highly stylized production. Through Mr. Hira's performance, the Japanese version excavates to the heart of Euripides, powerfully restating this story of the blackest revenge. The play is performed in Japanese, without translation; though one misses the Euripidean poetry (in one of the various English translations), there is no difficulty in following the emotions of the eternal story.

At its opening on Wednesday night at the Delacorte Theater in Central Park, the play had an elemental directness - in two senses of the word. Despite an almost steady rain, the play was performed in its entirety. The drizzle did not deter the Toho actors, but it certainly dampened their ornate costumes (and also the audience). One sidelight: the rain caused steam to emanate from Mr. Hira's costume. He seemed surrounded by a vaporous cloud, an evocative, though accidental metaphor for a Medea on fire.

Except for his deep masculine voice, Mr. Hira is a totally convincing Medea, in emotional depth an equal to many English-speaking actresses who have played the role. The actor moves authoritatively through the play, an avenging angel repeatedly tortured by conscience but undiscouraged in the plunge toward Medea's maniacal act.

The other actors, especially Hatsuo Yamaya's sympathetic Nurse and Masane Tsukayama's imperious Jason, also manage to master the cross-cultural techniques. There are several minor detours in regard to the performance. Medea's children - twinned, white-costumed cherubs forever interlocking their arms - are given, in their vocalization, a falsely comic dimension. Whenever they are on stage, they chatter nonsensically to one another.

The score is a collage of East and West, but the director might more effectively have held to Eastern music. By far the most plangent music is the surging sound of Japanese stringed instruments played in unison by the 16-man chorus. The music marches along with the chorus.

The director handles the chorus with a sculptural and balletic poise. In small and large groups, wearing flaring costumes, they look like massed winged creatures, watching in horror as Medea acts out their darkest fears. When Medea speaks, the chorus remains motionless, as Mr. Ninagawa artfully parallels dialogue and silence, movement and stasis.

Visually the conception is striking, filling the New York Shakespeare Festival theater with the sweep of an epic imagination. The evening leads inexorably to its tragic conclusion, as Medea snatches a knife and, without a flinch, rushes offstage to end the lives of her children. As we watch, Medea ascends in a chariot, in a final coup de théâtre, moving higher and higher over the stage until she seems to be flying into the still-threatening sky.

NOH: APRIL 24, 1993

In a stunning collaboration between theater and architecture and between diverse cultures over a period of centuries, the Temple of Dendur is being used as an environment for the presentation of Noh drama. The special three-performance series is a remarkable event both for the Metropolitan Museum of Art and for Japanese theater.

In previous engagements in New York, Noh has been seen on a traditional proscenium or concert stage. Performed in the open on a raised platform in front of this Egyptian temple (built in the first century B.C.), the plays gain theatrical and historical relevance. What might have seemed exotic turns out to be the most natural linkage. In this setting, the Kanze Noh Theater conjures a feeling close to Noh's spiritual source in the 14th and 15th centuries when plays were performed at shrines.

Rokuro Umewaka, the artistic director of the company, selected this location because its grandeur reminded him of an outdoor stage at the Parthenon where his father presented Noh plays. By intention, the performances are the director's "offering" to the Temple of Dendur. In its high vaulted surroundings, the temple is a magnificent setting for classical performance.

As dusk falls, the actors on stage are reflected in the greenhouse-style windows that face Central Park, giving the audience a double-image view. The reflections are like frescoes floating in air while the stage below resonates with visual and dramatic opulence.

The plays, which change nightly, are carefully chosen to underscore the variety of Noh, a lyrical theater in contrast to the more popular Kabuki. All three plays on opening night draw extensively from the Noh resources: the resplendent costumes and masks (a museum exhibition by themselves), hypnotic music and intricately stylized performance. There is no simultaneous translation, but if one reads the plot summaries in the program, the plays are not difficult to follow. Theatergoers can concentrate on the whole rather than on individual details.

Okina, the first play on Thursday, a choreographed religious rite, is the most expressive in terms of movement and sound. Approaching the stage on a long ramp, the actors slide their feet as if walking on air. Drumbeating and singing lead to dancing until the stage itself becomes a drum, as the actors stomp tympanic patterns in rhythm with the musicians.

After an intermission in which theatergoers can look at the antiquities in surrounding rooms, the actors return with a Kyogen comedy, traditionally presented between Noh dramas. In this one, a young man and his father visit the youth's prospective father-in-law but have to share a single hakama, or ceremonial robe. With the deft bumbling of silent clowns, Sengoro Shigeyama and Masakuni Shigeyama (who are themselves father and son) briskly switch the one costume and try to overcome their embarassment. Eventually, they rip the garment in half, a Solomonesque resolution to an Oriental dilemma.

The closing play chronicles the mystical journey of a priest in search of wisdom. More than the other works, this play, with its periods of exposition, demands patience from the audience. The rewards are plentiful, including Mr. Umewaka's own performance as an elderly wise man and god, and the fiercely caricatured masks worn by the actors portraying demons and dragons.

Throughout the performance, the Temple of Dendur is a silent sentinel. This is the ultimate in site-specific spaces. With the Kanze company in residence, time stands still and theater is transporting.

MOLIÈRE

THE MISER: MAY 18, 1990

HARTFORD - For Harpagon, the title character in *The Miser*, greed is not only good but it also essential for his well-being. In Mark Lamos's production of the play at Hartford Stage, Gerry Bamman makes it self-evident that the miser is as obsessive as he is egomaniacal, and, in so doing, the actor carries comedy to diabolical lengths.

The character is far more devoted to his money than he is to his son and daughter, and when his strong box is stolen, he is crushed beyond belief. At the climax of the play, he is told he can have his fortune back if he will let his son marry the woman he loves, the same woman the aged father had selected for himself.

Confronted with this choice - his money or a wife - Mr. Bamman takes a long Jack Benny-like pause, thinking it over and inducing hearty laughter from the audience before he decides where his interest lies. As the actor knows, Harpagon must end as he begins, as the meanest of skinflints, without any redeeming virtue.

Two seasons ago at Hartford Stage, Mr. Bamman played the complacent master of "The School for Wives." With his role in "The Miser," he reaffirms his comic franchise as a leading interpreter of Molière's self-important, self-deluding protagonists.

The production is fueled by the actor's antic spirit. He has a silent clown's gift for physical comedy as well as a drollness in handling his character's acerbic insults. Even when he is offstage, one can sense his proximity, as if he might leap through a curtain to uncover a devious counterplot.

When he is onstage, he is delightful, asserting his will (and his zeal for his weal). He is especially funny when he falls for the false flatterer Frosine. This wily matchmaker (Pamela Payton-Wright) easily convinces him that it would be impossible for a young woman to prefer a young man when Harpagon himself is available. "You are in your salad days," she tells him. Mr. Bamman looks more like a bowl of wilted lettuce.

Fawning will get Frosine everywhere when faced with an old fool like

Harpagon. He will accept any compliment, no matter how irrational, if it certifies his own lofty opinion of himself. Ms. Payton-Wright is amusing although her performance is perilously close to a Ruth Gordon imitation.

The miser's worthiest antagonist proves to be his son. At Hartford Stage, that role receives the evening's second most entertaining performance. The lanky Tom Wood, towering over his father (he has to stoop to be badgered), is as impetuous a swain as ever disobeyed the wishes of a parent.

Gabriella Diaz-Farrar is pert as the son's intended, a woman so vulnerable that she faints when she sees the old man to whom she is temporarily affianced. Marcus Giamatti and Ted van Griethuysen are adroit in other roles. Oddly, Mr. Giamatti as a scheming servant, is the only one in the company who speaks with a French accent.

Lightness and spontaneity are the mode as the actors sweep to the upbeat conclusion. Long-lost children are reunited with their parents, couples are bound together in bliss, and Harpagon once again embraces his true love, his strongbox. Mr. Bamman beams, his exasperation finally replaced by ecstasy: a perfect match of man and money.

JOHN O'KEEFFE

WILD OATS: JANUARY 4, 1980

WASHINGTON - Were anyone to ask what plays I would like to take with me to a desert island, high on the list would be John O'Keeffe's *Wild Oats*. However, in order to feel the full flavor of this rollicking 18th-century romance one would have to be accompanied by a troupe of actors, either the Royal Shakespeare Company or the company that Leonard Peters has put together for the current revival of the play at the Folger Theater Group. *Wild Oats* is not so much an emotion to be recollected in tranquillity as a live performance by a merry band of players.

I have now seen three productions of *Wild Oats*, at the R.S.C., New York's C.S.C., and the Folger, and each time the comedy seems as fresh as it is familiar. One laughs aloud at the convoluted escapades of the rogue hero, Jack Rover, and it is impossible not to become misty-eyed at the golden-hued denouement. This is a play in which someone is always staking his or her life on someone else's innocence, in which the righteous are wronged until the end when every single wrong is righted.

Clifford Williams's R.S.C. production, a rediscovery of this classic after years of neglect, gave Alan Howard one of his finest roles as Jack Rover. Christopher

Martin's CSC production last season proved that the play was foolproof fun. Mr. Peters's version in our nation's capital is, in a word, capital.

The Folger's wood-hewn Elizabethan stage, embellished by Russell Metheny's simple rustic design, is a perfect place for *Wild Oats*, and John Neville-Andrews is an inspired choice to play Rover. He is a comic hero, an itinerant actor as well as a "strolling gentleman" as in the work's subtitle. He is in and out of mischief. When he is struck by love for the Quaker heiress, Lady Amaranth, it is a thunderbolt from the skies and almost flattens him to the floor. Mr. Neville-Andrews accents the clownish side of the character, but he does not ignore Rover's impulsive sense of goodwill and his headstrong romantic inclinations. As a traveling actor, Rover has memorized a folio of Shakespeare. His dialogue is riddled with borrowings from the Bard, as adapted for his own uses - for flattery, for insults, to fill in the spaces.

It is Mr. Neville-Andrews's clever notion to imitate the characters that he is quoting. A line from *Hamlet*, and suddenly he is melancholy. A random sampling from *Richard III*, reflexively a hump appears on his back. The actor never misses a trick and occasionally he draws a trump card. With his angular features and madcap grin, he looks and reacts just a bit like a fugitive from a Monty Python show, convincingly demonstrating that John O'Keeffe and his strolling players may have been antecedents to the mirthful mania of these contemporary English satirists. Certainly the plot is as twisted and labyrinthine as in any modern lampoon.

Once we catch the drift, we are Mr. O'Keeffe's confidantes. We are swept away in a Sargasso Sea of devilish duplicity: we know that she knows that he doesn't yet know. Rover's long-lost mother's rodomontade recapitulation of her entire biography - love, abandonment, loss of child, destitution - takes about two minutes. Mikel Lambert delivers the history without pausing for a breath, as if she is a woman possessed. She seems taken by surprise by the story's conclusion. With justification, the audience breaks into applause.

Under Mr. Peters's direction, the principals strike the right balance between total immersion and self-mockery. Cara Duff-MacCormick is a charming Lady Amaranth. She even makes the woman's sense of propriety - actors are "profane stage players" until she meets one - seem honorable and humorous.

The climax of *Wild Oats* is like a crazy quilt of Shakespearean mistaken identity. True identities tumble with dizzying speed. Hypocrites are unmasked, villains exposed, lost sons and mothers reunited, prodigal fathers redeemed, paradise regained. *Wild Oats* is a splendiferous comedy.

ACKNOWLEDGMENTS

On at least one point, I agree with James Agate. It was he who said, "Anybody can write dramatic criticism; it takes a very clever fellow indeed to get it reprinted." It also takes a receptive publisher; my thanks go to Glenn Young for publishing this volume.

Thanks, too, to Clara Rotter and Carol Coburn who have greatly facilitated my life at the Times. Until her retirement, Clara was the bastion of the theater department at that newspaper. She was also the voice of the theater audience. Her pithy criticism would have made her an asset on Newsweek. My appreciation goes to my agent Owen Laster for his helpful advice and to Leslie Nipkow, a fine actress who took time out from her career to word-process this manuscript. And a round of applause for Ann and our son Ethan, intrepid companions on this voyage to the edge of theater.

I also want to thank the New York Times for allowing me to reprint the pieces that appeared there; and Newsweek and Jim O'Quinn at American Theater for their cooperation in reprinting pieces from those magazines. The review of *Who's Afraid of Virginia Woolf?* appeared in Newsweek and American Theater published the essays entitled "The Noble Look at Stratford-on-Avon," "Actors Put a New Spin on the Old Bard at Stratford," "Ghosts," "Design Marches On: the Prague Quadrennial" and "Actors Theater of Louisville: The Plays Tell the Tale." All other reviews and essays first appeared in the New York Times.

INDEX